Modern Compiler Design

Dick Grune • Kees van Reeuwijk • Henri E. Bal
Ceriel J.H. Jacobs • Koen Langendoen

Modern Compiler Design

Second Edition

Dick Grune
Vrije Universiteit
Amsterdam, The Netherlands

Ceriel J.H. Jacobs
Vrije Universiteit
Amsterdam, The Netherlands

Kees van Reeuwijk
Vrije Universiteit
Amsterdam, The Netherlands

Koen Langendoen
Delft University of Technology
Delft, The Netherlands

Henri E. Bal
Vrije Universiteit
Amsterdam, The Netherlands

Additional material to this book can be downloaded from http://extras.springer.com.

ISBN 978-1-4939-4472-9   ISBN 978-1-4614-4699-6 (eBook)
DOI 10.1007/978-1-4614-4699-6
Springer New York Heidelberg Dordrecht London

Printed on acid-free paper

Springer is part of Springer Science+Business Media (www.springer.com)

Preface

Twelve years have passed since the first edition of *Modern Compiler Design*. For many computer science subjects this would be more than a life time, but since compiler design is probably the most mature computer science subject, it is different. An adult person develops more slowly and differently than a toddler or a teenager, and so does compiler design. The present book reflects that.

Improvements to the book fall into two groups: presentation and content. The 'look and feel' of the book has been modernized, but more importantly we have rearranged significant parts of the book to present them in a more structured manner: large chapters have been split and the optimizing code generation techniques have been collected in a separate chapter. Based on reader feedback and experiences in teaching from this book, both by ourselves and others, material has been expanded, clarified, modified, or deleted in a large number of places. We hope that as a result of this the reader feels that the book does a better job of making compiler design and construction accessible.

The book adds new material to cover the developments in compiler design and construction over the last twelve years. Overall the standard compiling techniques and paradigms have stood the test of time, but still new and often surprising optimization techniques have been invented; existing ones have been improved; and old ones have gained prominence. Examples of the first are: procedural abstraction, in which routines are recognized in the code and replaced by routine calls to reduce size; binary rewriting, in which optimizations are applied to the binary code; and just-in-time compilation, in which parts of the compilation are delayed to improve the perceived speed of the program. An example of the second is a technique which extends optimal code generation through exhaustive search, previously available for tiny blocks only, to moderate-size basic blocks. And an example of the third is tail recursion removal, indispensable for the compilation of functional languages. These developments are mainly described in Chapter 9.

Although syntax analysis is the one but oldest branch of compiler construction (lexical analysis being the oldest), even in that area innovation has taken place. Generalized (non-deterministic) LR parsing, developed between 1984 and 1994, is now used in compilers. It is covered in Section 3.5.8.

New hardware requirements have necessitated new compiler developments. The main examples are the need for size reduction of the object code, both to fit the code into small embedded systems and to reduce transmission times; and for lower power consumption, to extend battery life and to reduce electricity bills. Dynamic memory allocation in embedded systems requires a balance between speed and thrift, and the question is how compiler design can help. These subjects are covered in Sections 9.2, 9.3, and 10.2.8, respectively.

With age comes legacy. There is much legacy code around, code which is so old that it can no longer be modified and recompiled with reasonable effort. If the source code is still available but there is no compiler any more, recompilation must start with a grammar of the source code. For fifty years programmers and compiler designers have used grammars to produce and analyze programs; now large legacy programs are used to produce grammars for them. The recovery of the grammar from legacy source code is discussed in Section 3.6. If just the binary executable program is left, it must be disassembled or even decompiled. For fifty years compiler designers have been called upon to design compilers and assemblers to convert source programs to binary code; now they are called upon to design disassemblers and decompilers, to roll back the assembly and compilation process. The required techniques are treated in Sections 8.4 and 8.5.

The bibliography

The literature list has been updated, but its usefulness is more limited than before, for two reasons. The first is that by the time it appears in print, the Internet can provide more up-to-date and more to-the-point information, in larger quantities, than a printed text can hope to achieve. It is our contention that anybody who has understood a larger part of the ideas explained in this book is able to evaluate Internet information on compiler design.

The second is that many of the papers we refer to are available only to those fortunate enough to have login facilities at an institute with sufficient budget to obtain subscriptions to the larger publishers; they are no longer available to just anyone who walks into a university library. Both phenomena point to paradigm shifts with which readers, authors, publishers and librarians will have to cope.

The structure of the book

This book is conceptually divided into two parts. The first, comprising Chapters 1 through 10, is concerned with techniques for program processing in general; it includes a chapter on memory management, both in the compiler and in the generated code. The second part, Chapters 11 through 14, covers the specific techniques required by the various programming paradigms. The interactions between the parts of the book are outlined in the adjacent table. The leftmost column shows the four phases of compiler construction: *analysis, context handling, synthesis,* and *run-time systems.* Chapters in this column cover both the manual and the automatic creation

of the pertinent software but tend to emphasize automatic generation. The other
columns show the four paradigms covered in this book; for each paradigm an example of a subject treated by each of the phases is shown. These chapters tend to
contain manual techniques only, all automatic techniques having been delegated to
Chapters 2 through 9.

	in imperative and object- oriented programs (Chapter 11)	in functional programs (Chapter 12)	in logic programs (Chapter 13)	in parallel/ distributed programs (Chapter 14)
How to do:				
analysis (Chapters 2 & 3)	—	—	—	—
context handling (Chapters 4 & 5)	identifier identification	polymorphic type checking	static rule matching	Linda static analysis
synthesis (Chapters 6–9)	code for while- statement	code for list comprehension	structure unification	marshaling
run-time systems (no chapter)	stack	reduction machine	Warren Abstract Machine	replication

The scientific mind would like the table to be nice and square, with all boxes
filled —in short "orthogonal"— but we see that the top right entries arc missing
and that there is no chapter for "run-time systems" in the leftmost column. The top
right entries would cover such things as the special subjects in the program text
analysis of logic languages, but present text analysis techniques are powerful and
flexible enough and languages similar enough to handle all language paradigms:
there is nothing to be said there, for lack of problems. The chapter missing from
the leftmost column would discuss manual and automatic techniques for creating
run-time systems. Unfortunately there is little or no theory on this subject: run-time
systems are still crafted by hand by programmers on an intuitive basis; there is
nothing to be said there, for lack of solutions.

Chapter 1 introduces the reader to compiler design by examining a simple traditional modular compiler/interpreter in detail. Several high-level aspects of compiler
construction are discussed, followed by a short history of compiler construction and
introductions to formal grammars and closure algorithms.

Chapters 2 and 3 treat the program text analysis phase of a compiler: the conversion of the program text to an abstract syntax tree. Techniques for lexical analysis,
lexical identification of tokens, and syntax analysis are discussed.

Chapters 4 and 5 cover the second phase of a compiler: context handling. Several methods of context handling are discussed: automated ones using attribute
grammars, manual ones using L-attributed and S-attributed grammars, and semi-
automated ones using symbolic interpretation and data-flow analysis.

Chapters 6 through 9 cover the synthesis phase of a compiler, covering both interpretation and code generation. The chapters on code generation are mainly concerned with machine code generation; the intermediate code required for paradigm-specific constructs is treated in Chapters 11 through 14.

Chapter 10 concerns memory management techniques, both for use in the compiler and in the generated program.

Chapters 11 through 14 address the special problems in compiling for the various paradigms – imperative, object-oriented, functional, logic, and parallel/distributed. Compilers for imperative and object-oriented programs are similar enough to be treated together in one chapter, Chapter 11.

Appendix B contains hints and answers to a selection of the exercises in the book. Such exercises are marked by a ▷ followed the page number on which the answer appears. A larger set of answers can be found on Springer's Internet page; the corresponding exercises are marked by ▷www.

Several subjects in this book are treated in a non-traditional way, and some words of justification may be in order.

Lexical analysis is based on the same dotted items that are traditionally reserved for bottom-up syntax analysis, rather than on Thompson's NFA construction. We see the dotted item as the essential tool in bottom-up pattern matching, unifying lexical analysis, LR syntax analysis, bottom-up code generation and peep-hole optimization. The traditional lexical algorithms are just low-level implementations of item manipulation. We consider the different treatment of lexical and syntax analysis to be a historical artifact. Also, the difference between the lexical and the syntax levels tends to disappear in modern software.

Considerable attention is being paid to attribute grammars, in spite of the fact that their impact on compiler design has been limited. Yet they are the only known way of automating context handling, and we hope that the present treatment will help to lower the threshold of their application.

Functions as first-class data are covered in much greater depth in this book than is usual in compiler design books. After a good start in Algol 60, functions lost much status as manipulatable data in languages like C, Pascal, and Ada, although Ada 95 rehabilitated them somewhat. The implementation of some modern concepts, for example functional and logic languages, iterators, and continuations, however, requires functions to be manipulated as normal data. The fundamental aspects of the implementation are covered in the chapter on imperative and object-oriented languages; specifics are given in the chapters on the various other paradigms.

Additional material, including more answers to exercises, and all diagrams and all code from the book, are available through Springer's Internet page.

Use as a course book

The book contains far too much material for a compiler design course of 13 lectures of two hours each, as given at our university, so a selection has to be made. An introductory, more traditional course can be obtained by including, for example,

Chapter 1;

Chapter 2 up to 2.7; 2.10; 2.11; Chapter 3 up to 3.4.5; 3.5 up to 3.5.7;

Chapter 4 up to 4.1.3; 4.2.1 up to 4.3; Chapter 5 up to 5.2.2; 5.3;

Chapter 6; Chapter 7 up to 9.1.1; 9.1.4 up to 9.1.4.4; 7.3;

Chapter 10 up to 10.1.2; 10.2 up to 10.2.4;

Chapter 11 up to 11.2.3.2; 11.2.4 up to 11.2.10; 11.4 up to 11.4.2.3.

A more advanced course would include all of Chapters 1 to 11, possibly excluding Chapter 4. This could be augmented by one of Chapters 12 to 14.

An advanced course would skip much of the introductory material and concentrate on the parts omitted in the introductory course, Chapter 4 and all of Chapters 10 to 14.

Acknowledgments

We owe many thanks to the following people, who supplied us with help, remarks, wishes, and food for thought for this Second Edition: Ingmar Alting, José Fortes, Bert Huijben, Jonathan Joubert, Sara Kalvala, Frank Lippes, Paul S. Moulson, Prasant K. Patra, Carlo Perassi, Marco Rossi, Mooly Sagiv, Gert Jan Schoneveld, Ajay Singh, Evert Wattel, and Freek Zindel. Their input ranged from simple corrections to detailed suggestions to massive criticism. Special thanks go to Stefanie Scherzinger, whose thorough and thoughtful criticism of our outline code format induced us to improve it considerably; any remaining imperfections should be attributed to stubbornness on the part of the authors. The presentation of the program code snippets in the book profited greatly from Carsten Heinz's listings package; we thank him for making the package available to the public.

We are grateful to Ann Kostant, Melissa Fearon, and Courtney Clark of Springer US, who, through fast and competent work, have cleared many obstacles that stood in the way of publishing this book. We thank them for their effort and pleasant cooperation.

We mourn the death of Irina Athanasiu, who did not live long enough to lend her expertise in embedded systems to this book.

We thank the Faculteit der Exacte Wetenschappen of the Vrije Universiteit for their support and the use of their equipment.

Amsterdam,   *Dick Grune*

March 2012   *Kees van Reeuwijk*

                                                                                       Henri E. Bal

                                                                                 Ceriel J.H. Jacobs

Delft,   *Koen G. Langendoen*

Abridged Preface to the First Edition (2000)

In the 1980s and 1990s, while the world was witnessing the rise of the PC and the Internet on the front pages of the daily newspapers, compiler design methods developed with less fanfare, developments seen mainly in the technical journals, and –more importantly– in the compilers that are used to process today's software. These developments were driven partly by the advent of new programming paradigms, partly by a better understanding of code generation techniques, and partly by the introduction of faster machines with large amounts of memory.

The field of programming languages has grown to include, besides the traditional imperative paradigm, the object-oriented, functional, logical, and parallel/distributed paradigms, which inspire novel compilation techniques and which often require more extensive run-time systems than do imperative languages. BURS techniques (Bottom-Up Rewriting Systems) have evolved into very powerful code generation techniques which cope superbly with the complex machine instruction sets of present-day machines. And the speed and memory size of modern machines allow compilation techniques and programming language features that were unthinkable before. Modern compiler design methods meet these challenges head-on.

The audience

Our audience are students with enough experience to have at least used a compiler occasionally and to have given some thought to the concept of compilation. When these students leave the university, they will have to be familiar with language processors for each of the modern paradigms, using modern techniques. Although curriculum requirements in many universities may have been lagging behind in this respect, graduates entering the job market cannot afford to ignore these developments.

Experience has shown us that a considerable number of techniques traditionally taught in compiler construction are special cases of more fundamental techniques. Often these special techniques work for imperative languages only; the fundamental techniques have a much wider application. An example is the stack as an optimized representation for activation records in strictly last-in-first-out languages. Therefore, this book

- focuses on principles and techniques of wide application, carefully distinguishing between the essential (= material that has a high chance of being useful to the student) and the incidental (= material that will benefit the student only in exceptional cases);
- provides a first level of implementation details and optimizations;
- augments the explanations by pointers for further study.

The student, after having finished the book, can expect to:

- have obtained a thorough understanding of the concepts of modern compiler design and construction, and some familiarity with their practical application;
- be able to start participating in the construction of a language processor for each of the modern paradigms with a minimal training period;
- be able to read the literature.

The first two provide a firm basis; the third provides potential for growth.

Acknowledgments

We owe many thanks to the following people, who were willing to spend time and effort on reading drafts of our book and to supply us with many useful and sometimes very detailed comments: Mirjam Bakker, Raoul Bhoedjang, Wilfred Dittmer, Thomer M. Gil, Ben N. Hasnai, Bert Huijben, Jaco A. Imthorn, John Romein, Tim Rühl, and the anonymous reviewers. We thank Ronald Veldema for the Pentium code segments.

We are grateful to Simon Plumtree, Gaynor Redvers-Mutton, Dawn Booth, and Jane Kerr of John Wiley & Sons Ltd, for their help and encouragement in writing this book. Lambert Meertens kindly provided information on an older ABC compiler, and Ralph Griswold on an Icon compiler.

We thank the Faculteit Wiskunde en Informatica (now part of the Faculteit der Exacte Wetenschappen) of the Vrije Universiteit for their support and the use of their equipment.

Dick Grune   dick@cs.vu.nl, http://www.cs.vu.nl/~dick

Henri E. Bal   bal@cs.vu.nl, http://www.cs.vu.nl/~bal

Ceriel J.H. Jacobs   ceriel@cs.vu.nl, http://www.cs.vu.nl/~ceriel

Koen G. Langendoen   koen@pds.twi.tudelft.nl, http://pds.twi.tudelft.nl/~koen

Amsterdam, May 2000

Contents

Part I From Program Text to Abstract Syntax Tree

Chapter 1
Introduction

In its most general form, a **compiler** is a program that accepts as input a program text in a certain language and produces as output a program text in another language, while preserving the meaning of that text. This process is called **translation**, as it would be if the texts were in natural languages. Almost all compilers translate from one input language, the **source language**, to one output language, the **target language**, only. One normally expects the source and target language to differ greatly: the source language could be C and the target language might be machine code for the Pentium processor series. The language the compiler itself is written in is the **implementation language**.

The main reason why one wants such a translation is that one has hardware on which one can "run" the translated program, or more precisely: have the hardware perform the actions described by the semantics of the program. After all, hardware is the only real source of computing power. Running a translated program often involves feeding it input data in some format, and will probably result in some output data in some other format. The input data can derive from a variety of sources; examples are files, keystrokes, and network packets. Likewise, the output can go to a variety of places; examples are files, screens, and printers.

To obtain the translated program, we run a compiler, which is just another program whose input is a file with the format of a program source text and whose output is a file with the format of executable code. A subtle point here is that the file containing the executable code is (almost) tacitly converted to a runnable program; on some operating systems this requires some action, for example setting the "execute" attribute.

To obtain the compiler, we run another compiler whose input consists of compiler source text and which will produce executable code for it, as it would for any program source text. This process of compiling and running a compiler is depicted in Figure 1.1; that compilers can and do compile compilers sounds more confusing than it is. When the source language is also the implementation language and the source text to be compiled is actually a new version of the compiler itself, the process is called **bootstrapping**. The term "bootstrapping" is traditionally attributed to a story of Baron von Münchhausen (1720–1797), although in the original story

1

the baron pulled himself from a swamp by his hair plait, rather than by his boot-straps [14].

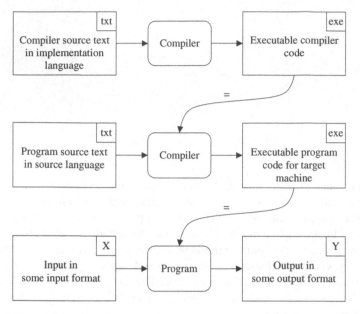

Fig. 1.1: Compiling and running a compiler

Compilation does not differ fundamentally from file conversion but it does differ in degree. The main aspect of conversion is that the input has a property called semantics—its "meaning"—which must be preserved by the process. The structure of the input and its semantics can be simple, as, for example in a file conversion program which converts EBCDIC to ASCII; they can be moderate, as in an WAV to MP3 converter, which has to preserve the acoustic impression, its semantics; or they can be considerable, as in a compiler, which has to faithfully express the semantics of the input program in an often extremely different output format. In the final analysis, a compiler is just a giant file conversion program.

The compiler can work its magic because of two factors:

- the input is in a language and consequently has a structure, which is described in the language reference manual;
- the semantics of the input is described in terms of and is attached to that same structure.

These factors enable the compiler to "understand" the program and to collect its semantics in a **semantic representation**. The same two factors exist with respect to the target language. This allows the compiler to rephrase the collected semantics in terms of the target language. How all this is done in detail is the subject of this book.

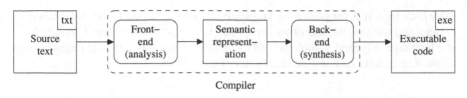

Compiler

Fig. 1.2: Conceptual structure of a compiler

The part of a compiler that performs the analysis of the source language text is called the **front-end**, and the part that does the target language synthesis is the **back-end**; see Figure 1.2. If the compiler has a very clean design, the front-end is totally unaware of the target language and the back-end is totally unaware of the source language: the only thing they have in common is knowledge of the semantic representation. There are technical reasons why such a strict separation is inefficient, and in practice even the best-structured compilers compromise.

The above description immediately suggests another mode of operation for a compiler: if all required input data are available, the compiler could *perform* the actions specified by the semantic representation rather than re-express them in a different form. The code-generating back-end is then replaced by an interpreting back-end, and the whole program is called an *interpreter*. There are several reasons for doing this, some fundamental and some more opportunistic.

One fundamental reason is that an interpreter is normally written in a high-level language and will therefore run on most machine types, whereas generated object code will only run on machines of the target type: in other words, portability is increased. Another is that writing an interpreter is much less work than writing a back-end.

A third reason for using an interpreter rather than a compiler is that performing the actions straight from the semantic representation allows better error checking and reporting. This is not fundamentally so, but is a consequence of the fact that compilers (front-end/back-end combinations) are expected to generate efficient code. As a result, most back-ends throw away any information that is not essential to the program execution in order to gain speed; this includes much information that could have been useful in giving good diagnostics, for example source code and its line numbers.

A fourth reason is the increased security that can be achieved by interpreters; this effect has played an important role in Java's rise to fame. Again, this increased security is not fundamental since there is no reason why compiled code could not do the same checks an interpreter can. Yet it is considerably easier to convince oneself that an interpreter does not play dirty tricks than that there are no booby traps hidden in binary executable code.

A fifth reason is the ease with which an interpreter can handle new program code generated by the running program itself. An interpreter can treat the new code exactly as all other code. Compiled code must, however, invoke a compiler (if available), and load and link the newly compiled code to the running program (if possible). In fact, if a programming language allows new code to be constructed in a running program, the use of an interpreter is almost unavoidable. Conversely, if the language is typically implemented by an interpreter, the language might as well allow new code to be constructed in a running program.

Why is a compiler called a compiler?

The original meaning of "to compile" is "to select representative material and add it to a collection"; makers of compilation CDs use the term in its proper meaning. In its early days programming language translation was viewed in the same way: when the input contained for example "a + b", a prefabricated code fragment "load a in register; add b to register" was selected and added to the output. A compiler compiled a list of code fragments to be added to the translated program. Today's compilers, especially those for the non-imperative programming paradigms, often perform much more radical transformations on the input program.

It should be pointed out that there is no fundamental difference between using a compiler and using an interpreter. In both cases the program text is processed into an intermediate form, which is then interpreted by some interpreting mechanism. In compilation,

- the program processing is considerable;
- the resulting intermediate form, machine-specific binary executable code, is low-level;
- the interpreting mechanism is the hardware CPU; and
- program execution is relatively fast.

In interpretation,

- the program processing is minimal to moderate;
- the resulting intermediate form, some system-specific data structure, is high- to medium-level;
- the interpreting mechanism is a (software) program; and
- program execution is relatively slow.

These relationships are summarized graphically in Figure 1.3. Section 7.5.1 shows how a fairly smooth shift from interpreter to compiler can be made.

After considering the question of why one should study compiler construction (Section 1.1) we will look at simple but complete demonstration compiler (Section 1.2); survey the structure of a more realistic compiler (Section 1.3); and consider possible compiler architectures (Section 1.4). This is followed by short sections on the properties of a good compiler (1.5), portability and retargetability (1.6), and the history of compiler construction (1.7). Next are two more theoretical subjects: an introduction to context-free grammars (Section 1.8), and a general closure algorithm (Section 1.9). A brief explanation of the various code forms used in the book (Section 1.10) concludes this introductory chapter.

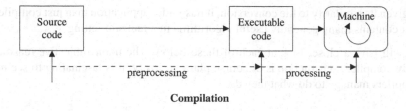

Compilation

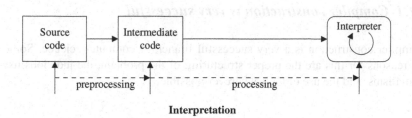

Interpretation

Fig. 1.3: Comparison of a compiler and an interpreter

Occasionally, the structure of the text will be summarized in a "roadmap", as shown for this chapter.

Roadmap

1.1 Why study compiler construction?

There are a number of objective reasons why studying compiler construction is a good idea:

- compiler construction is a very successful branch of computer science, and one of the earliest to earn that predicate;

- given its similarity to file conversion, it has wider application than just compilers;
- it contains many generally useful algorithms in a realistic setting.

We will have a closer look at each of these below. The main subjective reason to study compiler construction is of course plain curiosity: it is fascinating to see how compilers manage to do what they do.

1.1.1 Compiler construction is very successful

Compiler construction is a very successful branch of computer science. Some of the reasons for this are the proper structuring of the problem, the judicious use of formalisms, and the use of tools wherever possible.

1.1.1.1 Proper structuring of the problem

Compilers analyze their input, construct a semantic representation, and synthesize their output from it. This **analysis–synthesis paradigm** is very powerful and widely applicable. A program for tallying word lengths in a text could for example consist of a front-end which analyzes the text and constructs internally a table of (length, frequency) pairs, and a back-end which then prints this table. Extending this program, one could replace the text-analyzing front-end by a module that collects file sizes in a file system; alternatively, or additionally, one could replace the back-end by a module that produces a bar graph rather than a printed table; we use the word "module" here to emphasize the exchangeability of the parts. In total, four programs have already resulted, all centered around the semantic representation and each reusing lots of code from the others.

Likewise, without the strict separation of analysis and synthesis phases, programming languages and compiler construction would not be where they are today. Without it, each new language would require a completely new set of compilers for all interesting machines—or die for lack of support. With it, a new front-end for that language suffices, to be combined with the existing back-ends for the current machines: for L languages and M machines, L front-ends and M back-ends are needed, requiring $L + M$ modules, rather than $L \times M$ programs. See Figure 1.4.

It should be noted immediately, however, that this strict separation is not completely free of charge. If, for example, a front-end knows it is analyzing for a machine with special machine instructions for multi-way jumps, it can probably analyze case/switch statements so that they can benefit from these machine instructions. Similarly, if a back-end knows it is generating code for a language which has no nested routine declarations, it can generate simpler code for routine calls. Many professional compilers are integrated compilers for one programming language and one machine architecture, using a semantic representation which derives from the source language and which may already contain elements of the target machine.

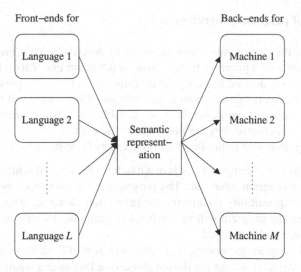

Fig. 1.4: Creating compilers for L languages and M machines

Still, the structuring has played and still plays a large role in the rapid introduction of new languages and new machines.

1.1.1.2 Judicious use of formalisms

For some parts of compiler construction excellent standardized formalisms have been developed, which greatly reduce the effort to produce these parts. The best examples are regular expressions and context-free grammars, used in lexical and syntactic analysis. Enough theory about these has been developed from the 1960s onwards to fill an entire course, but the practical aspects can be taught and understood without going too deeply into the theory. We will consider these formalisms and their applications in Chapters 2 and 3.

Attribute grammars are a formalism that can be used for handling the context, the long-distance relations in a program that link, for example, the use of a variable to its declaration. Since attribute grammars are capable of describing the full semantics of a language, their use can be extended to interpretation or code generation, although other techniques are perhaps more usual. There is much theory about them, but they are less well standardized than regular expressions and context-free grammars. Attribute grammars are covered in Section 4.1.

Manual object code generation for a given machine involves a lot of nitty-gritty programming, but the process can be automated, for example by using pattern matching and dynamic programming. Quite a number of formalisms have been designed for the description of target code, both at the assembly and the binary level, but none of these has gained wide acceptance to date and each compiler writing system has its own version. Automated code generation is treated in Section 9.1.4.

1.1.1.3 Use of program-generating tools

Once one has the proper formalism in which to describe what a program should do, one can generate a program from it, using a **program generator**. Examples are lexical analyzers generated from regular descriptions of the input, parsers generated from grammars (syntax descriptions), and code generators generated from machine descriptions. All these are generally more reliable and easier to debug than their handwritten counterparts; they are often more efficient too.

Generating programs rather than writing them by hand has several advantages:

* The input to a program generator is of a much higher level of abstraction than the handwritten program would be. The programmer needs to specify less, and the tools take responsibility for much error-prone housekeeping. This increases the chances that the program will be correct. For example, it would be cumbersome to write parse tables by hand.
* The use of program-generating tools allows increased flexibility and modifiability. For example, if during the design phase of a language a small change in the syntax is considered, a handwritten parser would be a major stumbling block to any such change. With a generated parser, one would just change the syntax description and generate a new parser.
* Pre-canned or tailored code can be added to the generated program, enhancing its power at hardly any cost. For example, input error handling is usually a difficult affair in handwritten parsers; a generated parser can include tailored error correction code with no effort on the part of the programmer.
* A formal description can sometimes be used to generate more than one type of program. For example, once we have written a grammar for a language with the purpose of generating a parser from it, we may use it to generate a syntax-directed editor, a special-purpose program text editor that guides and supports the user in editing programs in that language.

In summary, generated programs may be slightly more or slightly less efficient than handwritten ones, but generating them is so much more efficient than writing them by hand that whenever the possibility exists, generating a program is almost always to be preferred.

The technique of creating compilers by program-generating tools was pioneered by Brooker *et al.* in 1963 [51], and its importance has continually risen since. Programs that generate parts of a compiler are sometimes called **compiler compilers**, although this is clearly a misnomer. Yet, the term lingers on.

1.1.2 Compiler construction has a wide applicability

Compiler construction techniques can be and are applied outside compiler construction in its strictest sense. Alternatively, more programming can be considered compiler construction than one would traditionally assume. Examples are reading structured data, rapid introduction of new file formats, and general file conversion problems. Also, many programs use configuration or specification files which require processing that is very similar to compilation, if not just compilation under another name.

If input data has a clear structure it is generally possible to write a grammar for it. Using a parser generator, a parser can then be generated automatically. Such techniques can, for example, be applied to rapidly create "read" routines for HTML files, PostScript files, etc. This also facilitates the rapid introduction of new formats. Examples of file conversion systems that have profited considerably from compiler construction techniques are *TeX* text formatters, which convert *TeX* text to *dvi* format, and PostScript interpreters, which convert PostScript text to image rendering instructions for a specific printer.

1.1.3 Compilers contain generally useful algorithms

A third reason to study compiler construction lies in the generally useful data structures and algorithms compilers contain. Examples are hashing, precomputed tables, the stack mechanism, garbage collection, dynamic programming, and graph algorithms. Although each of these can be studied in isolation, it is educationally more valuable and satisfying to do so in a meaningful context.

1.2 A simple traditional modular compiler/interpreter

In this section we will show and discuss a simple demo compiler and interpreter, to introduce the concepts involved and to set the framework for the rest of the book. Turning to Figure 1.2, we see that the heart of a compiler is the semantic representation of the program being compiled. This semantic representation takes the form of a data structure, called the "intermediate code" of the compiler. There are many possibilities for the form of the intermediate code; two usual choices are linked lists of pseudo-instructions and annotated abstract syntax trees. We will concentrate here on the latter, since the semantics is primarily attached to the syntax tree.

1.2.1 The abstract syntax tree

The **syntax tree** of a program text is a data structure which shows precisely how the various segments of the program text are to be viewed in terms of the grammar. The syntax tree can be obtained through a process called "parsing"; in other words, parsing[1] is the process of structuring a text according to a given grammar. For this reason, syntax trees are also called **parse trees**; we will use the terms interchangeably, with a slight preference for "parse tree" when the emphasis is on the actual parsing. Conversely, parsing is also called **syntax analysis**, but this has the problem that there is no corresponding verb "to syntax-analyze". The parser can be written by hand if the grammar is very small and simple; for larger and/or more complicated grammars it can be generated by a parser generator. Parser generators are discussed in Chapter 3.

The exact form of the parse tree as required by the grammar is often not the most convenient one for further processing, so usually a modified form of it is used, called an **abstract syntax tree**, or **AST**. Detailed information about the semantics can be attached to the nodes in this tree through **annotations**, which are stored in additional data fields in the nodes; hence the term **annotated abstract syntax tree**. Since unannotated ASTs are of limited use, ASTs are always more or less annotated in practice, and the abbreviation "AST" is used also for annotated ASTs.

Examples of annotations are type information ("this assignment node concerns a Boolean array assignment") and optimization information ("this expression does not contain a function call"). The first kind is related to the semantics as described in the manual, and is used, among other things, for context error checking. The second kind is not related to anything in the manual but may be important for the code generation phase. The annotations in a node are also called the **attributes** of that node and since a node represents a grammar symbol, one also says that the grammar symbol has the corresponding attributes. It is the task of the *context handling* module to determine and place the annotations or attributes.

Figure 1.5 shows the expression b*b − 4*a*c as a parse tree; the grammar used for expression is similar to those found in the Pascal, Modula-2, or C manuals:

```
expression  →  expression '+' term | expression '−' term | term
term  →  term '*' factor | term '/' factor | factor
factor  →  identifier | constant | '(' expression ')'
```

Figure 1.6 shows the same expression as an AST and Figure 1.7 shows it as an annotated AST in which possible type and location information has been added. The precise nature of the information is not important at this point. What is important is that we see a shift in emphasis from syntactic structure to semantic contents.

Usually the grammar of a programming language is not specified in terms of input characters but of input "tokens". Examples of input tokens are identifiers (for example length or a5), strings ("Hello!", "!@#"), numbers (0, 123e−5), keywords (begin, real), compound operators (++, :=), separators (;, [), etc. Input tokens may be and sometimes must be separated by white space, which is otherwise ignored. So before feeding the input program text to the parser, it must be divided into tokens. Doing so is the task of the *lexical analyzer*; the activity itself is sometimes called "to tokenize", but the literary value of that word is doubtful.

---

[1] In linguistic and educational contexts, the verb "to parse" is also used for the determination of word classes: determining that in "to go by" the word "by" is an adverb and in "by the way" it is a preposition. In computer science the word is used exclusively to refer to syntax analysis.

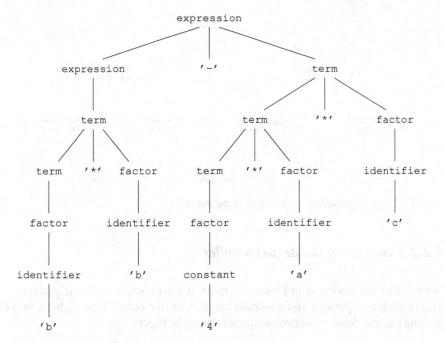

Fig. 1.5: The expression b*b – 4*a*c as a parse tree

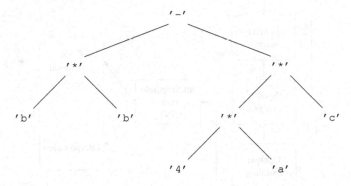

Fig. 1.6: The expression b*b – 4*a*c as an AST

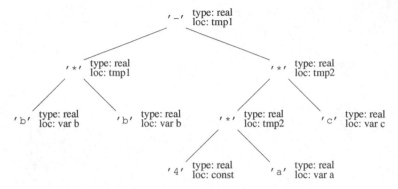

Fig. 1.7: The expression b*b – 4*a*c as an annotated AST

1.2.2 Structure of the demo compiler

We see that the front-end in Figure 1.2 must at least contain a lexical analyzer, a syntax analyzer (parser), and a context handler, in that order. This leads us to the structure of the demo compiler/interpreter shown in Figure 1.8.

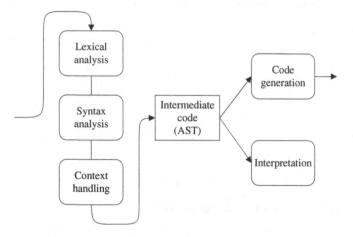

Fig. 1.8: Structure of the demo compiler/interpreter

The back-end allows two intuitively different implementations: a code generator and an interpreter. Both use the AST, the first for generating machine code, the second for performing the implied actions immediately.

1.2.3 The language for the demo compiler

To keep the example small and to avoid the host of detailed problems that marks much of compiler writing, we will base our demonstration compiler on **fully paren-thesized expressions** with operands of one digit. An arithmetic expression is "fully parenthesized" if each operator plus its operands is enclosed in a set of parentheses and no other parentheses occur. This makes parsing almost trivial, since each open parenthesis signals the start of a lower level in the parse tree and each close parenthesis signals the return to the previous, higher level: a fully parenthesized expression can be seen as a linear notation of a parse tree.

```
expression  →  digit | '(' expression operator expression ')'
operator    →  '+' | '*'
digit       →  '0' | '1' | '2' | '3' | '4' | '5' | '6' | '7' | '8' | '9'
```

Fig. 1.9: Grammar for simple fully parenthesized expressions

To simplify things even further, we will have only two operators, + and *. On the other hand, we will allow white space, including tabs and newlines, in the input. The grammar in Figure 1.9 produces such forms as **3**, **(5+8)**, and **(2*((3*4)+9))**.

Even this almost trivial language allows us to demonstrate the basic principles of both compiler and interpreter construction, with the exception of context handling: the language just has no context to handle.

```
#include   "parser.h"     /* for type AST_node */
#include   "backend.h"    /* for Process() */
#include   "error.h"      /* for Error() */

int main(void) {
    AST_node *icode;

    if (!Parse_program(&icode)) Error("No top−level expression");
    Process(icode);

    return 0;
}
```

Fig. 1.10: Driver for the demo compiler

Figure 1.10 shows the driver of the compiler/interpreter, in C. It starts by including the definition of the syntax analyzer, to obtain the definitions of type AST_node and of the routine Parse_program(), which reads the program and constructs the AST. Next it includes the definition of the back-end, to obtain the definition of the routine Process(), for which either a code generator or an interpreter can be linked in. It then calls the front-end and, if it succeeds, the back-end.

(It should be pointed out that the condensed layout used for the program texts in the following sections is not really favored by any of the authors but is solely intended to keep each program text on a single page. Also, the #include commands for various system routines have been omitted.)

1.2.4 Lexical analysis for the demo compiler

The tokens in our language are (,), +, *, and digit. Intuitively, these are five different tokens, but actually digit consists of ten tokens, for a total of 14. Our intuition is based on the fact that the parser does not care exactly which digit it sees; so as far as the parser is concerned, all digits are one and the same token: they form a token class. On the other hand, the back-end *is* interested in exactly which digit is present in the input, so we have to preserve the digit after all. We therefore split the information about a token into two parts, the class of the token and its representation. This is reflected in the definition of the type Token_type in Figure 1.11, which has two fields, one for the class of the token and one for its representation.

```
/* Define class constants */
/* Values 0—255 are reserved for ASCII characters */
#define    EoF      256
#define    DIGIT    257

typedef struct {int class; char repr;} Token_type;

extern Token_type Token;
extern void get_next_token(void);
```

Fig. 1.11: Header file lex.h for the demo lexical analyzer

For token classes that contain only one token which is also an ASCII character (for example +), the class is the ASCII value of the character itself. The class of digits is DIGIT, which is defined in lex.h as 257, and the repr field is set to the representation of the digit. The class of the pseudo-token end-of-file is EoF, which is defined as 256; it is useful to treat the end of the file as a genuine token. These numbers over 255 are chosen to avoid collisions with any ASCII values of single characters.

The representation of a token has at least two important uses. First, it is processed in one or more phases after the parser to produce semantic information; examples are a numeric value produced from an integer token, and an identification in some form from an identifier token. Second, it is used in error messages, to display the exact form of the token. In this role the representation is useful for all tokens, not just for those that carry semantic information, since it enables any part of the compiler to produce directly the correct printable version of any token.

The representation of a token is usually a string, implemented as a pointer, but in our demo compiler all tokens are single characters, so a field of type char suffices.

The implementation of the demo lexical analyzer, as shown in Figure 1.12, defines a global variable Token and a procedure get_next_token(). A call to get_next_token() skips possible layout characters (white space) and stores the next single character as a (class, repr) pair in Token. A global variable is appropriate here, since the corresponding input file is also global. In summary, a stream of tokens can be obtained by calling get_next_token() repeatedly.

```
#include    "lex.h"          /* for self check */
                                    /* PRIVATE */
static int Is_layout_char(int ch) {
    switch (ch) {
    case ' ': case '\t': case '\n': return 1;
    default:                        return 0;
    }
}
                                    /* PUBLIC */
Token_type Token;

void get_next_token(void) {
    int ch;

    /* get a non—layout character: */
    do {
        ch = getchar();
        if (ch < 0) {
            Token.class = EoF; Token.repr = '#';
            return;
        }
    } while (Is_layout_char(ch));

    /* classify it : */
    if ('0' <= ch && ch <= '9') {Token.class = DIGIT;}
    else {Token.class = ch;}

    Token.repr = ch;
}
```

Fig. 1.12: Lexical analyzer for the demo compiler

1.2.5 Syntax analysis for the demo compiler

It is the task of syntax analysis to structure the input into an AST. The grammar in Figure 1.9 is so simple that this can be done by two simple Boolean read routines, Parse_operator() for the non-terminal operator and Parse_expression() for the non-

terminal expression. Both routines are shown in Figure 1.13 and the driver of the
parser, which contains the initial call to Parse_expression(), is in Figure 1.14.

```
static int Parse_operator(Operator *oper) {
    if (Token.class == '+') {
        *oper = '+'; get_next_token(); return 1;
    }
    if (Token.class == '*') {
        *oper = '*'; get_next_token(); return 1;
    }
    return 0;
}

static int Parse_expression(Expression **expr_p) {
    Expression *expr = *expr_p = new_expression();

    /* try to parse a digit : */
    if (Token.class == DIGIT) {
        expr->type = 'D'; expr->value = Token.repr - '0';
        get_next_token();
        return 1;
    }

    /* try to parse a parenthesized expression: */
    if (Token.class == '(') {
        expr->type = 'P';
        get_next_token();
        if (!Parse_expression(&expr->left)) {
            Error("Missing expression");
        }
        if (!Parse_operator(&expr->oper)) {
            Error("Missing operator");
        }
        if (!Parse_expression(&expr->right)) {
            Error("Missing expression");
        }
        if (Token.class != ')') {
            Error("Missing )");
        }
        get_next_token();
        return 1;
    }

    /* failed on both attempts */
    free_expression(expr); return 0;
}
```

Fig. 1.13: Parsing routines for the demo compiler

Each of the routines tries to read the syntactic construct it is named after, using
the following strategy. The routine for the non-terminal N tries to read the alter-

```
#include    <stdlib .h>
#include    "lex.h"
#include    "error .h"      /* for Error() */
#include    "parser.h"      /* for self check */

                                    /* PRIVATE */
static  Expression *new_expression(void) {
    return (Expression *)malloc(sizeof (Expression));
}
static  void free_expression(Expression *expr) {free((void *)expr);}
static  int  Parse_operator(Operator *oper_p);
static  int  Parse_expression(Expression **expr_p);

                                    /* PUBLIC */
int  Parse_program(AST_node **icode_p) {
    Expression *expr;

    get_next_token();               /* start the lexical analyzer */
    if (Parse_expression(&expr)) {
        if (Token.class != EoF) {
            Error("Garbage after end of program");
        }
        *icode_p = expr;
        return 1;
    }
    return 0;
}
```

Fig. 1.14: Parser environment for the demo compiler

natives of N in order. For each alternative A it tries to read its first member A_1. If A_1 is found present, the routine assumes that A is the correct alternative and it then requires the presence of the other members of A. This assumption is not always warranted, which is why this parsing method is quite weak. But for the grammar of Figure 1.9 the assumption holds.

If the routine succeeds in reading the syntactic construct in this way, it yields a pointer to the corresponding AST as an output parameter, and returns a 1 for success; the output parameter is implemented as a pointer to the location where the output value must be stored, a usual technique in C. If the routine fails to find the first member of any alternative of N, it does not consume any input, does not set its output parameter, and returns a 0 for failure. And if it gets stuck in the middle it stops with a syntax error message.

The C template used for a rule

$$P \rightarrow A_1 A_2 \dots A_n \mid B_1 B_2 \dots \mid \dots$$

is presented in Figure 1.15. More detailed code is required if any of A_i, B_i, ..., is a terminal symbol; see the examples in Figure 1.13. An error in the input is detected when we require a certain syntactic construct and find it is not there. We then give

an error message by calling Error() with an appropriate message; this routine does
not return and terminates the program, after displaying the message to the user.

```
int P(...) {
    /* try to parse the alternative A₁ A₂ ... Aₙ */
    if (A₁(...)) {
        if (!A₂(...)) Error("Missing A₂");
        ...
        if (!Aₙ(...)) Error("Missing Aₙ");
        return 1;
    }
    /* try to parse the alternative B₁ B₂ ... */
    if (B₁(...)) {
        if (!B₂(...)) Error("Missing B₂");
        ...
        return 1;
    }
    ...
    /* failed to find any alternative of P */
    return 0;
}
```

Fig. 1.15: A C template for the grammar rule P → $A_1 A_2 \ldots A_n | B_1 B_2 \ldots | \ldots$

This approach to parsing is called "recursive descent parsing", because a set of
routines descend recursively to construct the parse tree. It is a rather weak parsing
method and makes for inferior error diagnostics, but is, if applicable at all, very simple to implement. Much stronger parsing methods are discussed in Chapter 3, but
recursive descent is sufficient for our present needs. The recursive descent parsing
presented here is not to be confused with the much stronger *predictive* recursive
descent parsing, which is discussed amply in Section 3.4.1. The latter is an implementation of LL(1) parsing, and includes having look-ahead sets to base decisions
on.

Although in theory we should have different node types for the ASTs of different
syntactic constructs, it is more convenient to group them in broad classes and have
only one node type for each of these classes. This is one of the differences between
the parse tree, which follows the grammar faithfully, and the AST, which serves the
convenience of the compiler writer. More in particular, in our example all nodes in
an expression are of type Expression, and, since we have only expressions, that is
the only possibility for the type of AST_node. To differentiate the nodes of type
Expression, each such node contains a type attribute, set with a characteristic value:
'D' for a digit and 'P' for a parenthesized expression. The type attribute tells us how
to interpret the fields in the rest of the node. Such interpretation is needed in the
code generator and the interpreter. The header file with the definition of node type
Expression is shown in Figure 1.16.

The syntax analysis module shown in Figure 1.14 defines a single Boolean routine Parse_program() which tries to read the program as an expression by calling

```
typedef int Operator;

typedef struct _expression {
    char type;                       /* 'D' or 'P' */
    int value;                       /* for 'D' */
    struct _expression *left, *right ; /* for 'P' */
    Operator oper;                   /* for 'P' */
} Expression;

typedef Expression AST_node;         /* the top node is an Expression */

extern int Parse_program(AST_node **);
```

Fig. 1.16: Parser header file for the demo compiler

Parse_expression() and, if it succeeds, converts the pointer to the expression to a pointer to AST_node, which it subsequently yields as its output parameter. It also checks if the input is indeed finished after the expression.

Figure 1.17 shows the AST that results from parsing the expression (2*((3*4)+9)). Depending on the value of the type attribute, a node contains either a value attribute or three attributes left, oper, and right. In the diagram, the non-applicable attributes have been crossed out in each node.

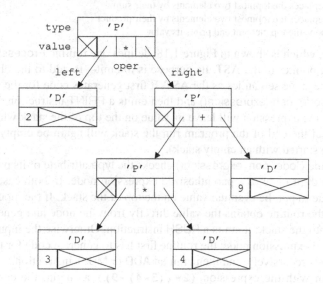

Fig. 1.17: An AST for the expression (2*((3*4)+9))

1.2.6 Context handling for the demo compiler

As mentioned before, there is no context to handle in our simple language. We could have introduced the need for some context handling in the form of a context check by allowing the logical values t and f as additional operands (for *true* and *false*) and defining + as *logical or* and * as *logical and*. The context check would then be that the operands must be either both numeric or both logical. Alternatively, we could have collected optimization information, for example by doing all arithmetic that can be done at compile time. Both would have required code that is very similar to that shown in the code generation and interpretation sections below. (Also, the optimization proposed above would have made the code generation and interpretation trivial!)

1.2.7 Code generation for the demo compiler

The code generator receives the AST (actually a pointer to it) and generates code from it for a simple stack machine. This machine has four instructions, which work on integers:

```
PUSH n   pushes the integer n onto the stack
ADD      replaces the topmost two elements by their sum
MULT     replaces the topmost two elements by their product
PRINT    pops the top element and prints its value
```

The module, which is shown in Figure 1.18, defines one routine Process() with one parameter, a pointer to the AST. Its purpose is to emit—to add to the object file—code with the same semantics as the AST. It first generates code for the expression by calling Code_gen_expression() and then emits a PRINT instruction. When run, the code for the expression will leave its value on the top of the stack where PRINT will find it; at the end of the program run the stack will again be empty (provided the machine started with an empty stack).

The routine Code_gen_expression() checks the type attribute of its parameter to see if it is a digit node or a parenthesized expression node. In both cases it has to generate code to put the eventual value on the top of the stack. If the input node is a digit node, the routine obtains the value directly from the node and generates code to push it onto the stack: it emits a PUSH instruction. Otherwise the input node is a parenthesized expression node; the routine first has to generate code for the left and right operands recursively, and then emit an ADD or MULT instruction.

When run with the expression **(2*((3*4)+9))** as input, the compiler that results from combining the above modules produces the following code:

```
#include    "parser.h"     /* for types AST_node and Expression */
#include    "backend.h"    /* for self check */
                           /* PRIVATE */
static void Code_gen_expression(Expression *expr) {
    switch (expr->type) {
    case 'D':
        printf ("PUSH %d\n", expr->value);
        break;
    case 'P':
        Code_gen_expression(expr->left);
        Code_gen_expression(expr->right);
        switch (expr->oper) {
        case '+': printf ("ADD\n"); break;
        case '*': printf ("MULT\n"); break;
        }
        break;
    }
}

                           /* PUBLIC */
void Process(AST_node *icode) {
    Code_gen_expression(icode); printf("PRINT\n");
}
```

Fig. 1.18: Code generation back-end for the demo compiler

```
PUSH 2
PUSH 3
PUSH 4
MULT
PUSH 9
ADD
MULT
PRINT
```

1.2.8 Interpretation for the demo compiler

The interpreter (see Figure 1.19) is very similar to the code generator. Both perform a depth-first scan of the AST, but where the code generator emits code to have the actions performed by a machine at a later time, the interpreter performs the actions right away. The extra set of braces ({...}) after case 'P': is needed because we need two local variables and the C language does not allow declarations in the case parts of a switch statement.

Note that the code generator code (Figure 1.18) and the interpreter code (Figure 1.19) share the same module definition file (called a "header file" in C), backend.h, shown in Figure 1.20. This is possible because they both implement the same interface: a single routine Process(AST_node *). Further on we will see an example of a different type of interpreter (Section 6.3) and two other code generators (Section

```
#include    "parser.h"      /* for types AST_node and Expression */
#include    "backend.h"     /* for self check */
                                   /* PRIVATE */
static int Interpret_expression(Expression *expr) {
    switch (expr->type) {
    case 'D':
        return expr->value;
        break;
    case 'P': {
        int e_left = Interpret_expression(expr->left);
        int e_right = Interpret_expression(expr->right);
        switch (expr->oper) {
        case '+': return e_left + e_right;
        case '*': return e_left * e_right;
        }}
        break;
    }
}
                                   /* PUBLIC */
void Process(AST_node *icode) {
    printf ("%d\n", Interpret_expression(icode));
}
```

Fig. 1.19: Interpreter back-end for the demo compiler

7.5.1), each using this same interface. Another module that implements the back-end interface meaningfully might be a module that displays the AST graphically. Each of these can be combined with the lexical and syntax modules, to produce a program processor.

```
extern void Process(AST_node *);
```

Fig. 1.20: Common back-end header for code generator and interpreter

1.3 The structure of a more realistic compiler

Figure 1.8 showed that in order to describe the demo compiler we had to decompose the front-end into three modules and that the back-end could stay as a single module. It will be clear that this is not sufficient for a real-world compiler. A more realistic picture is shown in Figure 1.21, in which front-end and back-end each consists of five modules. In addition to these, the compiler will contain modules for symbol table handling and error reporting; these modules will be called upon by almost all other modules.

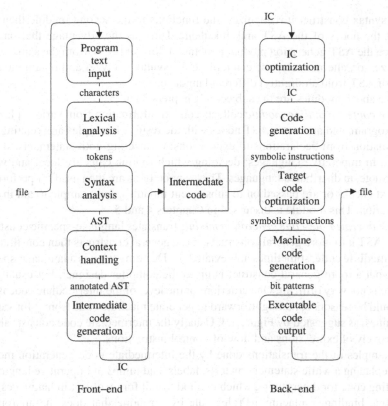

Fig. 1.21: Structure of a compiler

1.3.1 The structure

A short description of each of the modules follows, together with an indication of where the material is discussed in detail.

The *program text input module* finds the program text file, reads it efficiently, and turns it into a stream of characters, allowing for different kinds of newlines, escape codes, etc. It may also switch to other files, when these are to be included. This function may require cooperation with the operating system on the one hand and with the lexical analyzer on the other.

The *lexical analysis module* isolates tokens in the input stream and determines their class and representation. It can be written by hand or generated from a description of the tokens. Additionally, it may do some limited interpretation on some of the tokens, for example to see if an identifier is a macro identifier or a keyword (reserved word).

The *syntax analysis module* structures the stream of tokens into the corresponding abstract syntax tree (AST). Some syntax analyzers consist of two modules. The first one reads the token stream and calls a function from the second module for each syntax construct it recognizes; the functions in the second module then construct the nodes of the AST and link them. This has the advantage that one can replace the AST generation module to obtain a different AST from the same syntax analyzer, or, alternatively, one can replace the syntax analyzer and obtain the same type of AST from a (slightly) different language.

The above modules are the subject of Chapters 2 and 3.

The *context handling module* collects context information from various places in the program, and annotates AST nodes with the results. Examples are: relating type information from declarations to expressions; connecting goto statements to their labels, in imperative languages; deciding which routine calls are local and which are remote, in distributed languages. These annotations are then used for performing context checks or are passed on to subsequent modules, for example to aid in code generation. This module is discussed in Chapters 4 and 5.

The *intermediate-code generation module* translates language-specific constructs in the AST into more general constructs; these general constructs then constitute the **intermediate code**, sometimes abbreviated *IC*. Deciding what is a language-specific and what a more general construct is up to the compiler designer, but usually the choice is not very difficult. One criterion for the level of the intermediate code is that it should be reasonably straightforward to generate machine code from it for various machines, as suggested by Figure 1.4. Usually the intermediate code consists almost exclusively of expressions and flow-of-control instructions.

Examples of the translations done by the intermediate-code generation module are: replacing a while statement by tests, labels, and jumps in imperative languages; inserting code for determining which method to call for an object in languages with dynamic binding; replacing a Prolog rule by a routine that does the appropriate backtracking search. In each of these cases an alternative translation would be a call to a routine in the run-time system, with the appropriate parameters: the Prolog rule could stay in symbolic form and be interpreted by a run-time routine, a run-time routine could dynamically find the method to be called, and even the while statement could be performed by a run-time routine if the test and the body were converted to anonymous subroutines. Thus, the intermediate-code generation module is the place where the division of labor between in-line code and the run-time system is decided. This module is treated in Chapters 11 through 14, for the imperative, object-oriented, functional, logic, and parallel and distributed programming paradigms, respectively.

The *intermediate-code optimization module* performs preprocessing on the intermediate code, with the intention of improving the effectiveness of the code generation module. A straightforward example of preprocessing is constant folding, in which operations in expressions with known simple operands are performed. A more sophisticated example is in-lining, in which carefully chosen calls to some routines are replaced by the bodies of those routines, while at the same time substituting the parameters.

The *code generation module* rewrites the AST into a linear list of target machine instructions, in more or less symbolic form. To this end, it selects instructions for segments of the AST, allocates registers to hold data and arranges the instructions in the proper order.

The *target-code optimization module* considers the list of symbolic machine instructions and tries to optimize it by replacing sequences of machine instructions by faster or shorter sequences. It uses target-machine-specific properties.

The precise boundaries between intermediate-code optimization, code generation, and target-code optimization are floating: if the code generation is particularly good, little target-code optimization may be needed or even possible. Conversely, an optimization like constant folding can be done during code generation or even on the target code. Still, some optimizations fit better in one module than in another, and it is useful to distinguish the above three levels.

The *machine-code generation module* converts the symbolic machine instructions into the corresponding bit patterns. It determines machine addresses of program code and data and produces tables of constants and relocation tables.

The *executable-code output module* combines the encoded machine instructions, the constant tables, the relocation tables, and the headers, trailers, and other material required by the operating system into an executable code file. It may also apply code compression, usually for embedded or mobile systems.

The back-end modules are discussed in Chapters 6 through 9.

1.3.2 Run-time systems

There is one important component of a compiler that is traditionally left out of compiler structure pictures: the run-time system of the compiled programs. Some of the actions required by a running program will be of a general, language-dependent, and/or machine-dependent housekeeping nature; examples are code for allocating arrays, manipulating stack frames, and finding the proper method during method invocation in an object-oriented language. Although it is quite possible to generate code fragments for these actions wherever they are needed, these fragments are usually very repetitive and it is often more convenient to compile them once and store the result in library modules. These library modules together form the **run-time system**. Some imperative languages need only a minimal run-time system; others, especially the logic and distributed languages, may require run-time systems of considerable size, containing code for parameter unification, remote procedure call, task scheduling, etc. The parts of the run-time system needed by a specific program can be linked in by the linker when the complete object program is constructed, or even be linked in dynamically when the compiled program is called; object programs and linkers are explained in Chapter 8. If the back-end is an interpreter, the run-time system must be incorporated in it.

It should be pointed out that run-time systems are not only traditionally left out of compiler overview pictures like those in Figure 1.8 and Figure 1.21, they are also sometimes overlooked or underestimated in compiler construction planning. Given the fact that they may contain such beauties as printf(), malloc(), and concurrent task management, overlooking them is definitely inadvisable.

1.3.3 Short-cuts

It is by no means always necessary to implement all modules of the back-end:

*   Writing the modules for generating machine code and executable code can be avoided by using the local assembler, which is almost always available.
*   Writing the entire back-end can often be avoided by generating C code from the intermediate code. This exploits the fact that good C compilers are available on virtually any platform, which is why C is sometimes called, half jokingly, "The Machine-Independent Assembler". This is the usual approach taken by compilers for the more advanced paradigms, but it can certainly be recommended for first implementations of compilers for any new language.

The object code produced by the above "short-cuts" is often of good to excellent quality, but the increased compilation time may be a disadvantage. Most C compilers are quite substantial programs and calling them may well cost noticeable time; their availability may, however, make them worth it.

1.4 Compiler architectures

The internal architecture of compilers can differ considerably; unfortunately, terminology to describe the different types is lacking or confusing. Two architectural questions dominate the scene. One is concerned with the granularity of the data that is passed between the compiler modules: is it bits and pieces or is it the entire program? In other words, how wide is the compiler? The second concerns the flow of control between the compiler modules: which of the modules is the boss?

1.4.1 The width of the compiler

A compiler consists of a series of modules that transform, refine, and pass on information between them. Information passes mainly from the front to the end, from module M_n to module M_{n+1}. Each such consecutive pair of modules defines an interface, and although in the end all information has to pass through all these interfaces, the size of the chunks of information that are passed on makes a considerable difference to the structure of the compiler. Two reasonable choices for the size of the chunks of information are the smallest unit that is meaningful between the two modules; and the entire program. This leads to two types of compilers, neither of which seems to have a name; we will call them "narrow" and "broad" compilers, respectively.

A **narrow compiler** reads a small part of the program, typically a few tokens, processes the information obtained, produces a few bytes of object code if appropriate, discards most of the information about these tokens, and repeats this process until the end of the program text is reached.

A **broad compiler** reads the entire program and applies a series of transformations to it (lexical, syntactic, contextual, optimizing, code generating, etc.), which eventually result in the desired object code. This object code is then generally written to a file.

It will be clear that a broad compiler needs an amount of memory that is proportional to the size of the source program, which is the reason why this type has always been rather unpopular. Until the 1980s, a broad compiler was unthinkable, even in academia. A narrow compiler needs much less memory; its memory requirements are still linear in the length of the source program, but the proportionality constant is much lower since it gathers permanent information (for example about global variables) at a much slower rate.

From a theoretical, educational, and design point of view, broad compilers are preferable, since they represent a simpler model, more in line with the functional programming paradigm. A broad compiler consists of a series of function calls (Figure 1.22) whereas a narrow compiler consists of a typically imperative loop (Figure 1.23). In practice, "real" compilers are often implemented as narrow compilers. Still, a narrow compiler may compromise and have a broad component: it is quite natural for a C compiler to read each routine in the C program in its entirety, process it, and then discard all but the global information it has obtained.

```
Object code ←
    Assembly(
        CodeGeneration(
            ContextCheck(
                Parse(
                    Tokenize(
                        SourceCode
                    )
                )
            )
        )
    );
```

Fig. 1.22: Flow-of-control structure of a broad compiler

In the future we expect to see more broad compilers and fewer narrow ones. Most of the compilers for the new programming paradigms are already broad, since they often started out as interpreters. Since scarcity of memory will be less of a problem in the future, more and more imperative compilers will be broad. On the other hand, almost all compiler construction tools have been developed for the narrow model

while not Finished:
    Read some data D from the source code;
    Process D and produce the corresponding object code, if any;

Fig. 1.23: Flow-of-control structure of a narrow compiler

and thus favor it. Also, the narrow model is probably better for the task of writing a simple compiler for a simple language by hand, since it requires much less dynamic memory allocation.

Since the "field of vision" of a narrow compiler is, well, narrow, it is possible that it cannot manage all its transformations on the fly. Such compilers then write a partially transformed version of the program to disk and, often using a different program, continue with a second pass; occasionally even more passes are used. Not surprisingly, such a compiler is called a **2-pass** (or N-pass) compiler, or a **2-scan** (N-scan) compiler. If a distinction between these two terms is made, "2-scan" often indicates that the second pass actually re-reads (re-scans) the original program text, the difference being that it is now armed with information extracted during the first scan.

The major transformations performed by a compiler and shown in Figure 1.21 are sometimes called **phases**, giving rise to the term N**-phase compiler**, which is of course not the same as an N-pass compiler. Since on a very small machine each phase could very well correspond to one pass, these notions are sometimes confused.

With larger machines, better syntax analysis techniques and simpler programming language grammars, N-pass compilers with $N > 1$ are going out of fashion. It turns out that not only compilers but also people like to read their programs in one scan. This observation has led to syntactically stronger programming languages, which are correspondingly easier to process.

Many algorithms in a compiler use only local information; for these it makes little difference whether the compiler is broad or narrow. Where it does make a difference, we will show the broad method first and then explain the narrow method as an optimization, if appropriate.

1.4.2 Who's the boss?

In a broad compiler, control is not a problem: the modules run in sequence and each module has full control when it runs, both over the processor and over the data. A simple driver can activate the modules in the right order, as already shown in Figure 1.22. In a narrow compiler, things are more complicated. While pieces of data are moving forward from module to module, control has to shuttle forward and backward, to activate the proper module at the proper time. We will now examine the flow of control in narrow compilers in more detail.

The modules in a compiler are essentially "filters", reading chunks of information, processing them, and writing the result. Such filters are most easily programmed as loops which execute function calls to obtain chunks of information from the previous module and routine calls to write chunks of information to the next module. An example of a filter as a main loop is shown in Figure 1.24.

```
while ObtainedFromPreviousModule (Ch):
    if Ch = 'a':
        — See if there is another 'a':
        if ObtainedFromPreviousModule (Ch1):
            if Ch1 = 'a':
                — We have 'aa':
                OutputToNextModule ('b');
            else — Ch1 ≠ 'a':
                OutputToNextModule ('a');
                OutputToNextModule (Ch1);
        else — There were no more characters:
            OutputToNextModule ('a');
            exit;
    else — Ch ≠ 'a':
        OutputToNextModule (Ch);
```

Fig. 1.24: The filter aa → b as a main loop

It describes a simple filter which copies input characters to the output while replacing the sequence **aa** by **b**; the filter is representative of, but of course much simpler than, the kind of transformations performed by an actual compiler module. The reader may nevertheless be surprised at the complexity of the code, which is due to the requirements for the proper termination of the previous, the present, and the next module. The need for proper handling of end of input is, however, very much a fact of life in compiler construction and we cannot afford to sweep its complexities under the rug.

The filter obtains its input characters by calling upon its predecessor in the module sequence; such a call may succeed and yield a character, or it may fail. The transformed characters are passed on to the next module. Except for routine calls to the previous and the next module, control remains inside the while loop all the time, and no global variables are needed.

Although main loops are efficient, easy to program and easy to understand, they have one serious flaw which prevents them from being used as the universal programming model for compiler modules: a main loop does not interface well with another main loop in traditional programming languages. When we want to connect the main loop of Figure 1.24, which converts **aa** to **b**, to a similar one which converts **bb** to **c**, such that the output of the first becomes the input of the second, we need a transfer of control that leaves both environments intact.

The traditional function call creates a new environment for the callee and the subsequent return destroys the environment. So it cannot serve to link two main loops. A transfer of control that does possess the desired properties is the **coroutine call**, which involves having separate stacks for the two loops to preserve both environments. The coroutine mechanism also takes care of the end-of-input handling:

an attempt to obtain information from a module whose loop has terminated fails. A well-known implementation of the coroutine mechanism is the UNIX pipe, in which the two separate stacks reside in different processes and therefore in different address spaces; threads are another. (Implementation of coroutines in imperative languages is discussed in Section 11.3.8).

Although the coroutine mechanism was proposed by Conway [68] early in the history of compiler construction, the main stream programming languages used in compiler construction do not have this feature. In the absence of coroutines we have to choose one of our modules as the main loop in a narrow compiler and implement the other loops through trickery.

If we choose the **bb** → **c** filter as the main loop, it obtains the next character from the **aa** → **b** filter by calling the subroutine *ObtainedFromPreviousModule*. This means that we have to rewrite that filter as subroutine. This requires major surgery as shown by Figure 1.25, which contains our filter as a loop-less subroutine to be used before the main loop.

```
InputExhausted ← False;
CharacterStored ← False;
StoredCharacter ← Undefined;        — can never be an 'a'

function FilteredCharacter returning (a Boolean, a character):
    if InputExhausted: return (False, NoCharacter);
    else if CharacterStored:
        — It cannot be an 'a':
        CharacterStored ← False;
        return (True, StoredCharacter);
    else — not InputExhausted and not CharacterStored:
        if ObtainedFromPreviousModule (Ch):
            if Ch = 'a':
                — See if there is another 'a':
                if ObtainedFromPreviousModule (Ch1):
                    if Ch1 = 'a':
                        — We have 'aa':
                        return (True, 'b');
                    else — Ch1 ≠ 'a':
                        StoredCharacter ← Ch1;
                        CharacterStored ← True;
                        return (True, 'a');
                else — There were no more characters:
                    InputExhausted ← True;
                    return (True, 'a');
            else — Ch ≠ 'a':
                return (True, Ch);
        else — There were no more characters:
            InputExhausted ← True;
            return (False, NoCharacter);
```

Fig. 1.25: The filter aa → b as a pre-main subroutine module

We see that global variables are needed to record information that must remain available between two successive calls of the function. The variable *InputExhausted* records whether the previous call of the function returned from the position before the **exit** in Figure 1.24, and the variable *CharacterStored* records whether it returned from before outputting *Ch1*. Some additional code is required for proper end-of-input handling. Note that the code is 29 lines long as opposed to 15 for the main loop. An additional complication is that proper end-of-input handling requires that the filter be flushed by the using module when it has supplied its final chunk of information.

If we choose the **aa** → **b** filter as the main loop, similar considerations apply to the **bb** → **c** module, which must now be rewritten into a post-main loop-less subroutine module. Doing so is given as an exercise (Exercise 1.11). Figure B.1 shows that the transformation is similar to but differs in many details from that in Figure 1.25.

Looking at Figure 1.25 above and B.1 in the answers to the exercises, we see that the complication comes from having to save program state that originally resided on the stack. So it will be convenient to choose for the main loop the module that has the most state on the stack. That module will almost always be the parser; the code generator may gather more state, but it is usually stored in a global data structure rather than on the stack. This explains why we almost universally find the parser as the main module in a narrow compiler: in very simple-minded wording, the parser pulls the program text in through the lexical analyzer, and pushes the code out through the code generator.

1.5 Properties of a good compiler

The foremost property of a good compiler is of course that it generates correct code. A compiler that occasionally generates incorrect code is useless; a compiler that generates incorrect code once a year may seem useful but is dangerous.

It is also important that a compiler conform completely to the language specification. It may be tempting to implement a subset of the language, a superset or even what is sometimes sarcastically called an "extended subset", and users may even be grateful, but those same users will soon find that programs developed with such a compiler are much less portable than those written using a fully conforming compiler. (For more about the notion of "extended subset", see Exercise 1.13.)

Another property of a good compiler, one that is often overlooked, is that it should be able to handle programs of essentially arbitrary size, as far as available memory permits. It seems very reasonable to say that no sane programmer uses more than 32 parameters in a routine or more than 128 declarations in a block and that one may therefore allocate a fixed amount of space for each in the compiler. One should, however, keep in mind that programmers are not the only ones who write programs. Much software is generated by other programs, and such generated software may easily contain more than 128 declarations in one block—although more than 32 parameters to a routine seems excessive, even for a generated program; famous last words ... Especially any assumptions about limits on the number of cases in a case/switch statement are unwarranted: very large case statements are often used in the implementation of automatically generated parsers and code generators. Section 10.1.3.2 shows how the flexible memory allocation needed for handling programs of essentially arbitrary size can be achieved at an almost negligible increase in cost.

Compilation speed is an issue but not a major one. Small programs can be expected to compile in under a second on modern machines. Larger programming projects are usually organized in many relatively small subprograms, modules, library routines, etc., together called **compilation units**. Each of these compilation units can be compiled separately, and recompilation after program modification is usually restricted to the modified compilation units only. Also, compiler writers have traditionally been careful to keep their compilers "linear in the input", which means that the compilation time is a linear function of the length of the input file. This is even more important when generated programs are being compiled, since these can be of considerable length.

There are several possible sources of non-linearity in compilers. First, all linear-time parsing techniques are rather inconvenient, but the worry-free parsing techniques can be cubic in the size of the input in the worst case. Second, many code optimizations are potentially exponential in the size of the input, since often the best code can only be found by considering all possible combinations of machine instructions. Third, naive memory management can result in quadratic time consumption. Fortunately, good linear-time solutions or heuristics are available for all these problems.

Compiler size is almost never an issue anymore, with most computers having gigabytes of primary memory nowadays. Compiler size and speed are, however, of importance when programs call the compiler again at run time, as in just-in-time compilation.

The properties of good generated code are discussed in Section 7.1.

1.6 Portability and retargetability

A program is considered **portable** if it takes a limited and reasonable effort to make it run on different machine types. What constitutes "a limited and reasonable effort" is, of course, a matter of opinion, but today many programs can be ported by just editing the makefile to reflect the local situation and recompiling. And often even the task of adapting to the local situation can be automated, for example by using GNU's *autoconf*.

With compilers, machine dependence not only resides in the program itself, it resides also—perhaps even mainly—in the output. Therefore, with a compiler we have to consider a further form of machine independence: the ease with which it can be made to generate code for another machine. This is called the **retargetability** of the compiler, and must be distinguished from its **portability**. If the compiler

is written in a reasonably good style in a modern high-level language, good portability can be expected. Retargeting is achieved by replacing the entire back-end; the
retargetability is thus inversely related to the effort to create a new back-end.

In this context it is important to note that creating a new back-end does not necessarily mean writing one from scratch. Some of the code in a back-end is of course
machine-dependent, but much of it is not. If structured properly, some parts can be
reused from other back-ends and other parts can perhaps be generated from formalized machine-descriptions. This approach can reduce creating a back-end from a
major enterprise to a reasonable effort. With the proper tools, creating a back-end
for a new machine may cost between one and four programmer-months for an experienced compiler writer. Machine descriptions range in size between a few hundred
lines and many thousands of lines.

This concludes our introductory part on actually constructing a compiler. In the
remainder of this chapter we consider three further issues: the history of compiler
construction, formal grammars, and closure algorithms.

1.7 A short history of compiler construction

Three periods can be distinguished in the history of compiler construction: 1945–
1960, 1960–1975, and 1975–present. Of course, the years are approximate.

1.7.1 1945–1960: code generation

During this period programming languages developed relatively slowly and machines were idiosyncratic. The primary problem was how to generate code for a
given machine. The problem was exacerbated by the fact that assembly programming was held in high esteem, and high(er)-level languages and compilers were
looked at with a mixture of suspicion and awe: using a compiler was often called
"automatic programming". Proponents of high-level languages feared, not without
reason, that the idea of high-level programming would never catch on if compilers
produced code that was less efficient than what assembly programmers produced
by hand. The first FORTRAN compiler, written by Sheridan et al. in 1959 [260],
optimized heavily and was far ahead of its time in that respect.

1.7.2 1960–1975: parsing

The 1960s and 1970s saw a proliferation of new programming languages, and language designers began to believe that having a compiler for a new language quickly

was more important than having one that generated very efficient code. This shifted the emphasis in compiler construction from back-ends to front-ends. At the same time, studies in formal languages revealed a number of powerful techniques that could be applied profitably in front-end construction, notably in parser generation.

1.7.3 1975–present: code generation and code optimization; paradigms

From 1975 to the present, both the number of new languages proposed and the number of different machine types in regular use decreased, which reduced the need for quick-and-simple/quick-and-dirty compilers for new languages and/or machines. The greatest turmoil in language and machine design being over, people began to demand professional compilers that were reliable, efficient, both in use and in generated code, and preferably with pleasant user interfaces. This called for more attention to the quality of the generated code, which was easier now, since with the slower change in machines the expected lifetime of a code generator increased.

Also, at the same time new paradigms in programming were developed, with functional, logic, and distributed programming as the most prominent examples. Almost invariably, the run-time requirements of the corresponding languages far exceeded those of the imperative languages: automatic data allocation and dealloca-tion, list comprehensions, unification, remote procedure call, and many others, are features which require much run-time effort that corresponds to hardly any code in the program text. More and more, the emphasis shifts from "how to compile" to "what to compile to".

1.8 Grammars

Grammars, or more precisely **context-free grammars**, are the essential formalism for describing the structure of programs in a programming language. In principle the grammar of a language describes the syntactic structure only, but since the semantics of a language is defined in terms of the syntax, the grammar is also instrumental in the definition of the semantics.

There are other grammar types besides context-free grammars, but we will be mainly concerned with context-free grammars. We will also meet *regular gram-mars*, which more often go by the name of "regular expressions" and which result from a severe restriction on the context-free grammars; and *attribute grammars*, which are context-free grammars extended with parameters and code. Other types of grammars play only a marginal role in compiler construction. The term "context-free" is often abbreviated to **CF**. We will give here a brief summary of the features of CF grammars.

A "grammar" is a recipe for constructing elements of a set of strings of symbols. When applied to programming languages, the symbols are the tokens in the language, the strings of symbols are program texts, and the set of strings of symbols is the programming language. The string

BEGIN print ("Hi!") END

consists of 6 symbols (tokens) and could be an element of the set of strings of symbols generated by a programming language grammar, or in more normal words, be a program in some programming language. This cut-and-dried view of a programming language would be useless but for the fact that the strings are constructed in a structured fashion; and to this structure semantics can be attached.

1.8.1 The form of a grammar

A **grammar** consists of a set of production rules and a start symbol. Each production rule defines a named syntactic construct. A **production rule** consists of two parts, a left-hand side and a right-hand side, separated by a left-to-right arrow. The **left-hand side** is the name of the syntactic construct; the **right-hand side** shows a possible form of the syntactic construct. An example of a production rule is

expression → '(' expression operator expression ')'

The right-hand side of a production rule can contain two kinds of symbols, terminal symbols and non-terminal symbols. As the word says, a **terminal symbol** (or **terminal** for short) is an end point of the production process, and can be part of the strings produced by the grammar. A **non-terminal symbol** (or **non-terminal** for short) must occur as the left-hand side (the name) of one or more production rules, and cannot be part of the strings produced by the grammar. Terminals are also called **tokens**, especially when they are part of an input to be analyzed. Non-terminals and terminals together are called **grammar symbols**. The grammar symbols in the right-hand side of a rule are collectively called its **members**; when they occur as nodes in a syntax tree they are more often called its "children".

In discussing grammars, it is customary to use some conventions that allow the class of a symbol to be deduced from its typographical form.

* Non-terminals are denoted by capital letters, mostly A, B, C, and N.
* Terminals are denoted by lower-case letters near the end of the alphabet, mostly x, y, and z.
* Sequences of grammar symbols are denoted by Greek letters near the beginning of the alphabet, mostly α (alpha), β (beta), and γ (gamma).
* Lower-case letters near the beginning of the alphabet (a, b, c, etc.) stand for themselves, as terminals.
* The empty sequence is denoted by ε (epsilon).

1.8.2 The grammatical production process

The central data structure in the production process is the **sentential form**. It is usually described as a string of grammar symbols, and can then be thought of as representing a partially produced program text. For our purposes, however, we want to represent the syntactic structure of the program too. The syntactic structure can be added to the flat interpretation of a sentential form as a tree positioned above the sentential form so that the leaves of the tree are the grammar symbols. This combination is also called a **production tree**.

A string of terminals can be produced from a grammar by applying so-called production steps to a sentential form, as follows. The sentential form is initialized to a copy of the start symbol. Each **production step** finds a non-terminal N in the leaves of the sentential form, finds a production rule N $\rightarrow$ α with N as its left-hand side, and replaces the N in the sentential form with a tree having N as the root and the right-hand side of the production rule, α, as the leaf or leaves. When no more non-terminals can be found in the leaves of the sentential form, the production process is finished, and the leaves form a string of terminals in accordance with the grammar.

Using the conventions described above, we can write that the production process replaces the sentential form $\beta N \gamma$ by $\beta \alpha \gamma$.

The steps in the production process leading from the start symbol to a string of terminals are called the **derivation** of that string. Suppose our grammar consists of the four numbered production rules:

1. expression $\rightarrow$ '(' expression operator expression ')'
2. expression $\rightarrow$ '1'
3. operator $\rightarrow$ '+'
4. operator $\rightarrow$ '*'

in which the terminal symbols are surrounded by apostrophes and the non-terminals are identifiers, and suppose the start symbol is expression. Then the sequence of sentential forms shown in Figure 1.26 forms the derivation of the string (1*(1+1)). More in particular, it forms a **leftmost derivation**, a derivation in which it is always the leftmost non-terminal in the sentential form that is rewritten. An indication $R@P$ in the left margin in Figure 1.26 shows that grammar rule R is used to rewrite the non-terminal at position P. The resulting parse tree (in which the derivation order is no longer visible) is shown in Figure 1.27.

We see that recursion—the ability of a production rule to refer directly or indirectly to itself—is essential to the production process; without recursion, a grammar would produce only a finite set of strings.

The production process is kind enough to produce the program text together with the production tree, but then the program text is committed to a linear medium (paper, computer file) and the production tree gets stripped off in the process. Since we need the tree to find out the semantics of the program, we use a special program, called a "parser", to retrieve it. The systematic construction of parsers is treated in Chapter 3.

```
1@1   expression
2@2   '(' expression operator expression ')'
4@3   '(' '1' operator expression ')'
1@4   '(' '1' '*' expression ')'
2@5   '(' '1' '*' '(' expression operator expression ')' ')'
3@6   '(' '1' '*' '(' '1' operator expression ')' ')'
2@7   '(' '1' '*' '(' '1' '+' expression ')' ')'
      '(' '1' '*' '(' '1' '+' '1' ')' ')'
```

Fig. 1.26: Leftmost derivation of the string (1*(1+1))

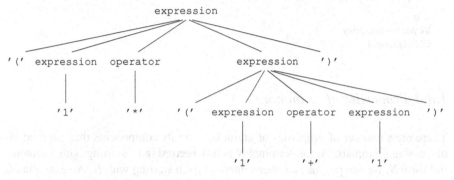

Fig. 1.27: Parse tree of the derivation in Figure 1.26

1.8.3 Extended forms of grammars

The single grammar rule format

non-terminal → zero or more grammar symbols

used above is sufficient in principle to specify any grammar, but in practice a richer notation is used. For one thing, it is usual to combine all rules with the same left-hand side into one rule: for example, the rules

N → α
N → β
N → γ

are combined into one rule

N → α | β | γ

in which the original right-hand sides are separated by vertical bars. In this form α, β, and γ are called the **alternatives** of N.

The format described so far is known as **BNF**, which may be considered an abbreviation of **Backus–Naur Form** or of **Backus Normal Form**. It is very suitable for expressing nesting and recursion, but less convenient for expressing repetition and optionality, although it can of course express repetition through recursion. To remedy this, three additional notations are introduced, each in the form of a postfix operator:

- R^+ indicates the occurrence of one or more Rs, to express repetition;
- $R^?$ indicates the occurrence of zero or one Rs, to express optionality; and
- R^* indicates the occurrence of zero or more Rs, to express optional repetition.

Parentheses may be needed if these postfix operators are to operate on more than one grammar symbol. The grammar notation that allows the above forms is called **EBNF**, for **Extended BNF**. An example is the grammar rule

parameter_list → ('IN' | 'OUT')$^?$ identifier (',' identifier)*

which produces program fragments like

a, b
IN year, month, day
OUT left, right

1.8.4 Properties of grammars

There are a number of properties of grammars and its components that are used in discussing grammars. A non-terminal N is **left-recursive** if, starting with a sentential form N, we can produce another sentential form starting with N. An example of direct left-recursion is

expression → expression '+' factor | factor

but we will meet other forms of left-recursion in Section 3.4.3. By extension, a grammar that contains one or more left-recursive rules is itself called left-recursive. **Right-recursion** also exists, but is less important.

A non-terminal N is **nullable** if, starting with a sentential form N, we can produce an empty sentential form ε. A grammar rule for a nullable non-terminal is called an ε-**rule**. Note that nullability need not be directly visible from the ε-rule.

A non-terminal N is **useless** if it can never produce a string of terminal symbols: any attempt to do so inevitably leads to a sentential that again contains N. A simple example is

expression → '+' expression | '−' expression

but less obvious examples can easily be constructed. Theoretically, useless non-terminals can just be ignored, but in real-world specifications they almost certainly signal a mistake on the part of the user; in the above example, it is likely that a third alternative, perhaps | factor, has been omitted. Grammar-processing software should check for useless non-terminals, and reject the grammar if they are present.

A grammar is **ambiguous** if it can produce two different production trees with the same leaves in the same order. That means that when we lose the production tree due to linearization of the program text we cannot reconstruct it unambiguously; and since the semantics derives from the production tree, we lose the semantics as well. So ambiguous grammars are to be avoided in the specification of programming languages, where attached semantics plays an important role.

1.8.5 The grammar formalism

Thoughts, ideas, definitions, and theorems about grammars are often expressed in a mathematical formalism. Some familiarity with this formalism is indispensable in reading books and articles about compiler construction, which is why we will briefly introduce it here. Much, much more can be found in any book on formal languages, for which see the Further Reading section of this chapter.

1.8.5.1 The definition of a grammar

The basic unit in formal grammars is the **symbol**. The only property of these symbols is that we can take two of them and compare them to see if they are the same. In this they are comparable to the values of an enumeration type. Like these, symbols are written as identifiers, or, in mathematical texts, as single letters, possibly with subscripts. Examples of symbols are N, x, procedure_body, assignment_symbol, t_k.

The next building unit of formal grammars is the *production rule*. Given two sets of symbols V_1 and V_2, a production rule is a pair

(N, α) such that $N \in V_1, \alpha \in V_2^*$

in which X^* means a sequence of zero or more elements of the set X. This means that a production rule is a pair consisting of an N which is an element of V_1 and a sequence α of elements of V_2. We call N the left-hand side and α the right-hand side. We do not normally write this as a pair (N, α) but rather as $N \rightarrow \alpha$; but technically it is a pair. The V in V_1 and V_2 stands for **vocabulary**.

Now we have the building units needed to define a grammar. A **context-free grammar** G is a 4-tuple

$G = (V_N, V_T, S, P)$

in which V_N and V_T are sets of symbols, S is a symbol, and P is a set of production rules. The elements of V_N are called the **non-terminal symbols**, those of V_T the **terminal symbols**, and S is called the **start symbol**. In programmer's terminology this means that a grammar is a record with four fields: the non-terminals, the terminals, the start symbol, and the production rules.

The previous paragraph defines only the *context-free* form of a grammar. To make it a real, acceptable grammar, it has to fulfill three **context conditions**:

(1) $V_N \cap V_T = \emptyset$

in which $\emptyset$ denotes the empty set and which means that V_N and V_T are not allowed to have symbols in common: we must be able to tell terminals and non-terminals apart;

(2) $S \in V_N$

which means that the start symbol must be a non-terminal; and

(3) $P \subseteq \{(N, \alpha) \mid N \in V_N, \alpha \in (V_N \cup V_T)^*\}$

which means that the left-hand side of each production rule must be a non-terminal and that the right-hand side may consist of both terminals and non-terminals but is not allowed to include any other symbols.

1.8.5.2 Definition of the language generated by a grammar

Sequences of symbols are called **strings**. A string may be derivable from another string in a grammar; more in particular, a string β is **directly derivable from** a string α, written as $\alpha \Rightarrow \beta$, if and only if there exist strings γ, δ_1, δ_2, and a non-terminal $N \in V_N$, such that

$$\alpha = \delta_1 N \delta_2, \quad \beta = \delta_1 \gamma \delta_2, \quad (N, \gamma) \in P$$

This means that if we have a string and we replace a non-terminal N in it by its right-hand side γ in a production rule, we get a string that is directly derivable from it. This replacement is called a **production step**. Of course, "replacement" is an imperative notion whereas the above definition is purely functional.

A string β is **derivable from** a string α, written as $\alpha \overset{*}{\Rightarrow} \beta$, if and only if $\alpha = \beta$ or there exists a string γ such that $\alpha \overset{*}{\Rightarrow} \gamma$ and $\gamma \Rightarrow \beta$. This means that a string is derivable from another string if we can reach the second string from the first through zero or more production steps.

A **sentential form** of a grammar G is defined as

$$\alpha \mid S \overset{*}{\Rightarrow} \alpha$$

which is any string that is derivable from the start symbol S of G. Note that α may be the empty string.

A **terminal production** of a grammar G is defined as a sentential form that does not contain non-terminals:

$$\alpha \mid S \overset{*}{\Rightarrow} \alpha \wedge \alpha \in V_T^*$$

which denotes a string derivable from S which is in V_T^*, the set of all strings that consist of terminal symbols only. Again, α may be the empty string.

The **language** $\mathscr{L}$ **generated by a grammar** G is defined as

$$\mathscr{L}(G) = \{\alpha \mid S \overset{*}{\Rightarrow} \alpha \wedge \alpha \in V_T^*\}$$

which is the set of all terminal productions of G. These terminal productions are called **sentences** in the language $\mathscr{L}(G)$. Terminal productions are the main *raison d'être* of grammars: if G is a grammar for a programming language, then $\mathscr{L}(G)$ is the set of all programs in that language that are correct in a context-free sense. This is because terminal symbols have another property in addition to their identity: they have a representation that can be typed, printed, etc. For example the representation of the assignment_symbol could be := or =, that of integer_type_symbol could be int, etc. By replacing all terminal symbols in a sentence by their representations and possibly mixing in some blank space and comments, we obtain a program. It is usually considered unsociable to have a terminal symbol that has an empty representation; it is only slightly less objectionable to have two different terminal symbols that share the same representation.

Since we are, in this book, more concerned with an intuitive understanding than with formal proofs, we will use this formalism sparingly or not at all.

1.9 Closure algorithms

Quite a number of algorithms in compiler construction start off by collecting some basic information items and then apply a set of rules to extend the information and/or draw conclusions from them. These "information-improving" algorithms share a common structure which does not show up well when the algorithms are treated in isolation; this makes them look more different than they really are. We will therefore treat here a simple representative of this class of algorithms, the construction of the calling graph of a program, and refer back to it from the following chapters.

1.9.1 A sample problem

The **calling graph** of a program is a directed graph which has a node for each routine (procedure or function) in the program and an arrow from node A to node B if routine A calls routine B directly or indirectly. Such a graph is useful to find out, for example, which routines are recursive and which routines can be expanded in-line inside other routines. Figure 1.28 shows the sample program in C, for which we will construct the calling graph; the diagram shows the procedure headings and the procedure calls only.

```
void P(void) {  ...  Q();  ...  S();  ...  }
void Q(void) {  ...  R();  ...  T();  ...  }
void R(void) {  ...  P();  }
void S(void) {  ...  }
void T(void) {  ...  }
```

Fig. 1.28: Sample C program used in the construction of a calling graph

When the calling graph is first constructed from the program text, it contains only the arrows for the direct calls, the calls to routine B that occur directly in the body of routine A; these are our basic information items. (We do not consider here calls of anonymous routines, routines passed as parameters, etc.; such calls can be handled too, but their problems have nothing to do with the algorithm being discussed here.)

The initial calling graph of the code in Figure 1.28 is given in Figure 1.29, and derives directly from that code.

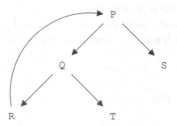

Fig. 1.29: Initial (direct) calling graph of the code in Figure 1.28

The initial calling graph is, however, of little immediate use since we are mainly interested in which routine calls which other routine directly or indirectly. For example, recursion may involve call chains from A to B to C back to A. To find these additional information items, we apply the following rule to the graph:

If there is an arrow from node A to node B and one from B to C,
make sure there is an arrow from A to C.

If we consider this rule as an algorithm (which it is not yet), this set-up computes the **transitive closure** of the relation "calls directly or indirectly". The transitivity axiom of the relation can be written as:

$$A \subseteq B \wedge B \subseteq C \rightarrow A \subseteq C$$

in which the operator $\subseteq$ should be read as "calls directly or indirectly". Now the statements "routine A is recursive" and "$A \subseteq A$" are equivalent.

The resulting calling graph of the code in Figure 1.28 is shown in Figure 1.30. We see that the recursion of the routines P, Q, and R has been brought into the open.

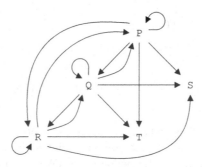

Fig. 1.30: Calling graph of the code in Figure 1.28

1.9.2 The components of a closure algorithm

In its general form, a **closure algorithm** exhibits the following three elements:

- Data definitions— definitions and semantics of the information items; these derive from the nature of the problem.
- Initializations— one or more rules for the initialization of the information items; these convert information from the specific problem into information items.
- Inference rules— one or more rules of the form: "If information items $I_1, I_2, \ldots$ are present then information item J must also be present". These rules may again refer to specific information from the problem at hand.

The rules are called **inference rules** because they tell us to infer the presence of information item J from the presence of information items $I_1, I_2, \ldots$. When all inferences have been drawn and all inferred information items have been added, we have obtained the closure of the initial item set. If we have specified our closure algorithm correctly, the final set contains the answers we are looking for. For example, if there is an arrow from node A to node A, routine A is recursive, and otherwise it is not. Depending on circumstances, we can also check for special, exceptional, or erroneous situations. Figure 1.31 shows recursion detection by calling graph analysis written in this format.

Data definitions:
   1. G, a directed graph with one node for each routine. The information items are arrows in G.
   2. An arrow from a node A to a node B means that routine A calls routine B directly or indirectly.

Initializations:
   If the body of a routine A contains a call to routine B, an arrow from A to B must be present.

Inference rules:
   If there is an arrow from node A to node B and one from B to C, an arrow from A to C must be present.

Fig. 1.31: Recursion detection as a closure algorithm

Two things must be noted about this format. The first is that it does specify which information items *must* be present but it does not specify which information items *must not* be present; nothing in the above prevents us from adding arbitrary information items. To remedy this, we add the requirement that we do not want any information items that are not required by any of the rules: we want the smallest set of information items that fulfills the rules in the closure algorithm. This constellation is called the **least fixed point** of the closure algorithm.

The second is that the closure algorithm as introduced above is not really an algorithm in that it does not specify when and how to apply the inference rules and when to stop; it is rather a declarative, Prolog-like specification of the requirements that follow from the problem, and "closure specification" would be a more proper term. Actually, it does not even correspond to an acceptable Prolog program: the Prolog program in Figure 1.32 gets into an infinite loop immediately.

```
calls (A, C) :− calls (A, B), calls (B, C).
calls (a, b).
calls (b, a).
:−? calls (a, a).
```

Fig. 1.32: A Prolog program corresponding to the closure algorithm of Figure 1.31

What we need is an implementation that will not miss any inferred information items, will not add any unnecessary information items, and will not get into an infinite loop. The most convenient implementation uses an iterative bottom-up algorithm and is treated below.

General closure algorithms may have inference rules of the form "If information items $I_1, I_2, \ldots$ are present then information item J must also be present", as explained above. If the inference rules are restricted to the form "If information items (A,B) and (B,C) are present then information item (A,C) must also be present", the algorithm is called a **transitive closure algorithm**. On the other hand, it is often useful to extend the possibilities for the inference rules and to allow them also to specify the replacement or removal of information items. The result is no longer a proper closure algorithm, but rather an arbitrary recursive function of the initial set, which may or may not have a fixed point. When operations like replacement and removal are allowed, it is quite easy to specify contradictions; an obvious example is "If A is present, A must not be present". Still, when handled properly such extended closure algorithms allow some information handling to be specified very efficiently. An example is the closure algorithm in Figure 3.23.

1.9.3 An iterative implementation of the closure algorithm

The usual way of implementing a closure algorithm is by repeated bottom-up sweep. In this approach, the information items are visited in some systematic fashion to find sets of items that fulfill a condition of an inference rule. When such a set is found, the corresponding inferred item is added, if it was not already there. Adding items may fulfill other conditions again, so we have to repeat the bottom-up sweeps until there are no more changes.

The exact order of investigation of items and conditions depends very much on the data structures and the inference rules. There is no generic closure algorithm in which the inference rules can be plugged in to obtain a specific closure algorithm; programmer ingenuity is still required. Figure 1.33 shows code for a bottom-up implementation of the transitive closure algorithm.

SomethingWasChanged ← True;

while SomethingWasChanged:
    SomethingWasChanged ← False;

    for each $Node_1$ **in** Graph:
        for each $Node_2$ **in** descendants of $Node_1$:
            for each $Node_3$ **in** descendants of $Node_2$:
                if there is no arrow from $Node_1$ to $Node_3$:
                    Add an arrow from $Node_1$ to $Node_3$;
                    SomethingWasChanged ← True;

Fig. 1.33: Outline of a bottom-up algorithm for transitive closure

A sweep consists of finding the nodes of the graph one by one, and for each node adding an arrow from it to all its descendants' descendants, as far as these are known at the moment. It is important to recognize the restriction "as far as the arrows are known at the moment" since this is what forces us to repeat the sweep until we find a sweep in which no more arrows are added. We are then sure that the descendants we know are all the descendants there are.

The algorithm seems quite inefficient. If the graph contains n nodes, the body of the outermost for-loop is repeated n times; each node can have at most n descendants, so the body of the second for-loop can be repeated n times, and the same applies to the third for-loop. Together this is $O(n^3)$ in the worst case. Each run of the while-loop adds at least one arc (except the last run), and since there are at most n^2 arcs to be added, it could in principle be repeated n^2 times in the worst case. So the total time complexity would seem to be $O(n^5)$, which is much too high to be used in a compiler.

There are, however, two effects that save the iterative bottom-up closure algorithm. The first is that the above worst cases cannot materialize all at the same time. For example, if all nodes have all other nodes for descendants, all arcs are already present and the algorithm finishes in one round. There is a well-known algorithm by Warshall [292] which does transitive closure in $O(n^3)$ time and $O(n^2)$ space, with very low multiplication constants for both time and space. Unfortunately it has the disadvantage that it *always* uses this $O(n^3)$ time and $O(n^2)$ space, and $O(n^3)$ time is still rather stiff in a compiler.

The second effect is that the graphs to which the closure algorithm is applied are usually sparse, which means that almost all nodes have only a few outgoing arcs. Also, long chains of arcs are usually rare. This changes the picture of the complexity of the algorithm completely. Let us say for example that the average fan-out of a routine is f, which means that a routine calls on average f other routines; and that the average calling depth is d, which means that on the average after d calls within calls we reach either a routine that does not call other routines or we get involved in recursion. Under these assumptions, the while-loop will be repeated on the average d times, since after d turns all required arcs will have been added. The outermost for-loop will still be repeated n times, but the second and third loops will be repeated

f times during the first turn of the while-loop, f^2 times during the second turn, f^3 times during the third turn, and so on, until the last turn, which takes f^d times. So on average the if-statement will be executed

$$n \times (f^2 + f^4 + f^6 + \ldots f^{2d}) = \frac{f^{2(d+1)} - f^2}{f^2 - 1} \times n$$

times. Although the constant factor can be considerable —for $f = 4$ and $d = 4$ it is almost 70 000— the main point is that the time complexity is now linear in the number of nodes, which suggests that the algorithm may be practical after all. This is borne out by experience, and by many measurements [270]. For non-sparse graphs, however, the time complexity of the bottom-up transitive closure algorithm is still $O(n^3)$.

In summary, although transitive closure has non-linear complexity in the general case, for sparse graphs the bottom-up algorithm is almost linear.

1.10 The code forms used in this book

Three kinds of code are presented in this book: sample input to the compiler, sample implementations of parts of the compiler, and outline code. We have seen an example of compiler input in the `3`, `(5+8)`, and `(2*((3*4)+9))` on page 13. Such text is presented in a `constant-width` computer font; the same font is used for the occasional textual output of a program.

Examples of compiler parts can be found in the many figures in Section 1.2 on the demo compiler. They are presented in a sans serif font.

In addition to being explained in words and by examples, the outline of an algorithm is sometimes sketched in an *outline code*; we have already seen an example in Figure 1.33. Outline code is shown in the same font as the main text of this book; segments of outline code in the running text are distinguished by presenting them in *italic*.

The outline code is an informal, reasonably high-level language. It has the advantage that it allows ignoring much of the problematic details that beset many real-world programming languages, including memory allocation and deallocation, type conversion, and declaration before use. We have chosen not to use an existing programming language, for several reasons:

- We emphasize the ideas behind the algorithms rather than their specific implementation, since we believe the ideas will serve for a longer period and will allow the compiler designer to make modifications more readily than a specific implementation would. This is not a cookbook for compiler construction, and supplying specific code might suggest that compilers can be constructed by copying code fragments from books.
- We do not want to be drawn into a C versus C++ versus Java versus other languages discussion. We emphasize ideas and principles, and we find each of these languages pretty unsuitable for high-level idea expression.

- Real-world code is much less intuitively readable, mainly due to historical syntax and memory allocation problems.

The rules of the outline code are not very fixed, but the following notes may help in reading the code.

Lines can end in a semicolon (;), which signals a command, or in a colon (:), which signals a control structure heading. The body of a control structure is indented by some white space with respect to its heading. The end of a control structure is evident from a return to a previous indentation level or from the end of the code segment; so there is no explicit **end** line.

The format of identifiers follows that of many modern programming languages. They start with a capital letter, and repeat the capital for each following word: *EndOfLine*. The same applies to selectors, except that the first letter is lower case: *RoadToNowhere.leftFork*.

A command can, among other things, be an English-language command starting with a verb; an example from Figure 1.33 is

    Add an arrow from Node$_1$ to Node$_3$;

Other possibilities are procedure calls, and the usual control structures: **if**, **while**, **return**, etc.

Long lines may be broken for reasons of page width; the continuation line or lines are indented by more white space. Broken lines can be recognized by the fact that they do not end in a colon or semicolon.

Comments start at -- and run to the end of the line.

1.11 Conclusion

This concludes our introduction to compiler writing. We have seen a toy interpreter and compiler that already show many of the features of a real compiler. A discussion of the general properties of compilers was followed by an introduction to context-free grammars and closure algorithms. Finally, the outline code used in this book was introduced. As in the other chapters, a summary, suggestions for further reading, and exercises follow.

Summary

- A compiler is a big file conversion program. The input format is called the source language, the output format is called the target language, and the language it is written in is the implementation language.
- One wants this file conversion because the result is in some sense more useful, like in any other conversion. Usually the target code can be run efficiently, on hardware.

- Target code need not be low-level, as in assembly code. Many compilers for high- and very high-level languages generate target code in C or C++.
- Target code need not be run on hardware, it can also be interpreted by an interpreter; in that case the conversion from source to target can be much simpler.
- Compilers can compile newer versions of themselves; this is called bootstrapping.
- Compiling works by first analyzing the source text to construct a semantic representation, and then synthesizing target code from this semantic representation. This analysis/synthesis paradigm is very powerful, and is also useful outside compiler construction.
- The usual form of the semantic representation is the AST, abstract syntax tree, which is the syntax tree of the input, with useful context and semantic annotations at the nodes.
- Large parts of compilers are generated automatically, using program generators written in special-purpose programming languages. These "tiny" languages are often based on formalisms; important formalisms are regular and context-free grammars (for program text analysis), attribute grammars (for context handling), and bottom-up tree rewriting systems (for code generation).
- The source code input consists of characters. Lexical analysis constructs tokens from the characters. Syntax analysis constructs a syntax tree from the tokens. Context handling checks and annotates the syntax tree. Code generation constructs target code from the annotated syntax tree. Usually the target code needs the support of a run-time system.
- Broad compilers have the entire AST at their disposal all the time; narrow compilers make do with the path from the node under consideration upwards to the top of the AST, plus information collected about the branches on the left of that path.
- The driving loop of a narrow compiler is usually inside the parser: it pulls tokens out of the lexical analyzer and pushes parse tree nodes to the code generator.
- A good compiler generates correct, truthful code, conforms exactly to the source language standard, is able to handle programs of virtually arbitrary size, and contains no quadratic or worse algorithms.
- A compiler that can easily be run on different platforms is portable; a compiler that can easily produce target code for different platforms is retargetable.
- Target code optimizations are attractive and useful, but dangerous. First make it correct, then make it fast.
- Over the years, emphasis in compiler construction has shifted from how to compile it to what to compile it into. Most of the how-to problems have been solved by automatic generation from formalisms.
- Context-free grammars and parsing allow us to recover the structure of the source program; this structure was lost when its text was linearized in the process of committing it to paper or text file.
- Many important algorithms in compiler construction are closure algorithms: information is propagated in a graph to collect more information, until no more

new information can be obtained at any node. The algorithms differ in what information is collected and how.

Further reading

The most famous compiler construction book ever is doubtlessly *Compilers: Principles, Techniques and Tools*, better known as "The Red Dragon Book" by Aho, Sethi and Ullman [4]; a second edition, by Aho, Lam, Sethi and Ullman [6], has appeared, and extends the Red Dragon book with many optimizations. There are few books that also treat compilers for programs in other paradigms than the imperative one. For a code-oriented treatment we mention Appel [18] and for a more formal treatment the four volumes by Wilhelm, Seidl and Hack [113, 300–302]. Srikant and Shankar's *Compiler Design Handbook* [264] provides insight in a gamut of advanced compiler design subjects, while the theoretical, formal basis of compiler design is presented by Meduna [189].

New developments in compiler construction are reported in journals, for example *ACM Transactions on Programming Languages and Systems*, *Software—Practice and Experience*, *ACM SIGPLAN Notices*, *Computer Languages*, and the more theoretical *Acta Informatica*; in the proceedings of conferences, for example *ACM SIGPLAN Conference on Programming Language Design and Implementation—PLDI*, *Conference on Object-Oriented Programming Systems, Languages and Applications—OOPSLA*, and *IEEE International Conference on Computer Languages—ICCL*; and in some editions of "Lecture Notes in Computer Science", more in particular the *Compiler Construction International Conference* and *Implementation of Functional Languages*.

Interpreters are the second-class citizens of the compiler construction world: everybody employs them, but hardly any author pays serious attention to them. There are a few exceptions, though. Griswold and Griswold [111] is the only textbook dedicated solely to interpreter construction, and a good one at that. Pagan [209] shows how thin the line between interpreters and compilers is.

The standard work on grammars and formal languages is still Hopcroft and Ullman [124]. A relatively easy introduction to the subject is provided by Linz [180]; a modern book with more scope and more mathematical rigor is by Sudkamp [269]. The most readable book on the subject is probably that by Révész [234].

Much has been written about transitive closure algorithms. Some interesting papers are by Feijs and van Ommering [99], Nuutila [206], Schnorr [254], Purdom Jr. [226], and Warshall [292]. Schnorr presents a sophisticated but still reasonably simple version of the iterative bottom-up algorithm shown in Section 1.9.3 and proves that its expected time requirement is linear in the sum of the number of nodes and the final number of edges. Warshall's algorithm is very famous and is treated in any text book on algorithms, for example Sedgewick [257] or Baase and Van Gelder [23].

The future of compiler research is discussed by Hall *et al.* [115] and Bates [33].

Exercises

1.1. (▷785) Compilers are often written in the language they implement. Identify advantages and disadvantages of this technique.

1.2. (▷www) Referring to Section 1.1.1.1, give additional examples of why a language front-end would need information about the target machine and why a back-end would need information about the source language.

1.3. Redo the demo compiler from Section 1.2 in your favorite programming language. Compare it to the version in this book.

1.4. Given the following incomplete grammar for a very simple segment of English:

```
Sentence   →  Subject Verb Object
Subject   →  Noun_Phrase
Object   →  Noun_Phrase
Noun_Phrase   →  Noun_Compound | Personal_Name | Personal_Pronoun
Noun_Compound   →  Article? Adjective_Sequence? Noun
...
```

(a) What is the parse tree for the sentence I see you, in which I and you are terminal productions of Personal_Pronoun and see is a terminal production of Verb?
(b) What would be a sensible AST for this parse tree?

1.5. Consider the demo compiler from Section 1.2. One property of a good compiler is that it is able to give good error messages, and good error messages require, at least, knowledge of the name of the input file and the line number in this file where an error occurred. Adapt the lexical analyzer from Section 1.2.4 to record these data in the nodes and use them to improve the quality of the error reporting.

1.6. (▷www) Implement the constant folding optimization discussed in Section 1.2.6: do all arithmetic at compile time.

1.7. (▷www) One module that is missing from Figure 1.21 is the error reporting module. Which of the modules shown would use the error reporting module and why?

1.8. Modify the code generator of Figure 1.18 to generate code in a language you are comfortable with –rather than PUSH, ADD, MULT and PRINT instructions– and compile and run that code.

1.9. (▷785) Where is the context that must be remembered between each cycle of the while loop in Figure 1.23 and the next?

1.10. Is the compiler implemented in Section 1.2 a narrow or a broad compiler?

1.11. (▷785) Construct the post-main version of the main-loop module in Figure 1.24.

1.12. For those who already know what a finite-state automaton (FSA) is: rewrite the pre-main and post-main versions of the aa → b filter using an FSA. You will notice that now the code is simpler: an FSA is a more efficient but less structured device for the storage of state than a set of global variables.

1.13. (▷785) What is an "extended subset" of a language? Why is the term usually used in a pejorative sense?

1.14. (▷www) The grammar for expression in Section 1.2.1 has:

expression → expression '+' term | expression '–' term | term

If we replaced this by

expression → expression '+' expression | expression '–' expression | term

the grammar would still produce the same language, but the replacement is not correct. What is wrong?

1.15. (▷www) Rewrite the EBNF rule

parameter_list → ('IN' | 'OUT')$^?$ identifier (',' identifier)*

from Section 1.8.3 to BNF.

1.16. (▷www) Given the grammar:

S → A | B | C
A → B | ε
B → x | C y
C → B C S

in which S is the start symbol.
(a) Name the non-terminals that are left-recursive, right-recursive, nullable, or useless, if any.
(b) What language does the grammar produce?
(c) Is the grammar ambiguous?

1.17. (▷www) Why could one want two or more terminal symbols with the same representation? Give an example.

1.18. (▷www) Why would it be considered bad design to have a terminal symbol with an empty representation?

1.19. (▷785) Refer to Section 1.8.5.1 on the definition of a grammar, condition (1). Why do we have to be able to tell terminals and non-terminals apart?

1.20. (▷785) Argue that there is only one "smallest set of information items" that fulfills the requirements of a closure specification.

1.21. *History of compiler construction*: Study Conway's 1963 paper [68] on the coroutine-based modularization of compilers, and write a summary of it.

Part I
From Program Text
to Abstract Syntax Tree

Chapter 2
Program Text to Tokens — Lexical Analysis

The front-end of a compiler starts with a stream of characters which constitute the program text, and is expected to create from it intermediate code that allows context handling and translation into target code. It does this by first recovering the syntactic structure of the program by parsing the program text according to the grammar of the language. Since the meaning of the program is defined in terms of its syntactic structure, possessing this structure allows the front-end to generate the corresponding intermediate code.

For example, suppose a language has constant definitions of the form

CONST pi = 3.14159265;
CONST pi_squared = pi * pi;

and that the grammar for such constant definitions is:

constant_definition → 'CONST' identifier '=' expression ';'

Here the apostrophes (") demarcate terminal symbols that appear unmodified in the program, and identifier and expression are non-terminals which refer to grammar rules supplied elsewhere.

The semantics of the constant definition could then be: "The occurrence of the constant definition in a block means that the expression in it is evaluated to give a value V and that the identifier in it will represent that value V in the rest of the block." (The actual wording will depend on the context of the given language.)

The syntactic analysis of the program text results in a syntax tree, which contains nodes representing the syntactic structures. Since the desired semantics is defined based on those nodes, it is reasonable to choose some form of the syntax tree as the intermediate code.

In practice, the actual syntax tree contains too many dead or uninteresting branches and a cleaned up version of it, the abstract syntax tree or AST, is more efficient. The difference between the two is pragmatic rather than fundamental, and the details depend on the good taste and design skills of the compiler writer. Consider the (oversimplified) grammar rule for expression in Figure 2.1. Then the actual syntax tree for

CONST pi_squared = pi * pi;

is

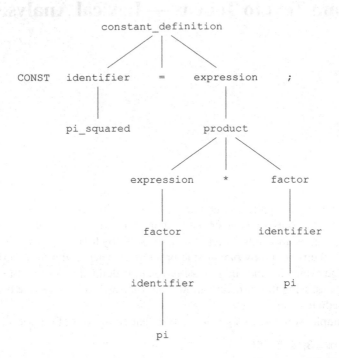

as specified by the grammar, and a possible abstract syntax tree could be:

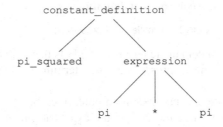

expression → product | factor
product → expression '*' factor
factor → number | identifier

Fig. 2.1: A very simple grammar for expression

The simplifications are possible because

1. the tokens 'CONST', '=', and ';' serve only to alert the reader and the parser to the presence of the constant definition, and do not have to be retained for further processing;

2. the semantics of identifier (in two different cases), expression, and factor are trivial (just passing on the value) and need not be recorded.

This means that nodes for constant_definition can be implemented in the compiler as records with two fields:

```
struct constant_definition {
    Identifier *CD_idf;
    Expression *CD_expr;
}
```

(in addition to some standard fields recording in which file and at what line the constant definition was found).

Another example of a useful difference between parse tree and AST is the combination of the node types for if-then-else and if-then into one node type if-then-else. An if-then node is represented by an if-then-else node, in which the else part has been supplemented as an empty statement, as shown in Figure 2.2.

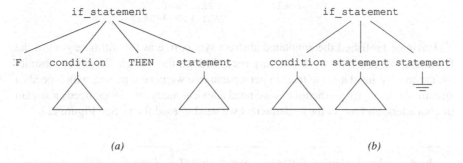

(a)   (b)

Fig. 2.2: Syntax tree (a) and abstract syntax tree (b) of an if-then statement

Noonan [205] gives a set of heuristic rules for deriving a good AST structure from a grammar. For an even more compact internal representation of the program than ASTs see Waddle [290].

The context handling module gathers information about the nodes and combines it with that of other nodes. This information serves to perform contextual checking and to assist in code generation. The abstract syntax tree adorned with these bits of information is called the *annotated abstract syntax tree*. Actually the abstract syntax tree passes through many stages of "annotatedness" during compilation. The degree of annotatedness starts out at almost zero, straight from parsing, and continues to grow even through code generation, in which, for example, actual memory addresses may be attached as annotations to nodes.

At the end of the context handling phase our AST might have the form

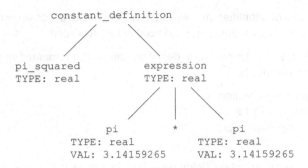

and after constant folding—the process of evaluating constant expressions in the
compiler rather than at run time—it might be

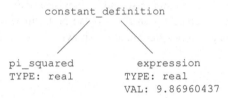

Having established the annotated abstract syntax tree as the ultimate goal of the
front-end, we can now work our way back through the design. To get an abstract
syntax tree we need a parse tree; to get a parse tree we need a parser, which needs a
stream of tokens; to get the tokens we need a lexical analyzer, which needs a stream
of characters, and to get these characters we need to read them. See Figure 2.3.

Fig. 2.3: Pipeline from input to annotated syntax tree

Some compiler systems come with a so-called structure editor and a program
management system which stores the programs in parsed form. It would seem that
such systems can do without much of the machinery described in this chapter, but
if they allow unstructured program text to be imported or allow such modifications
to the existing text that parts of it have to be reanalyzed from the character level on,
they still need the full apparatus.

The form of the tokens to be recognized by lexical analyzers is almost always
specified by "regular expressions" or "regular descriptions"; these are discussed in
Section 2.3. Taking these regular expressions as input, the lexical analyzers themselves can be written by hand, or, often more conveniently, generated automatically,
as explained in Sections 2.5 through 2.9. The applicability of lexical analyzers can
be increased considerably by allowing them to do a limited amount of symbol handling, as shown in Sections 2.10 through 2.12.

2.1 Reading the program text

The program reading module and the lexical analyzer are the only components of a compiler that get to see the entire program text. As a result, they do a lot of work in spite of their simplicity, and it is not unusual for 30% of the time spent in the front-end to be actually spent in the reading module and lexical analyzer. This is less surprising when we realize that the average line in a program may be some 30 to 50 characters long and may contain perhaps no more than 3 to 5 tokens. It is not uncommon for the number of items to be handled to be reduced by a factor of 10 between the input to the reading module and the input to the parser. We will therefore start by paying some attention to the reading process; we shall also focus on efficiency more in the input module and the lexical analyzer than elsewhere in the compiler.

2.1.1 Obtaining and storing the text

Program text consists of characters, but the use of the standard character-reading routines provided by the implementation language is often inadvisable: since these routines are intended for general purposes, it is likely that they are slower than necessary, and on some systems they may not even produce an exact copy of the characters the file contains. Older compilers featured buffering techniques, to speed up reading of the program file and to conserve memory at the same time. On modern machines the recommended method is to read the entire file with one system call. This is usually the fastest input method and obtaining the required amount of memory should not be a problem: modern machines have many megabytes of memory and even generated program files are seldom that large. Also, most operating systems allow the user to obtain the size of a file, so memory can be allocated completely before reading the file.

   In addition to speed, there is a second advantage to having the entire file in memory: it makes it easier to manage tokens of variable size. Examples of such tokens are identifiers, strings, numbers, and perhaps comments. Many of these need to be stored for further use by the compiler and allocating space for them is much easier if their sizes are known in advance. Suppose, for example, that a string is read using a routine that yields characters one by one. In this set-up, the incoming characters have to be stored in some temporary buffer until the end of the string is found; the size of this buffer is not known in advance. Only after the end of the string has been read can the final allocation of space for the string take place; and once we have the final destination we still have to copy the characters there. This may lead to complicated allocation techniques, or alternatively the compiler writer is tempted to impose arbitrary limits on the largest allowable string length; it also costs processing time for the copying operation.

With the entire file in memory, however, one can just note the position of the first string character, find the end, calculate the size, allocate space, and copy it. Or, if the input file stays in memory throughout the entire compilation, one could represent the string by a pointer to the first character and its length, thus avoiding all allocation and copying. Keeping the entire program text in memory has the additional advantage that error messages can easily show the precise code around the place of the problem.

2.1.2 The troublesome newline

There is some disagreement as to whether "newline" is a character or not, and if it is, what it looks like. Trivial as the question may seem, it can be a continuous source of background bother in writing and using the compiler. Several facts add to the confusion. First, each operating system has its own convention. In UNIX, the newline *is* a character, with the value of octal 12. In MS-DOS the newline is a combination of *two* characters, with values octal 15 and 12, in that order; the meaning of the reverse order and that of the characters in isolation is undefined. And in OS-370 the newline is not a character at all: a text file consists of lines called "logical records" and reading it produces a series of data structures, each containing a single line. Second, in those systems that seem to have a newline character, it is actually rather an end-of-line character, in that it does not occur at the beginning of the first line, but does occur at the end of the last line. Again, what happens when the last line is not terminated properly by a "newline character" is undefined. Last but not least, some people have strong opinions on the question, not all of them in agreement with the actual or the desired situation.

Probably the sanest attitude to this confusion is to convert the input to a fixed internal format as soon as possible. This keeps the operating-system-dependent part of the compiler to a minimum; some implementation languages already provide library routines that do this. The internal format must allow easy lexical analysis, for normal processing, and easy reproduction of the original program text, for error reporting. A convenient format is a single character array in which the lines are stored consecutively, each terminated by a newline character. But when the text file format of the operating system differs too much from this, such an array may be expensive to construct.

2.2 Lexical versus syntactic analysis

Having both a lexical and a syntax analysis requires one to decide where the border between the two lies. Lexical analysis produces tokens and syntax analysis consumes them, but what exactly is a token? Part of the answer comes from the language definition and part of it is design. A good guideline is "If it can be separated from its left and right neighbors by white space without changing the meaning, it's a token; otherwise it isn't." If white space is allowed between the colon and the equals sign in :=, it is two tokens, and each has to appear as a separate token in the grammar. If they have to stand next to each other, with nothing intervening, it is one token, and only one token occurs in the grammar. This does not mean that tokens cannot include white space: strings can, and they are tokens by the above rule, since adding white space in a string changes its meaning. Note that the quotes that demarcate the string are not tokens, since they cannot be separated from their neighboring characters by white space without changing the meaning.

Comments and white space are not tokens in that the syntax analyzer does not consume them. They are generally discarded by the lexical analyzer, but it is often useful to preserve them, to be able to show some program text surrounding an error.

From a pure need-to-know point of view, all the lexical analyzer has to supply in the struct Token are the class and repr fields as shown in Figure 1.11, but in practice it is very much worthwhile to also record the name of the file, line number, and character position in which the token was found (or actually where it started). Such information is invaluable for giving user-friendly error messages, which may surface much later on in the compiler, when the actual program text may be long discarded from memory.

2.3 Regular expressions and regular descriptions

The shapes of the tokens of a language may be described informally in the language manual, for example: "An identifier is a sequence of letters, digits, and underscores that starts with a letter; no two consecutive underscores are allowed in it, nor can it have a trailing underscore." Such a description is quite satisfactory for the user of the language, but for compiler construction purposes the shapes of the tokens are more usefully expressed in what are called "regular expressions". Regular expressions are well known from their use as search expressions in text editors, where for example the search expression ab* is used to find a text segment that consists of an a followed by zero or more bs.

A **regular expression** is a formula that describes a possibly infinite set of strings. Like a grammar, it can be viewed both as a recipe for generating these strings and as a pattern to match these strings. The above regular expression ab*, for example, generates the infinite set { a ab abb abbb ... }. When we have a string that can be generated by a given regular expression, we say that the regular expression **matches** the string.

Basic pattern	Matching string
x	The character x
.	Any character, usually except a newline
$[xyz\ldots]$	Any of the characters $x, y, z, \ldots$
Repetition operators:	
$R^?$	An R or nothing (= optionally an R)
R^*	Zero or more occurrences of R
R^+	One or more occurrences of R
Composition operators:	
$R_1\,R_2$	An R_1 followed by an R_2
$R_1	R_2$	Either an R_1 or an R_2
Grouping:	
(R)	R itself

Fig. 2.4: Components of regular expressions

The most basic regular expression is a pattern that matches just one character, and the simplest of these is the one that specifies that character explicitly; an example is the pattern a which matches the character a. There are two more basic patterns, one for matching a set of characters and one for matching all characters (usually with the exception of the end-of-line character, if it exists). These three basic patterns appear at the top of Figure 2.4. In this figure, $x, y, z, \ldots$ stand for any character and $R, R_1, R_2, \ldots$ stand for any regular expression.

A basic pattern can optionally be followed by a **repetition operator**; examples are b$^?$ for an optional b; b* for a possibly empty sequence of bs; and b$^+$ for a non-empty sequence of bs.

There are two **composition operators**. One is the invisible operator, which indicates concatenation; it occurs for example between the a and the b in ab*. The second is the | operator which separates alternatives; for example, ab*|cd$^?$ matches anything that is matched by ab* or alternatively by cd$^?$.

The repetition operators have the highest precedence (bind most tightly); next comes the concatenation operator; and the alternatives operator | has the lowest precedence. Parentheses can be used for grouping. For example, the regular expression ab*|cd$^?$ is equivalent to (a(b*))|(c(d$^?$)).

A more extensive set of operators might for example include a repetition operator of the form $Rm - n$, which stands for m to n repetitions of R, but such forms have limited usefulness and complicate the implementation of the lexical analyzer considerably.

2.3.1 Regular expressions and BNF/EBNF

A comparison with the right-hand sides of production rules in CF grammars suggests itself. We see that only the basic patterns are characteristic of regular expressions. Regular expressions share with the BNF notation the invisible concatenation operator and the alternatives operator, and with EBNF the repetition operators and parentheses.

2.3.2 Escape characters in regular expressions

The superscript operators *, +, and ? do not occur in widely available character set and on keyboards, so for computer input the characters *, +, ? are often used. This has the unfortunate consequence that these characters cannot be used to match themselves as actual characters. The same applies to the characters |, [,], (, and), which are used directly by the regular expression syntax. There is usually some trickery involving **escape characters** to force these characters to stand for themselves rather than being taken as operators or separators One example of such an escape character is the backslash, \, which is used as a prefix: * denotes the asterisk, \\ the backslash character itself, etc. Another is the quote, ", which is used to surround the escaped part: "*" denotes the asterisk, "+?" denotes a plus followed by a question mark, """" denotes the quote character itself, etc. As we can see, additional trickery is needed to represent the escape character itself.

It might have been more esthetically satisfying if the escape characters had been used to endow the normal characters *, +, ?, etc., with a special meaning rather than vice versa, but this is not the path that history has taken and the present situation presents no serious problems.

2.3.3 Regular descriptions

Regular expressions can easily become complicated and hard to understand; a more convenient alternative is the so-called regular description. A **regular description** is like a context-free grammar in EBNF, with the restriction that no non-terminal can be used before it has been fully defined.

As a result of this restriction, we can substitute the right-hand side of the first rule (which obviously cannot contain non-terminals) in the second and further rules, adding pairs of parentheses where needed to obey the precedences of the repetition operators. Now the right-hand side of the second rule will no longer contain non-terminals and can be substituted in the third and further rules, and so on; this technique, which is also used elsewhere, is called **forward substitution**, for obvious reasons. The last rule combines all the information of the previous rules and its right-hand side corresponds to the desired regular expression.

The regular description for the identifier defined at the beginning of this section is:

```
letter  →  [a–zA–Z]
digit  →  [0–9]
underscore  →  '_'
letter_or_digit  →  letter | digit
underscored_tail  →  underscore letter_or_digit+
identifier  →  letter letter_or_digit* underscored_tail*
```

It is relatively easy to see that this implements the restrictions about the use of the underscore: no two consecutive underscores and no trailing underscore.

The substitution process described above combines this into

identifier → [a–zA–Z] ([a–zA–Z] | [0–9])* (_ ([a–zA–Z] | [0–9])$^+$)*

which, after some simplification, reduces to:

identifier → [a–zA–Z][a–zA–Z0–9]*(_[a–zA–Z0–9]$^+$)*

The right-hand side is the regular expression for identifier. This is a clear case of conciseness versus readability.

2.4 Lexical analysis

Each token class of the source language is specified by a regular expression or regular description. Some tokens have a fixed shape and correspond to a simple regular expression; examples are :, :=, and =/=. Keywords also fall in this class, but are usually handled by a later lexical identification phase; this phase is discussed in Section 2.10. Other tokens can occur in many shapes and correspond to more complicated regular expressions; examples are identifiers and numbers. Strings and comments also fall in this class, but again they often require special treatment. The combination of token class name and regular expression is called a **token description**. An example is

```
assignment_symbol  →  :=
```

The basic task of a lexical analyzer is, given a set S of token descriptions and a position P in the input stream, to determine which of the regular expressions in S will match a segment of the input starting at P and what that segment is.

If there is more than one such segment, the lexical analyzer must have a disambiguating rule; normally the longest segment is the one we want. This is reasonable: if S contains the regular expressions =, =/, and =/=, and the input is **=/=**, we want the full **=/=** matched. This rule is known as the **maximal-munch** rule.

If the longest segment is matched by more than one regular expression in S, again tie-breaking is needed and we must assign priorities to the token descriptions in S. Since S is a set, this is somewhat awkward, and it is usual to rely on the textual order in which the token descriptions are supplied: the token that has been defined textually first in the token description file wins. To use this facility, the compiler writer has to specify the more specific token descriptions before the less specific ones: if any letter sequence is an identifier except xyzzy, then the following will do the job:

```
magic_symbol  →  xyzzy
identifier  →  [a–z]⁺
```

_____ **Roadmap** _____

2.5 Creating a lexical analyzer by hand

Lexical analyzers can be written by hand or generated automatically, in both cases based on the specification of the tokens through regular expressions; the required techniques are treated in this and the following section, respectively. Generated lexical analyzers in particular require large tables and it is profitable to consider methods to compress these tables (Section 2.7). Next, we discuss input error handling in lexical analyzers. An example of the use of a traditional lexical analyzer generator concludes the sections on the creation of lexical analyzers.

It is relatively easy to write a lexical analyzer by hand. Probably the best way is to start it with a case statement over the first character of the input. The first characters of the different tokens are often different, and such a case statement will split the analysis problem into many smaller problems, each of which can be solved with a few lines of ad hoc code. Such lexical analyzers can be quite efficient, but still require a lot of work, and may be difficult to modify.

Figures 2.5 through 2.12 contain the elements of a simple but non-trivial lexical analyzer that recognizes five classes of tokens: identifiers as defined above, integers, one-character tokens, and the token classes ERRONEOUS and EoF. As one-character tokens we accept the operators +, –, *, and /, and the separators ;, ,(comma), (,), {, and }, as an indication of what might be used in an actual programming language. We skip layout characters and comment; comment starts with a sharp character # and ends either at another # or at end of line. Single characters in the input not covered by any of the above are recognized as tokens of class ERRONEOUS. An alternative action would be to discard such characters with a warning or error message, but since it is likely that they represent some typing error for an actual token, it is probably better to pass them on to the parser to show that there was something there. Finally, since most parsers want to see an explicit end-of-file token, the pseudo-character end-of-input yields the real token of class EoF for end-of-file.

```
/* Define class constants; 0–255 reserved for ASCII characters: */
#define EoF           256
#define IDENTIFIER    257
#define INTEGER       258
#define ERRONEOUS     259

typedef struct {
    char *file_name;
    int line_number;
    int char_number;
} Position_in_File ;

typedef struct {
    int class;
    char *repr;
    Position_in_File pos;
} Token_Type;

extern Token_Type Token;

extern void start_lex (void);
extern void get_next_token(void);
```

Fig. 2.5: Header file lex.h of the handwritten lexical analyzer

Figure 2.5 shows that the Token_Type has been extended with a field for recording the position in the input at which the token starts; it also includes the definitions of the class constants. The lexical analyzer driver, shown in Figure 2.6, consists of declarations of local data to manage the input, a global declaration of Token, and the routines start_lex(), which starts the machine, and get_next_token(), which scans the input to obtain the next token and put its data in Token.

After skipping layout and comment, the routine get_next_token() (Figure 2.7) records the position of the token to be identified in the field Token.pos by calling note_token_position(); the code for this routine is not shown here. Next, get_next_token() takes a five-way split based on the present input character, a copy of which is stored in input_char. Three cases are treated on the spot; two more complicated cases are referred to routines. Finally, get_next_token() converts the chunk of the input which forms the token into a zero-terminated string by calling input_to_zstring() (not shown) and stores the result as the representation of the token. Creating a representation for the EoF token is slightly different since there is no corresponding chunk of input.

Figures 2.8 through 2.10 show the routines for skipping layout and recognizing identifiers and integers. Their main task is to move the variable dot just

```
#include    "input.h"         /* for get_input() */
#include    "lex.h"

/* PRIVATE */
static char *input;
static int dot;               /* dot position in input */
static int input_char;        /* character at dot position */

#define next_char()           (input_char = input[++dot])

/* PUBLIC */
Token_Type Token;

void start_lex (void) {
    input = get_input ();
    dot = 0; input_char = input[dot];
}
```

Fig. 2.6: Data and start-up of the handwritten lexical analyzer

```
void get_next_token(void) {
    int start_dot;

    skip_layout_and_comment();
    /* now we are at the start of a token or at end-of-file, so: */
    note_token_position();

    /* split on first character of the token */
    start_dot = dot;
    if (is_end_of_input(input_char)) {
        Token.class = EoF; Token.repr = "<EoF>"; return;
    }
    if ( is_letter (input_char)) { recognize_identifier ();}
    else
    if ( is_digit (input_char)) {recognize_integer ();}
    else
    if (is_operator(input_char) || is_separator(input_char)) {
        Token.class = input_char; next_char();
    }
    else {Token.class = ERRONEOUS; next_char();}

    Token.repr = input_to_zstring (start_dot, dot-start_dot);
}
```

Fig. 2.7: Main reading routine of the handwritten lexical analyzer

```
void skip_layout_and_comment(void) {
    while (is_layout(input_char)) {next_char();}
    while (is_comment_starter(input_char)) {
        next_char();
        while (!is_comment_stopper(input_char)) {
            if (is_end_of_input(input_char)) return;
            next_char();
        }
        next_char();
        while (is_layout(input_char)) {next_char();}
    }
}
```

Fig. 2.8: Skipping layout and comment in the handwritten lexical analyzer

```
void recognize_identifier (void) {
    Token.class = IDENTIFIER; next_char();

    while ( is_letter_or_digit (input_char)) {next_char();}

    while (is_underscore(input_char) && is_letter_or_digit (input[dot+1])) {
        next_char();
        while ( is_letter_or_digit (input_char)) {next_char();}
    }
}
```

Fig. 2.9: Recognizing an identifier in the handwritten lexical analyzer

past the end of the form they recognize. In addition, recognize_identifier() and recognize_integer() set the attribute Token.class.

```
void recognize_integer(void) {
    Token.class = INTEGER; next_char();
    while ( is_digit (input_char)) {next_char();}
}
```

Fig. 2.10: Recognizing an integer in the handwritten lexical analyzer

The routine get_next_token() and its subroutines frequently test the present input character to see whether it belongs to a certain class; examples are calls of is_letter(input_char) and is_digit(input_char). The routines used for this are defined as macros and are shown in Figure 2.11.

As an example of its use, Figure 2.12 shows a simple main program that calls get_next_token() repeatedly in a loop and prints the information found in Token. The loop terminates when a token with class EoF has been encountered and processed. Given the input #*# 8; ##abc__dd_8;zz_#/ it prints the results shown in Figure 2.13.

```
#define is_end_of_input(ch)       ((ch) == '\0')
#define is_layout(ch)             (!is_end_of_input(ch) && (ch) <= ' ')
#define is_comment_starter(ch) ((ch) == '#')
#define is_comment_stopper(ch) ((ch) == '#' || (ch) == '\n')

#define is_uc_letter(ch)          ('A' <= (ch) && (ch) <= 'Z')
#define is_lc_letter(ch)          ('a' <= (ch) && (ch) <= 'z')
#define is_letter(ch)             (is_uc_letter(ch) || is_lc_letter(ch))
#define is_digit(ch)              ('0' <= (ch) && (ch) <= '9')
#define is_letter_or_digit(ch)    (is_letter(ch) || is_digit(ch))
#define is_underscore(ch)         ((ch) == '_')

#define is_operator(ch)           (strchr("+-*/", (ch)) != 0)
#define is_separator(ch)          (strchr(" ;,(){} ", (ch)) != 0)
```

Fig. 2.11: Character classification in the handwritten lexical analyzer

```
#include    "lex.h"       /* for start_lex (), get_next_token() */

int main(void) {
    start_lex ();

    do {
        get_next_token();
        switch (Token.class) {
        case IDENTIFIER:   printf (" Identifier "); break;
        case INTEGER:      printf ("Integer"); break;
        case ERRONEOUS: printf("Erroneous token"); break;
        case EoF:          printf ("End-of-file pseudo-token"); break;
        default:           printf ("Operator or separator"); break;
        }
        printf (": %s\n", Token.repr);
    } while (Token.class != EoF);
    return 0;
}
```

Fig. 2.12: Driver for the handwritten lexical analyzer

```
Integer: 8
Operator or separator: ;
Identifier: abc
Erroneous token: _
Erroneous token: _
Identifier: dd_8
Operator or separator: ;
Identifier: zz
Erroneous token: _
End-of-file pseudo-token: <EoF>
```

Fig. 2.13: Sample results of the hand-written lexical analyzer

2.5.1 Optimization by precomputation

We see that often questions of the type is_letter(ch) are asked. These questions have the property that their input parameters are from a finite set and their result depends on the parameters only. This means that for given input parameters the answer will be the same every time. If the finite set defined by the parameters is small enough, we can compute all the answers in advance, store them in an array and replace the routine and macro calls by simple array indexing. This technique is called **precomputation** and the gains in speed achieved with it can be considerable. Often a special tool (program) is used which performs the precomputation and creates a new program containing the array and the replacements for the routine calls. Precomputation is closely linked to the use of program generation tools.

Precomputation can be applied not only in handwritten lexical analyzers but everywhere the conditions for its use are fulfilled. We will see several other examples in this book. It is especially appropriate here, in one of the places in a compiler where speed matters: roughly estimated, a program line contains perhaps 30 to 50 characters, and each of them has to be classified by the lexical analyzer.

Precomputation for character classification is almost trivial; most programmers do not even think of it as precomputation. Yet it exhibits some properties that are representative of the more serious applications of precomputation used elsewhere in compilers. One characteristic is that naive precomputation yields very large tables, which can then be compressed either by exploiting their structure or by more general means. We will see examples of both.

2.5.1.1 Naive precomputation

The input parameter to each of the macros of Figure 2.11 is an 8-bit character, which can have at most 256 values, and the outcome of the macro is one bit. This suggests representing the table of answers as an array A of 256 1-bit elements, in which element A[ch] contains the result for parameter ch. However, few languages offer 1-bit arrays, and if they do, accessing the elements on a byte-oriented machine is slow. So we decide to sacrifice 7×256 bits and allocate an array of 256 bytes for the answers. Figure 2.14 shows the relevant part of a naive table implementation of is_operator(), assuming that the ASCII character set is used. The answers are collected in the table is_operator_bit[]; the first 42 positions contain zeroes, then we get some ones in the proper ASCII positions and 208 more zeroes fill up the array to the full 256 positions. We could have relied on the C compiler to fill out the rest of the array, but it is neater to have them there explicitly, in case the language designer decides that (position 126) or ≥ (position 242 in some character codes) is an operator too. Similar arrays exist for the other 11 character classifying macros.

Another small complication arises from the fact that the ANSI C standard leaves it undefined whether the range of a char is 0 to 255 (unsigned char) or -128 to 127 (signed char). Since we want to use the input characters as indexes into arrays, we have to make sure the range is 0 to 255. Forcibly extracting the rightmost 8 bits by

```
#define is_operator(ch)          (is_operator_bit [(ch)&0377])

static const char is_operator_bit[256] = {
    0,                  /* position 0 */
    0, 0, ...           /* another 41 zeroes */
    1,                  /* '*', position 42 */
    1,                  /* '+' */
    0,
    1,                  /* '−' */
    0,
    1,                  /* '/', position 47 */
    0, 0, ...           /* 208 more zeroes */
};
```

Fig. 2.14: A naive table implementation of is_operator()

ANDing with the octal number 0377—which reads 11111111 in binary—solves the problem, at the expense of one more operation, as shown in Figure 2.14.

This technique is usually called **table lookup**, which is somewhat misleading since the term seems to suggest a process of looking through a table that may cost an amount of time linear in the size of the table. But since the table lookup is implemented by array indexing, its cost is constant, like that of the latter.

In C, the ctype package provides similar functions for the most usual subsets of the characters, but one cannot expect it to provide tests for sets like { '+' '−' '*' '/' }. One will have to create one's own, to match the requirements of the source language.

There are 12 character classifying macros in Figure 2.11, each occupying 256 bytes, totaling 3072 bytes. Now 3 kilobytes is not a problem in a compiler, but in other compiler construction applications naive tables are closer to 3 megabytes, 3 gigabytes or even 3 terabytes [90], and table compression is usually essential. We will show that even in this simple case we can easily compress the tables by more than a factor of ten.

2.5.1.2 Compressing the tables

We notice that the leftmost 7 bits of each byte in the arrays are always zero, and the idea suggests itself to use these bits to store outcomes of some of the other functions. The proper bit for a function can then be extracted by ANDing with a mask in which one bit is set to 1 at the proper bit position. Since there are 12 functions, we need 12 bit positions, or, rounded upwards, 2 bytes for each parameter value. This reduces the memory requirements to 512 bytes, a gain of a factor of 6, at the expense of one bitwise AND instruction.

If we go through the macros in Figure 2.14, however, we also notice that three macros test for one character only: is_end_of_input(), is_comment_starter(), and is_underscore(). Replacing the simple comparison performed by these macros by a table lookup would not bring in any gain, so these three macros are better left unchanged. This means they do not need a bit position in the table entries. Two macros define their classes as combinations of existing character classes: is_letter() and is_letter_or_digit(). These can be implemented by combining the masks for these existing classes, so we do not need separate bits for them either. In total we need only 7 bits per entry, which fits comfortably in one byte. A representative part of the implementation is shown in Figure 2.15. The memory requirements are now a single array of 256 bytes, charbits[].

```
#define UC_LETTER_MASK (1<<1) /* a 1 bit, shifted left 1 pos. */
#define LC_LETTER_MASK (1<<2) /* a 1 bit, shifted left 2 pos. */
#define OPERATOR_MASK (1<<5)

#define LETTER_MASK      (UC_LETTER_MASK | LC_LETTER_MASK)

#define bits_of(ch)          (charbits [( ch)&0377])

#define is_end_of_input(ch) ((ch) == '\0')

#define is_uc_letter(ch)    (bits_of(ch) & UC_LETTER_MASK)
#define is_lc_letter (ch)   (bits_of(ch) & LC_LETTER_MASK)
#define is_letter (ch)      (bits_of(ch) & LETTER_MASK)
#define is_operator(ch)     (bits_of(ch) & OPERATOR_MASK)

static const char charbits[256] = {
    0000,       /* position 0 */
    ...
    0040,       /* '*', position 42 */
    0040,       /* '+' */
    ...
    0000,       /* position 64 */
    0002,       /* 'A' */
    0002,       /* 'B' */

    0000,       /* position 96 */
    0004,       /* 'a' */
    0004,       /* 'b' */
    ...
    0000        /* position 255 */
};
```

Fig. 2.15: Efficient classification of characters (excerpt)

This technique exploits the particular structure of the arrays and their use; in Section 2.7 we will see a general compression technique. They both reduce the memory requirements enormously at the expense of a small loss in speed.

2.6 Creating a lexical analyzer automatically

The previous sections discussed techniques for writing a lexical analyzer by hand. An alternative method to obtain a lexical analyzer is to have it generated automatically from regular descriptions of the tokens. This approach creates lexical analyzers that are fast and easy to modify. We will consider the pertinent techniques in detail, first because automatically generated lexical analyzers are interesting and important in themselves and second because the techniques involved will be used again in syntax analysis and code generation.

A naive way to determine the longest matching token in the input is to try the regular expressions one by one, in textual order; when a regular expression matches the input, we note the token class and the length of the match, replacing shorter matches by longer ones as they are found. This gives us the textually first token among those that have the longest match. An outline of the code for n token descriptions is given in Figure 2.16; it is similar to that for a handwritten lexical analyzer. This process has two disadvantages: it is linearly dependent on the number of token classes, and it requires restarting the search process for each regular expression.

We will now develop an algorithm which does not require restarting and the speed of which does not depend on the number of token classes. For this, we first describe a peculiar implementation of the naive search, which still requires restarting. Then we show how to perform this search in parallel for all token classes while stepping through the input; the time required will still be proportional to the number of token classes, but restarting is not necessary: each character is viewed only once. Finally we will show that the results of the steps can be precomputed for every possible input character (but not for unbounded sequences of them!) so that the computations that depended on the number of token classes can be replaced by a table lookup. This eliminates the dependency on the number of token classes and improves the efficiency enormously.

(Token.class, Token.length) ← (0, 0); — Token is a global variable

— Try to match token description $T_1 \rightarrow R_1$:
for each Length **such that** the input matches $T_1 \rightarrow R_1$ over Length:
    if Length > Token.length:
        (Token.class, Token.length) ← (T_1, Length);

— Try to match token description $T_2 \rightarrow R_2$:
for each Length **such that** the input matches $T_2 \rightarrow R_2$ over Length:
    if Length > Token.length:
        (Token.class, Token.length) ← (T_2, Length);

...

for each Length **such that** the input matches $T_n \rightarrow R_n$ over Length:
    if Length > Token.length:
        (Token.class, Token.length) ← (T_n, Length);

if Token.length = 0:
    HandleNonMatchingCharacter();

Fig. 2.16: Outline of a naive generated lexical analyzer

2.6.1 Dotted items

Imagine we stop the attempt to match the input to a given token description before
it has either succeeded or failed. When we then study it, we see that we are dealing
with four components: the part of the input that has already been matched, the part
of the regular expression that has matched it, the part of the regular expression that
must still find a match, and the rest of the input which will hopefully provide that
match. A schematic view is shown in Figure 2.17.

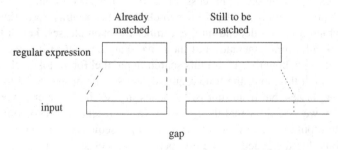

Fig. 2.17: Components of a token description and components of the input

The traditional and very convenient way to use these components is as follows.
The two parts of the regular expression are recombined into the original token description, with the gap marked by a dot •. Such a dotted token description has the
form

$$T \to \alpha\bullet\beta$$

and is called a **dotted item**, or an **item** for short. The dotted item is then viewed as positioned between the matched part of the input and the rest of the input, as shown schematically in Figure 2.18.

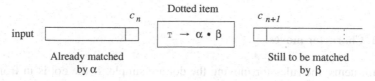

Fig. 2.18: The relation between a dotted item and the input

When attempting to match a given token description, the lexical analyzer constructs sets of dotted items between each consecutive pair of input characters. The presence of a dotted item $T \to \alpha\bullet\beta$ between two input characters c_n and c_{n+1} means that at this position the part α has already been matched by the characters between the start of the token and c_n, and that if part β is matched by a segment of the input starting with c_{n+1}, a token of class T will have been recognized. The dotted item at a given position represents a "hypothesis" about the presence of a token T in the input.

An item with the dot in front of a basic pattern is called a **shift item**, one with the dot at the end a **reduce item**; together they are called **basic items**. A non-basic item has the dot in front of a regular subexpression that corresponds to a repetition operator or a parenthesized subexpression.

What makes the dotted items extremely useful is that the item between c_n and c_{n+1} can be computed from the one between c_{n-1} and c_n, on the basis of c_n. The result of this computation can be zero, one or more than one item— in short, a set of items. So lexical analyzers record sets of items between the input characters.

Starting with a known item set at the beginning of the input and repeating the computation for each next character in the input, we obtain successive sets of items to be positioned between the characters of the input. When during this process we construct a reduce item, an item with the dot at the end, the corresponding token has been recognized in the input. This does not mean that the correct token has been found, since a longer token may still be ahead. So the recognition process must continue until all hypotheses have been refuted and there are no more items left in the item set. Then the token most recently recognized is the longest token. If there is more than one longest token, a tie-breaking rule is invoked; as we have seen, the code in Figure 2.16 implements the rule that the first among the longest tokens prevails.

This algorithm requires us to have a way of creating the initial item set and to compute a new item set from the previous one and an input character. Creating the initial item set is easy: since nothing has been recognized yet, it consists of the token description of the token we are hunting for, with the dot placed before the regular expression: $R \rightarrow \bullet\alpha$. We will now turn to the rules for computing a new item from a previous one and an input character. Since the old item is conceptually stored on the left of the input character and the new item on the right (as shown in Figure 2.18), the computation is usually called "moving the item over a character". Note that the regular expression in the item does not change in this process, only the dot in it moves.

2.6.1.1 Character moves

For shift items, the rules for moving the dot are simple. If the dot is in front of a character c and if the input has c at the next position, the item is transported to the other side and the dot is moved accordingly:

$$\boxed{\text{T} \rightarrow \alpha \bullet c \ \beta} \quad c \quad \Longrightarrow \quad c \quad \boxed{\text{T} \rightarrow \alpha \ c \bullet \beta}$$

And if the character after the dot and the character in the input are not equal, the item is not transported over the character at all: the hypothesis it contained is rejected. The character set pattern $[abc...]$ is treated similarly, except that it can match any one of the characters in the pattern.

If the dot in an item is in front of the basic pattern ., the item is always moved over the next character and the dot is moved accordingly, since the pattern . matches any character.

Since these rules involve moving items over characters, they are called **character moves**. Note that for example in the item $\text{T} \rightarrow \bullet a^*$, the dot is not in front of a basic pattern. It seems to be in front of the a, but that is an illusion: the a is enclosed in the scope of the repetition operator * and the item is actually $\text{T} \rightarrow \bullet(a^*)$.

2.6.1.2 ε-moves

A non-basic item cannot be moved directly over a character since there is no character set to test the input character against. The item must first be processed ("developed") until only basic items remain. The rules for this processing require us to indicate very precisely where the dot is located, and it becomes necessary to put parentheses around each part of the regular expression that is controlled by an operator.

An item in which the dot is in front of an operator-controlled pattern has to be replaced by one or more other items that express the meaning of the operator. The rules for this replacement are easy to determine. Suppose the dot is in front of an expression R followed by a star:

(1) : $T \rightarrow \alpha\bullet(R)^*\beta$

The star means that R may occur zero or more times in the input. So the item actually represents two items, one in which R is not present in the input, and one in which there is at least one R. The first has the form

(2) : $T \rightarrow \alpha(R)^* \bullet \beta$

and the second one:

(3) : $T \rightarrow \alpha(\bullet R)^* \beta$

Note that the parentheses are essential to express the difference between item (1) and item (3). Note also that the regular expression itself is not changed, only the position of the dot in it is.

When the dot in item (3) has finally moved to the end of R, there are again two possibilities: either this was the last occurrence of R or there is another one coming; therefore, the item

(4) : $T \rightarrow \alpha(R\bullet)^* \beta$

must be replaced by two items, (2) and (3).

When the dot has been moved to another place, it may of course end up in front of another non-basic pattern, in which case the process has to be repeated until there are only basic items left.

Figure 2.19 shows the rules for the operators from Figure 2.4. In analogy to the character moves which move items over characters, these rules can be viewed as moving items over the empty string. Since the empty string is represented as ε (epsilon), they are called ε-**moves**.

2.6.1.3 A sample run

To demonstrate the technique, we need a simpler example than the identifier used above. We assume that there are two token classes, integral_number and fixed_point_number. They are described by the regular expressions shown in Figure 2.20. If regular descriptions are provided as input to the lexical analyzer, these must first be converted to regular expressions. Note that the decimal point has been put between apostrophes, to prevent its interpretation as the basic pattern for "any character". The second definition says that fixed-point numbers need not start with a digit, but that at least one digit must follow the decimal point.

We now try to recognize the input **3.1;** using the regular expression

fixed_point_number $\rightarrow$ $([0\text{--}9])^*$ '.' $([0\text{--}9])^+$

We then observe the following chain of events. The initial item set is

fixed_point_number $\rightarrow$ $\bullet\,([0\text{--}9])^*$ '.' $([0\text{--}9])^+$

Since this is a non-basic pattern, it has to be developed using ε moves; this yields two items:

$$T \rightarrow \alpha \bullet (R)^* \beta \qquad \Rightarrow \; T \rightarrow \alpha(R)^* \bullet \beta$$
$$T \rightarrow \alpha(\bullet R)^* \beta$$

$$T \rightarrow \alpha(R\bullet)^* \beta \qquad \Rightarrow \; T \rightarrow \alpha(R)^* \bullet \beta$$
$$T \rightarrow \alpha(\bullet R)^* \beta$$

$$T \rightarrow \alpha \bullet (R)^+ \beta \qquad \Rightarrow \; T \rightarrow \alpha(\bullet R)^+ \beta$$

$$T \rightarrow \alpha(R\bullet)^+ \beta \qquad \Rightarrow \; T \rightarrow \alpha(R)^+ \bullet \beta$$
$$T \rightarrow \alpha(\bullet R)^+ \beta$$

$$T \rightarrow \alpha \bullet (R)^? \beta \qquad \Rightarrow \; T \rightarrow \alpha(R)^? \bullet \beta$$
$$T \rightarrow \alpha(\bullet R)^? \beta$$

$$T \rightarrow \alpha(R\bullet)^? \beta \qquad \Rightarrow \; T \rightarrow \alpha(R)^? \bullet \beta$$

$$T \rightarrow \alpha \bullet (R_1|R_2|\ldots)\beta \; \Rightarrow \; T \rightarrow \alpha(\bullet R_1|R_2|\ldots)\beta$$
$$T \rightarrow \alpha(R_1|\bullet R_2|\ldots)\beta$$
$$\ldots$$

$$T \rightarrow \alpha(R_1 \bullet |R_2|\ldots)\beta \; \Rightarrow \; T \rightarrow \alpha(R_1|R_2|\ldots)\bullet\beta$$
$$T \rightarrow \alpha(R_1|R_2\bullet|\ldots)\beta \; \Rightarrow \; T \rightarrow \alpha(R_1|R_2|\ldots)\bullet\beta$$
$$\ldots \qquad\qquad \ldots \; \ldots$$

Fig. 2.19: ε-move rules for the regular operators

integral_number $\rightarrow$ [0–9]$^+$
fixed_point_number $\rightarrow$ [0–9]*'.'[0–9]$^+$

Fig. 2.20: A simple set of regular expressions

fixed_point_number $\rightarrow$ ($\bullet$ [0–9])* '.' ([0–9])$^+$
fixed_point_number $\rightarrow$ ([0–9])* $\bullet$ '.' ([0–9])$^+$

The first item can be moved over the **3**, resulting in

fixed_point_number $\rightarrow$ ([0–9] $\bullet$)* '.' ([0–9])$^+$

but the second item is discarded. The new item develops into

fixed_point_number $\rightarrow$ ($\bullet$ [0–9])* '.' ([0–9])$^+$
fixed_point_number $\rightarrow$ ([0–9])* $\bullet$ '.' ([0–9])$^+$

Moving this set over the character ' . ' leaves only one item:

fixed_point_number $\rightarrow$ ([0–9])* '.' $\bullet$ ([0–9])$^+$

which develops into

fixed_point_number $\rightarrow$ ([0–9])* '.' ($\bullet$ [0–9])$^+$

This item can be moved over the **1**, which results in

fixed_point_number $\rightarrow$ ([0–9])* '.' ([0–9] $\bullet$)$^+$

This in turn develops into

fixed_point_number → ([0–9])* '.' (• [0–9])$^+$
fixed_point_number → ([0–9])* '.' ([0–9])$^+$ •   ← recognized

We note that the last item is a reduce item, so we have recognized a token; the token class is fixed_point_number. We record the token class and the end point, and continue the algorithm, to look for a longer matching sequence. We find, however, that neither of the items can be moved over the semicolon that follows the **3.1** in the input, so the process stops.

When a token is recognized, its class and its end point are recorded, and when a longer token is recognized later, this record is updated. Then, when the item set is exhausted and the process stops, this record is used to isolate and return the token found, and the input position is moved to the first character after the recognized token. So we return a token with token class fixed_point_number and representation 3.1, and the input position is moved to point at the semicolon.

2.6.2 Concurrent search

The above algorithm searches for one token class only, but it is trivial to modify it to search for all the token classes in the language simultaneously: just put all initial items for them in the initial item set. The input **3.1;** will now be processed as follows. The initial item set

integral_number → • ([0–9])$^+$
fixed_point_number → • ([0–9])* '.' ([0–9])$^+$

develops into

integral_number → (• [0–9])$^+$
fixed_point_number → (• [0–9])* '.' ([0–9])$^+$
fixed_point_number → ([0–9])* • '.' ([0–9])$^+$

Processing the **3** results in

integral_number → ([0–9] •)$^+$
fixed_point_number → ([0–9] •)* '.' ([0–9])$^+$

which develops into

integral_number → (• [0–9])$^+$
integral_number → ([0–9])$^+$ •   ← recognized
fixed_point_number → (• [0–9])* '.' ([0–9])$^+$
fixed_point_number → ([0–9])* • '.' ([0–9])$^+$

Processing the **.** results in

fixed_point_number → ([0–9])* '.' • ([0–9])$^+$

which develops into

fixed_point_number → ([0–9])* '.' (• [0–9])$^+$

Processing the **1** results in

$$\text{fixed\_point\_number} \rightarrow ([0\text{--}9])^* \text{'.'} ([0\text{--}9] \bullet)^+$$

which develops into

$$\text{fixed\_point\_number} \rightarrow ([0\text{--}9])^* \text{'.'} (\bullet [0\text{--}9])^+$$
$$\text{fixed\_point\_number} \rightarrow ([0\text{--}9])^* \text{'.'} ([0\text{--}9])^+ \bullet \qquad \leftarrow \text{recognized}$$

Processing the semicolon results in the empty set, and the process stops. Note that no integral_number items survive after the decimal point has been processed.

The need to record the latest recognized token is illustrated by the input **1 . g**, which may for example occur legally in FORTRAN, where .ge. is a possible form of the greater-than-or-equal operator. The scenario is then as follows. The initial item set

$$\text{integral\_number} \rightarrow \bullet ([0\text{--}9])^+$$
$$\text{fixed\_point\_number} \rightarrow \bullet ([0\text{--}9])^* \text{'.'} ([0\text{--}9])^+$$

develops into

$$\text{integral\_number} \rightarrow (\bullet [0\text{--}9])^+$$
$$\text{fixed\_point\_number} \rightarrow (\bullet [0\text{--}9])^* \text{'.'} ([0\text{--}9])^+$$
$$\text{fixed\_point\_number} \rightarrow ([0\text{--}9])^* \bullet \text{'.'} ([0\text{--}9])^+$$

Processing the **1** results in

$$\text{integral\_number} \rightarrow ([0\text{--}9] \bullet)^+$$
$$\text{fixed\_point\_number} \rightarrow ([0\text{--}9] \bullet)^* \text{'.'} ([0\text{--}9])^+$$

which develops into

$$\text{integral\_number} \rightarrow (\bullet [0\text{--}9])^+$$
$$\text{integral\_number} \rightarrow ([0\text{--}9])^+ \bullet \qquad \leftarrow \text{recognized}$$
$$\text{fixed\_point\_number} \rightarrow (\bullet [0\text{--}9])^* \text{'.'} ([0\text{--}9])^+$$
$$\text{fixed\_point\_number} \rightarrow ([0\text{--}9])^* \bullet \text{'.'} ([0\text{--}9])^+$$

Processing the **.** results in

$$\text{fixed\_point\_number} \rightarrow ([0\text{--}9])^* \text{'.'} \bullet ([0\text{--}9])^+$$

which develops into

$$\text{fixed\_point\_number} \rightarrow ([0\text{--}9])^* \text{'.'} (\bullet [0\text{--}9])^+$$

Processing the letter **g** results in the empty set, and the process stops. In this run, two characters have already been processed after the most recent token was recognized. So the read pointer has to be reset to the position of the point character, which turned out not to be a decimal point after all.

In principle the lexical analyzer must be able to reset the input over an arbitrarily long distance, but in practice it only has to back up over a few characters. Note that this backtracking is much easier if the entire input is in a single array in memory.

We now have a lexical analysis algorithm that processes each character once, except for those that the analyzer backed up over. An outline of the algorithm is given in Figure 2.21. The function *GetNextToken()* uses three functions that derive from the token descriptions of the language:

- *InitialItemSet()* (Figure 2.22), which supplies the initial item set;

```
import InputChar [1..];              --- as from the previous module
ReadIndex ← 1;                       --- the read index into InputChar [ ]

procedure GetNextToken:
    StartOfToken ← ReadIndex;
    EndOfLastToken ← Uninitialized;
    ClassOfLastToken ← Uninitialized;

    ItemSet ← InitialItemSet ();
    while ItemSet ≠ ∅:
        Ch ← InputChar [ReadIndex];
        ItemSet ← NextItemSet (ItemSet, Ch);
        Class ← ClassOfTokenRecognizedIn (ItemSet);
        if Class ≠ NoClass:
            ClassOfLastToken ← Class;
            EndOfLastToken ← ReadIndex;
        ReadIndex ← ReadIndex + 1;

    Token.class ← ClassOfLastToken;
    Token.repr ← InputChar [StartOfToken .. EndOfLastToken];
    ReadIndex ← EndOfLastToken + 1;
```

Fig. 2.21: Outline of a linear-time lexical analyzer

```
function InitialItemSet returning an item set:
    NewItemSet ← ∅;

    --- Initial contents—obtain from the language specification:
    for each token description T→R in the language specification:
        Insert item T→•R into NewItemSet;

    return ε-closure (NewItemSet);
```

Fig. 2.22: The function *InitialItemSet* for a lexical analyzer

```
function NextItemSet (ItemSet, Ch) returning an item set:
    NewItemSet ← ∅;

    --- Initial contents—obtain from character moves:
    for each item T→α•Bβ in ItemSet:
        if B is a basic pattern and B matches Ch:
            Insert item T→αB•β into NewItemSet;

    return ε-closure (NewItemSet);
```

Fig. 2.23: The function *NextItemSet()* for a lexical analyzer

function ε-closure (ItemSet) **returning** an item set:
　　ClosureSet ← the closure set produced by the
　　　　closure algorithm of Figure 2.25, passing the ItemSet to it;

　　— Filter out the interesting items:
　　NewItemSet ← ∅;
　　for each item I **in** ClosureSet:
　　　　if I is a basic item:
　　　　　　Insert I into NewItemSet;

　　return NewItemSet;

Fig. 2.24: The function ε-*closure()* for a lexical analyzer

Data definitions:
　　ClosureSet, a set of dotted items.

Initializations:
　　Put each item in *ItemSet* in *ClosureSet*.

Inference rules:
　　If an item in *ClosureSet* matches the left-hand side of one of the ε moves in Figure
　　2.19, the corresponding right-hand side must be present in *ClosureSet*.

Fig. 2.25: Closure algorithm for dotted items

- *NextItemSet(ItemSet, Ch)* (Figure 2.23), which yields the item set resulting from moving *ItemSet* over *Ch*;
- *ClassOfTokenRecognizedIn(ItemSet)*, which checks to see if any item in *ItemSet* is a reduce item, and if so, returns its token class. If there are several such items, it applies the appropriate tie-breaking rules. If there is none, it returns the value *NoClass*.

The functions *InitialItemSet()* and *NextItemSet()* are similar in structure. Both start by determining which items are to be part of the new item set for external reasons. *InitialItemSet()* does this by deriving them from the language specification, *NextItemSet()* by moving the previous items over the character *Ch*. Next, both functions determine which other items must be present due to the rules from Figure 2.19, by calling the function ε-*closure ()*. This function, which is shown in Figure 2.24, starts by applying a closure algorithm from Figure 2.25 to the *ItemSet* being processed. The inference rule of the closure algorithm adds items reachable from other items by ε-moves, until all such items have been found. For example, from the input item set

```
integral_number    → • ([0–9])+
fixed_point_number  → • ([0–9])* '.' ([0–9])+
```

it produces the item set

```
integral_number    → (• [0–9])+
fixed_point_number  → (• [0–9])* '.' ([0–9])+
fixed_point_number  → ([0–9])* • '.' ([0–9])+
```

We recognize the item sets from the example at the beginning of this section. The function ε-*closure* () then removes all non-basic items from the result and returns the cleaned-up ε-closure.

2.6.3 *Precomputing the item sets*

We have now constructed a lexical analyzer that will work in linear time, but considerable work is still being done for each character. In Section 2.5.1 we saw the beneficial effect of precomputing the values yielded by functions, and the question arises whether we can do the same here. Intuitively, the answer seems to be negative; although characters are a finite domain, we seem to know nothing about the domain of *ItemSet*. (The value of *InitialItemSet()* can obviously be precomputed, since it depends on the token descriptions only, but it is called only once for every token, and the gain would be very limited.) We know, however, that the domain is finite: there is a finite number of token descriptions in the language specification, there is a finite number of places where a dot can be put in a regular expression, so there is a finite number of dotted items. Consequently, there is a finite number of sets of items, which means that, at least in principle, we can precompute and tabulate the values of the functions *NextItemSet(ItemSet, Ch)* and *ClassOfTokenRecognizedIn(ItemSet)*.

There is a problem here, however: the domain not only needs to be finite, it has to be reasonably small too. Suppose there are 50 regular expressions (a reasonable number), with 4 places for the dot to go in each. So we have 200 different items, which can be combined into 2^{200} or about 1.6×10^{60} different sets. This seriously darkens the prospect of tabulating them all. We are, however, concerned only with item sets that can be reached by repeated applications of *NextItemSet()* to the initial item set: no other sets will occur in the lexical analyzer. Fortunately, most items cannot coexist with most other items in such an item set. The reason is that for two items to coexist in the same item set, their portions before the dots must be able to match the same string, the input recognized until that point. As an example, the items

```
some_token_1 → 'a' • 'x'
some_token_2 → 'b' • x
```

cannot coexist in the same item set, since the first item claims that the analyzer has just seen an a and the second claims that it has just seen a b, which is contradictory. Also, the item sets can contain basic items only. Both restrictions limit the number of items so severely, that for the above situation of 50 regular expressions, one can expect perhaps a few hundreds to a few thousands of item sets to be reachable, and experience has shown that tabulation is quite feasible.

The item set considered by the lexical analyzer at a given moment is called its **state**. The function *InitialItemSet()* provides its **initial state**, and the function *NextItemSet(ItemSet, Ch)* describes its **state transitions**; the function *NextItemSet()* is called a **transition function**. The algorithm itself is called a **finite-state automa-**

ton, or **FSA**. Since there are only a finite number of states, it is customary to number them, starting from S_0 for the initial state.

The question remains how to determine the set of reachable item sets. The answer is very simple: by just constructing them, starting from the initial item set; that item set is certainly reachable. For each character Ch in the character set we then compute the item set $NextItemSet(ItemSet, Ch)$. This process yields a number of new reachable item sets (and perhaps some old ones we have already met). We repeat the process for each of the new item sets, until no new item sets are generated anymore. Since the set of item sets is finite, this will eventually happen. This procedure is called the **subset algorithm**; it finds the reachable subsets of the set of all possible items, plus the transitions between them. It is depicted as a closure algorithm in Figure 2.26.

Data definitions:
   1. *States*, a set of states, where a "state" is a set of items.
   2. *Transitions*, a set of state transitions, where a "state transition" is a triple (start state, character, end state).

Initializations:
   1. Set *States* to contain a single state, *InitialItemSet( )*.
   2. Set *Transitions* to the empty set.

Inference rules:
   If *States* contains a state S, *States* must contain the state E and *Transitions* must contain the state transition (S, *Ch*, E) for each character *Ch* in the input character set, where E = *NextItemSet(S, Ch)*.

Fig. 2.26: The subset algorithm for lexical analyzers

For the two token descriptions above, we find the initial state *InitialItemSet( )*:

integral_number $\rightarrow$ ($\bullet$ [0–9])$^+$
fixed_point_number $\rightarrow$ ($\bullet$ [0–9])* '.' ([0–9])$^+$
fixed_point_number $\rightarrow$ ([0–9])* $\bullet$ '.' ([0–9])$^+$

We call this state S_0. For this example we consider only three character classes: digits, the decimal points and others—semicolons, parentheses, etc. We first compute $NextItemSet(S_0, \text{digit})$, which yields

integral_number $\rightarrow$ ($\bullet$ [0–9])$^+$
integral_number $\rightarrow$ ([0–9])$^+$ $\bullet$ $\leftarrow$ recognized
fixed_point_number $\rightarrow$ ($\bullet$ [0–9])* '.' ([0–9])$^+$
fixed_point_number $\rightarrow$ ([0–9])* $\bullet$ '.' ([0–9])$^+$

and which we call state S_1; the corresponding transition is (S_0, digit, S_1). Next we compute $NextItemSet(S_0, '.')$, which yields state S_2:

fixed_point_number $\rightarrow$ ([0–9])* '.' ($\bullet$ [0–9])$^+$

with the transition $(S_0, '.', S_2)$. The third possibility, $NextItemSet(S_0, \text{other})$ yields the empty set, which we call S_ω; this supplies transition $(S_0, \text{other}, S_\omega)$.

We have thus introduced three new sets, S_1, S_2, and S_ω, and we now have to apply the inference rule to each of them. *NextItemSet(S_1, digit)* yields

integral_number → (• [0–9])$^+$
integral_number → ([0–9])$^+$ •   ← recognized
fixed_point_number → (• [0–9])* '.' ([0–9])$^+$
fixed_point_number → ([0–9])* • '.' ([0–9])$^+$

which we recognize as the state S_1 we have already met. *NextItemSet(S_1, '.')* yields

fixed_point_number → ([0–9])* '.' (• [0–9])$^+$

which is our familiar state S_2. *NextItemSet(S_1, other)* yields the empty set S_ω, as does every move over the character class other.

We now turn to state S_2. *NextItemSet(S_2, digit)* yields

fixed_point_number → ([0–9])* '.' (• [0–9])$^+$
fixed_point_number → ([0–9])* '.' ([0–9])$^+$ •   ← recognized

which is new and which we call S_3. And *NextItemSet(S_2, '.')* yields S_ω.

It is easy to see that state S_3 allows a non-empty transition only on the digits, and then yields state S_3 again. No new states are generated, and our closure algorithm terminates after having generated five sets, out of a possible 64 (see Exercise 2.19).

The resulting transition table *NextState[State, Ch]* is given in Figure 2.27; note that we speak of *NextState* now rather than *NextItemSet* since the item sets are gone. The empty set S_ω is shown as a dash. As is usual, the states index the rows and the characters the columns. This figure also shows the token recognition table *ClassOfTokenRecognizedIn[State]*, which indicates which token is recognized in a given state, if any. It can be computed easily by examining the items in each state; it also applies tie-breaking rules if more than one token is recognized in a state.

	NextState [ ]			*ClassOfTokenRecognizedIn[ ]*
State	*Ch*			
	digit	point	other	
S_0	S_1	S_2	–	–
S_1	S_1	S_2	–	integral_number
S_2	S_3	–	–	–
S_3	S_3	–	–	fixed_point_number

Fig. 2.27: Transition table and recognition table for the regular expressions from Figure 2.20

It is customary to depict the states with their contents and their transitions in a **transition diagram**, as shown in Figure 2.28. Each bubble represents a state and shows the item set it contains. Transitions are shown as arrows labeled with the character that causes the transition. Recognized regular expressions are marked with an exclamation mark. To fit the items into the bubbles, some abbreviations have been used: D for [0–9], I for integral_number, and F for fixed_point_number.

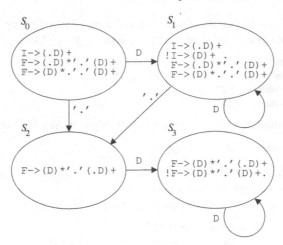

Fig. 2.28: Transition diagram of the states and transitions for Figure 2.20

2.6.4 The final lexical analyzer

Precomputing the item sets results in a lexical analyzer whose speed is independent of the number of regular expressions to be recognized. The code it uses is almost identical to that of the linear-time lexical analyzer of Figure 2.21. The only difference is that in the final lexical analyzer *InitialItemSet* is a constant and *NextItemSet[ ]* and *ClassOfTokenRecognizedIn[ ]* are constant arrays. For reference, the code for the routine *GetNextToken()* is shown in Figure 2.29.

```
procedure GetNextToken:
    StartOfToken ← ReadIndex;
    EndOfLastToken ← Uninitialized;
    ClassOfLastToken ← Uninitialized;

    ItemSet ← InitialItemSet;
    while ItemSet ≠ ∅:
        Ch ← InputChar [ReadIndex];
        ItemSet ← NextItemSet [ItemSet, Ch];
        Class ← ClassOfTokenRecognizedIn [ItemSet];
        if Class ≠ NoClass:
            ClassOfLastToken ← Class;
            EndOfLastToken ← ReadIndex;
        ReadIndex ← ReadIndex + 1;

    Token.class ← ClassOfLastToken;
    Token.repr ← InputChar [StartOfToken .. EndOfLastToken];
    ReadIndex ← EndOfLastToken + 1;
```

Fig. 2.29: Outline of an efficient linear-time routine *GetNextToken()*

We have now reached our goal of generating a very efficient lexical analyzer that needs only a few instructions for each input character and whose operation is independent of the number of token classes it has to recognize. The code shown in Figure 2.29 is the basic code that is generated by most modern lexical analyzer generators. An example of such a generator is *lex*, which is discussed briefly in Section 2.9.

It is interesting and in some sense satisfying to note that the same technique is used in computer virus scanners. Each computer virus is identified by a specific regular expression, its **signature**, and using a precomputed transition table allows the virus scanner to hunt for an arbitrary number of different viruses in the same time it would need to hunt for one virus.

2.6.5 Complexity of generating a lexical analyzer

The main component in the amount of work done by the lexical analyzer generator is proportional to the number of states of the FSA; if there are N_{FSA} states, N_{FSA} actions have to be performed to find them, and a table of size $N_{FSA} \times$ the number of characters has to be compressed. All other tasks—reading and parsing the regular descriptions, writing the driver—are negligible in comparison.

In principle it is possible to construct a regular expression that requires a number of states exponential in the length of the regular expression. An example is:

```
a_and_b_6_apart  →  .*a......b
```

which describes the longest token that ends in an a and a b, 6 places apart. To check this condition, the automaton will have to remember the positions of all as in the last 7 positions. There are $2^7 = 128$ different combinations of these positions. Since an FSA can distinguish different situations only by having a different state for each of them, it will have to have at least 128 different states. Increasing the distance between the a and the b by 1 doubles the number of states, which leads to exponential growth.

Fortunately, such regular expressions hardly ever occur in practical applications, and five to ten states per regular pattern are usual. As a result, almost all lexical analyzer generation is linear in the number of regular patterns.

2.6.6 Transitions to S_ω

Our attitude towards transitions to the **empty state** S_ω is ambivalent. On the one hand, transitions to S_ω are essential to the functioning of the lexical analyzer. They signal that the game is over and that the time has come to take stock of the results and isolate the token found. Also, proper understanding of some algorithms, theorems, and proofs in finite-state automata requires us to accept them as real transitions. On the other hand, it is customary and convenient to act, write, and speak as if these transitions do not exist. Traditionally, S_ω and transitions leading to it are left out of a transition diagram (see Figure 2.28), the corresponding entries in a transition table are left empty (see Figure 2.27), and we use phrases like "the state S has no transition on the character C" when actually S does have such a transition (of course it does) but it leads to S_ω.

We will conform to this convention, but in order to show the "real" situation, we show the transition diagram again in Figure 2.30, now with the omitted parts added.

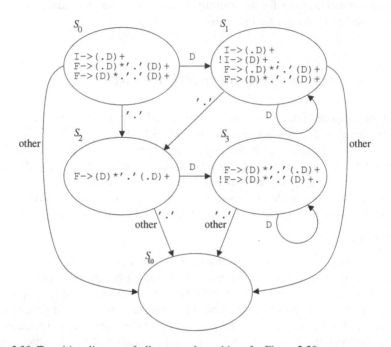

Fig. 2.30: Transition diagram of *all* states and transitions for Figure 2.20

2.6.7 Complexity of using a lexical analyzer

The time required to divide a program text into tokens seems linear in the length of that text, since the automaton constructed above seems to touch each character in the text only once. But in principle this is not true: since the recognition process may overshoot the end of the token while looking for a possible longer token, some characters will be touched more than once. Worse, the entire recognition process can be quadratic in the size of the input.

Suppose we want to recognize just two tokens:

```
single_a    → 'a'
a_string_plus_b    → 'a'*'b'
```

and suppose the input is a sequence of *n* **a**s, with no **b** anywhere. Then the input must be divided into *n* tokens single_a, but before recognizing each single_a, the lexical analyzer must hunt down the entire input to convince itself that there is no **b**. When it finds out so, it yields the token single_a and resets the *ReadIndex* back to *EndOfLastToken + 1*, which is actually *StartOfToken + 1* in this case. So recognizing the first single_a touches *n* characters, the second hunt touches *n* − 1 characters, the third *n* − 2 characters, etc., resulting in quadratic behavior of the lexical analyzer.

Fortunately, as in the previous section, such cases do not occur in programming languages. If the lexical analyzer has to scan right to the end of the text to find out what token it should recognize, then so will the human reader, and a programming language designed with two tokens as defined above would definitely have a less than average chance of survival. Also, Reps [233] describes a more complicated lexical analyzer that will divide the input stream into tokens in linear time.

2.7 Transition table compression

Transition tables are not arbitrary matrices; they exhibit a lot of structure. For one thing, when a token is being recognized, only very few characters will at any point continue that token; so most transitions lead to the empty set, and most entries in the table are empty. Such low-density transition tables are called **sparse**. Densities (fill ratios) of 5% or less are not unusual. For another, the states resulting from a move over a character *Ch* all contain exclusively items that indicate that a *Ch* has just been recognized, and there are not too many of these. So columns tend to contain only a few different values which, in addition, do not normally occur in other columns. The idea suggests itself to exploit this redundancy to compress the transition table. Now with a few hundred states, perhaps a hundred different characters, and say two or four bytes per entry, the average uncompressed lexical analysis transition table occupies perhaps a hundred kilobytes. On modern computers this is bearable, but parsing and code generation tables may be ten or a hundred times larger, and compressing them is still essential, so we will explain the techniques here.

The first idea that may occur to the reader is to apply compression algorithms of the Huffman or Lempel–Ziv variety to the transition table, in the same way they are used in well-known file compression programs. No doubt they would do an excellent job on the table, but they miss the point: the compressed table must still allow cheap access to *NextState[State, Ch]*, and digging up that value from a Lempel–Ziv compressed table would be most uncomfortable!

There is a rich collection of algorithms for compressing tables while leaving the accessibility intact, but none is optimal and each strikes a different compromise. As a result, it is an attractive field for the inventive mind. Most of the algorithms exist in several variants, and almost every one of them can be improved with some ingenuity. We will show here the simplest versions of the two most commonly used algorithms, row displacement and graph coloring.

All algorithms exploit the fact that a large percentage of the entries are empty by putting non-empty entries in those locations. How they do this differs from algorithm to algorithm. A problem is, however, that the so-called empty locations are not really empty but contain the number of the empty set S_ω. So we end up with locations containing both a non-empty state and S_ω (no location contains more than one non-empty state). When we access such a location we must be able to find out which of the two is our answer. Two solutions exist: mark the entries with enough information so we can know which is our answer, or make sure we never access the empty entries.

The implementation of the first solution depends on the details of the algorithm and will be covered below. The second solution is implemented by having a bit map with a single bit for each table entry, telling whether the entry is the empty set. Before accessing the compressed table we check the bit, and if we find the entry is empty we have got our answer; if not, we access the table after all, but now we know that what we find there is our answer. The bit map takes 1/16 or 1/32 of the size of the original uncompressed table, depending on the entry size; this is not good for our compression ratio. Also, extracting the correct bit from the bit map requires code that slows down the access. The advantage is that the subsequent table compression and its access are simplified. And surprisingly, having a bit map often requires less space than marking the entries.

2.7.1 Table compression by row displacement

Row displacement cuts the transition matrix into horizontal strips: each row becomes a strip. For the moment we assume we use a bit map *EmptyState[ ]* to weed out all access to empty states, so we can consider the empty entries to be really empty. Now the strips are packed in a one-dimensional array *Entry[ ]* of minimal length according to the rule that two entries can share the same location if either one of them is empty or both are the same. We also keep an array *Displacement[ ]* indexed by row number (state) to record the position at which we have packed the corresponding row in *Entry[ ]*.

Figure 2.31 shows the transition matrix from Figure 2.27 in reduced form; the first column contains the row (state) numbers, and is not part of the matrix. Slicing it yields four strips, $(1, -, 2)$, $(1, -, 2)$, $(3, -, -)$ and $(3, -, -)$, which can be fitted at displacements 0, 0, 1, 1 in an array of length 3, as shown in Figure 2.32. Ways of finding these displacements will be discussed in the next subsection.

The resulting data structures, including the bit map, are shown in Figure 2.33. We do not need to allocate room for the fourth, empty element in Figure 2.32, since it will never be accessed. The code for retrieving the value of *NextState[State, Ch]* is given in Figure 2.34.

```
state digit=1 other=2 point=3
0      1      -       2
1      1      -       2
2      3      -       -
3      3      -       -
```

Fig. 2.31: The transition matrix from Figure 2.27 in reduced form

```
0   1 - 2
1   1 - 2
2   3 - -
3   3 - -
    1 3 2 -
```

Fig. 2.32: Fitting the strips into one array

```
EmptyState [0..3][1..3] =
    ((0, 1, 0), (0, 1, 0), (0, 1, 1), (0, 1, 1));
Displacement[ 0..3] = (0, 0, 1, 1);
Entry [1..3] = (1, 3, 2);
```

Fig. 2.33: The transition matrix from Figure 2.27 in compressed form

```
if EmptyState [State][Ch]:
    NewState ← NoState;
else — entry in Entry [ ] is valid:
    NewState ← Entry [Displacement [State] + Ch];
```

Fig. 2.34: Code for *NewState ← NextState[State, Ch]*

Assuming two-byte entries, the uncompressed table occupied $12 \times 2 = 24$ bytes. In the compressed table, the bit map occupies 12 bits = 2 bytes, the array *Displacement[ ]* $4 \times 2 = 8$ bytes, and *Entry[ ]* $3 \times 2 = 6$ bytes, totaling 16 bytes. In this example the gain is less than spectacular, but on larger tables, especially on very large tables, the algorithm performs much better and compression ratios of 90–95% can be expected. This reduces a table of a hundred kilobytes to ten kilobytes or less.

Replacing the bit map with markings in the entries turns out to be a bad idea in our example, but we will show the technique anyway, since it performs much better on large tables and is often used in practice. The idea of marking is to extend an entry with index *[State, Ch]* with a field containing either the *State* or the *Ch*, and to check this field when we retrieve the entry. Marking with the state is easy to understand: the only entries marked with a state S in the compressed array are those that originate from the strip with the values for S, so if we find that the entry we retrieved is indeed marked with S we know it is from the correct state.

The same reasoning cannot be applied to marking with the character, since the character does not identify the strip. However, when we index the position found from *Displacement[State]* by a character C and we find there an entry marked C, we know that it originates from a strip starting at *Displacement[State]*. And if we make sure that no two strips have the same displacement, this identifies the strip. So we can also mark with the character, provided no two strips get the same displacement.

Since the state requires two bytes of storage and the character only one, we will choose marking by character (see Exercise 2.21 for the other choice). The strips now become $((1, 1), -, (2, 3))$, $((1, 1), -, (2, 3))$, $((3, 1), -, -)$ and $((3, 1), -, -)$, which can be fitted as shown in Figure 2.35. We see that we are severely hindered by the requirement that no two strips should get the same displacement. The complete data structures are shown in Figure 2.36. Since the sizes of the markings and the entries differ, we implement them in different arrays. The corresponding code is given in Figure 2.37. The array *Displacement[ ]* still occupies $4 \times 2 = 8$ bytes, *Mark[ ]* occupies $8 \times 1 = 8$ bytes, and *Entry[ ]* $6 \times 2 = 12$ bytes, totaling 28 bytes. We see that our gain has turned into a loss.

```
0 (1, 1)    –    (2, 3)
1        (1, 1)    –    (2, 3)
2                        (3, 1)    –    –
3                                  (3, 1) – –
  ─────────────────────────────────────────
  (1, 1) (1, 1) (2, 3) (2, 3) (3, 1) (3, 1) – –
```

Fig. 2.35: Fitting the strips with entries marked by character

```
Displacement [0..3] = (0, 1, 4, 5);
Mark [1..8] = (1, 1, 3, 3, 1, 1, 0, 0);
Entry [1..6] = (1, 1, 2, 2, 3, 3);
```

Fig. 2.36: The transition matrix compressed with marking by character

```
if Mark [Displacement [State] + Ch] ≠ Ch:
    NewState ← NoState;
else -- entry in Entry [ ] is valid:
    NewState ← Entry [Displacement [State] + Ch];
```

Fig. 2.37: Code for *NewState ← NextState[State, Ch]* for marking by character

As mentioned before, even the best compression algorithms do not work well on small-size data; there is just not enough redundancy there. Try compressing a 10-byte file with any of the well-known file compression programs!

2.7.1.1 Finding the best displacements

Finding those displacements that result in the shortest entry array is an NP-complete problem; see below for a short introduction to what "NP-complete" means. So we have to resort to heuristics to find sub-optimal solutions. One good heuristic is to sort the strips according to density, with the most dense (the one with the most non-empty entries) first. We now take an extensible array (see Section 10.1.3.2) of entries, in which we store the strips by **first-fit**. This means that we take the strips in decreasing order as sorted, and store each in the first position from the left in which it will fit without conflict. A conflict arises if both the array and the strip have non-empty entries at a certain position and these entries are different.

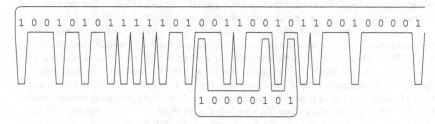

Fig. 2.38: A damaged comb finding room for its teeth

It is helpful to picture the non-empty entries as the remaining teeth on a damaged comb and the first-fit algorithm as finding the first place where we can stick in the comb with all its teeth going into holes left by the other combs; see Figure 2.38. This is why the row-displacement algorithm is sometimes called the **comb algorithm**.

The heuristic works because it does the difficult cases (the densely filled strips) first. The sparse and very sparse strips come later and can find room in the holes left by their big brothers. This philosophy underlies many fitting heuristics: fit the large objects first and put the small objects in the holes left over; this applies equally to packing vacation gear in a trunk and to strips in an array.

A more advanced table compression algorithm using row displacement is given by Driesen and Hölzle [89].

2.7.2 Table compression by graph coloring

There is another, less intuitive, technique to compress transition tables, which works better for large tables when used in combination with a bit map to check for empty entries. In this approach, we select a subset S from the total set of strips, such that we can combine all strips in S without displacement and without conflict: they can just be positioned all at the same location. This means that the non-empty positions in each strip in S avoid the non-empty positions in all the other strips or have identical values in those positions. It turns out that if the original table is large enough we can find many such subsets that result in packings in which no empty entries remain. The non-empty entries in the strips just fill all the space, and the packing is optimal.

NP-complete problems

As a rule, solving a problem is more difficult than verifying a solution, once it has been given. For example, sorting an array of n elements costs at least $O(n \ln n)$ operations, but verifying that an array is sorted can be done with $n - 1$ operations.

There is a large class of problems which nobody knows how to solve in less than exponential time, but for which verifying a given solution can be done in less than exponential time (in so-called **polynomial time**). Remarkably, all these problems are equivalent in the sense that each can be converted to any of the others without introducing exponential time dependency. Why this is so, again nobody knows. These problems are called the **NP-complete** problems, for "Nondeterministic-Polynomial". An example is "Give me a set of displacements that results in a packing of k entries or less" ($Prob(k)$).

In practice we are more interested in the optimization problem "Give me a set of displacements that results the smallest packing" (Opt) than in $Prob(k)$. Formally, this problem is not NP-complete, since when we are given the answer, we cannot check in polynomial time that it is optimal. But Opt is at least as difficult as $Prob(k)$, since once we have solved Opt we can immediately solve $Prob(k)$ for all values of k. On the other hand we can use $Prob(k)$ to solve Opt in $\ln n$ steps by using binary search, so Opt is not more difficult than $Prob(k)$, within a polynomial factor. We conclude that $Prob(k)$ and Opt are equally difficult within a polynomial factor, so by extension we can call Opt NP-complete too.

It is unlikely that an algorithm will be found that can solve NP-complete problems in less than exponential time, but fortunately this need not worry us too much, since for almost all of these problems good heuristic algorithms have been found, which yield answers that are good enough to work with. The first-fit decreasing heuristic for row displacement is an example.

A good introduction to NP-complete can be found in Baase and Van Gelder [23, Chapter 13]; the standard book on NP-complete problems is by Garey and Johnson [104].

The sets are determined by first constructing and then coloring a so-called **interference graph**, a graph in which each strip is a node and in which there is an edge between each pair of strips that cannot coexist in a subset because of conflicts. Figure 2.39(a) shows a fictitious but reasonably realistic transition table, and its interference graph is given in Figure 2.40.

	w	x	y	z		w	x	y	z		w	x	y	z
0	1	2	–	–	0	1	2	–	–					
1	3	–	4	–	1						3	–	4	–
2	1	–	–	6	2	1	–	–	6					
3	–	2	–	–	3	–	2	–	–					
4	–	–	–	5	4						–	–	–	5
5	1	–	4	–	5	1	–	4	–					
6	–	7	–	–	6						–	7	–	–
7	–	–	–	–	7						–	–	–	–
						1	2	4	6		3	7	4	5

(a)   (b)

Fig. 2.39: A transition table (a) and its compressed form packed by graph coloring (b)

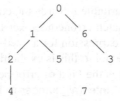

Fig. 2.40: Interference graph for the automaton of Figure 2.39(a)

This seemingly arbitrary technique hinges on the possibility of coloring a graph (almost) optimally. A graph is colored when colors have been assigned to its nodes, such that no two nodes that are connected by an edge have the same color; usually one wants to color the graph with the minimal number of different colors. The important point is that there are very good heuristic algorithms to almost always find the minimal number of colors; the problem of always finding the exact minimal number of colors is again NP-complete. We will discuss some of these algorithms in Section 9.1.5, where they are used for register allocation.

The relation of graph coloring to our subset selection problem is obvious: the strips correspond to nodes, the colors correspond to the subsets, and the edges prevent conflicting strips from ending up in the same subset. Without resorting to the more sophisticated heuristics explained in Section 9.1.5, we can easily see that the interference graph in Figure 2.40 can be colored with two colors. It happens to be a tree, and any tree can be colored with two colors, one for the even levels and one for the odd levels. This yields the packing as shown in Figure 2.39(b). The cost is $8 \times 2 = 16$ bytes for the entries, plus 32 bits = 4 bytes for the bit map, plus $8 \times 2 = 16$ bytes for the mapping from state to strip, totaling 36 bytes, against $32 \times 2 = 64$ bytes for the uncompressed matrix.

2.8 Error handling in lexical analyzers

The only error that can occur in the scheme described in Section 2.6.4 is that no regular expression matches the current input. This is easily remedied by specifying at the very end of the list of regular expressions a regular expression ., which matches any single character, and have it return a token *UnknownCharacter*. If no further action is taken, this token is then passed to the parser, which will reject it and enter its error recovery.

Depending on the quality of the error recovery of the parser this may or may not be a good idea, but it is likely that the resulting error message will not be very informative. Since the lexical analyzer usually includes an identification layer (see Section 2.10), the same layer can be used to catch and remove the *UnknownCharacter* token and give a more sensible error message.

If one wants to be more charitable towards the compiler user, one can add special regular expressions that match erroneous tokens that are likely to occur in the input. An example is a regular expression for a fixed-point number along the above lines that has no digits after the point; this is explicitly forbidden by the regular expressions in Figure 2.20, but it is the kind of error people make. If the grammar of the language does not allow an integral_number to be followed by a point in any position, we can adopt the specification

integral_number → [0–9]$^+$
fixed_point_number → [0–9]*'.'[0–9]$^+$
bad_fixed_point_number → [0–9]*'.'

This specification will produce the token bad_fixed_point_number on such erroneous input. The lexical identification layer can then give a warning or error message, append a character 0 to the end of *Token.repr* to turn it into a correct representation, and change *Token.class* to fixed_point_number.

Correcting the representation by appending a 0 is important, since it allows routines further on in the compiler to blindly accept token representations knowing that they are correct. This avoids inefficient checks in semantic routines or alternatively obscure crashes on incorrect compiler input.

It is in general imperative that phases that check incoming data for certain properties do not pass on any data that does not conform to those properties, even if that means patching the data and even if that patching is algorithmically inconvenient. The only alternative is to give up further processing altogether. Experience has shown that if the phases of a compiler do not adhere strictly to this rule, avoiding compiler crashes on incorrect programs is very difficult. Following this rule does not prevent all compiler crashes, but at least implies that for each incorrect program that causes a compiler crash, there is also a correct program that causes the same compiler crash.

The user-friendliness of a compiler shows mainly in the quality of its error reporting. As we indicated above, the user should at least be presented with a clear error message including the perceived cause of the error, the name of the input file, and the position in it. Giving a really good error cause description is often hard or impossible, due to the limited insight compilers have into incorrect programs. Pinpointing the error is aided by recording the file name and line number with every token and every node in the AST, as we did in Figure 2.5. More fancy reporting mechanisms, including showing parts of the syntax tree, may not have the beneficial effect the compiler writer may expect from them, but it may be useful to provide some visual display mechanism, for example opening a text editor at the point of the error.

2.9 A traditional lexical analyzer generator—*lex*

The best-known interface for a lexical analyzer generator is that of the UNIX program *lex*. In addition to the UNIX implementation, there are several freely available implementations that are for all practical purposes compatible with UNIX *lex*, for example GNU's *flex*. Although there are small differences between them, we will treat them here as identical. Some of these implementations use highly optimized versions of the algorithm explained above and are very efficient.

```
%{
#include    "lex.h"

Token_Type Token;
int line_number = 1;
%}

whitespace              [ \t]

 letter                 [a−zA−Z]
 digit                  [0−9]
 underscore             "_"
 letter_or_digit        ({ letter }|{ digit })
 underscored_tail       ({underscore}{ letter_or_digit }+)
 identifier             ({ letter }{ letter_or_digit }*{ underscored_tail}*)

 operator               [−+*/]
 separator              [;,(){}]

%%

 { digit }+                     {return INTEGER;}
 { identifier }                 {return IDENTIFIER;}
 {operator}|{ separator}        {return yytext [0];}
 #[^#\n]*#?                     {/* ignore comment */}
 {whitespace}                   {/* ignore whitespace */}
 \n                             {line_number++;}
 .                              {return ERRONEOUS;}

%%

void start_lex (void) {}

void get_next_token(void) {
    Token.class = yylex ();
    if  (Token.class == 0) {
        Token.class = EoF; Token.repr = "<EoF>"; return;
    }
    Token.pos.line_number = line_number;
    Token.repr = strdup(yytext );
}

int yywrap(void) {return 1;}
```

Fig. 2.41: *Lex* input for the token set used in Section 2.5

Figure 2.41 shows a lexical analyzer description in *lex* format for the same token set as used in Section 2.5. *Lex* input consists of three sections: one for regular definitions, one for pairs of regular expressions and code segments, and one for auxiliary C code. The program *lex* generates from it a file in C, which contains the declaration of a single routine, int yylex(void). The semantics of this routine is somewhat surprising, since it contains a built-in loop. When called, it starts isolating tokens from the input file according to the regular expressions in the second section, and for each token found it executes the C code associated with it. This code can find the representation of the token in the array char yytext[]. When the code executes a return statement with some value, the routine yylex() returns with that value; otherwise, yylex() proceeds to isolate the next token. This set-up is convenient for both retrieving and skipping tokens.

The three sections in the lexical analyzer description are separated by lines that contain the characters %% only. The first section contains regular definitions which correspond to those in Figure 2.20; only a little editing was required to conform to the *lex* format. The most prominent difference is the presence of braces ({...}) around the names of regular expressions when they are applied rather than defined. The section also includes the file lex.h to introduce definitions for the token classes; the presence of the C code is signaled to *lex* by the markers %{ and %}.

The second section contains the regular expressions for the token classes to be recognized together with their associated C code; again the regular expression names are enclosed in braces. We see that the code segments for integer, identifier, operator/separator, and unrecognized character stop the loop inside yylex() by returning with the token class as the return value. For the operator/separator class this is the first (and only) character in yytext[]. Comment and layout are skipped automatically by associating empty C code with them. The regular expression for the comment means: a # followed by anything except (^) the character # and end of line (\n), occurring zero or more times (*), and if that stops at a #, include the # as well.

To keep the interface clean, the only calls to yylex() occur in the third section. This section is written to fit in with the driver for the handwritten lexical analyzer from Figure 2.12. The routine start_lex() is empty since *lex* generated analyzers do not need to be started. The routine get_next_token() starts by calling yylex(). This call will skip layout and comments until it has recognized a real token, the class value of which is then returned. It also detects end of input, since yylex() returns the value 0 in that case. Finally, since the representation of the token in the array yytext[] will be overwritten by that of the next token, it is secured in *Token.repr*. The function yywrap() arranges the proper end-of-file handling; further details can be found in any *lex* manual, for example that by Levine, Mason and Brown [174].

The handwritten lexical analyzer of Section 2.5 recorded the position in the input file of the token delivered by tracking that position inside the routine next_char(). Unfortunately, we cannot do this in a reliable way in *lex*, for two reasons. First, some variants of *lex* read ahead arbitrary amounts of input before producing the first token; and second, some use the UNIX input routine fread() rather than getc() to obtain input. In both cases, the relation between the characters read and the token recognized is lost. We solve half the problem by explicitly counting lines in the *lex* code. To solve the entire problem and record also the character positions inside a line, we need to add code to measure and tally the lengths of all patterns recognized. We have not shown this in our code to avoid clutter.

This concludes our discussion of lexical analyzers proper. The basic purpose of the stream of tokens generated by a lexical analyzer in a compiler is to be passed on to a syntax analyzer. For purely practical reasons it is, however, convenient, to introduce additional layers between lexical and syntax analysis. These layers may assist in further identification of tokens (Section 2.10), macro processing and file inclusion (Section 2.12.1), conditional text inclusion (Section 2.12.2), and possibly generics (Section 2.12.3). We will now first turn to these intermediate layers.

2.10 Lexical identification of tokens

In a clean design, the only task of a lexical analyzer is isolating the text of the token and identifying its token class. The lexical analyzer then yields a stream of (token class, token representation) pairs. The token representation is carried through the syntax analyzer to the rest of the compiler, where it can be inspected to yield the appropriate semantic information. An example is the conversion of the representation 377#8 (octal 377 in Ada) to the integer value 255. In a broad compiler, a good place for this conversion would be in the initialization phase of the annotation of the syntax tree, where the annotations that derive from the tokens form the basis of further attributes.

In a narrow compiler, however, the best place to do computations on the token text is in the lexical analyzer. Such computations include simple conversions, as shown above, but also more elaborate actions, for example identifier identification. Traditionally, almost all compilers were narrow for lack of memory and did considerable semantic processing in the lexical analyzer: the integer value 255 stored in two bytes takes less space than the string representation "377#8". With modern machines the memory considerations have for the most part gone away, but language properties can force even a modern lexical analyzer to do some semantic processing. Three such properties concern identifiers that influence subsequent parsing, macro processing, and keywords.

In C and C++, typedef and class declarations introduce identifiers that influence the parsing of the subsequent text. In particular, in the scope of the declaration

    typedef int T;

the code fragment

    (T *)

is a cast which converts the subsequent expression to "pointer to T", and in the scope of the variable declaration

    int T;

it is an incorrect expression with a missing right operand to the multiplication sign. In C and C++ parsing can only continue when all previous identifiers have been identified sufficiently to decide if they are type identifiers or not.

We said "identified sufficiently" since in many languages we cannot do full identifier identification at this stage. Given the Ada declarations

   type Planet = (Mercury, Venus, Earth, Mars);
   type Goddess = (Juno, Venus, Minerva, Diana);

then in the code fragment

   for P **in** Mercury .. Venus **loop**

the identifier Venus denotes a planet, and in

   for G **in** Juno .. Venus **loop**

it denotes a goddess. This requires overloading resolution and the algorithm for this belongs in the context handling module rather than in the lexical analyzer. (Identification and overloading resolution are covered in Section 11.1.1.)

A second reason to have at least some identifier identification done by the lexical analyzer is related to macro processing. Many languages, including C, have a macro facility, which allows chunks of program text to be represented in the program by identifiers. Examples of parameterless macros are

   #define EoF   256
   #define DIGIT   257

from the lexical analyzer in Figure 1.11; a macro with parameters occurred in

   #define is_digit (c)   ('0' <= (c) && (c) <= '9')

The straightforward approach is to do the macro processing as a separate phase between reading the program and lexical analysis, but that means that each and every character in the program will be processed several times; also the intermediate result may be very large. See Exercise 2.25 for additional considerations. Section 2.12 shows that macro processing can be conveniently integrated into the reading module of the lexical analyzer, provided the lexical analyzer checks each identifier to see if it has been defined as a macro.

A third reason to do some identifier identification in the lexical analyzer stems from the existence of keywords. Most languages have a special set of tokens that look like identifiers but serve syntactic purposes: the keywords or reserved words. Examples are if, switch, case, etc. from Java and C, and begin, end, task, etc. from Ada. There is again a straightforward approach to deal with the problems that are caused by this, which is specifying each keyword as a separate regular expression to the lexical analyzer, textually before the regular expression for identifier. Doing so increases the size of the transition table considerably, however, which may not be acceptable.

These three problems can be solved by doing a limited amount of identifier identification in the lexical analyzer, just enough to serve the needs of the lexical analyzer and parser. Since identifier identification has many more links with the rest of the compiler than the lexical analyzer itself has, the process is best delegated to a separate module, the symbol table module. In practical terms this means that the routine *GetNextToken()*, which is our version of the routine get_next_token() described extensively above, is renamed to something like *GetNextSimpleToken()*, and that the real *GetNextToken()* takes on the structure shown in Figure 2.42. The procedure *SwitchToMacro()* does the fancy footwork needed to redirect further input to the macro body; see Section 2.12.1 for details.

```
function GetNextToken () returning a token:
    SimpleToken ← GetNextSimpleToken ();
    if SimpleToken.class = Identifier:
        SimpleToken ← IdentifyInSymbolTable (SimpleToken);
        — See if this has reset SimpleToken.class:
        if SimpleToken.class = Macro:
            SwitchToMacro (SimpleToken);
            return GetNextToken ();
        else — SimpleToken.class ≠ Macro:
            — Identifier or TypeIdentifier or Keyword:
            return SimpleToken;
    else — SimpleToken.class ≠ Identifier:
        return SimpleToken;
```

Fig. 2.42: A *GetNextToken()* that does lexical identification

Effectively this introduces a separate phase between the lexical analyzer proper and the parser, the **lexical identification phase**, as shown in Figure 2.43. Lexical identification is also called **screening** [81]. Once we have this mechanism in place, it can also render services in the implementation of generic declarations; this aspect is covered in Section 2.12.3. We will first consider implementation techniques for symbol tables, and then see how to do macro processing and file inclusion; the section on lexical analysis closes by examining the use of macro processing in implementing generic declarations.

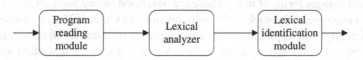

Fig. 2.43: Pipeline from input to lexical identification

2.11 Symbol tables

In its basic form a **symbol table** (or **name list**) is a mapping from an identifier onto an associated record which contains collected information about the identifier.

The name "symbol table" derives from the fact that identifiers were once called "symbols", and that the mapping is often implemented using a hash table.

The primary interface of a symbol table module consists of one single function:

```
function Identify (IdfName)
    returning a pointer to IdfInfo;
```

When called with an arbitrary string *IdfName* it returns a pointer to a record of type *IdfInfo*; when it is later called with that same string, it returns the same pointer, regardless of how often this is done and how many other calls of *Identify( )* intervene. The compiler writer chooses the record type *IdfInfo* so that all pertinent information that will ever need to be collected for an identifier can be stored in it.

It is important that the function *Identify( )* return a pointer to the record rather than a copy of the record, since we want to be able to update the record to collect information in it. In this respect *Identify( )* acts just like an array of records in C. If C allowed arrays to be indexed by strings, we could declare an array

```
struct   Identifier_info   Sym_table[""];
```

and use &Sym_table[Identifier_name] instead of *Identify(IdfName)*.

When used in a symbol table module for a C compiler, *IdfInfo* could, for example, contain pointers to the following pieces of information:

- the actual string (for error messages; see below)
- a macro definition (see Section 2.12)
- a keyword definition
- a list of type, variable and function definitions (see Section 11.1.1)
- a list of struct and union name definitions (see Section 11.1.1)
- a list of struct and union field selector definitions (see Section 11.1.1)

In practice, many of these pointers would be null for most of the identifiers.

This approach splits the problem of building a symbol table module into two problems: how to obtain the mapping from identifier string to information record, and how to design and maintain the information attached to the identifier string. For the first problem several data structures suggest themselves; examples are hash tables and various forms of trees. These are described in any book about data structures, for example Sedgewick [257] or Baase and Van Gelder [23]. The second problem is actually a set of problems, since many pieces of information about identifiers have to be collected and maintained, for a variety of reasons and often stemming from different parts of the compiler. We will treat these where they occur.

2.12 Macro processing and file inclusion

A **macro definition** defines an identifier as being a macro and having a certain string as a value; when the identifier occurs in the program text, its string value is to be substituted in its place. A macro definition can specify formal parameters, which have to be substituted by the actual parameters. An example in C is

#define is_capital (ch)   ('A' <= (ch) && (ch) <= 'Z')

which states that is_capital(ch) must be substituted by ('A' <= (ch) && (ch) <= 'Z')
with the proper substitution for ch. The parentheses around the expression and the
parameters serve to avoid precedence conflicts with operators outside the expression
or inside the parameters. A **call** (also called **application**) of this macro

is_capital (txt [i])

which supplies the actual parameter txt[i], is to be replaced by

('A' <= (txt [i]) && (txt [i]) <= 'Z')

The string value of the macro is kept in the macro field of the record associated
with the identifier. We assume here that there is only one level of macro definition,
in that each macro definition of an identifier *I* overwrites a previous definition of
I, regardless of scopes. If macro definitions are governed by scope in the source
language, the macro field will have to point to a stack (linked list) of definitions.

Many macro processors, including that of C, define a third substitution mechanism in addition to macro substitution and parameter substitution: **file inclusion**. A
file inclusion directive contains a file name, and possibly formal parameters; the corresponding file is retrieved from the file system and its contents are substituted for
the file inclusion directive, possibly after parameter substitution. In C, file inclusions
can nest to arbitrary depth.

Another text manipulation feature, related to the ones mentioned above, is **conditional compilation**. Actually, **conditional text inclusion** would be a better name,
but the feature is traditionally called conditional compilation. The text inclusion is
controlled by some form of if-statement recognizable to the macro processor and
the condition in it must be such that the macro processor can evaluate it. It may,
for example, test if a certain macro has been defined or compare two constants. If
the condition evaluates to true, the text up to the following macro processor ELSE
or END IF is included; nesting macro processor IF statements should be honored as
they are met in this process. And if the condition evaluates to false, the text up to
the following macro ELSE or END IF is skipped, but if an ELSE is present, the text
between it and the matching END IF is included instead. An example from C is

```
# ifdef    UNIX
char *file_name_separator = '/' ;
#else
# ifdef    MSDOS
char *file_name_separator = '\\' ;
#endif
#endif
```

Here the #ifdef UNIX tests if the macro UNIX has been defined. If so, the line
char *file_name_separator = '/'; is processed as program text, otherwise a test for
the presence of a macro MSDOS is done. If both tests fail, no program code results from the above example. The conditional compilation in C is line-oriented;
only complete lines can be included or skipped and each syntax fragment involved

in conditional compilation occupies a line of its own. All conditional compilation markers start with a # character at the beginning of a line, which makes them easy to spot.

Some macro processors allow even more elaborate text manipulation. The PL/I preprocessor features for-statements and procedures that will select and produce program text, in addition to if-statements. For example, the PL/I code

```
%DECLARE I FIXED;
%DO I := 1 TO 4; A(I) := I * (I − 1); %END;
%DEACTIVATE I;
```

in which the % sign marks macro keywords, produces the code

```
A(1) := 1 * (1 − 1);
A(2) := 2 * (2 − 1);
A(3) := 3 * (3 − 1);
A(4) := 4 * (4 − 1);
```

In fact, the PL/I preprocessor acts on segments of the parse tree rather than on sequences of characters, as the C preprocessor does. Similar techniques are used to generate structured document text, in for example SGML or XML, from templates.

2.12.1 The input buffer stack

All the above substitution and inclusion features can be implemented conveniently by a single mechanism: a **stack of input buffers**. Each stack element consists at least of a read pointer and an end-of-text pointer. If the text has been read in from a file, these pointers point into the corresponding buffer; this is the case for the initial input file and for included files. If the text is already present in memory, the pointers point there; this is the case for macros and parameters. The initial input file is at the bottom of the stack, and subsequent file inclusions, macro calls, and parameter substitutions are stacked on top of it. The actual input for the lexical analyzer is taken from the top input buffer, until it becomes exhausted; we know this has happened when the read pointer becomes equal to the end pointer. Then the input buffer is unstacked and reading continues on what is now the top buffer.

2.12.1.1 Back-calls

The input buffer stack is incorporated in the module for reading the input. It is controlled by information obtained in the lexical identification module, which is at least two steps further on in the pipeline. So, unfortunately we need up-calls, or rather back-calls, to signal macro substitution, which is recognized in the lexical identification module, back to the input module. See Figure 2.44.

It is easy to see that in a clean modularized system these back-calls cannot be written. We have seen that a lexical analyzer can overshoot the end of the token

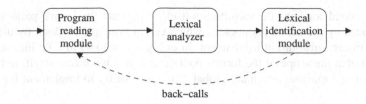

back–calls

Fig. 2.44: Pipeline from input to lexical identification, with feedback

by some characters, and these characters have already been obtained from the input module when the signal to do macro expansion arrives. This signal in fact requests the input module to insert text before characters it has already delivered. More in particular, if a macro mac has been defined as donald and the input reads **mac;**, the lexical analyzer requires to see the characters **m**, **a**, **c**, and **;** before it can recognize the identifier mac and pass it on. The lexical identification module then identifies mac as a macro and signals to the input module to insert the text donald right after the end of the characters **m**, **a**, and **c**. The input module cannot do this since it has already sent off the semicolon following these characters.

Fighting fire with fire, the problem is solved by introducing yet another back-call, one from the lexical analyzer to the input module, signaling that the lexical analyzer has backtracked over the semicolon. This is something the input module *can* implement, by just resetting a read pointer, since the characters are in a buffer in memory. This is another advantage of maintaining the entire program text in a single buffer. If a more complicated buffering scheme is used, caution must be exercised if the semicolon is the last character in an input buffer: exhausted buffers cannot be released until it is certain that no more backtracking back-calls for their contents will be issued. Depending on the nature of the tokens and the lexical analyzer, this may be difficult to ascertain.

All in all, the three modules have to be aware of each other's problems and internal functions; actually they form one integrated module. Still, the structure shown in Figure 2.44 is helpful in programming the module(s).

2.12.1.2 Parameters of macros

Handling the parameters requires some special care, on two counts. The first one is that one has to be careful to determine the extent of an actual parameter *before* any substitution has been applied to it. Otherwise the sequence

```
#define A      a,b
#define B(p)   p
B(A)
```

would cause B(A) to be replaced by B(a,b) which gives B two parameters instead of the required one.

The second concerns the substitution itself. It requires the formal parameters to be replaced by the actual parameters, which can in principle be done by using the normal macro-substitution mechanism. In doing so, one has to take into account, however, that the scope of the formal parameter is just the macro itself, unlike the scopes of real macros, which are global. So, when we try to implement the macro call

    is_capital (txt [i])

by simply defining its formal parameter and substituting its body:

    #define ch txt [i]
    ('A' <= (ch) && (ch) <= 'Z')

we may find that we have just redefined an existing macro ch. Also, the call is_capital(ch + 1) would produce

    #define ch ch + 1
    ('A' <= (ch) && (ch) <= 'Z')

with disastrous results.

One simple way to implement this is to generate a new name for each actual (not formal!) parameter. So the macro call

    is_capital (txt [i])

may be implemented as

    #define arg_00393   txt [i]
    ('A' <= (arg_00393) && (arg_00393) <= 'Z')

assuming that txt[i] happens to be the 393rd actual parameter in this run of the macro processor. Normal processing then turns this into

    ('A' <= (txt [i]) && (txt [i]) <= 'Z')

which is correct. A more efficient implementation that causes less clutter in the symbol table keeps a set of "local" macros with each buffer in the input buffer stack. These local macros apply to that buffer only; their values are set from the actual parameters.

Figure 2.45 shows the situation in which the above macro call occurs in an included file mac.h; the lexical analyzer has just read the [in the first substitution of the parameter.

Depending on the language definition, it may or may not be an error for a macro to be recursive or for a file to include itself; if the macro system also features conditional text inclusion, such recursion may be meaningful. A check for recursion can be made simply by stepping down the input buffer stack and comparing identifiers.

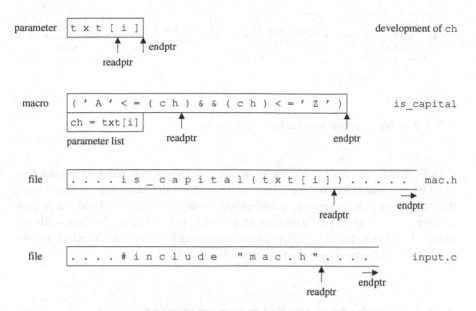

Fig. 2.45: An input buffer stack of include files, macro calls, and macro parameters

2.12.2 Conditional text inclusion

The actual logic of conditional text inclusion is usually simple to implement; the difficult question is where it fits in the character to token pipeline of Figure 2.44, or the input buffer stack of Figure 2.45. The answer varies considerably with the details of the mechanism.

Conditional text inclusion as described in the language manual is controlled by certain items in the text and acts on certain items in the text. The C preprocessor is controlled by tokens that are matched by the regular expression \n#[\n\t]*[a-z]+ (which describes tokens like #ifdef starting right after a newline). These tokens must be recognized by the tokenizing process, to prevent them from being recognized inside other tokens, for example inside comments. Also, the C preprocessor works on entire lines. The PL/I preprocessor is controlled by tokens of the form %[A-Z]* and works on tokens recognized in the usual way by the lexical analyzer.

The main point is that the place in the input pipeline where the control originates may differ from the place where the control is exerted, as was also the case in macro substitution. To make the interaction possible, interfaces must be present in both places.

So, in the C preprocessor, a layer must be inserted between the input module and the lexical analyzer. This layer must act on input lines, and must be able to perform functions like "skip lines up to and including a preprocessor #else line". It is controlled from the lexical identification module, as shown in Figure 2.46.

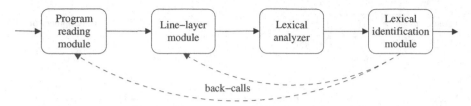

Fig. 2.46: Input pipeline, with line layer and feedback

A PL/I-like preprocessor is simpler in this respect: it is controlled by tokens supplied by the lexical identification layer and works on the same tokens. This means that all tokens from the lexical identification module can be stored and the preprocessing actions can be performed on the resulting list of tokens. No back-calls are required, and even the more advanced preprocessing features, which include repetition, can be performed conveniently on the list of tokens.

2.12.3 Generics by controlled macro processing

A *generic unit X* is a template from which an *X* can be created by instantiation; *X* can be a type, a routine, a module, an object definition, etc., depending on the language definition. Generally, parameters have to be supplied in an instantiation; these parameters are often of a kind that cannot normally be passed as parameters: types, modules, etc. For example, the code

```
GENERIC TYPE List_link (Type):
    FIELD Value: Type;
    FIELD Next: Pointer to List_link (Type);
```

declares a generic type for the links in linked lists of values; the type of the values is given by the generic parameter Type. The generic type declaration can be used in an actual type declaration to produce the desired type. A type for links to be used in linked lists of integers could be instantiated from this generic declaration by code like

```
TYPE Integer_list_link:
    INSTANTIATED List_link (Integer);
```

which supplies the generic parameter Integer to List_link. This instantiation would then act as if the programmer had written

```
TYPE Integer_list_link:
    FIELD Value: Integer;
    FIELD Next: Pointer to Integer_list_link;
```

Generic instantiation looks very much like parameterized text substitution, and treating a generic unit as some kind of parameterized macro is often the simplest way to implement generics. Usually generic substitution differs in detail from macro substitution. In our example we have to replace the text INSTANTIATED List_link(Integer) by the fields themselves, but List_link(Integer) by the name Integer_list_link.

The obvious disadvantage is that code is duplicated, which costs compilation time and run-time space. With nested generics, the cost can be exponential in the number of generic units. This can be a problem, especially if libraries use generics liberally.

For another way to handle generics that does not result in code duplication, see Section 11.5.3.2.

2.13 Conclusion

We have seen that lexical analyzers can conveniently be generated from the regular expressions that describe the tokens in the source language. Such generated lexical analyzers record their progress in sets of "items", regular expressions in which a dot separates the part already matched from the part still to be matched. It turned out that the results of all manipulations of these item sets can be precomputed during lexical analyzer generation, leading to finite-state automata or FSAs. Their implementation results in very efficient lexical analyzers, both in space, provided the transition tables are compressed, and in time.

Traditionally, lexical analysis and lexical analyzers are explained and implemented directly from the FSA or transition diagrams of the regular expressions [278], without introducing dotted items [93]. Dotted items, however, unify lexical and syntactic analysis and play an important role in tree-rewriting code generation, so we have based our explanation of lexical analysis on them.

We have seen that the output of a lexical analyzer is a sequence of tokens, (token class, token representation) pairs. The identifiers in this sequence often need some identification and further processing for the benefit of macro processing and subsequent syntax analysis. This processing is conveniently done in a lexical identification phase. We will now proceed to consider *syntax analysis*, also known as *parsing*.

Summary

- Lexical analysis turns a stream of characters into a stream of tokens; syntax analysis turns a stream of tokens into a parse tree, or, more probably, an abstract syntax tree. Together they undo the linearization the program suffered in being written out sequentially.
- An abstract syntax tree is a version of the syntax tree in which only the semantically important nodes are retained. What is "semantically important" is up to the compiler writer.

- Source program processing starts by reading the entire program into a character buffer. This simplifies memory management, token isolation, file position tracking, and error reporting.
- Standardize newline characters as soon as you see them.
- A token consists of a number (its class), and a string (its representation); it should also include position-tracking information.
- The form of the tokens in a source language is described by patterns in a special formalism; the patterns are called regular expressions. Complicated regular expressions can be simplified by naming parts of them and reusing the parts; a set of named regular expressions is called a regular description.
- A lexical analyzer is a repeating pattern matcher that will cut up the input stream into tokens matching the token patterns of the source language.
- Ambiguous patterns are resolved by accepting the longest match (maximal munch). If that fails, the order of the patterns is used to break the tie.
- Lexical analyzers can be written by hand or generated automatically, in both cases based on the specification of the tokens through regular expressions.
- Handwritten lexical analyzers make a first decision based on the first character of the token, and use ad-hoc code thereafter.
- The lexical analyzer is the only part of the compiler that sees each character of the source program; as a result, it performs an order of magnitude more actions that the rest of the compiler phases.
- Much computation in a lexical analyzer is done by side-effect-free functions on a finite domain. The results of such computations can be determined statically by precomputation and stored in a table. The computation can then be replaced by table lookup, greatly increasing the efficiency.
- The resulting tables require and allow table compression.
- Generated lexical analyzers represent their knowledge as a set of items. An item is a named fully parenthesized regular expression with a dot somewhere in it. The part before the dot matches the last part of the input scanned; the part after the dot must match the first part of the rest of the input for the item to succeed.
- Scanning one character results in an item being transformed into zero, one, or more new items. This transition is called a shift. The set of items kept by the lexical analyzer is transformed into another set of items by a shift over a character.
- The item sets are called states and the transformations are called state transitions.
- An item with the dot at the end, called a reduce item, signals a possible token found, but the end of a longer token may still be ahead. When the item set becomes empty, there are no more tokens to be expected, and the most recent reduce item identifies the token to be matched and reduced.
- All this item manipulation can be avoided by precomputing the states and their transitions. This is possible since there are a finite number of characters and a finite number of item sets; it becomes feasible when we limit the precomputation to those item sets that can occur in practice: the states.
- The states, the transition table, and the transition mechanism together are called a finite-state automaton, FSA.

- Generated lexical analyzers based on FSAs are very efficient, and are standard, although handwritten lexical analyzers can come close.
- Transition tables consist mainly of empty entries. They can be compressed by cutting them into strips, row-wise or column-wise, and fitting the values in one strip into the holes in other strips, by shifting one with respect to the other; the starting positions of the shifted strips are recorded and used to retrieve entries. Some trick must be applied to resolve the value/hole ambiguity.
- In another compression scheme, the strips are grouped into clusters, the members of which do not interfere with each other, using graph coloring techniques. All members of a cluster can then be superimposed.
- Often, identifiers recognized by the lexical analysis have to be identified further before being passed to the syntax analyzer. They are looked up in the symbol table. This identification can serve type identifier identification, keyword identification, macro processing, conditional compilation, and file inclusion.
- A symbol table is an extensible array of records indexed by strings. The string is the identifier and the corresponding record holds all information about the identifier.
- String-indexable arrays can be implemented efficiently using hashing.
- Macro substitution, macro parameter expansion, conditional compilation, and file inclusion can be implemented simultaneously using a single stack of input buffers.
- Often, generics can be implemented using file inclusion and macro processing. This makes generics a form of token insertion, between the lexical and the syntax analyzer.

Exercises

2.1. Section 2.1 advises to read the program text with a single system call. Actually, you usually need three: one to find out the size of the input file, one to allocate space for it, and one to read it. Write a program for your favorite operating system that reads a file into memory, and counts the number of occurrences of the character sequence abcabc. Try to make it as fast as possible. Note: the sequences may overlap.

2.2. On your favorite system and programming language, time the process of reading a large file using the language-supplied character read routine. Compare this time to asking the system for the size of the file, allocating the space, and reading the file using one call of the language-supplied mass read routine.

2.3. Using your favorite system and programming language, create a file of size 256 which contains all 256 different 8-bit characters. Read it character by character, and as a block. What do you get?

2.4. Somebody in a compiler construction project suggests solving the newline problem by systematically replacing all newlines by spaces, since they mean the same anyway. Why is this almost certainly wrong?

2.5. (▷786) Some programming languages, for example Algol 68, feature a token class similar to strings—the **format**. It is largely similar to the formats used in C printf() calls. For example, $3d$ described the formatting of an integer value in 3 digits. Additionally, numbers in formats may be dynamic expressions: integers formatted under $n(2*a)d$ will have $2*a$ digits. Design a lexical analyzer that will handle this. Hint 1: the dynamic expressions can, of course, contain function calls that have formats as parameters, recursively. Hint 2: this is not trivial.

2.6. (▷www) Give a regular expression for all sequences of 0s and 1s that (a) contain exactly 2 1s. (b) contain no consecutive 1s. (c) contain an even number of 1s.

2.7. Why would the dot pattern (.) usually exclude the newline (Figure 2.4)?

2.8. (▷786) What does the regular expression $a^{?*}$ mean? And a^{**}? Are these expressions erroneous? Are they ambiguous?

2.9. (from Stuart Broad) The following is a highly simplified grammar for URLs, assuming proper definitions for letter and digit.

```
URL  →  label | URL '.' label
label  →  letter '(' letgit_hyphen_string? letgit ')'?
letgit_hyphen_string  →
     letgit_hyphen | letgit_hyphen letgit_hyphen_string
letgit_hyphen  →  letgit | '-'
letgit  →  letter | digit
```

(a) Turn this grammar into a regular description. (b) Turn this regular description into a regular expression.

2.10. (▷www) Rewrite the skip_layout_and_comment routine of Figure 2.8 to allow for nested comments.

2.11. The comment skipping scheme of Figure 2.8 suffices for single-character comment-delimiters. However, multi-character comment-delimiters require some more attention. Write a skip_layout_and_comment routine for C, where comments are delimited by "/*" and "*/", and don't nest.

2.12. (▷786) Section 2.5.1.2 leaves us with a single array of 256 bytes, charbits[ ]. Since programs contain only ASCII characters in the range 32 through 126, plus newline and perhaps tab, somebody proposes to gain another factor of 2 and reduce the array to a length of 128. What is your reaction?

2.13. (▷www) Explain why is there a **for each** statement in Figure 2.16 rather than just:

if the input matches $T_1 → R_1$ over Length:
   ...

2.14. The text distinguishes "shift items" with the dot in front of a basic pattern, "reduce items" with the dot at the end, and "non-basic items" with the dot in front of a regular subexpression. What about items with the dot just before the closing parenthesis of a parenthesized subexpression?

2.15. (▷www) Suppose you are to extend an existing lexical analyzer generator with a basic pattern $\equiv$, which matches two consecutive occurrences of the same characters, for example aa, ==, or ,,. How would you implement this (not so) basic pattern?

2.16. (▷www) Argue the correctness of some of the dot motion rules of Figure 2.19.

2.17. (▷www) Some systems that use regular expressions, for example SGML, add a third composition operator, &, with $R_1 \& R_2$ meaning that both R_1 and R_2 must occur but that they may occur in any order; so $R_1 \& R_2$ is equivalent to $R_1 R_2 | R_2 R_1$. Show the ε-move rules for this composition operator in a fashion similar to those in Figure 2.19, starting from the item $T \rightarrow \alpha \bullet (R_1 \& R_2 \& \ldots \& R_n) \beta$.

$$T \rightarrow \alpha \bullet (R_1 \& R_2 \& \ldots \& R_n) \beta \Rightarrow T \rightarrow \alpha \bullet R_1 (R_2 \& R_3 \& \ldots \& R_n) \beta$$
$$T \rightarrow \alpha \bullet R_2 (R_1 \& R_3 \& \ldots \& R_n) \beta$$
$$\ldots$$
$$T \rightarrow \alpha \bullet R_n (R_1 \& R_2 \& \ldots \& R_{n-1}) \beta$$

2.18. (▷786) Show that the closure algorithm for dotted items (Figure 2.25) terminates.

2.19. (▷www) In Section 2.6.3, we claim that "our closure algorithm terminates after having generated five sets, out of a possible 64". Explain the 64.

2.20. The task is to isolate keywords in a file. A keyword is any sequence of letters delineated by apostrophes: 'begin' is the keyword **begin**.
(a) Construct by hand the FSA to do this. (Beware of non-letters between apostrophes.)
(b) Write regular expressions for the process, and construct the FSA. Compare it to the hand version.

2.21. (▷www) Pack the transition table of Figure 2.31 using marking by state (rather than by character, as shown in Figure 2.36).

2.22. Tables to be compressed often contain many rows that are similar. Examples are rows 0, 3, and 7 of Figure 3.42:

state	i	+	(	)	$	E	T
0	5			1	6	shift	
3	5	7		4	shift		
7	5	7		8	6	shift	

More empty entries—and thus more compressibility—can be obtained by assigning to one of the rows in such a group the role of "principal" and reducing the others to the difference with the principal. Taking row 7 for the principal, we can simplify the table to:

```
state principal i  +  (  )  $  E  T

  0         7              1
  3         7                    4
  7              5  7    8  6  shift
```

If, upon retrieval, an empty entry is obtained from a row that has a principal, the actual answer can be obtained from that principal. Fill in the details to turn this idea into an algorithm.

2.23. Compress the SLR(1) table of Figure 3.46 in two ways: using row displacement with marking by state, and using column displacement with marking by state.

2.24. (▷www) Use *lex, flex*, or a similar lexical analyzer generator to generate a filter that removes comment from C program files. One problem is that the comment starter /∗ may occur inside strings. Another is that comments may be arbitrarily long and most generated lexical analyzers store a token even if it is subsequently discarded, so removing comments requires arbitrarily large buffers, which are not supplied by all generated lexical analyzers. Hint: use the start condition feature of *lex* or *flex* to consume the comment line by line.

2.25. (▷786) An adviser to a compiler construction project insists that the programmatically correct way to do macro processing is in a separate phase between reading the program and lexical analysis. Show this person the errors of his or her ways.

2.26. In Section 2.12.1.1, we need a back-call because the process of recognizing the identifier mac overruns the end of the identifier by one character. The handwritten lexical analyzer in Section 2.5 also overruns the end of an identifier. Why do we not need a back-call there?

2.27. (▷www) Give a code segment (in some ad hoc notation) that uses N generic items and that will cause a piece of code to be generated 2^{N-1} times under generics by macro expansion.

2.28. (▷www) *History of lexical analysis*: Study Rabin and Scott's 1959 paper *Finite Automata and their Decision Problems* [228], and write a summary of it, with special attention to the "subset construction algorithm".

Chapter 3
Tokens to Syntax Tree — Syntax Analysis

There are two ways of doing parsing: top-down and bottom-up. For top-down parsers, one has the choice of writing them by hand or having them generated automatically, but bottom-up parsers can only be generated. In all three cases, the syntax structure to be recognized is specified using a context-free grammar; grammars were discussed in Section 1.8. Sections 3.2 and 3.5.10 detail considerations concerning error detection and error recovery in syntax analysis.

Grammars are an essential tool in language specification; they have several important aspects. First, a grammar serves to impose a structure on the linear sequence of tokens which is the program. This structure is all-important since the semantics of the program is specified in terms of the nodes in this structure. The process of finding the structure in the flat stream of tokens is called **parsing**, and a module that performs this task is a **parser**.

Second, using techniques from the field of formal languages, a parser can be constructed automatically from a grammar. This is a great help in compiler construction.

Third, grammars are a powerful documentation tool. They help programmers to write syntactically correct programs and provide answers to detailed questions about the syntax. They do the same for compiler writers.

There are two well-known and well-researched ways to do parsing, deterministic left-to-right top-down (the LL method) and deterministic left-to-right bottom-up (the LR and LALR methods), and a third, emerging, technique, generalized LR. **Left-to-right** means that the program text, or more precisely the sequence of tokens, is processed from left to right, one token at the time. Intuitively speaking, **deterministic** means that no searching is involved: each token brings the parser one step closer to the goal of constructing the syntax tree, and it is never necessary to undo one of these steps. The theory of formal languages provides a more rigorous definition. The terms top-down and bottom-up will be explained below.

The deterministic parsing methods have the advantage that they require an amount of time that is a linear function of the length of the input: they are **linear-time** methods. There is also another reason to require determinacy: a grammar for which a deterministic parser can be generated is guaranteed to be non-ambiguous, which is of course a very important property of a programming language grammar. Being non-ambiguous and allowing deterministic parsing are not exactly the same (the second implies the first but not vice versa), but requiring determinacy is technically the best non-ambiguity test we have.

Unfortunately, deterministic parsers do not solve all parsing problems: they work for restricted classes of grammars only. A grammar copied "as is" from a language manual has a very small chance of leading to a deterministic method, unless of course the language designer has taken pains to make the grammar match such a method. There are several ways to deal with this problem:

- transform the grammar so that it becomes amenable to a deterministic method;
- allow the user to "add" sufficient determinism;
- use a non-deterministic method.

Methods to transform the grammar are explained in Sections 3.4.3. The transformed grammar will assign syntax trees to at least some programs that differ from the original trees. This unavoidably causes some problems in further processing, since the semantics is described in terms of the original syntax trees. So grammar transformation methods must also create transformed semantic rules. Methods to add extra-grammatical determinism are described in Section 3.4.3.3 and 3.5.7. They use so-called "conflict resolvers," which specify decisions the parser cannot take. This can be convenient, but takes away some of the safety inherent in grammars.

Dropping the determinism—allowing searching to take place—results in algorithms that can handle practically all grammars. These algorithms are not linear-time and their time and space requirements vary. One such algorithm is "generalized LR", which is reasonably well-behaved when applied to programming language grammars. Generalized LR is most often used in (re)compiling legacy code for which no deterministic grammar exists. Generalized LR is treated in Section 3.5.8.

We will assume that the grammar of the programming language is non-ambiguous. This implies that to each input program there belongs either one syntax tree, and then the program is syntactically correct, or no syntax tree, and then the program contains one or more syntax errors.

3.1 Two classes of parsing methods

A parsing method constructs the syntax tree for a given sequence of tokens. Constructing the syntax tree means that a tree of nodes must be created and that these nodes must be labeled with grammar symbols, in such a way that:

- leaf nodes are labeled with terminals and inner nodes are labeled with non-terminals;
- the top node is labeled with the start symbol of the grammar;
- the children of an inner node labeled N correspond to the members of an alternative of N, in the same order as they occur in that alternative;
- the terminals labeling the leaf nodes correspond to the sequence of tokens, in the same order as they occur in the input.

Left-to-right parsing starts with the first few tokens of the input and a syntax tree, which initially consists of the top node only. The top node is labeled with the start symbol.

The parsing methods can be distinguished by the order in which they construct the nodes in the syntax tree: the top-down method constructs them in pre-order, the bottom-up methods in post-order. A short introduction to the terms "pre-order" and "post-order" can be found below. The top-down method starts at the top and constructs the tree downwards to match the tokens in the input; the bottom-up methods combine the tokens in the input into parts of the tree to finally construct the top node. The two methods do quite different things when they construct a node. We will first explain both methods in outline to show the similarities and then in enough detail to design a parser generator.

Note that there are three different notions involved here: *visiting a node*, which means doing something with the node that is significant to the algorithm in whose service the traversal is performed;*traversing a node*, which means visiting that node and traversing its subtrees in some order; and *traversing a tree*, which means traversing its top node, which will then recursively traverse the entire tree. "Visiting" belongs to the algorithm; "traversing" in both meanings belongs to the control mechanism. This separates two concerns and is the source of the usefulness of the tree traversal concept. In everyday speech these terms are often confused, though.

3.1.1 Principles of top-down parsing

A **top-down parser** begins by constructing the top node of the tree, which it knows to be labeled with the start symbol. It now constructs the nodes in the syntax tree in pre-order, which means that the top of a subtree is constructed before any of its lower nodes are.

When the top-down parser constructs a node, the label of the node itself is already known, say N; this is true for the top node and we will see that it is true for all other nodes as well. Using information from the input, the parser then determines the

Pre-order and post-order traversal

The terms *pre-order visit* and *post-order visit* describe recursive processes traversing trees and visiting the nodes of those tree. Such traversals are performed as part of some algorithms, for example to draw a picture of the tree.

When a process **visits a node** in a tree it performs a specific action on it: it can, for example, print information about the node. When a process **traverses a node** in a tree it does two things: it traverses the **subtrees** (also known as **children**) and it visits the node itself; the order in which it performs these actions is crucial and determines the nature of the traversal. A process **traverses a tree** by traversing its top node.

The traversal process starts at the top of the tree in both cases and eventually visits all nodes in the tree; the order in which the nodes are visited differs, though. When traversing a node N in **pre-order**, the process first visits the node N and then traverses N's subtrees in left-to-right order. When traversing a node N in **post-order**, the process first traverses N's subtrees in left-to-right order and then visits the node N. Other variants (multiple visits, mixing the visits inside the left-to-right traversal, deviating from the left-to-right traversal) are possible but less usual.

Although the difference between pre-order and post-order seems small when written down in two sentences, the effect is enormous. For example, the first node visited in pre-order is the top of the tree, in post-order it is its leftmost bottom-most leaf. Figure 3.1 shows the same tree, once with the nodes numbered in pre-order and once in post-order. Pre-order is generally used to distribute information over the tree, post-order to collect information from the tree.

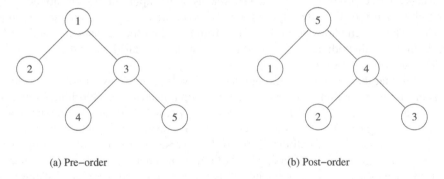

(a) Pre−order   (b) Post−order

Fig. 3.1: A tree with its nodes numbered in pre-order and post-order

correct alternative for N; how it can do this is explained in Section 3.4.1. Knowing which alternative applies, it knows the labels of all the children of this node labeled N. The parser then proceeds to construct the first child of N; note that it already knows its label. The process of determining the correct alternative for the leftmost child is repeated on the further levels, until a leftmost child is constructed that is a terminal symbol. The terminal then "matches" the first token t_1 in the program. This does not happen by accident: the top-down parser chooses the alternatives of the higher nodes precisely so that this will happen. We now know "why the first token is there," which syntax tree segment produced the first token.

The parser then leaves the terminal behind and continues by constructing the next node in pre-order; this could for example be the second child of the parent of the first token. See Figure 3.2, in which the large dot is the node that is being constructed, the smaller dots represent nodes that have already been constructed and the hollow dots indicate nodes whose labels are already known but which have not yet been constructed. Nothing is known about the rest of the parse tree yet, so that part is not shown. In summary, the main task of a top-down parser is to choose the correct alternatives for known non-terminals. Top-down parsing is treated in Sections 3.3 and 3.4.

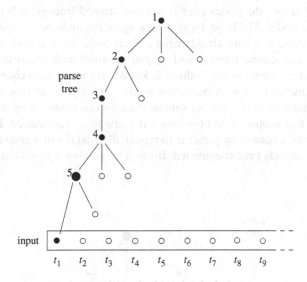

Fig. 3.2: A top-down parser recognizing the first token in the input

3.1.2 Principles of bottom-up parsing

The **bottom-up parsing method** constructs the nodes in the syntax tree in post-order: the top of a subtree is constructed after all of its lower nodes have been constructed. When a bottom-up parser constructs a node, all its children have already been constructed, and are present and known; the label of the node itself is also known. The parser then creates the node, labels it, and connects it to its children.

A bottom-up parser always constructs the node that is the top of the first complete subtree it meets when it proceeds from left to right through the input; a complete subtree is a tree all of whose children have already been constructed. Tokens are considered as subtrees of height 1 and are constructed as they are met. The new subtree must of course be chosen so as to be a subtree of the parse tree, but an obvious problem is that we do not know the parse tree yet; Section 3.5 explains how to deal with this.

The children of the first subtree to be constructed are leaf nodes only, labeled with terminals, and the node's correct alternative is chosen to match them. Next, the second subtree in the input is found all of whose children have already been constructed; the children of this node can involve non-leaf nodes now, created by earlier constructing of nodes. A node is constructed for it, with label and appropriate alternative. This process is repeated until finally all children of the top node have been constructed, after which the top node itself is constructed and the parsing is complete.

Figure 3.3 shows the parser after it has constructed (recognized) its first, second, and third nodes. The large dot indicates again the node being constructed, the smaller ones those that have already been constructed. The first node spans tokens t_3, t_4, and t_5; the second spans t_7 and t_8; and the third spans the first node, token t_6, and the second node. Nothing is known yet about the existence of other nodes, but branches have been drawn upward from tokens t_1 and t_2, since we know that they cannot be part of a smaller subtree than the one spanning tokens t_3 through t_8; otherwise that subtree would have been the first to be constructed. In summary, the main task of a bottom-up parser is to repeatedly find the first node all of whose children have already been constructed. Bottom-up parsing is treated in Section 3.5.

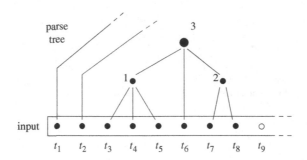

Fig. 3.3: A bottom-up parser constructing its first, second, and third nodes

3.2 Error detection and error recovery

An error is detected when the construction of the syntax tree fails; since both top-down and bottom-up parsing methods read the tokens from left to right, this occurs when processing a specific token. Then two questions arise: what error message to give to the user, and whether and how to proceed after the error.

The position at which the error is detected may be unrelated to the position of the actual error the user made. In the C fragment

x = a(p+q(− b(r−s);

the error is most probably the opening parenthesis after the q, which should have been a closing parenthesis, but almost all parsers will report two missing closing parentheses before the semicolon. It will be clear that it is next to impossible to spot this error at the right moment, since the segment x = a(p+q(−b(r−s) is correct with q a function and − a monadic minus. Some advanced error handling methods consider the entire program when producing error messages, but after 30 years these are still experimental, and are hardly ever found in compilers. The best one can expect from the efficient methods in use today is that they do not derail the parser any further. Sections 3.4.5 and 3.5.10 discuss such methods.

It has been suggested that with today's fast interactive systems, there is no point in continuing program processing after the first error has been detected, since the user can easily correct the error and then recompile in less time than it would take to read the next error message. But users like to have some idea of how many syntax errors there are left in their program; recompiling several times, each time expecting it to be the last time, is demoralizing. We therefore like to continue the parsing and give as many error messages as there are syntax errors. This means that we have to do error recovery.

There are two strategies for error recovery. One, called **error correction** modifies the input token stream and/or the parser's internal state so that parsing can continue; we will discuss below the question of whether the resulting parse tree will still be consistent. There is an almost infinite number of techniques to do this; some are simple to implement, others complicated, but all of them have a significant chance of derailing the parser and producing an avalanche of spurious error messages. The other, called **non-correcting error recovery**, does not modify the input stream, but rather discards all parser information and continues parsing the rest of the program with a grammar for "rest of program" [235]. If the parse succeeds, there were no more errors; if it fails it has certainly found another error. It may miss errors, though. It does not produce a parse tree for syntactically incorrect programs.

The grammar for "rest of program" for a language L is called the **suffix grammar** of L, since it generates all suffixes (tail ends) of all programs in L. Although the suffix grammar of a language L can be derived easily from the original grammar of L, suffix grammars can generally not be handled by any of the deterministic parsing techniques. They need stronger but slower parsing methods, which requires the presence of two parsers in the compiler. Non-correcting error recovery yields very reliable error detection and recovery, but is relatively difficult to implement. It is not often found in parser generators.

It is important that the parser never allows an inconsistent parse tree to be constructed, when given syntactically incorrect input. All error recovery should be either error-correcting and always produce parse trees that conform to the syntax, or be non-correcting and produce no parse trees for incorrect input.

As already explained in Section 2.8 where we were concerned with token representations, allowing inconsistent data to find their way into later phases in a compiler is asking for trouble, the more so when this data is the parse tree. Any subsequent phase working on an inconsistent parse tree may easily access absent nodes, apply algorithms to the wrong data structures, follow non-existent pointers, and get itself in all kinds of trouble, all of which happens far away from the place where the error occurred. Any error recovery technique should be designed and implemented so that it will under no circumstances produce an inconsistent parse tree; if it cannot avoid doing so for technical reasons, the implementation should stop further processing after the parsing phase. Non-correcting error recovery has to do this anyway, since it does not produce a parse tree at all for an incorrect program.

Most parser generators come with a built-in error detection and recovery mechanism, so the compiler writer has little say in the matter. Knowing how the error handling works may allow the compiler writer to make it behave in a more user-friendly way, however.

3.3 Creating a top-down parser manually

Given a non-terminal N and a token t at position p in the input, a top-down parser must decide which alternative of N must be applied so that the subtree headed by the node labeled N will be the correct subtree at position p. We do not know, however, how to tell that a tree is correct, but we do know when a tree is incorrect: when it has a different token than t as its leftmost leaf at position p. This provides us with a reasonable approximation to what a correct tree looks like: a tree that starts with t or is empty.

The most obvious way to decide on the right alternative for N is to have a (recursive) Boolean function which tests N's alternatives in succession and which succeeds when it finds an alternative that can produce a possible tree. To make the method deterministic, we decide not to do any backtracking: the first alternative that can produce a possible tree is assumed to be the correct alternative; needless to say, this assumption gets us into trouble occasionally. This approach results in a **recursive descent parser**; recursive descent parsers have for many years been popular with compiler writers and writing one may still be the simplest way to get a simple parser. The technique does have its limitations, though, as we will see.

3.3.1 Recursive descent parsing

Figure 3.5 shows a recursive descent parser for the grammar from Figure 3.4; the driver is shown in Figure 3.6. Since it lacks code for the construction of the parse tree, it is actually a recognizer. The grammar describes a very simple-minded kind of arithmetic expression, one in which the + operator is right-associative. It produces token strings like **IDENTIFIER + (IDENTIFIER + IDENTIFIER) EoF**, where EoF stands for end-of-file. The parser text shows an astonishingly direct relationship to the grammar for which it was written. This similarity is one of the great attractions of recursive descent parsing; the lazy Boolean operators && and || in C are especially suitable for expressing it.

```
input           → expression EoF
expression      → term rest_expression
term            → IDENTIFIER | parenthesized_expression
parenthesized_expression  → '(' expression ')'
rest_expression → '+' expression | ε
```

Fig. 3.4: A simple grammar for demonstrating top-down parsing

```
#include    "tokennumbers.h"

/* PARSER */
int input(void) {
    return expression() && require(token(EoF));
}

int expression(void) {
    return term() && require(rest_expression());
}

int term(void) {
    return token(IDENTIFIER) || parenthesized_expression();
}

int parenthesized_expression(void) {
    return token('(') && require(expression()) && require(token(')'));
}

int rest_expression(void) {
    return token('+') && require(expression()) || 1;
}

int token(int tk) {
    if (tk != Token.class) return 0;
    get_next_token(); return 1;
}

int require(int found) {
    if (!found) error ();
    return 1;
}
```

Fig. 3.5: A recursive descent recognizer for the grammar of Figure 3.4

```
#include    "lex.h"     /* for start_lex (), get_next_token(), Token */

/* DRIVER */
int  main(void) {
     start_lex ();  get_next_token();
     require(input ());
     return 0;
}

void error(void) {
     printf ("Error in expression\n");  exit (1);
}
```

Fig. 3.6: Driver for the recursive descent recognizer

Each rule N corresponds to an integer routine that returns 1 (true) if a terminal
production of N was found in the present position in the input stream, and then the
part of the input stream corresponding to this terminal production of N has been
consumed. Otherwise, no such terminal production of N was found, the routine
returns 0 (false) and no input was consumed. To this end, the routine tries each of
the alternatives of N in turn, to see if one of them is present. To see if an alternative
is present, the presence of its first member is tested, recursively. If it is there, the
alternative is considered the correct one, and the other members are required to be
present. If the first member is not there, no input has been consumed, and the routine
is free to test the next alternative. If none of the alternatives succeeds, N is not there,
the routine for N returns 0, and no input has been consumed, since no successful
call to a routine has been made. If a member is required to be present and it is not
found, there is a syntax error, which is reported, and the parser stops.

The routines for expression, term, and parenthesized_expression in Figure 3.5
are the direct result of this approach, and so is the routine token(). The rule for
rest_expression contains an empty alternative; since this can always be assumed to
be present, it can be represented simply by a 1 in the routine for rest_expression.
Notice that the precedence and the semantics of the lazy Boolean operators && and
|| give us exactly what we need.

3.3.2 Disadvantages of recursive descent parsing

In spite of their initial good looks, recursive descent parsers have a number of drawbacks. First, there is still some searching through the alternatives; the repeated testing of the global variable *Token.class* effectively implements repeated backtracking
over one token. Second, the method often fails to produce a correct parser. Third,
error handling leaves much to be desired. The second problem in particular is both-
ersome, as the following three examples will show.

1. Suppose we want to add an array element as a term:

> term → IDENTIFIER | indexed_element | parenthesized_expression
> indexed_element → IDENTIFIER '[' expression ']'

and create a recursive descent parser for the new grammar. We then find that the routine for indexed_element will never be tried: when the sequence IDENTIFIER '[' occurs in the input, the first alternative of term will succeed, consume the identifier, and leave the indigestible part '['expression']' in the input.

2. A similar but slightly different phenomenon occurs in the grammar of Figure 3.7, which produces **ab** and **aab**. A recursive recognizer for it contains the routines shown in Figure 3.8. This recognizer will not recognize ab, since A() will consume the a and require(token('a')) will fail. And when the order of the alternatives in A() is inverted, aab will not be recognized.

S → A 'a' 'b'
A → 'a' | ε

Fig. 3.7: A simple grammar with a FIRST/FOLLOW conflict

```
int S(void) {
    return A() && require(token('a')) && require(token('b'));
}
int A(void) {
    return token('a') || 1;
}
```

Fig. 3.8: A *faulty* recursive recognizer for grammar of Figure 3.7

3. Suppose we want to replace the + for addition by a – for subtraction. Then the right associativity expressed in the grammar from Figure 3.4 is no longer acceptable. This means that the rule for expression will now have to read:

> expression → expression '–' term | ...

If we construct the recursive descent routine for this, we get

```
int expression(void) {
    return expression() && require(token('−')) &&
        require(term()) || ...;
}
```

but a call to this routine is guaranteed to loop. Recursive descent parsers cannot handle left-recursive grammars, which is a serious disadvantage, since most programming language grammars are left-recursive in places.

3.4 Creating a top-down parser automatically

The principles of constructing a top-down parser automatically derive from those of writing one by hand, by applying precomputation. Grammars which allow this construction of a top-down parser to be performed are called LL(1) grammars, those that do not exhibit LL(1) conflicts. The LL(1) parsing mechanism represents a push-down automaton, as described in Section 3.4.4. An important aspect of a parser is its error recovery capability; manual and automatic techniques are discussed in Section 3.4.5. An example of the use of a traditional top-down parser generator concludes this section on the creation of top-down parsers.

———————————————— Roadmap ————————————————

In previous sections we have obtained considerable gains by using precomputation, and we can do the same here. When we look at the recursive descent parsing process in more detail, we see that each time a routine for N is called with the same token t as first token of the input, the same sequence of routines gets called and the same alternative of N is chosen. So we can precompute for each rule N the alternative that applies for each token t in the input. Once we have this information, we can use it in the routine for N to decide right away which alternative applies on the basis of the input token. One advantage is that this way we will no longer need to call other routines to find the answer, thus avoiding the search overhead. Another advantage is that, unexpectedly, it also provides a solution of sorts to the problems with the three examples above.

3.4.1 LL(1) parsing

When we examine the routines in Figure 3.5 closely, we observe that the final decision on the success or failure of, for example, the routine term() is made by comparing the input token to the first token produced by the alternatives of term(): IDENTIFIER and parenthesized_expression(). So we have to precompute the sets of first tokens produced by all alternatives in the grammar, their so-called **FIRST sets**. It is easy to see that in order to do so, we will also have to precompute the FIRST sets of all non-terminals; the FIRST sets of the terminals are obvious.

The FIRST set of an alternative α, FIRST(α), contains all terminals α can start with; if α can produce the empty string ε, this ε is included in the set FIRST(α). Finding FIRST(α) is trivial when α starts with a terminal, as it does for example in

parenthesized_expression → '(' expression ')'

but when α starts with a non-terminal, say N, we have to find FIRST(N). FIRST(N), however, is the union of the FIRST sets of its alternatives. So we have to determine the FIRST sets of the rules and the alternatives simultaneously in one algorithm.

The FIRST sets can be computed by the closure algorithm shown in Figure 3.9. The initializations set the FIRST sets of the terminals to contain the terminals as singletons, and set the FIRST set of the empty alternative to ε; all other FIRST sets start off empty. Notice the difference between the empty set { } and the singleton containing ε: $\{\varepsilon\}$. The first inference rule says that if α is an alternative of N, N can start with any token α can start with. The second inference rule says that an alternative α can start with any token its first member can start with, except ε. The case that the first member of α is nullable (in which case its FIRST set contains ε) is covered by the third rule. The third rule says that if the first member of α is nullable, α can start with any token the rest of the alternative after the first member (β) can start with. If α contains only one member, the rest of the alternative is the empty alternative and FIRST(α) contains ε, as per initialization 4.

Data definitions:
    1. Token sets called FIRST sets for all terminals, non-terminals and alternatives of non-terminals in G.
    2. A token set called FIRST for each alternative tail in G; an alternative tail is a sequence of zero or more grammar symbols α if $A\alpha$ is an alternative or alternative tail in G.

Initializations:
    1. For all terminals T, set FIRST(T) to $\{T\}$.
    2. For all non-terminals N, set FIRST(N) to $\{\}$.
    3. For all non-empty alternatives and alternative tails α, set FIRST(α) to $\{\}$.
    4. Set the FIRST set of all empty alternatives and alternative tails to $\{\varepsilon\}$.

Inference rules:
    1. For each rule $N\rightarrow\alpha$ in G, FIRST(N) must contain all tokens in FIRST(α), including ε if FIRST(α) contains it.
    2. For each alternative or alternative tail α of the form $A\beta$, FIRST(α) must contain all tokens in FIRST(A), excluding ε, should FIRST(A) contain it.
    3. For each alternative or alternative tail α of the form $A\beta$ and FIRST(A) contains ε, FIRST(α) must contain all tokens in FIRST(β), including ε if FIRST(β) contains it.

Fig. 3.9: Closure algorithm for computing the FIRST sets in a grammar G

The closure algorithm terminates since the FIRST sets can only grow in each application of an inference rule, and their largest possible contents is the set of all terminals and ε. In practice it terminates very quickly. The initial and final FIRST sets for our simple grammar are shown in Figures 3.10 and 3.11, respectively.

```
Rule / alternative (tail)        FIRST set
input                            { }
   expression EoF                { }
      EoF                        { EoF }

expression                       { }
   term rest_expression          { }
      rest_expression            { }

term                             { }
   IDENTIFIER                    { IDENTIFIER }
|
   parenthesized_expression { }

parenthesized_expression         { }
   '(' expression ')'            { '(' }
      expression ')'             { }
         ')'                     { ')' }

rest_expression                  { }
   '+' expression                { '+' }
      expression                 { }
|  ε                             { ε }
```

Fig. 3.10: The initial FIRST sets

```
Rule/alternative (tail)          FIRST set
input                            { IDENTIFIER  '(' }
   expression EoF                { IDENTIFIER  '(' }
      EoF                        { EoF }

expression                       { IDENTIFIER  '(' }
   term rest_expression          { IDENTIFIER  '(' }
      rest_expression            { '+' ε }

term                             { IDENTIFIER  '(' }
   IDENTIFIER                    { IDENTIFIER }
|
   parenthesized_expression { '(' }

parenthesized_expression         { '(' }
   '(' expression ')'            { '(' }
      expression ')'             { IDENTIFIER  '(' }
         ')'                     { ')' }

rest_expression                  { '+' ε }
   '+' expression                { '+' }
      expression                 { IDENTIFIER  '(' }
|  ε                             { ε }
```

Fig. 3.11: The final FIRST sets

The FIRST sets can now be used in the construction of a predictive parser, as shown in Figure 3.12. It is called a **predictive recursive descent parser** (or **predictive parser** for short) because it predicts the presence of a given alternative without trying to find out explicitly if it is there. Actually the term "predictive" is somewhat misleading: the parser does not predict, it knows for sure. Its "prediction" can only be wrong when there is a syntax error in the input.

We see that the code for each alternative is preceded by a case label based on its FIRST set: all testing is done on tokens only, using switch statements in C. The routine for a grammar rule will now only be called when it is certain that a terminal production of that rule starts at this point in the input (barring syntactically incorrect input), so it will always succeed and is represented by a procedure rather than by a Boolean function. This also applies to the routine token(), which now only has to match the input token or give an error message; the routine require() has disappeared.

3.4.1.1 LL(1) parsing with nullable alternatives

A complication arises with the case label for the empty alternative in rest_expression. Since it does not itself start with any token, how can we decide whether it is the correct alternative? We base our decision on the following consideration: when a non-terminal N produces a non-empty string we see a token that N can start with; when N produces an empty string we see a token that can follow N. So we choose the nullable alternative of N when we find ourselves looking at a token that can follow N.

This requires us to determine the set of tokens that can immediately follow a given non-terminal N; this set is called the **FOLLOW set** of N: FOLLOW(N). This FOLLOW(N) can be computed using an algorithm similar to that for FIRST(N); in this case we do not need FOLLOW sets of the separate alternatives, though. The closure algorithm for computing FOLLOW sets is given in Figure 3.13.

The algorithm starts by setting the FOLLOW sets of all non-terminals to the empty set, and uses the FIRST sets as obtained before. The first inference rule says that if a non-terminal N is followed by some alternative tail β, N can be followed by any token that β can start with. The second rule is more subtle: if β can produce the empty string, any token that can follow M can also follow N.

Figure 3.14 shows the result of this algorithm on the grammar of Figure 3.4. We see that FOLLOW(rest_expression) = { EoF ')' }, which supplies the case labels for the nullable alternative in the routine for rest_expression in Figure 3.12. The parser construction procedure described here is called **LL(1) parser generation**: "LL" because the parser works from Left to right identifying the nodes in what is called Leftmost derivation order, and "(1)" because all choices are based on a one-token look-ahead. A grammar that can be handled by this process is called an **LL(1) grammar** (but see the remark at the end of this section).

The above process describes only the bare bones of LL(1) parser generation: real-world LL(1) parser generators also have to worry about such things as

```
void input(void) {
    switch (Token.class) {
    case IDENTIFIER: case '(':
                            expression(); token(EoF); break;
    default:                error ();
    }
}

void expression(void) {
    switch (Token.class) {
    case IDENTIFIER: case '(':
                            term(); rest_expression(); break;
    default:                error ();
    }
}

void term(void) {
    switch (Token.class) {
    case IDENTIFIER:  token(IDENTIFIER); break;
    case '(':         parenthesized_expression(); break;
    default:          error ();
    }
}

void parenthesized_expression(void) {
    switch (Token.class) {
    case '(':         token('('); expression(); token(')'); break;
    default:          error ();
    }
}

void rest_expression(void) {
    switch (Token.class) {
    case '+':         token('+'); expression(); break;
    case EoF: case ')': break;
    default:          error ();
    }
}

void token(int tk) {
    if (tk != Token.class) error ();
    get_next_token();
}
```

Fig. 3.12: A predictive parser for the grammar of Figure 3.4

Data definitions:

1. Token sets called FOLLOW sets for all non-terminals in *G*.
2. Token sets called FIRST sets for all alternatives and alternative tails in *G*.

Initializations:

1. For all non-terminals *N*, set FOLLOW(*N*) to {}.
2. Set all FIRST sets to the values determined by the algorithm for FIRST sets.

Inference rules:

1. For each rule of the form $M\rightarrow\alpha N\beta$ in *G*, FOLLOW(*N*) must contain all tokens in FIRST(β), excluding ε, should FIRST(β) contain it.
2. For each rule of the form $M\rightarrow\alpha N\beta$ in *G* where FIRST(β) contains ε, FOLLOW(*N*) must contain all tokens in FOLLOW(*M*).

Fig. 3.13: Closure algorithm for the FOLLOW sets in grammar *G*

Rule	FIRST set		FOLLOW set
input	{ IDENTIFIER	'(' }	{ }
expression	{ IDENTIFIER	'(' }	{ EoF ')' }
term	{ IDENTIFIER	'(' }	{ '+' EoF ')' }
parenthesized_expression	{ '(' }		{ '+' EoF ')' }
rest_expression	{ '+' ε }		{ EoF ')' }

Fig. 3.14: The FIRST and FOLLOW sets for the grammar from Figure 3.4

- repetition operators in the grammar; these allow, for example, expression and rest_expression to be combined into

  expression → term ('+' term)*

  and complicate the algorithms for the computation of the FIRST and FOLLOW sets;
- detecting and reporting parsing conflicts (see below);
- including code for the creation of the syntax tree;
- including code and tables for syntax error recovery;
- optimizations; for example, the routine parenthesized_expression() in Figure 3.12 is only called when it has already been established that *Token.class* is (, so the test in the routine itself is superfluous.

Actually, technically speaking, the above grammar is **strongly LL(1)** and the parser generation process discussed yields **strong-LL(1) parsers**. There exists a more complicated **full-LL(1)** parser generation process, which is more powerful in theory, but it turns out that there are no full-LL(1) grammars that are not also strongly-LL(1), so the difference has no direct practical consequences and everybody calls "strong-LL(1) parsers" "LL(1) parsers". There is an indirect difference, though: since the full-LL(1) parser generation process collects more information, it allows better error recovery. But even this property is not usually exploited in compilers. Further details are given in Exercise 3.13.

3.4.2 LL(1) conflicts as an asset

We now return to the first of our three problems described at the end of Section
3.3.1: the addition of indexed_element to term. When we generate code for the new
grammar, we find that FIRST(indexed_element) is { IDENTIFIER }, and the code
for term becomes:

```
void term(void) {
    switch (Token.class) {
    case IDENTIFIER:    token(IDENTIFIER); break;
    case IDENTIFIER:    indexed_element(); break;
    case '(':           parenthesized_expression(); break;
    default :           error ();
    }
}
```

Two different cases are marked with the same case label, which clearly shows the
internal conflict the grammar suffers from: the C code will not even compile. Such a
conflict is called an **LL(1) conflict**, and grammars that are free from them are called
"LL(1) grammars". It is the task of the parser generator to check for such conflicts,
report them and refrain from generating a parser if any are found. The grammar in
Figure 3.4 is LL(1), but the grammar extended with the rule for indexed_element is
not: it contains an LL(1) conflict, more in particular a **FIRST/FIRST conflict**. For
this conflict, the parser generator could for example report: "Alternatives 1 and 2 of
term have a FIRST/FIRST conflict on token IDENTIFIER".

For the non-terminals in the grammar of Figure 3.7 we find the following FIRST
and FOLLOW sets:

Rule	FIRST set	FOLLOW set
S → A 'a' 'b'	{ 'a' }	{ }
A → 'a' | ε	{ 'a' ε }	{ 'a' }

This yields the parser shown in Figure 3.15. This parser is not LL(1) due to the
conflict in the routine for A. Here the first alternative of A is selected on input **a**,
since a is in FIRST(A), but the second alternative of A is also selected on input **a**,
since a is in FOLLOW(A): we have a **FIRST/FOLLOW conflict**.

Our third example concerned a left-recursive grammar:

```
expression  →  expression '-' term | ... .
```

This will certainly cause an LL(1) conflict, for the following reason: the FIRST set
of expression will contain the FIRST sets of its non-recursive alternatives (indicated
here by ...), but the recursive alternative starts with expression, so its FIRST set will
contain the FIRST sets of all the other alternatives: the left-recursive alternative will
have a FIRST/FIRST conflict with all the other alternatives.

We see that the LL(1) method predicts the alternative A_k for a non-terminal N
when the look-ahead token is in the set FIRST(A_k) if A_k is not nullable, or in

```
void S(void) {
    switch (Token.class) {
    case 'a':    A(); token('a'); token('b'); break;
    default:     error ();
    }
}

void A(void) {
    switch (Token.class) {
    case 'a':    token('a'); break;
    case 'a':    break;
    default:     error ();
    }
}
```

Fig. 3.15: A predictive parser for the grammar of Figure 3.7

FIRST(A_k) $\cup$ FOLLOW(N) if A_k is nullable. This information must allow the alternative A_k to be identified uniquely from among the other alternatives of N. This leads to the following three requirements for a grammar to be LL(1):

- No FIRST/FIRST conflicts: if FIRST(A_i) and FIRST(A_j) ($A_i \neq A_j$) of a non-terminal N have a token t in common, LL(1) cannot distinguish between A_i and A_j on look-ahead t.
- No FIRST/FOLLOW conflicts: if FIRST(A_i) of a non-terminal N with a nullable alternative A_j ($A_i \neq A_j$) has a token t in common with FOLLOW(N), LL(1) cannot distinguish between A_i and A_j on look-ahead t.
- No more than one nullable alternative per non-terminal: if a non-terminal N has two nullable alternatives A_i and A_j ($A_i \neq A_j$), LL(1) cannot distinguish between A_i and A_j on all tokens in FOLLOW(N).

Rather than creating a parser that does not work for certain look-aheads, as the recursive descent method would, LL(1) parser generation detects the LL(1) conflict(s) and generates no parser at all. This is safer than the more cavalier approach of the recursive descent method, but has a new disadvantage: it leaves the compiler writer to deal with LL(1) conflicts.

3.4.3 LL(1) conflicts as a liability

When a grammar is not LL(1)—and most are not—there are basically two options: use a stronger parsing method or make the grammar LL(1). Using a stronger parsing method is in principle preferable, since it allows us to leave the grammar intact. Two kinds of stronger parsing methods are available: enhanced LL(1) parsers, which are still top-down, and the bottom-up methods LALR(1) and LR(1). The problem with these is that they may not help: the grammar may not be amenable to any deterministic parsing method. Also, top-down parsers are more convenient to use than bottom-up parsers when context handling is involved, as we will see in Section 4.2.1. So there may be reason to resort to the second alternative: making the grammar LL(1). LL(1) parsers enhanced by dynamic conflict resolvers are treated in Section 3.4.3.3.

3.4.3.1 Making a grammar LL(1)

Making a grammar LL(1) means creating a new grammar which generates the same language as the original non-LL(1) grammar and which *is* LL(1). The advantage of the new grammar is that it can be used for automatic parser generation; the disadvantage is that it does not construct exactly the right syntax trees, so some semantic patching up will have to be done.

There is no hard and fast recipe for making a grammar LL(1); if there were, the parser generator could apply it and the problem would go away. In this section we present some tricks and guidelines. Applying them so that the damage to the resulting syntax tree is minimal requires judgment and ingenuity.

There are three main ways to remove LL(1) conflicts: left-factoring, substitution, and left-recursion removal.

Left-factoring can be applied when two alternatives start directly with the same grammar symbol, as in:

    term → IDENTIFIER | IDENTIFIER '[' expression ']' | ...

Here the common left factor IDENTIFIER is factored out, in the same way as for example the **x** can be factored out in **x∗y+x∗z**, leaving **x∗(y+z)**. The resulting grammar fragment is now LL(1), unless of course term itself can be followed by a [elsewhere in the grammar:

    term → IDENTIFIER after_identifier | ...
    after_identifier → '[' expression ']' | ε

or more concisely with a repetition operator:

    term → IDENTIFIER ('[' expression ']')$^?$ | ...

Substitution involves replacing a non-terminal N in a right-hand side α of a production rule by the alternatives of N. If N has n alternatives, the right-hand side α is replicated n times, and in each copy N is replaced by a different alternative. For example, the result of substituting the rule

    A → 'a' | B c | ε

in

    S → 'p' A q

is:

    S → 'p' a 'q' | 'p' B 'c' q | p q

In a sense, substitution is the opposite of factoring. It is used when the conflicting entities are not directly visible; this occurs in indirect conflicts and FIRST/FOLLOW conflicts. The grammar fragment

```
term          →  IDENTIFIER | indexed_element | parenthesized_expression
indexed_element  →  IDENTIFIER '[' expression ']'
```

exhibits an indirect FIRST/FIRST conflict on the token IDENTIFIER. Substitution of indexed_element in term turns it into a direct conflict, which can then be handled by left-factoring.

Something similar occurs in the grammar of Figure 3.7, which has a FIRST/-FOLLOW conflict. Substitution of A in S yields:

```
S  →  'a' 'a' 'b' | 'a' 'b'
```

which can again be made LL(1) by left-factoring.

Left-recursion removal can in principle be performed automatically. The algorithm removes all left-recursion from any grammar, but the problem is that it mangles the grammar beyond recognition. Careful application of the manual technique explained below will also work in most cases, and leave the grammar largely intact.

Three types of left-recursion must be distinguished:

- **direct left-recursion**, in which an alternative of N starts with N;
- **indirect left-recursion**, in which an alternative of N starts with A, an alternative of A starts with B, and so on, until finally an alternative in this chain brings us back to N;
- **hidden left-recursion**, in which an alternative of N starts with αN and α can produce ε.

Indirect and hidden left-recursion (and hidden indirect left-recursion!) can usually be turned into direct left-recursion by substitution. We will now see how to remove direct left-recursion.

We assume that only one alternative of the left-recursive rule N starts with N; if there are more, left-factoring will reduce them to one. Schematically, N has the form

$$N \rightarrow N\alpha|\beta$$

in which α represents whatever comes after the N in the left-recursive alternative and β represents the other alternatives. This rule produces the set of strings

$$
\begin{aligned}
&\beta \\
&\beta\alpha \\
&\beta\alpha\alpha \\
&\beta\alpha\alpha\alpha \\
&\beta\alpha\alpha\alpha\alpha \\
&\dots
\end{aligned}
$$

which immediately suggests the two non-left-recursive rules

$$
\begin{aligned}
N &\rightarrow \beta N\prime \\
N\prime &\rightarrow \alpha N\prime | \varepsilon
\end{aligned}
$$

in which N_t produces the repeating tail of N, the set $\{\alpha^n | n >= 0\}$. It is easy to verify that these two rules generate the same pattern as shown above.

This transformation gives us a technique to remove direct left-recursion. When we apply it to the traditional left-recursive definition of an arithmetic expression

expression → expression '–' term | term

we find that

N = expression
α = '–' term
β = term

So the non-left-recursive equivalent is:

expression → term expression_tail_option
expression_tail_option → '–' term expression_tail_option | ε

There is no guarantee that repeated application of the above techniques will result in an LL(1) grammar. A not unusual vicious circle is that removal of FIRST/FIRST conflicts through left-factoring results in nullable alternatives, which cause FIRST/-FOLLOW conflicts. Removing these through substitution causes new FIRST/FIRST conflicts, and so on. But for many grammars LL(1)-ness can be achieved relatively easily.

3.4.3.2 Undoing the semantic effects of grammar transformations

While it is often possible to transform our grammar into a new grammar that is acceptable by a parser generator and that generates the same language, the new grammar usually assigns a different structure to strings in the language than our original grammar did. Fortunately, in many cases we are not really interested in the structure but rather in the semantics implied by it. In those cases, it is often possible to move the semantics to so-called **marker rules**, syntax rules that always produce the empty string and whose only task consists of making sure that the right actions are executed at the right time. The trick is then to carry these marker rules along in the grammar transformations as if they were normal syntax rules.

It is convenient to collect all the semantics at the end of an alternative: it is the first place in which we are certain we have all the information. Following this technique, we can express the semantics of our traditional definition of arithmetic expressions as follows in a C-like notation:

expression(**int** *e) →
    expression(**int** *e) '–' term(**int** *t) {*e –= *t;}
| term(**int** *t) {*e = *t;}

We handle the semantics of the expressions as pointers to integers for our demonstration. The C fragments {*e –= *t;} and {*e = *t;} are the marker rules; the first subtracts the value obtained from term from that obtained from expression, and the second just copies the value obtained from term to the left-hand side. Note that the pointer to the result is shared between expression on the left and expression on the right; the initial application of the rule expression somewhere else in the grammar will have to supply a pointer to an integer variable.

Now we find that

N = expression(**int** *e)
α = '−' term(**int** *t) {*e −= *t;}
β = term(**int** *t) {*e = *t;}

So the semantically corrected non-left-recursive equivalent is

expression(**int** *e) →
    term(**int** *t) *e = *t; expression_tail_option(**int** *e)
expression_tail_option(**int** *e) →
    '−' term(**int** *t) *e −= *t; expression_tail_option(**int** *e) |

This makes sense: the C fragment {*e = *t;} now copies the value obtained from term to a location shared with expression_tail_option; the code {*e −= *t;} does effectively the same.

If the reader feels that all this is less than elegant patchwork, we agree. Still, the transformations can be performed almost mechanically and few errors are usually introduced. A somewhat less objectionable approach is to rig the markers so that the correct syntax tree is constructed in spite of the transformations, and to leave all semantic processing to the next phase, which can then proceed as if nothing out of the ordinary had happened. In Section 3.4.6.2 we show how this can be done in a traditional top-down parser generator.

3.4.3.3 Automatic conflict resolution

There are two ways in which LL parsers can be strengthened: by increasing the look-ahead and by allowing dynamic conflict resolvers. Distinguishing alternatives not by their first token but by their first two tokens is called **LL(2)**. It helps, for example, to differentiate between IDENTIFIER '(' (routine call), IDENTIFIER '[' (array element), IDENTIFIER 'of' (field selection), IDENTIFIER '+' (expression) and perhaps others. A disadvantage of LL(2) is that the parser code can get much bigger. On the other hand, only a few rules need the full power of the two-token look-ahead, so the problem can often be limited. The *ANTLR* parser generator [214] computes the required look-ahead for each rule separately: it is LL(k), for varying k. But no amount of look-ahead can resolve left-recursion.

Dynamic conflict resolvers are conditions expressed in some programming language that are attached to alternatives that would otherwise conflict. When the conflict arises during parsing, some of the conditions are evaluated to resolve it. The details depend on the parser generator.

The parser generator *LLgen* (which will be discussed in Section 3.4.6) requires a conflict resolver to be placed on the first of two conflicting alternatives. When the parser has to decide between the two, the condition is evaluated and if it yields true, the first alternative is considered to apply. If it yields false, the parser continues with the second alternative, which, of course, may be the first of another pair of conflicting alternatives.

An important question is: what information can be accessed by the dynamic conflict resolvers? After all, this information must be available dynamically during parsing, which may be a problem. The simplest information one can offer is no information. Remarkably, this already helps to solve, for example, the LL(1) conflict in the conditional statement in some languages. After left-factoring, the conditional statement in C may have the following form:

```
conditional_statement  →  'if' '(' expression ')' statement else_tail_option
else_tail_option  →  'else' statement | ε
statement  →  ... | conditional_statement | ...
```

in which the rule for else_tail_option has a FIRST/FOLLOW conflict. The reason is that it has an alternative that produces $ε$, and both its FIRST set and its FOLLOW set contain the token 'else'. The conflict materializes for example in the C statement

if (x > 0) **if** (y > 0) p = 0; **else** q = 0;

where the else could derive from the FIRST set of else_tail_option, in which case it belongs to the second if, or from its FOLLOW set, in which case the if (y > 0) p = 0; ends here and the else belongs to the first if. This is called the **dangling-else problem**. (Actually the grammar is ambiguous; see Section 3.5.9.)

Since the manual [150, § 3.2] says that an else must be associating the with the closest previous else-less if, the LL(1) conflict can be solved by attaching to the first alternative of else_tail_option a conflict resolver which always returns true:

```
else_tail_option  →  %if (1) 'else' statement | ε
```

The static conflict resolver %if (1) can be expressed more appropriately as %prefer in *LLgen*.

A more informative type of information that can be made available easily is one or more look-ahead tokens. Even one token can be very useful: supposing the lexical analyzer maintains a global variable ahead_token, we can write

```
basic_expression:
    %if (ahead_token == '(')          routine_call |
    %if (ahead_token == '[')             indexed_element |
    %if (ahead_token == OF_TOKEN ) field_selection |
                                            identifier
;
```

in which all four alternatives start with IDENTIFIER. This implements a poor man's LL(2) parser.

Narrow parsers—in which the actions attached to a node are performed as soon as the node becomes available—can consult much more information in conflict resolvers than broad compilers can, for example symbol table information. This way, the parsing process can be influenced by an arbitrarily remote context, and the parser is no longer context-free. It is not context-sensitive either in the technical sense of the word: it has become a fully-fledged program, of which determinacy and termination are no longer guaranteed. Dynamic conflict resolution is one of those features that, when abused, can lead to big problems, and when used with caution can be a great help.

3.4.4 The LL(1) push-down automaton

We have seen that in order to construct an LL(1) parser, we have to compute for each non-terminal N, which of its alternatives to predict for each token t in the input. We can arrange these results in a table; for the LL(1) parser of Figure 3.12, we get the table shown in Figure 3.16.

Top of stack/state:		Look-ahead token		
	IDENTIFIER	+	(	) EoF
input	expression EoF		expression EoF	
expression	term rest_expression		term rest_expression	
term	IDENTIFIER		parenthesized_ expression	
parenthesized_ expression			(expression)	
rest_expression		+ expression		ε ε

Fig. 3.16: Transition table for an LL(1) parser for the grammar of Figure 3.4

This table looks suspiciously like the transition tables we have seen in the table-controlled lexical analyzers. Even the meaning often seems the same: for example, in the state term, upon seeing a '(', we go to the state parenthesized_expression. Occasionally, there is a difference, though: in the state expression, upon seeing an IDENTIFIER, we go to a series of states, term and rest_expression. There is no provision for this in the original finite-state automaton, but we can keep very close to its original flavor by going to the state term and pushing the state rest_expression onto a stack for later treatment. If we consider the state term as the top of the stack, we have replaced the single state of the FSA by a stack of states. Such an automaton is called a **push-down automaton** or **PDA**. A push-down automaton as derived from LL(1) grammars by the above procedure is deterministic, which means that each entry in the transition table contains only one value: it does not have to try more than one alternative. The stack of states contains both non-terminals and terminals; together they form the prediction to which the present input must conform (or it contains a syntax error). This correspondence is depicted most clearly by showing the prediction stack horizontally above the present input, with the top of the stack at the left. Figure 3.17 shows such an arrangement; in it, the input was (i+i)+i where i is the character representation of the token IDENTIFIER, and the '(' has just been processed. It is easy to see how the elements on the prediction stack are going to match the input.

PredictionStack: expression ')' rest_expression EoF
Present input: IDENTIFIER '+' IDENTIFIER ')' '+' IDENTIFIER EoF

Fig. 3.17: Prediction stack and present input in a push-down automaton

A push-down automaton uses and modifies a push-down prediction stack and the input stream, and consults a transition table *PredictionTable[Non_terminal, Token]*. Only the top of the stack and the first token in the input stream are consulted by and affected by the algorithm. The table is two-dimensional and is indexed with non-terminals in one dimension and tokens in the other; the entry indexed with a non-terminal N and a token t either contains the alternative of N that must be predicted when the present input starts with t, or is empty.

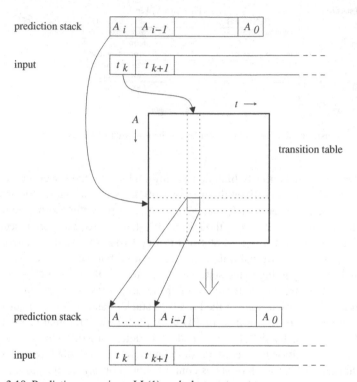

Fig. 3.18: Prediction move in an LL(1) push-down automaton

The automaton starts with the start symbol of the grammar as the only element on the prediction stack, and the token stream as the input. It knows two major and one minor types of moves; which one is applied depends on the top of the prediction stack:

- Prediction: The **prediction move** applies when the top of the prediction stack is a non-terminal N. N is removed (popped) from the stack, and the transition table entry *PredictionTable[N, t]* is looked up. If it contains no alternatives, we have found a syntax error in the input. If it contains one alternative of N, then this alternative is pushed onto the prediction stack. The LL(1) property guarantees that the entry will not contain more than one alternative. See Figure 3.18.

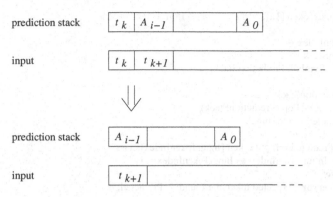

Fig. 3.19: Match move in an LL(1) push-down automaton

- Match: The **match move** applies when the top of the prediction stack is a terminal. It must be equal to the first token of the present input. If it is not, there is a syntax error; if it is, both tokens are removed. See Figure 3.19.
- Termination: Parsing terminates when the prediction stack is exhausted. If the input stream is also exhausted, the input has been parsed successfully; if it is not, there is a syntax error.

The push-down automaton repeats the above moves until it either finds a syntax error or terminates successfully. Note that the algorithm as described above does not construct a syntax tree; it is a recognizer only. If we want a syntax tree, we have to use the prediction move to construct nodes for the members of the alternative and connect them to the node that is being expanded. In the match move we have to attach the attributes of the input token to the syntax tree.

Unlike the code for the recursive descent parser and the recursive predictive parser, the code for the non-recursive predictive parser is independent of the language; all language dependence is concentrated in the *PredictionTable[ ]*. Outline code for the LL(1) push-down automaton is given in Figure 3.20, where ⊥ denotes the empty stack. It assumes that the input tokens reside in an array *InputToken[1..]*; if the tokens are actually obtained by calling a function like *NextInputToken()*, care has to be taken not to read beyond end-of-file. The algorithm terminates successfully when the prediction stack is empty; since the prediction stack can only become empty by matching the EoF token, we know that the input is empty as well. When the stack is not empty, the prediction on the top of it is examined. It is either a terminal, which then has to match the input token, or it is a non-terminal, which then has to lead to a prediction, taking the input token into account. If either of these requirements is not fulfilled, an error message follows; an error recovery algorithm may then be activated. Such algorithms are described in Section 3.4.5.

It is instructive to see how the automaton arrived at the state of Figure 3.17. Figure 3.21 shows all the moves.

Whether to use an LL(1) predictive parser or an LL(1) push-down automaton is mainly decided by the compiler writer's preference, the general structure of the

import InputToken [1..];   — from lexical analyzer

InputTokenIndex ← 1;
PredictionStack ← ⊥;
Push (StartSymbol, PredictionStack);

while PredictionStack ≠ ⊥:
      Predicted ← Pop (PredictionStack);
      if Predicted is a terminal:
            — Try a match move:
            if Predicted = InputToken [InputTokenIndex].class:
                  InputTokenIndex ← InputTokenIndex + 1; — matched
            else:
                  error "Expected token not found: ", Predicted;
      else — Predicted is a non-terminal:
            — Try a prediction move, using the input token as look-ahead:
            Prediction ← PredictionTable [Predicted, InputToken [InputTokenIndex]];
            if Prediction = ∅:
                  error "Token not expected: ", InputToken [InputTokenIndex]];
            else — Prediction ≠ ∅:
                  for each symbol S **in** Prediction **reversed**:
                        Push (S, PredictionStack);

Fig. 3.20: Predictive parsing with an LL(1) push-down automaton

Initial situation:
PredictionStack: input
Input: '(' IDENTIFIER '+' IDENTIFIER ')' '+' IDENTIFIER EoF

Prediction moves:
PredictionStack: expression EoF
PredictionStack: term rest_expression EoF
PredictionStack: parenthesized_expression rest_expression EoF
PredictionStack: '(' expression ')' rest_expression EoF
Input: '(' IDENTIFIER '+' IDENTIFIER ')' '+' IDENTIFIER EoF

Match move on '(':
PredictionStack: expression ')' rest_expression EoF
Input: IDENTIFIER '+' IDENTIFIER ')' '+' IDENTIFIER EoF

Fig. 3.21: The first few parsing moves for (i+i)+i

compiler, and the available software. A predictive parser is more usable in a narrow compiler since it makes combining semantic actions with parsing much easier. The push-down automaton is more important theoretically and much more is known about it; little of this, however, has found its way into compiler writing. Error handling may be easier in a push-down automaton: all available information lies on the stack, and since the stack is actually an array, the information can be inspected and modified directly; in predictive parsers it is hidden in the flow of control.

3.4.5 Error handling in LL parsers

We have two major concerns in syntactic error recovery: to avoid infinite loops and to avoid producing corrupt syntax trees. Neither of these dangers is imaginary. Many compiler writers, including the authors, have written ad-hoc error correction methods only to find that they looped on the very first error. The grammar

S → 'a' c | b S

provides a simple demonstration of the effect; it generates the language b*ac. Now suppose the actual input is c. The prediction is S, which, being a non-terminal, must be replaced by one of its alternatives, in a prediction move. The first alternative, ac, is rejected since the input does not start with a. The alternative bS fails too, since the input does not start with b either. To the naive mind this suggests a way out: predict bS anyhow, insert a b in front of the input, and give an error message "Token b inserted in line ...". The inserted b then gets matched to the predicted b, which seems to advance the parsing but in effect brings us back to the original situation. Needless to say, in practice such infinite loops originate from much less obvious interplay of grammar rules.

Faced with the impossibility of choosing a prediction, one can also decide to discard the non-terminal. This, however, will cause the parser to produce a corrupt syntax tree. To see why this is so, return to Figure 3.2 and imagine what would happen if we tried to "improve" the situation by deleting one of the nodes indicated by hollow dots.

A third possibility is to discard tokens from the input until a matching token is found: if you need a b, skip other tokens until you find a b. Although this is guaranteed not to loop, it has two severe problems. Indiscriminate skipping will often skip important structuring tokens like procedure or), after which our chances for a successful recovery are reduced to nil. Also, when the required token does not occur in the rest of the input at all, we are left with a non-empty prediction and an empty input, and it is not clear how to proceed from there.

A fourth possibility is inserting a non-terminal at the front of the prediction, to force a match, but this would again lead to a corrupt syntax tree.

So we need a better strategy, one that guarantees that at least one input token will be consumed to prevent looping and that nothing will be discarded from or inserted into the prediction stack, to prevent corrupting the syntax tree. We will now discuss such a strategy, the acceptable-set method.

3.4.5.1 The acceptable-set method

The **acceptable-set method** is actually a framework for systematically constructing a safe error recovery method [267]. It centers on an "acceptable set" of tokens, and consists of three steps, all of which are performed after the error has been detected. The three steps are:

- Step 1: construct the acceptable set A from the state of the parser, using some suitable algorithm C; it is required that A contain the end-of-file token;
- Step 2: discard tokens from the input stream until a token t_A from the set A is found;
- Step 3: resynchronize the parser by advancing it until it arrives in a state in which it consumes the token t_A from the input, using some suitable algorithm R; this prevents looping.

Algorithm C is a parameter to the method, and in principle it can be determined freely. The second step is fixed. Algorithm R, which is used in Step 3 to resynchronize the parser, must fit in with algorithm C used to construct the acceptable set. In practice this means that the algorithms C and R have to be designed together. The acceptable set is sometimes called the **follow set** and the technique **follow-set error recovery**, but to avoid confusion with the FOLLOW set described in Section 3.4.1 and the FOLLOW-set error recovery described below, we will not use these terms.

A wide range of algorithms presents itself for Step 1, but the two simplest possibilities, those that yield the singleton {end-of-file} or the set of all tokens, are unsuitable: all input and no input will be discarded, respectively, and in both cases it is difficult to see how to advance the parser to accept the token t_A. The next possibility is to take the empty algorithm for R. This means that the state of the parser must be corrected by Step 2 alone and so equates the acceptable set with the set of tokens that is correct at the moment the error is detected. Step 2 skips all tokens until a correct token is found, and parsing can continue immediately. The disadvantage is that this method has the tendency again to throw away important structuring tokens like procedure or), after which the situation is beyond redemption. The term **panic-mode** for this technique is quite appropriate.

Another option is to have the compiler writer determine the acceptable set by hand. If, for example, expressions in a language are always followed by), ;, or ,, we can store this set in a global variable *AcceptableSet* whenever we start parsing an expression. Then, when we detect an error, we skip the input until we find a token that is in *AcceptableSet* (Step 2), discard the fragment of the expression we have already parsed and insert a dummy expression in the parse tree (Step 3) and continue the parser. This is sometimes called the "acceptable-set method" in a more narrow sense.

Although it is not unusual in recursive descent parsers to have the acceptable sets chosen by hand, the choice can also be automated: use the FOLLOW sets of the non-terminals. This approach is called **FOLLOW-set error recovery** [117,216].

Both methods are relatively easy to implement but have the disadvantage that there is no guarantee that the parser can indeed consume the input token in Step 3. For example, if we are parsing a program in the language C and the input contains a(b + **int**; c), a syntax error is detected upon seeing the **int**, which is a keyword, not an identifier, in C. Since we are at that moment parsing an **expression**, the FOL-LOW set does not contain a token **int** but it does contain a semicolon. So the **int** is skipped in Step 2 but the semicolon is not. Then a dummy expression is inserted in Step 3 to replace b +, This leaves us with a(_dummy_expression_ ; c) in which the semicolon still cannot be consumed. The reason is that, although in general expressions may indeed be followed by semicolons, which is why the semicolon is in the FOLLOW set, expressions in parameter lists may not, since a closing parenthesis must intervene according to C syntax.

Another problem with FOLLOW sets is that they are often quite small; this results in skipping large chunks of text. So the FOLLOW set is both too large and not large enough to serve as the acceptable set. Both problems can be remedied to a large extent by basing the acceptable set on continuations, as explained in the next section.

3.4.5.2 A fully automatic acceptable-set method based on continuations

The push-down automaton implementation of an LL(1) parser shows clearly what material we have to work with when we encounter a syntax error: the prediction stack and the first few tokens of the rest of the input. More in detail, the situation looks as follows:

```
PredictionStack: A B C EoF
Input:           i ...
```

in which we assume for the moment that the prediction starts with a non-terminal, A. Since there is a syntax error, we know that A has no predicted alternative on the input token **i**, but to guarantee a correct parse tree, we have to make sure that the prediction on the stack comes true. Something similar applies if the prediction starts with a terminal.

Now suppose for a moment that the error occurred because the end of input has been reached; this simplifies our problem temporarily by reducing one of the participants, the rest of the input, to a single token, EoF. In this case we have no option but to construct the rest of the parse tree out of thin air, by coming up with predictions for the required non-terminals and by inserting the required terminals. Such a sequence of terminals that will completely fulfill the predictions on the stack is called a **continuation** of that stack [240].

A continuation can be constructed for a given stack by replacing each of the non-terminals on the stack by a terminal production of it. So there are almost always

infinitely many continuations of a given stack, and any of them leads to an acceptable set in the way explained below. For convenience and to minimize the number of
terminals we have to insert we prefer the shortest continuation: we want the shortest
way out. This shortest continuation can be obtained by predicting for each non-
terminal on the stack the alternative that produces the shortest string. How we find
the alternative that produces the shortest string is explained in the next subsection.

We now imagine feeding the chosen continuation to the parser. This will cause
a number of parser moves, leading to a sequence of stack configurations, the last
of which terminates the parsing process and completes the parse tree. The above
situation could, for example, develop as follows:

```
A B C EoF
p Q B C EoF  (say A → pQ is the shortest alternative of A)
Q B C EoF    (inserted p is matched)
q B C EoF    (say Q → q is the shortest alternative of Q)
B C EoF      (inserted q is matched)
...
EoF          (always-present EoF is matched)
ε            (the parsing process ends)
```

Each of these stack configurations has a FIRST set, which contains the tokens that
would be correct if that stack configuration were met. We take the union of all
these sets as the acceptable set of the original stack configuration A B C EoF. The
acceptable set contains all tokens in the shortest continuation plus the first tokens of
all side paths of that continuation. It is important to note that such acceptable sets
always include the EoF token; see Exercise 3.16.

We now return to our original problem, in which the rest of the input is still
present and starts with i. After having determined the acceptable set (Step 1), we do
the following:

• Step 2: skip unacceptable tokens: Zero or more tokens from the input are discarded in order, until we meet a token that is in the acceptable set. Since the
  token EoF is always acceptable, this step terminates. Note that we may not need
  to discard any tokens at all: the present input token may be acceptable in one of
  the other stack configurations.
• Step 3: resynchronize the parser: We continue parsing with a modified parser.
  This modified parser first tries the usual predict or match move. If this succeeds
  the parser is on the rails again and parsing can continue normally, but if the move
  fails, the modified parser proceeds as follows. For a non-terminal on the top of the
  prediction stack, it predicts the shortest alternative, and for a terminal it inserts
  the predicted token. Step 3 is repeated until a move succeeds and the parser is
  resynchronized.

Since the input token was in the "acceptable set", it is in the FIRST set of one of
the stack configurations constructed by the repeated Steps 3, so resynchronization
is guaranteed. The code can be found in Figure 3.22.

The parser has now accepted one token, and the parse tree is still correct, provided we produced the proper nodes for the non-terminals to be expanded and the

— Step 1: construct acceptable set:
AcceptableSet ← AcceptableSetFor (PredictionStack);

— Step 2: skip unacceptable tokens:
while InputToken [InputTokenIndex] ∉ AcceptableSet:
   report "Token skipped: ", InputToken [InputTokenIndex];
   InputTokenIndex ← InputTokenIndex + 1;

— Step 3: resynchronize the parser:
Resynchronized ← False;
while not Resynchronized:
   Predicted ← Pop (PredictionStack);
   if Predicted is a terminal:
      — Try a match move:
      if Predicted = InputToken [InputTokenIndex].class:
         InputTokenIndex ← InputTokenIndex + 1; — matched
         Resynchronized ← True;   — resynchronized!
      else — Predicted ≠ InputToken:
         Insert a token of class Predicted, including representation;
         report "Token inserted of class ", Predicted;
   else — Predicted is a non-terminal:
      — Do a prediction move:
      Prediction ← PredictionTable [Predicted, InputToken [InputTokenIndex]];
      if Prediction = ∅:
         Prediction ← ShortestProductionTable [Predicted];
      — Now Prediction ≠ ∅:
      for each symbol S **in** Prediction **reversed**:
         Push (S, PredictionStack);

Fig. 3.22: Acceptable-set error recovery in a predictive parser

tokens to be inserted. We see that this approach requires the user to supply a routine that will create the tokens to be inserted, with their representations, but such a routine is usually easy to write.

3.4.5.3 Finding the alternative with the shortest production

Each alternative of each non-terminal in a grammar defines in itself a language, a set of strings. We are interested here in the length of the shortest string in each of these languages. Once we have computed these, we know for each non-terminal which of its alternatives produces the shortest string; if two alternatives produce shortest strings of the same length, we simply choose one of them. We then use this information to fill the array *ShortestProductionTable[ ]*.

The lengths of the shortest productions of all alternatives of all non-terminals can be computed by the closure algorithm in Figure 3.23. It is based on the fact that the length of shortest productions of an alternative $N{\rightarrow}AB...$ is the sum of the lengths of the shortest productions of A, B, etc. The initializations 1b and 2b set the minimum lengths of empty alternatives to 0 and those of terminal symbols to

1. All other lengths are set to ∞, so any actual length found will be smaller. The first inference rule says that the shortest length of an alternative is the sum of the shortest lengths of its components; more complicated but fairly obvious rules apply if the alternative includes repetition operators. The second inference rule says that the shortest length of a non-terminal is the minimum of the shortest lengths of its alternatives. Note that we have implemented variables as (name, value) pairs.

Data definitions:
    1. A set of pairs of the form (production rule, integer).
    2a. A set of pairs of the form (non-terminal, integer).
    2b. A set of pairs of the form (terminal, integer).

Initializations:
    1a. For each production rule $N{\to}A_1\ldots A_n$ with $n > 0$ there is a pair $(N{\to}A_1\ldots A_n, \infty)$.
    1b. For each production rule $N{\to}\varepsilon$ there is a pair $(N{\to}\varepsilon, 0)$.
    2a. For each non-terminal N there is a pair (N, ∞).
    2b. For each terminal T there is a pair $(T, 1)$.

Inference rules:
    1. For each production rule $N{\to}A_1\ldots A_n$ with $n > 0$, if there are pairs (A_1, l_1) to (A_n, l_n) with all $l_i < \infty$, the pair $(N{\to}A_1\ldots A_n, l_N)$ must be replaced by a pair $(N{\to}A_1\ldots A_n, l_{new})$ where $l_{new} = \Sigma_{i=1}^n l_i$ provided $l_{new} < l_N$.
    2. For each non-terminal N, if there are one or more pairs of the form $(N{\to}\alpha, l_i)$ with $l_i < \infty$, the pair (N, l_N) must be replaced by (N, l_{new}) where l_{new} is the minimum of the l_is, provided $l_{new} < l_N$.

Fig. 3.23: Closure algorithm for computing lengths of shortest productions

Figure 3.24 shows the table *ShortestProductionTable[ ]* for the grammar of Figure 3.4. The recovery steps on parsing (i++i)+i are given in Figure 3.25. The figure starts at the point at which the error is discovered and continues until the parser is on the rails again. Upon detecting the error, we determine the acceptable set of the stack expression ')' rest_expression EoF to be { IDENTIFIER (+) EoF }. So, we see that we do not need to skip any tokens, since the + in the input is in the acceptable set: it is unacceptable to normal parsing but is acceptable to the error recovery. Replacing expression and term with their shortest productions brings the terminal IDENTIFIER to the top of the stack. Since it does not match the +, it has to be inserted. It will be matched instantaneously, which brings the non-terminal rest_expression to the top of the stack. Since that non-terminal has a normal prediction for the + symbol, the parser is on the rails again. We see that it has inserted an identifier between the two pluses.

3.4.6 A traditional top-down parser generator—LLgen

LLgen is the parser generator of the Amsterdam Compiler Kit [271]. It accepts as input a grammar that is more or less LL(1), interspersed with segments of C code.

Non-terminal	Alternative	Shortest length
input	expression EoF	2
expression	term rest_expression	1
term	IDENTIFIER	1
parenthesized_expression	'(' expression ')'	3
rest_expression	ε	0

Fig. 3.24: Shortest production table for the grammar of Figure 3.4

Error detected, since *PredictionTable [expression, '+']* is empty:
PredictionStack: expression ')' rest_expression EoF
Input: '+' IDENTIFIER ')' '+' IDENTIFIER EoF

Shortest production for expression:
PredictionStack: term rest_expression ')' rest_expression EoF
Input: '+' IDENTIFIER ')' '+' IDENTIFIER EoF

Shortest production for term:
PredictionStack: IDENTIFIER rest_expression ')' rest_expression EoF
Input: '+' IDENTIFIER ')' '+' IDENTIFIER EoF

Token IDENTIFIER inserted in the input and matched:
PredictionStack: rest_expression ')' rest_expression EoF
Input: '+' IDENTIFIER ')' '+' IDENTIFIER EoF

Normal prediction for rest_expression, resynchronized:
PredictionStack: '+' expression ')' rest_expression EoF
Input: '+' IDENTIFIER ')' '+' IDENTIFIER EoF

Fig. 3.25: Some steps in parsing (i++i)+i

The non-terminals in the grammar can have parameters, and rules can have local variables, both again expressed in C. Formally, the segments of C code correspond to anonymous ε-producing rules and are treated as such, but in practice an LL(1) grammar reads like a program with a flow of control that always chooses the right alternative. In this model, the C code is executed when the flow of control passes through it. In addition, *LLgen* features dynamic conflict resolvers as explained in Section 3.4.3, to cover the cases in which the input grammar is not entirely LL(1), and automatic error correction as explained in Section 3.4.5, which edits any syntactically incorrect program into a syntactically correct one.

The grammar may be distributed over multiple files, thus allowing a certain degree of modularity. Each module file may also contain C code that belongs specifically to that module; examples are definitions of routines that are called in the C segments in the grammar. *LLgen* translates each module file into a source file in C. It also generates source and include files which contain the parsing mechanism, the error correction mechanism and some auxiliary routines. Compiling these and linking the object files results in a parser.

Figure 3.26 shows the template from which *LLgen* generates code for the rule

```
void P(void) {
  repeat:
    switch(dot) {
    case FIRST(A\dn{1} A\dn{2} {\ldots} A\dn{n}):
        record_push(A2); .... record_push(An);
        {action_A0} A1();
        update_dot();
        record_pop(A2);
        {action_A1} A2();
        ....
        break;
    case FIRST(B\dn{1} {\ldots}):
    shortest_alternative :
        record_push (....);
        {action_B0} B1();
        ....
        break;
    case FIRST(....):
        ....
        break;
    default: /* error */
        if (solvable_by_skipping()) goto repeat;
        goto shortest_alternative;
    }
}
```

Fig. 3.26: Template used for P:{action_A0}A$_1${action_A1}A$_2${action_A2}...|{action_B0}B$_1$...|...;
by *LLgen*

```
P:
    {action_A0} A1 {action_A1} A2 {action_A2} ....
|   {action_B0} B1 ....
|   ....
;
```

which can be compared to Figure 1.15. The alternatives are identified by their FIRST
sets, using a switch statement. The calls to report_....() serve to register the stacking
and unstacking of nonterminals for the benefit of the error recovery from Section
3.4.5.2. The registering of the pushing of A1 and its immediately following popping
have been optimized away. The default case in the switch statement treats the absence of an expected token. If the error can be handled by skipping, another attempt
is made to parse P; otherwise the presence of the shortest production is forced.

3.4.6.1 An example with a transformed grammar

For a simple example of the application of *LLgen* we turn towards the minimal non-
left-recursive grammar for expressions that we derived in Section 3.4.3, and which
we repeat in Figure 3.27. We have completed the grammar by adding an equally

minimal rule for term, one that allows only identifiers having the value 1. In spite of its minimality, the grammar shows all the features we need for our example. It is convenient in *LLgen* to use the parameters for passing to a rule a pointer to the location in which the rule must deliver its result, as shown.

```
expression(int *e) →
    term(int *t) {*e = *t;}
    expression_tail_option(int *e)

expression_tail_option(int *e) →
    '−' term(int *t) {*e −= *t;}
    expression_tail_option(int *e)
|   ε

term(int *t) →  IDENTIFIER {*t = 1;};
```

Fig. 3.27: Minimal non-left-recursive grammar for expressions

We need only a few additions and modifications to turn these two rules into work-ing *LLgen* input, and the result is shown in Figure 3.28. The first thing we need are local variables to store the intermediate results. They are supplied as C code right after the parameters of the non-terminal: this is the {int t;} in the rules expression and expression_tail_option. We also need to modify the actual parameters to suit C syntax; the C code segments remain unchanged. Now the grammar rules themselves are in correct *LLgen* form.

Next, we need a start rule: main. It has one local variable, result, which receives the result of the expression, and whose value is printed when the expression has been parsed. Reading further upward, we find the **LLgen directive** %start, which tells the parser generator that main is the start symbol and that we want its rule converted into a C routine called Main_Program(). The directive %token registers IDENTIFIER as a token; otherwise *LLgen* would assume it to be a non-terminal from its use in the rule for term. Finally, the directive %lexical identifies the C rou-tine int get_next_token_class() as the entry point in the lexical analyzer from where to obtain the stream of tokens, or actually token classes. The code from Figure 3.28 resides in a file parser.g. *LLgen* converts this file to one called parser.c, which con-tains a recursive descent parser. The code is essentially similar to that in Figure 3.12, complicated slightly by the error recovery code. When compiled, it yields the desired parser.

The file parser.g also contains some auxiliary code, shown in Figure 3.29. The extra set of braces identifies the enclosed part as C code. The first item in the code is the mandatory C routine main(); it starts the lexical engine and then the generated parser, using the name specified in the %start directive. The rest of the code is dedicated almost exclusively to error recovery support.

LLgen requires the user to supply a routine, LLmessage(int) to assist in the error correction process. The routine LLmessage(int) is called by *LLgen* when an error has been detected. On the one hand, it allows the user to report the error, on the

```
%lexical get_next_token_class;
%token IDENTIFIER;

%start Main_Program, main;

main {int  result ;}:
    expression(&result)              { printf ("result  = %d\n", result );}
;

expression(int *e) {int  t ;}:
    term(&t)                         {*e = t ;}
    expression_tail_option(e)
;

expression_tail_option(int *e) {int  t ;}:
    ' −' term(&t)                    {*e −= t;}
    expression_tail_option(e)
|
;

term(int *t ):
    IDENTIFIER                       {*t = 1;}
;
```

Fig. 3.28: *LLgen* code for a parser for simple expressions

other it places an obligation on the user: when a token must be inserted, it is up to
the user to construct that token, including its attributes. The int parameter class to
LLmessage() falls into one of three categories:

- class > 0: It is the class of a token to be inserted. The user must arrange the
  situation as if a token of class class had just been read and the token that was
  actually read were still in the input. In other words, the token stream has to be
  pushed back over one token. If the lexical analyzer keeps a record of the input
  stream, this will require negotiations with the lexical analyzer.
- class = 0: The present token, whose class can be found in LLsymb, is skipped
  by *LLgen*. If the lexical analyzer keeps a record of the input stream, it must be
  notified; otherwise no further action is required from the user.
- class = −1: The parsing stack is exhausted, but *LLgen* found there is still input
  left. *LLgen* skips the rest of the input. Again, the user may want to inform the
  lexical analyzer.

The code for LLmessage() used in Figure 3.29 is shown in Figure 3.30.

Pushing back the input stream is the difficult part, but fortunately only one token
needs to be pushed back. We avoid negotiating with the lexical analyzer and implement a one-token buffer Last_Token in the routine get_next_token_class(), which
is the usual packaging of the lexical analyzer routine yielding the class of the token.
The use of this buffer is controlled by a flag Reissue_Last_Token, which is switched
on in the routine insert_token() when the token must be pushed back. When a call

```
{
#include    "lex.h"

int main(void) {
    start_lex (); Main_Program(); return 0;
}

Token_Type Last_Token;          /* error recovery support */
int Reissue_Last_Token = 0;     /* idem */

int get_next_token_class(void) {
    if (Reissue_Last_Token) {
        Token = Last_Token;
        Reissue_Last_Token = 0;
    }
    else get_next_token();
    return Token.class;
}

void insert_token(int token_class) {
    Last_Token = Token; Reissue_Last_Token = 1;
    Token.class = token_class;
    /* and set the attributes of Token, if any */
}

void print_token(int token_class) {
    switch (token_class) {
    case IDENTIFIER: printf("IDENTIFIER"); break;
    case EOFILE   :  printf ("<EoF>"); break;
    default       :  printf ("%c", token_class); break;
    }
}
}
```

Fig. 3.29: Auxiliary C code for a parser for simple expressions

of get_next_token_class() finds the flag on, it reissues the token and switches the flag off.

A sample run with the syntactically correct input **i-i-i** gives the output

```
result = -1
```

and a run with the incorrect input **i i-i** gives the messages

```
Token deleted: IDENTIFIER
result = 0
```

3.4.6.2 Constructing a correct parse tree with a transformed grammar

In Section 3.4.3.2 we suggested that it is possible to construct a correct parse tree even with a transformed grammar. Using techniques similar to the ones used above,

```
void LLmessage(int class) {
    switch (class) {
    default:
        insert_token(class);
        printf ("Missing token ");
        print_token(class);
        printf (" inserted in front of token ");
        print_token(LLsymb); printf ("\n");
        break;
    case 0:
        printf ("Token deleted: ");
        print_token(LLsymb); printf ("\n");
        break;
    case −1:
        printf ("End of input expected, but found token ");
        print_token(LLsymb); printf ("\n");
        break;
    }
}
```

Fig. 3.30: The routine LLmessage() required by *LLgen*

we will now indicate how to do this. The original grammar for simple expressions
with code for constructing parse trees can be found in Figure 3.31; the definitions of
the node types of the parse tree are given in Figure 3.32. Each rule creates the node
corresponding to its non-terminal, and has one parameter, a pointer to a location in
which to store the pointer to that node. This allows the node for a non-terminal N to
be allocated by the rule for N, but it also means that there is one level of indirection
more here than meets the eye: the node itself inside expression is represented by
the C expression (*ep) rather than by just ep. Memory for the node is allocated at
the beginning of each alternative using calls of new_expr(); this routine is defined
in Figure 3.32. Next the node type is set. The early allocation of the node allows
the further members of an alternative to write the pointers to their nodes in it. All
this hinges on the facility of C to manipulate addresses of fields inside records as
separate entities.

```
expression(struct expr **ep)  →
    {(*ep) = new_expr(); (*ep)->type = '−';}
    expression(&(*ep)->expr) '−' term(&(*ep)->term)
|   {(*ep) = new_expr(); (*ep)->type = 'T';}
    term(&(*ep)->term)

term(struct term **tp)  →
    {(*tp) = new_term(); (*tp)->type = 'I';}
    IDENTIFIER
```

Fig. 3.31: Original grammar with code for constructing a parse tree

```
struct expr {
    int type;                /* '−' or 'T' */
    struct expr *expr;       /* for '−' */
    struct term *term;       /* for '−' and 'T' */
};
#define new_expr() ((struct expr *)malloc(sizeof(struct expr)))

struct term {
    int type;                /* 'I' only */
};
#define new_term() ((struct term *)malloc(sizeof(struct term)))

extern void print_expr(struct expr *e);
extern void print_term(struct term *t);
```

Fig. 3.32: Data structures for the parse tree

The grammar in Figure 3.31 has a serious LL(1) problem: it exhibits hidden
left-recursion. The left-recursion of the rule expression is hidden by the C code
{(∗ep) = new_expr(); (∗ep)−>type = '−';}, which is a pseudo-rule producing ε. This
hidden left-recursion prevents us from applying the left-recursion removal technique
from Section 3.4.3. To turn the hidden left-recursion into visible left-recursion, we
move the C code to after expression; this requires storing the result of expression
temporarily in an auxiliary variable, e_aux. See Figure 3.33, which shows only the
new rule for expression; the one for term remains unchanged.

```
expression(struct expr **ep) →
    expression(ep)
    {struct expr *e_aux = (*ep);
        (*ep) = new_expr(); (*ep)−>type = '−'; (*ep)−>expr = e_aux;
    }
    '−' term(&(*ep)−>term)
|   {(*ep) = new_expr(); (*ep)−>type = 'T';}
    term(&(*ep)−>term)
```

Fig. 3.33: Visibly left-recursive grammar with code for constructing a parse tree

Now that we have turned the hidden left-recursion into direct left-recursion we
can apply the technique from Section 3.4.3. We find that

N = expression(struct expr ∗∗ep)

α =
```
    {   struct  expr *e_aux = (*ep);
        (*ep) = new_expr();
        (*ep)−>type = '−'; (*ep)−>expr = e_aux;
    }
    '−' term(&(*ep)−>term)
```

β =
    {(*ep) = new_expr(); (*ep)–>type = 'T';}
    term(&(*ep)–>term)

which results in the code shown in Figure 3.34. Figure 3.35 shows what the new code does. The rule expression_tail_option is called with the address (ep) of a pointer (*ep) to the top node collected thus far as a parameter (a). When another term is found in the input, the pointer to the node is held in the auxiliary variable e_aux (b), a new node is inserted above it (c), and the old node and the new term are connected to the new node, which is accessible through ep as the top of the new tree. This technique constructs proper parse trees in spite of the grammar transformation required for LL(1) parsing.

```
expression(struct expr **ep)  →
    {(*ep) = new_expr(); (*ep)->type = 'T';}
    term(&(*ep)->term)
    expression_tail_option(ep)

expression_tail_option(struct expr **ep)  →
    {struct expr *e_aux = (*ep);
        (*ep) = new_expr();
        (*ep)->type = '–'; (*ep)->expr = e_aux;
    }
    '–' term(&(*ep)->term)
    expression_tail_option(ep)
|   ε
```

Fig. 3.34: Adapted *LLgen* grammar with code for constructing a parse tree

A sample run with the input i–i–i yields (((I)–I)–I) ; here i is just an identifier and I is the printed representation of a token of the class IDENTIFIER.

3.5 Creating a bottom-up parser automatically

Unlike top-down parsing, for which only one practical technique is available— LL(1)—there are many bottom-up techniques. We will explain the principles using the fundamentally important but impractical LR(0) technique and consider the practically important LR(1) and LALR(1) techniques in some depth. Not all grammars allow the LR(1) or LALR(1) parser construction technique to result in a parser; those that do not are said to exhibit LR(1) or LALR(1) conflicts, and measures to deal with them are discussed in Section 3.5.7. Techniques to incorporate error handling in LR parsers are treated in Section 3.5.10. An example of the use of a traditional bottom-up parser generator concludes this section on the creation of bottom-up parsers.

The main task of a bottom-up parser is to find the leftmost node that has not yet been constructed but all of whose children *have* been constructed. This sequence of

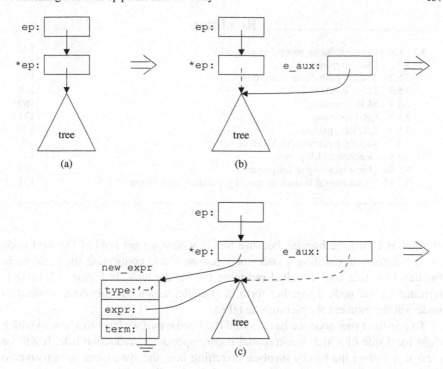

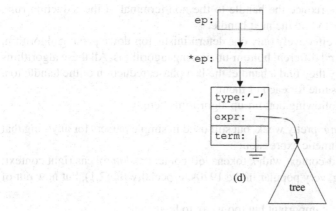

Fig. 3.35: Tree transformation performed by expression_tail_option

children is called the **handle**, because this is where we get hold of the next node to be constructed. Creating a node for a parent N and connecting the children in the handle to that node is called **reducing** the handle to N. In Figure 3.3, node 1, terminal t_6, and node 2 together form the handle, which has just been reduced to node 3 at the moment the picture was taken.

To construct that node we have to find the handle *and* we have to know to which right-hand side of which non-terminal it corresponds: its reduction rule. It will be clear that finding the handle involves searching both the syntax tree as constructed so far and the input. Once we have found the handle and its reduction rule, our troubles are over: we reduce the handle to the non-terminal of the reduction rule, and restart the parser to find the next handle.

Although there is effectively only one deterministic top-down parsing algorithm, LL(k), there are several different bottom-up parsing algorithms. All these algorithms differ only in the way they find a handle; the last phase, reduction of the handle to a non-terminal, is the same for each of them.

We mention the following bottom-up algorithms here:

- *precedence parsing*: pretty weak, but still used in simple parsers for anything that looks like an arithmetic expression;
- BC(k,m): bounded-context with k tokens left context and m tokens right context; reasonably strong, very popular in the 1970s, especially BC(2,1), but now out of fashion;
- *LR(0)*: theoretically important but too weak to be useful;
- *SLR(1)*: an upgraded version of LR(0), but still fairly weak;
- *LR(1)*: like LR(0) but both very powerful and very memory-consuming; and
- *LALR(1)*: a slightly watered-down version of LR(1), which is both powerful and usable: the workhorse of present-day bottom-up parsing.

We will first concentrate on LR(0), since it shows all the principles in a nutshell. The steps to LR(1) and from there to LALR(1) are then simple.

It turns out that finding a handle is not a simple thing to do, and all the above algorithms, with the possible exception of precedence parsing, require so much detail that it is humanly impossible to write a bottom-up parser by hand: all bottom-up parser writing is done by parser generator.

3.5.1 LR(0) parsing

One of the immediate advantages of bottom-up parsing is that it has no problems with left-recursion. We can therefore improve our grammar of Figure 3.4 so as to generate the proper left-associative syntax tree for the + operator. The result is left-recursive—see Figure 3.36. We have also removed the non-terminal parenthesized_expression by substituting it; the grammar is big enough as it is.

```
input       →  expression EoF
expression  →  term | expression '+' term
term        →  IDENTIFIER | '(' expression ')'
```

Fig. 3.36: A simple grammar for demonstrating bottom-up parsing

LR parsers are best explained using diagrams with item sets in them. To keep these diagrams manageable, it is customary to represent each non-terminal by a capital letter and each terminal by itself or by a single lower-case letter. The end-of-input token is traditionally represented by a dollar sign. This form of the grammar is shown in Figure 3.37; we have abbreviated the input to Z, to avoid confusion with the i, which stands for IDENTIFIER.

```
Z  →  E $
E  →  T | E '+' T
T  →  'i' | '(' E ')'
```

Fig. 3.37: An abbreviated form of the simple grammar for bottom-up parsing

In the beginning of our search for a handle, we have only a vague idea of what the handle can be and we need to keep track of many different hypotheses about it. In lexical analysis, we used dotted items to summarize the state of our search and sets of items to represent sets of hypotheses about the next token. LR parsing uses the same technique: item sets are kept in which each item is a hypothesis about the handle. Where in lexical analysis these item sets are situated between successive characters, here they are between successive grammar symbols. The presence of an **LR item** $N \rightarrow \alpha \bullet \beta$ between two grammar symbols means that we maintain the hypothesis of $\alpha\beta$ as a possible handle, that this $\alpha\beta$ is to be reduced to N when actually found applicable, and that the part α has already been recognized directly to the left of this point. When the dot reaches the right end of the item, as in $N \rightarrow \alpha\beta \bullet$, we have identified a handle. The members of the right-hand side $\alpha\beta$ have all been recognized, since the item has been obtained by moving the dot successively over each member of them. These members can now be collected as the children of a new node N. As with lexical analyzers, an item with the dot at the end is called a **reduce item**; the others are called **shift items**.

The various LR parsing methods differ in the exact form of their LR items, but not in their methods of using them. So there are LR(0) items, SLR(1) items, LR(1) items and LALR(1) items, and the methods of their construction differ, but there is essentially only one LR parsing algorithm.

We will now demonstrate how LR items are used to do bottom-up parsing. Assume the input is `i+i$`. First we are interested in the initial item set, the set of hypotheses about the handle we have before the first token. Initially, we know only one node of the tree: the top. This gives us the first possibility for the handle: Z→•E$, which means that if we manage to recognize an E followed by end-of-input, we have found a handle which we can reduce to Z, the top of the syntax tree. But since the dot is still at the beginning of the right-hand side, it also means that we have not seen any of these grammar symbols yet. The first we need to see is an E. The dot in front of the non-terminal E suggests that we may be looking for the wrong symbol at the moment and that the actual handle may derive from E. This adds two new items to the initial item set, one for each alternative of E: E→•T and E→•E+T, which describe two other hypotheses about the handle. Now we have a dot in front of another non-terminal T, which suggests that perhaps the handle derives from T. This adds two more items to the initial item set: T→•i and T→•(E). The item E→•E+T suggests also that the handle could derive from E, but we knew that already and that item introduces no new hypotheses. So our initial item set, s_0, contains five hypotheses about the handle:

```
Z  →  •E$
E  →  •T
E  →  •E+T
T  →  •i
T  →  •(E)
```

As with a lexical analyzer, the initial item set is positioned before the first input symbol:

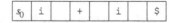

where we have left open spaces between the symbols for the future item sets.

Note that the four additional items in the item set s_0 are the result of ε-moves, moves made by the handle-searching automaton without consuming input. As before, the ε-moves are performed because the dot is in front of something that cannot be matched directly. The construction of the complete LR item is also very similar to that of a lexical item set: the initial contents of the item set are brought in from outside and the set is completed by applying an ε-closure algorithm. An ε-closure algorithm for LR item sets is given in Figure 3.38. To be more precise, it is the ε-closure algorithm for LR(0) item sets and s_0 is an LR(0) item set. Other ε-closure algorithms will be shown below.

Data definitions:
    S, a set of LR(0) items.

Initializations:
    S is prefilled externally with one or more LR(0) items.

Inference rules:
    For each item of the form $P \rightarrow \alpha \bullet N \beta$ in S and for each production rule $N \rightarrow \gamma$ in G, S
    must contain the item $N \rightarrow \bullet \gamma$.

Fig. 3.38: ε-closure algorithm for LR(0) item sets for a grammar G

The ε-closure algorithm expects the initial contents to be brought in from elsewhere. For the initial item set s_0 this consists of the item $Z \rightarrow \bullet S\$$, where S is the
start symbol of the grammar and $\$$ represents the end-of-input. The important part
is the inference rule: it predicts new handle hypotheses from the hypothesis that we
are looking for a certain non-terminal, and is sometimes called the **prediction rule**;
it corresponds to an ε-move, in that it allows the automaton to move to another state
without consuming input.

Note that the dotted items plus the prediction rule represent a top-down component in our bottom-up algorithm. The items in an item set form one or more sets
of top-down predictions about the handle, ultimately deriving from the start symbol. Since the predictions are kept here as hypotheses in a set rather than being
transformed immediately into syntax tree nodes as they are in the LL(1) algorithm,
left-recursion does not bother us here.

Using the same technique as with the lexical analyzer, we can now compute the
contents of the next item set s_1, the one between the i and the +. There is only one
item in s_0 in which the dot can be moved over an i: $T \rightarrow \bullet i$. Doing so gives us the initial
contents of the new item set s_1: { $T \rightarrow i \bullet$ }. Applying the prediction rule does not add
anything, so this is the new item set. Since it has the dot at the end, it is a reduce
item and indicates that we have found a handle. More precisely, it identifies i as the
handle, to be reduced to T using the rule $T \rightarrow i$. When we perform this reduction and
construct the corresponding part of the syntax tree, the input looks schematically as
follows:

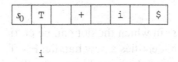

Having done one reduction, we restart the algorithm, which of course comes up
with the same value for s_0, but now we are looking at the non-terminal T rather than
at the unreduced i. There is only one item in s_0 in which the dot can be moved over
a T: $E \rightarrow \bullet T$. Doing so gives us the initial contents of a new value for s_1: { $E \rightarrow T \bullet$ }.
Again, applying the prediction rule does not add anything, so this is the new item
set; it contains one reduce item. After reduction by $E \rightarrow T$, the input looks as follows:

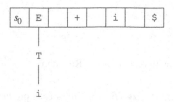

and it is quite satisfying to see the syntax tree grow. Restarting the algorithm, we finally get a really different initial value for s_1, the set

Z → E•$
E → E•+T

We now have:

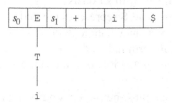

The next token in the input is a **+**. There is one item in s_1 that has the dot in front of a **+**: E→E•+T. So the initial contents of s_2 are { E→E+•T }. Applying the prediction rule yields two more items, for a total of three for s_2:

E → E+•T
T → •i
T → •(E)

Going through the same motions as with s_0 and again reducing the i to T, we get:

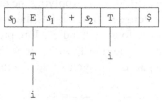

Now there is one item in s_2 in which the dot can be carried over a T: E→E+•T; this yields { E→E+T• }, which identifies a new handle, E + T, which is to be reduced to E. So we finally find a case in which our hypothesis that the handle might be E + T is correct. Remember that this hypothesis already occurs in the construction of s_0. Performing the reduction we get:

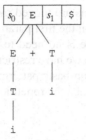

which brings us back to a value of s_1 that we have seen already:

    Z → E•$
    E → E•+T

Unlike last time, the next token in the input is now the end-of-input token $. Moving the dot over it gives us s_2, { Z→E$• }, which contains one item, a reduce item, shows that a handle has been found, and says that E $ must be reduced to Z:

This final reduction completes the syntax tree and ends the parsing process. Note how the LR parsing process (and any bottom-up parsing technique for that matter) structures the input, which is still there in its entirety.

3.5.1.1 Precomputing the item set

The above demonstration of LR parsing shows two major features that need to be discussed further: the computation of the item sets and the use of these sets. We will first turn to the computation of the item sets. The item sets of an LR parser show considerable similarities to those of a lexical analyzer. Their number is finite and not embarrassingly large and we can define routines *InitialItemSet( )* and *NextItemSet( )* with meanings corresponding to those in the lexical analyzer. We can therefore precompute the contents of all the reachable item sets and the values of *InitialItemSet( )* and *NextItemSet( )* for all their parameters. Even the bodies of the two routines for LR(0) items, shown in Figures 3.39 and 3.40, are similar to those for the lexical analyzer, as we can see when we compare them to the ones in Figures 2.22 and 2.23.

One difference is that LR item sets are moved over grammar symbols, rather than over characters. This is reflected in the first parameter of *NextItemSet()*, which now is a *Symbol*. Another is that there is no need to test if S is a basic pattern (compare Figure 2.23). This is because we have restricted ourselves here to grammars in BNF notation. So S cannot be a non-basic pattern; if, however, we allow EBNF, the code in Figure 3.40 will have to take the repetition and combination operators into account.

---

function InitialItemSet **returning** an item set:
    NewItemSet ← ∅;

    — Initial contents—obtain from the start symbol:
    for each production rule $S \rightarrow \alpha$ for the start symbol S:
        Insert item $S \rightarrow \bullet \alpha$ into NewItemSet;

    return ε-closure (NewItemSet);

Fig. 3.39: The routine *InitialItemSet* for an LR(0) parser

---

function NextItemSet (ItemSet, Symbol) **returning** an item set:
    NewItemSet ← ∅;

    — Initial contents—obtain from token moves:
    for each item $N \rightarrow \alpha \bullet S \beta$ **in** ItemSet:
        if S = Symbol:
            Insert item $N \rightarrow \alpha S \bullet \beta$ into NewItemSet;

    return ε-closure (NewItemSet);

Fig. 3.40: The routine *NextItemSet()* for an LR(0) parser

Calling *InitialItemSet()* yields S_0, and repeated application of *NextItemSet()* gives us the other reachable item sets, in an LR analog of the lexical subset algorithm explained in Section 2.6.3. The reachable item sets are shown, together with the transitions between them, in the transition diagram in Figure 3.41. The reduce items, the items that indicate that a handle has been found, are marked by a double rim. We recognize the sets S_0, S_5, S_6, S_1, S_3, S_4 and S_2 (in that order) from the parsing of i+i; the others will occur in parsing different inputs.

The transition table is shown in Figure 3.42. This tabular version of *NextItemSet()* is traditionally called the **GOTO table** in LR parsing. The empty entries stand for the empty set of hypotheses; if an empty set is obtained while searching for the handle, there is no hypothesis left, no handle can be found, and there is a syntax error. The empty set is also called the **error state**. It is quite representative that most of the GOTO table is empty; also the non-empty part shows considerable structure. Such LR tables are excellent candidates for transition table compression.

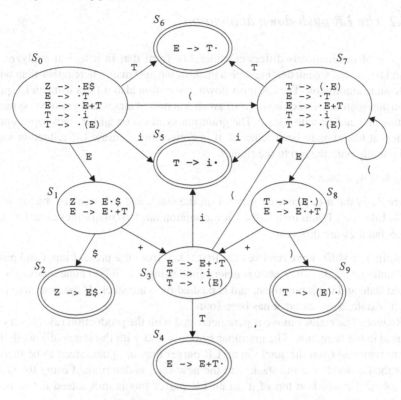

Fig. 3.41: Transition diagram for the LR(0) automaton for the grammar of Figure 3.37

	← GOTO table →						ACTION table
			symbol				
state	i	+	(	)	$	E	T	

state	i	+	(	)	$	E	T	
0	5		7			1	6	shift
1		3			2			shift
2								Z→E$
3	5		7				4	shift
4								E→E+T
5								T→i
6								E→T
7	5		7		8		6	shift
8		3		9				shift
9								T→(E)

Fig. 3.42: GOTO and ACTION tables for the LR(0) automaton for the grammar of Figure 3.37

3.5.2 The LR push-down automaton

The use of the item sets differs considerably from that in a lexical analyzer, the reason being that we are dealing with a push-down automaton here rather than with a finite-state automaton. The LR push-down automaton also differs from an LL push-down automaton. Its stack consists of an alternation of states and grammar symbols, starting and ending with a state. The grammar symbols on an LR stack represent the input that has already been reduced. It is convenient to draw LR reduction stacks horizontally with the top to the right:

$s_0 \, A_1 \, s_1 \, A_2 \ldots A_t \, s_t$

where A_n is the n-th grammar symbol on the stack and t designates the top of the stack. Like the LL automaton, the LR automaton has two major moves and a minor move, but they are different:

- Shift: The **shift move** removes the first token from the present input and pushes it onto the stack. A new state is determined using the GOTO table indexed by the old state and the input token, and is pushed onto the stack. If the new state is the error state, a syntax error has been found.
- Reduce: The **reduce move** is parameterized with the production rule $N \rightarrow \alpha$ to be used in the reduction. The grammar symbols in α with the states following them are removed from the stack; in an LR parser they are guaranteed to be there. N is then pushed onto the stack, and the new state is determined using the GOTO table and pushed on top of it. In an LR parser this is guaranteed not to be the error state.
- Termination: The input has been parsed successfully when it has been reduced to the start symbol. If there are tokens left in the input though, there is a syntax error.

The state on top of the stack in an LR(0) parser determines which of these moves is applied. The top state indexes the so-called **ACTION table**, which is comparable to *ClassOfTokenRecognizedIn()* in the lexical analyzer. Like the latter, it tells us whether we have found something or should go on shifting input tokens, and if we found something it tells us what it is. The ACTION table for our grammar is shown as the rightmost column in Figure 3.42. For states that have outgoing arrows it holds the entry "shift"; for states that contain exactly one reduce item, it holds the corresponding rule. We can now summarize our demonstration of the parsing of i+i in a few lines; see Figure 3.43.

The code for the LR(0) parser can be found in Figure 3.44. Comparison to Figure 3.20 shows a clear similarity to the LL push-down automaton, but there are also considerable differences. Whereas the stack of the LL automaton contains grammar symbols only, the stack of the LR automaton consists of an alternating sequence of states and grammar symbols, starting and ending with a state, as shown, for example, in Figure 3.43 and in many other figures. Parsing terminates when the entire input has been reduced to the start symbol of the grammar, and when that start symbol is followed on the stack by the end state; as with the LL(1) automaton this will

Stack	Input	Action
S_0	i + i $	shift
S_0 i S_5	+ i $	reduce by T→i
S_0 T S_6	+ i $	reduce by E→T
S_0 E S_1	+ i $	shift
S_0 E S_1 + S_3	i $	shift
S_0 E S_1 + S_3 i S_5	$	reduce by T→i
S_0 E S_1 + S_3 T S_4	$	reduce by E→E+T
S_0 E S_1	$	shift
S_0 E S_1 $ S_2		reduce by Z→E$
S_0 Z		stop

Fig. 3.43: LR(0) parsing of the input i+i

happen only when the EoF token has also been reduced. Otherwise, the state on top of the stack is looked up in the ACTION table. This results in "shift", "reduce using rule $N→\alpha$", or "erroneous". If the new state is "erroneous" there was a syntax error; this cannot happen in an LR(0) parser, but the possibility is mentioned here for compatibility with other LR parsers. For "shift", the next input token is stacked and a new state is stacked on top of it. For "reduce", the grammar symbols in α are popped off the stack, including the intervening states. The non-terminal N is then pushed onto the stack, and a new state is determined by consulting the GOTO table and stacked on top of it. This new state cannot be "erroneous" in any LR parser (see Exercise 3.19).

Above we stated that bottom-up parsing, unlike top-down parsing, has no problems with left-recursion. On the other hand, bottom-up parsing has a slight problem with right-recursive rules, in that the stack may grow proportionally to the size of the input program; maximum stack size is normally proportional to the logarithm of the program size. This is mainly a problem with parsers with a fixed stack size; since parsing time is already linear in the size of the input, adding another linear component does not much degrade parsing speed. Some details of the problem are considered in Exercise 3.22.

3.5.3 LR(0) conflicts

The above LR(0) method would appear to be a fail-safe method to create a deterministic parser for any grammar, but appearances are deceptive in this case: we selected the grammar carefully for the example to work. We can make a transition diagram for any grammar and we can make a GOTO table for any grammar, but we cannot make a deterministic ACTION table for just any grammar. The innocuous-looking sentence about the construction of the ACTION table may have warned the reader; we repeat it here: 'For states that have outgoing arrows it holds the entry "shift"; for states that contain exactly one reduce item, it holds the corresponding rule.' This points to two problems: some states may have both outgoing arrows *and* reduce

import InputToken [1..];   — from the lexical analyzer

InputTokenIndex ← 1;
ReductionStack ← ⊥;
Push (StartState, ReductionStack);

while ReductionStack ≠ {StartState, StartSymbol, EndState}:
    State ← TopOf (ReductionStack);
    Action ← ActionTable [State];
    if Action = "shift":
        — Do a shift move:
        ShiftedToken ← InputToken [InputTokenIndex];
        InputTokenIndex ← InputTokenIndex + 1; — shifted
        Push (ShiftedToken, ReductionStack);
        NewState ← GotoTable [State, ShiftedToken.class];
        Push (NewState, ReductionStack); can be ∅
    else if Action = ("reduce", $N{\to}\alpha$):
        — Do a reduction move:
        Pop the symbols of α from ReductionStack;
        State ← TopOf (ReductionStack); update State
        Push (N, ReductionStack);
        NewState ← GotoTable [State, N];
        Push (NewState, ReductionStack); cannot be ∅
    else — Action = ∅:
        error "Error at token ", InputToken [InputTokenIndex];

Fig. 3.44: LR(0) parsing with a push-down automaton

items; and some states may contain more than one reduce item. The first situation is called a **shift-reduce conflict**, the second a **reduce-reduce conflict**. In both cases the ACTION table contains entries with multiple values and the algorithm is no longer deterministic. If the ACTION table produced from a grammar in the above way is deterministic (conflict-free), the grammar is called an **LR(0) grammar**.

Very few grammars are LR(0). For example, no grammar with an ε-rule can be LR(0). Suppose the grammar contains the production rule A→ε. Then an item A→• will be predicted by any item of the form $P{\to}\alpha{\bullet}A\beta$. The first is a reduce item, the second has an arrow on A, so we have a shift-reduce conflict. And ε-rules are very frequent in grammars.

Even modest extensions to our example grammar cause trouble. Suppose we extend it to allow array elements in expressions, by adding the production rule T→i[E]. When we construct the transition diagram, we meet the item set corresponding to S_5:

T → i•
T → i•[E]

and we have a shift-reduce conflict on our hands: the ACTION table requires both a shift and a reduce, and the grammar is no longer LR(0).

Or suppose we want to allow assignments in the input by adding the rules Z→V:=E\$ and V→i, where V stands for variable; we want a separate rule for V, since its semantics differs from that of T→i. Now we find the item set corresponding to S_5 to be

T → i•
V → i•

and we have a reduce-reduce conflict. These are very common cases.

Note that states that do not contain reduce items cannot cause conflicts: reduce items are required both for shift-reduce and for reduce-reduce conflicts. For more about the non-existence of shift-shift conflicts see Exercise 3.20.

For a run-of-the-mill programming language grammar, one can expect the LR(0) automaton to have some thousands of states. With, say, 50 tokens in the language and 2 or 4 bytes to represent an entry, the ACTION/GOTO table will require some hundreds of kilobytes. Table compression will reduce this to some tens of kilobytes. So the good news is that LR(0) tables claim only a moderate amount of memory; the bad news is that LR(0) tables are almost certainly full of conflicts.

The above examples show that the LR(0) method is just too weak to be useful. This is caused by the fact that we try to decide from the transition diagram alone what action to perform, and that we ignore the input: the ACTION table construction uses a zero-token look-ahead, hence the name LR(0). There are basically three ways to use a one-token look-ahead, SLR(1), LR(1), and LALR(1). All three methods use a two-dimensional ACTION table, indexed by the state on the top of the stack and the first token of the present input. The construction of the states and the table differ, though.

3.5.4 SLR(1) parsing

The SLR(1) (for Simple LR(1)) [80] parsing method has little practical significance these days, but we treat it here because we can explain it in a few lines at this stage and because it provides a good stepping stone to the far more important LR(1) method. For one thing it allows us to show a two-dimensional ACTION table of manageable proportions.

The SLR(1) method is based on the consideration that a handle should not be reduced to a non-terminal N if the look-ahead is a token that cannot follow N: a reduce item $N→\alpha\bullet$ is applicable only if the look-ahead is in FOLLOW(N). Consequently, SLR(1) has the same transition diagram as LR(0) for a given grammar, the same GOTO table, but a different ACTION table.

Based on this rule and on the FOLLOW sets

FOLLOW(Z) = { \$ }
FOLLOW(E) = {) + \$ }
FOLLOW(T) = {) + \$ }

state	look-ahead token				
	i	+	(	)	$
0	shift		shift		
1		shift			shift
2					Z→E$
3	shift		shift		
4		E→E+T		E→E+T	E→E+T
5		T→i		T→i	T→i
6		E→T		E→T	E→T
7	shift		shift		
8		shift		shift	
9		T→(E)		T→(E)	T→(E)

Fig. 3.45: ACTION table for the SLR(1) automaton for the grammar of Figure 3.37

we can construct the SLR(1) ACTION table for the grammar of Figure 3.37. The result is shown in Figure 3.45, in which a reduction to a non-terminal N is indicated only for look-ahead tokens in FOLLOW(N).

When we compare the ACTION table in Figure 3.45 to the GOTO table from Figure 3.42, we see that the columns marked with non-terminals are missing; non-terminals do not occur in the input and they do not figure in look-aheads. Where the ACTION table has "shift", the GOTO table has a state number; where the ACTION table has a reduction, the GOTO table is empty. It is customary to superimpose the ACTION and GOTO tables in the implementation. The combined ACTION/GOTO table has shift entries of the form sN, which mean "shift to state N"; reduce entries rN, which mean "reduce using rule number N"; and of course empty entries which mean syntax errors. The ACTION/GOTO table is also called the **parse table**. It is shown in Figure 3.46, in which the following numbering of the grammar rules is used:

1: Z → E $
2: E → T
3: E → E + T
4: T → i
5: T → (E)

Note that each alternative counts as a separate rule. Also note that there is a lot of structure in the ACTION/GOTO table, which can be exploited by a compression algorithm.

It should be emphasized that in spite of their visual similarity the GOTO and ACTION tables are fundamentally different. The GOTO table is indexed by a state and one grammar symbol that resides on the stack, whereas the ACTION table is indexed by a state and a look-ahead token that resides in the input. That they can be superimposed in the case of a one-token look-ahead is more or less accidental, and the trick is not available for look-ahead lengths other than 1.

When we now introduce a grammar rule T→i[E], we find that the shift-reduce conflict has gone away. The reduce item T→i• applies only when the look-ahead is

```
            stack symbol/look-ahead token
    state i   +   (   )   $   E   T
      0  s5      s7          s1 s6
      1      s3      s2
      2              r1
      3  s5      s7              s4
      4      r3      r3 r3
      5      r4      r4 r4
      6      r2      r2 r2
      7  s5      s7          s8 s6
      8      s3      s9
      9      r5      r5 r5
```

Fig. 3.46: ACTION/GOTO table for the SLR(1) automaton for the grammar of Figure 3.37

one of ')', '+', and '$', so the ACTION table can freely specify a shift for '['. The
SLR(1) table will now contain the line

```
state i +    ( )    [    ]    $
  5    T→i  T→i  shift T→i T→i
```

Note the reduction on], since] is in the new FOLLOW(T). The ACTION table is
deterministic and the grammar is SLR(1).

It will be clear that the SLR(1) automaton has the same number of states as the
LR(0) automaton for the same grammar. Also, the ACTION/GOTO table of the
SLR(1) automaton has the same size as the GOTO table of the LR(0) automaton,
but it has fewer empty entries.

Experience has shown that SLR(1) is a considerable improvement over LR(0),
but is still far inferior to LR(1) or LALR(1). It was a popular method for some years
in the early 1970s, mainly because its parsing tables are the same size as those of
LR(0). It has now been almost completely superseded by LALR(1).

3.5.5 LR(1) parsing

The reason why conflict resolution by FOLLOW set does not work nearly as well
as one might wish is that it replaces the look-ahead of a single item of a rule N in a
given LR state by FOLLOW set of N, which is the union of all the look-aheads of all
alternatives of N in all states. LR(1) item sets are more discriminating: a look-ahead
set is kept with each separate item, to be used to resolve conflicts when a reduce
item has been reached. This greatly increases the strength of the parser, but also the
size of its parse tables.

The LR(1) technique will be demonstrated using the rather artificial grammar
shown in Figure 3.47. The grammar has been chosen because, first, it is not LL(1)
or SLR(1), so these simpler techniques are ruled out, and second, it is both LR(1)
and LALR(1), but the two automata differ.

```
S  →  A | 'x' 'b'
A  →  'a' A 'b' | B
B  →  'x'
```

Fig. 3.47: Grammar for demonstrating the LR(1) technique

The grammar produces the language { **xb**, **a^{n}xb^n** | $n >= 0$}. This language can of course be parsed by much simpler means, but that is beside the point: if semantics is attached to the rules of the grammar of Figure 3.47, we want a structuring of the input in terms of that grammar and of no other.

It is easy to see that the grammar is not LL(1): x is in FIRST(B), so it is in FIRST(A), and S exhibits a FIRST/FIRST conflict on x.

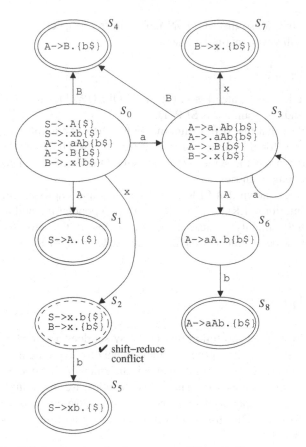

Fig. 3.48: The SLR(1) automaton for the grammar of Figure 3.47

The grammar is not SLR(1) either, which we can see from the SLR(1) automaton shown in Figure 3.48. Since the SLR(1) technique bases its decision to reduce using an item $N{\rightarrow}\alpha{\bullet}$ on the FOLLOW set of N, these FOLLOW sets have been added to each item in set braces. We see that state S_2 contains both a shift item, on b, and a reduce item, B$\rightarrow$x·b{$}. The SLR(1) technique tries to solve this conflict by restricting the reduction to those look-aheads that are in FOLLOW(B). Unfortunately, however, b is in FOLLOW(A), so it is also in FOLLOW(B), resulting in an SLR(1) shift-reduce conflict.

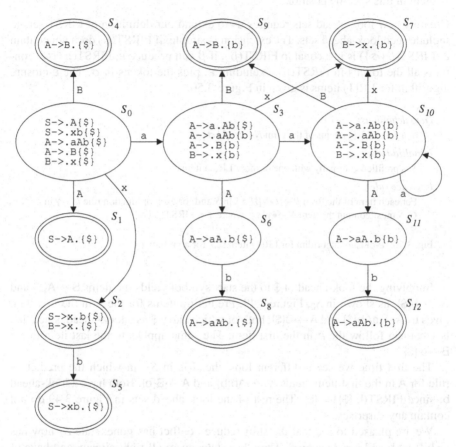

Fig. 3.49: The LR(1) automaton for the grammar of Figure 3.47

The LR(1) technique does not rely on FOLLOW sets, but rather keeps the specific look-ahead with each item. We will write an LR(1) item thus: $N{\rightarrow}\alpha{\bullet}\beta\{\sigma\}$, in which σ is the set of tokens that can follow this specific item. When the dot has reached the end of the item, as in $N{\rightarrow}\alpha\beta{\bullet}\{\sigma\}$, the item is an acceptable reduce item only if the look-ahead at that moment is in σ; otherwise the item is ignored.

The rules for determining the look-ahead sets are simple. The look-ahead sets of existing items do not change; only when a new item is created, a new look-ahead set must be determined. There are two situations in which this happens.

- When creating the initial item set: The look-ahead set of the initial items in the initial item set S_0 contains only one token, the end-of-file token (denoted by \$), since that is the only token that can follow the start symbol of the grammar.
- When doing ε-moves: The prediction rule creates new items for the alternatives of N in the presence of items of the form $P{\rightarrow}\alpha{\bullet}N\beta\{\sigma\}$; the look-ahead set of each of these items is FIRST($\beta\{\sigma\}$), since that is what can follow this specific item in this specific position.

Creating new look-ahead sets requires us to extend our definition of FIRST sets to include such look-ahead sets. The extension is simple: if FIRST(β) does not contain ε, FIRST($\beta\{\sigma\}$) is just equal to FIRST(β); if β can produce ε, FIRST($\beta\{\sigma\}$) contains all the tokens in FIRST(β), excluding ε, plus the tokens in σ. The ε-closure algorithm for LR(1) items is given in Figure 3.50.

Data definitions:
    S, a set of LR(1) items of the form $N{\rightarrow}\alpha{\bullet}\beta\{\sigma\}$.

Initializations:
    S is prefilled externally with one or more LR(1) items.

Inference rules:
    For each item of the form $P{\rightarrow}\alpha{\bullet}N\beta\{\sigma\}$ in S and for each production rule $N{\rightarrow}\gamma$ in G, S must contain the item $N{\rightarrow}{\bullet}\gamma\{\tau\}$, where $\tau = $ FIRST($\beta\{\sigma\}$).

Fig. 3.50: ε-closure algorithm for LR(1) item sets for a grammar G

Supplying the look-ahead of \$ to the start symbol yields the items S→•A{\$} and S→•xb{\$}, as shown in S_0, Figure 3.49. Predicting items for the A in the first item gives us A→•aAb{\$} and A→•B{\$}, both of which carry \$ as a look-ahead, since that is what can follow the A in the first item. The same applies to the last item in S_0: B→•x{\$}.

The first time we see a different look-ahead is in S_3, in which the prediction rule for A in the first item yields A→•aAb{b} and A→•B{b}. Both have a look-ahead b, since FIRST(b {\$}) = {b}. The rest of the look-ahead sets in Figure 3.49 do not contain any surprises.

We are pleased to see that the shift-reduce conflict has gone: state S_2 now has a shift on b and a reduce on \$. The other states were all right already and have of course not been spoiled by shrinking the look-ahead set. So the grammar of Figure 3.47 is LR(1).

The code for the LR(1) automaton is shown in Figure 3.51. The only difference with the LR(0) automaton in Figure 3.44 is that the *ActionTable* is now indexed by the state *and* the look-ahead symbol. The pattern of Figure 3.51 can also be used in a straightforward fashion for LR(k) parsers for $k > 1$, by simply indexing the ACTION table with more look-ahead symbols. Of course, the ACTION table must have been constructed accordingly.

We see that the LR(1) automaton is more discriminating than the SLR(1) automaton. In fact, it is so strong that any language that *can* be parsed from left to right with

```
import InputToken [1..];              — from the lexical analyzer

InputTokenIndex ← 1;
ReductionStack ← ⊥;
Push (StartState, ReductionStack);

while ReductionStack ≠ {StartState, StartSymbol, EndState}:
    State ← TopOf (ReductionStack);
    LookAhead ← InputToken [InputTokenIndex].class;
    Action ← ActionTable [State, LookAhead];
    if Action = "shift":
        — Do a shift move:
        ShiftedToken ← InputToken [InputTokenIndex];
        InputTokenIndex ← InputTokenIndex + 1; — shifted
        Push (ShiftedToken, ReductionStack);
        NewState ← GotoTable [State, ShiftedToken.class];
        Push (NewState, ReductionStack); cannot be ∅
    else if Action = ("reduce", N→α):
        — Do a reduction move:
        Pop the symbols of α from ReductionStack;
        State ← TopOf (ReductionStack); update State
        Push (N, ReductionStack);
        NewState ← GotoTable [State, N];
        Push (NewState, ReductionStack); cannot be ∅
    else — Action = ∅:
        error "Error at token ", InputToken [InputTokenIndex];
```

Fig. 3.51: LR(1) parsing with a push-down automaton

a one-token look-ahead in linear time can be parsed using the LR(1) method: LR(1) is the strongest possible linear left-to-right parsing method. The reason for this is that it can be shown [155] that the set of LR items implements the best possible breadth-first search for handles.

It is possible to define an LR(k) parser, with $k > 1$, which does a k-token look-ahead. This change affects the ACTION table only: rather than being indexed by a state and a look-ahead token it is indexed by a state and a look-ahead string of length k. The GOTO table remains unchanged. It is still indexed by a state and one stack symbol, since the symbol in the GOTO table is not a look-ahead; it already resides on the stack. LR($k > 1$) parsers are stronger than LR(1) parsers, but only marginally so. If a grammar is not LR(1), chances are slim that it *is* LR(2). Also, it can be proved that any language that can be expressed by an LR($k > 1$) grammar can be expressed by an LR(1) grammar. LR($k > 1$) parsing has some theoretical significance but has never become popular.

The increased parsing power of the LR(1) technique does not come entirely free of charge: LR(1) parsing tables are one or two orders of magnitude larger than SLR(1) parsing tables. Whereas the average compressed SLR(1) automaton for a programming language will require some tens of kilobytes of memory, LR(1) tables may require some megabytes of memory, with perhaps ten times that amount required during the construction of the table. This may present little problem in

present-day computers, but traditionally compiler writers have been unable or un-
willing to use that much memory just for parsing, and ways to reduce the LR(1)
memory requirements have been sought. This has resulted in the discovery of
LALR(1) parsing. Needless to say, memory requirements for LR(k) ACTION tables with $k > 1$ are again orders of magnitude larger.

A different implementation of LR(1) that reduces the table sizes somewhat has
been presented by Fortes Gálvez [100].

3.5.6 LALR(1) parsing

When we look carefully at the states in the LR(1) automaton in Figure 3.49, we see
that some of the item sets are very similar to some other sets. More in particular, S_3
and S_{10} are similar in that they are equal if one ignores the look-ahead sets, and so
are S_4 and S_9, S_6 and S_{11}, and S_8 and S_{12}. What remains of the item set of an LR(1)
state when one ignores the look-ahead sets is called the **core** of the LR(1) state. For
example, the core of state S_2 in Figure 3.49 is

    S → x•b
    B → x•

All cores of LR(1) states correspond to LR(0) states. The reason for this is that
the contents of the cores are determined only by the results of shifts allowed from
other states. These shifts are determined by the GOTO table and are not influenced
by the look-aheads. So, given an LR(1) state whose core is an LR(0) state, shifts
from the item set in it will produce new LR(1) states whose cores are again LR(0)
states, regardless of look-aheads. We see that the LR(1) states are split-up versions
of LR(0) states.

Of course this fine split is the source of the power of the LR(1) automaton, but this
power is not needed in each and every state. For example, we could easily combine
states S_8 and S_{12} into one new state $S_{8,12}$ holding one item A→aAb•{b$}, without
in the least compromising the discriminatory power of the LR(1) automaton. Note
that we combine states with the same cores only, and we do this by adding the look-
ahead sets of the corresponding items they contain.

Next we lead the transitions away from the old states and to the new state. In
our example, the transitions on b in S_6 and S_{11} leading to S_8 and S_{12} respectively,
are moved to lead to $S_{8,12}$. The states S_8 and S_{12} can then be removed, reducing the
number of states by 1.

Continuing this way, we can reduce the number of states considerably. Due to
the possibility of cycles in the LR(1) transition diagrams, the actual algorithm for
doing so is much more complicated than shown here [211], but since it is not used
in practice, we will not give it in detail.

It would seem that if one goes on combining states in the fashion described above,
one would very soon combine two (or more) states into a new state that would have
a conflict, since after all we are gradually throwing away the look-ahead information that we have just built up to avoid such conflicts. It turns out that for the average

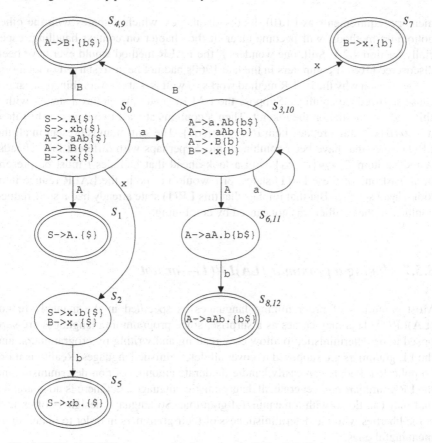

Fig. 3.52: The LALR(1) automaton for the grammar of Figure 3.47

programming language grammar this is not true. Better still, one can almost always afford to combine all states with identical cores, thus reducing the number of states to that of the SLR(1)—and LR(0)—automaton. The automaton obtained by combining all states of an LR(1) automaton that have the same cores is the **LALR(1) automaton.**

The LALR(1) automaton for the grammar of Figure 3.47 is shown in Figure 3.52. We see that our wholesale combining of states has done no damage: the automaton is still conflict-free, and the grammar is LALR(1), as promised. The item B→x•{$} in S_2 has retained its look-ahead $, which distinguishes it from the shift on b. The item for B that does have a look-ahead of b (since b is in FOLLOW(B), such an item must exist) sits safely in state S_7. The contexts in which these two reductions take place differ so much that the LALR(1) method can keep them apart.

It is surprising how well the LALR(1) method works. It is probably the most popular parsing method today, and has been so for at least thirty years. It combines power—it is only marginally weaker than LR(1)—with efficiency—it has the same memory requirements as LR(0). Its disadvantages, which it shares with the other bottom-up methods, will become clear in the chapter on context handling, especially Section 4.2.1. Still, one wonders if the LALR method would ever have been discovered [165] if computers in the late 1960s had not been so starved of memory.

One reason why the LALR method works so well is that state combination cannot cause shift-reduce conflicts. Suppose the LALR(1) automaton has a state S with a shift-reduce conflict on the token t. Then S contains at least two items, a shift item $A \rightarrow \alpha \bullet t \beta \{\sigma\}$ and a reduce item $B \rightarrow \gamma \bullet \{\sigma_1 t \sigma_2\}$. The shift item is present in all the LR(1) states that have been combined into S, perhaps with different look-aheads. A reduce item $B \rightarrow \gamma \bullet \{\sigma_3 t \sigma_4\}$ with a look-ahead that includes t must be present in at least one of these LR(1) states, or t would not be in the LALR reduce item look-ahead set of S. But that implies that this LR(1) state already had a shift-reduce conflict, so the conflict was not caused by combining.

3.5.7 Making a grammar (LA)LR(1)—or not

Most grammars of programming languages as specified in the manual are not (LA)LR(1). This may comes as a surprise, since programming languages are supposed to be deterministic, to allow easy reading and writing by programmers; and the LR grammars are supposed to cover all deterministic languages. Reality is more complicated. People can easily handle moderate amounts of non-determinism; and the LR grammars *can* generate all deterministic languages, but there is no guarantee that they can do so with a meaningful grammar. So language designers often take some liberties with the deterministicness of their grammars in order to obtain more meaningful ones.

A simple example is the declaration of integer and real variables in a language:

```
declaration  →  int_decl | real_decl
int_decl  →  int_var_seq 'int'
real_decl  →  real_var_seq 'real'
int_var_seq  →  int_var_seq int_var | int_var
real_var_seq  →  real_var_seq real_var | real_var
int_var  →  IDENTIFIER
real_var  →  IDENTIFIER
```

This grammar shows clearly that integer declarations declare integer variables, and real declarations declare real ones; it also allows the compiler to directly enter the variables into the symbol table with their correct types. But the grammar is not (LA)LR(k) for any k, since the tokens 'int' or 'real', which are needed to decide whether to reduce an IDENTIFIER to int_var or real_var, can be arbitrarily far ahead in the input. This does not bother the programmer or reader, who have no trouble understanding declarations like:

```
        i  j  k  p  q  r  'int'
        dist  height  'real'
```

but it does bother the LALR(1) parser generator, which finds a reduce-reduce conflict.

As with making a grammar LL(1) (Section 3.4.3.1) there is no general technique to make a grammar deterministic; and since LALR(1) is not sensitive to left-factoring and substitution and does not need left-recursion removal, the techniques used for LL(1) conflicts cannot help us here. Still, sometimes reduce-reduce conflicts can be resolved by combining some rules, since this allows the LR parser to postpone the reductions. In the above case we can combine int_var → IDENTI-FIER and real_var → IDENTIFIER into var → IDENTIFIER, and propagate the combination upwards, resulting in the grammar

```
declaration → int_decl | real_decl
int_decl → int_var_seq 'int'
real_decl → real_var_seq 'real'
int_var_seq → var_seq
real_var_seq → var_seq
var_seq → var_seq var | var
var → IDENTIFIER
```

which *is* LALR(1). A disadvantage is that we now have to enter the variable names into the symbol table without a type indication and come back later (upon the reduction of var_seq) to set the type.

In view of the difficulty of making a grammar LR, and since it is preferable anyhow to keep the grammar in tact to avoid the need for semantic transformations, almost all LR parser generators include ways to resolve LR conflicts. A problem with dynamic conflict resolvers is that very little useful information is available dynamically in LR parsers, since the actions of a rule are not performed until after the rule has been reduced. So LR parser generators stick to static conflict resolvers only: simple rules to resolve shift-reduce and reduce-reduce conflicts.

3.5.7.1 Resolving shift-reduce conflicts automatically

Shift-reduce conflicts are traditionally solved in an LR parser generator by the same maximal-munch rule as is used in lexical analyzers: the longest possible sequence of grammar symbols is taken for reduction. This is very simple to implement: in a shift-reduce conflict do the shift. Note that if there is more than one shift-reduce conflict in the same state, this criterion solves them all. As with the lexical analyzer, this almost always does what one wants.

We can see this rule in action in the way LR parser generators handle the dangling else. We again use the grammar fragment for the conditional statement in C

```
if_statement → 'if' '(' expression ')' statement
if_else_statement → 'if' '(' expression ')' statement 'else' statement
conditional_statement → if_statement | if_else_statement
statement → ... | conditional_statement | ...
```

and consider the statement

```
if (x > 0) if (y > 0) p = 0; else q = 0;
```

When during parsing we are between the) and the if, we are in a state which contains at least the items

```
statement → • conditional_statement { ... 'else' ... }
conditional_statement → • if_statement { ... 'else' ... }
conditional_statement → • if_else_statement { ... 'else' ... }
if_statement → • 'if' '(' expression ')' statement { ... 'else' ... }
if_else_statement → • 'if' '(' expression ')' statement 'else' statement { ... 'else' ... }
```

Then, continuing our parsing, we arrive in a state S between the ; and the else, in which at least the following two items remain:

```
if_statement → 'if' '(' expression ')' statement • { ... 'else' ... }
if_else_statement → 'if' '(' expression ')' statement • 'else' statement { ... 'else' ... }
```

We see that this state has a shift-reduce conflict on the token else.

If we now resolve the shift-reduce conflict by shifting the else, it will be paired with the latest if without an else, thus conforming to the C manual.

Another useful technique for resolving shift-reduce conflicts is the use of precedences between tokens. The word "precedence" is used here in the traditional sense, in which, for example, the multiplication sign has a higher precedence than the plus sign; the notion may be extended to other tokens as well in parsers. This method can be applied only if the reduce item in the conflict ends in a token followed by at most one non-terminal, but many do. In that case we have the following situation which has a shift-reduce conflict on t:

$$P \rightarrow \alpha \bullet t \beta \{...\} \quad \text{(the shift item)}$$
$$Q \rightarrow \gamma u R \bullet \{...t...\} \text{ (the reduce item)}$$

where R is either empty or one non-terminal. Now, if the look-ahead is t, we perform one of the following three actions:

1. if symbol u has a higher precedence than symbol t, we reduce; this yields a node Q containing u and leaves t outside of it to the right;
2. if t has a higher precedence than u, we shift; this continues with the node for P which will contain t when recognized eventually, and leaves u out of it to the left;
3. if both have equal precedence, we also shift (but see Exercise 3.25).

This method requires the precedence information to be supplied by the user of the parser generator. It allows considerable control over the resolution of shift-reduce conflicts. Note that the dangling else problem can also be solved by giving the else token the same precedence as the) token; then we do not have to rely on a built-in preference for shifting in a shift-reduce conflict.

3.5.7.2 Resolving reduce-reduce conflicts automatically

A reduce-reduce conflict corresponds to the situation in a lexical analyzer in which the longest token still matches more than one pattern. The most common built-in resolution rule is the same as in lexical analyzers: the textually first grammar rule in the parser generator input wins. This is easy to implement and allows the programmer some influence on the resolution. It is often but by no means always satisfactory. Note, for example, that it does not and even cannot solve the int_var versus real_var reduce-reduce conflict.

3.5.8 Generalized LR parsing

Although the chances for a grammar to be (LA)LR(1) are much larger than those of being SLR(1) or LL(1), there are several occasions on which one meets a grammar that is not (LA)LR(1). Many official grammars of programming languages are not (LA)LR(1), but these are often easily handled, as explained in Section 3.5.7. Especially grammars for legacy code can be stubbornly non-deterministic. The reason is sometimes that the language in which the code was written was developed in an era when grammar-based compilers were not yet mainstream, for example early versions of Fortran and COBOL; another reason can be that the code was developed on a compiler which implemented ad-hoc language extensions. For the analysis and (re)compilation of such code a parsing method stronger than LR(1) is very helpful; one such method is generalized LR.

3.5.8.1 The basic GLR algorithm

The basic principle of **generalized LR** (or **GLR** for short) is very simple: if the ACTION table specifies more than one action, we just copy the parser stack and its partially constructed parse tree as often as needed and apply each specified action to a different copy. We then continue with multiple parsing stacks; if, on a subsequent token, one or more of the stacks require more than one action, we copy these again and proceed as above. If at some stage a stack and token combination result in an empty GOTO table entry, that stack is abandoned. If that results in the removal of the last stack the input was in error at that point. If at the end of the parsing one stack (which then contains the start symbol) remains, the program was unambiguous and the corresponding parse tree can be delivered. If more than one stack remains, the program was ambiguous with respect to the given grammar; all parse trees are available for further analysis, based, for example, on context conditions. With this approach the parser can handle almost all grammars (see Exercise 3.27 for grammars this method cannot handle).

This wholesale copying of parse stacks and trees may seem very wasteful and inefficient, but, as we shall see below in Section 3.5.8.2, several optimizations are possible, and a good implementation of GLR is perhaps a factor of 2 or 3 slower than a deterministic parser, for most grammars. What is more, its efficiency is not too dependent on the degree of non-determinism in the LR automaton. This implies that a GLR parser works almost as efficiently with an LR(0) or SLR(1) table as with an LALR(1) table; using an LR(1) table is even detrimental, due to its much larger size. So, most GLR parser generators use one of the simpler table types.

We will use the following grammar to demonstrate the technique:

Z → E $
E → T | E M T
M → '*' | ε
T → 'i' | 'n'

It is a variant of the grammar for simple expressions in Figure 3.37, in which 'i' represents identifiers and 'n' numbers. It captures the feature that the multiplication sign in an arithmetic expression may be left out; this allows the programmer to write expressions in a more algebra-like notation: **2x, x(x+1)**, etc. It is a feature that one might well find in legacy code. We will use an LR(0) table, the transition diagram of which is shown in Figure 3.53. The ACTION table is not deterministic, since the entry for S_4 contains both "shift" and "reduce by M→ε".

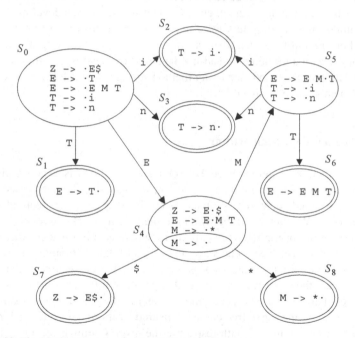

Fig. 3.53: The LR(0) automaton for the GLR demo grammar

The actions of the parser on an input text like **2x** are shown in Figure 3.54. This input is represented by the token string **ni**. The first three steps reduce the **n** to a E, which brings the non-deterministic state S_4 to the top of the stack. We duplicate the stack, obtaining stacks 1.1 and 1.2. First we perform all required reductions; in our case that amounts to the reduction M→ε on stack 1.1. Now both stacks have states on top that (also) specify a shift: S_5 and S_4. After performing a shift on both stacks, we find that the GOTO table for the combination [S_4, **i**] on stack 1.2 indicates an error. So we reject stack 1.2 and continue with stack 1.1 only. The rest of the parsing proceeds as usual.

Stack #	Stack contents	Rest of input	Action
1.	S_0	n i $	shift
1.	S_0 n S_3	i $	reduce by T→n
1.	S_0 T S_1	i $	reduce by E→T
1.	S_0 E S_4	i $	duplicate
1.1	S_0 E S_4	i $	reduce by M→ε
1.1.	S_0 E S_4 M S_5	i $	shift
1.2.	S_0 E S_4	i $	shift
1.1.	S_0 E S_4 M S_5 i S_2	$	reduce by T→i
1.2.	S_0 E S_4 i	$	error
1.1.	S_0 E S_4 M S_5 T S_6	$	reduce by E→E M T
1.1.	S_0 E S_4	$	shift
1.1.	S_0 E S_4 $ S_7		reduce by Z→E$
1.1.	S_0 Z		stop

Fig. 3.54: GLR parsing of the string **ni**

Note that performing all reductions first leaves all stacks with states on top which specify a shift. This allows us to do the shift for all stacks simultaneously, so the input remains in sync for all stacks. This avoids copying the input as well when the stacks and partial parse trees are copied.

In principle the algorithm as described here has exponential complexity; in practice it is efficient enough so the GNU parser generator *bison* uses it as its GLR algorithm. The efficiency can be further improved and the exponential sting removed by the two optimizations discussed in the next section.

3.5.8.2 Optimizations for GLR parsers

The first optimization is easily demonstrated in the process of Figure 3.54. We implement the stack as a linked list, and when we meet a non-deterministic state on top, we duplicate that state only, obtaining a forked stack:

$$\begin{matrix} 1 \\ 1 \end{matrix} S_0 \leftarrow E \begin{matrix} \swarrow S_4 \\ \nwarrow S_4 \end{matrix} \qquad \begin{matrix} \text{i \$ reduce by M}\to\varepsilon \\ \text{i \$ shift} \end{matrix}$$

This saves copying the entire stack, but comes at a price: if we have to do a reduction it may reduce a segment of the stack that includes a fork point. In that case we have to copy enough of the stack so the required segment becomes available.

After the reduction on stack 1.1 and the subsequent shift on both we get:

$$\begin{matrix} 1 \\ 1 \end{matrix} S_0 \leftarrow E \begin{matrix} \swarrow S_4 \leftarrow M \leftarrow S_5 \\ \nwarrow S_4 \end{matrix} \qquad \begin{matrix} \text{i \$ shift} \\ \text{i \$ shift} \end{matrix}$$

$$\begin{matrix} 1 \\ 1 \end{matrix} S_0 \leftarrow E \begin{matrix} \swarrow S_4 \leftarrow M \leftarrow S_5 \leftarrow i \leftarrow S_2 \\ \nwarrow S_4 \leftarrow i \end{matrix} \qquad \begin{matrix} \text{\$ reduce by T}\to\text{i} \\ \text{\$ error} \end{matrix}$$

When we now want to discard stack 1.2 we only need to remove the top two elements:

$$1\ S_0 \leftarrow E \leftarrow S_4 \leftarrow M \leftarrow S_5 \leftarrow i \leftarrow S_2 \qquad \text{\$ reduce by T}\to\text{i}$$

and parsing proceeds as usual.

To demonstrate the second optimization, a much larger example would be needed, so a sketch will have to suffice. When there are many forks in the stack and, consequently there are many tops of stack, it often happens that two or more top states are the same. These are then combined, causing joins in the stack; this limits the number of possible tops of stack to the number of states in the LR automaton, and results in stack configurations which resemble shunting-yard tracks:

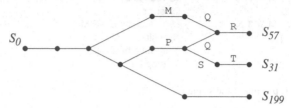

This optimization reduces the time complexity of the algorithm to some grammar-dependent polynomial in the length of the input.

We may have to undo some of these combinations when doing reductions. Suppose we have to do a reduction by $T \rightarrow PQR$ on state S_{57} in the above picture. To do so, we have to undo the sharing of S_{57} and the state below it, and copy the segment containing P:

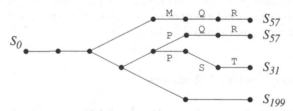

We can now do the reduction $T \rightarrow PQR$ and use the GOTO table to obtain the state to put on top. Suppose this turns out to be S_{31}; it must then be combined with the existing S_{31}:

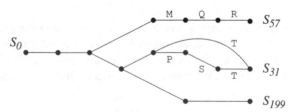

We see that a single reduction can change the appearance of a forked stack completely.

More detailed explanations of GLR parsing and its optimizations can be found in Grune and Jacobs [112, Sct. 11.1] and Rekers [232].

GLL parsing It is also possible to construct a **generalized LL (GLL)** parser, but, surprisingly, this is much more difficult. The main reason is that in a naive implementation a left-recursive grammar rule causes an infinite number of stacks to be copied, but there are also subtler problems, due to ε-rules. A possible advantage of GLL parsing is the closer relationship of the parser to the grammar than is possible with LR parsing. This may make debugging the grammar easier, but there is not yet enough experience with GLL parsing to tell.

Grune and Jacobs [112, Sct. 11.2] explain in detail the problems of GLL parsing, together with possible solutions. Scott and Johnstone [256] describe a practical way to construct a GLL parser from templates, much like *LLgen* does for LL(1) parsing (Figure 3.26).

3.5.9 Making a grammar unambiguous

Generalized LR solves all our parsing problems; actually, it solves them a little too well, since for an ambiguous grammar it will easily produce multiple parse trees, specifying multiple semantics, which is not acceptable in a compiler. There are two ways to solve this problem. The first is to check the parse trees from the produced set against further syntactic or perhaps context-dependent conditions, and reject those that fail. A problem with this approach is that it does not guarantee that only one tree will remain; another is that the parser can produce exponentially many parse trees, unless a very specific and complicated data structure is chosen for them. The second is to make the grammar unambiguous.

There is no algorithm to make a grammar unambiguous, so we have to resort to heuristics, as with making a grammar LL(1) or LALR(1). Where LL(1) conflicts could often be eliminated by left-factoring, substitution, and left-recursion removal, and LALR(1) conflicts could sometimes be removed by combining rules, ambiguity is not sensitive to any grammar rewriting: removing all but one of the rules that cause the ambiguity is the only option. To do so these rules must first be brought to the surface.

Once again we will use the grammar fragment for the conditional statement in C, which we repeat here in Figure 3.55, and concentrate now on its ambiguity. The

```
conditional_statement → if_statement | if_else_statement
if_statement → 'if' '(' expression ')' statement
if_else_statement → 'if' '(' expression ')' statement 'else' statement
statement → ... | conditional_statement | ...
```

Fig. 3.55: Standard, ambiguous, grammar for the conditional statement

statement

    if (x > 0) **if** (y > 0) p = 0; **else** q = 0;

has two parsings:

```
if  (x > 0) {  if  (y > 0) p = 0;  else  q = 0; }
if  (x > 0) {  if  (y > 0) p = 0; }  else  q = 0;
```

and the manual defines the first as the correct one.

For ease of manipulation and to save paper we rewrite the grammar to

```
C  →  'if' B S 'else' S
C  →  'if' B S
S  →  C
S  →  R
```

in which we expanded the alternatives into separate rules, and abbreviated conditional_statement, statement, and '(' expression ')' to C, S, and B, respectively, and the rest of statement to R.

First we substitute the C, which serves naming purposes only:

```
S  →  'if' B S 'else' S
S  →  'if' B S
S  →  R
```

Since the ambiguity shows itself in the Ss after the Bs, we substitute them with the production rules for S; this yields $2 \times 3 = 6$ rules:

```
S  →  'if' B 'if' B S 'else' S 'else' S
S  →  'if' B 'if' B S 'else' S
S  →  'if' B R 'else' S

S  →  'if' B 'if' B S 'else' S
S  →  'if' B 'if' B S
S  →  'if' B R

S  →  R
```

Now the ambiguity has been brought to the surface, in the form of the second and fourth rule, which are identical. When we follow the derivation we see that the second rule is in error, since its derivation associates the 'else' with the first 'if'. So we remove this rule.

When we now try to undo the substitution of the S, we see that we can do so in the second group of three rules, but not in the first. There we have to isolate a shorter rule, which we shall call T:

```
T  →  'if' B S 'else' S
T  →  R

S  →  'if' B T 'else' S
S  →  'if' B S
S  →  R
```

Unfortunately the grammar is still ambiguous, as the two parsings

```
if  (x > 0) {  if  (y > 0) {  if  (z > 0) p = 0;  else  q = 0; }  else  r = 0; }
if  (x > 0) {  if  (y > 0) {  if  (z > 0) p = 0; }  else  q = 0; }  else  r = 0;
```

attest; the second one is incorrect. When we follow the production process for these statements, we see that the ambiguity is caused by T allowing the full S, including S → 'if' B S, in front of the 'else'. When we correct this, we find another ambiguity:

if $(x > 0)$ { if $(y > 0)$ p = 0; else { if $(z > 0)$ q = 0; } } else r = 0;
if $(x > 0)$ { if $(y > 0)$ p = 0; else { if $(z > 0)$ q = 0; else r = 0 } };

More analysis reveals that the cause is the fact that T can end in S, which can then produce an else-less conditional statement, which can subsequently associate a following 'else' with the wrong 'if'. Correcting this yields the grammar

T → 'if' B T 'else' T
T → R

S → 'if' B T 'else' S
S → 'if' B S
S → R

This grammar is unambiguous; the proof is surprisingly simple: feeding it to an LALR parser generator shows that it is LALR(1), and thus unambiguous.

Looking back we see that in T we have constructed a sub-rule of S that cannot be continued by an 'else', and which can thus be used in other grammar rules in front of an 'else'; in short, it is "else-proof". With this terminology we can now give the final unambiguous grammar for the conditional statement, shown in Figure 3.56.

```
conditional_statement →
        'if' '(' expression ')' else_proof_statement 'else' statement |
        'if' '(' expression ')' statement
statement → ... | conditional_statement | ...
else_proof_conditional_statement →
        'if' '(' expression ')' else_proof_statement 'else' else_proof_statement
else_proof_statement → ... | else_proof_conditional_statement | ...
```

Fig. 3.56: Unambiguous grammar for the conditional statement

To finish the job we need to prove that the grammar of Figure 3.56 produces the same language as that of Figure 3.55, that is, that we have not lost any terminal productions.

The original grammar produces a sequence of 'if's and 'else's, such that there are never more 'else's than 'if's, and we only have to show that (1) the unambiguous grammar produces 'if's in the same places as the ambiguous one, and (2) it preserves the above restriction; its unambiguity then guarantees that the correct parsing results. Both conditions can easily be verified by comparing the grammars.

3.5.10 Error handling in LR parsers

When an LR parser finds a syntax error, it has a reduction stack and an input token, such that the ACTION table entry for the top of the stack s_t and the input token t_x is empty:

$$s_0 A_1 s_1 A_2 \ldots A_t s_t \qquad t_x$$

To recover from the error we need to reach a situation in which this is no longer true. Since two parties are involved, the stack and the input, we can consider modifying either or both, but just as in Section 3.4.5, modifying the stack endangers our chances of obtaining a correct syntax tree. Actually, things are even worse in an LR parser, since removing states and grammar symbols from the reduction stack implies throwing away parts of the syntax tree that have already been found to be correct.

There are many proposed techniques to do repairs, almost all of them moderately successful at best. Some even search the states on the stack and the next few input tokens combinatorially to find the most promising match [37, 188].

3.5.10.1 Recovery without modifying the stack

One would prefer not to modify the stack, but this is difficult. Several techniques have been proposed.

If the top state s_t allows a shift or reduction on a token, say t_r, one can insert this t_r, and perform the shift or reduction. Unfortunately, this has a good chance of bringing us back to a situation with the same top state s_t, and since the rest of the input has not changed, history will repeat itself.

We have seen that the acceptable-set techniques from Section 3.4.5 avoid modifying the stack, so they suggest themselves for LR parsers too, but they are less successful there. A naive approach is to take the set of correct tokens as the acceptable set. This causes the parser to discard tokens from the input one by one until a token is found that does have an entry in the ACTION/GOTO table, so parsing *can* continue, but this panic-mode error recovery tends to throw away important tokens, and yields bad results. An approach similar to the one based on continuations, described for LL parsers in Section 3.4.5, is possible, but the corresponding algorithm is much more complicated for LR parsers [240].

All in all, practical error recovery techniques in LR parsers tend to modify the stack.

3.5.10.2 Recovery with stack modification

The best known method is the one used by the LALR(1) parser generator *yacc* [224]. The method requires some non-terminals to be chosen as **error-recovering non-terminals**; these are usually the "big names" from the grammar: declaration, expression, etc. If a syntax error is detected while constructing a node for an error-recovering non-terminal, say R, the idea is to give up the entire attempt to construct that node, construct a dummy node instead that has the proper attributes, and discard tokens from the input until one is found that indicates the end of the damaged production of R in the input. Needless to say, finding the end of the damaged production is the risky part.

This idea is implemented as follows. The grammar writer adds the alternative erroneous to the right-hand side of one or more non-terminals, thereby marking them as non-terminals that are licensed to produce a dummy syntax subtree. During the construction of the LR states, each state that contains an item of the form

$$N \rightarrow \alpha\bullet R\beta$$

in which R is an error-recovering non-terminal, is marked as "error-recovering".

When a syntax error occurs, the top of the stack exhibits a state s_x and the present input starts with a token t_x, such that ACTION$[s_x, t_x]$ is empty. See Figure 3.57, in which we assume that R was defined as

R → G H I | erroneous

and that we have already recognized and reduced the G and H. The pseudo-terminal erroneous_R represents the dummy node that is allowed as an alternative of R.

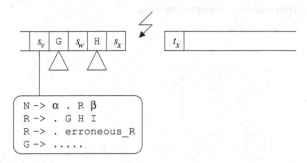

Fig. 3.57: LR error recovery—detecting the error

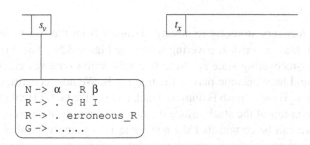

Fig. 3.58: LR error recovery—finding an error recovery state

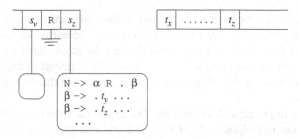

Fig. 3.59: LR error recovery—repairing the stack

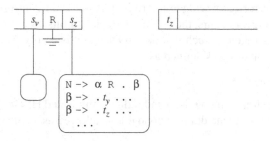

Fig. 3.60: LR error recovery—repairing the input

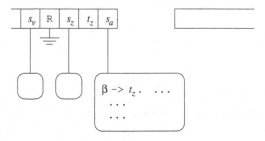

Fig. 3.61: LR error recovery—restarting the parser

The error recovery starts by removing elements from the top of the stack one by one until it finds an error-recovering state. See Figure 3.58, where the algorithm finds the error-recovering state s_v. Note that this action removes correctly parsed nodes that could have become part of the tree for R. We now construct the dummy node erroneous_R for R, push R onto the stack and use the GOTO table to determine the new state on top of the stack. Since the error-recovering state contains the item $N\rightarrow\alpha\bullet R\beta$, we can be certain that the new state is not empty, as shown in Figure 3.59. The new state s_z defines a set of acceptable tokens, tokens for which the row ACTION[$s_z,\ldots$] contains a non-empty entry; these are the tokens that are acceptable in s_z. We then discard tokens from the input until we find a token t_z that is in the acceptable set and can therefore follow R. This action attempts to remove the rest of the production of R from the input; see Figure 3.60. Now at least one parsing step can be taken, since ACTION[s_z, t_z] is not empty. This prevents looping. The final situation is depicted in Figure 3.61.

The procedure described here cannot loop, restricts the damage to the syntax tree to a known place and has a reasonable chance of getting the parser on the rails again. There is a risk, however, that it will discard an important token and derail the parser further. Also, the rest of the compiler must be based on the grammar as extended with the alternatives erroneous in all error-recovering non-terminals. In the above example that means that all code that processes nodes of type R must allow the possibility that the node is actually a dummy node erroneous_R.

3.5.11 A traditional bottom-up parser generator—yacc/bison

Probably the most famous parser generator is *yacc*, which started as a UNIX utility in the mid-1970s and has since seen more than twenty years of service in many compilation and conversion projects. *Yacc* is an LALR(1) parser generator. The name stands for "Yet Another Compiler Compiler", but it is not a compiler compiler in that it generates parsers rather than compilers. From the late 1990s on it has gradually been replaced by a *yacc* look-alike called *bison*, provided by GNU, which generates ANSI C rather than C. The *yacc* code shown in this section has been tested using *bison*.

The most striking difference between top-down and bottom-up parsing is that where top-down parsing determines the correct alternative right at the beginning and then works its way through it, bottom-up parsing considers collections of alternatives simultaneously and only decides at the last possible moment on the correct alternative. Although this openness of mind increases the strength of the method considerably, it makes it much more difficult to execute code. In fact code can only be executed safely at the end of an alternative, when its applicability has been firmly established. This also rules out the use of parameters since it would be unclear when (or even whether) to evaluate them and to pass them on.

Yacc's approach to this is to associate with each member exactly one parameter, which should be set by that member when it has been recognized. By induction, this means that when the entire alternative of a non-terminal N has been recognized, all parameters of its members are in place and can be used to construct the parameter for N. The parameters are named $1, $2, ... $n, for the n members of an alternative; the count includes terminal symbols. The parameter associated with the rule non-terminals itself is $$. The full *yacc* code for constructing parse trees for simple expressions is shown in Figure 3.62. The code at the end of the first alternative of expression allocates a new node and yields its address as the parameter for expression. Next, it sets the type and the two pointer fields to the parameter of the first member and the third member, respectively. The second member is the terminal symbol '–'; its parameter is not used. The code segments in the second alternative of expression and in term are similar.

```
%union {
    struct expr *expr;
    struct term *term;
}

%type <expr> expression;
%type <term> term;

%token IDENTIFIER

%start main

%%

main:
    expression        {print_expr($1);  printf ("\n");}
    ;

expression:
    expression '–' term
                      {$$ = new_expr(); $$->type = '–'; $$->expr = $1; $$->term = $3;}
    |
    term              {$$ = new_expr(); $$->type = 'T'; $$->term = $1;}
    ;

term:
    IDENTIFIER        {$$ = new_term(); $$->type = 'I';}
    ;

%%
```

Fig. 3.62: *Yacc* code for constructing parse trees

All this raises questions about the types of the parameters. Since the parameters are implemented as an array that parallels the LALR(1) parsing stack, they all have to be of the same type. This is inconvenient, because the user will want to associate different data structures with different non-terminals. A way out is provided by implementing the parameters as unions of the various data structures. *Yacc* is aware of this and allows the union to be defined by the user, through a %union keyword. Referring to Figure 3.62, we see two structures declared inside the %union, with tags expr and term. The %type statements associate the entry tagged expr in the union with the non-terminal expression and the entry term with the non-terminal term. This allows *yacc* and *bison* to generate type-correct C code without using casts.

The commands %token IDENTIFIER and %start main are similar to those explained for *LLgen*. The separator %% marks the start of the grammar proper. The

second occurrence of %% ends the grammar and starts auxiliary C code. This code
is very simple and is shown in Figure 3.63.

```
#include    "lex.h"

int main(void) {
    start_lex ();
    yyparse();              /* routine generated by yacc */
    return 0;
}

int yylex(void) {
    get_next_token();
    return Token.class;
}

int
yyerror(const char *msg) {
    fprintf (stderr, "%s\n", msg);
    return 0;
}
```

Fig. 3.63: Auxiliary code for the *yacc* parser for simple expressions

The generated parser produces the same output as the *LLgen* example on correct
input. The output for the incorrect input **i i-i** is:

```
(I)
parse error
```

3.6 Recovering grammars from legacy code

Grammars are the foundations of compiler design. From the early 1970s on the
grammars were supplied through programming language manuals, but many programs still in use today are written in languages invented before that era. So when
we want to construct a modern compiler to port such programs to a modern platform the grammar we need may not be available. And the problems do not end with
the early 1970s. Many programs written in modern standard languages are developed on compilers which actually implement dialects or supersets of those standard
languages. In addition many programs are written in local or ad-hoc languages,
sometimes with poor or non-existing documentation. In 1998 Jones [134] estimated
the number of such languages in use in industry at about 500, plus about 200 proprietary languages. All these programs conform to grammars which may not be
available explicitly. With hardware changes and staff turnover, chances are high that
these programs can no longer be modified and recompiled with reasonable effort,
which makes them **legacy code**.

The first step in remedying this situation is to recover the correct grammar; this is the subject of this section. Unavoidably, recovering a grammar from whatever can be found in the field is more an art than a science. Still, the work can be structured; Lämmel and Verhoef [166] distinguish five levels of grammar quality, each next level derived by specific actions from the previous one. We will illustrate their approach using a fictional report of a grammar recovering project, starting from some documentation of mixed quality and a large body of code containing millions of lines of code, and ending with an LALR(1) grammar for that code body.

Most examples in this book are perhaps two or three orders of magnitude smaller than what one may encounter in the real world. Given the nature of legacy code recovery it will not surprise the reader that the following example is easily six orders of magnitude (10^6 times) smaller than a real project; still it shows many realistic traits.

The process starts with the construction of a **level 0** grammar from whatever documentation can be found: paper manuals, on-line manuals, old compiler (parser) code, pretty-printers, test-set generation tools, interviews with (former) programmers, etc. For our fictional project this yielded the following information:

```
bool_expr: (expr AND)+ expr
if_statement: IF cond_expr THEN statement
statement:: assignment | BEGIN statements END | if_statement
assignation: dest := expr
dest -> idf | idf [ expr ]
expr: ( expr oper )* expr | dest | idf ( expr )
<command> == <block> | <conditional> | <expression>
```

Several features catch the eye: the format of the grammar rules is not uniform; there are regular-language repetition operators, which are not accepted by many parser generators; parentheses are used both for the grouping of symbols in the grammar and as tokens in function calls in the language; and some rules occur multiple times, with small variations. The first three problems, being linear in the number of rules, can be dealt with by manual editing. The multiple occurrence problem is at least quadratic, so with hundreds of rules it can be difficult to sort out; Lämmel and Zaytsev [167] describe software to assist in the process. We decide that the rules

```
statement:: assignment | BEGIN statements END | if_statement
<command> == <block> | <conditional> | <expression>
```

describe the same grammatical category, and we merge them into

```
statement: assignment | BEGIN statements END | if_statement | expression
```

We also find that there is no rule for the start symbol program; inspection of examples in the manual suggests

```
program: PROG statements END
```

This yields a **level 1** grammar, the first grammar in standard format:

```
program   → PROG statements END
bool_expr  → expr AND expr | bool_expr AND expr
if_statement  → IF cond_expr THEN statement
statement  → assignment | BEGIN statements END | if_statement | expression
assignation  → dest ':=' expr
dest  → idf | idf '[' expr ']'
expr  → expr oper expr | dest | idf '(' expr ')'
```

The level 1 grammar contains a number of unused symbols, called **top symbols** because they label the tops of production trees, and a number of undefined symbols, called **bottom symbols**. The top symbols are program, bool_expr, statement, and assignation; the bottom symbols are AND, BEGIN, END, IF, PROG, THEN, assignment, cond_expr, expression, idf, oper, and statements. Only one top symbol can remain, program. The others must be paired with appropriate bottom symbols. The names suggest that assignation is the same as assignment, and bool_expr the same as cond_expr; and since one of the manuals states that "statements are separated by semicolons", statement and statements can be paired through the rule

```
statements  → statements ';' statement | statement
```

The bottom symbol expression is probably the same as expr. Inspection of program examples revealed that the operators '+' and '–' are in use. The remaining bottom symbols are suspected to be terminals. This yields our **level 2** grammar, the first grammar in which the only top symbol is the start symbol and the only bottom symbols are terminals:

```
program   → PROG statements END
bool_expr  → expr AND expr | bool_expr AND expr
if_statement  → IF cond_expr THEN statement
statement  → assignment | BEGIN statements END | if_statement | expression
assignation  → dest ':=' expr
dest  → idf | idf '[' expr ']'
expr  → expr oper expr | dest | idf '(' expr ')'
assignment  → assignation
cond_expr  → bool_expr
expression  → expr
statements  → statements ';' statement | statement
oper  → '+' | '–'
```

terminal symbols: AND, BEGIN, END, IF, PROG, THEN, idf

Note that we did not substitute the pairings; this is because they are tentative, and are more easily modified and updated if the nonterminals involved have separate rules.

This grammar is completed by supplying regular expressions for the terminal symbols. The manual shows that keywords consist of capital letters, between apostrophes:

```
AND  → 'AND'
BEGIN  → 'BEGIN'
END  → 'END'
IF  → 'IF'
PROG  → 'PROG'
THEN  → 'THEN'
```

The only more complex terminal is idf:

idf → LETTER idf | LETTER

Again we leave them in as rules. Integrating them into the level 2 grammar gives us a **level 3** grammar, the first complete grammar.

This level 3 grammar is then tested and refined against several millions of lines of code, called the "code body". It is represented here by

'PROG' a(i) := start; 'IF' a[i] 'THEN' 'BGN' b := F(i) + i − j; 'END' 'End'

Since our grammar has no special properties which would allow the use of simpler parser, we use a generalized LR parser (Section 3.5.8) in this phase, which works with any grammar. When during normal compilation we find a syntax error, the program being compiled is in error; when during grammar recovery we find a syntax error, it is the grammar that needs correction.

Many syntax errors were found, the first one occurring at the first (. Indeed a function call cannot be the destination of an assignment, so why is it in the code body? It turns out that an appendix to a manual contains the phase "Due to character representation problems on some data input equipment the compiler allows square brackets to be replaced by round ones." Such were the problems of the 1960s and 70s. So we extend the rule for dest:

dest → idf | idf '[' expr ']' | idf '(' expr ')'

Next the parsing gets stuck at the 'THEN'. This is more puzzling. Upon inspection it turns out that bool_expr requires at least one 'AND', and is not a correct match for cond_expr. It seems the 1972 language designer thought: "It's only Boolean if it contains a Boolean operator". We follow this reasoning and extend cond_expr with expr, rather than adapting bool_expr.

The next parsing error occurs at the G of 'BGN'. Inspection of some of the code body shows that the original compiler allowed some abbreviations of the keywords. These were not documented, but extracting all keywords from the code body and sorting and counting them using the Unix commands sort | uniq −c provided a useful list. In fact, the official way to start a program was apparently with 'PROGRAM', rather than with 'PROG'.

The next problem is caused by the right-most semicolon in the code body. Much of the code body used the semicolon as a terminator rather than as a separator, and the original compiler accepted that. The rule for statements was modified to be equally accommodating, by renaming the original nonterminal to statements_proper and allowing an optional trailing semicolon in the new nonterminal statements.

A second problem with keywords was signaled at the n of the keyword 'End'. Apparently keywords are treated as case-insensitive, a feature which is not easily handled in a CF grammar. So a lexical (*flex*-based) scan was added, which solves this keyword problem in an inelegant but relatively simple way:

```
\'[Aa][Nn][Dd]\'               return AND;
\'[Bb][Ee][Gg][Ii][Nn]\'       return BEGIN;
\'[Bb][Gg][Nn]\'               return BEGIN;
\'[Ee][Nn][Dd]\'               return END;
\'[Ii][Ff]\'                   return IF;
\'[Pp][Rr][Oo][Gg][Rr][Aa][Mm]\' return PROGRAM;
\'[Pp][Rr][Oo][Gg]\'           return PROGRAM;
\'[Tt][Hh][Ee][Nn]\'           return THEN;
```

With these modifications in place the entire code body parsed correctly, and we have obtained our **level 4** grammar, which we present in *bison* format in Figure 3.64.

```
%glr-parser
%token AND BEGIN END IF PROGRAM THEN
%token LETTER
%%

program:            PROGRAM statements END ;
bool_expr:          expr AND expr | bool_expr AND expr ;
if_statement:       IF cond_expr THEN statement ;
statement:          assignment | BEGIN statements END |
                    if_statement | expression ;
assignation:        dest ':' '=' expr ;
dest:               idf | idf '[' expr ']' | idf '(' expr ')' ;
expr:               expr oper expr %merge <dummy> |
                    dest %merge <dummy>| idf '(' expr ')' %merge <dummy>;
assignment:         assignation ;
cond_expr:          bool_expr | expr ;
expression:         expr ;
statements:         statements_proper | statements_proper ';' ;
statements_proper:  statements_proper ';' statement | statement ;
oper:               '+' | '-' ;
idf :               LETTER idf | LETTER ;
%%
```

Fig. 3.64: The GLR level 4 grammar in *bison* format

The %glr-parser directive activates *bison*'s GLR feature. The %merge directives in the rule for expr tell *bison* how to merge the semantics of two stacks when an ambiguity is found in the input; leaving them out causes the ambiguity to be reported as an error. Since an ambiguity is not an error when recovering a grammar, we supply the %merge directives, and since at this stage we are not interested in semantics, we declare the merge operation as dummy.

To reach the next level we need to remove the ambiguities. Forms like F(i) are produced twice, once directly through expr and once through dest in expr. The ambiguity can be removed by deleting the alternative idf '(' expr ')' from expr (or, more in line with Section 3.5.9: 1. substitute dest in expr to bring the ambiguity to the surface; 2. delete all but one occurrence of the ambiguity-causing alternative; 3. roll back the substitution):

expr → expr oper expr %merge <dummy>| dest
dest → idf | idf '[' expr ']' | idf '(' expr ')'

Now it is easier to eliminate the second ambiguity, the double parsing of F(i)–i+j as (F(i)–i)+j or as F(i)–(i+j), where the first parsing is the correct one. The rule

expr → expr oper expr | dest

produces a sequence (dest oper)* dest. The grammar must produce a left-associative parsing for this, which is achieved by the rule

expr → expr oper dest | dest

Now all %merge directives have been eliminated, which allows us to conclude that we have obtained a **level 5** grammar, an unambiguous grammar for the entire code body.[1] Note that although there are no formal proofs for unambiguity, in grammar recovery there is an empirical proof: parsing of the entire code body by *bison* with a grammar without %merge directives.

The above tests were done with a generalized LR parser, but further development of the compiler and the code body (which was the purpose of the exercise in the first place) requires a deterministic, linear-time parser. Fortunately the level 5 grammar is already LALR(1), as running it through the non-GLR version of *bison* shows. The final LALR(1) **level 6** grammar in *bison* format is shown in Figure 3.65.

```
%token AND BEGIN END IF PROGRAM THEN
%token LETTER
%%

program:              PROGRAM statements END ;
statements:           statements_proper | statements_proper ';' ;
statements_proper:    statements_proper ';' statement | statement ;
statement:            assignment | BEGIN statements END |
                      if_statement | expression ;
assignment:           assignation ;
assignation:          dest ':' '=' expr ;
if_statement:         IF cond_expr THEN statement ;
cond_expr:            bool_expr | expr ;
bool_expr:            expr AND expr | bool_expr AND expr ;
expression:           expr ;
expr:                 expr oper dest | dest ;
dest:                 idf | idf '[' expr ']' | idf '(' expr ')' ;
idf :                 LETTER idf | LETTER ;
oper:                 '+' | '−' ;
%%
```

Fig. 3.65: The LALR(1) level 6 grammar in *bison* format

In summary, most of the work on the grammar is done manually, often with the aid of a grammar editing system. All processing of the code body is done using

---

[1] Lämmel and Verhoef [166] use a different, unrelated definition of level 5.

generalized LR and/or (LA)LR(1) parsers; the code body itself is never modified, except perhaps for converting it to a modern character code. Experience shows that a grammar of a real-world language can be recovered in a short time, not exceeding a small number of weeks (see for example Biswas and Aggarwal [42] or Lämmel and Verhoef [166]). The recovery levels of the grammar are summarized in the table in Figure 3.66.

Level	Properties
level 0	consists of collected information
level 1	is a grammar in uniform format
level 2	is a complete grammar
level 3	includes a complete lexical description
level 4	parses the entire code body
level 5	is unambiguous
level 6	is deterministic, (LA)LR(1)

Fig. 3.66: The recovery levels of a grammar

3.7 Conclusion

This concludes our discussion of the first stage of the compilation process—textual analysis: the conversion from characters in a source file to abstract syntax tree. We have seen that the conversion takes places in two major steps separated by a minor one. The major steps first assemble the input characters into tokens (lexical analysis) and then structure the sequence of tokens into a parse tree (syntax analysis). Between the two major steps, some assorted language-dependent character and token manipulation may take place, to perform preliminary identifier identification, macro processing, file inclusion, and conditional assembly (screening). Both major steps are based on more or less automated pattern matching, using regular expressions and context-free grammars respectively. Important algorithms in both steps use "items", which are simple data structures used to record partial pattern matches. We have also seen that the main unsolved problem in textual analysis is the handling of syntactically incorrect input; only ad-hoc techniques are available. A very high-level view of the relationships of the techniques is given in Figure 3.67.

	Lexical analysis	Syntax analysis
Top-down	Decision on first character: manual method	Decision on first token: LL(1) method
Bottom-up	Decision on reduce items: finite-state automata	Decision on reduce items: LR techniques

Fig. 3.67: A very high-level view of program text analysis techniques

Summary

- There are two ways of doing parsing: top-down and bottom-up. Top-down parsing tries to mimic the program production process; bottom-up parsing tries to roll
  back the program production process.
- Top-down parsers can be written manually or be generated automatically from a
  context-free grammar.
- A handwritten top-down parser consists of a set of recursive routines, each routine corresponding closely to a rule in the grammar. Such a parser is called a
  recursive descent parser. This technique works for a restricted set of grammars
  only; the restrictions are not easily checked by hand.
- Generated top-down parsers use precomputation of the decisions that predictive
  recursive descent parsers take dynamically. Unambiguous transition tables are
  obtained for LL(1) grammars only.
- Construction of the table is based on the FIRST and FOLLOW sets of the non-
  terminals. FIRST(N) contains all tokens any production of N can start with, and ε
  if N produces the empty string. FOLLOW(N) contains all tokens that can follow
  any production of N.
- The transition table can be incorporated in a recursive descent parser to yield a
  predictive parser, in which the parsing stack coincides with the routine calling
  stack; or be used in an LL(1) push-down automaton, in which the stack is an
  explicit array.
- LL(1) conflicts can be removed by left-factoring, substitution, and left-recursion
  removal in the grammar, and can be resolved by having dynamic conflict resolvers in the LL(1) parser generator.
- LL(1) parsers can recover from syntax errors by plotting a shortest path out,
  deleting tokens from the rest of the input until one is found that is acceptable on
  that path, and then following that path until that token can be accepted. This is
  called acceptable-set error recovery.
- Bottom-up parsers work by repeatedly identifying a handle. The handle is the list
  of children of the last node that was expanded in producing the program. Once
  found, the bottom-up parser reduces it to the parent node and repeats the process.
- Finding the handle is the problem; there are many approximative techniques.
- The LR parsing techniques use item sets of proposed handles. Their behavior
  with respect to shift (over a token) is similar, their reduction decision criteria
  differ.
- In LR(0) parsing any reduce item (= item with the dot at the end) causes a reduction. In SLR(1) parsing a reduce item $N{\rightarrow}\alpha{\bullet}$ causes a reduction only if the
  look-ahead token is in the FOLLOW set of N. In LR(1) parsing a reduce item
  $N{\rightarrow}\alpha{\bullet}\{\sigma\}$ causes a reduction only if the look-ahead token is in σ, a small set
  of tokens computed especially for that occurrence of the item.
- Like the generated lexical analyzer, the LR parser can perform a shift over the
  next token or a reduce by a given grammar rule. The decision is found by consulting the ACTION table, which can be produced by precomputation on the
  item sets. If a shift is prescribed, the new state can be found by consulting the

GOTO table, which can be precomputed in the same way. For LR parsers with a one-token look-ahead, the ACTION and GOTO tables can be superimposed.

- The LALR(1) item sets and tables are obtained by combining those LR(1) item sets that differ in look-ahead sets only. This reduces the table sizes to those of LR(0) parsers, but, remarkably, keeps almost all parsing power.
- An LR item set has a shift-reduce conflict if one item in it orders a shift and another a reduce, taking look-ahead into account. An LR item set has a reduce-reduce conflict if two items in it order two different reduces, taking look-ahead into account.
- LR shift-reduce conflicts can be resolved by always preferring shift over reduce; LR reduce-reduce conflicts can be resolved by accepting the longest sequence of tokens for the reduce action. The precedence of operators can also help.
- Generalized LR (GLR) solves the non-determinism left in a non-deterministic LR parser by making multiple copies of the stack, and applying the required actions to the individual stacks. Stacks that are found to lead to an error are abandoned. The stacks can be combined at their heads and at their tails for efficiency; reductions may require this combining to be undone partially.
- Ambiguous grammars can sometimes be made unambiguous by developing the rule that causes the ambiguity until it becomes explicit; then all rules causing the ambiguity except are removed, and the developing action is rolled back partially.
- Error recovery in an LR parser is difficult, since much of the information it gathers is of a tentative nature. In one approach, some non-terminals are declared error-recovering by the compiler writer. When an error occurs, states are removed from the stack until a state is uncovered that allows a shift on an error-recovering non-terminal R; next, a dummy node R is inserted; finally, input tokens are skipped until one is found that is acceptable in the new state. This attempts to remove all traces of the production of R and replaces it with a dummy R.
- A grammar can be recovered from legacy code in several steps, in which the code body is the guide and the grammar is adapted to it by manual and semi-automated means, using generalized LR and (LA)LR(1) parsers.

Further reading

The use of finite-state automata for lexical analysis was first described by Johnson *et al.* [130] and the use of LL(1) was first described by Lewis and Stearns [176], although in both cases the ideas were older. LR(k) parsing was invented by Knuth [155].

Lexical analysis and parsing are covered to varying degrees in all compiler design books, but few books are dedicated solely to them. We mention here a practice-oriented book by Grune and Jacobs [112], and two theoretical books, one by Sippu and Soisalon-Soininen [262] and the other by Aho and Ullman [5], both in two volumes. A book by Chapman [57] gives a detailed treatment of LR parsing.

There are a number of good to excellent commercial and public domain lexical analyzer generators and parser generators. Information about them can be found in the postings in the *comp.compilers usenet newsgroup*, which are much more up to date than any printed text can be.

Exercises

3.1. Add parse tree constructing code to the recursive descent recognizer of Figure 3.5.

3.2. (a) Construct a (non-predictive) recursive descent parser for the grammar S → '(' S ')' | ')'. Will it parse correctly?
(b) Repeat for S → '('S')' | ε.
(c) Repeat for S → '('S')' | ')' | ε.

3.3. (▷www) Why is the correct associativity of the addition operator + (in the grammar of Figure 3.4) less important than that of the subtraction operator –?

3.4. (▷787) Naive recursive descent parsing of expressions with n levels of precedence requires n routines in the generated parser. Devise a technique to combine the n routines into one routine, which gets the precedence as a parameter. Modify this code to replace recursive calls to the same precedence level by repetition, so that only calls to parse expressions of higher precedence remain.

3.5. Add parse tree constructing code to the predictive recognizer in Figure 3.12.

3.6. (▷www) Naively generated predictive parsers often contain useless code. For example, the entire switch mechanism in the routine parenthesized_expression() in Figure 3.12 is superfluous, and so is the default: error(); case in the routine term(). Design rules to eliminate these inefficiencies.

3.7. Answer the questions of Exercise 3.2 for a predictive recursive descent parser.

3.8. (▷787) (a) Devise the criteria for a grammar to allow parsing with a non-predictive recursive descent parser. Call such a grammar **NPRD**.
(b) Would you create a predictive or non-predictive recursive descent parser for an NPRD grammar?

3.9. The grammar in Figure 3.68 describes a simplified version of declarations in C.

(a) Show how this grammar produces the declaration long int i = {1, 2};
(b) Make this grammar LL(1) under the—unrealistic—assumption that expression is a single token.
(c) Retrieve the full grammar of the variable declaration in C from the manual and make it LL(1). (Much more difficult.)

```
declaration  →  decl_specifiers init_declarator? ';'
decl_specifiers  →  type_specifier decl_specifiers?
type_specifier  →  'int' | 'long'
init_declarator  →  declarator initializer?
declarator  →  IDENTIFIER | declarator '(' ')' | declarator '[' ']'
initializer  →
        '=' expression
      | '=' '{' initializer_list '}' | '=' '{' initializer_list ',' '}'
initializer_list  →
        expression
      | initializer_list ',' initializer_list | '{' initializer_list '}'
```

Fig. 3.68: A simplified grammar for declarations in C

3.10. (a) Construct the transition table of the LL(1) push-down automaton for the grammar

```
S → A B C
A → 'a' A | C
B → 'b'
C → c
```

(b) Repeat, but with the above definition of B replaced by

$$B → 'b' | \varepsilon$$

3.11. Complete the parsing started in Figure 3.21.

3.12. (▷787) Determine where exactly the prediction stack is located in a predictive parser.

3.13. (▷www) *Full-LL(1), advanced parsing topic*:
(a) The LL(1) method described in this book uses the FOLLOW set of a non-terminal N to decide when to predict a nullable production of N. As in the SLR(1) method, the FOLLOW set is too coarse an approximation since it includes any token that can ever follow N, whereas we are interested in the set of tokens that can follow N on the actual prediction stack during parsing. Give a simple grammar in which this makes a difference.
(b) We can easily find the exact token set that can actually follow the top non-terminal T on the prediction stack [T, α]: it is FIRST(α). How can we use this exact token set to improve our prediction?
(c) We can incorporate the exact follow set of each prediction stack entry into the LL(1) push-down automaton by expanding the prediction stack entries to (grammar symbol, token set) pairs. In analogy to the LR(1) automaton, these token sets are called "look-ahead sets". Design rules for computing the look-ahead sets in the predictions for the stack element (N, σ) for production rules $N→\beta$.
(d) The LL(1) method that uses the look-aheads described here rather than the FOL-LOW set is called "full-LL(1)". Show that full-LL(1) provides better error detection than strong-LL(1), in the sense that it will not incorrectly predict a nullable alternative. Give an example using the grammar from part (a).

(e) Show that there is no full-LL(1) grammar that is not also strong-LL(1). Hint: try to construct a grammar that has a FIRST/FOLLOW conflict when using the FOLLOW set, such that the conflict goes away in all situations when using the full-LL(1) look-ahead set.

(f) Show that there *are* full-LL(2) grammars that are not strong-LL(2). Hint: consider a non-terminal with two alternatives, one producing the empty string and one producing one token.

3.14. (▷www) Using the grammar of Figure 3.4 and some tables provided in the text, determine the acceptable set of the LL(1) parsing stack parenthesized_expression rest_expression EoF.

3.15. (▷787) Consider the automatic computation of the acceptable set based on continuations, as explained in Section 3.4.5. The text suggests that upon finding an error, the parser goes through all the motions it would go through if the input were exhausted. This sounds cumbersome and it is. Devise a simpler method to compute the acceptable set. Hint 1: use precomputation. Hint 2: note that the order in which the symbols sit on the stack is immaterial for the value of the acceptable set.

3.16. (▷www) Explain why the acceptable set of a prediction stack configuration α will always contain the EoF token.

3.17. *Project*: Find rules for the conversion described in the Section on constructing correct parse trees with transformed grammars (3.4.6.2) that allow the conversion to be automated, or show that this cannot be done.

3.18. Compute the LR(0) item sets and their transitions for the grammar S $\rightarrow$ '('S')' | '('. (Note: '(', not ')' in the second alternative.)

3.19. (▷787) (a) Show that when the ACTION table in an LR parser calls for a "reduce using rule $N{\rightarrow}\alpha$", the top of the stack does indeed contain the members of α in the correct order.

(b) Show that when the reduce move has been performed by replacing α by N, the new state to be stacked on top of it cannot be "erroneous" in an LR parser.

3.20. (▷787) Explain why there cannot be **shift-shift conflicts** in an LR automaton.

3.21. (▷www) Construct the LR(0), SLR(1), LR(1), and LALR(1) automata for the grammar

   S $\rightarrow$ 'x' S 'x' | x

3.22. (▷788) At the end of Section 3.5.2 we note in passing that right-recursion causes linear stack size in bottom-up parsers. Explain why this is so. More in particular, show that when parsing the string x^n using the grammar S$\rightarrow$xS|x the stack will grow at least to n elements. Also, is there a difference in behavior in this respect between LR(0), SLR(1), LR(1), and LALR(1) parsing?

3.23. (▷www) Which of the following pairs of items can coexist in an LR item set?
(a) A → P • Q and B → Q P • (b) A → P • Q and B → P Q • (c) A → • x and B → x •
(d) A → P • Q and B → P • Q (e) A → P • Q and A → • Q

3.24. (a) Can

    A → P • Q
    P → • 'p'
    Q → • p

be an item set in an LR automaton?
(b) Repeat for the item set

    A → P • P
    A → P • Q
    P → • 'p'
    Q → • p

(c) Show that no look-ahead can make the item set in part (b) conflict-free.

3.25. (▷788) Refer to Section 3.5.7.1, where precedence information about operators is used to help resolve shift-reduce conflicts. In addition to having precedences,
operators can be left- or right-associative. For example, the expression a+b+c must
be grouped as (a+b)+c, but a**b**c, in which the ** represents the exponentiation
operator, must be grouped as a**(b**c), a convention arising from the fact that
(a**b)**c would simply be equal to a**(b*c). So, addition is left-associative and
exponentiation is right-associative. Incorporate associativity into the shift-reduce
conflict-resolving rules stated in the text.

3.26. (a) Show that the grammar for type in some programming language, shown in
Figure 3.69, exhibits a reduce-reduce conflict.

```
type              →  actual_type | virtual_type
actual_type       →  actual_basic_type actual_size
virtual_type      →  virtual_basic_type virtual_size
actual_basic_type →  'int' | 'char'
actual_size       →  '[' NUMBER ']'
virtual_basic_type →  'int' | 'char' | 'void'
virtual_size      →  '[' ']'
```

Fig. 3.69: Sample grammar for type

(b) Make the grammar LALR(1); check your answer using an LALR(1) parser generator.
(c) Add code that constructs the proper parse tree in spite of the transformation.

3.27. (▷788) The GLR method described in Section 3.5.8 finds all parse trees for
a given input. This suggests a characterization of the set of grammars GLR cannot
handle. Find this characterization.

3.28. (▷www) The grammar

```
expression  →  expression oper expression %merge <decide> | term
oper  →  '+' | '−' | '*' | '/' | ↑
term  →  identifier
```

is a simpler version of the grammar on page 10. It is richer, in that it allows many more operators, but it is ambiguous. Construct a parser for it using *bison* and its GLR facility; more in particular, write the decide(YYSTYPE x0, YYSTYPE x1) routine (see the *bison* manual) required by *bison*'s %merge mechanism, to do the disambiguation in such a way that the traditional precedences and associativities of the operators are obeyed.

3.29. (▷788) This exercise shows the danger of using a textual description in lieu of a syntactic description (a grammar). The C manual (Kernighan and Ritchie [150, § 3.2]) states with respect to the dangling else "This [ambiguity] is resolved by associating the 'else' with the closest previous 'else'-less 'if'". If implemented literally this fails. Show how.

3.30. (▷www) Consider a variant of the grammar from Figure 3.47 in which A is error-recovering:

```
S  →  A | 'x' 'b'
A  →  'a' A 'b' | B | erroneous
B  →  x
```

How will the LR(1) parser for this grammar react to empty input? What will the resulting parse tree be?

3.31. (▷788) LR error recovery with stack modification throws away trees that have already been constructed. What happens to pointers that already point into these trees from elsewhere?

3.32. (▷788) Constructing a suffix grammar is easy. For example, the suffix rule for the non-terminal A → B C D is:

```
A_suffix  →  B_suffix C D | C D | C_suffix D | D | D_suffix
```

Using this technique, construct the suffix grammar for the grammar of Figure 3.36. Try to make the resulting suffix grammar LALR(1) and check this property using an LALR(1) parser generator. Use the resulting parser to recognize tails of productions of the grammar of Figure 3.36.

3.33. *History of parsing*: Study Samelson and Bauer's 1960 paper [248], which introduces the use of a stack in parsing, and write a summary of it.

Part II
Annotating
the Abstract Syntax Tree

Chapter 4
Grammar-based Context Handling

The lexical analysis and parsing described in Chapters 2 and 3, applied to a program text, result in an abstract syntax tree (AST) with a minimal but important degree of annotation: the *Token.class* and *Token.repr* attributes supplied by the lexical analyzer as the initial attributes of the terminals in the leaf nodes of the AST. For example, a token representing an integer has the class "integer" and its value derives from the token representation; a token representing an identifier has the class "identifier", but completion of further attributes may have to wait until the identification mechanism has done its work.

Lexical analysis and parsing together perform the context-free processing of the source program, which means that they analyze and check features that can be analyzed and checked either locally or in a nesting fashion. Other features, for example checking the number of parameters in a call to a routine against the number of parameters in its declaration, do not fall into this category. They require establishing and checking long-range relationships, which is the domain of context handling.

Context handling is required for two different purposes: to collect information for semantic processing and to check context conditions imposed by the language specification. For example, the *Java Language Specification* [108, 3rd edition, page 527] specifies that:

> Each local variable and every blank final field must have a definitely assigned value when any access of its value occurs.

This restriction cannot be enforced by just looking at a single part of the AST. The compiler has to collect information from the entire program to verify this restriction.

In an extremely clean compiler, two different phases would be assigned to this: first all language-required context checking would be done, then the input program would be declared contextually correct, and only then would the collection of other information start. The techniques used are, however, exactly the same, and it would be artificial to distinguish the two aspects on a technical level. After all, when we try to find out if a given array parameter A to a routine has more than one dimension, it makes no difference whether we do so because the language forbids multi-dimensional array parameters and we have to give an error message if A has more than one dimension, or because we can generate simpler code if we find that *A* has only one dimension.

The data needed for these analyses and checks is stored as attributes in the nodes of the AST. Whether they are physically stored there or actually reside elsewhere, for example in a symbol table or even in the local variables of an analyzing routine, is more or less immaterial for the basic concepts, although convenience and efficiency considerations may of course dictate one implementation or another. Since our prime focus in this book is on understanding the algorithms involved rather than on their implementation, we will treat the attributes as residing in the corresponding node.

The context-handling phase performs its task by computing all attributes and checking all context conditions. As was the case with parsers, one can write the code for the context-handling phase by hand or have it generated from a more high-level specification. The most usual higher-level specification form is the *attribute grammar*. However, the use of attribute grammars for context handling is much less widespread than that of context-free grammars for syntax handling: context-handling modules are still often written by hand. Two possible reasons why this is so come to mind. The first is that attribute grammars are based on the "data-flow paradigm" of programming, a paradigm in which values can be computed in essentially arbitrary order, provided that the input values needed for their computations have already been computed. This paradigm, although not really weird, is somewhat unusual, and may be perceived as an obstacle. A second reason might be that the gap between what can be achieved automatically and what can be achieved manually is smaller with attribute grammars than with context-free grammars, so the gain is less.

Still, attribute grammars allow one to stay much closer to the context conditions as stated in a programming language manual than ad-hoc programming does. This is very important in the construction of compilers for many modern programming languages, for example C++, Ada, and Java, since these languages have large and often repetitive sets of context conditions, which have to be checked rigorously. Any reduction in the required manual conversion of the text of these context conditions will simplify the construction of the compiler and increase the reliability of the result; attribute grammars can provide such a reduction.

We will first discuss attribute grammars in this chapter, and then some manual methods in Chapter 5. We have chosen this order because the manual methods can often be viewed as simplified forms of attribute grammar methods, even though, historically, they were invented earlier.

4.1 Attribute grammars

The computations required by context handling can be specified inside the context-free grammar that is already being used for parsing; this results in an **attribute grammar**. To express these computations, the context-free grammar is extended with two features, one for data and one for computing:

Roadmap

- For each *grammar symbol S*, terminal or non-terminal, zero or more attributes are specified, each with a name and a type, like the fields in a record; these are **formal attributes**, since, like formal parameters, they consist of a name and a type only. Room for the actual attributes is allocated automatically in each node that is created for S in the abstract syntax tree. The attributes are used to hold information about the semantics attached to that specific node. So, all nodes in the AST that correspond to the same grammar symbol S have the same formal attributes, but their values—the actual attributes—may differ.

- With each *production rule $N \rightarrow M_1 \ldots M_n$*, a set of computation rules are associated —the **attribute evaluation rules**— which express some of the attribute values of the left-hand side N and the members of the right-hand side M_i in terms of other attributes values of these. These evaluation rules also check the context conditions and issue warning and error messages. Note that evaluation rules are associated with production rules rather than with non-terminals. This is reasonable since the evaluation rules are concerned with the attributes of the members M_i, which are production-rule-specific.

In addition, the attributes have to fulfill the following requirement:

- The attributes of each grammar symbol N are divided into two groups, called **synthesized attributes** and **inherited attributes**; the evaluation rules for all production rules of N can count on the values of the inherited attributes of N to be set by the parent node, and have themselves the obligation to set the synthesized attributes of N. Note that the requirement concerns grammar symbols rather than production rules. This is again reasonable, since in any position in the AST in which an N node produced by one production rule for N occurs, a node produced by any other production rule of N may occur and they should all have the same attribute structure.

The requirements apply to all alternatives of all grammar symbols, and more in particular to all M_is in the production rule $N \rightarrow M_1 \ldots M_n$. As a result, the evaluation rules for a production rule $N \rightarrow M_1 \ldots M_n$ can count on the values of the synthesized attributes of M_i to be set by M_i, and have the obligation to set the inherited attributes of M_i, for all $1 <= i <= n$. The division of attributes into synthesized and inherited is not a logical necessity (see Exercise 4.2), but it is very useful and is an integral part of all theory about attribute grammars.

4.1.1 The attribute evaluator

It is the task of an *attribute evaluator* to activate the evaluation rules in such an order as to set all attribute values in a given AST, without using a value before it has been computed. The paradigm of the attribute evaluator is that of a data-flow machine: a computation is performed only when all the values it depends on have been determined. Initially, the only attributes that have values belong to terminal symbols; these are synthesized attributes and their values derive directly from the program text. These synthesized attributes then become accessible to the evaluation rules of their parent nodes, where they allow further computations, both for the synthesized attributes of the parent and for the inherited attributes of the children of the parent. The attribute evaluator continues to propagate the values until all attributes have obtained their values. This will happen eventually, provided there is no cycle in the computations.

The attribute evaluation process within a node is summarized in Figure 4.1. It depicts the four nodes that originate from a production rule A → B C D. The inherited and synthesized attributes for each node have been indicated schematically to the left and the right of the symbol name. The arrows symbolize the data flow, as explained in the next paragraph. The picture is a simplification: in addition to the attributes, the node for A will also contain three pointers which connect it to its children, the nodes for B, C, and D, and possibly a pointer that connects it back to its parent. These pointers have been omitted in Figure 4.1, to avoid clutter.

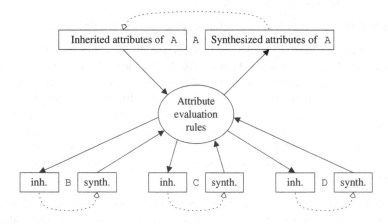

Fig. 4.1: Data flow in a node with attributes

The evaluation rules for the production rule A → B C D have the obligation to set the values of the attributes at the ends of the outgoing arrows in two directions: upwards to the synthesized attributes of A, and downwards to the inherited attributes of B, C, and D. In turn the evaluation rules can count on the parent of A to supply information downward by setting the inherited attributes of A, and on A's children B, C, and D to supply information upward by setting their synthesized attributes, as indicated by the incoming arrows.

In total this results in data flow from the inherited to the synthesized attributes of A. Since the same rules apply to B, C, and D, they too provide data flow from their inherited to their synthesized attributes, under control of their respective attribute evaluation rules. This data flow is shown as dotted arrows in Figure 4.1. We also observe that the attribute evaluation rules of A can cause data to flow from the synthesized attributes of B to its inherited attributes, perhaps even passing through C and/or D. Similarly, A can expect data to flow from its synthesized attributes to its inherited attributes, through its parent. This data flow too is shown as a dotted arrow in the diagram.

It seems reasonable to call the inherited attributes input parameters and the synthesized attributes output parameters, but some caution is required. Input and output suggest some temporal order, with input coming before output, but it is quite possible for some of the synthesized attributes to be set before some of the inherited ones. Still, the similarity is strong, and we will meet below variants of the general attribute grammars in which the terms "input parameters" and "output parameters" are fully justified.

A simple example of a practical attribute grammar rule is shown in Figure 4.2; it describes the declaration of constants in a Pascal-like language. The grammar part is in a fairly representative notation, the rules part is in a format similar to that used in the algorithm outlines in this book. The attribute grammar uses the non-terminals *Defined_identifier* and *Expression*, the headings of which are also shown.

```
Constant_definition (INH oldSymbolTable, SYN newSymbolTable) →
    'CONST' Defined_identifier '=' Expression ';'
    attribute rules:
        Expression.symbolTable ← Constant_definition.oldSymbolTable;
        Constant_definition.newSymbolTable ←
            UpdatedSymbolTable (
                Constant_definition.oldSymbolTable,
                Defined_identifier.name,
                CheckedTypeOfConstant_definition (Expression.type),
                Expression.value
            );

Defined_identifier (SYN name) → ...

Expression (INH symbolTable, SYN type, SYN value) → ...
```

Fig. 4.2: A simple attribute rule for *Constant_definition*

The attribute grammar shows that nodes created for the grammar rule *Constant_definition* have two attributes, *oldSymbolTable* and *newSymbolTable*. The first is an inherited attribute and represents the symbol table before the application of the constant definition, and the second is a synthesized attribute representing the symbol table after the identifier has been entered into it.

Next comes the only alternative of the grammar rule for *Constant_definition*, followed by a segment containing attribute evaluation rules. The first evaluation rule sets the inherited attribute symbol table of *Expression* equal to the inherited attribute *Constant_definition.oldSymbolTable*, so the evaluation rules for *Expression* can consult it to determine the synthesized attributes *type* and *value* of *Expression*. We see that symbol names from the grammar can be used as identifiers in the evaluation rules: the identifier *Expression* stands for any node created for the rule *Expression*, and the attributes of that node are accessed as if they were fields in a record—which in fact they are in most implementations.

The second evaluation rule creates a new symbol table and assigns it to *Constant_definition.newSymbolTable*. It does this by calling a function, *UpdatedSymbolTable()*, which has the declaration

```
function UpdatedSymbolTable (
    Symbol table, Name, Type, Value
) returning a symbol table;
```

It takes the *Symbol table* and adds to it a constant identifier with the given *Name*, *Type*, and *Value*, if that is possible; it then returns the new symbol table. If the constant identifier cannot be added to the symbol table because of context conditions—there may be another identifier there already with the same name and the same scope—the routine gives an error message and returns the unmodified symbol table.

A number of details require more explanation. First, note that, although the order of the two evaluation rules in Figure 4.2 seems very natural, it is in fact immaterial: the execution order of the evaluation rules is not determined by their textual position but rather by the availability of their operands.

Second, the non-terminal *Defined_identifier* is used rather than just *Identifier*. The reason is that there is actually a great difference between the two: a defining occurrence of an identifier has only one thing to contribute: its name; an applied occurrence of an identifier, on the other hand, brings in a wealth of information in addition to its name: scope information, type, kind (whether it is a constant, variable, parameter, field selector, etc.), possibly a value, allocation information, etc.

Third, we use a function call *CheckedTypeOfConstant_definition (Expression.type)* instead of just *Expression.type*. The function allows us to perform a context check on the type of the constant definition. Such a check may be needed in a language that forbids constant definitions of certain classes of types, for example unions. If the check succeeds, the original *Expression.type* is returned; if it fails, an error message is given and the routine returns a special value, Erroneous_Type. This filtering of values is done to prevent inappropriate attribute values from getting into the system and causing trouble later on in the compiler. Similar considerations prompted us to return the old symbol table rather than a corrupted one in the case of a duplicate identifier in the call of *UpdatedSymbolTable( )* above.

There is some disagreement on whether the start symbol and terminal symbols are different from other symbols with respect to attributes. In the original theory as published by Knuth [156], the start symbol has no inherited attributes, and terminal symbols have no attributes at all. The idea was that the AST has a certain semantics, which would emerge as the synthesized attribute of the start symbol. Since this semantics is independent of the environment, there is nothing to inherit. Terminal symbols serve syntactic purposes most of the time and then have no semantics. Where they do have semantics, as for example digits do, each terminal symbol is supposed to identify a separate alternative and separate attribute rules are associated with each of them.

In practice, however, there are good reasons besides orthogonality to allow both types of attributes to both the start symbol and terminal symbols. The start symbol may need inherited attributes to supply, for example, definitions from standard libraries, or details about the machine for which to generate code; and terminals symbols already have synthesized attributes in the form of their representations. The conversion from representation to synthesized attribute could be controlled by an inherited attribute, so it is reasonable for terminal symbols to have inherited attributes.

We will now look into means of evaluating the attributes. One problem with this is the possibility of an infinite loop in the computations. Normally it is the responsibility of the programmer—in this case the compiler writer—not to write infinite loops, but when one provides a high-level mechanism, one hopes to be able to give a bit more support. And this is indeed possible: there is an algorithm for loop detection in attribute grammars. We will have a look at it in Section 4.1.3.2; remarkably, it also leads to a more effective way of attribute evaluation. Our main tool in understanding these algorithms is the "dependency graph", which we will discuss in the following section.

4.1.2 Dependency graphs

Each node in a syntax tree corresponds to a production rule $N{\rightarrow}M_1...M_n$; it is labeled with the symbol N and contains the attributes of N and n pointers to nodes, labeled with M_1 through M_n. It is useful and customary to depict the data flow in a node for a given production rule by a simple diagram, called a **dependency graph**. The inherited attributes of N are represented by named boxes on the left of the label and synthesized attributes by named boxes on the right. The diagram for an alternative consists of two levels, the top depicting the left-hand side of the grammar rule and the bottom the right-hand side. The top level shows one non-terminal with attributes, the bottom level zero or more grammar symbols, also with attributes. Data flow is indicated by arrows leading from the source attributes to the destination attributes.

Figure 4.3 shows the dependency graph for the only production rule for *Constant_definition*; note that the dependency graph is based on the abstract syntax tree. The short incoming and outgoing arrows are not part of the dependency graph but indicate the communication of this node with the surrounding nodes. Actually, the use of the term "dependency graph" for diagrams like the one in Figure 4.3 is misleading: the arrows show the data flow, not the dependency, since the latter points in the other direction. If data flows from variable *a* to variable *b*, then *b* is **dependent on** *a*. Also, data dependencies are sometimes given in the form of pairs; a pair (a, b) means "b depends on a", but it is often more useful to read it as "data flows from a to b" or as "a is **prerequisite to** b". Unfortunately, "dependency graph" is the standard term for the graph of the attribute data flow (see, for example, Aho, Sethi and Ullman [4, page 284]), and in order to avoid heaping confusion on confusion we will follow this convention. In short, an attribute dependency graph contains data-flow arrows.

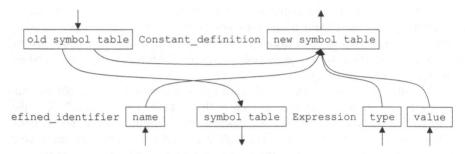

Fig. 4.3: Dependency graph of the rule for *Constant_definition* from Figure 4.2

Expression (**INH** symbolTable, **SYN** type, **SYN** value) →
    Number
    attribute rules:
        Expression.type ← Number.type;
        Expression.value ← Number.value;

Fig. 4.4: Trivial attribute grammar for *Expression*

Using the trivial attribute grammar for *Expression* from Figure 4.4, we can now construct the complete data-flow graph for the *Constant_definition*

CONST pi = 3.14159265;

The result is shown in Figure 4.5. Normally, the semantics of an expression depends on the contents of the symbol table, which is why the symbol table is an inherited attribute of *Expression*. The semantics of a number, however, is independent of the symbol table; this explains the arrow going nowhere in the middle of the diagram in our example.

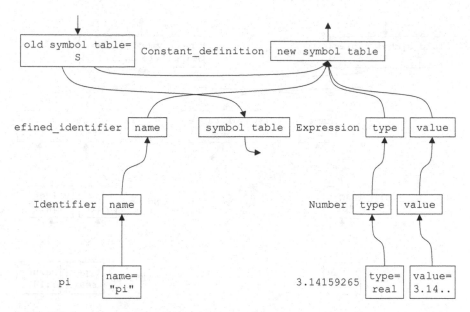

Fig. 4.5: Sample attributed syntax tree with data flow

4.1.3 Attribute evaluation

To make the above approach work, we need a system that will

- create the abstract syntax tree,
- allocate space for the attributes in each node in the tree,
- fill the attributes of the terminals in the tree with values derived from the representations of the terminals,
- execute evaluation rules of the nodes to assign values to attributes until no new values can be assigned, and do this in the right order, so that no attribute value will be used before it is available and that each attribute will get a value once,
- detect when it cannot do so.

Such a system is called an **attribute evaluator**. Figure 4.6 shows the attributed syntax tree from Figure 4.5 after attribute evaluation has been performed.

We have seen that a grammar rule in an attribute grammar consists of a syntax segment, which, in addition to the BNF items, supplies a declaration for the attributes, and a rules segment for each alternative, specified at the end of the latter. See Figure 4.2. The BNF segment is straightforward, but a question arises as to exactly what the attribute evaluator user can and has to write in the rules segment. The answer depends very much on the attribute system one uses.

Simple systems allow only assignments of the form

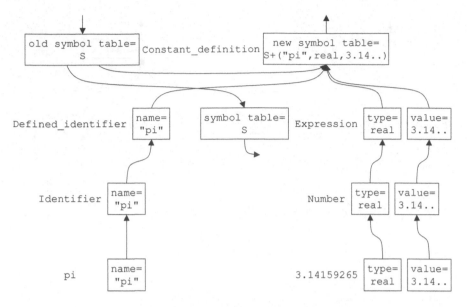

Fig. 4.6: The attributed syntax tree from Figure 4.5 after attribute evaluation

$$attribute_1 := func_1(attribute_{1,1}, \; attribute_{1,2}, \; \ldots)$$

$$attribute_2 := func_2(attribute_{2,1}, \; attribute_{2,2}, \; \ldots)$$

. . .

as in the example above. This makes it very easy for the system to check that the code fulfills its obligations of setting all synthesized attributes of the left-hand side and all inherited attributes of all members of the right-hand side. The actual context handling and semantic processing is delegated to the functions $func_1()$, $func_2()$, etc., which are written in some language external to the attribute grammar system, for example C.

More elaborate systems allow actual programming language features to be used in the rules segment, including if, while, and case statements, local variables called **local attributes**, etc. Some systems have their own programming language for this, which makes checking the obligations relatively easy, but forces the user to learn yet another language (and the implementer to implement one!). Other systems use an existing language, for example C, which is easier for user and implementer but makes it difficult or impossible for the system to see where exactly attributes are set and used.

The naive and at the same time most general way of implementing attribute evaluation is just to implement the data-flow machine. There are many ways to implement the data-flow machine of attribute grammars, some very ingenious; see, for example, Katayama [147] and Jourdan [137].

We will stick to being naive and use the following technique: visit all nodes of the data-flow graph, performing all possible assignments in each node when we visit it, and repeat this process until all synthesized attributes of the root have been given a value. An assignment is possible when all attributes needed for the assignment have already been given a value. It will be clear that this algorithm is wasteful of computer time, but for educational purposes it has several advantages. First, it shows convincingly that general attribute evaluation is indeed algorithmically possible; second, it is relatively easy to implement; and third, it provides a good stepping stone to more realistic attribute evaluation.

The method is an example of **dynamic attribute evaluation**, since the order in which the attributes are evaluated is determined dynamically, at run time of the compiler; this is opposed to **static attribute evaluation**, where the evaluation order is fixed in advance during compiler generation. (The term "static attribute evaluation order" would actually be more appropriate, since it is the evaluation *order* that is static rather than the evaluation.)

```
Number    → Digit_Seq Base_Tag
Digit_Seq → Digit_Seq Digit | Digit
Digit     → Digit_Token          -- 0 1 2 3 4 5 6 7 8 9
Base_Tag  → 'B' | 'D'
```

Fig. 4.7: A context-free grammar for octal and decimal numbers

4.1.3.1 A dynamic attribute evaluator

The strength of attribute grammars lies in the fact that they can transport information from anywhere in the parse tree to anywhere else, in a controlled way. To demonstrate the attribute evaluation method, we use a simple attribute grammar that exploits this possibility. It is shown in Figure 4.8 and calculates the value of integral numbers, in octal or decimal notation; the context-free version is given in Figure 4.7. If the number, which consists of a sequence of *Digit*s, is followed by a *Base_Tag* 'B' it is to be interpreted as octal; if followed by a 'D' it is decimal. So 17B has the value 15, 17D has the value 17 and 18B is an error. Each *Digit* and the *Base_Tag* are all considered separate tokens for this example. The point is that the processing of the *Digit*s depends on a token (B or D) elsewhere, which means that the information of the *Base_Tag* must be distributed over all the digits. This models the distribution of information from any node in the AST to any other node.

The multiplication and addition in the rules section of the first alternative of *Digit_Seq* in Figure 4.8 do the real work. The index [1] in *Digit_Seq[1]* is needed to distinguish this *Digit_Seq* from the *Digit_Seq* in the header. A context check is done in the attribute rules for *Digit* to make sure that the digit found lies within the range of the base indicated. Contextually improper input is detected and corrected by passing the value of the digit through a testing function *CheckedDigitValue*, the code

Number(**SYN** value) →
  Digit_Seq Base_Tag
  attribute rules:
    Digit_Seq.base ← Base_Tag.base;
    Number.value ← Digit_Seq.value;

Digit_Seq(**INH** base, **SYN** value) →
  Digit_Seq [1] Digit
  attribute rules:
    Digit_Seq [1].base ← Digit_Seq.base;
    Digit.base ← Digit_Seq.base;
    Digit_Seq.value ← Digit_Seq [1].value × Digit_Seq.base + Digit.value;
|
  Digit
  attribute rules:
    Digit.base ← Digit_Seq.base;
    Digit_Seq.value ← Digit.value;

Digit(**INH** base, **SYN** value) →
  Digit_Token
  attribute rules:
    Digit.value ← CheckedDigitValue (
      Value_of (Digit_Token.repr [0]) – Value_of ('0'), base
    );

Base_Tag(**SYN** base) →
  'B'
  attribute rules:
    Base_Tag.base ← 8;
|
  'D'
  attribute rules:
    Base_Tag.base ← 10;

Fig. 4.8: An attribute grammar for octal and decimal numbers

function CheckedDigitValue (TokenValue, Base) **returning** an integer:
  if TokenValue < Base: **return** TokenValue;
  else –– TokenValue >= Base:
    error "Token " TokenValue " cannot be a digit in base " Base;
    return Base – 1;

Fig. 4.9: The function *CheckedDigitValue*

of which is shown in Figure 4.9. For example, the input **18B** draws the error message **Token 8 cannot be a digit in base 8**, and the attributes are reset to show the situation that would result from the correct input **17B**, thus safeguarding the rest of the compiler against contextually incorrect data.

The dependency graphs of *Number*, *Digit_Seq*, *Digit*, and *Base_Tag* can be found in Figures 4.10 through 4.13.

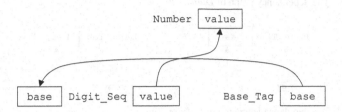

Fig. 4.10: The dependency graph of *Number*

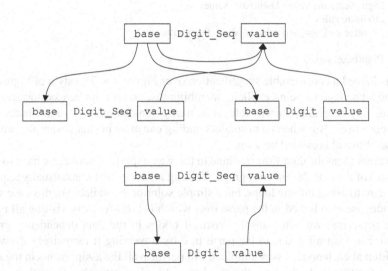

Fig. 4.11: The two dependency graphs of *Digit_Seq*

The attribute grammar code as given in Figure 4.8 is very heavy and verbose. In particular, many of the qualifiers (text parts like the *Digit_Seq.* in *Digit_Seq.base*) could be inferred from the contexts and many assignments are just copy operations between attributes of the same name in different nodes. Practical attribute grammars have abbreviation techniques for these and other repetitive code structures, and in such a system the rule for *Digit_Seq* could, for example, look as follows:

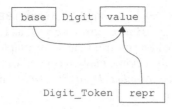

Fig. 4.12: The dependency graph of *Digit*

Fig. 4.13: The two dependency graphs of *Base_Tag*

Digit_Seq(**INH** base, **SYN** value) →
    Digit_Seq(base, value) Digit(base, value)
    attribute rules:
        value ← Digit_Seq.value × base + Digit.value;
|
    Digit(base, value)

This is indeed a considerable simplification over Figure 4.8. The style of Figure 4.8 has the advantage of being explicit, unambiguous, and not influenced towards any particular system, and is preferable when many non-terminals have attributes with identical names. But when no misunderstanding can arise in small examples we will use the above abbreviated notation.

To implement the data-flow machine in the way explained above, we have to visit all nodes of the data dependency graph. Visiting all nodes of a graph usually requires some care to avoid infinite loops, but a simple solution is available in this case since the nodes are also linked in the parse tree, which is loop-free. By visiting all nodes in the parse tree we automatically visit all nodes in the data dependency graph, and we can visit all nodes in the parse tree by traversing it recursively. Now our algorithm at each node is very simple: try to perform all the assignments in the rules section for that node, traverse the children, and when returning from them again try to perform all the assignments in the rules section. The pre-visit assignments propagate inherited attribute values downwards; the post-visit assignments harvest the synthesized attributes of the children and propagate them upwards.

Outline code for the evaluation of nodes representing the first alternative of *Digit_Seq* is given in Figure 4.14. The code consists of two routines, one, *EvaluateForDigit_SeqAlternative_1*, which organizes the assignment attempts and the recursive traversals, and one, *PropagateForDigit_SeqAlternative_1*, which attempts the actual assignments. Both get two parameters: a pointer to the *Digit_Seq* node itself and a pointer, *Digit_SeqAlt_1*, to a record containing the pointers to the children of the node. The type of this pointer is digit_seqAlt_1Node, since we

```
procedure EvaluateForDigit_SeqAlternative_1 (
    pointer to digit_seqNode Digit_Seq,
    pointer to digit_seqAlt_1Node Digit_SeqAlt_1
):
    -- Propagate attributes:
    PropagateForDigit_SeqAlternative_1 (Digit_Seq, Digit_SeqAlt_1);

    -- Traverse subtrees:
    EvaluateForDigit_Seq (Digit_SeqAlt_1.digit_Seq);
    EvaluateForDigit (Digit_SeqAlt_1.digit);

    -- Propagate attributes:
    PropagateForDigit_SeqAlternative_1 (Digit_Seq, Digit_SeqAlt_1);

procedure PropagateForDigit_SeqAlternative_1 (
    pointer to digit_seqNode Digit_Seq,
    pointer to digit_seqAlt_1Node Digit_SeqAlt_1
):
    if Digit_SeqAlt_1.digit_Seq.base is not set and Digit_Seq.base is set:
        Digit_SeqAlt_1.digit_Seq.base ← Digit_Seq.base;

    if Digit_SeqAlt_1.digit.base is not set and Digit_Seq.base is set:
        Digit_SeqAlt_1.digit.base ← Digit_Seq.base;

    if Digit_Seq.value is not set
            and Digit_SeqAlt_1.digit_Seq.value is set
            and Digit_Seq.base is set
            and Digit_SeqAlt_1.digit.value is set:
        Digit_Seq.value ←
            Digit_SeqAlt_1.digit_Seq.value × Digit_Seq.base
            + Digit_SeqAlt_1.digit.value;
```

Fig. 4.14: Data-flow code for the first alternative of *Digit_Seq*

are working on nodes that represent the first alternative of the grammar rule for *Digit_Seq*. The two pointers represent the two levels in dependency graph diagrams like the one in Figure 4.3.

The routine *EvaluateForDigit_SeqAlternative_1* is called by a routine *EvaluateForDigit_Seq* when this routine finds that the *Digit_Seq* node it is called for derives its first alternative. The code in *EvaluateForDigit_SeqAlternative_1* is straightforward. The first IF statement in *PropagateForDigit_SeqAlternative_1* corresponds to the assignment

```
Digit_Seq [1].base ← Digit_Seq.base;
```

in the rules section of *Digit_Seq* in Figure 4.8. It shows the same assignment, now expressed as

```
Digit_SeqAlt_1.digit_Seq.base ← Digit_Seq.base;
```

but preceded by a test for appropriateness. The assignment is appropriate only if the destination value has not yet been set and the source value(s) are available. A more elaborate version of the same principle can be seen in the third IF statement. All this means, of course, that attributes have to be implemented in such a way that one can test if their values have been set.

The overall driver, shown in Figure 4.15, calls the routine *EvaluateForNumber* repeatedly, until the attribute *Number.value* is set. Each such call will cause a complete recursive traversal of the syntax tree, transporting values down and up as available. For a "normal" attribute grammar, this process converges in a few rounds. Actually, for the present example it always stops after two rounds, since the traversals work from left to right and the grammar describes a two-pass process. A call of the resulting program with input **567B** prints

```
EvaluateForNumber called
EvaluateForNumber called
Number.value = 375
```

The above data-flow implementation, charming as it is, has a number of drawbacks. First, if there is a cycle in the computations, the attribute evaluator will loop. Second, the produced code may not be large, but it does a lot of work; with some restrictions on the attribute grammar, much simpler evaluation techniques become possible. There is much theory about both problems, and we will discuss the essentials of them in Sections 4.1.3.2 and 4.1.5.

> **procedure** Driver:
>   **while** Number.value is not set:
>   **report** "EvaluateForNumber called" report progress
>   EvaluateForNumber (Number);
>
>   — Print one attribute:
>   **report** "Number.value = ", Number.value;

Fig. 4.15: Driver for the data-flow code

There is another, almost equally naive, method of dynamic attribute evaluation, which we want to mention here, since it shows an upper bound for the time required to do dynamic attribute evaluation. In this method, we link all attributes in the parse tree into a linked list, sort this linked list topologically according to the data dependencies, and perform the assignments in the sorted order. If there are n attributes and d data dependencies, sorting them topologically costs $O(n + d)$; the subsequent assignments cost $O(n)$. The topological sort will also reveal any (dynamic) cycles. For more about topological sort, see below.

4.1.3.2 Cycle handling

To prevent the attribute evaluator from looping, cycles in the evaluation computations must be detected. We must distinguish between static and dynamic cycle detection. In dynamic cycle detection, the cycle is detected during the evaluation of the

Topological sort

The difference between normal sorting and topological sorting is that the normal sort works with a comparison operator that yields the values "smaller", "equal", and "larger", whereas the comparison operator of the topological sort can also yield the value "don't care": normal sorting uses a total ordering, topological sorting a partial ordering. Element that compare as "don't care" may occur in any order in the ordered result.

The topological sort is especially useful when the comparison represents a dependency of some kind: the ordered result will be such that no element in it is dependent on a later element and each element will be preceded by all its prerequisites. This means that the elements can be produced, computed, assigned, or whatever, in their topological order.

Topological sort can be performed recursively in time proportional to $O(n + d)$, where n is the number of elements and d the number of dependencies, as follows. Take an arbitrary element not yet in the ordered result, recursively find all elements it is dependent on, and put these in the ordered result in the proper order. Now we can append the element we started with, since all elements it depends on precede it. Repeat until all elements are in the ordered result. For an outline algorithm see Figure 4.16, where ⊢ denotes the empty list. It assumes that the set of nodes that a given node is dependent on can be found in a time proportional to the size of that set.

```
function TopologicalSort (a set Set) returning a list:
    List ← ⊢;
    while there is a Node in Set but not in List:
        Append Node and its predecessors to List;
    return List;

procedure Append Node and its predecessors to List:
    -- First append the predecessors of Node:
    for each N in the Set of nodes that Node is dependent on:
        if N ∉ List:
            Append N and its predecessors to List;
    Append Node to List;
```

Fig. 4.16: Outline code for a simple implementation of topological sort

attributes in an actual syntax tree; it shows that there is a cycle in a particular tree. Static cycle detection looks at the attribute grammar and from it deduces whether any tree that it produces can ever exhibit a cycle: it covers all trees. In other words: if dynamic cycle detection finds that there is no cycle in a particular tree, then all we know is that that particular tree has no cycle; if static cycle detection finds that there is no cycle in an attribute grammar, then we know that no tree produced by that grammar will ever exhibit a cycle. Clearly static cycle detection is much more valuable than dynamic cycle detection; unsurprisingly, it is also much more difficult.

Dynamic cycle detection There is a simple way to dynamically detect a cycle in the above data-flow implementation, but it is inelegant: if the syntax tree has N attributes and more than N rounds are found to be required for obtaining an answer, there must be a cycle. The reasoning is simple: if there is no cycle, each round will compute at least one attribute value, so the process will terminate after at most

N rounds; if it does not, there is a cycle. Even though this brute-force approach works, the general problem with dynamic cycle detection remains: in the end we have to give an error message saying something like "Compiler failure due to a data dependency cycle in the attribute grammar", which is embarrassing. It is far preferable to do static cycle checking; if we reject during compiler construction any attribute grammar that can ever produce a cycle, we will not be caught in the above situation.

Static cycle checking As a first step in designing an algorithm to detect the possibility of an attribute dependency cycle in any tree produced by a given attribute grammar, we ask ourselves how such a cycle can exist at all. A cycle cannot originate directly from a dependency graph of a production rule P, for the following reason. The attribute evaluation rules assign values to one set of attributes, the inherited attributes of the children of P and the synthesized attributes of P, while using another set of attributes, the values of the synthesized attributes of the children of P and the inherited attributes of P. And these two sets are disjoint, have no element in common, so no cycle can exist.

For an attribute dependency cycle to exist, the data flow has to leave the node, pass through some part of the tree and return to the node, perhaps repeat this process several times to different parts of the tree and then return to the attribute it started from. It can leave downward through an inherited attribute of a child, into the tree that hangs from this node and then it must return from that tree through a synthesized attribute of that child, or it can leave towards the parent through one of its synthesized attributes, into the rest of the tree, after which it must return from the parent through one of its inherited attributes. Or it can do both in succession, repeatedly, in any combination.

Figure 4.17 shows a long, possibly circular, data-flow path. It starts from an inherited attribute of node N, descends into the tree below N, passes twice through one of the subtrees at the bottom and once through the other, climbs back to a synthesized attribute of N, continues to climb into the rest of the tree, where it first passes through a sibling tree of N at the left and then through one at the right, after which it returns to node N, where it lands at an inherited attribute. If this is the same inherited attribute the data flow started from, there is a dependency cycle in this particular tree. The main point is that to form a dependency cycle the data flow has to leave the node, sneak its way through the tree and return to the same attribute. It is this behavior that we want to catch at compiler construction time.

Figure 4.17 shows that there are two kinds of dependencies between the attributes of a non-terminal N: from inherited to synthesized and from synthesized to inherited. The first is called an **IS-dependency** and stems from all the subtrees that can be found under N; there are infinitely many of these, so we need a summary of the dependencies they can generate. The second is called an **SI-dependency** and originates from all the trees of which N can be a node; there are again infinitely many of these. The summary of the dependencies between the attributes of a non-terminal can be collected in an **IS-SI graph**, an example of which is shown in Figure 4.18. Since IS-dependencies stem from things that happen below nodes for N and SI-

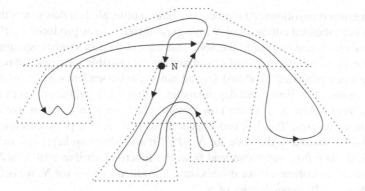

Fig. 4.17: A fairly long, possibly circular, data-flow path

dependencies from things that happen above nodes for *N*, it is convenient to draw
the dependencies (in data-flow direction!) in those same positions.

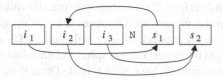

Fig. 4.18: An example of an IS-SI graph

The IS-SI graphs are used as follows to find cycles in the attribute dependencies
of a grammar. Suppose we are given the dependency graph for a production rule
$N \rightarrow PQ$ (see Figure 4.19), and the complete IS-SI graphs of the children *P* and *Q*
in it, then we can obtain the IS-dependencies of *N* caused by $N \rightarrow PQ$ by adding the
dependencies in the IS-SI graphs of *P* and *Q* to the dependency graph of $N \rightarrow PQ$
and taking the transitive closure of the dependencies. This transitive closure uses
the inference rule that if data flows from attribute *a* to attribute *b* and from attribute
b to attribute *c*, then data flows from attribute *a* to attribute *c*.

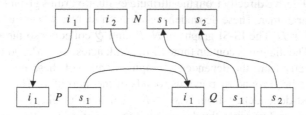

Fig. 4.19: The dependency graph for the production rule $N \rightarrow PQ$

The reason is as follows. At attribute evaluation time, all data flow enters the node through the inherited attributes of N, may pass through trees produced by P and/or Q, in any order, and emerge to the node and may end up in synthesized attributes. Since the IS-SI graphs of P and Q summarize all possible data paths through all possible trees produced by P and Q, and since the dependency graph of $N{\rightarrow}PQ$ already showed the fixed direct dependencies within that rule, the effects of all data paths in trees below $N{\rightarrow}PQ$ are now known. Next we take the transitive closure of the dependencies. This has two effects: first, if there is a possible cycle in the tree below N including the node for $N{\rightarrow}PQ$, it will show up here; and second, it gives us all data-flow paths that lead from the inherited attributes of N in $N{\rightarrow}PQ$ to synthesized attributes. If we do this for all production rules for N, we obtain the complete set of IS-dependencies of N.

Likewise, if we had all dependency graphs of all production rules in which N is a child, and the complete IS-SI graphs of all the other non-terminals in those production rules, we could in the same manner detect any cycle that runs through a tree of which N is a child, and obtain all SI-dependencies of N. Together this leads to the IS-SI graph of N and the detection of all cycles involving N.

Initially, however, we do not have any complete IS-SI graphs. So we start with empty IS-SI graphs and perform the transitive closure algorithm on each production rule in turn and repeat this process until no more changes occur to the IS-SI graphs. The first sweep through the production rules will find all IS- and SI-dependencies that follow directly from the dependency graphs, and each following sweep will collect more dependencies, until all have been found. Then, if no IS-SI graph exhibits a cycle, the attribute grammar is non-cyclic and is incapable of producing an AST with a circular attribute dependency path. We will examine the algorithm more in detail and then see why it cannot miss any dependencies.

An outline of the algorithm is given in Figure 4.20, where we denote the IS-SI graph of a symbol S by IS-SI_Graph[S]. It examines each production rule in turn, takes a copy of its dependency graph, merges in the dependencies already known through the IS-SI graphs of the non-terminal and its children, and takes the transitive closure of the dependencies. If a cycle is discovered, an error message is given. Then the algorithm updates the IS-SI graphs of the non-terminal and its children with any newly discovered dependencies. If any IS-SI graph changes as a result of this, the process is repeated, since still more dependencies might be discovered.

Figures 4.19 through 4.23 show the actions of one such step. The dependencies in Figure 4.19 derive directly from the attribute evaluation rules given for $N{\rightarrow}PQ$ in the attribute grammar. These dependencies are immutable, so we make a working copy of them in D. The IS-SI graphs of N, P, and Q collected so far are shown in Figure 4.21. The diagrams contain three IS-dependencies, in N, P, and Q; these may originate directly from the dependency graphs of rules of these non-terminals, or they may have been found by previous rounds of the algorithm. The diagrams also contain one SI-dependency, from $N.s_1$ to $N.i_2$; it must originate from a previous round of the algorithm, since the dependency graphs of rules for a non-terminal do not contain assignments to the inherited attributes of that non-terminal. The value of the synthesized attribute $Q.s_1$ does not depend on any input to Q, so it is either

— Initialization step:
for each terminal T **in** AttributeGrammar:
    IS-SI_Graph $[T] \leftarrow T$'s dependency graph;

for each non-terminal N **in** AttributeGrammar:
    IS-SI_Graph $[N] \leftarrow$ the empty set;

— Closure step:
SomethingWasChanged $\leftarrow$ True;

while SomethingWasChanged:
    SomethingWasChanged $\leftarrow$ False;

    for each production rule $P = M_0 \rightarrow M_1 \ldots M_n$ **in** AttributeGrammar:
        — Construct the dependency graph copy D:
        $D \leftarrow$ a copy of the dependency graph of P;
        — Add the dependencies already found for $M_{i=0\ldots n}$:
        for each M **in** $M_0 \ldots M_n$:
            for each dependency d **in** IS-SI_Graph $[M]$:
                Insert d in D;

        — Use the dependency graph D:
        Compute all induced dependencies in D by transitive closure;
        if D contains a cycle:
            error "Cycle found in production", P;
        — Propagate the newly discovered dependencies:
        for each M **in** $M_0 \ldots M_n$:
            for each d **in** D **such that** the attributes in d are attributes of M:
                if $d \notin$ IS-SI_Graph $[M]$:
                    Insert d into IS-SI_Graph $[M]$;
                    SomethingWasChanged $\leftarrow$ True;

Fig. 4.20: Outline of the strong-cyclicity test for an attribute grammar

generated inside Q or derives from a terminal symbol in Q; this is shown as an arrow starting from nowhere.

The dotted lines in Figure 4.22 show the result of merging the IS-SI graphs of N, P, and Q into the copy D. Taking the transitive closure adds many more dependencies, but to avoid clutter, we have drawn only those that connect two attributes of the same non-terminal. There are two of these, one IS-dependency from $N.i_1$ to $N.s_2$ (because of the path $N.i_1 \rightarrow P.i_1 \rightarrow P.s_1 \rightarrow Q.i_1 \rightarrow Q.s_2 \rightarrow N.s_2$), and one SI-dependency from $Q.s_1$ to $Q.i_1$ (because of the path $Q.s_1 \rightarrow N.s_1 \rightarrow N.i_2 \rightarrow Q.i_1$). These are added to the IS-SI graphs of N and Q, respectively, resulting in the IS-SI graphs shown in Figure 4.23.

We now want to show that the algorithm of Figure 4.20 cannot miss cycles that might occur; the algorithm may, however, sometimes detect cycles that cannot occur in actual trees, as we will see below. Suppose the algorithm has declared the attribute grammar to be cycle-free, and we still find a tree T with a cyclic attribute dependency path P in it. We shall now show that this leads to a contradiction. We

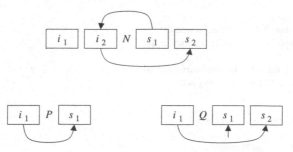

Fig. 4.21: The IS-SI graphs of N, P, and Q collected so far

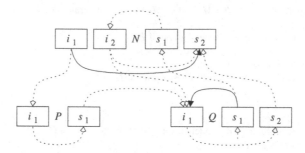

Fig. 4.22: Transitive closure over the dependencies of N, P, Q and D

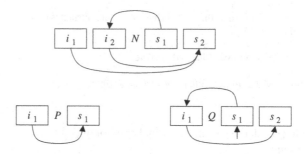

Fig. 4.23: The new IS-SI graphs of N, P, and Q

first take an arbitrary node N on the path, and consider the parts of the path inside N. If the path does not leave N anywhere, it just follows the dependencies of the dependency graph of N; since the path is circular, the dependency graph of N itself must contain a cycle, which is impossible. So the path has to leave the node somewhere. It does so through an attribute of the parent or a child node, and then returns through another attribute of that same node; there may be more than one node with that property. Now for at least one of these nodes, the attributes connected by the path leaving and returning to N are not connected by a dependency arc in the IS-SI graph of N: if *all* were connected they would form a cycle in the IS-SI graph, which would have been detected. Call the node G, and the attributes A_1 and A_2.

Next we shift our attention to node G. A_1 and A_2 cannot be connected in the IS-SI graph of G, since if they were the dependency would have been copied to the IS-SI graph of N. So it is obvious that the dependency between A_1 and A_2 cannot be a direct dependency in the dependency graph of G. We are forced to conclude that the path continues and that G too must have at least one parent or child node H, different from N, through which the circular path leaves G and returns to it, through attributes that are not connected by a dependency arc in the IS-SI graph of G: if they were all connected the transitive closure step would have added the dependency between A_1 and A_2.

The same reasoning applies to H, and so on. This procedure crosses off all nodes as possible sources of circularity, so the hypothetical circular path P cannot exist, which leads to our claim that the algorithm of Figure 4.20 cannot miss cycles.

An attribute grammar in which no cycles are detected by the algorithm of Figure 4.20 is called **strongly non-cyclic**. The algorithm presented here is actually too pessimistic about cyclicity and may detect cycles where none can materialize. The reason is that the algorithm assumes that when the data flow from an attribute of node N passes through N's child M_k more than once, it can find a different subtree there on each occasion. This is the result of merging into D in Figure 4.20 the IS-SI graph of M_k, which represents the data flow through all possible subtrees for M_k. This assumption is clearly incorrect, and it occasionally allows dependencies to be detected that cannot occur in an actual tree, leading to false cyclicity messages.

A correct algorithm exists, and uses a *set* of IS-SI graphs for each non-terminal, rather than a single IS-SI graph. Each IS-SI graph in the set describes a combination of dependencies that can actually occur in a tree; the union of the IS-SI graphs in the set of IS-SI graphs for N yields the single IS-SI graph used for N in the algorithm of Figure 4.20, much in the same way as the union of the look-ahead sets of the items for N in an LR(1) parser yields the FOLLOW set of N. In principle, the correct algorithm is exponential in the maximum number of members in any grammar rule, but tests [229] have shown that cyclicity testing for practical attribute grammars is quite feasible. A grammar that shows no cycles under the correct algorithm is called **non-cyclic**. Almost all grammars that are non-cyclic are also strongly non-cyclic, so in practice the simpler, heuristic, algorithm of Figure 4.20 is completely satisfactory. Still, it is not difficult to construct a non-cyclic but not strongly non-cyclic attribute grammar, as is shown in Exercise 4.5.

The data-flow technique from Section 4.1.3 enables us to create very general attribute evaluators easily, and the circularity test shown here allows us to make sure that they will not loop. It is, however, felt that this full generality is not always necessary and that there is room for less general but much more efficient attribute evaluation methods. We will cover three levels of simplification: multi-visit attribute grammars (Section 4.1.5), L-attributed grammars (Section 4.2.1), and S-attributed grammars (Section 4.2.2). The latter two are specially important since they do not need the full syntax tree to be stored, and are therefore suitable for narrow compilers.

4.1.4 Attribute allocation

So far we have assumed that the attributes of a node are allocated in that node, like fields in a record. For simple attributes—integers, pointers to types, etc.—this is satisfactory, but for large values, for example the environment, this is clearly undesirable. The easiest solution is to implement the routine that updates the environment such that it delivers a pointer to the new environment. This pointer can then point to a pair containing the update and the pointer to the old environment; this pair would be stored in global memory, hidden from the attribute grammar. The implementation suggested here requires a lookup time linear in the size of the environment, but better solutions are available.

Another problem is that many attributes are just copies of other attributes on a higher or lower level in the syntax tree, and that much information is replicated many times, requiring time for the copying and using up memory. Choosing a good form for the abstract syntax tree already alleviates the problem considerably. Many attributes are used in a stack-like fashion only and can be allocated very profitably on a stack [129]. Also, there is extensive literature on techniques for reducing the memory requirements further [9, 94, 98, 145].

Simpler attribute allocation mechanisms are possible for the more restricted attribute grammar types discussed below.

4.1.5 Multi-visit attribute grammars

Now that we have seen a solution to the cyclicity problem for attribute grammars, we turn to their efficiency problems. The dynamic evaluation of attributes exhibits some serious inefficiencies: values must repeatedly be tested for availability; the complicated flow of control causes much overhead; and repeated traversals over the syntax tree may be needed to obtain all desired attribute values.

4.1.5.1 Multi-visits

The above problems can be avoided by having a fixed evaluation sequence, implemented as program code, for each production rule of each non-terminal N; this implements a form of *static attribute evaluation*. The task of such a code sequence is to evaluate the attributes of a node P, which represents production rule $N \rightarrow M_1 M_2 \ldots$. The attribute values needed to do so can be obtained in two ways:

- The code can visit a child C of P to obtain the values of some of C's synthesized attributes while supplying some of C's inherited attribute values to enable C to compute those synthesized attributes.

- It can leave for the parent of P to obtain the values of some of P's own inherited attributes while supplying some of P's own synthesized attributes to enable the parent to compute those inherited attributes.

Since there is no point in computing an attribute before it is needed, the computation of the required attributes can be placed just before the point at which the flow of control leaves the node for the parent or for a child. So there are basically two kinds of visits:

Supply a set of inherited attribute values to a child M_i
Visit child M_i
Harvest a set of synthesized attribute values supplied by M_i

and

Supply a set of synthesized attribute values to the parent
Visit the parent
Harvest a set of inherited attribute values supplied by the parent

This reduces the possibilities for the visiting code of a production rule $N \to M_1 \ldots M_n$ to the outline shown in Figure 4.24.

This scheme is called **multi-visit attribute evaluation**: the flow of control pays multiple visits to each node, according to a scheme fixed at compiler generation time. It can be implemented as a tree-walker, which executes the code sequentially and moves the flow of control to the children or the parent as indicated; it will need a stack to leave to the correct position in the parent. Alternatively, and more usually, multi-visit attribute evaluation is implemented by recursive descent. Each visit from the parent is then implemented as a separate routine, a **visiting routine**, which evaluates the appropriate attribute rules and calls the appropriate visit routines of the children. In this implementation, the "leave to parent" at the end of each visit is implemented as a return statement and the leave stack is accommodated in the return stack.

Figure 4.25 shows a diagram of the i-th visit to a node for the production rule $N \to M_1 M_2 \ldots$, during which the routine for that node visits two of its children, M_k and M_l. The flow of control is indicated by the numbered dotted arrows, the data flow by the solid arrows. In analogy to the notation IN_i for the set of inherited attributes to be supplied to N on the i-th visit, the notation $(IM_k)_i$ indicates the set of inherited attributes to be supplied to M_k on the i-th visit. The parent of the node has prepared for the visit by computing the inherited attributes in the set IN_i, and these are supplied to the node for N (1).

Assuming that the first thing the i-th visit to a node of that type has to do is to perform the h-th visit to M_k (2), the routine computes the inherited attributes $(IM_k)_h$ (3), using the data dependencies from the dependency graph for the production rule $N \to M_1 M_2 \ldots$. These are passed to the node of type M_k, and its h-th visiting routine is called (4). This call returns with the synthesized attributes $(SM_k)_h$ set (5). One of these is combined with an attribute value from IN_i to produce the inherited attributes $(IM_l)_j$ (7) for the j-th visit to M_l (6). This visit (8) supplies back the values of the attributes in $(SM_l)_j$ (9). Finally the synthesized attributes in SN_i are computed (10), and the routine returns (11). Note that during the visits to M_k and M_l the flow of

— Visit 1 from the parent: flow of control from parent enters here.
— The parent has set some inherited attributes, the set IN_1.

— Visit some children M_k, M_l, ...:

Compute some inherited attributes of M_k, the set $(IM_k)_1$;
Visit M_k for the first time;
— M_k returns with some of its synthesized attributes evaluated.

Compute some inherited attributes of M_l, the set $(IM_l)_1$;
Visit M_l for the first time;
— M_l returns with some of its synthesized attributes evaluated.

... — Perhaps visit some more children, including possibly M_k or
— M_l again, while supplying the proper inherited attributes
— and obtaining synthesized attributes in return.

— End of the visits to children.

Compute some of N's synthesized attributes, the set SN_1;
Leave to the parent;
— End of visit 1 from the parent.

— Visit 2 from the parent: flow of control re-enters here.
— The parent has set some inherited attributes, the set IN_2.

... — Again visit some children while supplying inherited
— attributes and obtaining synthesized attributes in return.

Compute some of N's synthesized attributes, the set SN_2;
Leave to the parent;
— End of visit 2 from the parent.

... — Perhaps code for some more visits $3..n$ from the parent,
— supplying sets IN_3 to IN_n and yielding sets SN_3 to SN_n.

Fig. 4.24: Outline code for multi-visit attribute evaluation

control ((4) and (8)) and the data flow (solid arrows) coincide; this is because we cannot see what happens inside these visits.

An important observation about the sets $IN_{1..n}$ and $SN_{1..n}$ is in order here. IN_i is associated with the start of the i-th visit by the parent and SN_i with the i-th leave to the parent. The parent of the node for N must of course adhere to this interface, but the parent does not know which production rule for N has produced the child it is about to visit. So the sets $IN_{1..n}$ and $SN_{1..n}$ must be the same for all production rules for N: they are a property of the non-terminal N rather than of each separate production rule for N.

Similarly, all visiting routines for production rules in the grammar that contain the non-terminal N in the right-hand side must call the visiting routines of N in the same order $1..n$. If N occurs more than once in one production rule, each occurrence

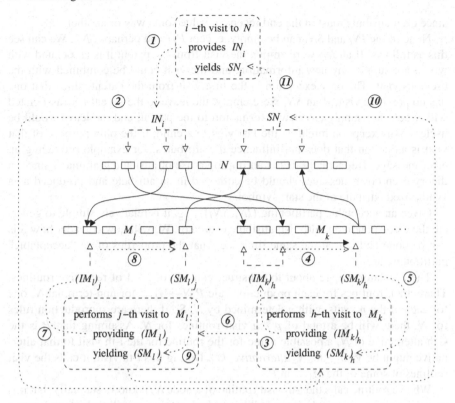

Fig. 4.25: The i-th visit to a node N, visiting two children, M_k and M_l

must get its own visiting sequence, which must consist of routine calls in that same order $1..n$.

It should also be pointed out that there is no reason why one single visiting routine could not visit a child more than once. The visits can even be consecutive, if dependencies in other production rules require more than one visit in general.

To obtain a multi-visit attribute evaluator, we will first show that once we know acceptable IN and SN sets for all non-terminals we can construct a multi-visit attribute evaluator, and we will then see how to obtain such sets.

4.1.5.2 Attribute partitionings

The above outline of the multiple visits to a node for a production rule $N \rightarrow M_1 M_2 \ldots$ partitions the attributes of N into a list of pairs of sets of attributes: $(IN_1, SN_1), (IN_2, SN_2), \ldots, (IN_n, SN_n)$ for what is called an n-visit. Visit i uses the attributes in IN_i, which were set by the parent, visits some children some number of times in some order, and returns after having set the attributes in SN_i. The sets $IN_{1..n}$ must contain all inherited attributes of N, and $SN_{1..n}$ all its synthesized attributes, since each attribute must in the end receive a value some way or another.

None of the IN_i and SN_i can be empty, except IN_1 and perhaps SN_n. We can see this as follows. If an IN_i were empty, the visit from the parent it is associated with would not supply any new information, and the visit could be combined with the previous visit. The only exception is the first visit from the parent, since that one has no previous visit. If an SN_i were empty, the leave to the parent it is associated with would not supply any new information to the parent, and the leave would be useless. An exception might be the last visit to a child, if the only purpose of that visit is an action that does not influence the attributes, for example producing an error message. But actually that is an improper use of attribute grammars, since in theory even error messages should be collected in an attribute and produced as a synthesized attribute of the start symbol.

Given an acceptable partitioning $(IN_i, SN_i)_{i=1..n}$, it is relatively simple to generate the corresponding multi-visit attribute evaluator. We will now consider how this can be done and will at the same time see what the properties of an "acceptable" partitioning are.

The evaluator we are about to construct consists of a set of recursive routines. There are n routines for each production rule $P\ N{\rightarrow}M_1\ldots$ for non-terminal N, one for each of the n visits, with n determined by N. So if there are p production rules for N, there will be a total of $p \times n$ visit routines for N. Assuming that P is the k-th alternative of N, a possible name for the routine for the i-th visit to that alternative might be $Visit\_i\_to\_N\_alternative\_k()$. During this i-th visit, it calls the visit routines of some of the $M_1\ldots$ in P.

When a routine calls the i-th visit routine of a node N, it knows statically that it is called for a node of type N, but it still has to find out dynamically which alternative of N is represented by this particular node. Only then can the routine for the i-the visit to the k-th alternative of N be called. So the routine $Visit\_i\_to\_N()$ contains calls to the routines $Visit\_i\_to\_N\_alternative\_k()$ as shown in Figure 4.26, for all required values of k.

```
procedure Visit_i_to_N (Node):
    --- Node is an N-node
    select Node.type:
        case alternative_1:
            Visit_i_to_N_alternative_1 (Node);
        ...
        case alternative_k:
            Visit_i_to_N_alternative_k (Node);
        ...
```

Fig. 4.26: Structure of an i-th visit routine for N

We will now discuss how we can determine which visit routines to call in which order inside a visiting routine $Visit\_i\_to\_N\_alternative\_k()$, based on information gathered during the generation of the routines $Visit\_h\_to\_N()$ for $1 <= h < i$, and knowledge of IN_i.

When we are about to generate the routine $Visit\_i\_to\_N\_alternative\_k()$, we have already generated the corresponding visit routines for visits $< i$. From these we know the numbers of the last visits generated to any of the children $M_1 \ldots$ of this alternative of N, so for each M_x we have a $next\_visit\_number_{M_x}$, which tells us the number of the next required visit to M_x.

We also know what attribute values of N and its children have already been evaluated as a result of previous visits; we call this set E, for "evaluated". And last but not least we know IN_i. We add IN_i to E, since the attributes in it were evaluated by the parent of N.

We now check to see if there is any child M_x whose next required visit routine can be called; we designate the visit number of this routine by j and its value is given by $next\_visit\_number_{M_x}$. Whether the routine can be called can be determined as follows. The j-th visit to M_x requires the inherited attributes in $(IM_x)_j$ to be available. Part of them may be in E, part of them must still be computed using the attribute evaluation rules of P. These rules may require the values of other attributes, and so on. If all these attributes are in E or can be computed from attributes that are in E, the routine $Visit\_j\_to\_M_x()$ can be called. If so, we generate code for the evaluation of the required attributes and for the call to $Visit\_j\_to\_M_x()$. The routine $Visit\_j\_to\_M_x()$ itself has a form similar to that in Figure 4.26, and has to be generated too.

When the code we are now generating is run and the call to the visit routine returns, it will have set the values of the attributes in $(SM_x)_j$. We can therefore add these to E, and repeat the process with the enlarged E.

When no more code for visits to children can be generated, we are about to end the generation of the routine $Visit\_i\_to\_N\_alternative\_k()$, but before doing so we have to generate code to evaluate the attributes in SN_i to return them to the parent. But here we meet a problem: we can do so only if those evaluations are allowed by the dependencies in P between the attributes; otherwise the code generation for the multi-visit attribute evaluator gets stuck. And there is no a priori reason why all the previous evaluations would allow the attributes in SN_i to be computed at precisely this moment.

This leads us to the definition of **acceptable partitioning**: a partitioning is acceptable if the attribute evaluator generation process based on it can be completed without getting stuck. So we have shown what we claimed above: having an acceptable partitioning allows us to generate a multi-visit attribute evaluator.

Unfortunately, this only solves half the problem: it is not at all obvious how to obtain an acceptable partitioning for an attribute grammar. To solve the other half of the problem, we start by observing that the heart of the problem is the interaction between the attribute dependencies and the order imposed by the given partitioning. The partitioning forces the attributes to be evaluated in a particular order, and as such constitutes an additional set of data dependencies. More in particular, all attributes of N in IN_i must be evaluated before all those in SN_i, and all attributes in SN_i must be evaluated before all those in IN_{i+1}. So, by using the given partitioning, we effectively introduce the corresponding data dependencies.

To test the acceptability of the given partitioning, we add the data dependencies from the partitioning to the data dependency graphs of the productions of N, for all non-terminals N, and then run the cycle-testing algorithm of Figure 4.20 again, to see if the overall attribute system is still cycle-free. If the algorithm finds a cycle, the set of partitionings is not acceptable, but if there are no cycles, the corresponding code adheres both to the visit sequence requirements *and* to the data dependencies in the attribute evaluation rules. And this is the kind of code we are after.

Most attribute grammars have at least one acceptable set of partitionings. This is not surprising since a grammar symbol N usually represents some kind of semantic unit, connecting some input concept to some output concept, and it is to be expected that in each production rule for N the information flows roughly in the same way.

Now we know what an acceptable partitioning is and how to recognize one; the question is how to get one, since it is fairly clear that a random partitioning will almost certainly cause cycles. Going through all possible partitionings is possible in theory, since all sets are finite and non-empty, but the algorithm would take many times the lifetime of the universe even for a simple grammar; it only shows that the problem is solvable. Fortunately, there is a heuristic that will in the large majority of cases find an acceptable partitioning and that runs in linear time: the construction algorithm for *ordered attribute evaluators*. This construction is based on late evaluation ordering of the attributes in the IS-SI graphs we have already computed above in our test for non-cyclicity.

4.1.5.3 Ordered attribute grammars

Since the IS-SI graph of N contains only arrows from inherited to synthesized attributes and vice versa, it is already close to a partitioning for N. Any partitioning for N must of course conform to the IS-SI graph, but the IS-SI graph does not generally determine a partitioning completely. For example, the IS-SI graph of Figure 4.18 allows two partitionings: $(\{I_1, I_3\}, \{S_1\})$, $(\{I_2\}, \{S_2\})$ and $(\{I_1\}, \{S_1\})$, $(\{I_2, I_3\}, \{S_2\})$. Now the idea behind ordered attribute grammars is that the later an attribute is evaluated, the smaller the chance that its evaluation will cause a cycle. This suggests that the second partitioning is preferable.

This late evaluation idea is used as follows to derive a partitioning from an IS-SI graph. We want attributes to be evaluated as late as possible; the attribute evaluated last cannot have any other attribute being dependent on it, so its node in the IS-SI graph cannot have outgoing data-flow arrows. This observation can be used to find the synthesized attributes in SN_{last}; note that we cannot write SN_n since we do not know yet the value of n, the number of visits required. SN_{last} contains all synthesized attributes in the IS-SI graph on which no other attributes depend; these are exactly those that have no outgoing arrows. Next, we remove the attributes in SN_{last} from the IS-SI graph. This exposes a layer of inherited attributes that have no outgoing data-flow arrows; these make up IN_{last}, and are removed from the IS-SI graph. This process is repeated for the pair $(IN_{last-1}, SN_{last-1})$, and so on, until the IS-SI graph has been consumed completely. Note that this makes all the sets in the partitioning non-empty except perhaps for IN_1, the last set to be created: it may find the IS-SI graph empty already. We observe that this algorithm indeed produces the partitioning $(\{I_1\}, \{S_1\}), (\{I_2, I_3\}, \{S_2\})$ for the IS-SI graph of Figure 4.18.

The above algorithms can be performed without problems for any strongly cycle-free attribute grammar, and will provide us with attribute partitionings for all symbols in the grammar. Moreover, the partitioning for each non-terminal N conforms to the IS-SI graph for N since it was derived from it. So, adding the data dependencies arising from the partition to the IS-SI graph of N will not cause any direct cycle inside that IS-SI graph to be created. But still the fact remains that dependencies are added, and these may cause larger cycles, cycles involving more than one non-terminal to arise. So, before we can start generating code, we have to run our cycle-testing algorithm again. If the test does not find any cycles, the grammar is an **ordered attribute grammar** and the partitionings can be used to generate attribute evaluation code. This code will

- not loop on any parse tree, since the final set of IS-SI graphs was shown to be cycle-free;
- never use an attribute whose value has not yet been set, since the moment an attribute is used is determined by the partitionings and the partitionings conform to the IS-SI graphs and so to the dependencies;
- evaluate the correct values before each visit to a node and before each return from it, since the code scheme in Figure 4.24 obeys the partitioning.

Very many, not to say almost all, attribute grammars that one writes naturally turn out to be ordered, which makes the notion of an ordered attribute grammar a very useful one.

We have explained the technique using terms like the k-th visit out of n visits, which somehow suggests that considerable numbers of visits may occur. We found it advantageous to imagine that for a while, while trying to understand the algorithms, since thinking so made it easier to focus on the general case. But in practice visit numbers larger than 3 are rare; most of the nodes need to be visited only once, some may need two visits, a small minority may need three visits, and in most attribute grammars no node needs to be visited four times. Of course it is possible to construct a grammar with a non-terminal X whose nodes require, say, 10 visits, but one should realize that its partition consists of 20 non-overlapping sets, $IN_{1..10}$ and $SN_{1..10}$, and that only set IN_1 may be empty. So X will have to have at least 9 inherited attributes and 10 synthesized attributes. This is not the kind of non-terminal one normally meets during compiler construction.

4.1.5.4 The ordered attribute grammar for the octal/decimal example

We will now apply the ordered attribute grammar technique to our attribute grammar of Figure 4.8, to obtain a multi-visit attribute evaluator for that grammar. We will at the same time show how the order of the calls to visit routines inside one *Visit_i_to_N_alternative_k()* routine is determined.

The IS-SI graphs of the non-terminals in the grammar, *Number*, *Digit_Seq*, *Digit*, and *Base_Tag*, are constructed easily; the results are shown in Figure 4.27.

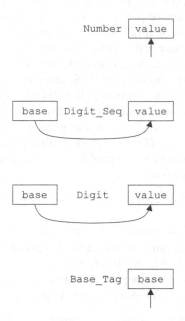

Fig. 4.27: The IS-SI graphs of the non-terminals from grammar 4.8

We find no cycles during their construction and see that there are no SI-dependencies: this reflects the fact that no non-terminal has a synthesized attribute whose value is propagated through the rest of the tree to return to the node it originates from.

The next step is to construct the partitionings. Again this is easy to do, since each IS-SI graph contains at most one inherited and one synthesized attribute. The table in Figure 4.28 shows the results.

	IN_1	SN_1
Number		value
Digit_Seq	base	value
Digit	base	value
Base_Tag		base

Fig. 4.28: Partitionings of the attributes of grammar 4.8

As we have seen above, the j-th visit to a node of type M_x in Figure 4.24 is a building block for setting the attributes in $(SM_x)_j$:

— Require the attributes needed to compute the
— attributes in $(IM_x)_j$ to be set;
Compute the set $(IM_x)_j$;
Visit child M_x for the j-th time;
— Child M_x returns with the set $(SM_x)_j$ evaluated.

but it can only be applied in an environment in which the values of the attributes in $(IM_x)_j$ are available or can be evaluated.

With this knowledge we can now construct the code for the first (and only) visit to nodes of the type *Number*. *Number* has only one alternative *NumberAlternative_1*, so the code we are about to generate will be part of a routine *Visit_1_to_NumberAlternative_1()*.

The alternative consists of a *Digit_Seq* and a *Base_Tag*. The set E of attributes that have already been evaluated is empty at this point and *next_visit_number*$_{Digit\_Seq}$ and *next_visit_number*$_{Base\_Tag}$ are both zero. The building block for visiting *Digit_Seq* is

— Requires NumberAlt_1.base_Tag.base to be set.
— Compute the attributes in IN_1 of Digit_Seq (), the set { base }:
NumberAlt_1.digit_Seq.base ← NumberAlt_1.base_Tag.base;
— Visit Digit_Seq for the first time:
Visit_1_to_Digit_Seq (NumberAlt_1.digit_Seq);
— Digit_Seq returns with its SN_1, the set { value }, evaluated;
— it supplies NumberAlt_1.digit_Seq.value.

and the one for *Base_Tag* is

— Requires nothing.
— Compute the attributes in IN_1 of Base_Tag (), the set { }:
— Visit Base_Tag for the first time:
Visit_1_to_Base_Tag (NumberAlt_1.base_Tag);
— Base_Tag returns with its SN_1, the set { base }, evaluated;
— it supplies NumberAlt_1.base_Tag.base.

Their data requirements have been shown as comments in the first line; they derive from the set IN_1 of *Digit_Seq* and *Base_Tag*, as transformed by the data dependencies of the attribute evaluation rules. For example, IN_1 of *Digit_Seq* says that the first visit requires *NumberAlt_1.digit_Seq.base* to be set. The attribute evaluation rule for this is

NumberAlt_1.digit_Seq.base ← NumberAlt_1.base_Tag.base;

whose data dependency requires *NumberAlt_1.base_Tag.base* to be set. But the value of *NumberAlt_1.base_Tag.base* is not in E at the moment, so the building block for visiting *Digit_Seq* cannot be generated at this moment.

Next we turn to the building block for visiting *Base_Tag*, also shown above. This building block requires no attribute values to be available, so we can generate code for it. The set SN_1 of *Base_Tag* shows that the building block sets the value of *NumberAlt_1.base_Tag.base*, so *NumberAlt_1.base_Tag.base* is added to E. This frees the way for the building block for visiting *Digit_Seq*, code for which is generated next. The set SN_1 of *Digit_Seq* consists of the attribute *value*, so we can add *NumberAlt_1.digit_Seq.value* to E.

There are no more visits to generate code for, and we now have to wrap up the routine *Visit_1_to_NumberAlternative_1()*. The set *SN*₁ of *Number* contains the attribute *value*, so code for setting *Number.value* must be generated. The attribute evaluation rule in Figure 4.8 shows that *Number.value* is just a copy of *NumberAlt_1.digit_Seq.value*, which is available, since it is in *E*. So the code can be generated and the attribute grammar turns out to be an ordered attribute grammar, at least as far as *Number* is concerned.

All these considerations result in the code of Figure 4.29. Note that we have effectively been doing a topological sort on the building blocks, using the data dependencies to compare building blocks.

```
procedure Visit_1_to_NumberAlternative_1 (
    pointer to number node Number,
    pointer to number alt_1Node NumberAlt_1
):
—— Visit 1 from the parent: flow of control from the parent enters here.
—— The parent has set the attributes in IN₁ of Number, the set { }.

    —— Visit some children:

    —— Compute the attributes in IN₁ of Base_Tag (), the set { }:
    —— Visit Base_Tag for the first time:
    Visit_1_to_Base_Tag (NumberAlt_1.base_Tag);
    —— Base_Tag returns with its SN₁, the set { base }, evaluated.

    —— Compute the attributes in IN₁ of Digit_Seq (), the set { base }:
    NumberAlt_1.digit_Seq.base ← NumberAlt_1.base_Tag.base;
    —— Visit Digit_Seq for the first time:
    Visit_1_to_Digit_Seq (NumberAlt_1.digit_Seq);
    —— Digit_Seq returns with its SN₁, the set { value }, evaluated.

    —— End of the visits to children.

    —— Compute the attributes in SN₁ of Number, the set { value }:
    Number.value ← NumberAlt_1.digit_Seq.value;
```

Fig. 4.29: Visiting code for *Number* nodes

For good measure, and to allow comparison with the corresponding routine for the data-flow machine in Figure 4.14, we give the code for visiting the first alternative of *Digit_Seq* in Figure 4.30. In this routine, the order in which the two children are visited is immaterial, since the data dependencies are obeyed both in the order (*Digit_Seq, Digit*) and in the order (*Digit, Digit_Seq*).

Similar conflict-free constructions are possible for *Digit* and *Base_Tag*, so the grammar of Figure 4.8 *is* indeed an ordered attribute grammar, and we have constructed automatically an attribute evaluator for it. The above code indeed visits each node of the integer number only once.

```
procedure Visit_1_to_Digit_SeqAlternative_1 (
    pointer to digit_seqNode Digit_Seq,
    pointer to digit_seqAlt_1Node Digit_SeqAlt_1
):
```
— Visit 1 from the parent: flow of control from the parent enters here.
— The parent has set the attributes in IN_1 of Digit_Seq, the set { base }.

— Visit some children:

— Compute the attributes in IN_1 of Digit_Seq (), the set { base }:
```
Digit_SeqAlt_1.digit_Seq.base ← Digit_Seq.base;
```
— Visit Digit_Seq for the first time:
```
Visit_1_to_Digit_Seq (Digit_SeqAlt_1.digit_Seq);
```
— Digit_Seq returns with its SN_1, the set { value }, evaluated.

— Compute the attributes in IN_1 of Digit (), the set { base }:
```
Digit_SeqAlt_1.digit.base ← Digit_Seq.base;
```
— Visit Digit for the first time:
```
Visit_1_to_Digit (Digit_SeqAlt_1.digit);
```
— Digit returns with its SN_1, the set { value }, evaluated.

— End of the visits to children.

— Compute the attributes in SN_1 of Digit_Seq, the set { value }:
```
Digit_Seq.value ←
    Digit_SeqAlt_1.digit_Seq.value × Digit_Seq.base +
    Digit_SeqAlt_1.digit.value;
```

Fig. 4.30: Visiting code for *Digit_SeqAlternative_1* nodes

Of course, numbers of the form $[0–9]^+[BD]$ can be and normally are handled by the lexical analyzer, but that is beside the point. The point is, however, that

- the grammar for *Number* is representative of those language constructs in which information from further on in the text must be used,
- the algorithms for ordered attribute evaluation have found out automatically that no node needs to be visited more than once in this case, provided they are visited in the right order.

See Exercises 4.6 and 4.7 for situations in which more than one visit *is* necessary.

The above construction was driven by the contents of the partitioning sets and the data dependencies of the attribute evaluation rules. This suggests a somewhat simpler way of constructing the evaluator while avoiding testing the partitionings for being appropriate:

- Construct the IS-SI graphs while testing for circularities.
- Construct from the IS-SI graphs the partitionings using late evaluation.
- Construct the code for the visiting routines, starting from the obligation to set the attributes in SN_k and working backwards from there, using the data dependencies and the *IN* and *SN* sets of the building blocks supplied by the other visit routines as our guideline. If we can construct all visit routine bodies without violating the

data dependencies, we have proved that the grammar was ordered and have at the same time obtained the multi-visit attribute evaluation code.

This technique is more in line with the usual compiler construction approach: just try to generate correct efficient code; if you can you win, no questions asked.

Farrow [97] discusses a more complicated technique that creates attribute evaluators for almost any non-cyclic attribute grammar, ordered or not. Rodriguez-Cerezo *et al.* [239] supply templates for the generation of attribute evaluators for arbitrary non-cyclic attribute grammars.

4.1.6 Summary of the types of attribute grammars

There are a series of restrictions that reduce the most general attribute grammars to ordered attribute grammars. The important point about these restrictions is that they increase considerably the algorithmic tractability of the grammars but are almost no obstacle to the compiler writer who uses the attribute grammar.

The first restriction is that all synthesized attributes of a production and all inherited attributes of its children must get values assigned to them in the production. Without this restriction, the attribute grammar is not even well-formed.

The second is that no tree produced by the grammar may have a cycle in the attribute dependencies. This property is tested by constructing for each non-terminal N, a summary, the IS-SI graph set, of the data-flow possibilities through all subtrees deriving from N. The test for this property is exponential in the number of attributes in a non-terminal and identifies non-cyclic attribute grammars. In spite of its exponential time requirement the test is feasible for "normal" attribute grammars on present-day computers.

The third restriction is that the grammar still be non-cyclic even if a single IS-SI graph is used per non-terminal rather than an IS-SI graph *set*. The test for this property is linear in the number of attributes in a non-terminal and identifies strongly non-cyclic attribute grammars.

The fourth restriction requires that the attributes can be evaluated using the fixed multi-visit scheme of Figure 4.24. This leads to multi-visit attribute grammars. Such grammars have a partitioning for the attributes of each non-terminal, as described above. Testing whether an attribute grammar is multi-visit is exponential in the total number of attributes in the worst case, and therefore prohibitively expensive (in the worst case).

The fifth restriction is that the partitioning constructed heuristically using the late evaluation criterion turn out to be acceptable and not create any new cycles. This leads to ordered attribute grammars. The test is $O(n^2)$ where n is the number of attributes per non-terminal if implemented naively, and $O(n \ln n)$ in theory, but since n is usually small, this makes little difference.

Each of these restrictions is a real restriction, in that the class it defines is a proper subclass of the class above it. So there are grammars that are non-cyclic but not strongly non-cyclic, strongly non-cyclic but not multi-visit, and multi-visit but not ordered. But these "difference" classes are very small and for all practical purposes the above classes form a single class, "the attribute grammars".

4.2 Restricted attribute grammars

In the following two sections we will discuss two classes of attribute grammars that result from far more serious restrictions: the "L-attributed grammars", in which an inherited attribute of a child of a non-terminal N may depend only on synthesized attributes of children to the left of it in the production rule for N and on the inherited attributes of N itself; and the "S-attributed grammars", which cannot have inherited attributes at all.

4.2.1 L-attributed grammars

The parsing process constructs the nodes in the syntax tree in left-to-right order: first the parent node and then the children in top-down parsing; and first the children and then the parent node in bottom-up parsing. It is interesting to consider attribute grammars that can match this behavior: attribute grammars which allow the attributes to be evaluated in one left-to-right traversal of the syntax tree. Such grammars are called **L-attributed grammars**. An L-attributed grammar is characterized by the fact that no dependency graph of any of its production rules has a data-flow arrow that points from a child to that child or to a child to the left of it. Many programming language grammars are L-attributed; this is not surprising, since the left-to-right information flow inherent in them helps programmers in reading and understanding the resulting programs. An example is the dependency graph of the rule for *Constant_definition* in Figure 4.3, in which no information flows from *Expression* to *Defined_identifier*. The human reader, like the parser and the attribute evaluator, arrives at a *Constant_definition* with a symbol table, sees the defined identifier and the expression, combines the two in the symbol table, and leaves the *Constant_definition* behind. An example of an attribute grammar that is not L-attributed is the *Number* grammar from Figure 4.8: the data-flow arrow for *base* points to the left, and in principle the reader has to read the entire digit sequence to find the B or D which tells how to interpret the sequence. Only the fact that a human reader can grasp the entire number in one glance saves him or her from this effort; computers are less fortunate.

The L-attributed property has an important consequence for the processing of the syntax tree: once work on a node has started, no part of the compiler will need to return to one of the node's siblings on the left to do processing there. The parser is finished with them, and all their attributes have been computed already. Only the data that the nodes contain in the form of synthesized attributes are still important. Figure 4.31 shows part of a parse tree for an L-attributed grammar.

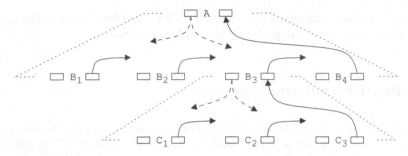

Fig. 4.31: Data flow in part of a parse tree for an L-attributed grammar

We assume that the attribute evaluator is working on node C_2, which is the second child of node B_3, which is the third child of node A; whether A is the top or the child of another node is immaterial. The upward arrows represent the data flow of the synthesized attributes of the children; they all point to the right or to the synthesized attributes of the parent. All inherited attributes are already available when work on a node starts, and can be passed to any child that needs them. They are shown as downward arrows in the diagram.

Figure 4.31 shows that when the evaluator is working on node C_2, only two sets of attributes play a role:

- all attributes of the nodes that lie on the path from the top to the node being processed: C_2, B_3, and A,
- the synthesized attributes of the left siblings of those nodes: C_1, B_1, B_2, and any left siblings of A not shown in the diagram.

More in particular, no role is played by the children of the left siblings of C_2, B_3, and A, since all computations in them have already been performed and the results are summarized in their synthesized attributes. Nor do the right siblings of C_2, B_3, and A play a role, since their synthesized attributes have no influence yet.

The attributes of C_2, B_3, and A reside in the corresponding nodes; work on these nodes has already started but has not yet finished. The same is not true for the left siblings of C_2, B_3, and A, since the work on them is finished; all that is left of them are their synthesized attributes. Now, if we could find a place to store the data synthesized by these left siblings, we could discard each node in left-to-right order, after the parser has created it and the attribute evaluator has computed its attributes. That would mean that we do not need to construct the entire syntax tree but can always restrict ourselves to the nodes that lie on the path from the top to the node being processed. Everything to the left of that path has been processed and, except for the synthesized attributes of the left siblings, discarded; everything to the right of it has not been touched yet.

A place to store the synthesized attributes of left siblings is easily found: we store them in the parent node. The inherited attributes remain in the nodes they belong to and their values are transported down along the path from the top to the node being processed. This structure is exactly what top-down parsing provides.

This correspondence allows us to write the attribute processing code between the various members, to be performed when parsing passes through.

4.2.1.1 L-attributed grammars and top-down parsers

An example of a system for handling L-attributed grammars is *LLgen*; *LLgen* was explained in Section 3.4.6, but the sample code in Figure 3.28 featured synthesized attributes only, representing the values of the expression and its subexpressions. Figure 4.32 includes an inherited attribute as well: a symbol table which contains the representations of some identifiers, together with the integer values associated with these identifiers.

This symbol table is produced as a synthesized attribute by the non-terminal declarations in the rule main, which processes one or more identifier declarations. The symbol table is then passed as an inherited attribute down through expression and expression_tail_option, to be used finally in term to look up the value of the identifier found. This results in the synthesized attribute *t, which is then passed on upwards. For example, the input **b = 9, c = 5; b−c**, passed to the program produced by *LLgen* from the grammar in Figure 4.32, yields the output **result = 4**. Note that synthesized attributes in *LLgen* are implemented as pointers passed as inherited attributes, but this is purely an implementation trick of *LLgen* to accommodate the C language, which does not feature output parameters.

The coordination of parsing and attribute evaluation is a great simplification compared to multi-visit attribute evaluation, but is of course applicable to a much smaller class of attribute grammars. Many attribute grammars can be doctored to become L-attributed grammars, and it is up to the compiler constructor to decide whether to leave the grammar intact and use an ordered attribute evaluator generator or to modify the grammar to adapt it to a system like *LLgen*. In earlier days much of compiler design consisted of finding ways to allow the—implicit—attribute grammar to be handled by a handwritten left-to-right evaluator, to avoid handwritten multi-visit processing.

The L-attributed technique allows a more technical definition of a narrow compiler than the one given in Section 1.4.1. A *narrow compiler* is a compiler, based formally or informally on some form of L-attributed grammar, that does not save substantially more information than that which is present on the path from the top to the node being processed. In most cases, the length of that path is proportional to ln n, where n is the length of the program, whereas the size of the entire AST is proportional to n. This, and the intuitive appeal of L-attributed grammars, explains the popularity of narrow compilers.

4.2.1.2 L-attributed grammars and bottom-up parsers

We have seen that the attribute evaluation in L-attributed grammars can be incorporated conveniently in top-down parsing, but its implementation using bottom-up

```
{
#include    "symbol_table.h"
}

%lexical get_next_token_class;
%token IDENTIFIER;
%token DIGIT;

%start Main_Program, main;

main {symbol_table sym_tab; int result ;}:
    {init_symbol_table(&sym_tab);}
    declarations(sym_tab)
    expression(sym_tab, &result)
    { printf ("result = %d\n", result );}
;

declarations(symbol_table sym_tab):
    declaration(sym_tab) [ ',' declaration(sym_tab) ]* ';'
;

declaration(symbol_table sym_tab) {symbol_entry *sym_ent;}:
    IDENTIFIER {sym_ent = look_up(sym_tab, Token.repr);}
    '=' DIGIT {sym_ent->value = Token.repr - '0';}
;

expression(symbol_table sym_tab; int *e) {int t ;}:
    term(sym_tab, &t)                {*e = t ;}
    expression_tail_option(sym_tab, e)
;

expression_tail_option(symbol_table sym_tab; int *e) {int t ;}:
    '-' term(sym_tab, &t)           {*e -= t;}
    expression_tail_option(sym_tab, e)
|
;

term(symbol_table sym_tab; int *t):
    IDENTIFIER     {*t = look_up(sym_tab, Token.repr)->value;}
;
```

Fig. 4.32: *LLgen* code for an L-attributed grammar for simple expressions

parsing is less obvious. In fact, it seems impossible. The problem lies in the inherited attributes, which must be passed down from parent nodes to children nodes. The problem is that in bottom-up parsing the parent nodes are identified and created only *after* all of their children have been processed, so there is just no place from where to pass down any inherited attributes when they are needed. Yet the most famous LALR(1) parser generator *yacc* and its cousin *bison* do it anyway, and it is interesting to see how they accomplish this feat.

As explained in Section 3.5.2, a bottom-up parser has a stack of shifted terminals and reduced non-terminals; we parallel this stack with an attribute stack which contains the attributes of each stack element in that same order. The problem is to fill the inherited attributes, since code has to be executed for it. Code in a bottom-up parser can only be executed at the end of an alternative, when the corresponding item has been fully recognized and is being reduced. But now we want to execute code in the middle:

A → B {C.inh_attr := f(B.syn_attr);} C

where B.syn_attr is a synthesized attribute of B and C.inh_attr is an inherited attribute of C. The trick is to attach the code to an ε-rule introduced for the purpose, say A_action1:

A → B A_action1 C
A_action1 → ε {C.inh_attr ':=' f(B.syn_attr);}

Yacc does this automatically and also remembers the context of A_action1, so B.syn_attr1 and C.inh_attr1 can be identified in spite of them having been lifted out of their scopes by the above transformation.

Now the code in A_action1 is at the end of an alternative and can be executed when the item A_action1 → ε • is reduced. This works, but the problem is that after this transformation the grammar may no longer be LALR(1): introducing ε-rules is bad for bottom-up parsers. The parser will work only if the item

A → B • C

is the only one in the set of hypotheses at that point. Only then can the parser be confident that this is the item and that the code can be executed. This also ensures that the parent node is A, so the parser knows already it is going to construct a parent node A. These are severe requirements. Fortunately, there are many grammars with only a small number of inherited attributes, so the method is still useful.

There are a number of additional tricks to get cooperation between attribute evaluation and bottom-up parsing. One is to lay out the attribute stack so that the one and only synthesized attribute of one node is in the same position as the one and only inherited attribute of the next node. This way no code needs to be executed in between and the problem of executing code in the middle of a grammar rule is avoided. See the *yacc* or *bison* manual for details and notation.

4.2.2 S-attributed grammars

If inherited attributes are a problem, let's get rid of them. This gives **S-attributed grammars**, which are characterized by having no inherited attributes at all. It is remarkable how much can still be done within this restriction. In fact, anything that can be done in an L-attributed grammar can be done in an S-attributed grammar, as we will show in Section 4.2.3.

Now life is easy for bottom-up parsers. Each child node stacks its synthesized attributes, and the code at the end of an alternative of the parent scoops them all up, processes them, and replaces them by the resulting synthesized attributes of the parent. A typical example of an S-attributed grammar can be found in the *yacc* code in Figure 3.62. The code at the end of the first alternative of expression:

   {$$ = new_expr(); $$−>type = '−'; $$−>expr = $1; $$−>term = $3;}

picks up the synthesized attributes of the children, $1 and $3, and combines them into the synthesized attribute of the parent, $$. For historical reasons, *yacc* grammar rules each have exactly one synthesized attribute; if more than one synthesized attribute has to be returned, they have to be combined into a record, which then forms the only attribute. This is comparable to functions allowing only one return value in most programming languages.

4.2.3 Equivalence of L-attributed and S-attributed grammars

It is relatively easy to convert an L-attributed grammar into an S-attributed grammar, but, as is usual with grammar transformations, this conversion does not improve its looks. The basic trick is to delay any computation that cannot be done now to a later moment when it *can* be done. More in particular, any computation that would need inherited attributes is replaced by the creation of a data structure specifying that computation and all its synthesized attributes. This data structure (or a pointer to it) is passed on as a synthesized attribute up to the level where the missing inherited attributes are available, either as constants or as synthesized attributes of nodes at that level. Then we do the computation.

The traditional example of this technique is the processing of variable declaration in a C-like language; an example of such a declaration is int i, j;. When inherited attributes are available, this processing can be described easily by the L-attributed grammar in Figure 4.33. Here the rule Type_Declarator produces a synthesized attribute type, which is then passed on as an inherited attribute to Declared_Idf_Sequence and Declared_Idf. It is combined in the latter with the representation provided by Idf, and the combination is added to the symbol table.

In the absence of inherited attributes, Declared_Idf can do only one thing: yield repr as a synthesized attribute, as shown in Figure 4.34. The various reprs resulting from the occurrences of Declared_Idf in Declared_Idf_Sequence are collected into a data structure, which is yielded as the synthesized attribute reprList. Finally this list

```
Declaration →
    Type_Declarator(type) Declared_Idf_Sequence(type) ';'

Declared_Idf_Sequence(INH type) →
    Declared_Idf(type)
|
    Declared_Idf_Sequence(type) ',' Declared_Idf(type)

Declared_Idf(INH type) →
    Idf(repr)
    attribute rules:
        AddToSymbolTable (repr, type);
```

Fig. 4.33: Sketch of an L-attributed grammar for Declaration

reaches the level on which the type is known and where the delayed computations can be performed.

```
Declaration →
    Type_Declarator(type) Declared_Idf_Sequence(reprList) ';'
    attribute rules:
        for each repr in reprList:
            AddToSymbolTable (repr, type);

Declared_Idf_Sequence(SYN reprList) →
    Declared_Idf(repr)
    attribute rules:
        reprList ← ConvertToList (repr);
|
    Declared_Idf_Sequence(oldReprList) ',' Declared_Idf(repr)
    attribute rules:
        reprList ← AppendToList (oldReprList, repr);
;

Declared_Idf(SYN repr) →
    Idf(repr)
;
```

Fig. 4.34: Sketch of an S-attributed grammar for Declaration

It will be clear that this technique can in principle be used to eliminate all inherited attributes at the expense of introducing more synthesized attributes and moving more code up the tree. In this way, any L-attributed grammar can be converted into an S-attributed one. Of course, in some cases, some of the attribute code will have to be moved right to the top of the tree, in which case the conversion automatically creates a separate postprocessing phase. This shows that in principle one scan over the input is enough.

The transformation from L-attributed to S-attributed grammar seems attractive: it allows stronger, bottom-up, parsing methods to be used for the more convenient

L-attributed grammars. Unfortunately, the transformation is practically feasible for small problems only, and serious problems soon arise. For example, attempts to eliminate the entire symbol table as an inherited attribute (as used in Figure 4.2) lead to a scheme in which at the end of each visibility range the identifiers used in it are compared to those declared in it, and any identifiers not accounted for are passed on upwards to surrounding visibility ranges. Also, much information has to be carried around to provide relevant error messages. See Exercise 4.12 for a possibility to automate the process. Note that the code in Figures 4.33 and 4.34 dodges the problem by having the symbol table as a hidden variable, outside the domain of attribute grammars.

4.3 Extended grammar notations and attribute grammars

Notations like E.attr for an attribute deriving from grammar symbol E break down if there is more than one E in the grammar rule. A possible solution is to use E[1], E[2], etc., for the children and E for the non-terminal itself, as we did for Digit_Seq in Figure 4.8. More serious problems arise when the right-hand side is allowed to contain regular expressions over the grammar symbols, as in EBNF notation. Given an attribute grammar rule

```
Declaration_Sequence(SYN symbol table) →
    Declaration*
    attribute rules:
        . . .
```

it is less than clear how the attribute evaluation code could access the symbol tables produced by the individual Declarations, to combine them into a single symbol table. Actually, it is not even clear exactly what kind of node must be generated for a rule with a variable number of children. As a result, most general attribute grammar systems do not allow EBNF-like notations. If the system has its own attribute rule language, another option is to extend this language with data access operations to match the EBNF extensions.

L-attributed and S-attributed grammars have fewer problems here, since one can just write the pertinent code inside the repeated part. This approach is taken in *LLgen* and a possible form of the above rule for Declaration_Sequence in *LLgen* would be

```
Declaration_Sequence(struct Symbol_Table *Symbol_Table)
        { struct  Symbol_Table st;}:
        {Clear_Symbol_Table(Symbol_Table);}
        [    Declaration(&st)
            {Merge_Symbol_Tables(Symbol_Table, &st);}
        ]*
    ;
```

given proper declarations of the routines Clear_Symbol_Table() and Merge_Symbol_Tables(). Note that *LLgen* uses square brackets [] for the grouping of grammatical constructs, to avoid confusion with the parentheses () used for passing attributes to rules.

4.4 Conclusion

This concludes our discussion of grammar-based context handling. In this approach, the context is stored in attributes, and the grammatical basis allows the processing to be completely automatic (for attribute grammars) or largely automatic (for L- and S-attributed grammars). Figure 4.35 summarizes the possible attribute value flow through the AST for ordered attribute grammars, L-attributed grammars, and S-attributed grammars. Values may flow along branches from anywhere to anywhere in ordered attribute grammars, up one branch and then down the next in L-attributed grammars, and upward only in S-attributed grammars.

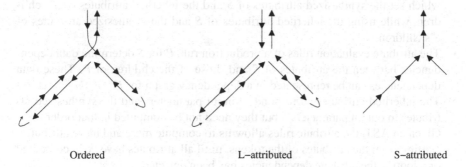

Ordered   L–attributed   S–attributed

Fig. 4.35: Pictorial comparison of three types of attribute grammars

In the next chapter we will now discuss some manual methods, in which the context is stored in ad-hoc data structures, not intimately connected with the grammar rules. Of course most of the data structures are still associated with nodes of the AST, since the AST is the only representation of the program that we have.

Summary

Summary—Attribute grammars

• Lexical analysis establishes local relationships between characters, syntax analysis establishes nesting relationships between tokens, and context handling establishes long-range relationships between AST nodes.

- Conceptually, the data about these long-range relationships is stored in the attributes of the nodes; implementation-wise, part of it may be stored in symbol tables and other tables.
- All context handling is based on a data-flow machine and all context-handling techniques are ways to implement that data-flow machine.
- The starting information for context handling is the AST and the classes and representations of the tokens that are its leaves.
- Context handlers can be written by hand or generated automatically from attribute grammars.
- Each non-terminal and terminal in an attribute grammar has its own specific set of formal attributes.
- A formal attribute is a named property. An (actual) attribute is a named property and its value; it is a (name, value) pair.
- Each node for a non-terminal and terminal S in an AST has the formal attributes of S; their values may and usually will differ.
- With each production rule for S, a set of attribute evaluation rules is associated, which set the synthesized attributes of S and the inherited attributes of S's children, while using the inherited attributes of S and the synthesized attributes of S's children.
- The attribute evaluation rules of a production rule P for S determine data dependencies between the attributes of S and those of the children of P. These data dependencies can be represented in a dependency graph for P.
- The inherited attributes correspond to input parameters and the synthesized attributes to output parameters—but they need not be computed in that order.
- Given an AST, the attribute rules allow us to compute more and more attributes, starting from the attributes of the tokens, until all attributes have been computed or a loop in the attribute dependencies has been detected.
- A naive way of implementing the attribute evaluation process is to visit all nodes repeatedly and execute at each visit the attribute rules that have the property that the attribute values they use are available and the attribute values they set are not yet available. This is dynamic attribute evaluation.
- Dynamic attribute evaluation is inefficient and its naive implementation does not terminate if there is a cycle in the attribute dependencies.
- Static attribute evaluation determines the attribute evaluation order of any AST at compiler construction time, rather than at compiler run time. It is efficient and detects cycles at compiler generation time, but is more complicated.
- Static attribute evaluation order determination is based on IS-SI graphs and late evaluation by topological sort. All these properties of the attribute grammar can be determined at compiler construction time.
- The nodes in the IS-SI graph of a non-terminal N are the attributes of N, and the arrows in it represent the summarized data dependencies between them. The arrows are summaries of all data dependencies that can result from any tree in which a node for N occurs. The important point is that this summary can be determined at compiler construction time, long before any AST is actually constructed.

- The IS-SI graph of N depends on the dependency graphs of the production rules in which N occurs and the IS-SI graphs of the other non-terminals in these production rules. This defines recurrence relations between all IS-SI graphs in the grammar. The recurrence relations are solved by transitive closure to determine all IS-SI graphs.
- If there is an evaluation cycle in the attribute grammar, an attribute will depend on itself, and at least one of the IS-SI graphs will exhibit a cycle. This provides cycle detection at compiler construction time; it allows avoiding constructing compilers that will loop on some programs.
- A multi-visit attribute evaluator visits a node for non-terminal N one or more times; the number is fixed at compiler construction time. At the start of the i-th visit, some inherited attributes have been freshly set, the set IN_i; at the end some synthesized attributes have been freshly set, the set SN_i. This defines an attribute partitioning $\{(IN_i, SN_i)\}_{i=1..n}\}$ for each non-terminal N, leading to an n-visit. The IN_i together comprise all inherited attributes of N, the SN_i all synthesized attributes.
- Given an acceptable partitioning, multi-visit code can be generated for the k-th alternative of non-terminal N, as follows. Given the already evaluated attributes, we try to find a child whose IN set allows the next visit to it. If there is one, we generate code for it. Its SN set now enlarges our set of already evaluated attributes, and we repeat the process. When done, we try to generate evaluation code for SN of this visit to this alternative of N. If the partitioning is acceptable, we can do so without violating data dependencies.
- Partitionings can be seen as additional data dependencies, which have to be merged with the original data dependencies. If the result is still cycle-free, the partitioning is acceptable.
- Any partitioning of the IS-SI graph of a non-terminal N will allow all routines for N to be generated, and could therefore be part of the required acceptable partitioning. Using a specific one, however, creates additional dependencies for other non-terminals, which may cause cycles in any of their dependency graphs. So we have to choose the partitioning of the IS-SI graph carefully.
- In an ordered attribute grammar, late partitioning of all IS-SI graphs yields an acceptable partitioning.
- In late partitioning, all synthesized attributes on which no other attributes depend are evaluated last. They are immediately preceded by all inherited attributes on which only attributes depend that will be evaluated later, and so on.
- Once we have obtained our late partitioning, the cycle-testing algorithm can test it for us, or we can generate code and see if the process gets stuck. If it does get stuck, the attribute grammar was not an ordered attribute grammar.

Summary—L- and S-attributed grammars

- An L-attributed grammar is an attribute grammar in which no dependency graph of any of its production rules has a data-flow arrow that points from an attribute to an attribute to the left of it. L-attributed grammars allow the attributes to be evaluated in one left-to-right traversal of the syntax tree.
- Many programming language grammars are L-attributed.
- L-attributed ASTs can be processed with only the information on the path from the present node to the top, plus information collected about the nodes on the left of this path. This is exactly what a narrow compiler provides.
- L-attributed grammar processing can be incorporated conveniently in top-down parsing. L-attributed processing during bottom-up parsing requires assorted trickery, since there is no path to the top in such parsers.
- S-attributed grammars have no inherited attributes at all.
- In an S-attributed grammar, attributes need to be retained only for non-terminal nodes that have not yet been reduced to other non-terminals. These are exactly the non-terminals on the stack of a bottom-up parser.
- Everything that can be done in an L-attributed grammar can be done in an S-attribute grammar: just package any computation you cannot do for lack of an inherited attribute into a data structure, pass it as a synthesized attribute, and do it when you can.

Further reading

Synthesized attributes have probably been used since the day grammars were invented, but the usefulness and manageability of inherited attributes was first shown by Knuth [156, 157].

Whereas there are many parser generators, attribute evaluator generators are much rarer. The first practical one for ordered attribute grammars was constructed by Kastens *et al.* [146]. Several more modern ones can be found on the Internet. For an overview of possible attribute evaluation methods see Alblas [10].

Exercises

4.1. (▷www) For each of the following items, indicate whether it belongs to a non-terminal or to a production rule of a non-terminal.
(a) inherited attribute;
(b) synthesized attribute;
(c) attribute evaluation rule;
(d) dependency graph;

(e) IS-SI graph;
(f) visiting routine;
(g) node in an AST;
(h) child pointer in an AST.

4.2. (▷788) The division into synthesized and inherited attributes is presented as a requirement on attribute grammars in the beginning of this chapter. Explore what happens when this requirement is dropped.

4.3. (▷www) What happens with the topological sort algorithm of Figure 4.16 when there is a cycle in the dependencies? Modify the algorithm so that it detects cycles.

4.4. (▷www) Consider the attribute grammar of Figure 4.36. Construct the IS-SI graph of A and show that the grammar contains a cycle.

```
S(SYN s) →
    A(i1, s1)
    attribute rules:
        i1 ← s1;
        s ← s1;

A(INH i1, SYN s1) →
    A(i2, s2) 'a'
    attribute rules:
        i2 ← i1;
        s1 ← s2;
  |
    B(i2, s2)
    attribute rules:
        i2 ← i1;
        s1 ← s2;

B(INH i, SYN s) →
    'b'
    attribute rules: s ← i;
```

Fig. 4.36: Attribute grammar for Exercise 4.4

4.5. (▷789) Construct an attribute grammar that is non-cyclic but not strongly non-cyclic, so the algorithm of Figure 4.20 will find a cycle but the cycle cannot materialize. Hint: the code for rule S visits its only child A twice; there are two rules for A, each with one production only; neither production causes a cycle when visited twice, but visiting one and then the other causes a—false—cycle.

4.6. (▷www) Given the attributed non-terminal

S(**INH** i1, i2, **SYN** s1, s2) →
   T U
   attribute rules:
      T.i ← f1(S.i1, U.s);
      U.i ← f2(S.i2);
      S.s1 ← f3(T.s);
      S.s2 ← f4(U.s);

draw its dependency graph. Given the IS-SI graphs for T and U shown in Figure
4.37 and given that the final IS-SI graph for S contains no SI arrows, answer the
following questions:

Fig. 4.37: IS-SI graphs for T and U

(a) Construct the complete IS-SI graph of S.
(b) Construct the late evaluation partition for S.
(c) How many visits does S require? Construct the contents of the visiting routine
or routines.

4.7. (▷www) Consider the grammar and graphs given in the previous exercise and
replace the datum that the IS-SI graph of S contains no SI arrows by the datum that
the IS-SI graph contains exactly one SI arrow, from S.s2 to S.i1. Draw the complete
IS-SI graph of S and answer the same three questions as above.

4.8. (▷789) Like all notations that try to describe repetition by using the symbol ...,
Figure 4.24 is wrong in some border cases. In fact, k can be equal to l, in which case
the line "Visit M_l for the first time;" is wrong since actually M_k is being visited for
the second time. How can k be equal to l and why cannot the two visits be combined
into one?

4.9. (▷www) Give an L-attributed grammar for *Number*, similar to the attribute
grammar of Figure 4.8.

4.10. (▷www) Consider the rule for S in Exercise 4.6. Convert it to being L-
attributed, using the technique explained in Section 4.2.3 for converting from L-
attributed to S-attributed.

4.11. Implement the effect of the *LLgen* code from Figure 4.32 in *yacc*.

4.12. (▷www) *Project*: As shown in Section 4.2.3, L-attributed grammars can be
converted by hand to S-attributed, thereby allowing stronger parsing methods in
narrow compilers. The conversion requires delayed computations of synthesized attributes to be returned instead of their values, which is very troublesome. A language
in which routines are first-class values would alleviate that problem.

Choose a language T with routines as first-class values. Design a simple language L for L-attributed grammars in which the evaluation rules are expressed in T. L-attributed grammars in L will be the input to your software. Design, and possibly write, a converter from L to a version of L in which there are no more inherited attributes. These S-attributed grammars are the output of your software, and can be processed by a T speaking version of Bison or another LALR(1) parser generator, if one exists. For hints see the Answer section.

4.13. *History of attribute grammars*: Study Knuth's 1968 paper [156], which introduces inherited attributes, and summarize its main points.

Chapter 5
Manual Context Handling

Although attribute grammars allow us to generate context processing programs automatically, their level of automation has not yet reached that of lexical analyzer and parser generators, and much context processing programming is still done at a lower level, by writing code in a traditional language like C or C++. We will give here two non-automatic methods to collect context information from the AST; one is completely manual and the other uses some reusable software. Whether this collected information is then stored in the nodes (as with an attribute grammar), stored in compiler tables, or consumed immediately is immaterial here: since it is all handy-work, it is up to the compiler writer to decide where to put the information.

The two methods are "symbolic interpretation" and "data-flow equations". Both start from the AST as produced by the syntax analysis, possibly already annotated to a certain extent, but both require more flow-of-control information than the AST holds initially. In particular, we need to know for each node its possible flow-of-control successor or successors. Although it is in principle possible to determine these successors while collecting and checking the context information, it is much more convenient to have the flow-of-control available in each node in the form of successor pointers. These pointers link the nodes in the AST together in an additional data structure, the "control-flow graph".

5.1 Threading the AST

The **control-flow graph** can be constructed statically by **threading** the tree, as follows. A threading routine exists for each node type; the threading routine for a node type T gets a pointer to the node N to be processed as a parameter, determines which production rule of N describes the node, and calls the threading routines of its children, in a recursive traversal of the AST. The set of routines maintains a global variable *LastNodePointer*, which points to the last node processed on the control-flow path, the dynamically last node. When a new node N on the control path is met during the recursive traversal, its address is stored in *LastNodePointer.successor* and *LastNodePointer* is made to point to N.

Using this technique, the threading routine for a binary expression could, for example, have the following form:

```
procedure ThreadBinaryExpression (ExprNodePointer):
    ThreadExpression (ExprNodePointer.left operand);
    ThreadExpression (ExprNodePointer.right operand);

    — link this node to the dynamically last node:
    LastNodePointer.successor ← ExprNodePointer;
    — make this node the new dynamically last node:
    LastNodePointer ← ExprNodePointer;
```

This makes the present node the successor of the last node of the right operand and then registers it as the next dynamically last node.

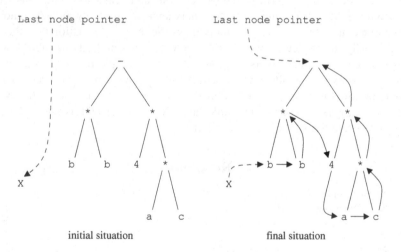

Fig. 5.1: Control flow graph for the expression b*b – 4*a*c

Figure 5.1 shows the threading of the AST for the expression b*b – 4*a*c; the pointers that make up the AST are shown as solid lines and the control-flow graph is shown using arrows. Initially *LastNodePointer* points to some node, say X. Next the threading process enters the AST at the top – node and recurses downwards to the leftmost b node N_b. Here a pointer to N_b is stored in *X.successor* and *LastNodePointer* is made to point to N_b. The process continues depth-first over the entire AST until it ends at the top – node, where *LastNodePointer* is set to that node. So statically the – node is the first node, but dynamically, at run time, the leftmost b is the first node.

Threading code in C for the demo compiler from Section 1.2 is shown in Figure 5.2. The threading code for a node representing a digit is trivial, that for a binary expression node derives directly from the code for *ThreadBinaryExpression* given above. Since there is no first dynamically last node, a dummy node is used to play that role temporarily. At the end of the threading, the thread is terminated properly; its start is retrieved from the dummy node and stored in the global variable Thread_start, to be used by a subsequent interpreter or code generator.

```
#include    "parser.h"      /* for types AST_node and Expression */
#include    "thread.h"      /* for self check */
                                            /* PRIVATE */
static AST_node *Last_node;

static void Thread_expression(Expression *expr) {
    switch (expr->type) {
    case 'D':
        Last_node->successor = expr; Last_node = expr;
        break;
    case 'P':
        Thread_expression(expr->left);
        Thread_expression(expr->right);
        Last_node->successor = expr; Last_node = expr;
        break;
    }
}
                                            /* PUBLIC */
AST_node *Thread_start;

void Thread_AST(AST_node *icode) {
    AST_node Dummy_node;

    Last_node = &Dummy_node; Thread_expression(icode);
    Last_node->successor = (AST_node *)0;
    Thread_start = Dummy_node.successor;
}
```

Fig. 5.2: Threading code for the demo compiler from Section 1.2

There are complications if the flow of control exits in more than one place from the tree below a node. For example, with the if-statement there are two problems. The first is that the node that corresponds to the run-time then/else decision has two successors rather than one, and the second is that when we reach the node dynamically following the entire if-statement, its address must be recorded in the dynamically last nodes of both the then-part and the else-part. So a single variable *LastNodePointer* is no longer sufficient.

The first problem can only be solved by just storing two successor pointers in the if-node; this makes the if-node different from the other nodes, but in any graph that is more complicated than a linked list, some node will have to store more than one pointer. One way to solve the second problem is to replace *LastNodePointer* by a set of last nodes, each of which will be filled in when the dynamically next node in the control-flow path is found. But it is often more convenient to construct a special join node to merge the diverging flow of control. Such a node is then part of the control-flow graph without being part of the AST; we will see in Section 5.2 that it can play a useful role in context checking.

The threading routine for an if-statement could then have the form shown in Figure 5.3. The if-node passed as a parameter has two successor pointers, true successor and false successor. Note that these differ from the then part and else part pointers; the part pointers point to the tops of the corresponding syntax subtrees, the successor pointers point to the dynamically first nodes in these subtrees. The code starts by threading the expression which is the condition in the if-statement; next, the if-node itself is linked in as the dynamically next node, *LastNodePointer* having been set by *ThreadExpression* to point to the dynamically last node in the expression. To prepare for processing the then- and else-parts, an End_if node is created, to be used to combine the control flows from both branches of the if-statement and to serve as a link to the node that dynamically follows the if-statement.

Since the if-node does not have a single *successor* field, it cannot be used as a last node, so we use a local auxiliary node *AuxLastNode* to catch the pointers to the dynamically first nodes in the then- and else-parts. The call of *ThreadBlock(IfNode.thenPart)* will put the pointer to its dynamically first node in *AuxLastNode*, from where it is picked up and assigned to *IfNode.trueSuccessor* by the next statement. Finally, the end of the then-part will have the end-if-join node set as its successor.

Given the AST from Figure 5.4, the routine will thread it as shown in Figure 5.5. Note that the *LastNodePointer* pointer has been moved to point to the end-if-join node.

Threading the AST can also be expressed by means of an attribute grammar. The successor pointers are then implemented as inherited attributes. Moreover, each node has an additional synthesized attribute that is set by the evaluation rules to the pointer to the first node to be executed in the tree.

The threading rules for an if-statement are given in Figure 5.6. In this example we assume that there is a special node type *Condition* (as suggested by the grammar), the semantics of which is to evaluate the Boolean expression and to direct the flow of control to true successor or false successor, as the case may be.

It is often useful to implement the control-flow graph as a doubly-linked graph, a graph in which each link consists of a pointer pair: one from the node to the successor and one from the successor to the node. This way, each node contains a set

procedure ThreadIfStatement (IfNodePointer):
    ThreadExpression (IfNodePointer.condition);
    LastNodePointer.successor ← IfNodePointer;

    EndIfJoinNode ← GenerateJoinNode ();

    LastNodePointer ← address of a local node AuxLastNode;
    ThreadBlock (IfNodePointer.thenPart);
    IfNodePointer.trueSuccessor ← AuxLastNode.successor;
    LastNodePointer.successor ← address of EndIfJoinNode;

    LastNodePointer ← address of AuxLastNode;
    ThreadBlock (IfNodePointer.elsePart);
    IfNodePointer.falseSuccessor ← AuxLastNode.successor;
    LastNodePointer.successor ← address of EndIfJoinNode;

    LastNodePointer ← address of EndIfJoinNode;

Fig. 5.3: Sample threading routine for if-statements

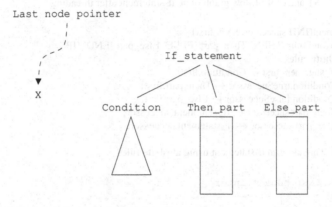

Fig. 5.4: AST of an if-statement before threading

of pointers to its dynamic successor(s) and a set of pointers to its dynamic predecessor(s). This arrangement gives the algorithms working on the control graph great freedom of movement, which will prove especially useful when processing dataflow equations. The doubly-linked control-flow graph of an if-statement is shown in Figure 5.7.

No threading is possible in a narrow compiler, for the simple reason that there is no AST to thread. Correspondingly less context handling can be done than in a broad compiler. Still, since parsing of programs in imperative languages tends to follow the flow of control, some checking can be done. Also, context handling that cannot be avoided, for example strong type checking, is usually based on information collected in the symbol table.

Now that we have seen means to construct the complete control-flow graph of a program, we are in a position to discuss two manual methods of context handling:

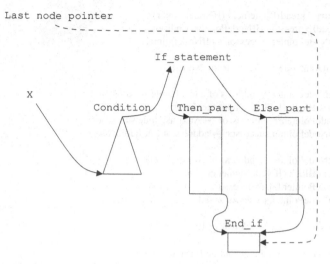

Fig. 5.5: AST and control-flow graph of an if-statement after threading

If_statement(**INH** successor, **SYN** first) →
    'IF' Condition 'THEN' Then_part 'ELSE' Else_part 'END' 'IF'
    attribute rules:
        If_statement.first ← Condition.first;
        Condition.trueSuccessor ← Then_part.first;
        Condition.falseSuccessor ← Else_part.first;
        Then_part.successor ← If_statement.successor;
        Else_part.successor ← If_statement.successor;

Fig. 5.6: Threading an if-statement using attribute rules

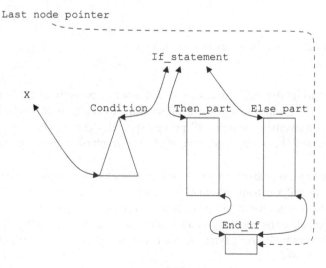

Fig. 5.7: AST and doubly-linked control-flow graph of an if-statement

symbolic interpretation, which tries to mimic the behavior of the program at run time in order to collect context information, and *data-flow equations*, which is a semi-automated restricted form of symbolic interpretation.

As said before, the purpose of the context handling is twofold: 1. context checking, and 2. information gathering for code generation and optimization. Examples of context checks are tests to determine if routines are indeed called with the same number of parameters they are declared with, and if the type of the expression in an if-statement is indeed Boolean. In addition they may include heuristic tests, for example for detecting the use of an uninitialized variable, if that is not disallowed by the language specification, or the occurrence of an infinite loop. Examples of information gathered for code generation and optimization are determining if a + operator works on integer or floating point values, and finding out that a variable is actually a constant, that a given routine is always called with the same second parameter, or that a code segment is unreachable and can never be executed.

5.2 Symbolic interpretation

When a program is executed, the control follows one possible path through the control-flow graph. The code executed at the nodes is not the rules code of the attribute grammar, which represents (compile-time) context relations, but code that represents the (run-time) semantics of the node. For example, the attribute evaluation code in the if-statement in Figure 5.6 is mainly concerned with updating the AST and with passing around information about the if-statement. At run time, however, the code executed by an if-statement node is the simple jump to the then- or else-part depending on a condition bit computed just before.

The run-time behavior of the code at each node is determined by the values of the variables it finds at run time upon entering the code, and the behavior determines these values again upon leaving the code. Much contextual information about variables can be deduced statically by simulating this run-time process at compile time in a technique called **symbolic interpretation** or **simulation on the stack**. To do so, we attach a **stack representation** to each arrow in the control-flow graph. In principle, this compile-time representation of the run-time stack holds an entry for each identifier visible at that point in the program, regardless of whether the corresponding entity will indeed be put on the stack at run time. In practice we are mostly interested in variables and constants, so most entries will concern these. The entry summarizes all compile-time information we have about the variable or the constant, at the moment that at run time the control is following the arrow in the control graph. Such information could, for example, tell whether it has been initialized or not, or even what its value is. The stack representations at the entry to a node and at its exit are connected by the semantics of that node.

Figure 5.8 shows the stack representations in the control flow graph of an if-statement similar to the one in Figure 5.5. We assume that we arrive with a stack containing two variables, x and y, and that the stack representation indicates that x is initialized and y has the value 5; so we can be certain that when the program is run and the flow of control arrives at the if-statement, x will be initialized and y will have the value 5. We also assume that the condition is y > 0. The flow of control arrives first at the node for y and leaves it with the value of y put on the stack. Next it comes to the 0, which gets stacked, and then to the operator >, which unstacks both operands and replaces them by the value true. Note that all these actions can be performed at compile time thanks to the fact that the value of y is known. Now we arrive at the if-node, which unstacks the condition and uses the value to decide that only the then-part will ever be executed; the else-part can be marked as unreachable and no code will need to be generated for it. Still, we depart for both branches, armed with the same stack representation, and we check them both, since it is usual to give compile-time error messages even for errors that occur in unreachable code.

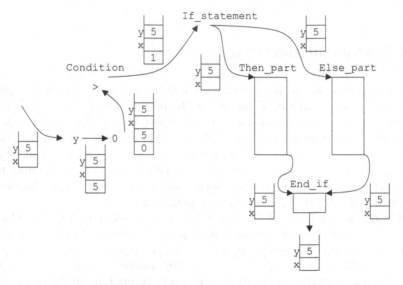

Fig. 5.8: Stack representations in the control-flow graph of an if-statement

The outline of a routine *SymbolicallyInterpretIfStatement* is given in Figure 5.9. It receives two parameters, describing the stack representation and the "if" node. First it symbolically interprets the condition. This yields a new stack representation, which holds the condition on top. The condition is unstacked, and the resulting stack representation is then used to obtain the stack representations at the ends of the then- and the else-parts. Finally the routine merges these stack representations and yields the resulting stack representation.

The actual code will contain more details. For example, it will have to check for the presence of the else-part, since the original if-statement may have been if-then only. Also, depending on how the stack representation is implemented it may need to be copied to pass one copy to each branch of the if-statement.

```
function SymbolicallyInterpretIfStatement (
    StackRepresentation, IfNode
) returning a stack representation:
    NewStackRepresentation ←
        SymbolicallyInterpretCondition (
            StackRepresentation, IfNode.condition
        );
    DiscardTopEntryFrom (NewStackRepresentation);
    return MergeStackRepresentations (
        SymbolicallyInterpretStatementSequence (
            NewStackRepresentation, IfNode.thenPart
        ),
        SymbolicallyInterpretStatementSequence (
            NewStackRepresentation, IfNode.elsePart
        )
    );
```

Fig. 5.9: Outline of a routine *SymbolicallyInterpretIfStatement*

It will be clear that many properties can be propagated in this way through the control-flow graph, and that the information obtained can be very useful both for doing context checks and for doing optimizations. In fact, this is how some implementations of the C context checking program *lint* work.

Symbolic interpretation in one form or another was already used in the 1960s (for example, Naur [199] used symbolic interpretation to do type checking in AL-GOL 60) but was not described in the mainstream literature until the mid-1970s [153]; it was just one of those things one did.

We will now consider the check for uninitialized variables in more detail, using two variants of symbolic interpretation. The first, simple symbolic interpretation, works in one scan from routine entrance to routine exit and applies to structured programs and specific properties only; a program is structured when it consists of flow-of-control structures with one entry point and one exit point only. The second variant, full symbolic interpretation, works in the presence of any kind of flow of control and for a wider range of properties.

The fundamental difference between the two is that simple symbolic interpretation follows the AST closely: for each node it analyzes its children once, in the order in which they occur in the syntax, and the stack representations are processed as L-attributes. This restricts the method to structured programs only, and to simple properties, but allows it to be applied in a narrow compiler. Full symbolic interpretation, on the other hand, follows the threading of the AST as computed in Section 5.1. This obviously requires the entire AST and since the threading of the AST may and usually will contain cycles, a closure algorithm is needed to compute the full required information. In short, the difference between full and simple symbolic interpretation is same as that between general attribute grammars and L-attributed grammars.

5.2.1 Simple symbolic interpretation

To check for the use of uninitialized variables using **simple symbolic interpretation**, we make a compile-time representation of the local stack of a routine (and possibly of its parameter stack) and follow this representation through the entire routine. Such a representation can be implemented conveniently as a linked list of names and properties pairs, a "property list".

The list starts off as empty, or, if there are parameters, as initialized with the parameters with their properties: Initialized for IN and INOUT parameters and Uninitialized for OUT parameters. We also maintain a **return list**, in which we combine the stack representations as found at return statements and routine exit.

We then follow the arrows in the control-flow graph, all the while updating our list. The precise actions required at each node type depend of course on the semantics of the source language, but are usually fairly obvious. We will therefore indicate them only briefly here.

When a declaration is met, the declared name is added to the list, with the appropriate status: Initialized if there was an initialization in the declaration, and Uninitialized otherwise.

When the flow of control splits, for example in an if-statement node, a copy is made of the original list; one copy is followed on its route through the then-part, the other through the else-part; and at the end-if node the two lists are merged. Merging is trivial except when a variable obtained a value in one branch but not in the other. In that case the status of the variable is set to MayBeInitialized. The status MayBeInitialized is equal to Uninitialized for most purposes since one cannot rely on the value being present at run time, but a different error message can be given for its use. Note that the status should actually be called MayBeInitializedAndAlsoMayNotBeInitialized. The same technique applies to case statements.

When an assignment is met, the status of the destination variable is set to Initialized, after processing the source expression first, since it may contain the same variable.

When the value of a variable is used, usually in an expression, its status is checked, and if it is not Initialized, a message is given: an error message if the status is Uninitialized, since the error is certain to happen when the code is executed and a warning for MayBeInitialized, since the code may actually still be all right. An example of C code with this property is

```
/* y is  still  uninitialized here */
if (x >= 0) {y = 0;}
if (x > 0) {z = y ;}
```

Here the status of y after the first statement is MayBeInitialized. This causes a warning concerning the use of y in the second statement, but the error cannot materialize, since the controlled part of the second statement will only be executed if x > 0. In that case the controlled part of the first statement will also have been executed, initializing y.

When we meet a node describing a routine call, we need not do anything at all in principle: we are considering information on the run-time stack only, and the called routine cannot touch our run-time stack. If, however, the routine has IN and/or IN-OUT parameters, these have to be treated as if they were used in an expression, and any INOUT and OUT parameters have to be treated as destinations in an assignment.

When we meet a for-statement, we pass through the computations of the bounds and the initialization of the controlled variable. We then make a copy of the list, which we call the **loop-exit list**. This list collects the information in force at the exit of the loop. We pass the original list through the body of the for-statement, and combine the result with the loop-exit list, as shown in Figure 5.10. The combination with the loop-exit list represents the possibility that the loop body was executed zero times. Note that we ignore here the back jump to the beginning of the for-statement—the possibility that the loop body was executed more than once. We will see below why this is allowed.

When we find an exit-loop statement inside a loop, we merge the list we have collected at that moment into the loop-exit list. We then continue with the empty list. When we find an exit-loop statement outside any loop, we give an error message.

When we find a return statement, we merge the present list into the return list, and continue with the empty list. We do the same when we reach the end of the routine, since a return statement is implied there. When all stack representations have been computed, we check the return list to see if all OUT parameters have obtained a value, and give an error message if they have not.

Finally, when we reach the end node of the routine, we check all variable identifiers in the list. If one has the status Uninitialized, it was never initialized, and a warning can be given.

The above technique can be refined in many ways. Bounds in for-statements are often constants, either literal or named. If so, their values will often prove that the loop will be performed at least once. In that case the original list should not be merged into the exit list, to avoid inappropriate messages. The same applies to the well-known C idioms for infinite loops:

```
for (;;) ...
while (1) ...
```

Once we have a system of symbolic interpretation in place in our compiler, we can easily extend it to fit special requirements of and possibilities offered by the source language. One possibility is to do similar accounting to see if a variable, constant, field selector, etc. is used at all. A second possibility is to replace the status Initialized by the value, the range, or even the set of values the variable may hold, a technique called **constant propagation**. This information can be used for at least two purposes: to identify variables that are actually used as constants in languages that do not have constant declarations, and to get a tighter grip on the tests in for- and while-loops. Both may improve the code that can be generated. Yet another, more substantial, possibility is to do last-def analysis, as discussed in Section 5.2.3.

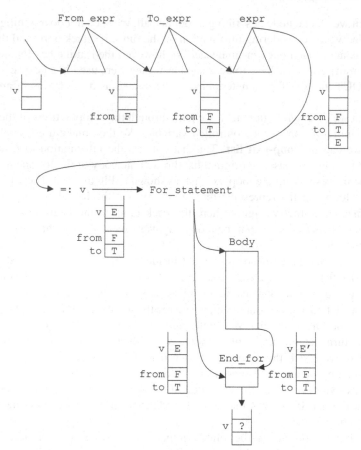

Fig. 5.10: Stack representations in the control-flow graph of a for-statement

When we try to implement constant propagation using the above technique, however, we run into problems. Consider the segment of a C program in Figure 5.11.
Applying the above simple symbolic interpretation technique yields that i has the
value 0 at the if-statement, so the test i > 0 can be evaluated at compile time and
yields 0 (false). Consequently, an optimizer might conclude that the body of the if-
statement, the call to printf(), can be removed since it will not be executed. This is
patently wrong.

It is therefore interesting to examine the situations in which, and the kind of
properties for which, simple symbolic interpretation as explained above will work.
Basically, there are four requirements for simple symbolic interpretation to work;
motivation for these requirements will be given below.

1. The program must consist of flow-of-control structures with one entry point and
   one exit point only.

```
    int  i = 0;

    while (some condition) {
        if  (i > 0)  printf ("Loop reentered: i = %d\n", i );
        i++;
    }
```

Fig. 5.11: Value set analysis in the presence of a loop statement

2. The values of the property must form a lattice, which means that the values can
   be ordered in a sequence $v_1..v_n$ such that there is no operation that will transform
   v_j into v_i with $i < j$; we will write $v_i < v_j$ for all $i < j$.
3. The result of merging two values must be at least as large as the smaller of the
   two.
4. An action taken on v_i in a given situation must make any action taken on v_j in
   that same situation superfluous, for $v_i <= v_j$.

The first requirement allows each control structure to be treated in isolation, with
the property being analyzed well-defined at the entry point of the structure and at its
exit. The other three requirements allow us to ignore the jump back to the beginning
of looping control structures, as we can see as follows. We call the value of the
property at the entrance of the loop body v_{in} and that at the exit is v_{out}. Requirement
2 guarantees that $v_{in} <= v_{out}$. Requirement 3 guarantees that when we merge the
v_{out} from the end of the first round through the loop back into v_{in} to obtain a value
v_{new} at the start of a second round, then $v_{new} >= v_{in}$. If we were now to scan the loop
body for the second time, we would undertake actions based on v_{new}. But it follows
from requirement 4 that all these actions are superfluous because of the actions
already performed during the first round, since $v_{new} >= v_{in}$. So there is no point in
performing a second scan through the loop body, nor is there a need to consider the
jump back to the beginning of the loop construct.

The initialization property with values v_1 = Uninitialized, v_2 = MayBeInitialized,
and v_3 = Initialized fulfills these requirements, since the initialization status can only
progress from left to right over these values and the actions on Uninitialized (error
messages) render those on MayBeInitialized superfluous (warning messages), which
again supersede those on Initialized (none).

If these four requirements are not fulfilled, it is necessary to perform full symbolic interpretation, which avoids the above short-cuts. We will now discuss this
technique, using the presence of jumps as an example.

5.2.2 Full symbolic interpretation

Goto statements cannot be handled by simple symbolic interpretation, since they
violate requirement 1 in the previous section. To handle goto statements, we need
full symbolic interpretation. Full symbolic interpretation consists of performing the

simple symbolic interpretation algorithm repeatedly until no more changes in the values of the properties occur, in closure algorithm fashion. We will now consider the details of our example.

We need an additional separate list for each label in the routine; these lists start off empty. We perform the simple symbolic interpretation algorithm as usual, taking into account the special actions needed at jumps and labels. Each time we meet a jump to a label L, we merge our present list into L's list and continue with the empty list. When we meet the label L itself, we merge in our present list, and continue with the merged list. This assembles in the list for L the merger of the situations at all positions from where L can be reached; this is what we can count on in terms of statuses of variables at label L—but not quite!

If we first meet the label L and then a jump to it, the list at L was not complete, since it may be going to be modified by that jump. So when we are at the end of the routine, we have to run the simple symbolic interpretation algorithm again, using the lists we have already assembled for the labels. We have to repeat this, until nothing changes any more. Only then can we be certain that we have found all paths by which a variable can be uninitialized at a given label.

Data definitions:
   Stack representations, with entries for every item we are interested in.

Initializations:
   1. Empty stack representations are attached to all arrows in the control flow graph residing in the threaded AST.
   2. Some stack representations at strategic points are initialized in accordance with properties of the source language; for example, the stack representations of input parameters are initialized to Initialized.

Inference rules:
   For each node type, source language dependent rules allow inferences to be made, adding information to the stack representation on the outgoing arrows based on those on the incoming arrows and the node itself, and vice versa.

Fig. 5.12: Full symbolic interpretation as a closure algorithm

---

There are several things to note here. The first is that full symbolic interpretation is a closure algorithm, an outline of which is shown in Figure 5.12; actually it is a family of closure algorithms, the details of which depend on the node types, source language rules, etc. Note that the inference rules allow information to be inferred backwards, from outgoing arrow to incoming arrow; an example is "there is no function call on any path from here to the end of the routine." Implemented naively, such inference rules lead to considerable inefficiency, and the situation is re-examined in Section 5.5.

The second is that in full symbolic interpretation we have to postpone the actions on the initialization status until all information has been obtained, unlike the case of simple symbolic interpretation, where requirement 4 allowed us to act immediately. A separate traversal at the end of the algorithm is needed to perform the actions.

Next we note that the simple symbolic interpretation algorithm without jumps can be run in one scan, simultaneously with the rest of the processing in a narrow compiler and that the full algorithm *with* the jumps cannot: the tree for the routine has to be visited repeatedly. So, checking initialization in the presence of jumps is fundamentally more difficult than in their absence.

But the most important thing to note is that although full symbolic interpretation removes almost all the requirements listed in the previous section, it does not solve all problems. We want the algorithm to terminate, but it is not at all certain it does. When trying naively to establish the set of values possible for i in Figure 5.11, we first find the set { 0 }. The statement i++ then turns this into the set { 0, 1 }. Merging this with the { 0 } at the loop entrance yields { 0, 1 }. The statement i++ now turns this into the set { 0, 1, 2 }, and so on, and the process never terminates.

The formal requirements to be imposed on the property examined have been analyzed by Wegbreit [293]; the precise requirements are fairly complicated, but in practice it is usually not difficult to see if a certain property can be determined. It is evident that the property "the complete set of possible values" of a variable cannot be determined at compile time in all cases. A good approximation is "a set of at most two values, or any value". The set of two values allows a source language variable that is used as a Boolean to be recognized in a language that does not feature Booleans. If we use this property in the analysis of the code in Figure 5.11, we find successively the property values { 0 }, { 0, 1 }, and "any value" for i. This last property value does not change any more, and the process terminates.

Symbolic interpretation need not be restricted to intermediate code: Regehr and Reid [231] show how to apply symbolic interpretation to object code of which the source code is not available, for a variety of purposes. We quote the following actions from their paper: analyzing worst-case execution time; showing type safety; inserting dynamic safety checks; obfuscating the program; optimizing the code; analyzing worst-case stack depth; validating the compiler output; finding viruses; and decompiling the program.

A sophisticated treatment of generalized constant propagation, both intraprocedural and interprocedural, is given by Verbrugge, Co and Hendren [287], with special attention to convergence. See Exercise 5.9 for an analysis of constant propagation by symbolic interpretation and by data-flow equations.

5.2.3 Last-def analysis

Last-def analysis attaches to each use of a variable V pointers to all the places where the present value of V could have come from; these are the last places where the value of V has been defined before arriving at this use of V along any path in the control-flow graph. Hence the term "last def", short for "last definition". It is also called **reaching-definitions analysis**. The word "definition" is used here rather than "assignment" because there are other language constructs besides assignments that cause the value of a variable to be changed: a variable can be passed as an OUT parameter to a routine, it can occur in a read statement in some languages, its address can have been taken, turned into a pointer and a definition of the value under that or a similar pointer can take place, etc. All these rank as "definitions".

A definition of a variable V in a node n is said to reach a node p where V is used, if there is a path through the control-flow graph on which the value of V is not redefined. This explains the name "reaching definitions analysis": the definitions reaching each node are determined.

Last-def information is useful for code generation, in particular for register allocation. The information can be obtained by full symbolic interpretation, as follows. A set of last defs is kept for each variable V in the stack representation. If an assignment to V is encountered at a node n, the set is replaced by the singleton $\{n\}$; if two stack representations are merged, for example in an end-if node, the union of the sets is formed, and propagated as the new last-def information of V. Similar rules apply for loops and other flow-of-control constructs.

Full symbolic interpretation is required since last-def information violates requirement 4 above: going through a loop body for the first time, we may not have seen all last-defs yet, since an assignment to a variable V at the end of a loop body may be part of the last-def set in the use of V at the beginning of the loop body, and actions taken on insufficient information do not make later actions superfluous.

5.3 Data-flow equations

Data-flow equations are a half-way automation of full symbolic interpretation, in which the stack representation is replaced by a collection of sets, the semantics of a node is described more formally, and the interpretation is replaced by a built-in and fixed propagation mechanism.

Two set variables are associated with each node N in the control-flow graph, the input set $IN(N)$ and the output set $OUT(N)$. Together they replace the stack representations; both start off empty and are computed by the propagation mechanism. For each node N two constant sets $GEN(N)$ and $KILL(N)$ are defined, which describe the semantics of the node. Their contents are derived from the information in the node. The IN and OUT sets contain static information about the run-time situation at the node; examples are "Variable x is equal to 1 here", "There has not been a remote procedure call in any path from the routine entry to here", "Definitions for the variable y reach here from nodes N_1 and N_2", and "Global variable line_count has been modified since routine entry". We see that the sets can contain any information that the stack representations in symbolic interpretation can contain, and other pieces of information as well.

Since the interpretation mechanism is missing in the data-flow approach, nodes whose semantics modify the stack size are not handled easily in setting up the data-flow equations. Prime examples are the nodes occurring in expressions: a node + will remove two entries from the stack and then push one entry onto it. There is no reasonable way to express this in the data-flow equations. The practical solution to this problem is to combine groups of control flow nodes into single data-flow nodes, such that the data-flow nodes have no net stack effect. The most obvious example is the assignment, which consists of a control-flow graph resulting from the source expression, a variable node representing the destination, and the assignment node itself. For data-flow equations this entire set of control-flow nodes is considered a single node, with one *IN*, *OUT*, *GEN*, and *KILL* set. Figure 5.13(a) shows the control-flow graph of the assignment x := y + 3; Figure 5.13(b) shows the assignment as a single node.

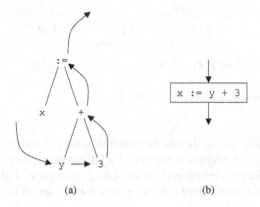

(a)   (b)

Fig. 5.13: An assignment as a full control-flow graph and as a single node

Traditionally, *IN* and *OUT* sets are defined only at the beginnings and ends of basic blocks, and data-flow equations are used only to connect the output conditions of basic blocks to the input conditions of other basic blocks. (A basic block is a sequence of assignments with the flow of control entering at the beginning of the first assignment and leaving the end of the last assignment; basic blocks are treated more extensively in Section 9.1.2.) In this approach, a different mechanism is used to combine the information about the assignments inside the basic block, and since that mechanism has to deal with assignments only, it can be simpler than general data-flow equations. Any such mechanism is, however, a simplification of or equivalent to the data-flow equation mechanism, and any combination of information about the assignments can be expressed in *IN*, *OUT*, *GEN*, and *KILL* sets. We will therefore use the more general approach here and consider the AST node rather than the basic block as the unit of data-flow information specification.

5.3.1 Setting up the data-flow equations

When control passes through node N at run time, the state of the program is probably changed. This change corresponds at compile time to the removal of some information items from the set at N and the addition of some other items. It is convenient to keep these two sets separated. The set $KILL(N)$ contains the items removed by the node N and the set $GEN(N)$ contains the items added by the node. A typical example of an information item in a GEN set is "Variable x is equal to variable y here" for the assignment node x:=y. The same node has the item "Variable x is equal to any value here" in its $KILL$ set, which is actually a finite representation of an infinite set of items. How such items are used will be shown in the next paragraph.

The actual data-flow equations are the same for all nodes and are shown in Figure 5.14.

$$IN(N) \;=\; \bigcup_{M=\text{dynamic predecessor of } N} OUT(M)$$

$$OUT(N) \;=\; (IN(N) \setminus KILL(N)) \cup GEN(N)$$

Fig. 5.14: Data-flow equations for a node N

The first equation tells us that the information at the entrance to a node N is equal to the union of the information at the exit of all dynamic predecessors of N. This is obviously true, since no information is lost going from the end of a predecessor of a node to that node itself. More colorful names for this union are the **meet** or **join operator**.

The second equation means that the information at the exit of a node N is in principle equal to that at the entrance, except that all information in the $KILL$ set has been removed from it and all information from the GEN set has been added to it. The order of removing and adding is important: first the information being invalidated must be removed, then the new information must be added.

Suppose, for example, we arrive at a node x:=y with the IN set { "Variable x is equal to 0 here" }. The $KILL$ set of the node contains the item "Variable x is equal to any value here", the GEN set contains "Variable x is equal to y here". First, all items in the IN set that are also in the $KILL$ set are erased. The item "Variable x is equal to any value here" represents an infinite number of items, including "Variable x is equal to 0 here", so this item is erased. Next, the items from the GEN set are added; there is only one item there, "Variable x is equal to y here". So the OUT set is { "Variable x is equal to y here" }.

The data-flow equations from Figure 5.14 seem to imply that the sets are just normal sets and that the $\cup$ symbol and the $\setminus$ symbol represent the usual set union and set difference operations, but the above explanation already suggests otherwise. Indeed the $\cup$ and $\setminus$ symbols should be read more properly as information union and information difference operators, and their exact workings depend very much on the kind of information they process. For example, if the information items are of the form "Variable V may be uninitialized here", the $\cup$ in the first data-flow equation can be interpreted as a set union, since V can be uninitialized at a given node N if it can be uninitialized at the exit of even one of N's predecessors. But if the information items say "Variable V is guaranteed to have a value here", the $\cup$ operator must be interpreted as set intersection, since for the value of V to be guaranteed at node N it must be guaranteed at the exits of *all* its predecessors. And merging information items of the type "The value of variable x lies between i and j" requires special code that has little to do with set unions. Still, it is often possible to choose the semantics of the information items so that $\cup$ can be implemented as set union and $\backslash$ as set difference, as shown below. We shall therefore stick to the traditional notation of Figure 5.14. For a more liberal interpretation see Morel [195], who incorporates the different meanings of information union and information difference in a single theory, extends it to global optimization, and applies it to suppress some run-time checks in Ada.

There is a third data-flow equation in addition to the two shown in Figure 5.14— although the term "zeroth data-flow equation" would probably be more appropriate. It defines the *IN* set of the first node of the routine as the set of information items established by the parameters of the routine. More in particular, each IN and INOUT parameter gives rise to an item "Parameter P_i has a value here". It is convenient to add control-flow arrows from all return statements in the routine to the end node of the routine, and to make the *OUT* sets of the return statements, which are normally empty, equal to their *IN* sets. The *KILL* set of the end node contains any item concerned with variables local to the routine. This way the routine has one entry point and one exit point, and all information valid at routine exit is collected in the *OUT* set of the end node; see Figure 5.15.

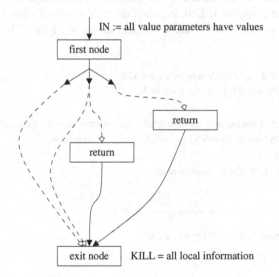

Fig. 5.15: Data-flow details at routine entry and exit

This streamlining of the external aspects of the data flow of a routine is helpful in interprocedural data-flow analysis, as we will see below.

The combining, sifting, and adding of information items described above may look cumbersome, but techniques exist to create very efficient implementations. In practice, most of the information items are Boolean in nature: "Variable x has been given a value here" is an example. Such items can be stored in one bit each, packed efficiently in machine words, and manipulated using Boolean instructions. This approach leads to an extremely efficient implementation, an example of which we will see below.

More complicated items are manipulated using ad-hoc code. If it is, for example, decided that information items of the type "Variable x has a value in the range M to N here" are required, data representations for such items in the sets and for the ranges they refer to must be designed, and data-flow code must be written that knows how to create, merge, and examine such ranges. So, usually the IN, OUT, $KILL$, and GEN sets contain bit sets that are manipulated by Boolean machine instructions, and, in addition to these, perhaps some ad-hoc items that are manipulated by ad-hoc code.

5.3.2 Solving the data-flow equations

The first data-flow equation tells us how to obtain the IN set of all nodes when we know the OUT sets of all nodes, and the second data-flow equation tells us how to obtain the OUT set of a node if we know its IN set (and its GEN and $KILL$ sets, but they are constants). This suggests the almost trivial closure algorithm for establishing the values of all IN and OUT sets shown in Figure 5.16.

Data definitions:
    1. Constant $KILL$ and GEN sets for each node.
    2. Variable IN and OUT sets for each node.

Initializations:
    1. The IN set of the top node is initialized with information established externally.
    2. For all other nodes N, $IN(N)$ and $OUT(N)$ are set to empty.

Inference rules:
    1. For any node N, $IN(N)$ must contain

$$\bigcup_{M=\text{dynamic predecessor of } N} OUT(M)$$

    2. For any node N, $OUT(N)$ must contain

$$(IN(N) \setminus KILL(N)) \cup GEN(N)$$

Fig. 5.16: Closure algorithm for solving the data-flow equations

The closure algorithm can be implemented by traversing the control graph repeatedly and computing the IN and OUT sets of the nodes visited. Once we have performed a complete traversal of the control-flow graph in which no *IN* or *OUT* set changed, we have found the solution to the set of equations. We then know the values of the *IN* sets of all nodes and can use this information for context checking and code generation. Note that the predecessors of a node are easy to find if the control graph is doubly-linked, as described in Section 5.1 and shown in Figure 5.7.

Figures 5.17 through Figure 5.19 show data-flow propagation through an if-statement, using bit patterns to represent the information. The meanings of the bits shown in Figure 5.17 have been chosen so that the information union in the data-flow equations can be implemented as a Boolean OR, and the information difference as a set difference; the set difference is in turn implemented as a Boolean AND NOT. The initialization status of a variable is coded in two bits; the first means "may be uninitialized", the second means "may be initialized".

Figure 5.18 gives examples of their application. For example, if the first bit is on and the second is off, the possibility of being uninitialized is left open but the possibility of being initialized is excluded; so the variable is guaranteed to be unini-tialized. This corresponds to the status Uninitialized in Section 5.2.1. Note that the negation of "may be initialized" is not "may be uninitialized" nor "may not be initialized"—it is "cannot be initialized"; trivalent logic is not easily expressed in natural language. If both bits are on, both possibilities are present; this corresponds to the status MayBeInitialized in Section 5.2.1. Both bits cannot be off at the same time: it cannot be that it is impossible for the variable to be uninitialized and also impossible to be initialized at the same time; or put more simply, there is no fourth possibility in trivalent logic.

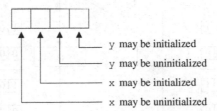

Fig. 5.17: Bit patterns for properties of the variables x and y

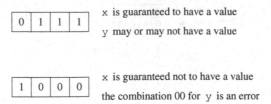

Fig. 5.18: Examples of bit patterns for properties of the variables x and y

Figure 5.19 shows how the bits and the information they carry are propagated through both branches of the if-statement

if y > 0 **then** x := y **else** y := 0 **end if** ;

Admittedly it is hard to think of a program in which this statement would occur, since it does not have any reasonable effect, but examples that are both illustrative and reasonable are much larger. We assume that x is uninitialized at the entry to this statement and that y is initialized. So the bit pattern at entry is 1001. Since the decision node does not affect either variable, this pattern is still the same at the exit. When the first data-flow equation is used to construct the *IN* set of x:=y, it combines the sets from all the predecessors of this node, of which there is only one, the decision node. So the *IN* set of x:=y is again 1001. Its *KILL* and *GEN* sets reflect the fact that the node represents an assignment to x; it also uses y, but that usage does not affect the bits for y. So its *KILL* set is 1000, which tells us to remove the possibility that x is uninitialized, and does not affect y; and its *GEN* set is 0100, which tells us to add the possibility that x is initialized. Using the second data-flow equation, they yield the new *OUT* set of the node, 0101, in which both x and y are guaranteed to be initialized.

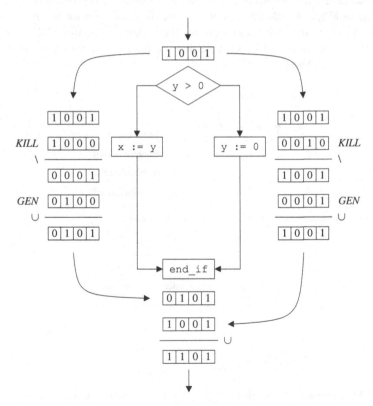

Fig. 5.19: Data-flow propagation through an if-statement

Similar but slightly different things happen in the right branch, since there the assignment is to y. The first data-flow equation for the end-if node requires us to combine the bit patterns at all its predecessors. The final result is the bit pattern 1101, which says that x may or may not be initialized and that y is initialized.

The above description assumes that we visit all the nodes by traversing the control-flow graph, much in the same way as we did in symbolic interpretation, but it is important to note that this is in no way necessary and is useful for efficiency only. Since all actions are purely local, we can visit the nodes in any permutation we like, as long as we stick to the rule that we repeat our visits until nothing changes any more. Still, since the data-flow equations transport information in the direction of the control flow, it is convenient to follow the latter.

Note that the data-flow algorithm in itself collects information only. It does no checking and gives no error messages or warnings. A subsequent traversal, or more likely several subsequent traversals are needed to utilize the information. One such traversal can check for the use of uninitialized variables. Suppose the if-statement in Figure 5.19 is followed by a node z:=x; the traversal visiting this node will then find the *IN* set to be the bit pattern 1101, the first two bits of which mean that x may or may not be initialized. Since the node uses the value of x, a message saying something like "Variable x may not have a value in assignment z:=x" can be issued.

5.4 Interprocedural data-flow analysis

Interprocedural data flow is the data flow between routines, as opposed to that inside routines. Such data flows in two directions, from the caller to the callee in a routine call, and from callee to caller in a return statement. The resulting information seldom serves context checking and is mostly useful for optimization purposes.

Symbolic interpretation can handle both kinds of information. One can collect information about the parameters of all calls to a given routine *R* by extracting it from the stack representations at the calls. This information can then be used to set the stack representations of the IN and INOUT parameters of *R*, and carried into the routine by symbolic interpretation of *R*. A useful piece of information uncovered by combining the stack representations at all calls to *R* could, for example, be that its second parameter always has the value 0. It is almost certain that this information can be used in the symbolic interpretation of *R*, to simplify the code generated for *R*. In fact, *R* can be instantiated for the case that its second parameter is 0.

Now one might wonder why a programmer would endow a routine with a parameter and then always supply the same value for it, and whether it is reasonable for the compiler writer to spend effort to detect such cases. Actually, there are two good reasons why such a situation might arise. First, the routine may have been written for a more general application and be reused in the present source code in a more restricted context. Second, the routine may have served abstraction only and is called only once.

About the only information that can be passed backwards from the called routine to the caller by symbolic interpretation is that an INOUT or OUT parameter is always set to a given value, but this is less probable.

The same techniques can be applied when processing data-flow equations. Routines usually have a unique entry node, and the set-up shown in Figure 5.15 provides each routine with a unique exit node. Collected information from the *IN* sets of all calls can be entered as the *IN* set of the entry node, and the *OUT* set of the exit node can be returned as the *OUT* set of the calls.

Information about global variables is especially interesting in this case. If, for example, an information item "No global variable has been read or written" is entered in the *IN* set of the entry node of a routine R and it survives until its exit node, we seem to have shown that R has no side effects and that its result depends exclusively on its parameters. But our conclusion is only correct if the same analysis is also done for all routines called directly or indirectly by R and the results are fed back to R. If one of the routines does access a global variable, the information item will not show up in its *OUT* set of the exit node, and if we feed back the results to the caller and repeat this process, eventually it will disappear from the *OUT* sets of the exit nodes of all routines that directly or indirectly access a global variable.

One problem with interprocedural data-flow analysis is that we may not know which routine is being called in a given call. For example, the call may invoke a routine under a pointer, or a virtual function in an object-oriented language; the first type of call is also known as an "indirect routine call". In both cases, the call can invoke any of a set of routines, rather than one specific routine. We will call this set the "candidate set"; the smaller the candidate set, the better the quality of the data-flow analysis will be. In the case of an indirect call to a routine of type T, it is a safe approach to assume the candidate set to contain the set of all routines of type T, but often we can do better: if we can obtain a list of all routines of type T whose addresses are ever taken by the program, we can restrict the candidate set to these. The candidate set for a call to a virtual function V is the set of all functions that override V. In both cases, symbolic execution may be able to restrict the candidate set even further.

A second problem with interprocedural data-flow analysis is that it works best when we have all control-flow graphs of all routines in the entire program at our disposal; only then are we certain that we see all calls to a given routine. Having all control-flow graphs available at the same moment, however, conflicts with separate compilation of modules or packages. After all, the point in separate compilation is that only a small part of the program needs to be available. Also, the control-flow graphs of libraries are usually not available. Both problems can be solved to a certain extent by having the compiler produce files with control-flow graph information in addition to the usual compiler output. Most libraries do not contain calls to user programs, which reduces the problem, but some do: a memory allocation package might, for example, call a user routine ReportInsufficientMemory when it runs irreparably out of memory.

5.5 Carrying the information upstream—live analysis

Both symbolic interpretation and data-flow equations follow information as it flows "forward" through the control-flow graph; they collect information from the preceding nodes and can deposit it at the present node. Mathematically speaking, this statement is nonsense, since there is no concept of "forward" in a graph: one can easily run in circles. Still, control-flow graphs are a special kind of graph in that they have one specific entry node and one specific exit node; this does give them a general notion of direction.

There are some items of interest that can be determined best (or only) by following the control-flow backwards. One prominent example of such information is the liveness of variables. A variable is **live** at a given node N in the control-flow graph if the value it holds is used on at least one path further through the control-flow graph from N; otherwise it is dead. Note that we are concerned with the use of a particular *value* of V, rather than with the use of the variable V itself. As a result, a variable can have more than one live range, each starting at an assignment of a value to the variable and ending at a node at which the value is used for the last time.

During code generation it is important to know if a variable is live or dead at a given node in the code, since if it is dead, the memory allocated to it can be reused. This is especially important if the variable resides in a register, since from that given node on, the register can be used for other purposes. For another application, suppose that the variable contains a pointer and that the compiled program uses garbage collection in its memory management. It is then advantageous to generate code that assigns a null pointer to the variable as soon as it becomes dead, since this may allow the garbage collector to free the memory the original pointer pointed to.

The start of the live range of a variable V is marked by a node that contains a definition of V, where "definition" is used in the sense of defining V's value, as in Section 5.2.3. The end of the live range is marked by a node that contains the last use of the value of V, in the sense that on no path from that node will the value be used again. The problem is that this node is hard to recognize, since there is nothing special about it. We only know that a node contains the last use of the value of V if on all paths from that node we either reach the end of the scope of V or meet the start of another live range.

Information about the future use of variable values cannot be obtained in a straightforward way using the above methods of symbolic interpretation or data-flow equations. Fortunately, the methods can be modified so they can solve this and other "backward flow" problems and we will discuss these modifications in the following two sections. We demonstrate the techniques using the C code segment from Figure 5.20.

The assignments x = ... and y = ... define the values of x and y; the print statements use the values of the variables shown. Code fragments indicated by ... do not define any values and are subject to the restrictions shown in the accompanying comments. For an assignment, such a restriction applies to the source (right-hand side).

```
{   int x = 5;           /* code fragment 0, initializes  x */
    print (x);           /* code fragment 1, uses x */
    if  (...)  {
        ...              /* code fragment 2, does not use x */
        print (x);       /* code fragment 3, uses x */
        ...              /* code fragment 4, does not use x */
    } else {
        int  y;
        ...              /* code fragment 5, does not use x,y */
        print (x+3);     /* code fragment 6, uses x, but not y */
        ...              /* code fragment 7, does not use x,y */
        y = ...;         /* code fragment 8, does not use x,y */
        ...              /* code fragment 9, does not use x,y */
        print (y);       /* code fragment 10, uses y but not x */
        ...              /* code fragment 11, does not use x,y */
    }
    x = ...;             /* code fragment 12, does not use x */
    ...                  /* code fragment 13, does not use x */
    print (x*x);         /* code fragment 14, uses x */
    ...                  /* code fragment 15, does not use x */
}
```

Fig. 5.20: A segment of C code to demonstrate live analysis

5.5.1 Live analysis by symbolic interpretation

Since symbolic interpretation follows the control-flow graph, it has no way of look-ing ahead and finding out if there is another use of the value of a given variable V, and so it has no way to set some isLastUseOfV attribute of the node it is visiting. The general solution to this kind of problem is to collect the addresses of the values we cannot compute and to fill them in when we can. Such lists of addresses are called **backpatch lists** and the activity of filling in values when the time is ripe is called **backpatching**.

In this case backpatching means that for each variable V we keep in our stack representation a set of pointers to nodes that contain the latest, most recent uses of the value of V; note that when looking backwards from a node we can have more than one most recent use, provided they are along different paths. Now, when we arrive at a node that uses the value of V, we set the attributes isLastUseOfV of the nodes in the backpatch list for V to false and set the same attribute of the present node to true. The rationale is that we assume that each use is the last use, until we are proven wrong by a subsequent use.

It is in the nature of backpatching that both the pointer sets and the attributes referred to by the pointers in these sets change as the algorithm progresses. We will therefore supply a few snapshots to demonstrate the algorithm.

Part of the control-flow graph for the block from Figure 5.20 with live analysis using backpatch lists for the first few nodes is given in Figure 5.21. It shows an attribute LU_x for "Last Use of x" in node 1; this attribute has been set to true, since the node uses x and we know of no later use yet. The stack representation contains a variable BPLU_x for "Backpatch list for the Last Use of x". Initially its value is the empty set, but when the symbolic interpretation passes node 1, it is set equal to a singleton containing a pointer to node 1. For the moment we follow the true branch of the if-statement, still carrying the variable BPLU_x in our stack representation. When the symbolic interpretation reaches the node print(x) (node 3) and finds a new use of the variable x, the attribute LU_x of the node under the pointer in BPLU_x (node 1) is set to false and subsequently BPLU_x itself is set equal to the singleton {3}. The new situation is depicted in Figure 5.22.

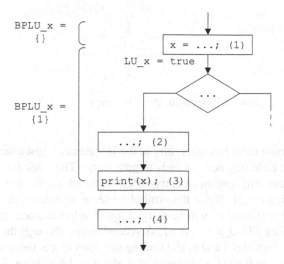

Fig. 5.21: The first few steps in live analysis for Figure 5.20 using backpatch lists

Figure 5.23 shows the situation after the symbolic interpretation has also finished the false branch of the if-statement. It has entered the false branch with a second copy of the stack representation, the first one having gone down the true branch. Passing the node print(x+3) (node 6) has caused the LU_x attribute of node 1 to be set to false for the second time. Furthermore, the LU_y attributes of nodes 8 and 10 have been set in a fashion similar to that of nodes 1, 2, and 3, using a backpatch list BPLU_y. The two stack representations merge at the end-if node, which results in BPLU_x now holding a set of two pointers, {3, 6} and in BPLU_y being removed due to leaving the scope of y. If we were now to find another use of x, the LU_x attributes of both nodes 3 and 6 would be cleared. But the next node, node 12, is an assignment to x that does not use x in the source expression. So the stack representation variable BPLU_x gets reset to {12}, and the LU_x attributes of nodes 3 and 6 remain set to true, thus signaling two last uses. The rest of the process is straightforward and is not shown.

Live analysis in the presence of jumps can be performed by the same technique as used in Section 5.2.2 for checking the use of uninitialized variables in the presence

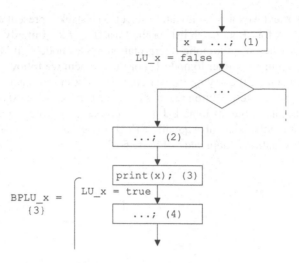

Fig. 5.22: Live analysis for Figure 5.20, after a few steps

of jumps. Suppose there is a label retry at the if-statement, just after code fragment 1, and suppose code fragment 11 ends in goto retry;. The stack representation kept for the label retry will contain an entry BPLU_x, which on the first pass will be set to {1} as in Figure 5.21. When the symbolic execution reaches the goto retry;, the value of BPLU_x at node 11 will be merged into that in the stack representation for retry, thus setting BPLU_x to {1, 6}. A second round through the algorithm will carry this value to nodes 3 and 6, and finding new uses of x at these nodes will cause the algorithm to set the LU_x attributes of nodes 1 and 6 to false. So the algorithm correctly determines that the use of x in node 6 is no longer the last use.

5.5.2 *Live analysis by data-flow equations*

Information about what happens further on in the control-flow graph can only be obtained by following the graph backwards. To this end we need a backwards-operating version of the data-flow equations, as shown in Figure 5.24.

Basically, the sets *IN* and *OUT* have changed roles and "predecessor" has changed to "successor". Note that the *KILL* information still has to be erased first, before the *GEN* information is merged in. Nodes that assign a value to *V* have *KILL* = { "*V* is live here" } and an empty *GEN* set, and nodes that use the value of *V* have an empty *KILL* set and a *GEN* set { "*V* is live here" }.

The control-flow graph for the block from Figure 5.20 with live analysis using backward data-flow equations is given in Figure 5.25. We implement the *OUT* and *IN* sets as two bits, the first one meaning "x is live here" and the second meaning "y is live here". To get a uniform representation of the information sets, we maintain a

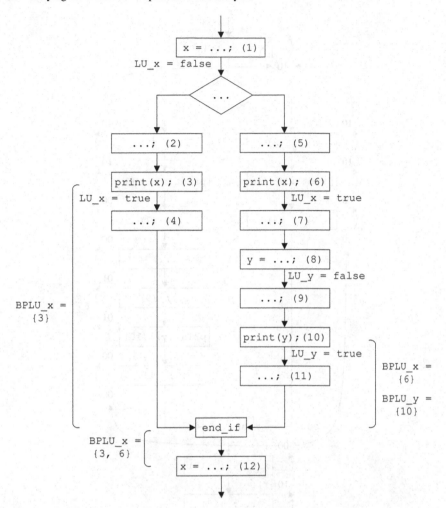

Fig. 5.23: Live analysis for Figure 5.20, merging at the end-if node

$$OUT(N) = \bigcup_{M=\text{dynamic successor of } N} IN(M)$$

$$IN(N) = (OUT(N) \setminus KILL(N)) \cup GEN(N)$$

Fig. 5.24: Backwards data-flow equations for a node N

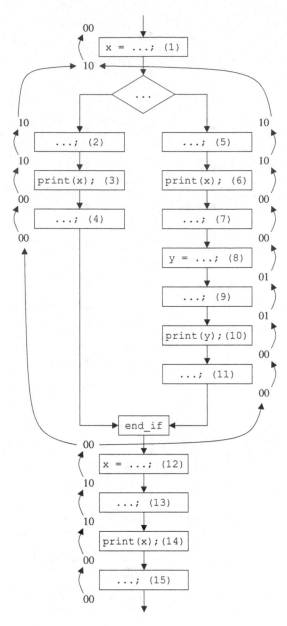

Fig. 5.25: Live analysis for Figure 5.20 using backward data-flow equations

bit for each variable declared in the routine even in nodes where the variable does not exist.

We start by setting the bits in the *OUT* set of the bottom-most node in Figure 5.25 to 00: the first bit is 0 because x certainly is not live at the end of its scope, and the second bit is 0 because y does not exist there. Following the control-flow graph backwards, we find that the first change comes at the node for print(x∗x). This node uses x, so its *GEN* set contains the item "x is live here", or, in bits, 10. Applying the second data-flow equation shown above, we find that the *IN* set of this node becomes 10. The next node that effects a change is an assignment to x; this makes its *GEN* set empty, and its *KILL* set contains the item "x is live here". After application of the second data-flow equation, the *IN* set is 00, as shown in Figure 5.25. Continuing this way, we propagate the bits upwards, splitting them at the end-if node and merging them at the if-node, until we reach the beginning of the block with the bits 00.

Several observations are in order here.

- The union in the data-flow equations can be implemented as a simple Boolean OR, since if a variable is live along one path from a node it is live at that node.
- Normally, when we reach the top node of the scope of a variable, its liveness in the *IN* set is equal to 0, since a variable should not be live at the very top of its scope; if we find its liveness to be 1, its value may be used before it has been set, and a warning message can be given.
- The nodes with the last use of the value of a variable *V* can be recognized by having a 1 for the liveness of *V* in the *IN* set and a 0 in the *OUT* set.
- If we find a node with an assignment to a variable *V* and the liveness of *V* is 0 both in the *IN* set and the *OUT* set, the assignment can be deleted, since no node is going to use the result. Note that the source expression in the assignment can only be deleted simultaneously if we can prove it has no side effects.
- It is important to note that the diagram does not contain the bit combination 11, so there is no node at which both variables are live. This means that they can share the same register or memory location. Indeed, the live range of x in the right branch of the if-statement stops at the statement print(x+3) and does not overlap the live range of y.

5.6 Symbolic interpretation versus data-flow equations

It is interesting to compare the merits of symbolic interpretation and data-flow equations. Symbolic interpretation is more intuitive and appealing in simple cases (well-structured flow graphs); data-flow equations can retrieve more information and can handle complicated cases ("bad" flow graphs) better. Symbolic interpretation can handle the flow of information inside expressions more easily than data-flow equations can. Symbolic interpretation fits in nicely with narrow compilers and L-attributed grammars, since only slightly more is needed than what is already available in the nodes from the top to the node where the processing is going on. Data-flow equations require the entire flow graph to be in memory (which is why it can handle complicated cases) and require all attributes to be present in all nodes (which is why it collects more information). Symbolic interpretation *can* handle arbitrary flow graphs, but the algorithm begins to approach that of data-flow equations and loses much of its attraction.

An unusual approach to data-flow analysis, based on a grammatical paradigm different from that of the attribute grammars, is given by Uhl and Horspool [282], in which the kinds of information to be gathered by data-flow analysis must be specified and the processing is automatic.

5.7 Conclusion

This concludes our discussion of context-handling methods. We have seen that they serve to annotate the AST of the source program with information that can be obtained by combining bits of information from arbitrarily far away in the AST, in short, from the context. These annotations are required for checking the contextual correctness of the source program and for the intermediate and low-level code generation processes that must follow.

The manual context-handling methods are based on abstract symbolic interpretation, and come mainly in three variants: full symbolic interpretation on the stack, simple symbolic interpretation, and data-flow equations.

Summary

- The two major manual methods for context handling are symbolic interpretation (simulation on the stack) and data-flow equations. Both need the control-flow graph rather than the AST.
- The control-flow graph can be obtained by threading the AST; the thread is an additional pointer in each node that points to the dynamic successor of that node. Some trickery is needed if a node has more than one dynamic successor.
- The AST can be threaded by a recursive visit which keeps a pointer to the dynamically last node. When reaching a new node the thread in the dynamically last node is updated and the new node becomes the dynamically last node.
- Symbolic interpretation works by simulating the dynamic behavior of the global data of the program and the local data of each of the routines at compile time. The possibilities for such a simulation are limited, but still useful information can be obtained.
- In symbolic interpretation, a symbolic version of the activation record of the routine to be analyzed is constructed, the stack representation. A similar representation of the global data may be used.

- Where the run-time global and stack representations contain the actual values of the variables in them, the symbolic representations contain properties of those variables, for example initialization status.
- Symbolic interpretation follows the control-flow graph from routine entrance to routine exit and records the changes in the properties of the variables.
- Simple symbolic interpretation follows the control-flow graph in one top-to-bottom left-to-right scan; this works for structured programs and a very restricted set of properties only. Full symbolic interpretation keeps following the control-flow graph until the properties in the symbolic representations converge; this works for any control structure and a wider—but still limited—set of properties.
- The difference between full and simple symbolic interpretation is the same as that between general attribute grammars and L-attributed grammars.
- Last-def analysis attaches to each node N representing a variable V, the set of pointers to the nodes of those assignments that result in setting the value of V at N. Last-def analysis can be done by full symbolic interpretation.
- A variable is "live" at a given node if its value is used on at least one path through the control-flow graph starting from that node.
- Live analysis requires information to be propagated backwards along the flow of control, from an assignment to a variable to its last preceding use: the variable is dead in the area in between.
- Information can be passed backwards during symbolic interpretation by propagating forwards a pointer to the node that needs the information and filling in the information when it is found, using that pointer. This is called backpatching.
- The other manual context-handling method, data-flow equations, is actually semi-automatic: data-flow equations are set up using handwritten code, the equations are then solved automatically, and the results are interpreted by handwritten code.
- In data-flow equations, two sets of properties are attached to each node, its IN set and its OUT set.
- The IN set of a node I is determined as the union of the OUT sets of the dynamic predecessors of I—all nodes whose outgoing flow of control leads to I.
- The OUT set of a node I is determined by its IN set, transformed by the actions inside the node. These transformations are formalized as the removal of the node's $KILL$ set from its IN set, followed by the addition of its GEN set. In principle, the $KILL$ and GEN sets are constants of the node under consideration.
- If the properties in the IN, OUT, $KILL$, and GEN sets are implemented as bits, the set union and set difference operations in the data-flow equations can be implemented very efficiently as bit array manipulations.
- Given the IN set at the entrance to the routine and the $KILL$ and GEN sets of all nodes, all other IN sets and the OUT set can be computed by a simple closure algorithm: the information is propagated until nothing changes any more.
- In another variant of data-flow equations, information is propagated backwards. Here the OUT set of a node I is determined as the union of the IN sets of the dynamic successors of I, and the IN set of a node I is determined by its OUT set, transformed by the actions inside the node.

- Live analysis can be done naturally using backwards data-flow equations.
- Interprocedural data-flow is the data flow between routines, as opposed to that inside routines.
- Interprocedural data-flow analysis can obtain information about the IN and IN-OUT parameters of a routine R by collecting their states in all stack representations at calls to R in all routines. Transitive closure over the complete program must be done to obtain the full information.

Further reading

Extensive information about many aspects of data-flow analysis can be found in Muchnick and Jones [198]. Since context handling and analysis is generally done for the purpose of optimization, most of the algorithms are discussed in literature about optimization, pointers to which can be found in the "Further reading" section of Chapter 9, on page 456.

Exercises

5.1. (▷www) Give the AST after threading of the while statement with syntax

```
while_statement  →
    'WHILE' condition 'DO' statements ';'
```

as shown in Figure 5.5 for the if-statement.

5.2. (▷www) Give the AST after threading of the repeat statement with syntax

```
repeat_statement  →
    'REPEAT' statements 'UNTIL' condition ';'
```

as shown in Figure 5.5 for the if-statement.

5.3. (▷790) The global variable LastNode can be eliminated from the threading mechanism described in Section 5.1 by using the technique from Figure 5.6: pass one or more successor pointers to each threading routine and let each threading routine return a pointer to its dynamically first node. Implement threading for the demo compiler of Section 1.2 using this technique.

5.4. (▷www) Describe the simple symbolic interpretation of a while statement.

5.5. (▷www) Describe the simple symbolic interpretation of a repeat-until statement.

5.6. (▷790) Some source language constructs require temporary variables to be allocated, for example to keep bounds and counters in for-loops, for temporary results in complicated arithmetic expressions, etc. The temporary variables from code segments that cannot be active simultaneously can overlap: if, for example, the then-part of an if-statement requires one temporary variable and the else-part requires one temporary variable too, we can allocate them in the same location and need only one temporary variable.

What variable(s) should be used in the stack representation to determine the maximum number of temporary variables in a routine by symbolic interpretation? Can the computation be performed by *simple* symbolic interpretation?

5.7. (▷790) Section 5.2.2 states that each time we meet a jump to a label L, we merge our present stack representation list into L's list and continue with the empty list. Somebody argues that this is wrong when we are symbolically interpreting the then-part of an if-statement and the then-part ends in a jump. We would then continue to process the else-part starting with an empty list, which is clearly wrong. Where is the error in this reasoning?

5.8. (▷www) Can simple symbolic interpretation be done in a time linear in the size of the source program? Can full symbolic interpretation? Can the data-flow equations be solved in linear time?

5.9. (▷790) Why is full symbolic interpretation required to determine the property "X is constant with value V"? Why is simple symbolic interpretation using a 3-point lattice with v_1 = "X is uninitialized", v_2 = "X is constant with value V", and v_3 = "X is variable" not enough?

5.10. (▷www) Why cannot the data-flow equations be used to determine the property "X is constant with value V"?

5.11. (▷www) The text in Section 5.3.1 treats the assignment statement only, but consider the routine call. Given the declaration of the routine in terms of IN and OUT parameters, what *KILL* and *GEN* sets should be used for a routine call node?

5.12. (▷790) What is the status of x in the assignment x := y in Figure 5.19 in the event that y is uninitialized? Is this reasonable? Discuss the pros and cons of the present situation.

5.13. (▷www) An optimization technique called **code hoisting** moves expressions to the earliest point beyond which they would always be evaluated. An expression that is always evaluated beyond a given point is called **very busy** at that point. Once it is known at which points an expression is very busy, the evaluation of that expression can be moved to the earliest of those points. Determining these points is a backwards data-flow problem.
(a) Give the general data-flow equations to determine the points at which an expression is very busy.
(b) Consider the example in Figure 5.26. Give the *KILL* and *GEN* sets for the expression x∗x.

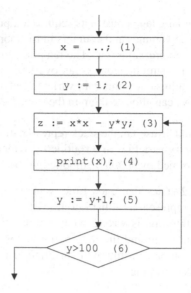

Fig. 5.26: Example program for a very busy expression

(c) Solve the data-flow equations for the expression x*x. What optimization becomes possible?

5.14. (▷791) Show that live analysis cannot be implemented by the forwards-operating data-flow equations mechanism of Section 5.3.1.

5.15. *History of context analysis*: Study Naur's 1965 paper on the checking of operand types in ALGOL 60 by symbolic interpretation [199], and write a summary of it.

Chapter 6
Interpretation

The previous chapters have provided us with an annotated syntax tree, either explicitly available as a data structure in memory in a broad compiler or implicitly available during parsing in a narrow compiler. This annotated syntax tree still bears very much the traces of the source language and the programming paradigm it belongs to: higher-level constructs like for-loops, method calls, list comprehensions, logic variables, and parallel select statements are all still directly represented by nodes and subtrees. Yet we have seen that the methods used to obtain the annotated syntax tree are largely language- and paradigm-independent.

The next step in processing the AST is its transformation to intermediate code, as suggested in Figure 1.21 and repeated in Figure 6.1. The AST as supplied by the context handling module is full of nodes that reflect the specific semantic concepts of the source language. As explained in Section 1.3, the intermediate code generation serves to reduce the set of these specific node types to a small set of general concepts that can be implemented easily on actual machines. Intermediate code generation finds the language-characteristic nodes and subtrees in the AST and rewrites them into (= replaces them by) subtrees that employ only a small number of features, each of which corresponds rather closely to a set of machine instructions. The resulting tree should probably be called an **intermediate code tree**, but it is usual to still call it an AST when no confusion can arise.

The standard intermediate code tree features are

- expressions, including assignments,
- routine calls, procedure headings, and return statements, and
- conditional and unconditional jumps.

In addition there will be administrative features, such as memory allocation for global variables, activation record allocation, and module linkage information. The details are up to the compiler writer or the tool designer. Intermediate code generation usually increases the size of the AST, but it reduces the conceptual complexity: the entire range of high-level concepts of the language is replaced by a few rather low-level concepts.

It will be clear that the specifics of these transformations and the run-time features they require are for a large part language- and paradigm-dependent —although of course the techniques by which they are applied will often be similar. For this reason the transformation specifics and run-time issues have been deferred to Chapters 11 through 14. This leaves us free to continue in this chapter with the largely machine- and paradigm-*in*dependent processing of the intermediate code. The situation is summarized in Figure 6.1.

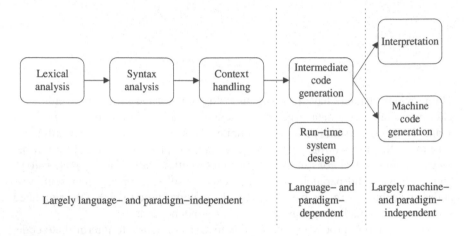

Fig. 6.1: The status of the various modules in compiler construction

In processing the intermediate code, the choice is between little preprocessing followed by execution on an interpreter, and much preprocessing, in the form of machine code generation, followed by execution on hardware. We will first discuss two types of interpreters (Chapter 6) and then turn to code generation, the latter at several levels of sophistication (Chapters 7 and 9).

In principle the methods in the following chapters expect intermediate code of the above simplified nature as input, but in practice the applicability of the methods is more complicated. For one thing, an interpreter may not require all language features to be removed: it may, for example, be able to interpret a for-loop node directly. Or the designer may decide to integrate intermediate code generation and target code generation, in which case a for-loop subtree will be rewritten directly to target code.

Code generation transforms the AST into a list of symbolic target machine instructions, which is still several steps away from an executable binary file. This gap is bridged by assemblers (Chapter 8, which also covers disassemblers). The code generation techniques from Chapter 7 are restricted to simple code with few optimizations. Further optimizations and optimizations for small code size, power-efficient code, fast turn-around time and platform-independence are covered in Chapter 9.

A sobering thought: whatever the processing method, writing the run-time system and library routines used by the programs will be a substantial part of the work. Little advice can be given on this; most of it is just coding, and usually there is a lot of it. It is surprising how much semantics programming language designers manage to stash away in innocent-looking library routines, especially formatting print routines.

6.1 Interpreters

The simplest way to have the actions expressed by the source program performed is to process the AST using an "interpreter". An **interpreter** is a program that considers the nodes of the AST in the correct order and performs the actions prescribed for those nodes by the semantics of the language. Note that unlike compilation, this requires the presence of the input data needed for the program. Note also that an interpreter performs essentially the same actions as the CPU of the computer, except that it works on AST nodes rather than on machine instructions: a CPU considers the instructions of the machine program in the correct order and performs the actions prescribed for those instructions by the semantics of the machine.

Interpreters come in two varieties: recursive and iterative. A recursive interpreter works directly on the AST and requires less preprocessing than an iterative interpreter, which works on a linearized version of the AST.

6.2 Recursive interpreters

A **recursive interpreter** has an interpreting routine for each node type in the AST. Such an interpreting routine calls other similar routines, depending on its children; it essentially does what it says in the language definition manual. This architecture is possible because the meaning of a language construct is defined as a function of the meanings of its components. For example, the meaning of an if-statement is defined by the meanings of the condition, the then-part, and the else-part it contains, plus a short paragraph in the manual that ties them together. This structure is reflected faithfully in a recursive interpreter, as can be seen in the routine in Figure 6.4, which first interprets the condition and then, depending on the outcome, interprets the then-part or the else-part; since the then and else-parts can again contain if-statements, the interpreter routine for if-statements will be recursive, as will many other interpreter routines. The interpretation of the entire program starts by calling the interpretation routine for Program with the top node of the AST as a parameter. We have already seen a very simple recursive interpreter in Section 1.2.8; its code was shown in Figure 1.19.

An important ingredient in a recursive interpreter is the **uniform self-identifying data representation**. The interpreter has to manipulate data values defined in the program being interpreted, but the types and sizes of these values are not known at the time the interpreter is written. This makes it necessary to implement these values in the interpreter as variable-size records that specify the type of the run-time value, its size, and the run-time value itself. A pointer to such a record can then serve as "the value" during interpretation.

As an example, Figure 6.2 shows a value of type Complex_Number as the programmer sees it; Figure 6.3 shows a possible representation of the same value in a recursive interpreter. The fields that correspond to run-time values are marked with a V in the top left corner; each of them is self-identifying through its type field. The data representation consists of two parts, the value-specific part and the part that is common to all values of the type Complex_Number. The first part provides the actual value of the instance; the second part describes the type of the value, which is the same for all values of type Complex_Number. These data structures will contain additional information in an actual interpreter, specifying for example source program file names and line numbers at which the value or the type originated.

re:	3.0
im:	4.0

Fig. 6.2: A value of type Complex_Number as the programmer sees it

The pointer is part of the value and should never be copied separately: if a copy is required, the entire record must be copied, and the pointer to the result is the new value. If the record contains other values, these must also be copied. In a recursive interpreter, which is slow anyway, it is probably worthwhile to stick to this representation even for the most basic values, as for example integers and Booleans. Doing so makes processing and reporting much more easy and uniform.

Another important feature is the **status indicator**; it is used to direct the flow of control. Its primary component is the mode of operation of the interpreter. This is an enumeration value; its normal value is something like *NormalMode*, indicating sequential flow of control, but other values are available, to indicate jumps, exceptions, function returns, and possibly other forms of flow of control. Its second component is a value in the wider sense of the word, to supply more information about the non-sequential flow of control. This may be a value for the mode *ReturnMode*, an exception name plus possible values for the mode *ExceptionMode*, and a label for *JumpMode*. The status indicator should also contain the file name and the line

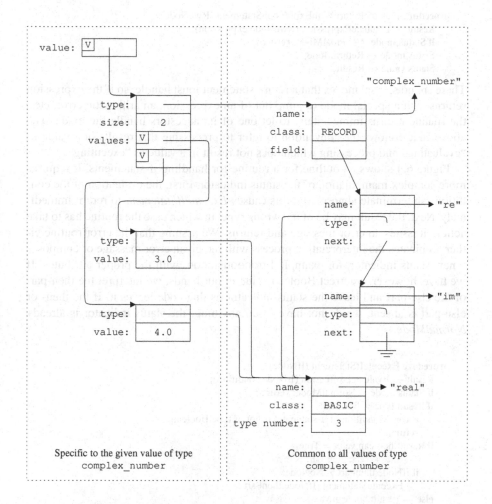

Fig. 6.3: A representation of the value of Figure 6.2 in a recursive interpreter.

number of the text in which the status indicator was created, and possibly other debugging information.

Each interpreting routine checks the status indicator after each call to another routine, to see how to carry on. If the status indicator is *NormalMode*, the routine carries on normally. Otherwise, it checks to see if the mode is one that it should handle; if it is, it does so, but if it is not, the routine returns immediately, to let one of the parent routines handle the mode.

For example, the interpreting routine for the C return-with-expression statement will evaluate the expression in it and combine it with the mode value *ReturnMode* into a status indicator, provided the status returned by the evaluation of the expression is *NormalMode* (Rwe stands for *ReturnWithExpression*):

```
procedure ExecuteReturnWithExpressionStatement (RweNode):
    Result ← EvaluateExpression (RweNode.expression);
    if Status.mode ≠ NormalMode: return;
    Status.mode ← ReturnMode;
    Status.value ← Result;
```

There are no special modes that a return statement must handle, so if the expression returns with a special mode (a jump out of an expression, an arithmetic error, etc.) the routine returns immediately, to let one of its ancestors handle the mode. The above code follows the convention to refer to processing that results in a value as "evaluating" and processing which does not result in a value as "executing".

Figure 6.4 shows an outline for a routine for handling if-statements. It requires more complex manipulation of the status indicator. First, the evaluation of the condition can terminate abnormally; this causes *ExecuteIfStatement* to return immediately. Next, the result may be of the wrong type, in which case the routine has to take action: it issues an error message and returns. We assume that the error routine either terminates the interpretation process with the given error message or composes a new status indicator, for example ErroneousMode, with the proper attributes. If we have, however, a correct Boolean value in our hands, we interpret the then-part or the else-part and leave the status indicator as that code leaves it. If the then- or else-part is absent, we do not have to do anything: the status indicator is already *NormalMode*.

```
procedure ExecuteIfStatement (IfNode):
    Result ← EvaluateExpression (IfNode.condition);
    if Status.mode ≠ NormalMode: return;
    if Result.type ≠ Boolean:
        error "Condition in if-statement is not of type Boolean";
        return;
    if Result.boolean.value = True:
        –– Check if the then-part is there:
        if IfNode.thenPart ≠ NoNode:
            ExecuteStatement (IfNode.thenPart);
    else –– Result.boolean.value = False:
        –– Check if the else-part is there:
        if IfNode.elsePart ≠ NoNode:
            ExecuteStatement (IfNode.elsePart);
```

Fig. 6.4: Outline of a routine for recursively interpreting an if-statement

For the sake of brevity the error message in the code above is kept short, but a real interpreter should give a far more helpful message containing at least the actual type of the condition expression and the location in the source code of the problem. One advantage of an interpreter is that this information is readily available.

Variables, named constants, and other named entities are handled by entering them into the symbol table, in the way they are described in the manual. Generally it is useful to attach additional data to the entry. For example, if the manual entry for "declaration of a variable V of type T" states that room should be allocated for it, we allocate the required room on the heap and enter into the symbol table under the name V a record of a type called something like Declarable, which could have the following fields:

- a pointer to the name V
- the file name and line number of its declaration
- an indication of the kind of the declarable (variable, constant, etc.)
- a pointer to the type T
- a pointer to newly allocated room for the value of V
- a bit telling whether or not V has been initialized, if known
- one or more scope- and stack-related pointers, depending on the language
- perhaps other data, depending on the language

The variable V is then accessed by looking up the name V in the symbol table; effectively, the name V is the address of the variable V.

If the language specifies so, a stack can be kept by the interpreter, but a symbol table organization like the one shown in Figure 11.2 allows us to use the symbol table as a stack mechanism. Anonymous values, created for example for the parameters of a routine call in the source language, can also be entered, using generated names. In fact, with some dexterity, the symbol table can be used for all data allocation.

A recursive interpreter can be written relatively quickly, and is useful for rapid prototyping; it is not the architecture of choice for a heavy-duty interpreter. A secondary but important advantage is that it can help the language designer to debug the design of the language and its description. Disadvantages are the speed of execution, which may be a factor of 1000 or more lower than what could be achieved with a compiler, and the lack of static context checking: code that is not executed will not be tested. Speed can be improved by doing judicious memoizing: if it is known, for example, from the identification rules of the language that an identifier in a given expression will always be identified with the same type (which is true in almost all languages) then the type of an identifier can be memoized in its node in the syntax tree. If needed, full static context checking can be achieved by doing full attribute evaluation before starting the interpretation; the results can also generally be used to speed up the interpretation. For a short introduction to memoization, see below.

6.3 Iterative interpreters

The structure of an **iterative interpreter** is much closer to that of a CPU than that of a recursive interpreter. It consists of a flat loop over a case statement which contains a code segment for each node type; the code segment for a given node type implements the semantics of that node type, as described in the language definition manual. It requires a fully annotated and threaded AST, and maintains an **active-node pointer**, which points to the node to be interpreted, the **active node**. The iterative interpreter runs the code segment for the node pointed at by the active-node pointer;

Memoization

Memoization is a dynamic version of precomputation. Whereas in precomputation we compute the results of a function F for all its possible parameters before the function F has ever been called, in memoizing we monitor the actual calls to F, record the parameters and the result, and find the result by table lookup when a call for F with the same parameters comes along again. In both cases we restrict ourselves to pure functions—functions whose results do not depend on external values and that have no side effects. Such functions always yield the same result for a given set of input parameters, and therefore it is safe to use a memoized result instead of evaluating the function again.

The usual implementation is such that the function remembers the values of the parameters it has been called with, together with the results it has yielded for them, using a hash table or some other efficient data structure. Upon each call, it checks to see if these parameters have already occurred before, and if so it immediately returns the stored answer.

Looking up a value in a dynamically created data structure may not be as fast as array indexing, but the point is that looking up an answer can be done in constant time, whereas the time needed for evaluating a function may be erratic.

Memoization is especially valuable in algorithms on graphs in which properties of nodes depending on those of other nodes have to be established, a very frequent case. Such algorithms can store the property of a node in the node itself, once it has been established by the algorithm. If the property is needed again, it can be retrieved from the node rather than recomputed. This technique can often turn an algorithm with exponential time complexity into a linear one, as is shown, for example, in Exercise 6.1.

at the end, this code sets the active-node pointer to another node, its successor, thus leading the interpreter to that node, the code of which is then run, etc. The active-node pointer is comparable to the instruction pointer in a CPU, except that it is set explicitly rather than incremented implicitly.

Figure 6.5 shows the outline of the main loop of an iterative interpreter. It contains only one statement, a case statement which selects the proper code segment for the active node, based on its type. One code segment is shown, the one for if-statements. We see that it is simpler than the corresponding recursive code in Figure 6.4: the condition code has already been evaluated since it precedes the if node in the threaded AST; it is not necessary to check the type of the condition code since the full annotation has done full type checking; and calling the interpreter for the proper branch of the if-statement is replaced by setting the active-node pointer correctly. Code segments for the other nodes are usually equally straightforward.

The data structures inside an iterative interpreter resemble much more those inside a compiled program than those inside a recursive interpreter. There will be an array holding the global data of the source program, if the source language allows these. If the source language is stack-oriented, the iterative interpreter will maintain a stack, on which local variables are allocated. Variables and other entities have addresses, which are offsets in these memory arrays. Stacking and scope information, if applicable, is placed on the stack. The symbol table is not used, except perhaps to give better error messages. The stack can be conveniently implemented as an extensible array, as explained in Section 10.1.3.2.

```
while ActiveNode.type ≠ EndOfProgramType:
    select ActiveNode.type:
        case ...
        case IfType:
            — We arrive here after the condition has been evaluated;
            — the Boolean result is on the working stack.
            Value ← Pop (WorkingStack);
            if Value.boolean.value = True:
                ActiveNode ← ActiveNode.trueSuccessor;
            else — Value.boolean.value = False:
                if ActiveNode.falseSuccessor ≠ NoNode:
                    ActiveNode ← ActiveNode.falseSuccessor;
                else — ActiveNode.falseSuccessor = NoNode:
                    ActiveNode ← ActiveNode.successor;
        case ...
```

Fig. 6.5: Sketch of the main loop of an iterative interpreter, showing the code for an if-statement

Figure 6.6 shows an iterative interpreter for the demo compiler of Section 1.2. Its structure is based on Figure 6.5, and consists of one "large" loop controlled by the active-node pointer. Since there is only one node type in our demo compiler, *Expression*, the body of the loop is simple. It is very similar to the code in Figure 1.19, except that the values are retrieved from and delivered onto the stack, using *Pop()* and *Push()*, rather than being yielded and returned by function calls. Note that the interpreter starts by threading the tree, in the routine *Process()*.

The iterative interpreter usually has much more information about the run-time events inside a program than a compiled program does, but less than a recursive interpreter. A recursive interpreter can maintain an arbitrary amount of information for a variable by storing it in the symbol table, whereas an iterative interpreter only has a value at a given address. This can be largely remedied by having **shadow memory** in the form of arrays, parallel to the memory arrays maintained by the interpreter. Each byte in the shadow array holds properties of the corresponding byte in the memory array. Examples of such properties are: "This byte is uninitialized", "This byte is a non-first byte of a pointer", "This byte belongs to a read-only array", "This byte is part of the routine call linkage", etc. The 256 different values provided by one byte for this are usually enough but not ample, and some clever packing may be required.

The shadow data can be used for interpret-time checking, for example to detect the use of uninitialized memory, incorrectly aligned data access, overwriting read-only and system data, and other mishaps, in languages in which these cannot be excluded by static context checking. An advantage of the shadow memory is that it can be disabled easily, when faster processing is desired. An implementation of shadow memory in an object code interpreter is described by Nethercote and Seward [200].

Some iterative interpreters also store the AST in a single array; there are several reasons for doing so, actually none of them of overriding importance. One reason is

```
#include    "parser.h"     /* for types AST_node and Expression */
#include    "thread.h"     /* for Thread_AST() and Thread_start */
#include    "stack.h"      /* for Push() and Pop() */
#include    "backend.h"    /* for self check */
                                            /* PRIVATE */
static AST_node *Active_node_pointer;

static void Interpret_iteratively (void) {
    while (Active_node_pointer != 0) {
        /* there is only one node type, Expression: */
        Expression *expr = Active_node_pointer;
        switch (expr->type) {
        case 'D':
            Push(expr->value);
            break;
        case 'P': {
            int e_left = Pop(); int e_right = Pop();
            switch (expr->oper) {
            case '+': Push(e_left + e_right); break;
            case '*': Push(e_left * e_right); break;
            }}
            break;
        }
        Active_node_pointer = Active_node_pointer->successor;
    }
    printf ("%d\n", Pop());        /* print the result */
}
                                            /* PUBLIC */
void Process(AST_node *icode) {
    Thread_AST(icode); Active_node_pointer = Thread_start;
    Interpret_iteratively ();
}
```

Fig. 6.6: An iterative interpreter for the demo compiler of Section 1.2

that storing the AST in a single array makes it easier to write it to a file; this allows
the program to be interpreted more than once without recreating the AST from the
source text every time. Another is that a more compact representation is possible this
way. The construction of the AST usually puts the successor of a node right after
that node. If this happens often enough it becomes profitable to omit the successor
pointer from the nodes and appoint the node following a node N implicitly as the
successor of N. This necessitates explicit jumps whenever a node is not immediately
followed by its successor or has more than one successor. The three forms of storing
an AST are shown in Figures 6.7 and 6.8. A third reason may be purely historical and
conceptual: an iterative interpreter mimics a CPU working on a compiled program
and the AST array mimics the compiled program.

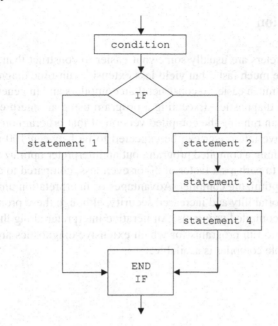

Fig. 6.7: An AST stored as a graph

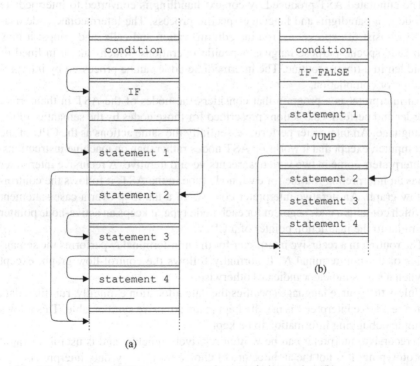

Fig. 6.8: Storing the AST in an array (a) and as pseudo-instructions (b)

6.4 Conclusion

Iterative interpreters are usually somewhat easier to construct than recursive interpreters; they are much faster but yield less extensive run-time diagnostics. Iterative interpreters are much easier to construct than compilers and in general allow far superior run-time diagnostics. Executing a program using an interpreter is, however, much slower than running the compiled version of that program on a real machine. Using an iterative interpreter can be expected to be between 100 and 1000 times slower than running a compiled program, but an interpreter optimized for speed can reduce the loss to perhaps a factor of 30 or even less, compared to a program compiled with an optimizing compiler. Advantages of interpretation unrelated to speed are increased portability and increased security, although these properties may also be achieved in compiled programs. An iterative interpreter along the above lines is the best means to run programs for which extensive diagnostics are desired or for which no suitable compiler is available.

Summary

- The annotated AST produced by context handling is converted to intermediate code in a paradigm- and language-specific process. The intermediate code usually consist of expressions, routine administration and calls, and jumps; it may include special-purpose language-specific operations, which can be in-lined or hidden in a library routine. The intermediate code can be processed by interpretation or compilation.
- An interpreter is a program that considers the nodes of the AST in the correct order and performs the actions prescribed for those nodes by the semantics of the language. An interpreter performs essentially the same actions as the CPU of the computer, except that it works on AST nodes rather than on machine instructions.
- Interpreters come in two varieties: recursive and iterative. A recursive interpreter has an interpreting routine for each node type in the AST; it follows the control-flow graph. An iterative interpreter consists of a flat loop over a case statement which contains a code segment for each node type; it keeps an active-node pointer similar to the instruction pointer of a CPU.
- The routine in a recursive interpreter for the non-terminal N performs the semantics of the non-terminal N. It normally follows the control-flow graph, except when a status indicator indicates otherwise.
- Unless the source language specifies the data allocation explicitly, run-time data in a recursive interpreter is usually kept in an extensive symbol table. This allows ample debugging information to be kept.
- A recursive interpreter can be written relatively quickly, and is useful for rapid prototyping; it is not the architecture of choice for a heavy-duty interpreter.
- The run-time data in an iterative interpreter are kept in arrays that represent the global data area and the activation records of the routines, in a form that is close

to that of a compiled program.

- Additional information about the run-time data in an iterative interpreter can be kept in shadow arrays that parallel the data arrays. These shadow arrays can be of assistance in detecting the use of uninitialized data, the improper use of data, alignment errors, attempts to overwrite protected or system area data, etc.
- Using an iterative interpreter can be expected to be between 30 and 100 times slower than running a compiled program, but an interpreter optimized for speed can reduce the loss to perhaps a factor 10.

Further reading

Books and general discussions on interpreter design are rare, unfortunately. The most prominent examples are by Griswold and Griswold [111], who describe an Icon interpreter in detail, and by Klint [154], who describes a variety of interpreter types. Much valuable information can still be found in the *Proceedings of the SIG-PLAN '87 Symposium on Interpreters and Interpretive Techniques* (1987). With the advent of Java and rapid prototyping, many papers on interpreters have been written recently, often in the journal *Software, Practice & Experience*.

Exercises

6.1. (▷www) This is an exercise in memoization, which is not properly a compiler

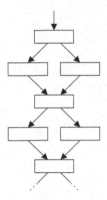

Fig. 6.9: Test graph for recursive descent marking

construction subject, but the exercise is still instructive. Given a directed acyclic graph G and a node N in it, design and implement an algorithm for finding the shortest distance from N to a leaf of G by recursive descent, where a leaf is a node with no outgoing arcs. Test your implementation on a large graph of the structure shown in Figure 6.9.

6.2. (▷www) Extend the iterative interpreter in Figure 6.5 with code for operators.

6.3. (▷www) Iterative interpreters are much faster than recursive interpreters, but yield less extensive run-time diagnostics. Explain. Compiled code gives even poorer error messages. Explain.

6.4. (▷www) *History of interpreters*: Study McCarthy's 1960 paper on LISP [186], and write a summary with special attention to the interpreter. Or

For those who read German: Study what may very well be the first book on compiler construction, Rutishauser's 1952 book [244], and write a summary with special attention to the described equivalence of interpretation and compilation.

Chapter 7
Code Generation

We will now turn to the generation of target code from the AST. Although simple code generation is possible, the generation of good code is a field full of snags and snares, and it requires considerable care. We will therefore start with a discussion of the desired properties of generated code.

7.1 Properties of generated code

The desired properties of generated code are complete correctness, high speed, small size, and low energy consumption, roughly in that order unless the application situation dictates otherwise. Correctness is obtained through the use of proper compilation techniques, and high speed, small size, and low energy consumption may to a certain extent be achieved by optimization techniques.

7.1.1 Correctness

Correctness may be the most important property of generated code, it is also its most vulnerable one. The compiler writer's main weapon against incorrect code is the "small semantics-preserving transformation": the huge and effectively incomprehensible transformation from source code to binary object code is decomposed into many small semantics-preserving transformations, each small enough to be understood locally and perhaps even be proven correct.

Probably the most impressive example of such a semantics-preserving transformation is the BURS tree rewriting technique from Section 9.1.4, in which subtrees from the AST are replaced by machine instructions representing the same semantics, thus gradually reducing the AST to a list of machine instructions. A very simple example of a semantics-preserving transformation is transforming the tree for a+0 to that for a.

Unfortunately this picture is too rosy: many useful transformations, especially the optimizing ones, preserve the semantics only under special conditions. Checking that these conditions hold often requires extensive analysis of the AST and it is here that the problems arise. Analyzing the code to determine which transformations can be safely applied is typically the more labor-intensive part of the compiler, and also the more error-prone: it is all too easy to overlook special cases in which some otherwise beneficial and clever transformation would generate incorrect code or the code analyzer would give a wrong answer. Compiler writers have learned the hard way to implement test suites to verify that all these transformations are correct, and stay correct when the compiler is developed further.

Next to correctness, important properties of generated code are speed, code size, and energy consumption. The relative importance of these properties depends very much on the situation in which the code is used.

7.1.2 Speed

There are several ways for the compiler designer to produce faster code. The most important ones are:

- We can design code transformations that yield faster code or, even better, no code at all, and do the analysis needed for their correct application. These are the traditional optimizations, and this chapter and Chapter 9 contain many examples.
- We can evaluate part of the program already during compilation. Quite reasonably, this is called "partial evaluation". Its simplest form is the evaluation of constant expressions at compile time, but a much more general technique is discussed in Section 7.5.1.2, and a practical example is shown in Section 13.5.2.
- We can duplicate code segments in line rather than jump to them. Examples are replacing a function call by the body of the called function ("function in-lining"), described in Section 7.3.3; and unrolling a loop statement by repeating the loop

body, as described on page 586 in the subsection on optimizations in Section 11.4.1.3. It would seem that the gain is meager, but often the expanded code allows new optimizations.

Two of the most powerful speed optimizations are outside the realm of compiler design: using a more efficient algorithm; and writing the program in assembly language. There is no doubt that very fast code can be obtained in assembly language, but some very heavily optimizing compilers generate code of comparable quality; still, a competent and gifted assembly programmer is probably unbeatable. The disadvantages are that it requires a lot of very specialized work to write, maintain and update an assembly language program, and that even if one spends all the effort the program runs on a specific processor type only.

Straightforward translation from high-level language to machine language usually does not result in very efficient code. Moderately advanced optimization techniques will perhaps provide a factor of three speed improvement over very naive code generation; implementing such optimizations may take about the same amount of time as the entire compiler writing project. Gaining another factor of two or even three over this may be possible through extensive and aggressive optimization; one can expect to spend many times the original effort on an optimization phase of this nature. In this chapter we will concentrate on the basic and a few of the moderately advanced optimizing code generation techniques.

7.1.3 Size

In an increasing number of applications code size matters. The main examples are code for embedded applications as found in cars, remote controls, smart cards, etc., where available memory size restricts code size; and programs that need to be downloaded to –usually mobile– equipment, where reduced code size is important to keep transmission times low.

Often just adapting the traditional speed optimization techniques to code size fails to produce significant size reductions, so other techniques are needed. These include aggressive suppression of unused code; use of special hardware; threaded code (Section 7.5.1.1); procedural abstraction (Section 7.3.3); and assorted code compression techniques (Section 9.2.2).

Size optimizations are discussed in Section 9.2.

7.1.4 Power consumption

Electrical power management consists of two components. The first is the saving of energy, to increase operation time in battery-powered equipment, and to reduce the electricity bill of wall-powered computers. The second is limiting peak heat dissipation, in all computers large and small, to protect the processor. The traditional optimizations for performance turn out be to a good first approximation for power optimizations, if only for the simple reason that if a program is faster, it finishes sooner and has less time to spend energy. The actual picture is more complicated; a sketch of it is given in Section 9.3.

7.1.5 About optimizations

Optimizations are attractive: much research in compiler construction is concerned with them, and compiler writers regularly see all kinds of opportunities for optimizations. It should, however, be kept in mind that implementing optimizations is the last phase in compiler construction: unlike correctness, optimizations *are* an add-on feature. In programming, it is easier to make a correct program fast than a fast program correct; likewise it is easier to make correct generated object code fast than to make fast generated object code correct.

There is another reason besides correctness why we tend to focus on the unoptimized algorithm in this book: some traditional algorithms are actually optimized versions of more basic algorithms. Sometimes the basic algorithm has wider applicability than the optimized version and in any case the basic version will provide us with more insight and freedom of design than the already optimized version.

An example in point is the stack in implementations of imperative languages. At any moment the stack holds the pertinent data —administration, parameters, and local data— for each active routine, a routine that has been called and has not yet terminated. This set of data is called the "activation record" of this activation of the routine. Traditionally, activation records are found only on the stack, and only the one on the top of the stack represents a running routine; we consider the stack as the primary mechanism of which activation records are just parts. It is, however, profitable to recognize the activation record as the primary item: it arises naturally when a routine is called ("activated") since it is obvious that its pertinent data has to be stored somewhere. Its allocation on a stack is just an optimization that happens to be possible in many—but not all—imperative and object-oriented languages. From this point of view it is easier to understand the implementation of those languages for which stack allocation is not a good optimization: imperative languages with coroutines or Ada-like tasks, object-oriented languages with active Smalltalk-like objects, functional languages, Icon, etc.

Probably the best attitude towards optimization is to first understand and implement the basic structure and algorithm, then see what optimizations the actual situation allows, determine which are worthwhile, and then implement some of them, in cost-benefit order. In situations in which the need for optimization is obvious from the start, as for example in code generators, the basic structure would include a framework for these optimizations. This framework can then be filled in as the project progresses.

Another consideration is the compiler time doing the optimizations takes. Slowing down every compilation for a rare optimization is usually not a good investment. Occasionally it might be worth it though, for example if it allows code to be squeezed into smaller memory in an embedded system.

7.2 Introduction to code generation

Compilation produces object code from the intermediate code tree through a process called **code generation**. The basis of code generation is the systematic replacement of nodes and subtrees of the AST by target code segments, in such a way that the semantics is preserved. This replacement process is called **tree rewriting**. It is followed by a linearization phase, which produces a linear sequence of instructions from the rewritten AST. The linearization is controlled by the data-flow and flow-of-control requirements of the target code segments, and is called **scheduling**. The mental image of the gradual transformation from AST into target code, during which at each stage the semantics remains unchanged conceptually, is a powerful aid in designing correct code generators. Tree rewriting is also applied in other file conversion problems, for example for the conversion of SGML and XML texts to displayable format [163].

As a demonstration of code generation by tree rewriting, suppose we have constructed the AST for the expression

a := (b[4*c + d] * 2) + 9;

in which a, c, and d are integer variables and b is a byte array in memory. The AST is shown on the left in Figure 7.1.

Suppose, moreover, that the compiler has decided that the variables a, c, and d are in the registers R_a, R_c, and R_d, and that the array indexing operator [for byte arrays has been expanded into an addition and a memory access mem. The AST in that situation is shown on the right in Figure 7.1.

On the machine side we assume the existence of two machine instructions:

- Load_Elem_Addr A[R_i],c,R_d, which loads the address of the R_i-th element of the array at A into R_d, where the size of the elements of the array is c bytes;
- Load_Offset_Elem (A+R_o)[R_i],c,R_d, which loads the contents of the R_i-th element of the array at A plus offset R_o into R_d, where the other parameters have the same meanings as above.

These instructions are representative of the Intel x86 instructions leal and movsbl. We represent these instructions in the form of ASTs as well, as shown in Figure 7.2.

Now we can first replace the bottom right part of the original AST by Load_Offset_Elem (b+R_d)[R_c],4,R_t, obtained from the second instruction by equating A with b, R_o with R_d, R_i with R_c, c with 4, and using a temporary register R_t as the result register:

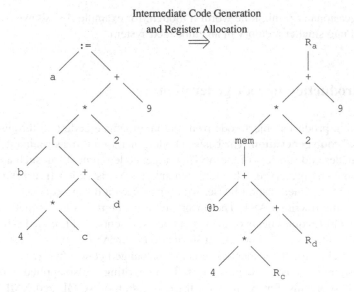

Fig. 7.1: Two ASTs for the expression a := (b[4*c + d] * 2) + 9

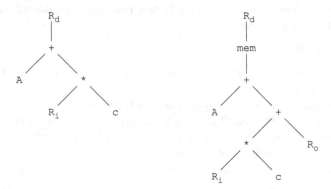

Load_Elem_Addr A[R$_i$],c,R$_d$ Load_Offset_Elem (A+R$_o$)[R$_i$],c,R$_d$

Fig. 7.2: Two sample instructions with their ASTs

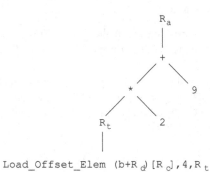

Load_Offset_Elem (b+R$_d$)[R$_c$],4,R$_t$

Next we replace the top part by the instruction Load_Elem_Addr 9[R_t],2,R_a obtained from the first instruction by equating A with 9, R_i with R_t, c with 2, and using the register R_a which holds the variable a as the result register:

$$R_a$$

$$|$$

Load_Elem_Addr 9[R $_t$],2,R $_a$

Load_Offset_Elem (b+R $_d$)[R $_c$],4,R $_t$

Note that the fixed address of the (pseudo-)array in the Load_Elem_Addr instruction is specified explicitly as 9. Scheduling is now trivial and yields the object code sequence

    Load_Offset_Elem (b+R$_d$)[R$_c$],4,R$_t$
    Load_Elem_Addr   9[R$_t$],2,R$_a$

which is indeed a quite satisfactory translation of the AST of Figure 7.1.

7.2.1 The structure of code generation

This depiction of the code generation process is still very scanty and leaves three questions unanswered: how did we find the subtrees to be replaced, where did the register R_t come from, and why were the instructions scheduled the way they were? These are indeed the three main issues in code generation:

1. *Instruction selection*: which part of the AST will be rewritten with which template, using which substitutions for the instruction parameters?
2. *Register allocation*: what computational results are kept in registers? Note that it is not certain that there will be enough registers for all values used and results obtained.
3. *Instruction scheduling*: which part of the code is will be executed first and which later?

One would like code generation to produce the most efficient translation possible for a given AST according to certain criteria, but the problem is that these three issues are interrelated. The strongest correlation exists between issues 1 and 2: the instructions selected affect the number and types of the required registers, and the available registers affect the choices for the selected instructions. As to instruction scheduling, any topological ordering of the instructions that is consistent with the flow-of-control and data dependencies is acceptable as far as correctness is concerned, but some orderings allow better instruction selection than others.

If one considers these three issues as three dimensions that together span a three-dimensional search space, it can be shown that to find the optimum translation for an AST essentially the entire space has to be searched: optimal code generation is

NP-complete and requires exhaustive search [53]. With perhaps 5 to 10 selectable instructions for a given node and perhaps 5 registers to choose from, this soon yields tens of possibilities for every node in the AST. To find the optimum, each of these possibilities has to be combined with each of the tens of possibilities for all other nodes, and each of the resulting combinations has to be evaluated against the criteria for code optimality, a truly Herculean task.

Therefore one compromises (on efficiency, never on correctness!), by restricting the problem. There are three traditional ways to restrict the code generation problem:

1. consider only small parts of the AST at a time;
2. assume that the target machine is simpler than it actually is, by disregarding some of its complicating features;
3. limit the possibilities in the three issues by having conventions for their use.

An example of the first restriction can be found in narrow compilers: they read a single expression, generate code for it and go on to the next expression. An example of the second type of restriction is the decision not to use the advanced addressing modes available in the target machine. And an example of the third restriction is the convention to use, say, registers R1, R2, and R3 for parameter transfer and R4 through R7 for intermediate results in expressions. Each of these restrictions cuts away a very large slice from the search space, thus making the code generation process more manageable, but it will be clear that in each case we may lose opportunities for optimization.

Efficient code generation algorithms exist for many combinations of restrictions, some of them with refinements of great sophistication. We will discuss a representative sample in Sections 9.1.2 to 9.1.5.

An extreme application of the first restriction is supercompilation, in which the size of the code to be translated is so severely limited that exhaustive search becomes feasible. This technique and its remarkable results are discussed briefly in Section 9.1.6.

7.2.2 The structure of the code generator

When generating code, it is often profitable to preprocess the intermediate code, in order to do efficiency-increasing AST transformations. Examples are the removal of +0 and ×1 in arithmetic expressions, and the in-lining of routines. Preprocessing the intermediate code is treated in Section 7.3.

Likewise it is often profitable to postprocess the generated code to remove some of the remaining inefficiencies. An example is the removal of the load instruction in sequences like

```
Store_Reg  R1,p
Load_Mem   p,R1
```

Postprocessing the generated code is treated in Section 7.6.

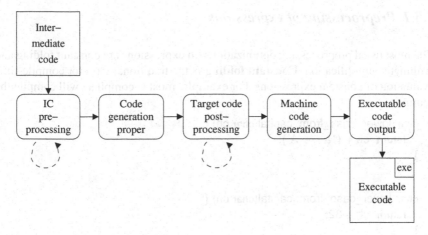

Fig. 7.3: Overall structure of a code generator

In summary: code generation is performed in three phases, as shown in Figure 7.3:

- preprocessing, in which AST node patterns are replaced by other ("better") AST node patterns,
- code generation proper, in which AST node patterns are replaced by target code sequences, and
- postprocessing, in which target code sequences are replaced by other ("better") target code sequences, using peephole optimization.

Both pre- and postprocessing tend to create new opportunities for themselves to be applied, so in some compilers these processes are performed more than once.

7.3 Preprocessing the intermediate code

We have seen that the intermediate code originates from source-language-dependent intermediate code generation, which removes most source-language-specific features and performs the specific optimizations required by these. For example, loops and case statements have been removed from imperative programs, pattern matching from functional programs, and unification from logic programs, and the optimizations involving them have been done. Basically, only expressions, if-statements, and routines remain. So preprocessing the intermediate code concentrates on these.

7.3.1 Preprocessing of expressions

The most usual preprocessing optimizations on expressions are constant folding and arithmetic simplification. **Constant folding** is the traditional term for compile-time evaluation of constant expressions. For example, most C compilers will compile the routine

```
char lower_case_from_capital(char ch) {
    return ch + ('a' − 'A');
}
```

as

```
char lower_case_from_capital(char ch) {
    return ch + 32;
}
```

since 'a' has the integer value 97 and 'A' is 65.

Some compilers will apply commutativity and associativity rules to expressions, in order to find constant expression. Such compilers will even fold the constants in

```
char lower_case_from_capital(char ch) {
    return ch + 'a' − 'A';
}
```

in spite of the fact that both constants do not share a node in the expression.

Constant folding is one of the simplest and most effective optimizations. Although programmers usually will not write constant expressions directly, constant expressions may arise from character constants, macro processing, symbolic interpretation, and intermediate code generation. **Arithmetic simplification** replaces expensive arithmetic operations by cheaper ones. Figure 7.4 shows a number of possible transformations; E represents a (sub)expression, V a variable, << the left-shift operator, and ** the exponentiation operator. We assume that multiplying is more expensive that addition and shifting together but cheaper than exponentiation, which is true for most machines. Transformations that replace an operation by a simpler one are called **strength reductions**; operations that can be removed completely are called **null sequences**. Some care has to be taken in strength reductions, to see that the semantics do not change in the process. For example, the multiply operation on a machine may work differently with respect to integer overflow than the shift operation does.

Constant folding and arithmetic simplification are performed easily during construction of the AST of the expression or in any tree visit afterwards. Since they are basically tree rewritings they can also be implemented using the BURS techniques from Section 9.1.4; these techniques then allow a constant folding and arithmetic simplification phase to be generated from specifications. In principle, constant folding can be viewed as an extreme case of arithmetic simplification.

Detailed algorithms for the reduction of multiplication to addition are supplied by Cocke and Kennedy [64]; generalized operator strength reduction is discussed in depth by Paige and Koenig [212].

operation	⇒ replacement
E * 2 ** n	⇒ E << n
2 * V	⇒ V + V
3 * V	⇒ (V << 1) + V
V ** 2	⇒ V * V
E + 0	⇒ E
E * 1	⇒ E
E ** 1	⇒ E
1 ** E	⇒ 1

Fig. 7.4: Some transformations for arithmetic simplification

7.3.2 Preprocessing of if-statements and goto statements

When the condition in an if-then-else statement turns out to be a constant, we can delete the code of the branch that will never be executed. This process is a form of **dead code elimination**. Another example of dead code elimination is the removal of a routine that is never called. Also, if a goto or return statement is followed by code that has no incoming data flow (for example because it does not carry a label), that code is dead and can be eliminated.

7.3.3 Preprocessing of routines

The major preprocessing actions that can be applied to routines are in-lining and cloning. The idea of **in-lining** is to replace a call to a routine R in the AST of a routine S by the body of R. To this end, a copy is made of the AST of R and this copy is attached to the AST of S in the place of the call. Somewhat surprisingly, routines R and S may be the same, since only one call is replaced by each in-lining step. One might be inclined to also replace the parameters in-line, in macro substitution fashion, but this is usually wrong; it is necessary to implement the parameter transfer in the way it is defined in the source language. So the call node in S is replaced by some nodes which do the parameter transfer properly, a block that results from copying the block inside routine R, and some nodes that handle the return value, if applicable.

As an example, the C routine print_square() in Figure 7.5 has been in-lined in Figure 7.6. Note that the naive macro substitution printf("square = %d\n", i++*i++) would be incorrect, since it would increase i twice. If static analysis has shown that there are no other calls to print_square(), the code of the routine can be eliminated, but this may not be easy to determine, especially not in the presence of separate compilation.

The obvious advantage of in-lining is that it eliminates the routine call mechanism, which may be expensive on some machines, but its greatest gain lies in the

```
void S {
    ...
    print_square(i++);
    ...
}

void print_square(int n) {
    printf ("square = %d\n", n*n);
}
```

Fig. 7.5: C code with a routine to be in-lined

```
void S {
    ...
    {int n = i++; printf ("square = %d\n", n*n);}
    ...
}

void print_square(int n) {
    printf ("square = %d\n", n*n);
}
```

Fig. 7.6: C code with the routine in-lined

fact that it often opens the door to many new optimizations, especially the more advanced ones. For example, the call print_square(3) is in-lined to

```
{ int n = 3;  printf ("square = %d\n", n*n);}
```

which is transformed by constant propagation into

```
{ int n = 3;  printf ("square = %d\n", 3*3);}
```

Constant folding then turns this into

```
{ int n = 3;  printf ("square = %d\n", 9);}
```

and code generation for basic blocks finds that the variable n is not needed and generates something like

```
SetPar_Const "square = %d\n",0
SetPar_Const 9,1
Call            printf
```

where SetPar_Const c,i sets the i-th parameter to c.

In-lining does not always live up to the expectations of the implementers; see, for example, Cooper, Hall and Torczon [69]. The reason is that in-lining can complicate the program text to such an extent that some otherwise effective optimizations fail; also, information needed for optimization can be lost in the process. Extensive in-lining can, for example, create very large expressions, which may require more registers than are available, resulting in a degradation in performance. Also, duplicating the code of a routine may increase the load on the instruction cache. These are examples of conflicting optimizations.

Using proper heuristics in-lining can give speed-ups of between 2 and 30%. See, for example, Cooper *et al.* [70] and Zhou *et al.* [313], who also cater for hard upper memory size limits, as they occur in embedded systems.

Cloning is similar to in-lining in that a copy of a routine is made, but rather than using the copy to replace a call, it is used to create a new routine in which one or more parameters have been replaced by constants. The cloning of a routine R is useful when static analysis shows that R is often called with the same constant parameter or parameters. Cloning is also known as **specialization**.

Suppose for example that the routine

```
double power_series(int n, double a [], double x) {
    double result = 0.0;
    int p;
    for (p = 0; p < n; p++) result += a[p] * (x ** p);
    return result ;
}
```

which computes $\sum_{p=0}^{n} a_p x^p$, is called with x set to 1.0. Cloning it for this parameter yields the new routine

```
double power_series_x_1(int n, double a []) {
    double result = 0.0;
    int p;
    for (p = 0; p < n; p++) result += a[p] * (1.0 ** p);
    return result ;
}
```

and arithmetic simplification reduces this to

```
double power_series_x_1(int n, double a []) {
    double result = 0.0;
    int p;
    for (p = 0; p < n; p++) result += a[p];
    return result ;
}
```

Each call of the form power_series(n, a, 1.0) is then replaced by a call power_series_x_1(n, a), and a more efficient program results. Note that the transformation is useful even if there is only one such call. Note also that in cloning the constant parameter *can* be substituted in macro fashion, since it is constant and cannot have side effects.

A large proportion of the calls with constant parameters concerns calls to library routines, and cloning is most effective when the complete program is being optimized, including the library routines.

7.3.4 Procedural abstraction

In-lining and cloning increase speed, which is almost always a good thing, but also increase code size, which is usually not a problem. In some applications, however, mainly in embedded systems, code size is much more important than speed. In these applications it is desirable to perform the inverse process, one which finds multiple occurrences of tree segments in an AST and replaces them by routine calls. This process is called **outlining**, or, more usually and to avoid confusion, **procedural abstraction**; it is much less straightforward than in-lining.

There is usually ample opportunity for finding repeating tree segments, partly because programmers often use template-like programming constructions ("programming idioms"), and partly because intermediate code generation tends to expand specific language constructs into standard translations. Now it could be argued that perhaps these specific language constructs should not have been expanded in the first place, but actually this expansion can be beneficial, since it allows repeating combinations of such translations, perhaps even combined with programming idioms, to be recognized.

The following is a relatively simple, relatively effective algorithm for procedural abstraction. Each node in the AST is the top of a subtree, and for each pair of nodes (N, M) the algorithm finds the largest top segment the subtrees of N and M have in common. This largest top segment T is easily found by two simultaneous depth-first scans starting from N and M, which stop and backtrack when they find differing nodes or when one scan encounters the top node of the other scan. The latter condition is necessary to prevent identifying overlapping segments. This results in a tuple $((N,M),T)$ for each pair N and M. Together they form the set of common top segments, C. Note that in the tuple $((N,M),T)$, N and M indicate the nodes *with* their positions in the AST, whereas T just indicates the extent of the identified segment.

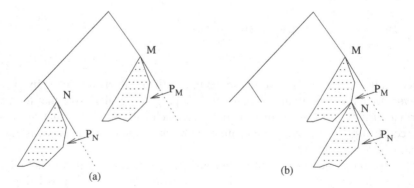

Fig. 7.7: Finding a procedure to abstract

Figure 7.7(a) gives a snapshot of the algorithm in action. Pointers P_N and P_M are used for the depth-first scans from N and M, respectively. The dotted areas have already been recognized as part of the subtree T; the areas to the right of the pointers will be compared next. Figure 7.7(b) shows a situation in which the scans stop because the scan pointer of one node (P_M) happens to hit the other node (N). The scans will then backtrack over that node and continue to attempt to find the largest common subtree.

When the set of common top segments C is complete, the most profitable $((N,M),T)$ in it is chosen to be abstracted into a procedure. Several routines are then constructed: one, R_T, for T, and one for each subtree $N_1...N_n$, $M_1...M_n$ hanging from N and M; note that the same number (n) of trees hang from N and M. Nodes N and M are then removed from the AST, including their subtrees, and replaced by routine calls $R_T(R_{N_1}...R_{N_n})$ and $R_T(R_{M_1}...R_{M_n})$, respectively, where R_{N_k} is the routine constructed for subtree N_k, and likewise for R_{M_k}. This process is then repeated until the required size is obtained or no profitable segment can be found any more.

An example of the transformation is shown in Figure 7.8. On the left we see the original AST. On the right we have the reduced main AST, in which the occurrences of T have been replaced by routine calls (a); the routine generated for T with its routine entry code, exit code, and calls to its parameters X and Y (b); and the routines generated for the parameters P, Q, R, and S, each with its entry and exit code (c).

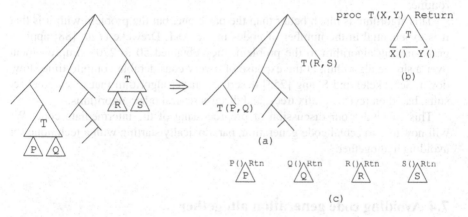

Fig. 7.8: Procedural abstraction

The algorithm requires us to select the "most profitable" of the common top segments. To make this more explicit, we have to consider where the profit comes from. We gain the number of nodes in T, once, but we lose on the new connections we have to make: the two routine calls $R_T(R_{N_1}...R_{N_n})$ and $R_T(R_{M_1}...R_{M_n})$; routine entries and exits for $R_{N_1}...R_{N_n},R_{M_1}...R_{M_n}$; and the calls to these routines inside R_T. Note that the subtrees must be passed to R_T as unevaluated routines rather than by value, since we have no idea how or if R_T is going to use them, or even if they have values at all.

The above algorithm has several flaws. First of all, our metric is faulty: the algorithm minimizes the number of nodes, whereas we want to minimize the code size. The problem can be mitigated somewhat by estimating the code size of each node, but with a strong code generator such an estimate is full of uncertainty. Therefore procedural abstraction is often applied to the generated assembly code, but that approach has problems of its own; see Section 7.6.2.

Second, the complexity of the algorithm is $O(k^3)$, where k is the number of nodes in the AST (k^2 for the pairs, and k for the maximum size of the subtree), which suggests a problem. Fortunately most tests for the equality of nodes will fail, so the $O(k)$ component does not usually materialize; but the $O(k^2)$ remains.

Third, the algorithm finds duplicate occurrences, not multiple occurrences, and there could easily be three or more occurrences of T in the AST. This case is simple to catch: if we find that C also contains the tuple $((N,M_1),T)$ in addition to $((N,M),T)$, we know that a call R_T can also be used to replace the T-shaped subtree at M_1. More worrying is the possibility that if we had made T one or more nodes smaller, we might have matched many more tree segments and made a much larger profit. To remedy this we need to keep *all* tree segments for N and M, rather than just the largest. C will then contain elements $((N_1,M_1),T_1)$, $((N_1,M_1),T_2)$, ..., $((N_i,M_j),T_k)$, ... The algorithm now considers each T_i in turn, collects all elements in which it occurs and computes the profit. Again the most profitable one is then turned into a routine.

This algorithm is much better than the basic one, but the problem with it is that it is exponential in the number of nodes in the AST. Dreweke *et al.* [88] apply a graph-mining algorithm to the problem; they obtained 50 to 270% improvement over a simple algorithm, at the expense of a very considerable compile-time slowdown. Schaekeler and Shang [253] describe a faster algorithm that gives good results, based on reverse prefix trees, and discuss several other algorithms.

This concludes our discussion of preprocessing of the intermediate code. We will now turn to actual code generation, paradoxically starting with a technique for avoiding it altogether.

7.4 Avoiding code generation altogether

Writing a code generator is a fascinating enterprise, but it is also far from trivial, and it is good to examine options on making it as simple as possible or even not do it at all.

Surprisingly, we can avoid code generation entirely and still please our customers to a certain degree, if we have an interpreter for the source language. The trick is to incorporate the AST of the source program P and the interpreter into one executable program file, E. This can be achieved by "freezing" the interpreter just before it begins its task of interpreting the AST, if the operating system allows doing so, or by copying and combining code segments and data structures. Calling the executable E starts the interpreter exactly at the point it was frozen, so the interpreter starts interpreting the AST of P. The result is that the frozen interpreter plus AST acts precisely as a compiled program.

This admittedly bizarre scheme allows a compiler to be constructed almost overnight if an interpreter is available, which makes it a good way to do rapid prototyping. Also, it makes the change from interpreter to compiler transparent to the user. In the introduction of a new language, it is very important that the users have access to the full standard compiler interface, right from day one. First working with an interpreter and then having to update all the makefiles when the real compiler arrives, because of changes in the command line calling convention, generates very little goodwill. Occasionally, faking a compiler is a valid option.

We will now turn to actual code generation. This chapter covers only trivial and simple code generation techniques. There exist innumerable optimization techniques; some of the more important ones are discussed in Chapter 9.

7.5 Code generation proper

As we have seen at the beginning of this chapter, the nodes in an intermediate code tree fall mainly in one of three classes: administration, expressions, and flow-of-control. The administration nodes correspond, for example, to declarations, module structure indications, etc. Normally, little or no code corresponds to them in the object code, although they may contain expressions that have to be evaluated. Also, in some cases module linkage may require code at run time to call the initialization parts of the modules in the right order (see Section 11.5.2). Still, the code needed for administration nodes is minimal and almost always trivial.

Flow-of-control nodes describe a variety of features: simple skipping deriving from if-then statements, multi-way choice deriving from case statements, computed gotos, function calls, exception handling, method application, Prolog rule selection, RPC (remote procedure calls), etc. If we are translating to real hardware rather than into a language that will undergo further processing, the corresponding target instructions are usually restricted to variants of the unconditional and conditional jump and the stacking routine call and return. For traditional languages, the semantics given by the language manual for each of the flow-of-control features can often be expressed easily in terms of the target machine, perhaps with the exception of non-local gotos—jumps that leave a routine. The more modern paradigms often require forms of flow of control that are more easily implemented in library routines than mapped directly onto the hardware. An example is determining the next Prolog clause the head of which matches a given goal. It is often profitable to expand these library routines in-line by substituting their ASTs in the program AST; this results in a much larger AST without the advanced flow-of-control features. This simplified AST is then subjected to more traditional processing. In any case, the nature of the code required for the flow-of-control nodes depends very much on the paradigm of the source language. We will therefore cover this subject again in each of the chapters on paradigm-specific compilation.

Expressions occur in all paradigms. They can occur explicitly in the code in all but the logic languages, but they can also be inserted as the translation of higher-level language constructs, for example array indexing. Many of the nodes for which code is to be generated belong to expressions, and most optimizations are concerned with these.

7.5.1 Trivial code generation

There is a strong relationship between iterative interpretation and code generation: an iterative interpreter contains code segments that perform the actions required by the nodes in the AST; a compiler generates code segments that perform the actions required by the nodes in the AST. This observation suggests a naive, trivial way to produce code: for each node in the AST, generate the code segment that the iterative interpreter contains for it. This essentially replaces the active-node pointer by the machine instruction pointer. To make this work, some details have to be seen to. First, the data structure definitions and auxiliary routines of the interpreter must be copied into the generated code; second, care must be taken to sequence the code properly, in accordance with the flow of control in the AST. Both are usually easy to do.

Figure 7.9 shows the results of this process applied to the iterative interpreter of Figure 6.6. Each case part now consists of a single print statement which produces the code executed by the interpreter. Note that the #include "stack.h" directive, which made the stack handling module available to the interpreter in Figure 6.6, is now part of the generated code. A call of the code generator of Figure 7.9 with the source program (7*(1+5)) yields the code shown in Figure 7.10; compiled and run, the code indeed prints the answer 42. The code in Figure 7.10 has been edited slightly for layout.

At first sight it may seem pointless to compile C code to C code, and we agree that the code thus obtained is inefficient, but still several points have been made:

- Compilation has taken place in a real sense, since arbitrarily more complicated source programs will result in the same "flat" and uncomplicated kind of code.
- The code generator was obtained with minimal effort.
- It is easy to see that the process can be repeated for much more complicated source languages, for example those representing advanced and experimental paradigms.

Also, if code with this structure is fed to a compiler that does aggressive optimization, often quite bearable object code results. Indeed, the full optimizing version of the GNU C compiler *gcc* removes all code resulting from the switch statements from Figure 7.10.

There are two directions into which this idea has been developed; both attempt to address the "stupidity" of the above code. The first has led to threaded code, a technique for obtaining very small object programs, the second to partial evaluation,

```
#include   "parser.h"      /* for types AST_node and Expression */
#include   "thread.h"      /* for Thread_AST() and Thread_start */
#include   "backend.h"     /* for self check */
                                     /* PRIVATE */
static AST_node *Active_node_pointer;

static void Trivial_code_generation(void) {
    printf ("#include    \"stack.h\"\n int main(void) {\n");
    while (Active_node_pointer != 0) {
        /* there is only one node type, Expression: */
        Expression *expr = Active_node_pointer;
        switch (expr->type) {
        case 'D':
            printf ("Push(%d);\n", expr->value);
            break;
        case 'P':
            printf (" {\n\
                int e_left = Pop(); int e_right = Pop();\n\
                switch (%d) {\n\
                case '+': Push(e_left + e_right); break;\n\
                case '*': Push(e_left * e_right); break;\n\
                }}\n",
                expr->oper
            );
            break;
        }
        Active_node_pointer = Active_node_pointer->successor;
    }
    printf (" printf (\"%%d\\n\", Pop()); /* print the result */\n");
    printf ("return 0;}\n");
}
                                     /* PUBLIC */
void Process(AST_node *icode) {
    Thread_AST(icode); Active_node_pointer = Thread_start;
    Trivial_code_generation();
}
```

Fig. 7.9: A trivial code generator for the demo compiler of Section 1.2

a very powerful and general but unfortunately still poorly understood technique that
can sometimes achieve spectacular speed-ups.

7.5.1.1 Threaded code

The code of Figure 7.10 is very repetitive, since it has been generated from a limited
number of code segments, and the idea suggests itself to pack the code segments into
routines, possibly with parameters. The resulting code then consists of a library of
routines derived directly from the interpreter and a list of routine calls derived from
the source program. Such a list of routine calls is called **threaded code**; the term has

```
#include    "stack.h"
int main(void) {
Push(7);
Push(1);
Push(5);
{
    int e_left = Pop(); int e_right = Pop();
    switch (43) {
    case '+': Push(e_left + e_right); break;
    case '*': Push(e_left * e_right); break;
    }}
{
    int e_left = Pop(); int e_right = Pop();
    switch (42) {
    case '+': Push(e_left + e_right); break;
    case '*': Push(e_left * e_right); break;
    }}
printf ("%d\n", Pop()); /* print the result */
return 0;}
```

Fig. 7.10: Code for **(7*(1+5))** generated by the code generator of Figure 7.9

nothing to do with the threading of the AST. Threaded code for the source program
(7*(1+5)) is shown in Figure 7.11, based on the assumption that we have introduced a routine *Expression_D* for the case 'D' in the interpreter, and *Expression_P*
for the case 'P', as shown in Figure 7.12. Only those interpreter routines that are
actually used by a particular source program need to be included in the threaded
code.

```
#include    "expression.h"
#include    "threaded.i"
```

Fig. 7.11: Possible threaded code for **(7*(1+5))**

The characteristic advantage of threaded code is that it is small. It is mainly used
in process control and embedded systems, to control hardware with very limited
processing power, for example toy electronics. The language Forth allows one to
write threaded code by hand, but threaded code can also be generated very well
from higher-level languages. Threaded code was first researched by Bell for the
PDP-11 [34] and has since been applied in a variety of contexts [82, 202, 236].

If the ultimate in code size reduction is desired, the routines can be numbered
and the list of calls can be replaced by an array of routine numbers; if there are no
more than 256 different routines, one byte per call suffices (see Exercise 7.5). Since
each routine has a known number of parameters and since all parameters derive
from fields in the AST and are thus constants known to the code generator, the
parameters can be incorporated into the threaded code. A small interpreter is now

```
#include   "stack.h"

void Expression_D(int digit) {
    Push(digit);
}

void Expression_P(int oper) {
    int  e_left  = Pop();  int  e_right = Pop();
    switch (oper) {
    case '+': Push(e_left + e_right);  break;
    case '*': Push(e_left * e_right);  break;
    }
}

void Print (void) {
    printf ("%d\n", Pop());
}
```

Fig. 7.12: Routines for the threaded code for **(7*(1+5))**

needed to activate the routines in the order prescribed by the threaded code. By now the distinction between interpretation and code generation has become completely blurred.

Actually, the above technique only yields the penultimate in code size reduction. Since the code segments from the interpreter generally use fewer features than the code in the source program, they too can be translated to threaded code, leaving only some ten to twenty primitive routines, which load and store variables, perform arithmetic and Boolean operations, effect jumps, etc. This results in extremely compact code. Also note that only the primitive routines need to be present in machine code; all the rest of the program including the interpreter is machine-independent.

7.5.1.2 Partial evaluation

When we look at the code in Figure 7.10, we see that the code generator generates a lot of code it could have executed itself; prime examples are the switch statements over constant values. It is usually not very difficult to modify the code generator by hand so that it is more discriminating about what code it *performs* and what code it *generates*. Figure 7.13 shows a case 'P' part in which the switch statement is performed at code generation time. The code resulting for **(7*(1+5))** is in Figure 7.14, again slightly edited for layout.

The process of performing part of a computation while generating code for the rest of the computation is called **partial evaluation**. It is a very general and powerful technique for program simplification and optimization, but its automatic application to real-world programs is still outside our reach. Many researchers believe that many of the existing optimization techniques are special cases of partial evaluation and that a better knowledge of it would allow us to obtain very powerful optimiz-

```
case 'P':
    printf ("{\nint  e_left  = Pop();  int  e_right = Pop();\n");
    switch (expr−>oper) {
    case '+':  printf ("Push(e_left + e_right );\n");  break;
    case '*':  printf ("Push(e_left * e_right );\n");  break;
    }
    printf ("}\n");
    break;
```

Fig. 7.13: Partial evaluation in a segment of the code generator

```
#include    "stack.h"
int  main(void) {
Push(7);
Push(1);
Push(5);
{int  e_left  = Pop();  int  e_right = Pop();  Push(e_left + e_right );}
{int  e_left  = Pop();  int  e_right = Pop();  Push(e_left * e_right );}
printf ("%d\n", Pop());  /* print the result */
return 0;}
```

Fig. 7.14: Code for **(7∗(1+5))** generated by the code generator of Figure 7.13

ers, thus simplifying compilation, program generation, and even program design. Considerable research is being put into it, most of it concentrated on the functional languages. For a real-world example of the use of partial evaluation for optimized code generation, see Section 13.5. Much closer to home, we note that the compile-time execution of the main loop of the iterative interpreter in Figure 6.6, which leads directly to the code generator of Figure 7.9, is a case of partial evaluation: the loop is performed now, code is generated for all the rest, to be performed later.

Partially evaluating code has an Escher-like[1] quality about it: it has to be viewed at two levels. Figures 7.15 and 7.16 show the foreground (run-now) and background (run-later) view of Figure 7.13.

```
case 'P':
    printf ("{\nint  e_left = Pop();  int  e_right = Pop();\n");
    switch (expr−>oper) {
    case '+':  printf ("Push(e_left + e_right );\n");  break;
    case '*':  printf ("Push(e_left * e_right );\n");  break;
    }
    printf ("}\n");
    break;
```

Fig. 7.15: Foreground (run-now) view of partially evaluating code

---

[1] M.C. (Maurits Cornelis) Escher (1898–1972), Dutch artist known for his intriguing and ambiguous drawings and paintings.

```
case 'P':
    printf (" {\nint e_left = Pop(); int e_right = Pop();\n");
    switch (expr->oper) {
    case '+':  printf ("Push(e_left + e_right );\n"); break;
    case '*':  printf ("Push(e_left * e_right );\n"); break;
    }
    printf (" }\n");
    break;
```

Fig. 7.16: Background (run-later) view of partially evaluating code

For a detailed description of how to convert an interpreter into a compiler see Pagan [209]. Extensive discussions of partial evaluation can be found in the book by Jones, Gomard and Sestoft [135], which applies partial evaluation to the general problem of program generation, and the more compiler-construction oriented book by Pagan [210]. An extensive example of generating an object code segment by manual partial evaluation can be found in Section 13.5.2.

7.5.2 Simple code generation

In simple code generation, a fixed translation to the target code is chosen for each possible node type. During code generation, the nodes in the AST are rewritten to their translations, and the AST is scheduled by following the data flow inside expressions and the flow of control elsewhere. Since the correctness of this composition of translations depends very much on the interface conventions between each of the translations, it is important to keep these interface conventions simple; but, as usual, more complicated interface conventions allow more efficient translations.

Simple code generation requires local decisions only, and is therefore especially suitable for narrow compilers. With respect to machine types, it is particularly suitable for two somewhat similar machine models, the pure stack machine and the pure register machine.

A **pure stack machine** uses a stack to store and manipulate values; it has no registers. It has two types of instructions, those that move or copy values between the top of the stack and elsewhere, and those that do operations on the top element or elements of the stack. The stack machine has two important data administration pointers: the stack pointer SP, which points to the top of the stack, and the base pointer BP, which points to the beginning of the region on the stack where the local variables are stored; see Figure 7.17. It may have other data administration pointers, for example a pointer to the global data area and a stack area limit pointer, but these play no direct role in simple code generation.

For our explanation we assume a very simple stack machine, one in which all stack entries are of type integer and which features only the machine instructions summarized in Figure 7.18. We also ignore the problems with stack overflow here; on many machines stack overflow is detected by the hardware and results in a syn-

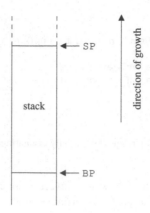

Fig. 7.17: Data administration in a simple stack machine

chronous interrupt, which allows the operating system to increase the stack size.

Instruction	Actions
Push_Const c	SP:=SP+1; stack[SP]:=c;
Push_Local i	SP:=SP+1; stack[SP]:=stack[BP+i];
Store_Local i	stack[BP+i]:=stack[SP]; SP:=SP−1;
Add_Top2	stack[SP−1]:=stack[SP−1]+stack[SP]; SP:=SP−1;
Subtr_Top2	stack[SP−1]:=stack[SP−1]−stack[SP]; SP:=SP−1;
Mult_Top2	stack[SP−1]:=stack[SP−1]×stack[SP]; SP:=SP−1;

Fig. 7.18: Stack machine instructions

Push_Const c pushes the constant c (incorporated in the machine instruction) onto the top of the stack; this action raises the stack pointer by 1. Push_Local i pushes a copy of the value of the i-th local variable on the top of the stack; i is incorporated in the machine instruction, but BP is added to it before it is used as an index to a stack element; this raises the stack pointer by 1. Store_Local i removes the top element from the stack and stores its value in the i-th local variable; this lowers the stack pointer by 1. Add_Top2 removes the top two elements from the stack, adds their values and pushes the result back onto the stack; this action lowers the stack pointer by 1. Subtr_Top2 and Mult_Top2 do similar things; note the order of the operands in Subtr_Top2: the deeper stack entry is the left operand since it was pushed first.

Suppose p is a local variable; then the code for p:=p+5 is

```
Push_Local  #p  −− Push value of #p-th local onto stack.
Push_Const 5   −− Push value 5 onto stack.
Add_Top2       −− Add top two elements.
Store_Local #p −− Pop and store result back in #p-th local.
```

in which #p is the position number of p among the local variables. Note that the operands of the machine instructions are all compile-time constants: the operand of Push_Local and Store_Local is not the *value* of p—which is a run-time quantity—but the *number* of p among the local variables.

The stack machine model has been made popular by the DEC PDP-11 and VAX machines. Since all modern machines, with the exception of RISC machines, have stack instructions, this model still has wide applicability. Its main disadvantage is that on a modern machine it is not very efficient.

A **pure register machine** has a memory to store values in, a set of registers to perform operations on, and two sets of instructions. One set contains instructions to copy values between the memory and a register. The instructions in the other set perform operations on the values in two registers and leave the result in one of them. In our simple register machine we assume that all registers store values of type integer; the instructions are summarized in Figure 7.19.

Instruction	Actions
Load_Const c,R_n	$R_n:=c$;
Load_Mem x,R_n	$R_n:=x$;
Store_Reg R_n,x	$x:=R_n$;
Add_Reg R_m,R_n	$R_n:=R_n+R_m$;
Subtr_Reg R_m,R_n	$R_n:=R_n-R_m$;
Mult_Reg R_m,R_n	$R_n:=R_n\times R_m$;

Fig. 7.19: Register machine instructions

The machine instruction names used here consist of two parts. The first part can be Load_, Add_, Subtr_, or Mult_, all of which imply a register as the target, or Store_, which implies a memory location as the target. The second part specifies the type of the source; it can be Const, Reg, or Mem. For example, an instruction Add_Const 5,R3 would add the constant 5 to the contents of register 3. The above instruction names have been chosen for their explanatory value; they do not derive from any assembly language. Each assembler has its own set of instruction names, most of them very abbreviated.

Two more remarks are in order here. The first is that the rightmost operand in the instructions is the destination of the operation, in accordance with most assembly languages. Note that this is a property of those assembly languages, not of the machine instructions themselves. In two-register instructions, the destination register doubles as the first source register of the operation during execution; this *is* a property of the machine instructions of a pure register machine.

The second remark is that the above notation Load_Mem x,R_n with semantics $R_n:=x$ is misleading. We should actually have written

Load_Mem &x,R_n $R_n:=*(\&x)$;

in which &x is the address of x in memory. Just as we have to write Push_Local #b, in which #b is the variable number of b, to push the value of b onto the stack, we should, in principle, write Load_Mem &x,R1 to load the value of x into R1. The reason is of course that machine instructions can contain constants only: the load-constant instruction contains the constant value directly, the load-memory and store-memory instructions contain constant addresses that allow them to access the values of the variables. But traditionally assembly languages consider the address indication & to be implicit in the load and store instructions, making forms like Load_Mem x,R1 the normal way of loading the value of a variable into a register; its semantics is $R_n:=*(\&x)$, in which the address operator & is provided by the assembler or compiler at compile time and the dereference operator * by the instruction at run time.

The code for p:=p+5 on a register-memory machine would be:

```
Load_Mem  p,R1
Load_Const 5,R2
Add_Reg    R2,R1
Store_Reg  R1,p
```

in which p represents the address of the variable p. Since all modern machines have registers, the model is very relevant. Its efficiency is good, but its main problem is that the number of registers is limited.

7.5.2.1 Simple code generation for a stack machine

We will now see how we can generate stack machine code for arithmetic expressions. As an example we take the expression b*b – 4*(a*c); its AST is shown in Figure 7.20.

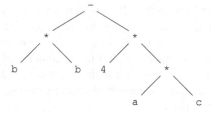

Fig. 7.20: The abstract syntax tree for b*b – 4*(a*c)

Next we consider the ASTs that belong to the stack machine instructions from Figure 7.18.

Under the interface convention that operands are supplied to and retrieved from the top of the stack, their ASTs are trivial: each machine instruction corresponds exactly to one node in the expression AST; see Figure 7.21. As a result, the rewriting of the tree is also trivial: each node is replaced by its straightforward translation; see Figure 7.22, in which #a, #b, and #c are the variable numbers (stack positions) of a, b, and c.

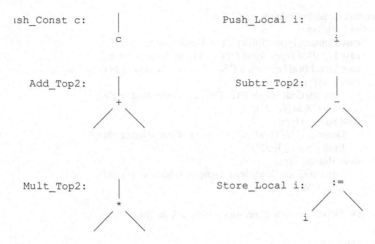

Fig. 7.21: The abstract syntax trees for the stack machine instructions

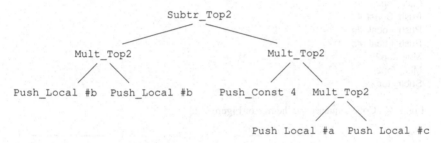

Fig. 7.22: The abstract syntax tree for b*b − 4*(a*c) rewritten

The only thing that is left to be done is to order the instructions. The conventions that an operand leaves its result on the top of the stack and that an operation may only be issued when its operand(s) are on the top of the stack immediately suggest a simple evaluation order: depth-first visit. Depth-first visit has the property that it first visits all the children of a node and then immediately afterwards the node itself; since the children have put their results on the stack (as per convention) the parent can now find them there and can use them to produce its own result. In other words, depth-first visit coincides with the data-flow arrows in the AST of an expression. So we arrive at the code generation algorithm shown in Figure 7.23, in which the procedure *Emit()* produces its parameter(s) in the proper instruction format.

Applying this algorithm to the top node in Figure 7.22 yields the code sequence shown in Figure 7.24. The successive stack configurations that occur when this sequence is executed are shown in Figure 7.25, in which the values appear in their symbolic form. The part of the stack on which expressions are evaluated is called the "working stack"; it is treated more extensively in Section 11.3.1.

procedure GenerateCode (Node):
  select Node.type:
    case ConstantType: Emit ("Push_Const" Node.value);
    case LocalVarType: Emit ("Push_Local" Node.number);
    case StoreLocalType: Emit ("Store_Local" Node.number);
    case AddType:
      GenerateCode (Node.left); GenerateCode (Node.right);
      Emit ("Add_Top2");
    case SubtractType:
      GenerateCode (Node.left); GenerateCode (Node.right);
      Emit ("Subtr_Top2");
    case MultiplyType:
      GenerateCode (Node.left); GenerateCode (Node.right);
      Emit ("Mult_Top2");

Fig. 7.23: Depth-first code generation for a stack machine

```
Push_Local  #b
Push_Local  #b
Mult_Top2
Push_Const 4
Push_Local  #a
Push_Local  #c
Mult_Top2
Mult_Top2
Subtr_Top2
```

Fig. 7.24: Code sequence for the tree of Figure 7.22

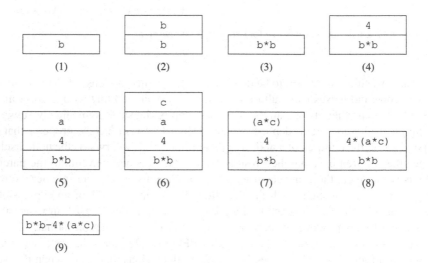

Fig. 7.25: Successive stack configurations for b*b − 4*(a*c)

7.5.2.2 Simple code generation for a register machine

Much of what was said about code generation for the stack machine applies to the register machine as well. The ASTs of the machine instructions from Figure 7.19 can be found in Figure 7.26.

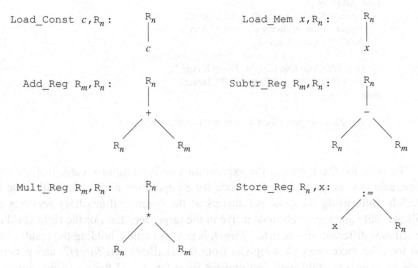

Fig. 7.26: The abstract syntax trees for the register machine instructions

The main difference with Figure 7.21 is that here the inputs and outputs are mentioned explicitly, as numbered registers. The interface conventions are that, except for the result of the top instruction, the output register of an instruction must be used immediately as an input register of the parent instruction in the AST, and that, for the moment at least, the two input registers of an instruction must be different.

Note that as a result of the convention to name the destination last in assembly instructions, the two-operand instructions mention their operands in an order reversed from that which appears in the ASTs: these instructions mention their second source register first, since the first register is the same as the destination, which is mentioned second. Unfortunately, this may occasionally lead to some confusion.

We use depth-first code generation again, but this time we have to contend with registers. A simple way to structure this problem is to decree that in the evaluation of each node in the expression tree, the result of the expression is expected in a given register, the **target register**, and that a given set of **auxiliary registers** is available to help get it there. We require the result of the top node to be delivered in R1 and observe that all registers except R1 are available as auxiliary registers.

Register allocation is now easy; see Figure 7.27, in which *Target* is a register number and *Aux* is a set of register numbers. Less accurately, we will refer to *Target* as a register and to *Aux* as a set of registers.

```
procedure GenerateCode (Node, a register Target, a register set Aux):
    select Node.type:
        case ConstantType:
            Emit ("Load_Const " Node.value ",R" Target);
        case VariableType:
            Emit ("Load_Mem " Node.address ",R" Target);
        case ...
        case AddType:
            GenerateCode (Node.left, Target, Aux);
            Target2 ← an arbitrary element of Aux;
            Aux2 ← Aux \ Target2;
                -- the \ denotes the set difference operation
            GenerateCode (Node.right, Target2, Aux2);
            Emit ("Add_Reg R" Target2 ",R" Target);
        case ...
```

Fig. 7.27: Simple code generation with register allocation

The code for the leaves in the expression tree is straightforward: just emit the code, using the target register. The code for an operation node starts with code for the left child, using the same parameters as the parent: all auxiliary registers are still available and the result must arrive in the target register. For the right child the situation is different: one register, *Target*, is now occupied, holding the result of the left tree. We therefore pick a register from the auxiliary set, *Target2*, and generate code for the right child with that register for a target and the remaining registers as auxiliaries. Now we have our results in *Target* and *Target2*, respectively, and we emit the code for the operation. This leaves the result in *Target* and frees *Target2*. So when we leave the routine, all auxiliary registers are free again. Since this situation applies at all nodes, our code generation works.

Actually, no set manipulation is necessary in this case, because the set can be implemented as a stack of registers. Rather than picking an arbitrary register, we pick the top of the register stack for *Target2*, which leaves us the rest of the stack for *Aux2*. Since the register stack is actually a stack of the numbers 1 to the number of available registers, a single integer suffices to represent it. The combined code generation/register allocation code is shown in Figure 7.28.

The code it generates is shown in Figure 7.29. Figure 7.30 shows the contents of the registers during the execution of this code. The similarity with Figure 7.25 is immediate: the registers act as a working stack.

Weighted register allocation It is somewhat disappointing to see that 4 registers are required for the expression where 3 would do. (The inefficiency of loading b twice is dealt with in the subsection on common subexpression elimination in Section 9.1.2.1.) The reason is that one register gets tied up holding the value 4 while the subtree a∗c is being computed. If we had treated the right subtree first, 3 registers would have sufficed, as is shown in Figure 7.31.

Indeed, one register fewer is available for the second child than for the first child, since that register is in use to hold the result of the first child. So it is advantageous

```
procedure GenerateCode (Node, a register number Target):
    select Node.type:
        case ConstantType:
            Emit ("Load_Const " Node.value ",R" Target);
        case VariableType:
            Emit ("Load_Mem " Node.address ",R" Target);
        case ...
        case AddType:
            GenerateCode (Node.left, Target);
            GenerateCode (Node.right, Target+1);
            Emit ("Add_Reg R" Target+1 ",R" Target);
        case ...
```

Fig. 7.28: Simple code generation with register numbering

```
Load_Mem   b,R1
Load_Mem   b,R2
Mult_Reg   R2,R1
Load_Const 4,R2
Load_Mem   a,R3
Load_Mem   c,R4
Mult_Reg   R4,R3
Mult_Reg   R3,R2
Subtr_Reg  R2,R1
```

Fig. 7.29: Register machine code for the expression b*b – 4*(a*c)

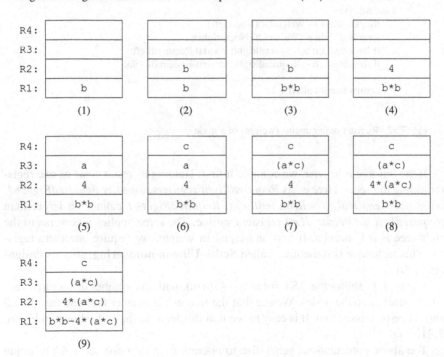

Fig. 7.30: Successive register contents for b*b – 4*(a*c)

```
Load_Mem   b,R1
Load_Mem   b,R2
Mult_Reg   R2,R1
Load_Mem   a,R2
Load_Mem   c,R3
Mult_Reg   R3,R2
Load_Const 4,R3
Mult_Reg   R3,R2
Subtr_Reg  R2,R1
```

Fig. 7.31: Weighted register machine code for the expression b*b – 4*(a*c)

to generate the code for the child that requires the most registers first. In an obvious analogy, we will call the number of registers required by a node its **weight**. Since the weight of each leaf is known and the weight of a node can be computed from the weights of its children, the weight of a subtree can be determined simply by a depth-first prescan, as shown in Figure 7.32.

```
function WeightOf (Node) returning an integer:
    select Node.type:
        case ConstantType: return 1;
        case VariableType: return 1;
        case ...
        case AddType:
            RequiredLeft ← WeightOf (Node.left);
            RequiredRight ← WeightOf (Node.right);
            if RequiredLeft > RequiredRight: return RequiredLeft;
            if RequiredLeft < RequiredRight: return RequiredRight;
            --- At this point we know RequiredLeft = RequiredRight
            return RequiredLeft + 1;
        case ...
```

Fig. 7.32: Register requirements (weight) of a node

If the left tree is heavier, we compile it first. Holding its result costs us one register, doing the second tree costs *RequiredRight* registers, together *RequiredRight+1*, but since *RequiredLeft* > *RequiredRight*, *RequiredRight+1* cannot be larger than *RequiredLeft*, so *RequiredLeft* registers suffice. The same applies vice versa to the right tree if *it* is heavier. If both are equal in weight, we require one extra register. This technique is sometimes called **Sethi–Ullman numbering**, after its designers [259].

Figure 7.33 shows the AST for b*b – 4*(a*c), with the number of required registers attached to the nodes. We see that the tree a*c is heavier than the tree 4, and should be processed first. It is easy to see that this leads to the code shown in Figure 7.31.

The above computations generalize to operations with n operands. An example of such an operation is a routine call with n parameters, under the not unusual con-

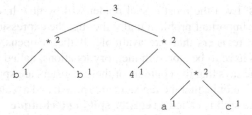

Fig. 7.33: AST for b*b – 4*(a*c) with register weights

vention that all parameters must be passed in registers (for n smaller than some reasonable number). Based on the argument that each finished operand takes away one register, registers will be used most economically if the parameter trees are sorted according to weight, the heaviest first, and processed in that order [17]. If the sorted order is $E_1 \ldots E_n$, then the compilation of tree 1 requires $E_1 + 0$ registers, that of tree 2 requires $E_2 + 1$ registers, and that of tree n requires $E_n + n - 1$ registers. The total number of required registers for the node is the maximum of these terms, in a formula $\max_{k=1}^{n}(E_k + k - 1)$. For $n = 2$ this reduces to the IF-statements in Figure 7.32.

Suppose, for example, we have a routine with three parameters, to be delivered in registers R1, R2, and R3, with actual parameters of weights $W_1 = 1$, $W_2 = 4$, and $W_3 = 2$. By sorting the weights, we conclude that we must process the parameters in the order 2, 3, 1. The computation

Parameter number (N)	2 3 1	
Sorted weight of parameter N	4 2 1	
Registers occupied when starting parameter N	0 1 2	
Maximum needed for parameter N	4 3 3	
Overall maximum	4	

shows that we need 4 registers for the code generation of the parameters. Since we now require the first expression to deliver its result in register 2, we can no longer use a simple stack in the code of Figure 7.28, but must rather use a set, as in the original code of Figure 7.27. The process and its results are shown in Figure 7.34.

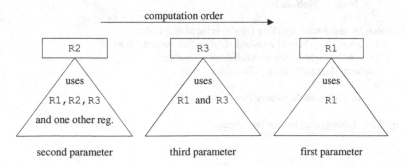

Fig. 7.34: Evaluation order of three parameter trees

Spilling registers Even the most casual reader will by now have noticed that we have swept a very important problem under the rug: the expression to be translated may require more registers than are available. If that happens, one or more values from registers have to be stored in memory locations, called temporaries, to be retrieved later. One says that the contents of these registers are spilled, or, less accurately but more commonly, that the registers are spilled; and a technique of choosing which register(s) to spill is called a **register spilling technique**.

There is no best register spilling technique (except for exhaustive search), and new techniques and improvements to old techniques are still being developed. The simple method we will describe here is based on the observation that the tree for a very complicated expression has a top region in which the weights are higher than the number of registers we have. From this top region a number of trees dangle, the weights of which are equal to or smaller than the number of registers. We can detach these trees from the original tree and assign their values to temporary variables. This leaves us with a set of temporary variables with expressions for which we *can* generate code since we have enough registers, plus a substantially reduced original tree, to which we repeat the process. An outline of the code is shown in Figure 7.35.

```
procedure GenerateCodeForLargeTrees (Node, TargetRegister):
    AuxiliaryRegisterSet ← AvailableRegisterSet \ TargetRegister;

    while Node ≠ NoNode:
        Compute the weights of all nodes of the tree Node;
        TreeNode ← MaximalNonLargeTree (Node);
        GenerateCode (TreeNode, TargetRegister, AuxiliaryRegisterSet);

        if TreeNode ≠ Node:
            TempLoc ← NextFreeTemporaryLocation();
            Emit ("Store R" TargetRegister ",T" TempLoc);
            Replace TreeNode by a reference to TempLoc;
            Return any temporary locations in the tree of TreeNode
                to the pool of free temporary locations;
        else — TreeNode = Node:
            Return any temporary locations in the tree of Node
                to the pool of free temporary locations;
            Node ← NoNode;

function MaximalNonLargeTree (Node) returning a node:
    if Node.weight ≤ Size of AvailableRegisterSet: return Node;
    if Node.left.weight > Size of AvailableRegisterSet:
        return MaximalNonLargeTree (Node.left);
    else — Node.right.weight ≥ Size of AvailableRegisterSet:
        return MaximalNonLargeTree (Node.right);
```

Fig. 7.35: Code generation for large trees

The method uses the set of available registers and a pool of temporary variables in memory. The main routine repeatedly finds a subtree that can be compiled using no more than the available registers, and generates code for it which yields the result in *TargetRegister*. If the subtree was the entire tree, the code generation process is complete. Otherwise, a temporary location is chosen, code for moving the contents of *TargetRegister* to that location is emitted, and the subtree is replaced by a reference to that temporary location. (If replacing the subtree is impossible because the expression tree is an unalterable part of an AST, we have to make a copy first.) The process of compiling subtrees continues until the entire tree has been consumed.

The auxiliary function *MaximalNonLargeTree(Node)* returns the largest subtree of the given node that can be evaluated using registers only. It first checks if the tree of its parameter *Node* can already be compiled with the available registers; if so, the non-large tree has been found. Otherwise, at least one of the children of *Node* must require at least all the available registers. The function then looks for a non-large tree in the left or the right child; since the register requirements decrease going down the tree, it will eventually succeed.

Figure 7.36 shows the code generated for our sample tree when compiled with 2 registers. Only one register is spilled, to temporary variable T1.

```
Load_Mem    a,R1
Load_Mem    c,R2
Mult_Reg    R2,R1
Load_Const  4,R2
Mult_Reg    R2,R1
Store_Reg   R1,T1
Load_Mem    b,R1
Load_Mem    b,R2
Mult_Reg    R2,R1
Load_Mem    T1,R2
Subtr_Reg   R2,R1
```

Fig. 7.36: Code generated for b*b − 4*(a*c) with only 2 registers

A few words may be said about the number of registers that a compiler designer should reserve for expressions. Experience shows [312] that for handwritten programs 4 or 5 registers are enough to avoid spilling almost completely. A problem is, however, that generated programs can and indeed do contain arbitrarily complex expressions, for which 4 or 5 registers will not suffice. Considering that such generated programs would probably cause spilling even if much larger numbers of registers were set aside for expressions, reserving 4 or 5 registers still seems a good policy.

Machines with register-memory operations In addition to the pure register machine instructions described above, many register machines have instructions for combining the contents of a register with that of a memory location. An example is an instruction Add_Mem X,R1 for adding the contents of memory location X to R1. The above techniques are easily adapted to include these new instructions. For example, a memory location as a right operand now requires zero registers rather than one; this reduces the weights of the trees. The new tree is shown in Figure 7.37 and the resulting new code in Figure 7.38. We see that the algorithm now produces code for the subtree 4∗a∗c first, and that the produced code differs completely from that in Figure 7.31.

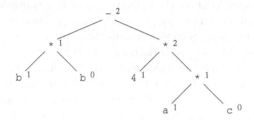

Fig. 7.37: Register-weighted tree for a memory-register machine

```
Load_Const  4,R2
Load_Mem    a,R1
Mult_Mem    c,R1
Mult_Reg    R1,R2
Load_Mem    b,R1
Mult_Mem    b,R1
Subtr_Reg   R2,R1
```

Fig. 7.38: Code for the register-weighted tree for a memory-register machine

Procedure-wide register allocation There are a few simple techniques for allocating registers for the entire routine we are compiling. The simplest is to set aside a fixed number of registers L for the first L local variables and to use the rest of the available registers as working registers for the evaluation of expressions. Available registers are those that are not needed for fixed administrative tasks (stack limit pointer, heap pointer, activation record base pointer, etc.).

With a little bit of effort we can do better; if we set aside L registers for local variables, giving them to the first L such variables is not the only option. For example, the C language allows local variables to have the storage attribute **register**, and priority can be given to these variables when handing out registers. A more sophisticated approach is to use usage counts [103]. A **usage count** is an estimate of how frequently a variable is used. The idea is that it is best to keep the most frequently used variables in registers. Frequency estimates can be obtained from static or dynamic profiles. See the sidebar for more on profiling information.

A problem with these and all other procedure-wide register allocation schemes is that they assign a register to a variable even in those regions of the routine in which the variable is not used. In Section 9.1.5 we will see a method to solve this problem.

Profiling information

The honest, labor-intensive way of obtaining statistical information about code usage is by dynamic profiling. Statements are inserted, manually or automatically, into the program, which produce a record of which parts of the code are executed: the program is **instrumented**. The program is then run on a representative set of input data and the records are gathered and condensed into the desired statistical usage data.

In practice it is simpler to do static profiling, based on the simple control flow traffic rule which says that the amount of traffic entering a node equals the amount leaving it; this is the flow-of-control equivalent of Kirchhoff's laws of electric circuits [159]. The stream entering a procedure body is set to, say, 1. At if-statements we guess that 70% of the incoming stream passes through the then-part and 30% through the else-part; loops are (re)entered 9 out of 10 times; etc. This yields a set of linear equations, which can be solved, resulting in usage estimates for all the basic blocks. See Exercises 7.9 and 7.10.

Evaluation of simple code generation Quite generally speaking and as a very rough estimate, simple code generation loses about a factor of three over a reasonable good optimizing compiler. This badly quantified statement means that it would be surprising if reasonable optimization effort did not bring a factor of two of improvement, and that it would be equally surprising if an improvement factor of six could be reached without extensive effort. Section 9.1 discuses a number of techniques that yield good optimization with reasonable effort. In a highly optimization compiler these would be supplemented by many small but often complicated refinements, each yielding a speed-up of a few percent.

We will now continue with the next phase in the compilation process, the postprocessing of the generated code, leaving further optimizations to Chapter 9.

7.6 Postprocessing the generated code

Many of the optimizations possible on the intermediate code can also be performed on the generated code if so preferred, for example arithmetic simplification, dead code removal and short-circuiting jumps to jumps. We will discus here two techniques: peephole optimization, which is specific to generated code; and procedural abstraction, which we saw applied to intermediate code in Section 7.3.4, but which differs somewhat when applied to generated code.

7.6.1 Peephole optimization

Even moderately sophisticated code generation techniques can produce stupid instruction sequences like

```
    Load_Reg R1,R2
    Load_Reg R2,R1
or
    Store_Reg R1,n
    Load_Mem n,R1
```

One way of remedying this situation is to do postprocessing in the form of peephole optimization. **Peephole optimization** replaces sequences of symbolic machine instructions in its input by more efficient sequences. This raises two questions: what instruction sequences are we going to replace, and by what other instruction sequences; and how do we find the instructions to be replaced? The two questions can be answered independently.

7.6.1.1 Creating replacement patterns

The instruction sequence to be replaced and its replacements can be specified in a **replacement pattern**. A replacement pattern consists of three components: a pattern instruction list with parameters, the left-hand side; conditions on those parameters; and a replacement instruction list with parameters, the right-hand side. A replacement pattern is applicable if the instructions in the pattern list match an instruction sequence in the input, with parameters that fulfill the conditions. Its application consists of replacing the matched instructions by the instructions in the replacement list, with the parameters substituted. Usual lengths for patterns lists are one, two, three, or perhaps even more instructions; the replacement list will normally be shorter.

An example in some ad-hoc notation is

Load_Reg R_a,R_b; Load_Reg R_c,R_d | $R_a=R_d$, $R_b=R_c$ $\Rightarrow$ Load_Reg R_a,R_b

which says that if we find the first two Load_Reg instructions in the input such that (|) they refer to the same but reversed register pair, we should replace them ($\Rightarrow$) by the third instruction.

It is tempting to construct a full set of replacement patterns for a given machine, which can be applied to any sequence of symbolic machine instructions to obtain a more efficient sequence, but there are several problems with this idea.

The first is that instruction sequences that do *exactly* the same as other instruction sequences are rarer than one might think. For example, suppose a machine has an integer increment instruction Increment R_n, which increments the contents of register R_n by 1. Before accepting it as a replacement for Add_Const 1,R_n we have to verify that both instructions affect the condition registers of the machine in the same way and react to integer overflow in the same way. If there is any difference, the replacement cannot be accepted in a general-purpose peephole optimizer. If, however, the peephole optimizer is special-purpose *and* is used after a code generator that is known not to use condition registers *and* is used for a language that declares the effect of integer overflow undefined, the replacement can be accepted without problems.

The second problem is that we would often like to accept replacements that patently do not do the same thing as the original. For example, we would like to replace the sequence Load_Const 1,R$_m$; Add_Reg R$_m$,R$_n$ by Increment R$_n$, but this is incorrect since the first instruction sequence leaves R$_m$ set to 1 and the second does not affect that register. If, however, the code generator is kind enough to indicate that the second use of R$_m$ is its last use, the replacement is correct. This could be expressed in the replacement pattern

Load_Const 1,R$_a$; Add_Reg R$_b$,R$_c$ | R$_a$ = R$_b$, is_last_use(R$_b$) $\Rightarrow$
    Increment R$_c$

Last-use information may be readily obtained when the code is being generated, but will not be available to a general-purpose peephole optimizer.

The third problem is that code generators usually have a very limited repertoire of instruction sequences, and a general-purpose peephole optimizer contains many patterns that will just never match anything that is generated.

Replacement patterns can be created by hand or generated by a program. For simple postprocessing, a handwritten replacement pattern set suffices. Such a set can be constructed by somebody with a good knowledge of the machine in question, by just reading pages of generated code. Good replacement patterns then easily suggest themselves. Experience shows [272] that about a hundred patterns are sufficient to take care of almost all correctable inefficiencies left by a relatively simple code generator. Experience has also shown [73] that searching for clever peephole optimizations is entertaining but of doubtful use: the most useful optimizations are generally obvious.

Replacement patterns can also be derived automatically from machine descriptions, in a process similar to code generation by bottom-up tree rewriting. Two, three, or more instruction trees are combined into one tree, and the best possible rewrite for it is obtained. If this rewrite has a lower total cost than the original instructions, we have found a replacement pattern. The process is described by Davidson and Fraser [71].

This automatic process is especially useful for the more outlandish applications of peephole optimization. An example is the use of peephole optimization to subsume the entire code generation phase from intermediate code to machine instructions [295]. In this process, the instructions of the intermediate code and the target machine instructions together are considered instructions of a single imaginary machine, with the proviso that any intermediate code instruction is more expensive than any sequence of machine instructions. A peephole optimizer is then used to optimize the intermediate code instructions away. The peephole optimizer is generated automatically from descriptions of both the intermediate and the machine instructions. This combines code generation and peephole optimization and works because any rewrite of any intermediate instructions to machine instructions is already an improvement. It also shows the interchangeability of some compiler construction techniques.

7.6.1.2 Locating and replacing instructions

We will now turn to techniques for locating instruction sequences in the target instruction list that match any of a list of replacement patterns; once found, the sequence must be replaced by the indicated replacement. A point of consideration is that this replacement may cause a new pattern to appear that starts somewhat earlier in the target instruction list, and the algorithm must be capable of catching this new pattern as well.

Some peephole optimizers allow labels and jumps inside replacement patterns:

GOTO La; Lb: | La = Lb ⇒ Lb:

but most peephole optimizers restrict the left-hand side of a replacement pattern to a sequence of instructions with the property that the flow of control is guaranteed to enter at the first instruction and to leave at the end of the last instruction. These are exactly the requirements for a basic block, and most peephole optimization is done on the code produced for basic blocks.

The linearized code from the basic block is scanned to find left-hand sides of patterns. When a left-hand side is found, its applicability is checked using the conditions attached to the replacement pattern, and if it applies, the matched instructions are replaced by those in the right-hand side. The process is then repeated to see if more left-hand sides of patterns can be found.

The total result of all replacements depends on the order in which left-hand sides are identified, but as usual, finding the least-cost result is an NP-complete problem. A simple heuristic scheduling technique is to find the first place in a left-to-right scan at which a matching left-hand side is found and then replace the longest possible match. The scanner must then back up a few instructions, to allow for the possibility that the replacement together with the preceding instructions match another left-hand side.

We have already met a technique that will do multiple pattern matching efficiently, choose the longest match, and avoid backing up—using an FSA; and that is what most peephole optimizers do. Since we have already discussed several pattern matching algorithms, we will describe this one only briefly here.

The dotted items involved in the matching operation consist of the pattern instruction lists of the replacement patterns, without the attached parameters; the dot may be positioned between two pattern instructions or at the end. We denote an item by $P_1 \ldots \bullet \ldots P_k$, with P_i for the i-th instruction in the pattern, and the input by $I_1 \ldots I_N$. The set of items kept between the two input instructions I_n and I_{n+1} contains all dotted items $P_1 \ldots P_k \bullet P_{k+1} \ldots$ for which $P_1 \ldots P_k$ matches $I_{n-k+1} \ldots I_n$. To move this set over the instruction I_{n+1}, we keep only the items for which P_{k+1} matches I_{n+1}, and we add all new items $P_1 \bullet \ldots$ for which P_1 matches I_{n+1}. When we find an item with the dot at the end, we have found a matching pattern and only then are we going to check the condition attached to it. If more than one pattern matches, including conditions, we choose the longest.

After having replaced the pattern instructions by the replacement instructions, we can start our scan at the first replacing instruction, since the item set just before it summarizes all partly matching patterns at that point. No backing up over previous instructions is required.

7.6.1.3 Evaluation of peephole optimization

The importance of a peephole optimizer is inversely proportional to the quality of the code yielded by the code generation phase. A good code generator requires little peephole optimization, but a naive code generator can benefit greatly from a good peephole optimizer. Some compiler writers [72, 73] report good quality compilers from naive code generation followed by aggressive peephole optimization.

7.6.2 Procedural abstraction of assembly code

In Section 7.3.4 we saw that the fundamental problem with applying procedural abstraction to the intermediate code is that it by definition uses the wrong metric: it minimizes the number of nodes rather than code size. This suggests applying it to the generated code, which is what is often done.

The basic algorithm is similar to that in Section 7.3.4, in spite of the fact that the intermediate code is a tree of nodes and the generated code is a linear list of machine instructions: for each pair of positions (n, m) in the list, determine the longest non-overlapping sequence of matching instructions following them. The most profitable of the longest sequences is then turned into a subroutine, and the process is repeated until no more candidates are found.

In Section 7.3.4 nodes matched when they were equal and parameters were found as trees hanging from the matched subtree. In the present algorithm instructions match when they are equal or differ in a non-register operand only. For example, Load_Mem T51,R_3 and Load_Mem x,R_3 match, but Load_Reg R_1,R_3 and Load_Mem R_2,R_3 do not.

The idea is to turn the sequence into a routine and to compensate for the differences by turning the differing operands into parameters. To this end a mapping is created while comparing the sequences for a pair (n, m), consisting of pairs of differing operands; for the above example, upon accepting the first match it would contain (T51,x).

The longer the sequence, the more profitable it is, but the longer the mapping, the less profitable the sequence is. So a compromise is necessary here; since each entry in the mapping corresponds to one parameter, one may even decide to stop constructing the sequence when the size of the mapping exceeds a given limit, say 3 entries.

Figure 7.39 shows an example. On the left we see the original machine code sequence, in which the sequence X; Load_Mem T51,R_3; Y matches the sequence X; Load_Mem x,R_3; Y. On the right we see the reduced program. A routine R47 has been created for the common sequences, and in the reduced program these se-

quences have been replaced by instructions for setting the parameter and calling
R47. The code for that routine retrieves the parameter and stores it in R_3. The gain
is the size of the common sequence, minus the size of the SetPar, Call, and Return
instructions.

In this example the parameter has been passed by value. This is actually an optimization; if either T51 or x is used in the sequence X, the parameter must be passed
by reference, and more complicated code is needed.

```
       .                              .
       .                              .
       .                              .
  X    (does not use T51 or x)    SetPar T51,1
  Load_Mem T51,R₃                 Call R47
  Y                                    .
       .                              .
       .                              .
       .                         SetPar x,1
  X    (does not use T51 or x)    Call R47
  Load_Mem x,R₃          ⇒            .
  Y                                    .
       .                              .
       .                              .
       .                    R47:
                                  X
                                  Load_Par 1,R₃
                                  Y
                                  Return
```

Fig. 7.39: Repeated code sequence transformed into a routine

Although this algorithm uses the correct metric, the other problems with the algorithm as applied to the AST still exist: the complexity is still $O(k^3)$, and recognizing
multiple occurrences of a subsequence is complicated. There exist linear-time algorithms for finding a longest common substring (McCreight [187], Ukkonen [283]),
but it is very difficult to integrate these with collecting a mapping. Runeson, Nyström and Jan Sjödin [243] describe a number of techniques to obtain reasonable
compilation times.

A better optimization is available if the last instruction in the common sequence
is a jump or return instruction, and the mapping is empty. In that case we can just
replace one sequence by a jump to the other, no parameter passing or routine linkage
required. This optimization is called **cross-jumping** or **tail merging**. Opportunities
for cross-jumping can be found more easily by starting from two jump instructions
to the same label or two return instructions, and working backwards from them
as long as the instructions match, or until the sequences threaten to overlap. This
process is then repeated until no more sequences are found that can be replaced by
jumps.

7.7 Machine code generation

The result of the above compilation efforts is that our source program has been transformed into a linearized list of target machine instructions in some symbolic format.
A usual representation is an array or a linked list of records, each describing a machine instruction in a format that was decided by the compiler writer; this format
has nothing to do with the actual bit patterns of the real machine instructions. The
purpose of compilation is, however, to obtain an executable object file with semantics corresponding to that of the source program. Such an object file contains the bit
patterns of the machine instructions described by the output of the code generation
process, embedded in binary-encoded information that is partly program-dependent
and partly operating-system-dependent. For example, the headers and trailers are
OS-dependent, information about calls to library routines are program-dependent,
and the format in which this information is specified is again OS-dependent.

So the task of target machine code generation is the conversion of the symbolic
target code in compiler-internal format into a machine object file. Since instruction
selection, register allocation, and instruction scheduling have already been done, this
conversion is straightforward in principle. But writing code for it is a lot of work,
and since it involves specifying hundreds of bit patterns, error-prone work at that. In
short, it should be avoided; fortunately that is easy to do, and highly recommended.

Almost all systems feature at least one assembler, a program that accepts lists of
symbolic machine code instructions and surrounding information in character code
format and generates objects files from them. These human-readable lists of symbolic machine instructions are called **assembly code**; the machine instructions we
have seen above were in some imaginary assembly code. So by generating assembly
code as the last stage of our code generation process we can avoid writing the target
machine code generation part of the compiler and capitalize on the work of the people who wrote the assembler. In addition to reducing the amount of work involved
in the construction of our compiler we also gain a useful interface for checking and
debugging the generated code: its output in readable assembly code.

It is true that writing the assembly output to file and calling another program
to finish the job slows down the compilation process, but the costs are often far
outweighed by the software-engineering benefits. Even if no assembler is available,
as may be the case for an experimental machine, it is probably worth while to first
write the assembler and then use it as the final step in the compilation process. Doing
so partitions the work, provides an interface useful in constructing the compiler, and
yields an assembler, which is a useful program in its own right and which can also
be used for other compilers.

If a C or C++ compiler is available on the target platform, it is possible and often
attractive to take this idea a step further, by changing to existing software earlier in
the compiling process: rather than generating intermediate code from the annotated
AST we generate C or C++ code from it, which we then feed to the existing C or
C++ compiler. The latter does all optimization and target machine code generation,
and usually does it very well. We name C and C++ here, since these are probably
the languages with the best, the most optimizing, and the most widely available

compilers at this moment. This is where C has earned its name as the platform-independent assembly language.

Code generation into a higher-level language than assembly language is especially attractive for compilers for non-imperative languages, and many compilers for functional, logical, distributed, and special-purpose languages produce C code in their final step. But the approach can also be useful for imperative and object-oriented languages: one of the first C++ compilers produced C code and even a heavily checking and profiling compiler for C itself could generate C code in which all checking and profiling has been made explicit. In each of these situations the savings in effort and gains in platform-independence are enormous. On the down side, using C as the target language produces compiled programs that may be up to a factor of two slower than those generated directly in assembly or machine code.

Lemkin [173] gives a case study of C as a target language for a compiler for the functional language SAIL, and Tarditi, Lee and Acharya [274] discuss the use of C for translating Standard ML.

If, for some reason, the compiler should do its own object file generation, the same techniques can be applied as those used in an assembler. The construction of assemblers is discussed in Chapter 8.

7.8 Conclusion

The basic process of code generation is tree rewriting: nodes or sets of nodes are replaced by nodes or sets of nodes that embody the same semantics but are closer to the hardware. The end result may be assembler code, but C, C–– (Peyton Jones, Ramsey, and Reig [221]), LLVM (Lattner, [170]), and perhaps others, are viable options too.

It is often profitable to preprocess the input AST, in order to do efficiency-increasing AST transformations, and to postprocess the generated code to remove some of the inefficiencies left by the code generation process. Code generation and preprocessing is usually done by tree rewriting, and postprocessing by pattern recognition.

Summary

- Code generation converts the intermediate code into symbolic machine instructions in a paradigm-independent, language-independent, and largely machine-independent process. The symbolic machine instructions are then converted to some suitable low-level code: C code, assembly code, machine code.
- The basis of code generation is the systematic replacement of nodes and subtrees of the AST by target code segments, in such a way that the semantics is pre-

served. It is followed by a scheduling phase, which produces a linear sequence of instructions from the rewritten AST.

- The replacement process is called tree rewriting. The scheduling is controlled by the data-flow and flow-of-control requirements of the target code segments.
- The three main issues in code generation are instruction selection, register allocation, and instruction scheduling.
- Finding the optimal combination is NP-complete in the general case. There are three ways to simplify the code generation problem: 1. consider only small parts of the AST at a time; 2. simplify the target machine; 3. restrict the interfaces between code segments.
- Code generation is performed in three phases: 1. preprocessing, in which some AST node patterns are replaced by other ("better") AST node patterns, using program transformations; 2. code generation proper, in which all AST node patterns are replaced by target code sequences, using tree rewriting; 3. postprocessing, in which some target code sequences are replaced by other ("better") target code sequences, using peephole optimization.
- Pre- and postprocessing may be performed repeatedly.
- Before converting the intermediate code to target code it may be preprocessed to improve efficiency. Examples of simple preprocessing are constant folding and arithmetic simplification. Care has to be taken that arithmetic overflow conditions are translated faithfully by preprocessing, if the source language semantics requires so.
- More extensive preprocessing can be done on routines: they can be in-lined or cloned.
- In in-lining a call to a routine is replaced by the body of the routine called. This saves the calling and return sequences and opens the way for further optimizations. Care has to be taken to preserve the semantics of the parameter transfer.
- In cloning, a copy C of a routine R is made, in which the value of a parameter P is fixed to the value V; all calls to R in which the parameter P has the value V are replaced by calls to the copy C. Often a much better translation can be produced for the copy C than for the original routine R.
- Procedural abstraction is the reverse of in-lining in that it replaces multiple occurrences of tree segments by routine calls to a routine derived from the common tree segment. Such multiple occurrences are found by examining the subtrees of pairs of nodes. The non-matching subtrees of these subtrees are processed as parameters to the derived routine.
- The simplest way to obtain code is to generate for each node of the AST the code segment an iterative interpreter would execute for it. If the target code is C or C++, all optimizations can be left to the C or C++ compiler. This process turns an interpreter into a compiler with a minimum of investment.
- Rather than repeating a code segment many times, routine calls to a single copy in a library can be generated, reducing the size of the object code considerably. This technique is called threaded code. The object size reduction may be important for embedded systems.

- An even larger reduction in object size can be achieved by numbering the library routines and storing the program as a list of these numbers. All target machine dependency is now concentrated in the library routines.
- Going in the other direction, the repeated code segments may each be partially evaluated in their contexts, leading to more efficient code.
- In simple code generation, a fixed translation to the target code is chosen for each possible node type. These translations are based on mutual interface conventions.
- Simple code generation requires local decisions only, and is therefore especially suitable for narrow compilers.
- Simple code generation for a register machine rewrites each expression node by a single machine instruction; this takes care of instruction selection. The interface convention is that the output register of one instruction must be used immediately as an input register of the parent instruction.
- Code for expressions on a register machine can be generated by a depth-first recursive visit; this takes care of instruction scheduling. The recursive routines carry two additional parameters: the register in which the result must be delivered and the set of free registers; this takes care of register allocation.
- Since each operand that is not processed immediately ties up one register, it is advantageous to compile code first for the operand that needs the most registers. This need, called the weight of the node, or its Sethi–Ullman number, can be computed in a depth-first visit.
- When an expression needs more registers than available, we need to spill one or more registers to memory. There is no best register spilling technique, except for exhaustive search, which is usually not feasible. So we resort to heuristics.
- In one heuristic, we isolate maximal subexpressions that can be compiled with the available registers, compile them and store the results in temporary variables. This reduces the original tree, to which we repeat the process.
- The machine registers are divided into four groups by the compiler designer: those needed for administration purposes, those reserved for parameter transfer, those reserved for expression evaluation, and those used to store local variables. Usually, the size of each set is fixed, and some of these sets may be empty.
- Often, the set of registers reserved for local variables is smaller than the set of candidates. Heuristics include first come first served, register hints from the programmer, and usage counts obtained by static or dynamic profiling. A more advanced heuristic uses graph coloring.
- Some sub-optimal symbolic machine code sequences produced by the code generation process can be removed by peephole optimization, in which fixed parameterized sequences are replaced by other, better, fixed parameterized sequences. About a hundred replacement patterns are sufficient to take care of almost all correctable inefficiencies left by a relatively simple code generator.
- Replaceable sequences in the instruction stream are recognized using an FSA based on the replacement patterns in the peephole optimizer. The FSA recognizer identifies the longest possible sequence, as it does in a lexical analyzer. The sequence is then replaced and scanning resumes.

- Procedural abstraction can also be applied to generated code. A longest common subsequence is found in which the instructions are equal or differ in an operand only. The occurrences of the subsequence are then replaced by routine calls to a routine derived from the subsequence, and the differing operands are passed as parameters.
- When two subsequences are identical and end in a jump or return instruction, one can be replaced by a jump to the other; this is called "cross-jumping". Such sequences can be found easily by starting from the end.
- Code generation yields a list of symbolic machine instructions, which is still several steps away from a executable binary program. In most compilers, these steps are delegated to the local assembler.

Further reading

The annual *ACM SIGPLAN Conferences on Programming Language Design and Implementation, PLDI* is a continuous source of information on code generation in general. A complete compiler, the retargetable C compiler *lcc*, is described by Fraser and Hanson [101]. For further reading on optimized code generation, see the corresponding section in Chapter 9, on page 456.

Exercises

7.1. On some processors, multiplication is extremely expensive, and it is worthwhile to replace all multiplications with a constant by a combination of left-shifts, additions, and/or subtractions. Assume that our register machine of Figure 7.19 has an additional instruction:

    Shift_Left c,Rn   Rn:=Rn<<c;

which shifts the contents of R_n over $|c|$ bits, to the right if $c < 0$, and to the left otherwise. Write a routine that generates code for this machine to multiply R0 with a positive value multiplier given as a parameter, without using the Mult_Reg instruction. The routine should leave the result in R1.

Hint: scoop up sequences of all 1s, then all 0s, in the binary representation of multiplier, starting from the right.

7.2. (▷www) What is the result of in-lining the call P(0) to the C routine

```
void P(int i) {
    if (i < 1) return ; else Q();
}
```

(a) immediately after the substitution?

(b) after constant propagation?
(c) after constant folding?
(d) after dead code elimination?
(e) What other optimization (not covered in the book) would be needed to eliminate the sequence entirely? How could the required information be obtained?

7.3. In addition to the tuple $((N,M),T)$ the naive algorithm on page 326 also produces the tuples $((M,N),T)$, $((N,N),T)$, and $((M,M),T)$, causing it to do more than twice the work it needs to. Give a simple trick to avoid this inefficiency.

7.4. (▷791) Explain how a self-extracting archive works (a self-extracting archive is a program that, when executed, extracts the contents of the archive that it represents).

7.5. (▷791) Section 7.5.1.1 outlines how the threaded code of Figure 7.11 can be reduced by numbering the routines and coding the list of calls as an array of routine numbers. Show such a coding scheme and the corresponding interpreter.

7.6. (▷www) Generating threaded code as discussed in Section 7.5.1.1 reduces the possibilities for partial evaluation as discussed in Section 7.5.1.2, because the switch is in the *Expression_P* routine. Find a way to prevent this problem.

7.7. (▷www) The weight of a tree, as discussed in Section 7.5.2.2, can also be used to reduce the maximum stack height when generating code for the stack machine of Section 7.5.2.1.
(a) How?
(b) Give the resulting code sequence for the AST of Figure 7.20.

7.8. (▷www) The subsection on machines with register-memory operations on page 347 explains informally how the weight function must be revised in the presence of instructions for combining the contents of a register with that of a memory location. Give the revised version of the weight function in Figure 7.32.

7.9. (▷791) The code of the C routine of Figure 7.40 corresponds to the flow graph of Figure 7.41. The weights for static profiling have been marked by the letters a to q. Set up the traffic flow equations for this flow graph, under the following assumptions. At an if-node 70% of the traffic goes to the then-part and 30% goes to the else-part; a loop body is (re)entered 9 out of 10 times; in a switch statement, all cases get the same traffic, except the default case, which gets half.

7.10. (▷www) Using the same techniques as in Exercise 7.9, draw the flow graph for the nested loop

```
while  (...)  {
    A;
    while  (...)  {
        B;
    }
}
```

Set up the traffic equations and solve them.

```
void Routine(void) {
    if (...) {
        while (...) {
            A;
        }
    }
    else {
        switch (...) {
            case: ...: B; break;
            case: ...: C; break;
        }
    }
}
```

Fig. 7.40: Routine code for static profiling

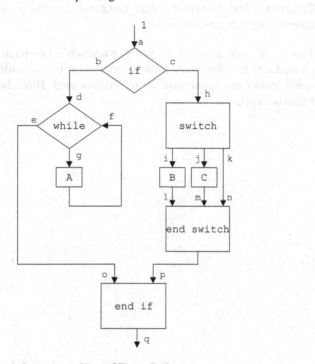

Fig. 7.41: Flow graph for static profiling of Figure 7.40

7.11. For a processor of your choice, find out the exact semantics of the Add_Const 1,R_n and Increment R_n instructions, find out where they differ and write a complete replacement pattern in the style shown in Section 7.6.1.1 for Increment R_C.

7.12. Given a simple, one-register processor, with, among others, an instruction Add_Constant c, which adds a constant c to the only, implicit, register. Two obvious peephole optimization patterns are

```
Add_Constant c; Add_Constant d ⇒ Add_Constant c+d
Add_Constant 0 ⇒
```

Show how the FSA recognizer and replacer described in Section 7.6.1.2 completely removes the instruction sequence Add_Constant 1; Add_Constant 2; Add_Constant −3. Show all states of the recognizer during the transformation.

7.13. *History of code generation*: Study Anderson's two-page 1964 paper [12], which introduces a rudimentary form of bottom-up tree-rewriting for code generation, and identify and summarize the techniques used. Hint: the summary will be longer than the paper.

Chapter 8
Assemblers, Disassemblers, Linkers, and Loaders

An assembler, like a compiler, is a converter from source code to target code, so many of the usual compiler construction techniques are applicable in assembler construction; they include lexical analysis, symbol table management, and back-patching. There are differences too, though, resulting from the relative simplicity of the source format and the relative complexity of the target format.

8.1 The tasks of an assembler

Assemblers are best understood by realizing that even the output of an assembler is still several steps away from a target program ready to run on a computer. To understand the tasks of an assembler, we will start from an execution-ready program and work our way backwards.

8.1.1 The running program

A running program consists of four components: a code segment, a stack segment, a data segment, and a set of registers. The contents of the **code segment** derive from the source code and are usually immutable; the code segment itself is often extendible to allow dynamic linking. The contents of the **stack segment** are mutable and start off empty. Those of the **data segment** are also mutable and are prefilled from the literals and strings from the source program. The contents of the registers usually start off uninitialized or zeroed.

The code and the data relate to each other through addresses of locations in the segments. These addresses are stored in the machine instructions and in the prefilled part of the data segment. Most operating systems will set the registers of the hardware memory manager unit of the machine in such a way that the address spaces

of the code and data segments start at zero for each running program, regardless of
where these segments are located in real memory.

8.1.2 The executable code file

A run of a program is initiated by loading the contents of an executable code file
into memory, using a **loader**. The loader is usually an integrated part of the operating system, which makes it next to invisible, and its activation is implicit in calling
a program, but we should not forget that it is there. As part of the operating system, it has special privileges. All initialized parts of the program derive from the
executable code file, in which all addresses should be based on segments starting
at zero. The loader reads these segments from the executable code file and copies
them to suitable memory segments; it then creates a stack segment, and jumps to a
predetermined location in the code segment, to start the program. So the executable
code file must contain a code segment and a data segment; it may also contain other
indications, for example the initial stack size and the execution start address.

8.1.3 Object files and linkage

The executable code file derives from combining one or more program object files
and probably some library object files, and is constructed by a **linker**. The linker
is a normal user program, without any privileges. All operating systems provide at
least one, and most traditional compilers use this standard linker, but an increasing number of compiling systems come with their own linker. The reason is that a
specialized linker can check that the proper versions of various object modules are
used, something the standard linker, usually designed for FORTRAN and COBOL,
cannot do.

Each object file carries its own code and data segment contents, and it is the task
of the linker to combine these into the one code segment and one data segment of
the executable code file. The linker does this in the obvious way, by making copies
of the segments, concatenating them, and writing them to the executable code file,
but there are two complications here. (Needless to say, the object file generator and
the linker have to agree on the format of the object files.)

The first complication concerns the addresses inside code and data segments. The
code and data in the object files relate to each other through addresses, the same way
those in the executable code file do, but since the object files were created without
knowing how they will be linked into an executable code file, the address space
of each code or data segment of each object file starts at zero. This means that all
addresses inside the copies of all object files except the first one have to be adjusted
to their actual positions when code and data segments from different object files are
linked together.

Suppose, for example, that the length of the code segment in the first object file a.o is 1000 bytes. Then the second code segment, deriving from object file b.o, will start at the location with machine address 1000. All its internal addresses were originally computed with 0 as start address, however, so all its internal addresses will now have to be increased by 1000. To do this, the linker must know which positions in the object segments contain addresses, and whether the addresses refer to the code segment or to the data segment. This information is called **relocation information**. There are basically two formats in which relocation information can be provided in an object file: in the form of bit maps, in which some bits correspond to each position in the object code and data segments at which an address may be located, and in the form of a linked list. Bit maps are more usual for this purpose. Note that code segments and data segments may contain addresses in code segments and data segments, in any combination.

The second complication is that code and data segments in object files may contain addresses of locations in other program object files or in library object files. A location L in an object file, whose address can be used in other object files, is marked with an **external symbol**, also called an **external name**; an external symbol looks like an identifier. The location L itself is called an **external entry point**. Object files can refer to L by using an **external reference** to the external symbol of L. Object files contain information about the external symbols they refer to and the external symbols for which they provide entry points. This information is stored in an **external symbol table**.

For example, if an object file a.o contains a call to the routine printf at location 500, the file contains the explicit information in the external symbol table that it refers to the external symbol printf at location 500. And if the library object file printf.o has the body of printf starting at location 100, the file contains the explicit information in the external symbol table that it features the external entry point printf at address 100. It is the task of the linker to combine these two pieces of information and to update the address at location 500 in the copy of the code segment of file a.o to the address of location 100 in the copy of printf.o, once the position of this copy with respect to the other copies has been established.

The linking process for three code segments is depicted in Figure 8.1; the segments derive from the object files a.o, b.o, and printf.o mentioned above. The length of the code segment of b.o is assumed to be 3000 bytes and that of printf.o 500 bytes. The code segment for b.o contains three internal addresses, which refer to locations 1600, 250, and 400, relative to the beginning of the segment; this is indicated in the diagram by having relocation bit maps along the code and data segments, in which the bits corresponding to locations 1600, 250, and 400 are marked with a C for "Code". The code segment for a.o contains one external address, of the external symbol printf as described above. The code segment for printf.o contains one external entry point, the location of printf. The code segments for a.o and printf.o will probably also contain many internal addresses, but these have been ignored here.

Segments usually contain a high percentage of internal addresses, much higher than shown in the diagram, and relocation information for internal addresses requires only a few bits. This explains why relocation bit maps are more efficient than linked lists for this purpose.

The linking process first concatenates the segments. It then updates the internal addresses in the copies of a.o, b.o, and printf.o by adding the positions of those segments to them; it finds the positions of the addresses by scanning the relocation maps, which also indicate if the address refers to the code segment or the data segment. Finally it stores the external address of printf, which computes to 4100 (=1000+3000+100), at location 100, as shown.

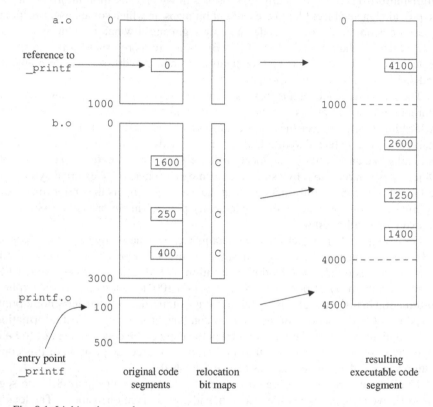

Fig. 8.1: Linking three code segments

We see that an object file needs to contain at least four components: the code segment, the data segment, the relocation bit map, and the external symbol table.

8.1.4 Alignment requirements and endianness

Although almost every processor nowadays uses addresses that represent (8-bit) bytes, there are often **alignment requirements** for some or all memory accesses. For example, a 16-bit (2-byte) aligned address points to data whose address is a multiple of 2. Modern processors require 16, 32, or even 64-bit aligned addresses. Requirements may differ for different types. For example, a processor might require 32-bit alignment for 32-bit words and instructions, 16-bit alignment for 16-bit words, and no particular alignment for bytes. If such restrictions are violated, the penalty is slower memory access or a processor fault, depending on the processor. So the compiler or assembler may need to do **padding** to honor these requirements, by inserting unused memory segments for data and no-op instructions for code.

Another important issue is the exact order in which data is stored in memory. For the bits in a byte there is nowadays a nearly universal convention, but there are two popular choices for storing multi-byte values. First, values can be stored with the least significant byte first, so that for hexadecimal number 1234 the byte 34 has the lowest address, and the value 12 has the address after that. This storage convention is called **little-endian**. It is also possible to place the most significant byte first, so that the byte 12 has the lowest address. This storage convention is called **big-endian**. There are no important reasons to choose one **endianness** over the other[1], but since conversion from one form to another takes some time and forgetting to convert can introduce subtle bugs, most architectures pick one of the two and stick to it.

We are now in a position to discuss issues in the construction of assemblers and linkers. We will not go into the construction of loaders, since they hardly require any special techniques and are almost universally supplied with the operating system.

8.2 Assembler design issues

An assembler converts from symbolic machine code to binary machine code, and from symbolic data to binary data. In principle the conversion is one to one; for example the 80x86 assembler instruction

    addl %edx,%ecx

which does a 32-bit addition of the contents of the %edx register to the %ecx register, is converted to the binary data

    0000 0001 11 010 001 (binary) = 01 D1 (hexadecimal)

The byte 0000 0001 is the operation code of the operation addl, the next two bits 11 mark the instruction as register-to-register, and the trailing two groups of three bits 010 and 001 are the translations of %edx and %ecx. It is more usual to write the binary translation in hexadecimal; as shown above, the instruction is 01D1 in this notation. The binary translations can be looked up in tables built into the assembler. In some assembly languages, there are some minor complications due to the overloading of instruction names, which have to be resolved by considering the types of the operands. The bytes of the translated instructions are packed closely, with no-op

---

[1] The insignificance of the choice is implied in the naming: it refers to *Gulliver's Travels* by Jonathan Swift, which describes a war between people who break eggs from the small or the big end to eat them.

instructions inserted if alignment requirements would leave gaps. A **no-op instruction** is a one-byte machine instruction that does nothing (except perhaps waste a machine cycle).

The conversion of symbolic data to binary data involves converting, for example, the two-byte integer 666 to hexadecimal 9A02 (again on an 80x86, which is a little-endian machine), the double-length (8-byte) floating point number 3.1415927 to hex 97D17E5AFB210940, and the two-byte string "PC" to hex 5043. Note that the string in assembly code is not extended with a null byte; the null-byte terminated string is a C convention, and language-specific conventions have no place in an assembler. So the C string "PC" must be translated by the code generator to "PC\0" in symbolic assembly code; the assembler will then translate this to hex 504300.

The main problem in constructing an assembler lies in the handling of addresses. Two kinds of addresses are distinguished: internal addresses, referring to locations in the same segment; and external addresses, referring to locations in segments in other object files.

8.2.1 Handling internal addresses

References to locations in the same code or data segment take the form of identifiers in the assembly code; an example is shown in Figure 8.2. The fragment starts with material for the data segment (.data), which contains a location of 4 bytes (.long) aligned on a 8-byte boundary, filled with the value 666 and labeled with the identifier var1. Next comes material for the code segment (.code) which contains, among other instructions, a 4-byte addition from the location labeled var1 to register %eax, a jump to label label1, and the definition of the label label1.

```
.data
        ...
        .align 8
var1:
        .long 666
        ...
.code
        ...
        addl var1,%eax
        ...
        jmp label1
        ...
label1:
        ...
        ...
```

Fig. 8.2: Assembly code fragment with internal symbols

The assembler reads the assembly code and assembles the bytes for the data and the code segments into two different arrays. When the assembler reads the fragment from Figure 8.2, it first meets the .data directive, which directs it to start assembling into the data array. It translates the source material for the data segment to binary, stores the result in the data array, and records the addresses of the locations at which the labels fall. For example, if the label var1 turns out to label location 400 in the data segment, the assembler records the value of the label var1 as the pair (data, 400). Note that in the assembler the value of var1 is 400; to obtain the value of the program variable var1, the identifier var1 must be used in a memory-reading instruction, for example addl var1,%eax.

Next, the assembler meets the .code directive, after which it switches to assembling into the code array. While translating the code segment, the assembler finds the instruction addl var1,%eax, for which it assembles the proper binary pattern and register indication, plus the value of the data segment label var1, 400. It stores the result in the array in which the code segment is being assembled. In addition, it marks the location of this instruction as "relocatable to the data segment" in the relocation bit map. When the assembler encounters the instruction jmp label1, however, it cannot do something similar, since the value of label1 is not yet known.

There are two solutions to this problem: backpatching and two-scans assembly. When using *backpatching*, the assembler keeps a backpatch list for each label whose value is not yet known. The backpatch list for a label L contains the addresses $A_1...A_n$ of the locations in the code and data segments being assembled, into which the value of L must eventually be stored. When an applied occurrence of the label L is encountered and the assembler decides that the value of L must be assembled into a location A_i, the address A_i is inserted in the backpatch list for L and the location at A_i is zeroed. The resulting arrangement is shown in Figure 8.3, which depicts the assembly code, the assembled binary code, and one backpatch list, for the label label1. When finally the defining occurrence of L is found, the address of the position it labels is determined and assigned to L as its value. Next the backpatch list is processed, and for each entry A_k, the value of L is stored in the location addressed by A_k.

In *two-scans assembly*, the assembler processes its input file twice. The purpose of the first scan is to determine the values of all labels. To this end, the assembler goes through the conversion process described above, but without actually assembling any code: the assembler just keeps track of where everything would go. During this process it meets the defining occurrences of all labels. For each label L, the assembler can record in its symbol table the value of L, since that value derives from the position that L is found to label. During the second scan, the values of all labels are known and the actual translation can take place without problems.

Some additional complications may occur if the assembly language supports features like macro processing, multiple segments, labels in expressions, etc., but these are mostly of an administrative nature.

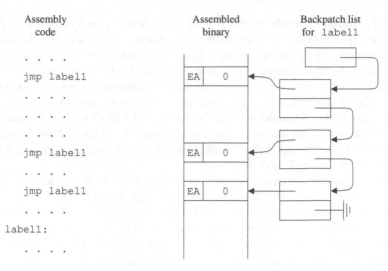

Fig. 8.3: A backpatch list for labels

8.2.2 Handling external addresses

The external symbol and address information of an object file is summarized in its external symbol table, an example of which is shown in Figure 8.4. The table specifies, among other things, that the data segment has an entry point named options at location 50, the code segment has an entry point named main at location 100, the code segment refers to an external entry point printf at location 500, etc. Also there is a reference to an external entry point named file_list at location 4 in the data segment. Note that the meaning of the numbers in the address column is completely different for entry points and references. For entry points, the number is the value of the entry point symbol; for references, the number is the address where the value of the referred entry point must be stored.

The external symbol table can be constructed easily while the rest of the translation is being done. The assembler then produces a binary version of it and places it in the proper position in the object file, together with the code and data segments, the relocation bit maps, and possibly further header and trailer material.

Additionally the linker can create tables for the debugging of the translated program, using information supplied by the compiler. In fact, many compilers can generate enough information to allow a debugger to find the exact variables and statements that originated from a particular code fragment.

External symbol	Type	Address
options	entry point	50 data
main	entry point	100 code
printf	reference	500 code
atoi	reference	600 code
printf	reference	650 code
exit	reference	700 code
msg_list	entry point	300 data
Out_Of_Memory	entry point	800 code
fprintf	reference	900 code
exit	reference	950 code
file_list	reference	4 data

Fig. 8.4: Example of an external symbol table

8.3 Linker design issues

The basic operation of a linker is simple: it reads each object file and appends each of the four components to the proper one of four lists. This yields one code segment, one data segment, one relocation bit map, and one external symbol table, each consisting of the concatenation of the corresponding components of the object files. In addition the linker retains information about the lengths and positions of the various components. It is now straightforward to do the relocation of the internal addresses and the linking of the external addresses; this resolves all addresses. The linker then writes the code and data segments to a file, the executable code file; optionally it can append the external symbol table and debugging information. This finishes the translation process that we started in the first line of Chapter 2!

Real-world linkers are often more complicated than described above, and constructing one is not a particularly simple task. There are several reasons for this. One is that the actual situation around object modules is much hairier than shown here: many object file formats have features for repeated initialized data, special arithmetic operations on relocatable addresses, conditional external symbol resolution, etc. Another is that linkers often have to wade through large libraries to find the required external entry points, and advanced symbol table techniques are used to speed up the process. A third is that users tend to think that linking, like garbage collection, should not take time, so there is pressure on the linker writer to produce a blindingly fast linker.

One obvious source of inefficiency is the processing of the external symbol table. For each entry point in it, the entire table must be scanned to find entries with the same symbol, which can then be processed. This leads to a process that requires a time $O(n^2)$ where n is the number of entries in the combined external symbol table. Scanning the symbol table for each symbol can be avoided by sorting it first; this brings all entries concerning the same symbol together, so they can be processed efficiently.

8.4 Disassembly

Now that we have managed to put together an executable binary file, the inquisitive mind immediately asks "Can we also take it apart again?" Yes, we can, up to a point, but why would we? One reason might be that we have an old but useful program, a so called "legacy program", for which we do not have the source code, and we want to make –hopefully small– changes to it. Less obvious is an extreme postprocessing technique that has become popular recently: disassemble the binary code, construct an overall dependency graph, possibly apply optimizations and security tests to it, possibly insert dynamic security checks and measurement code, and then reassemble it into a binary executable. This technique is called **binary rewriting** and its power lies in the fact that the executable binary contains all the pertinent code so there are no calls to routines that cannot be examined. An example of a binary rewriting system is *Valgrind*; see Nethercote and Seward [201]. Examples of applications are given by De Sutter, De Bus, and De Bosschere [75], who use binary rewriting to optimize code size; and Debray, Muth, and Watterson [78], who use it for optimizing power consumption.

There is also great interest in disassembly in both the software security and the software piracy world, for obvious reasons. We will not go into that aspect here.

We have to distinguish between *disassembly* and *decompilation*. **Disassembly** starts from the executable binary and yields a program in an assembly language. Usually the idea is to modify and reassemble this program. Using the best present-day disassembly techniques one can expect all or almost all routines in a large program to be disassembled successfully. Decompilation starts from the executable binary or assembly code and yields a program in a higher-level language. Usually the idea is to examine this program to gain an understanding of its functioning; often recompilation is possible only after spending serious manual effort on the code.

We will see that this distinction is actually too coarse — at least four levels of recovered code must be distinguished: assembler code; unstructured control-flow graph; structured control flow graph; and high-level language code.

A large part of an executable binary can be disassembled relatively easily, but properly disassembling the rest may take considerable effort and be very machine-specific. We will therefore restrict ourselves to the basics of disassembly and decompilation.

8.4.1 Distinguishing between instructions and data

Although most assembly languages have separate instruction (code) and data segments, the assembled program may very well contain data in the code segment. Examples are the in-line data for some instructions and null bytes for alignment. So the first problem in disassembly is to distinguish between instructions and data in the sequence of bytes the disassembler is presented with. More in particular, we need to know at precisely which addresses instructions start in order to decode them properly; and for the data we would like to know their types, so we can decode their values correctly.

The only datum we have initially is the start address (entry point) of the binary program, and we are sure it points to an instruction. We analyse this instruction and from its nature we draw conclusions about other addresses. We continue this process until no new conclusions can be drawn. The basic—closure—algorithm is given in Figure 8.5. Jump instructions include routine call and return, in addition to the conditional and unconditional jump. Note that no inference rule is given for the return instruction. The algorithm is often implemented as a depth-first recursive scan rather than as a breadth-first closure algorithm and is then called "recursive traversal". The basic algorithm works for programs that do not perform indirect addressing or self-modification.

Data definitions:

   1. A_I, the set of addresses at which an instruction starts; each such address is possibly associated with a label.

   2. A_D, the set of addresses at which a data item starts; each such address is associated with a label and a type.

Initializations:

A_I is filled with the start address of the binary program. A_D is empty.

Inference rules:

For each address A in A_I decode the instruction at A and call it I.

   1. If I is not a jump instruction, the address following I must be in A_I.

   2. If I is an unconditional jump, conditional jump or routine call instruction to the address L, L must be in A_I, associated with a label different from all other labels.

   3. If I is a conditional jump or routine call instruction, the address following I must be in A_I.

   4. If I accesses data at address L and uses it as type T, L must be in A_D, associated with label different from all other labels and type T.

Fig. 8.5: The basic disassembly algorithm

Next we use the information in A_I and A_D to convert the binary sequence to assembly code, starting from the beginning. For each address A we meet that is in A_I, we produce symbolic code for the instruction I we find at A, preceded by the label if it has one; if I contains one or more addresses, they will be in A_I or A_D, and have labels, so the labels can be produced in I. For each address A we meet that is in A_D, we produce properly formatted data for the bit pattern we find at A, preceded by its label.

If we are lucky and the external symbol table is still available, we can identify at least some of the addresses and replace their labels by the original names, thus improving the readability of the resulting assembly program.

Many addresses of locations in the analyzed segments will not be in A_I or A_D, for the simple reason that they point in the middle of an instruction or data item; others may be absent because they address unreachable code or unused data. Some addresses may occur more than once in A_D, with different types. This shows that the location is used for multiple purposes by the program; it could be a union, or reflect tricky programming. It is also possible that an address is both in A_I and in A_D. This means that the program uses instructions as data and/or vice versa; although performing much more analysis may allow such a program to be disassembled correctly, it is often more convenient to flag such occurrences for manual inspection; if there are not too many such problems a competent assembly language programmer can usually figure out what the intended code is. The same situation arises when a bit pattern at an address in A_I does not correspond to an instruction.

8.4.2 Disassembly with indirection

Almost all programs use indirect addresses, addresses obtained by computation rather than deriving directly from the instruction, and the above approach does not identify such addresses. We will first discuss this problem for instruction addresses.

The main sources of indirect instruction addresses are the translations of switches and computed routine calls. Figure 8.7 shows two possible intermediate code translations of the switch code of Figure 8.6. Both translations use switch tables; the code in the middle column is common to both. The column on the left uses a table of jump instructions, into which the flow of control is led; the one on the right uses a table of addresses, which are picked up and applied in an indirect jump. The instruction GOTO_INDEXED reg,L_jump_table jumps to L_jump_table[reg]; GOTO_INDIRECT reg jumps to mem[reg].

```
switch (ch) {
  case ' ' :  code to handle space; break;
  case '!' :  code to handle exclamation mark; break;
    .
    .
    .
  case '~' :  code to handle tilde ;  break;
}
```

Fig. 8.6: C switch code for translation

Figure 8.8 shows a possible translation for the computed routine call

(pic.width > pic.height ? show_landscape : show_portrait)(pic);

The question is now how we obtain the information that L032, L033, ..., L127, L0, L1, L_show_landscape, and L_show_portrait are instruction addresses and should be in A_I. In the general case this problem cannot be solved, but we will show here two techniques, one for switch tables and one for routine pointers, that will often produce the desired answers. Both require a form of control flow analysis, but obtaining the control flow graph is problematic since at this point the full code is not yet available.

```
/* common code */
reg := ch;
IF reg < 32 GOTO L_default;
IF reg > 127 GOTO L_default;
reg := reg - 32; /* slide to zero */
```

```
/* jump table */                        /* address table */
                                        reg := reg + L_address_table;
GOTO_INDEXED reg,L_jump_table;   GOTO_INDIRECT reg;
L_jump_table:                           L_address_table:
    GOTO L032;                              L032;
    GOTO L033;                              L033;
    .                                       .
    .                                       .
    .                                       .
    GOTO L127;                              L127;

    L032:  code to handle space; GOTO L_default;
    L033:  code to handle exclamation mark; GOTO L_default;
    .
    .
    L127:  code to handle tilde; GOTO L_default;
    L_default:
```

Fig. 8.7: Two possible translations of a C switch statement

```
reg1 := pic.width - pic.height;
IF reg1 > 0 GOTO L0;
reg2 := L_show_portrait;
GOTO L1;
L0: reg2 := L_show_landscape;
L1: LOAD_PARAM pic;
    CALL_REG reg2;
```

Fig. 8.8: Possible translation for a computed routine call

The presence of a switch table is signaled by the occurrence of an indexed jump J on a register, R, and we can be almost certain that it is preceded by code to load this R. The segment of the program that determines the value of R at the position J is called the **program slice** of R at J; one can imagine it as the slice of the program pie with its point at R in J. Program slices are useful for program understanding, debugging and optimizing. In the general case they can be determined by setting up data-flow equations similar to those in Section 5.3 and solving them; see Weiser [294]. For our purpose we can use a simpler approach.

First we scan backwards through the already disassembled code to find the instruction I_R that set R. We repeat this process for the registers in I_R from which R is set, and so on, but we stop after a register is loaded from memory or when we reach the beginning of the routine or the program. We now scan forwards, symbolically interpreting the instructions to create symbolic expressions for the registers.

Suppose, for example, that the forward scan yields the instruction sequence

```
Load_Mem   SP-12,R1
Load_Const 8,R2
Add_Reg    R2,R1
```

This sequence is first rewritten as

```
R1 := mem[SP-12];
R2 := 8;
R1 := R1 + R2;
```

and then turned into

```
R1 := mem[SP-12] + 8;
```

by forward substitution.

If all goes well, this leaves us with a short sequence of conditional jumps followed by the indexed jump, all with expressions as parameters. Since the function of this sequence is the same in all cases – testing boundaries, finding the switch table, and indexing it – there are only very few patterns for it, and a simple pattern match suffices to find the right one. The constants in the sequence are then matched to the parameters in the pattern. This supplies the position and size of the switch table; we can then extract the addresses from the table, and insert them in A_I. For details see Cifuentes and Van Emmerik [61], who found that there are basically only three patterns. And if all did not go well, the code can be flagged for manual inspection, or more analysis can be performed, as described in the following paragraphs.

The code in Figure 8.8 loads the addresses of L_show_landscape or L_show_portrait into a register, which means that they occur as addresses in Load_Addr instructions. Load_Addr instructions, however, are usually used to load *data* addresses, so we need to do symbolic interpretation to find the use of the loaded value(s). Again the problem is the incomplete control-flow graph, and to complete it we need just the information we are trying to extract from it. This chicken-and-egg problem can be handled by introducing an **Unknown node** in the control-flow graph, which is the source and the destination of jumps we know nothing about; the Unknown node is also graphically, but not very accurately, called the "hell node".

All jumps on registers follow edges leading into the Unknown node; if we are doing interprocedural control flow analysis outgoing edges from the Unknown node lead to all code positions after routine jumps. This is the most conservative flow-of-control assumption. For the incoming edges we assume that all registers are live; for the outgoing edges we assume that all registers have unknown contents. This is the most conservative data-flow assumption.

With the introduction of the Unknown node the control-flow graph is technically complete and we can start our traditional symbolic interpretation algorithm, in which we try to obtain the value sets for all registers at all positions, as described in Section 5.2.2. If all goes well, we will then find that some edges which went initially into the Unknown node actually should be rerouted to normal nodes, and that some of its outgoing edges actually originate from normal nodes. More in particular, symbolic interpretation of the code in Figure 8.8 shows immediately that reg2 holds the address value set { L_show_landscape, L_show_portrait }, and since reg2 is used in a CALL_REG instruction, these addresses belong in A_I.

We can now replace the edge from the CALL_REG instruction by edges leading to L_show_landscape and L_show_portrait. We then run the symbolic interpretation algorithm again, to find more edges that can be upgraded. Addresses to data can be discovered in the same process.

The technique sketched here is described extensively by De Sutter *et al.* [76].

8.4.3 Disassembly with relocation information

The situation is much better when the relocation information produced by the assembler is still available. As we saw in Section 8.1.3, the relocation bit map tells for every byte position if it is relocatable and if so whether it pertains to the code segment or the data segment. So scanning the relocation bit map we can easily find the addresses in instructions and insert them in A_I or A_D. The algorithm in Figure 8.5 then does the rest. But even with the relocation information present, most disassemblers still construct the control-flow graph, to obtain better information on routine boundaries and data types.

8.5 Decompilation

Decompilation takes the level-raising process a step further: it attempts to derive code in a high-level programming language from assembler or binary code. The main reason for doing this is to obtain a form of a legacy program which can be understood, modified, and recompiled, possibly for a different platform. Depending on the exact needs, different levels of decompilation can be distinguished; we will see that for the higher levels the difference between compilation and decompilation begin to fade.

We will sketch the decompilation process using the sample program segment from Figure 8.9, in the following setting. The original program, written in some source language L, derives from the outline code in 8.9(a). The routines *ReadInt(out n)*, *WriteInt(in n)*, and *IsEven(in n)* are built-in system routines and *DoOddInt(in n)* is a routine from elsewhere in the program. The program was translated into binary code, and was much later disassembled into the assembly code in 8.9(b), using the techniques described above. The routines *ReadInt*, *WriteInt*, *IsEven*, and *DoOddInt* were identified by the labels R_088, R_089, R_067, and R_374, respectively, but that mapping is not yet known at this point. The target language of the decompilation will be C.

The lowest level of decompilation just replaces each assembly instruction with the semantically equivalent C code. This yields the code given in Figure 8.10(a); the registers R1, R2, and R3 are declared as global variables. The machine condition

```
                                   L_043:
                                          Load_Addr   V_722,R3
                                          SetPar_Reg  R3,0
                                          Call        R_088
                                          Goto_False  L_044
                                          Load_Reg    V_722,R1
                                          Load_Const  0,R2
                                          Comp_Neq    R1,R2
     while ReadInt (n):                   Goto_False  L_043
       if n ≠ 0:                          SetPar_Reg  R1,0
         if IsEven (n):                   Call        R_067
           WriteInt (n / 2);              Goto_False  L_045
         else:                            Load_Reg    2,R2
           DoOddInt (n);                  Div_Reg     R2,R1
       (a)                                SetPar_     R1,0
                                          Call        R_089
                                          Goto        L_043
                                   L_045:
                                          SetPar_     R1,0
                                          Call        R_374
                                          Goto        L_043
                                   L_044:
                                            (b)
```

Fig. 8.9: Unknown program (a) and its disassembled translation (b)

register has been modeled as a global variable C, and the assembly code parameter transfer mechanism has been implemented with an additional register-like global variable P1. One could call this the "register level". In spite of its very low-level appearance the code of Figure 8.10(a) already compiles and runs correctly. If the sole purpose is recompilation for a different system this level of decompilation may be enough.

If, however, modifications need to be made, a more palatable version is desirable. The next level is obtained by a simple form of symbolic interpretation combined with forward substitution. The code in Figure 8.10(a) can easily be interpreted symbolically by using the goto statements as the arrows in a conceptual flow graph. A symbolic expression is built up for each register during this process, and the expression is substituted wherever the register is used. This results in the code of Figure 8.10(b). One could call this the "if-goto level". The actual process is more complicated: unused register expressions need to be removed, register expressions used multiple times need to be assigned to variables, etc.; the details are described by Johnstone and Scott [133].

If the goal of the decompilation is a better understanding of the program, or if a major revision of it is required, a better readable, structured version is needed, preferably without any goto statements. Basically, the structuring is achieved by a form of bottom-up rewriting (BURS) for graphs, in which the control-flow graph of the if-goto level derived above is rewritten using the control structures of the target language as patterns.

```
                int V_017;                        int V_017;

    L_043:                            L_043:
                R3 = &V_017;
                P1 = R3;
                C = R_088(P1);
                if  (C == 0) goto L_044;          if  (!R_088(&V_017)) goto L_044;
                R1 = V_017;
                R2 = 0;
                C =  (R1 != R2);
                if  (C == 0) goto L_043;          if  (!( V_017 != 0)) goto L_043;
                P1 = R1;
                C = R_067(P1);
                if  (C == 0) goto L_045;          if  (!R_067(V_017)) goto L_045;
                R2 = 2;
                R1 = R1 / R2;
                P1 = R1;
                C = R_089(P1);                    R_089(V_017 / 2);
                goto L_043;                       goto L_043;
    L_045:                            L_045:
                P1 = R1;
                C = R_374(P1);                    R_374(V_017);
                goto L_043;                       goto L_043;
    L_044:                            L_044:
```

        (a)   (b)

Fig. 8.10: Result of naive decompilation (a) and subsequent forward substitution (b)

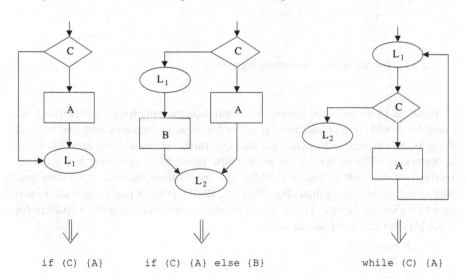

    if (C) {A}   if (C) {A} else {B}   while (C) {A}

Fig. 8.11: Some decompilation patterns for C

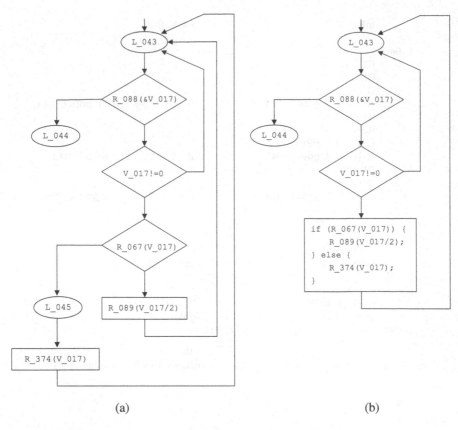

(a)   (b)

Fig. 8.12: Two stages in the decompilation process

Figure 8.11 shows three sample decompilation patterns for C; a real-world de-compiler would contain additional patterns for switch statements with and without defaults, repeat-until statements, negated condition statements, the lazy && and || operators, etc. Figure 8.12(a) shows the flow graph to be rewritten; it derives directly from the code in Figure 8.10(b). The labels from the code have been preserved to help in pattern matching. We use a BURS process that assigns the lowest cost to the largest pattern. The first identification it will make is with the pattern for if (C) {A} else {B}, using the equalities:

```
C  = R_067(V_017)
A  = R_089(V_017/2)
L₁ = L_045
B  = R_374(V_017)
L₂ = L_043
```

The rewriting step then substitutes the parameters thus obtained into the pattern and replaces the original nodes with one node containing the result of that substitution; this yields the control-flow graph in Figure 8.12(b).

```
    int V_017;                              int i;

    while (R_088(&V_017)) {                 while (ReadInt(&i)) {
      if ((V_017 != 0)) {                     if ((i != 0)) {
      if (R_067(V_017)) {                       if (IsEven(i)) {
          R_089(V_017 / 2);                         WriteInt(i / 2);
      } else {                                  } else {
          R_374(V_017);                             R_374(i);
      }                                         }
      }                                       }
    }                                       }
  L_044:
```

      (a)   (b)

Fig. 8.13: The decompiled text after restructuring (a) and with some name substitution (b)

Two more rewritings reduce the graph to a single node (except for the label L_044), which contains the code of Figure 8.13(a). At that point it might be possible to identify the functions of R_088, R_089, R_067, as *ReadInt*, *WriteInt*, and *IsEven*, respectively, by manually analysing the code attached to these labels. And since V_017 seems to be the only variable in the code, it may perhaps be given a more usual name, i for example. This leads to the code in Figure 8.13(b). If the binary code still holds the symbol table (name list) we might be able to do better or even much better.

It will be clear that many issues have been swept under the rug in the above sketch, some of considerable weight. For one thing, the BURS technique as explained in Section 9.1.4 is applicable to trees only, and here it is applied to graphs. The tree technique can be adapted to graphs, but since there are far fewer program construct patterns than machine instruction patterns, simpler search techniques can often be used. For another, the rewriting patterns may not suffice to rewrite the graph. However, the control-flow graphs obtained in decompilation are not arbitrary graphs in that they derive from what was at one time a program written by a person, and neither are the rewriting patterns arbitrary. As a result decompilation graphs occuring in practice can for the larger part be rewritten easily with most of the high-level language patterns. If the process gets stuck, there are several possibilities, including rewriting one or more arcs to goto statements; duplicating parts of the graph; and introducing state variables.

The above rewriting technique is from Lichtblau [179]. It is interesting to see that almost the same BURS process that converted the control-flow graph to assembly code in Section 9.1.4 is used here to convert it to high-level language code. This shows that the control-flow graph is the "real" program, of which the assembly code and the high-level language code are two possible representations for different purposes.

Cifuentes [60] gives an explicit algorithm to structure any graph into regions with one entry point only. These regions are then matched to the control structures of the target language; if the match fails, a goto is used. Cifuentes and Gough [62] describe the entire decompilation process from MSDOS .exe file to C program in reasonable detail. Vigna [288] discusses disassembly and semantic analysis of obfuscated binary code, with an eye to malware detection. The problem of the reconstruction of data types in the decompiled code is treated by Dolgova and Chernov [86].

Decompilation of Java bytecode is easier than that of native assembler code, since it contains more information, but also more difficult since the target code (Java) is more complicated. Several books treat the problem in depth, for example Nolan [204]. Gomez-Zamalloa *et al.* [107] exploit the intriguing idea of doing decompilation of low-level code by partially evaluating (Section 7.5.1.2) an interpreter for that code with the code as input. Using this technique they obtain a decompiler for full sequential Java bytecode into Prolog.

8.6 Conclusion

This concludes our discussion of the last step in compiler construction, the transformation of the fully annotated AST to an executable binary file.

In an extremely high-level view of compiler construction, one can say that textual analysis is done by pattern matching, context handling by data-flow machine, and object code synthesis (code generation) again by pattern matching. Many of the algorithms used in compilation can conveniently be expressed as closure algorithms, as can those in disassembly. Decompilation can be viewed as compilation towards a high-level language.

Summary

- The assembler translates the symbolic instructions generated for a source code module to a relocatable binary object file. The linker combines some relocatable binary files and probably some library object files into an executable binary program file. The loader loads the contents of the executable binary program file into memory and starts the execution of the program.
- The code and data segments of a relocatable object file consist of binary code derived directly from the symbolic instructions. Since some machine instruction require special alignment, it may be necessary to insert no-ops in the relocatable object code.
- Relocatable binary object files contain code segments, data segments, relocation information, and external linkage information.
- The memory addresses in a relocatable binary object file are computed as if the file were loaded at position 0 in memory. The relocation information lists the positions of the addresses that have to be updated when the file is loaded in a different position, as it usually will be.

- Obtaining the relocation information is in principle a two-scan process. The second scan can be avoided by backpatching the relocatable addresses as soon as their values are determined. The relocation information is usually implemented as a bit map.
- An external entry point marks a given location in a relocatable binary file as available from other relocatable binary files. An external entry point in one module can be accessed by an external reference in a different, or even the same, module.
- The external linkage information is usually implemented as an array of records.
- The linker combines the code segments and the data segments of its input files, converts relative addresses to absolute addresses using the relocation and external linkage information, and links in library modules to satisfy left-over external references.
- Linking results in an executable code file, consisting of one code segment and one data segment. The relocation bit maps and external symbol tables are gone, having served their purpose. This finishes the translation process.
- In an extremely high-level view of compiler construction, one can say that textual analysis is done by pattern matching, context handling by data-flow machine, and object code synthesis (code generation) again by pattern matching.
- Disassembly converts binary to assembly code; decompilation converts it to high-level language code.
- Instruction and data addresses, badly distinguishable in binary code, are told apart by inference and symbolic interpretation. Both can be applied to the incomplete control-flow graph by introducing an Unknown node.
- Decompilation progresses in four steps: assembly instruction to HLL code; register removal through forward substitution; construction of the control-flow graph; rewriting of the control-flow graph using bottom-up rewriting with patterns corresponding to control structures from the HLL; name substitution, as far as possible.
- The use of bottom-up rewriting both to convert the control-flow into assembly code and to convert it into high-level language suggest that the control-flow graph is the "real" program, with assembly code and the high-level language code being two possible representations.

Further reading

As with interpreters, reading material on assembler design is not abundant; we mention Saloman [246] as one of the few books.

Linkers and loaders have long lived in the undergrowth of compilers and operating systems; yet they are getting more important with each new programming language and more complicated with each new operating system. Levine's book [175] was the first book in 20 years to give serious attention to them and the first ever to be dedicated exclusively to them.

Exercises

8.1. Learn to use the local assembler, for example by writing, assembling and running a program that prints the tables of multiplication from 1 to 10.

8.2. (▷791) Many processors have **program-counter relative addressing** modes and/or instructions. They may, for example, have a jump instruction that adds a constant to the program counter (PC). What is the advantage of such instructions and addressing modes?

8.3. (▷www) Many processors have conditional jump instructions only for conditional jumps with a limited range. For example, the target of the jump may not be further than 128 bytes away from the current program counter. Sometimes, an assembler for such a processor still allows unlimited conditional jumps. How can such an unlimited conditional jump be implemented?

8.4. Find and study documentation on the object file format of a compiler system that you use regularly. In particular, read the sections on the symbol table format and the relocation information.

8.5. Compile the C-code

```
void copystring(char *s1, const char *s2) {
      while (*s1++ = *s2++) {}
}
```

and disassemble the result by hand.

8.6. *History of assemblers*: Study Wheeler's 1950 paper *Programme organization and initial orders for the EDSAC* [297], and write a summary with special attention to the Initial Program Loading and relocation facilities.

Chapter 9
Optimization Techniques

The code generation techniques described in Chapter 7 are simple, and generate straightforward unoptimized code, which may be sufficient for rapid prototyping or demonstration purposes, but which will not satisfy the modern user. In this chapter we will look at many optimization techniques. Since optimal code generation is in general NP-complete, many of the algorithms used are heuristic, but some, for example BURS, yield provably optimal results in restricted situations.

The general optimization algorithms in Section 9.1 aim at the over-all improvement of the code, with speed as their main target. Next are two sections discussing optimizations which address specific issues: code size reduction, and energy saving and power reduction. They are followed by a section on just-in-time (JIT) compilation; this optimization tries to improve the entire process of running a program, including machine and platform independence, compile time, and run time. The chapter closes with a discussion about the relationship between compilers and computer architectures.

9.1 General optimization

As explained in Section 7.2, instruction selection, register allocation, and instruction scheduling are intertwined, and finding the optimal rewriting of the AST with available instruction templates is NP-complete [3, 53]. We present here some techniques that address part or parts of the problem. The first, "compilation by symbolic interpretation", tries to combine the three components of code generation by performing them simultaneously during one or more symbolic interpretation scans. The second, "basic blocks", is mainly concerned with optimization, instruction selection, and instruction scheduling in limited parts of the AST. The third, "bottom-up tree rewriting", discussed in Section 9.1.4, shows how a very good instruction selector can be generated automatically for very general instruction sets and cost functions, under the assumption that enough registers are available. The fourth, "register allocation by graph coloring", discussed in Section 9.1.5, explains a good and very general heuristic for register allocation. And the fifth, "supercompilation", discussed in Section 9.1.6, shows how exhaustive search can yield optimal code for small routines. In an actual compiler some of these techniques would be combined with each other and/or with ad-hoc approaches.

We treat the algorithms in their basic form; the literature on code generation contains many, many more algorithms, often of a very advanced nature. Careful application of the techniques described in these sections will yield a reasonably optimizing compiler but not more than that. The production of a top-quality code generator is a subject that could easily fill an entire book. In fact, the book actually exists and is by Muchnick [197].

9.1.1 Compilation by symbolic interpretation

There are a host of techniques in code generation that derive more or less directly from the symbolic interpretation technique discussed in Section 5.2. Most of them are used to improve one of the simple code generation techniques, but it is also possible to employ compilation by symbolic interpretation as a full code generation technique. We briefly discuss these techniques here, between the simple and the more advanced compilation techniques.

As we recall, the idea of symbolic interpretation was to have an approximate representation of the stack at the entry of each node and to transform it into an approximate representation at the exit of the node. The stack representation was approximate in that it usually recorded information items like "x is initialized" rather than "x has the value 3", where x is a variable on the stack. The reason for using an approximation is, of course, that it is often impossible to obtain the exact stack representation at compile time. After the assignment x:=read_real() we know that x has been initialized, but we have no way of knowing its value.

Compilation by symbolic interpretation (also known as **compilation on the stack**) uses the same technique but does keep the representation exact by generating code for all values that cannot be computed at compile time. To this end the representation is extended to include the stack, the machine registers, and perhaps some memory locations; we will call such a representation a **register and variable descriptor** or **regvar descriptor** for short. Now, if the effect of a node can be represented exactly in the regvar descriptor, we do so. This is, for example, the case for assignments with a known constant: the effect of the assignment x:=3 can be recorded exactly in the regvar descriptor as "x = 3".

If, however, we cannot, for some reason, record the effect of a node exactly in the regvar descriptor, we solve the problem by generating code for the node and record *its* effect in the regvar descriptor. When confronted with an assignment x:=read_real() we are forced to generate code for it. Suppose in our compiler we call a function by using a Call instruction and suppose further that we have decided that a function returns its result in register R1. We then generate the code Call read_real and record in the regvar descriptor "The value of x is in R1". Together they implement the effect of the node x:=read_real() exactly.

In this way, the regvar descriptor gets to contain detailed information about which registers are free, what each of the other registers contains, where the present values of the local and temporary variables can be found, etc. These data can then be used to produce better code for the next node. Consider, for example, the code segment x:=read_real(); y:=x * x. At entry to the second assignment, the regvar descriptor contains "The value of x is in R1". Suppose register R4 is free. Now the second assignment can be translated simply as Load_Reg R1,R4; Mult_Reg R1,R4, which enters a second item into the regvar descriptor, "The value of y is in R4". Note that the resulting code

```
Call      read_real
Load_Reg  R1,R4
Mult_Reg  R1,R4
```

does not access the memory locations of x and y at all. If we have sufficient registers, the values of x and y will never have to be stored in memory. This technique combines very well with live analysis: when we leave the live range of a variable, we can delete all information about it from the regvar description, which will probably free a register.

Note that a register can contain the value of more than one variable: after a:=b:=<expression>, the register that received the value of the expression contains the present values of both a and b. Likewise the value of a variable can sometimes be found in more than one place: after the generated code Load_Mem x,R3, the value of x can be found both in the location x and in register R3.

The regvar descriptor can be implemented as a set of information items as suggested above, but it is more usual to base its implementation on the fact that the regvar descriptor has to answer three questions:

- where can the value of a variable V be found?
- what does register R contain?
- which registers are free?

It is traditionally implemented as a set of three data structures:

- a table of **register descriptors**, addressed by register numbers, whose n-th entry contains information on what register n contains;
- a table of **variable descriptors** (also known as **address descriptors**), addressed by variable names, whose entry V contains information indicating where the value of variable V can be found; and
- a set of free registers.

The advantage is that answers to questions are available directly, the disadvantage is that inserting and removing information may require updating three data structures. When this technique concentrates mainly on the registers, it is called **register tracking**.

9.1.2 Code generation for basic blocks

Goto statements, routine calls, and other breaks in the flow of control are complicating factors in code generation. This is certainly so in narrow compilers, in which neither the code from which a jump to the present code may have originated nor the code to which control is transferred is available, so no analysis can be done. But it is also true in a broad compiler: the required code may be available (or in the case of a routine it may not), but information about contents of registers and memory locations will still have to be merged at the join nodes in the flow of control, and, as explained in Section 5.2.1, this merge may have to be performed iteratively. Such join nodes occur in many places even in well-structured programs and in the absence of user-written jumps: the join node of the flow of control from the then-part and the else-part at the end of an if-else statement is an example.

The desire to do code generation in more "quiet" parts of the AST has led to the idea of basic blocks. A **basic block** is a part of the control graph that contains no splits (jumps) or combines (labels). It is usual to consider only **maximal basic blocks**, basic blocks which cannot be extended by including adjacent nodes without violating the definition of a basic block. A maximal basic block starts at a label or at the beginning of the routine and ends just before a jump or jump-like node or label or the end of the routine. A routine call terminates a basic block, after the parameters have been evaluated and stored in their required locations. Since jumps have been excluded, the control flow inside a basic block cannot contain cycles.

In the imperative languages, basic blocks consist exclusively of expressions and assignments, which follow each other sequentially. In practice this is also true for functional and logic languages, since when they are compiled, imperative code is generated for them.

The effect of an assignment in a basic block may be local to that block, in which case the resulting value is not used anywhere else and the variable is dead at the end of the basic block, or it may be non-local, in which case the variable is an output variable of the basic block. In general, one needs to do routine-wide live analysis to obtain this information, but sometimes simpler means suffice: the scope rules of C tell us that at the end of the basic block in Figure 9.1, n is dead.

```
{   int n;

    n = a + 1;
    x = b + n*n + c;
    n = n + 1;
    y = d * n;
}
```

Fig. 9.1: Sample basic block in C

If we do not have this information (as is likely in a narrow compiler) we have to assume that all variables are live at basic block end; they are all output variables. Similarly, last-def analysis (as explained in Section 5.2.3) can give us information about the values of input variables to a basic block. Both types of information can allow us to generate better code; of the two, knowledge about the output variables is more important.

A basic block is usually required to deliver its results in specific places: variables in specified memory locations and routine parameters in specified registers or places on the stack.

We will now look at one way to generate code for a basic block. Our code generation proceeds in two steps. First we convert the AST and the control flow implied in it into a dependency graph; unlike the AST the dependency graph is a **DAG**, a directed acyclic graph. We then rewrite the dependency graph to code.

We use the basic block of Figure 9.1 as an example; its AST is shown in Figure 9.2. It is convenient to draw the AST for an assignment with the source as the left branch and the destination as the right branch; to emphasize the inversion, we write the traditional assignment operator := as =:.

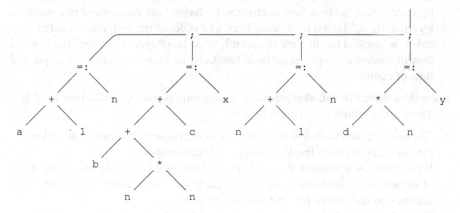

Fig. 9.2: AST of the sample basic block

The C program text in Figure 9.1 shows clearly that n is a local variable and is dead at block exit. We assume that the values of x and y are used elsewhere: x and y are live at block exit; it is immaterial whether we know this because of a preceding live analysis or just assume it because we know nothing about them.

9.1.2.1 From AST to dependency graph

Until now, we have threaded ASTs to obtain control-flow graphs, which are then used to make certain that code is generated in the right order. But the restrictions imposed by the control-flow graph are often more severe than necessary: actually only the data dependencies have to be obeyed. For example, the control-flow graph for a + b defines that a must be evaluated before b, whereas the data dependency allows a and b to be evaluated in any order. As a result, it is easier to generate good code from a data dependency graph than from a control-flow graph. Although in both cases any topological ordering consistent with the interface conventions of the templates is acceptable, the control flow graph generally defines the order precisely and leaves no freedom to the topological ordering, whereas the data dependency graph often leaves considerable freedom.

One of the most important properties of a basic block is that its AST including its control-flow graph is acyclic and can easily be converted into a data dependency graph, which is advantageous for code generation.

There are two main sources of data dependencies in the AST of a basic block:

- data flow inside expressions. The resulting data dependencies come in two varieties, downward from an assignment operator to the destination, and upward from the operands to all other operators. The generated code must implement this data flow (and of course the operations on these data).
- data flow from values assigned to variables to the use of the values of these variables in further nodes. The resulting data dependencies need not be supported by code, since the data flow is effected by having the data stored in a machine location, from where it is retrieved later. The order of the assignments to the variables, as implied by the flow of control, must be obeyed, however. The implied flow of control is simple, since basic blocks by definition contain only sequential flow of control.

For a third source of data dependencies, concerning pointers, see Section 9.1.2.3.

Three observations are in order here:

- The order of the evaluation of operations in expressions is immaterial, as long as the data dependencies inside the expressions are respected.
- If the value of a variable V is used more than once in a basic block, the order of these uses is immaterial, as long as each use comes after the assignment it depends on and before the next assignment to V.
- The order in which the assignments to variables are executed is immaterial, provided that the data dependencies established above are respected.

These considerations give us a simple algorithm to convert the AST of a basic block to a data dependency graph:

1. Replace the arcs that connect the nodes in the AST of the basic block by data dependency arrows. The arrows between assignment nodes and their destinations in the expressions in the AST point from destination node to assignment node; the other arrows point from the parent nodes downward. As already explained in the second paragraph of Section 4.1.2, the data dependency arrows point against the data flow.
2. Insert a data dependency arrow from each variable V used as an operand to the assignment that set its value, or to the beginning of the basic block if V was an input variable. This dependency reflects the fact that a value stays in a variable until replaced. Note that this introduces operand nodes with data dependencies.
3. Insert a data dependency arrow from each assignment to a variable V to all the previous uses of V, if present. This dependency reflects the fact that an assignment to a variable replaces the old value of that variable.
4. Designate the nodes that describe the output values as roots of the graph. From a data dependency point of view, they are the primary interesting results from which all other interesting results derive.
5. Remove the ;-nodes and their arrows. The effects of the flow of control specified by them have been taken over by the data dependencies added in steps 2 and 3.

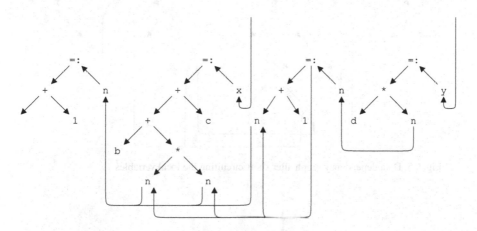

Fig. 9.3: Data dependency graph for the sample basic block

Figure 9.3 shows the resulting data dependency graph.

Next, we realize that an assignment in the data dependency graph just passes on the value and can be short-circuited; possible dependencies of the assignment move to its destination. The result of this modification is shown in Figure 9.4. Also, local variables serve no other purpose than to pass on values, and can be short-circuited as well; possible dependencies of the variable move to the operator that uses the variable. The result of this modification is shown in Figure 9.5. Finally, we can eliminate from the graph all nodes not reachable through at least one of the

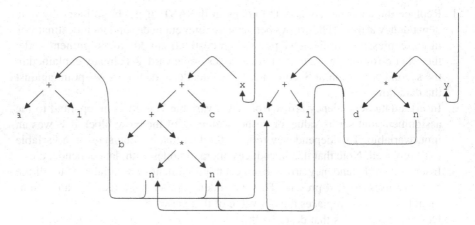

Fig. 9.4: Data dependency graph after short-circuiting the assignments

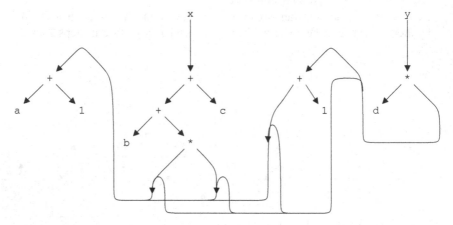

Fig. 9.5: Data dependency graph after short-circuiting the local variables

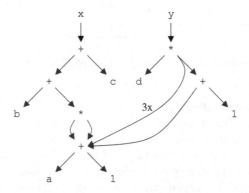

Fig. 9.6: Cleaned-up data dependency graph for the sample basic block

roots; this does not affect our sample graph. These simplifications yield the final data dependency graph redrawn in Figure 9.6.

Note that the only roots to the graph are the external dependencies for x and y. Note also that if we happened to know that x and y were dead at block exit too, the entire data dependency graph would disappear automatically.

Figure 9.6 has the pleasant property that it specifies the semantics of the basic block precisely: all required nodes and data dependencies are present and no node or data dependency is superfluous.

```
{   int n, n1;

    n = a + 1;
    x = b + n*n + c;
    n1 = n + 1;
    y = d * n1;
}
```

Fig. 9.7: The basic block of Fig. 9.1 in SSA form

Considerable simplification can often be obtained by transforming the basic block to **Static Single Assignment** (**SSA**) form. As the name suggests, in an SSA basic block each variable is only assigned to in one place. Any basic block can be transformed to this form by introducing new variables. For example, Figure 9.7 shows the SSA form of the basic block of Figure 9.1. The introduction of the new variables does not change the behavior of the basic block.

Since in SSA form a variable is always assigned exactly once, data dependency analysis becomes almost trivial: a variable is never available before it is assigned, and is always available after it has been assigned. If a variable is never used, its assignment can be eliminated.

To represent more than a single basic block, for example an if- or while statement, SSA analysis traditionally uses an approximation: if necessary, a ϕ function is used to represent different possible values. For example:

```
if (n < 0) {
    x = 3;
} else {
    x = 4;
}
```

is represented in SSA form as:

```
x = φ(3,4);
```

where the ϕ function is a "choice" function that simply lists possible values at a particular point in the program. Using a ϕ function for expression approximation is a reasonable compromise between just saying Unknown, which is unhelpful, and exactly specifying the value, which is only possible with the original program code, and hence is cumbersome. Using the ϕ function, the semantics of a large block of code can be represented as a list of assignments.

Before going into techniques of converting the dependency graph into efficient machine instructions, however, we have to discuss two further issues concerning basic blocks and dependency graphs. The first is an important optimization, *common subexpression elimination*, and the second is the traditional representation of basic blocks and dependency graphs as *triples*.

Common subexpression elimination Experience has shown that many basic blocks contain **common subexpressions**, subexpressions that occur more than once in the basic block and evaluate to the same value at each occurrence. Common subexpressions originate from repeated subexpressions in the source code, for example

```
x = a*a + 2*a*b + b*b;
y = a*a − 2*a*b + b*b;
```

which contains three common subexpressions. This may come as a surprise to C or Java programmers, who are used to factor out common subexpressions almost without thinking:

```
double sum_sqrs = a*a + b*b;
double cross_prod = 2*a*b;
x = sum_sqrs + cross_prod;
y = sum_sqrs − cross_prod;
```

but such solutions are less convenient in a language that does not allow variable declarations in sub-blocks. Also, common subexpressions can be generated by the intermediate code generation phase for many constructs in many languages, including C. For example, the C expression a[i] + b[i], in which a and b are arrays of 4-byte integers, is translated into

```
*(a + 4*i) + *(b + 4*i)
```

which features the common subexpression 4*i.

Identifying and combining common subexpressions for the purpose of computing them only once is useful, since doing so results in smaller and faster code, but this only works when the value of the expression is the same at each occurrence. Equal subexpressions in a basic block are not necessarily common subexpressions. For example, the source code

```
x = a*a + 2*a*b + b*b;
a = b = 0;
y = a*a − 2*a*b + b*b;
```

still contains three pairs of equal subexpressions, but they no longer evaluate to the same value, due to the intervening assignments, and do not qualify as "common subexpressions". The effect of the assignments cannot be seen easily in the AST, but shows up immediately in the data dependency graph of the basic block, since the as and bs in the third line have different dependencies from those in the first line.

This means that common subexpressions cannot be detected right away in the AST, but their detection has to wait until the data dependency graph has been constructed.

Once we have the data dependency graph, finding the common subexpressions is simple. The rule is that two nodes that have the operands, the operator, and the dependencies in common can be combined into one node. This reduces the number of operands, and thus the number of machine instructions to be generated. Note that we have already met a simple version of this rule: two nodes that have the operand and its dependencies in common can be combined into one node. It was this rule that allowed us to short-circuit the assignments and eliminate the variable n in the transformation from Figure 9.3 to Figure 9.6.

Consider the basic block in Figure 9.8, which was derived from the one in Figure 9.1 by replacing n by n*n in the third assignment.

```
{   int n;

    n = a + 1;
    x = b + n*n + c;    /* subexpression n*n ... */
    n = n*n + 1;        /* ... in common */
    y = d * n;
}
```

Fig. 9.8: Basic block in C with common subexpression

Figure 9.9 shows its data dependency graph at the moment that the common variables with identical dependencies have already been eliminated; it is similar to Figure 9.6, with the additional St node. This graph contains two nodes with identical operators (*), identical operands (the + node), and identical data dependencies, again on the + node. The two nodes can be combined (Figure 9.10), resulting in the elimination of the common subexpression.

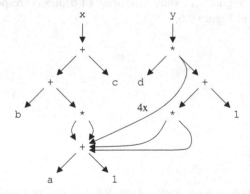

Fig. 9.9: Data dependency graph with common subexpression

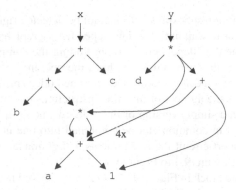

Fig. 9.10: Cleaned-up data dependency graph with common subexpression eliminated

Detecting that two or more nodes in a graph are the same is usually implemented by storing some representation of each node in a hash table. If the hash value of a node depends on its operands, its operator, and its dependencies, common nodes will hash to the same value. As is usual with hashing algorithms, an additional check is needed to see if they really fulfill the requirements.

As with almost all optimization techniques, the usefulness of common subexpression elimination depends on the source language and the source program, and it is difficult to give figures, but most compiler writers find it useful enough to include it in their compilers.

The triples representation of the data dependency graph   Traditionally, data dependency graphs are implemented as arrays of triples. A **triple** is a record with three fields representing an operator with its two operands, and corresponds to an operator node in the data dependency graph. If the operator is monadic, the second operand is left empty. The operands can be constants, variables, and indexes to other triples. These indexes to other triples replace the pointers that connect the nodes in the data dependency graph. Figure 9.11 shows the array of triples corresponding to the data dependency graph of Figure 9.6.

position	triple
1	a + 1
2	@1 * @1
3	b + @2
4	@3 + c
5	@4 =: x
6	@1 + 1
7	d * @6
8	@7 =: y

Fig. 9.11: The data dependency graph of Figure 9.6 as an array of triples

9.1.2.2 From dependency graph to code

Generating instructions from a data dependency graph is very similar to doing so from an AST: the nodes are rewritten by machine instruction templates and the result is linearized by scheduling. The main difference is that the data dependency graph allows much more leeway in the order of the instructions than the AST, since the latter reflects the full sequential specification inherent in imperative languages. So we will try to exploit this greater freedom. In this section we assume a "register-memory machine", a machine with reg op:= mem instructions in addition to the reg op:= reg instructions of the pure register machine, and we restrict our generated code to such instructions, to reduce the complexity of the code generation. The available machine instructions allow most of the nodes to be rewritten simply by a single appropriate machine instruction, and we can concentrate on instruction scheduling and register allocation. We will turn to the scheduling first, and leave the register allocation to the next subsection.

Scheduling of the data dependency graph We have seen in Section 7.2.1 that any scheduling obtained by a topological ordering of the instructions is acceptable as far as correctness is concerned, but that for optimization purposes some orderings are better than others. In the absence of other criteria, two scheduling techniques suggest themselves, corresponding to early evaluation and to late evaluation, respectively. In the early evaluation scheduling, code for a node is issued as soon as the code for all of its operands has been issued. In the late evaluation scheduling, code for a node is issued as late as possible. It turns out that early evaluation scheduling tends to require more registers than late evaluation scheduling. The reason is clear: early evaluation scheduling creates values as soon as possible, which may be long before they are used, and these values have to be kept in registers. We will therefore concentrate on late evaluation scheduling.

It is useful to distinguish between the notion of "late" evaluation used here and the more common notion of "lazy" evaluation. The difference is that "lazy evaluation" implies that we hope to avoid the action at all, which is clearly advantageous; in "late evaluation" we know beforehand that we will have to perform the action anyway, but we find it advantageous to perform it as late as possible, usually because fewer resources are tied up that way. The same considerations applied in Section 4.1.5.3, where we tried to evaluate the attributes as late as possible.

Even within the late evaluation scheduling there is still a lot of freedom, and we will exploit this freedom to adapt the scheduling to the character of our machine instructions. We observe that register-memory machines allow very efficient "ladder" sequences like

```
Load_Mem  a,R1
Add_Mem   b,R1
Mult_Mem  c,R1
Subtr_Mem d,R1
```

for the expression $(((a+b)*c)-d)$, and we would like our scheduling algorithm to produce such sequences. To this end we first define an **available ladder sequence** in a data dependency graph:

1. Each root node of the graph is an available ladder sequence.
2. If an available ladder sequence S ends in an operation node N whose left operand is an operation node L, then S extended with L is also an available ladder sequence.
3. If an available ladder sequence S ends in an operation node N whose operator is commutative—meaning that the left and right operand can be interchanged without affecting the result—and whose right operand is an operation node R, then S extended with R is also an available ladder sequence.

In other words, available ladder sequences start at root nodes, continue normally along left operands but may continue along the right operand for commutative operators, may stop anywhere, and must stop at leaves.

Code generated for a given ladder sequence starts at its last node, by loading a leaf variable if the sequence ends before a leaf, or by loading an intermediate value if the sequence ends earlier. Working backwards along the sequence, code is then generated for each of the operation nodes. Finally the resulting value is stored as indicated in the root node. For example, the code generated for the ladder sequence x, +, + in Figure 9.6 would be

```
Load_Mem b,R1
Add_Reg   I1,R1
Add_Mem   c,R1
Store_Reg R1,x
```

assuming that the anonymous right operand of the + is available in some register I1 (for "Intermediate 1"). The actual rewriting is shown in Figure 9.12.

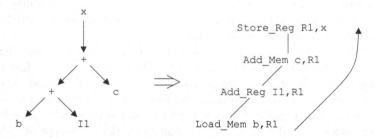

Fig. 9.12: Rewriting and scheduling a ladder sequence

The following simple heuristic scheduling algorithm tries to combine the identification of such ladder sequences with late evaluation. Basically, it repeatedly finds a ladder sequence from among those that could be issued last, issues code for it, and removes it from the graph. As a result, the instructions are identified in reverse order and the last instruction of the entire sequence is the first to be determined. To delay the issues of register allocation, we will use pseudo-registers during the scheduling phase. **Pseudo-registers** are like normal registers, except that we assume that there are enough of them. We will see in the next subsection how the pseudo-registers can be mapped onto real registers or memory locations. However, the register used inside the ladder sequence must be a real register or the whole plan fails, so we do not want to run the risk that it gets assigned to memory during register allocation. Fortunately, since the ladder register is loaded at the beginning of the resulting code sequence and is stored at the end of the code sequence, the live ranges of the registers in the different ladders do not overlap, and the same real register, for example R1, can be used for each of them.

The algorithm consists of the following five steps:

1. Find an available ladder sequence S of maximum length that has the property that none of its nodes has more than one incoming data dependency.
2. If any operand of a node N in S is not a leaf but another node M not in S, associate a new pseudo-register R with M if it does not have one already; use R as the operand in the code generated for N and make M an additional root of the dependency graph.
3. Generate code for the ladder sequence S, using R1 as the ladder register.
4. Remove the ladder sequence S from the data dependency graph.
5. Repeat steps 1 through 4 until the entire data dependency graph has been consumed and rewritten to code.

In step 1 we want to select a ladder sequence for which we can generate code immediately in a last-to-first sense. The intermediate values in a ladder sequence can only be used by code that will be executed later. Since we generate code from last to first, we cannot generate the code for a ladder sequence S until all code that uses intermediate values from S has already been generated. So any sequence that has incoming data dependencies will have to wait until the code that causes the dependencies has been generated and removed from the dependency graph, together with its dependencies. This explains the "incoming data dependency" part in step 1. It is advantageous to use a ladder sequence that cannot be extended without violating the property in step 1; hence the "maximum length". Using a sequence that ends earlier is not incorrect, but results in code to be generated that includes useless intermediate values. Step 2 does a simple-minded form of register allocation. The other steps speak for themselves.

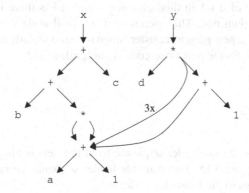

Fig. 9.13: Cleaned-up data dependency graph for the sample basic block

Returning to Figure 9.6, which is repeated here for convenience (Figure 9.13), we see that there are two available ladder sequences without multiple incoming data dependencies: x, +, +, *, in which we have followed the right operand of the second addition; and y, *, +. It makes no difference to the algorithm which one we process first; we will start here with the sequence y, *, +, on the weak grounds that we are generating code last-to-first, and y is the rightmost root of the dependency graph. The left operand of the node + in the sequence y, *, + is not a leaf but another node, the + of a + 1, and we associate the first free pseudo-register X1 with it. We make X1 an additional root of the dependency graph. So we obtain the following code:

```
Load_Reg  X1,R1
Add_Const 1,R1
Mult_Mem  d,R1
Store_Reg R1,y
```

Figure 9.14 shows the dependency graph after the above ladder sequence has been removed.

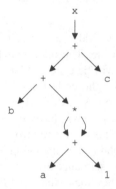

Fig. 9.14: Data dependency graph after removal of the first ladder sequence

The next available ladder sequence comprises the nodes x, +, +, *. We cannot include the + node of a + 1 in this sequence, since it has three incoming data dependencies rather than one. The operands of the final node * are not leaves, but they do not require a new pseudo-register, since they are already associated with the pseudo-register X1. So the generated code is straightforward:

```
Load_Reg  X1,R1
Mult_Reg  X1,R1
Add_Mem   b,R1
Add_Mem   c,R1
Store_Reg R1,x
```

Removal of this second ladder sequence from the dependency graph yields the graph shown in Figure 9.15. The available ladder sequence comprises both nodes: X1 and +; it rewrites to the following code:

Fig. 9.15: Data dependency graph after removal of the second ladder sequence

```
Load_Mem a,R1
Add_Const 1,R1
Load_Reg  R1,X1
```

Removing the above ladder sequence removes all nodes from the dependency graph, and we have completed this stage of the code generation. The result is in Figure 9.16.

```
Load_Mem a,R1
Add_Const 1,R1
Load_Reg  R1,X1

Load_Reg  X1,R1
Mult_Reg  X1,R1
Add_Mem   b,R1
Add_Mem   c,R1
Store_Reg R1,x

Load_Reg  X1,R1
Add_Const 1,R1
Mult_Mem  d,R1
Store_Reg R1,y
```

Fig. 9.16: Pseudo-register target code generated for the basic block

Register allocation for the scheduled code One thing remains to be done: the pseudo-registers have to be mapped onto real registers or, failing that, to memory locations. There are several ways to do so. One simple method, which requires no further analysis, is the following. We map the pseudo-registers onto real registers in the order of appearance, and when we run out of registers, we map the remaining ones onto memory locations. Note that mapping pseudo-registers to memory locations is consistent with their usage in the instructions. For a machine with at least two registers, R1 and R2, the resulting code is shown in Figure 9.17.

Note the instruction sequence Load_Reg R1,R2; Load_Reg R2,R1, in which the second instruction effectively does nothing. Such "stupid" instructions are generated often during code generation, usually on the boundary between two segments of the code. There are at least three ways to deal with such instructions: improving the code generation algorithm; doing *register tracking*, as explained in the last paragraph of Section 9.1.1; and doing *peephole optimization*, as explained in Section 7.6.1.

```
Load_Mem  a,R1
Add_Const 1,R1
Load_Reg  R1,R2

Load_Reg  R2,R1
Mult_Reg  R2,R1
Add_Mem   b,R1
Add_Mem   c,R1
Store_Reg R1,x

Load_Reg  R2,R1
Add_Const 1,R1
Mult_Mem  d,R1
Store_Reg R1,y
```

Fig. 9.17: Code generated for the program segment of Figure 9.1

A more general and better way to map pseudo-registers onto real ones involves doing more analysis. Now that the dependency graph has been linearized
by scheduling we can apply *live analysis*, as described in Section 5.5, to determine
the live ranges of the pseudo-registers, and apply the algorithms from Section 9.1.5
to do register allocation.

For comparison, the code generated by the full optimizing version of the GNU C
compiler *gcc* is shown in Figure 9.18, converted to the notation used in this chapter. We see that is has avoided both Load_Reg R2,R1 instructions, possibly using
register tracking.

```
Load_Mem  a,R1
Add_Const 1,R1
Load_Reg  R1,R2

Mult_Reg  R1,R2
Add_Mem   b,R2
Add_Mem   c,R2
Store_Reg R2,x

Add_Const 1,R1
Mult_Mem  d,R1
Store_Reg R1,y
```

Fig. 9.18: Code generated by the GNU C compiler, *gcc*

9.1.2.3 Code optimization in the presence of pointers

Pointers cause two different problems for the dependency graph construction in the
above sections. First, assignment under a pointer may change the value of a variable

in a subsequent expression: in

```
a = x * y;
*p = 3;
b = x * y;
```

x * y is not a common subexpression if p happens to point to x or y. Second, the value retrieved from under a pointer may change after an assignment: in

```
a = *p * q;
b = 3;
c = *p * q;
```

*p * q is not a common subexpression if p happens to point to b.

Static data-flow analysis may help to determine if the interference condition holds, but that does not solve the problem entirely. If we find that the condition holds, or if, in the more usual case, we cannot determine that it does not hold, we have to take the interference into account in the dependency graph construction. If we do this, the subsequent code generation algorithm of Section 9.1.2.2 will automatically generate correct code for the basic block.

The interference caused by an assignment under a pointer in an expression can be incorporated in the dependency graph by recognizing that it makes any variable used in a subsequent expression dependent on that assignment. These extra data dependencies can be added to the dependency graph. Likewise, the result of retrieving a value from under a pointer is dependent on all preceding assignments.

Figure 9.19 shows a basic block similar to that in Figure 9.1, except that the second assignment assigns *under* x rather than to x. The data dependency graph in Figure 9.20 features two additional data dependencies, leading from the variables n and d in the third and fourth expression to the assignment under the pointer. The assignment itself is marked with a *; note that the x is a normal input operand to this assignment operation, and that its data dependency is downward.

```
{ int n;

    n = a + 1;
    *x = b + n*n + c;
    n = n + 1;
    y = d * n;
}
```

Fig. 9.19: Sample basic block with an assignment under a pointer

Since the n in the third expression has more data dependencies than the ones in expression two, it is not a common subexpression, and cannot be combined with the other two. As a result, the variable n cannot be eliminated, as shown in the cleaned-up dependency graph, Figure 9.21. Where the dependency graph of Figure 9.6 had an available ladder sequence x, +, +, *, this sequence is now not available since

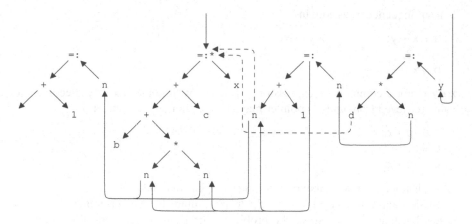

Fig. 9.20: Data dependency graph with an assignment under a pointer

the top operator =:* has an incoming data dependence. The only available sequence
is now y, *, +. Producing the corresponding code and removing the sequence also
removes the data dependency on the =:* node. This makes the sequence =:*, +, +, *
available, which stops before including the node n, since the latter has two incoming
data dependencies. The remaining sequence is n, =:, +. The resulting code can be
found in Figure 9.22.

The code features a pseudo-instruction

Instruction	Actions
Store_Indirect_Mem R_n,x	$*x := R_n$;

which stores the contents of register R_n under the pointer found in memory location x. It is unlikely that a machine would have such an instruction, but the ladder sequence algorithm requires the right operand to be a constant or variable.
On most machines the instruction would have to be expanded to something like
Load_Mem x,R_d; Store_Indirect_Reg R_n,R_d, where R_d holds the address of the
destination.

We see that the code differs from that in Figure 9.16 in that no pseudo-registers
were needed and some register-register instructions have been replaced by more
expensive memory-register instructions.

In the absence of full data-flow analysis, some simple rules can be used to restrict
the set of dependencies that have to be added. For example, if a variable is of the
register storage class in C, no pointer to it can be obtained, so no assignment under
a pointer can affect it. The same applies to local variables in languages in which no
pointers to local variables can be obtained. Also, if the source language has strong
typing, one can restrict the added dependencies to variables of the same type as that
of the pointer under which the assignment took place, since that type defines the set
of variables an assignment can possibly affect.

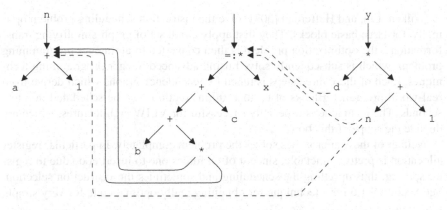

Fig. 9.21: Cleaned-up data dependency graph with an assignment under a pointer

Load_Mem	a,R1
Add_Const	1,R1
Store_Reg	R1,n
Load_Mem	n,R1
Mult_Mem	n,R1
Add_Mem	b,R1
Add_Mem	c,R1
Store_Indirect_Mem	R1,x
Load_Mem	n,R1
Add_Const	1,R1
Mult_Mem	d,R1
Store_Reg	R1,y

Fig. 9.22: Target code generated for the basic block of Figure 9.19

9.1.3 Almost optimal code generation

The above algorithms for code generation from DAGs resulting from basic blocks use heuristics, and often yield sub-optimal code. The prospects for feasible optimal code generation for DAGs are not good. To produce really optimal code, the code generator must choose the right combination of instruction selection, instruction scheduling, and register allocation; and, as said before, that problem is NP-complete. NP-complete problems almost certainly require exhaustive search; and exhaustive search is almost always prohibitively expensive. This has not kept some researchers from trying anyway. We will briefly describe some of their results.

Keßler and Bednarski [151] apply exhaustive search to basic blocks of tens of instructions, using dynamic programming to keep reasonable compilation times. Their algorithm handles instruction selection and instruction scheduling only; register allocation is done independently on the finished schedule, and thus may not be optimal.

Wilken, Liu, and Heffernan [303] solve the instruction scheduling problem optimally, for large basic blocks. They first apply a rich set of graph-simplifying transformations; the optimization problem is then converted to an integer programming
problem, which is subsequently solved using advanced integer programming techniques. Each of these three steps is tuned to dependency graphs which derive from
real-world programs. Blocks of up to 1000 instructions can be scheduled in a few
seconds. The technique is especially successful for VLIW architectures, which are
outside the scope of this book.

Neither of these approaches solves the problem completely. In particular register
allocation is pretty intractable, since it often forces one to insert code due to register spilling, thus upsetting the scheduling and sometimes the instruction selection.
See Section 9.1.6 for a technique for obtaining really optimal code for very simple
functions.

This concludes our discussion of optimized code generation for basic blocks. We
will now turn to a very efficient method to generate optimal code for expressions.

9.1.4 BURS code generation and dynamic programming

In Section 9.1.2.2 we have shown how bottom-up tree rewriting can convert an AST
for an arithmetic expression into an instruction tree which can then be scheduled.
In our example we used only very simple machine instructions, with the result that
the tree rewriting process was completely deterministic. In practice, however, machines often have a great variety of instructions, simple ones and complicated ones,
and better code can be generated if all available instructions are utilized. Machines
often have several hundred different machine instructions, often each with ten or
more addressing modes, and it would be very advantageous if code generators for
such machines could be derived from a concise machine description rather than be
written by hand. It turns out that the combination of bottom-up pattern matching
and dynamic programming explained below allows precisely that. The technique is
known as BURS, Bottom-Up Rewriting System.

Figure 9.23 shows a small set of instructions of a varied nature; the set is more
or less representative of modern machines, large enough to show the principles involved and small enough to make the explanation manageable. For each instruction
we show the AST it represents, its semantics in the form of a formula, its cost of
execution measured in arbitrary units, its name, both abbreviated and in full, and a
number which will serve as an identifying label in our pattern matching algorithm.
Since we will be matching partial trees as well, each node in the AST of an instruction has been given a label: for each instruction, the simple label goes to its top node
and the other nodes are labeled with compound labels, according to some scheme.
For example, the Mult_Scaled_Reg instruction has label #8 and its only subnode is
labeled #8.1. We will call the AST of an instruction a **pattern tree**, because we will
use these ASTs as patterns in a pattern matching algorithm.

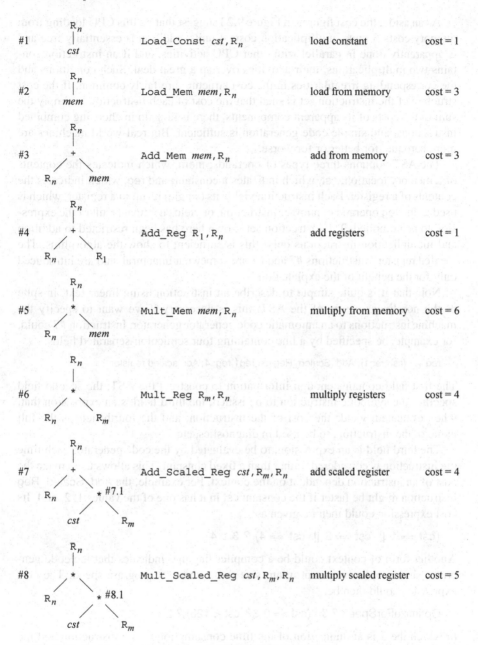

#		Instruction	Description	Cost
#1	R_n | cst	Load_Const cst, R_n	load constant	cost = 1
#2	R_n | mem	Load_Mem mem, R_n	load from memory	cost = 3
#3	R_n + / mem	Add_Mem mem, R_n	add from memory	cost = 3
#4	R_n + / R_n R_1	Add_Reg R_1, R_n	add registers	cost = 1
#5	R_n * / R_n mem	Mult_Mem mem, R_n	multiply from memory	cost = 6
#6	R_n * / R_n R_m	Mult_Reg R_m, R_n	multiply registers	cost = 4
#7	R_n + / R_n *#7.1 / cst R_m	Add_Scaled_Reg cst, R_m, R_n	add scaled register	cost = 4
#8	R_n * / R_n *#8.1 / cst R_m	Mult_Scaled_Reg cst, R_m, R_n	multiply scaled register	cost = 5

Fig. 9.23: Sample instruction patterns for BURS code generation

As an aside, the cost figures in Figure 9.23 suggest that on this CPU loading from memory costs 3 units, multiplication costs 4 units, addition is essentially free and is apparently done in parallel with other CPU activities, and if an instruction contains two multiplications, their activities overlap a great deal. Such conditions and the corresponding irregularities in the cost structure are fairly common. If the cost structure of the instruction set is such that the cost of each instruction is simply the sum of the costs of its apparent components, there is no gain in choosing combined instructions, and simple code generation is sufficient. But real-world machines are more baroque, for better or for worse.

The AST contains three types of operands: mem, which indicates the contents of a memory location; cst, which indicates a constant; and reg, which indicates the contents of a register. Each instruction yields its (single) result in a register, which is used as the reg operand of another instruction, or yields the final result of the expression to be compiled. The instruction set shown here has been restricted to addition and multiplication instructions only; this is sufficient to show the algorithms. The "scaled register" instructions #7 and #8 are somewhat unnatural, and are introduced only for the benefit of the explanation.

Note that it is quite simple to describe an instruction using linear text, in spite of the non-linear nature of the AST; this is necessary if we want to specify the machine instructions to an automatic code generator generator. Instruction #7 could, for example, be specified by a line containing four semicolon-separated fields:

reg +:= (cst*reg1); Add_Scaled_Reg cst,reg1,reg; 4; Add scaled register

The first field contains enough information to construct the AST; the second field specifies the symbolic instruction to be issued; the third field is an expression that, when evaluated, yields the cost of the instruction; and the fourth field is the full name of the instruction, to be used in diagnostics, etc.

The third field is an expression, to be evaluated by the code generator each time the instruction is considered, rather than a fixed constant. This allows us to make the cost of an instruction dependent on the context. For example, the Add_Scaled_Reg instruction might be faster if the constant cst in it has one of the values 1, 2, or 4. Its cost expression could then be given as:

(cst == 1 || cst == 2 || cst == 4) ? 3 : 4

Another form of context could be a compiler flag that indicates that the code generator should optimize for program size rather than for program speed. The cost expression could then be:

OptimizeForSpeed ? 3 : (cst >= 0 && cst < 128) ? 2 : 5

in which the 3 is an indication of the time consumption of the instruction and the 2 and 5 are the instruction sizes for small and non-small values of cst, respectively (these numbers suggest that cst is stored in one byte if it fits in 7 bits and in 4 bytes otherwise, a not unusual arrangement).

The expression AST we are going to generate code for is given in Figure 9.24; a and b are memory locations. To distinguish this AST from the ASTs of the instructions, we will call it the **input tree**. A rewrite of the input tree in terms of the instructions is described by attaching the instruction node labels to the nodes of the input tree. It is easy to see that there are many possible rewrites of our input tree using the pattern trees of Figure 9.23.

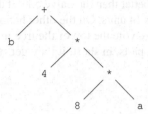

Fig. 9.24: Example input tree for the BURS code generation

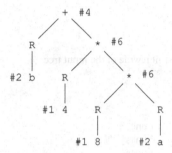

Fig. 9.25: Naive rewrite of the input tree

For example, Figure 9.25 shows a naive rewrite, which employs the pattern trees #1, #2, #4, and #6 only; these correspond to those of a pure register machine. The naive rewrite results in 7 instructions and its cost is 17 units, using the data from Figure 9.23. Its scheduling, as obtained following the weighted register allocation technique from Section 7.5.2.2, is shown in Figure 9.26.

```
Load_Const 8,R1    ; 1 unit
Load_Mem   a,R2    ; 3 units
Mult_Reg   R2,R1   ; 4 units
Load_Const 4,R2    ; 1 unit
Mult_Reg   R1,R2   ; 4 units
Load_Mem   b,R1    ; 3 units
Add_Reg    R2,R1   ; 1 unit
           Total   = 17 units
```

Fig. 9.26: Code resulting from the naive rewrite

Figure 9.27 illustrates another rewrite possibility. This one was obtained by applying a top-down largest-fit algorithm: starting from the top, the largest instruction that would fit the operators in the tree was chosen, and the operands were made to conform to the requirements of that instruction. This forces b to be loaded into a register, etc. This rewrite is better than the naive one: it uses 4 instructions, as shown in Figure 9.28, and its cost is 14 units. On the other hand, the top-down largest-fit algorithm might conceivably rewrite the top of the tree in such a way that no rewrites can be found for the bottom parts; in short, it may get stuck.

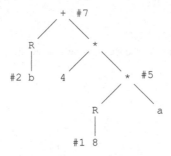

Fig. 9.27: Top-down largest-fit rewrite of the input tree

```
Load_Const      8,R1      ; 1 unit
Mult_Mem        a,R1      ; 6 units
Load_Mem        b,R2      ; 3 units
Add_Scaled_Reg 4,R1,R2  ; 4 units
                Total   = 14 units
```

Fig. 9.28: Code resulting from the top-down largest-fit rewrite

This discussion identifies two main problems:

1. How do we find all possible rewrites, and how do we represent them? It will be clear that we do not fancy listing them all!
2. How do we find the best/cheapest rewrite among all possibilities, preferably in time linear in the size of the expression to be translated?

Problem 1 can be solved by a form of bottom-up pattern matching and problem 2 by a form of dynamic programming. This technique is known as a **bottom-up rewriting system**, abbreviated **BURS**. More in particular, the code is generated in three scans over the input tree:

1. an **instruction-collecting scan**: this scan is bottom-up and identifies possible instructions for each node by pattern matching;
2. an **instruction-selecting scan**: this scan is top-down and selects at each node one instruction out of the possible instructions collected during the previous scan;

3. a **code-generating scan**: this scan is again bottom-up and emits the instructions in the correct order.

Each of the scans can be implemented as a recursive visit, the first and the third ones as post-order visits and the second as a pre-order visit.

The instruction-collecting scan is the most interesting, and four variants will be developed here. The first variant finds all possible instructions using item sets (Section 9.1.4.1), the second finds all possible instructions using a tree automaton (Section 9.1.4.2). The third consists of the first variant followed by a bottom-up scan that identifies the best possible instructions using dynamic programming, (Section 9.1.4.3), and the final one combines the second and the third into a single efficient bottom-up scan (Section 9.1.4.4).

9.1.4.1 Bottom-up pattern matching

The algorithm for **bottom-up pattern matching** is in essence a tree version of the lexical analysis algorithm from Section 2.6.1.

In the lexical analysis algorithm, we recorded between each pair of characters a set of items. Each item was a regular expression of a token, in which a position was marked by a dot. This dot separated the part we had already recognized from the part we still hoped to recognize.

In our tree matching algorithm, we record at the top of each node in the input tree (in bottom-up order) a set of instruction tree node labels. Each such label indicates one node in one pattern tree of a machine instruction, as described at the beginning of Section 9.1.4.

The idea is that when label L of pattern tree I is present in the label set at node N in the input tree, then the tree or subtree below L in the pattern tree I (including the node L) can be used to rewrite node N, with node L matching node N. Moreover, we hope to be able to match the entire tree I to the part of the input tree of which N heads a subtree. Also, if the label designates the top of a pattern tree rather than a subtree, we have recognized a full pattern tree, and thus an instruction. One can say that the pattern tree corresponds to a regular expression and that the label points to the dot in it.

An instruction leaves the result of the expression in a certain location, usually a register. This location determines which instructions can accept the result as an operand. For example, if the recognized instruction leaves its result in a register, its top node cannot be the operand of an instruction that requires that operand to be in a memory location. Although the label alone determines completely the type of the location in which the result is delivered, it is convenient to show the result location explicitly with the label, by using the notation $L \rightarrow location$.

All this is depicted in Figure 9.29, using instruction number #7 as an example. The presence of a label #7$\rightarrow$reg in a node means that that node can be the top of instruction number #7, and that that instruction will yield its result in a register. The notation #7$\rightarrow$reg can be seen as shorthand for the **dotted tree** of Figure 9.29(a). When the label designates a subnode, there is no result to be delivered, and we

write the compound label thus: #7.1; this notation is shorthand for the dotted tree of
Figure 9.29(b). When there is no instruction to rewrite, we omit the instruction: the
label →cst means that the node *is* a constant.

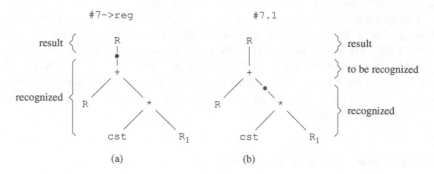

Fig. 9.29: The dotted trees corresponding to #7→reg and to #7.1

In the lexical analysis algorithm, we computed the item set after a character from
the item set before that character and the character itself. In the tree matching algorithm we compute the label set at a node from the label sets at the children of that
node and the operator in the node itself.

There are substantial differences between the algorithms too. The most obvious
one is, of course, that the first operates on a list of characters, and the second on a
tree. Another is that in lexical analysis we recognize the longest possible token starting at a given position; we then make that decision final and restart the automaton in
its initial state. In tree matching we keep all possibilities in parallel until the bottom-
up process reaches the top of the input tree and we leave the decision-making to the
next phase. Outline code for this bottom-up pattern recognition algorithm can be
found in Figure 9.30 and the corresponding type definitions in Figure 9.31.

The results of applying this algorithm to the input tree from Figure 9.24 are
shown in Figure 9.32. They have been obtained as follows. The bottom-up algorithm starts by visiting the node containing b. The routine *LabelSetForVariable()*
first constructs the label →mem and then scans the set of pattern trees for nodes that
could match this node: the operand should be a memory location and the operation
should be Load. It finds only one such pattern: the variable can be rewritten to a
register using instruction #2. So there are two labels here, →mem and #2→reg.

The rewrite possibilities for the node with the constant 4 result in two labels too:
→cst for the constant itself and #1→reg for rewriting to register using instruction
#1. The label sets for nodes 8 and a are obtained similarly.

The lower * node is next and its label set is more interesting. We scan the set of
pattern trees again for nodes that could match this node: their top nodes should be *
and they should have two operands. We find five such nodes: #5, #6, #7.1, #8, and
#8.1. First we see that we can match our node to the top node of pattern tree #5:

```
procedure BottomUpPatternMatching (Node):
    if Node is an operation:
        BottomUpPatternMatching (Node.left);
        BottomUpPatternMatching (Node.right);
        Node.labelSet ← LabelSetFor (Node);
    else if Node is a constant:
        Node.labelSet ← LabelSetForConstant ();
    else -- Node is a variable:
        Node.labelSet ← LabelSetForVariable ();

function LabelSetFor (Node) returning a label set:
    LabelSet ← ∅;
    for each Label in MachineLabelSet:
        for each LeftLabel in Node.left.labelSet:
            for each RightLabel in Node.right.labelSet:
                if Label.operator = Node.operator
                    and Label.firstOperand = LeftLabel.result
                    and Label.secondOperand = RightLabel.result:
                    Insert Label into LabelSet;
    return LabelSet;

function LabelSetForConstant () returning a label set:
    LabelSet ← { (NoOperator, NoLocation, NoLocation, "Constant") };
    for each Label in the MachineLabelSet:
        if Label.operator = "Load" and Label.firstOperand = "Constant":
            Insert Label into LabelSet;
    return LabelSet;

function LabelSetForVariable () returning a label set:
    LabelSet ← { (NoOperator, NoLocation, NoLocation, "Memory") };
    for each Label in the MachineLabelSet:
        if Label.operator = "Load" and Label.firstOperand = "Memory":
            Insert Label into LabelSet;
    return LabelSet;
```

Fig. 9.30: Outline code for bottom-up pattern matching in trees

```
type operator: "Load", '+', '*';
type location: "Constant", "Memory", "Register", a label;

type label:                           -- a node in a pattern tree
    field operator: operator;
    field firstOperand: location;
    field secondOperand: location;
    field result: location;
```

Fig. 9.31: Types for bottom-up pattern recognition in trees

- its left operand is required to be a register, and indeed the label #1→reg at the node with constant 8 in the input tree shows that a register can be found as its left operand;
- its right operand is required to be a memory location, the presence of which in the input tree is confirmed by the label →mem in the node with variable a.

This match results in the addition of a label #5→reg to our node.

Next we match our node to the top node of instruction #6: the right operand is now required to be a register, and the label #2→reg at the node with variable a shows that one can be made available. Next we recognize the subnode #7.1 of pattern tree #7, since it requires a constant for its left operand, which is confirmed by the label →cst at the 8 node, and a register as its right operand, which is also there; this adds the label #7.1. By the same reasoning we recognize subnode #8.1, but we fail to match node #8 to our node: its left operand is a register, which is available at the 4 node, but its right operand is marked #8.1, and #8.1 is not in the label set of the a node.

The next node to be visited by the bottom-up pattern matcher is the higher * node, where the situation is similar to that at the lower * node, and where we immediately recognize the top node of instructions #6 and the subnode #7.1. But here we also recognize the top node of instruction #8: the left operand of this top node is a register, which is available, and its right operand is #8.1, which is indeed in the label set of the right operand of the lower * node. Since the left operand allows a constant and the right operand allows a register, we also include subnode #8.1.

Recognizing the top nodes of instructions #4 and #7 for the top node of the input tree is now easy.

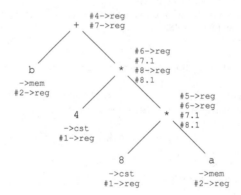

Fig. 9.32: Label sets resulting from bottom-up pattern matching

What we have obtained in the above instruction-collecting scan is an annotation of the nodes of the input tree with sets of possible rewriting instructions (Figure 9.32). This annotation can serve as a concise recipe for constructing tree rewrites using a subsequent top-down scan. The top node of the input tree gives us the choice of rewriting it by instruction #4 or by instruction #7. We could, for example, decide to rewrite by #7. This forces the b node and the lower ∗ node to be rewritten to registers and the higher ∗ node and the 4 node to remain in place. The label set at the b node supplies only one rewriting to register: by instruction #2, but that at the lower ∗ node allows two possibilities: instruction #5 or instruction #6. Choosing instruction #5 results in the rewrite shown in Figure 9.27; choosing instruction #6 causes an additional rewrite of the a node using instruction #2. We have thus succeeded in obtaining a succinct representation of all possible rewrites of the input tree.

Theoretically, it is possible for the pattern set to be insufficient to match a given input tree. This then leads to an empty set of rewrite labels at some node, in which case the matching process will get stuck. In practice, however, this is a non-problem since all real machines have so many "small" instructions that they alone will suffice to rewrite any expression tree completely. Note, for example, that the instructions #1, #2, #4, and #6 alone are already capable of rewriting any expression tree consisting of constants, variables, additions, and multiplications. Also, the BURS automaton construction algorithm discussed in Section 9.1.4.4 allows us to detect this situation statically, at compiler construction time.

9.1.4.2 Bottom-up pattern matching, efficiently

It is important to note that the algorithm sketched above performs at each node an amount of work that is independent of the size of the input tree. Also, the amount of space used to store the label set is limited by the number of possible labels and is also independent of the size of the input tree. Consequently, the algorithm is linear in the size of the input tree, both in time and in space.

On the other hand, both the work done and the space required are proportional to the size of the instruction set, which can be considerable, and we would like to remove this dependency. Techniques from the lexical analysis scene prove again valuable; more in particular we can precompute all possible matches at code generator generation time, essentially using the same techniques as in the generation of lexical analyzers.

Since there is only a finite number of nodes in the set of pattern trees (which is supplied by the compiler writer in the form of a machine description), there is only a finite number of label sets. So, given the operator of *Node* in *LabelSetFor (Node)* and the two label sets of its operands, we can precompute the resulting label set, in a fashion similar to that of the subset algorithm for lexical analyzers in Section 2.6.3 and Figure 2.26.

The initial label sets are supplied by the functions *LabelSetForConstant ()* and *LabelSetForVariable ()*, which yield constant results. (Real-world machines might add sets for the stack pointer serving as an operand, etc.) Using the locations in these label sets as operands, we check all nodes in the pattern trees to see if they could work with zero or more of these operands. If they can, we note the relation and add the resulting label set to our set of label sets. We then repeat the process with our enlarged set of label sets, and continue until the process converges and no changes occur any more. Only a very small fraction of the theoretically possible label sets are realized in this process.

The label sets are then replaced by numbers, the states. Rather than storing a label set at each node of the input tree we store a state; this reduces the space needed in each node for storing operand label set information to a constant and quite small amount. The result is a three-dimensional table, indexed by operator, left operand state, and right operand state; the indexed element contains the state of the possible matches at the operator.

This reduces the time needed for pattern matching at each node to that of simple table indexing in a transition table; the simplified code is shown in Figure 9.33. As with lexical analysis, the table algorithm uses constant and small amounts of time and space per node. In analogy to the finite-state automaton (FSA) used in lexical analysis, which goes through the character list and computes new states from old states and input characters using a table lookup, a program that goes through a tree and computes new states from old states and operators at the nodes using table indexing, is called a **finite-state tree automaton**.

```
procedure BottomUpPatternMatching (Node):
    if Node is an operation:
        BottomUpPatternMatching (Node.left);
        BottomUpPatternMatching (Node.right);
        Node.state ← NextState [Node.operator, Node.left.state, Node.right.state];
    else if Node is a constant:
        Node.state ← StateForConstant;
    else -- Node is a variable:
        Node.state ← StateForVariable;
```

Fig. 9.33: Outline code for efficient bottom-up pattern matching in trees

With, say, a hundred operators and some thousand states, the three-dimensional table would have some hundred million entries. Fortunately almost all of these are empty, and the table can be compressed considerably. If the pattern matching algorithm ever retrieves an empty entry, the original set of patterns was insufficient to rewrite the given input tree.

The above description applies only to pattern trees and input trees that are strictly binary, but this restriction can easily be circumvented. Unary operators can be accommodated by using the non-existing state 0 as the second operand, and nodes with more than two children can be split into spines of binary nodes. This simplifies the algorithms without slowing them down seriously.

9.1.4.3 Instruction selection by dynamic programming

Now that we have an efficient representation for all possible rewrites, as developed in Section 9.1.4.1, we can turn our attention to the problem of selecting the "best" one from this set. Our final goal is to get the value of the input expression into a register at minimal cost. A naive approach would be to examine the top node of the input tree to see by which instructions it can be rewritten, and to take each one in turn, construct the rest of the rewrite, calculate its cost, and take the minimum. Constructing the rest of the rewrite after the first instruction has been chosen involves repeating this process for subnodes recursively. When we are, for example, calculating the cost of rewrite starting with instruction #7, we are among other things interested in the cheapest way to get the value of the expression at the higher * node into a register, to supply the second operand to instruction #7.

This naive algorithm effectively forces us to enumerate all possible trees, an activity we would like to avoid since there can be exponentially many of them. When we follow the steps of the algorithm on larger trees, we see that we often recompute the optimal rewrites of the lower nodes in the tree. We could prevent this by doing memoization on the results obtained for the nodes, but it is easier to just precompute these results in a bottom-up scan, as follows.

For each node in our bottom-up scan, we examine the possible rewrites as determined by the instruction-collecting scan, and for each rewriting instruction we establish its cost by adding the cost of the instruction to the minimal costs of getting the operands in the places in which the instruction requires them to be. We then record the best rewrite in the node, with its cost, in the form of a label with cost indication. For example, we will write the rewrite label #5→reg with cost 7 units as #5→reg@7. The minimal costs of the operands are known because they were precomputed by the same algorithm, which visited the corresponding nodes earlier, due to the bottom-up nature of the scan. The only thing still needed to get the process started is knowing the minimal costs of the leaf nodes, but since a leaf node has no operands, its cost is equal to the cost of the instruction, if one is required to load the value, and zero otherwise.

As with the original instruction-collecting scan (as shown in Figure 9.32), this bottom-up scan starts at the b node; refer to Figure 9.34. There is only one way to get the value in a register, by using instruction #2, and the cost is 3; leaving it in memory costs 0. The situation at the 4 and 8 nodes is also simple (load to register by instruction #1, cost = 1, or leave as constant), and that at the a node is equal to that at the b node. But the lower * node carries four entries, #5→reg, #6→reg, #7.1, and #8.1, resulting in the following possibilities:

- A rewrite with pattern tree #5 (= instruction #5) requires the left operand to be placed in a register, which costs 1 unit; it requires its right operand to be in memory, where it already resides; and it costs 6 units itself: together 7 units. This results in the label #5→reg@7.
- A rewrite with pattern tree #6 again requires the left operand to be placed in a register, at cost 1; it requires its right operand to be placed in a register too, which costs 3 units; and it costs 4 units itself: together 8 units. This results in the label #6→reg@8.
- The labels #7.1 and #8.1 do not correspond with top nodes of expression trees and cannot get a value into a register, so no cost is attached to them.

We see that there are two ways to get the value of the subtree at the lower * node into a register, one costing 7 units and the other 8. We keep only the cheaper possibility, the one with instruction #5, and we record its rewrite pattern and its cost in the node. We do not have to keep the rewrite possibility with instruction #6, since it can never be part of a minimal cost rewrite of the input tree.

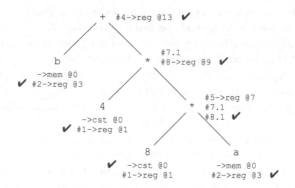

Fig. 9.34: Bottom-up pattern matching with costs

A similar situation obtains at the higher * node: it can be rewritten by instruction #6 at cost 1 (left operand) + 7 (right operand) + 4 (instruction) = 12, or by instruction #8 at cost 1 (left operand) + 3 (right operand) + 5 (instruction) = 9. The choice is obvious: we keep instruction #8 and reject instruction #6. At the top node we get again two possibilities: instruction #4 at cost 3 (left operand) + 9 (right operand) + 1 (instruction) = 13, or by instruction #7 at cost 3 (left operand) + 7 (right operand) + 4 (instruction) = 14. The choice is again clear: we keep instruction #4 and reject instruction #7.

Now we have only one rewrite possibility for each location at each node, and we are certain that it is the cheapest rewrite possible, given the instruction set. Still, some nodes have more than one instruction attached to them, and the next step is to remove this ambiguity in a top-down instruction-selecting scan, similar to the one described in Section 9.1.4.1. First we consider the result location required at the top of the input tree, which will almost always be a register. Based on this information, we choose the rewriting instruction that includes the top node and puts its result in the required location. This decision forces the locations of some lower operand nodes, which in turn decides the rewrite instructions of these nodes, and so on.

The top node is rewritten using instruction #4, which requires two register operands. This requirement forces the decision to load b into a register, and selects instruction #8 for the higher * node. The latter requires a register, a constant, and a register, which decides the instructions for the 4, 8, and a nodes: 4 and a are to be put into registers, but 8 remains a constant. The labels involved in the actual rewrite have been checked in Figure 9.34.

The only thing that is left to do is to schedule the rewritten tree into an instruction sequence: the code-generation scan in our code generation scheme. As explained in

Section 7.5.2.2, we can do this by a recursive process which for each node generates code for its heavier operand first, followed by code for the lighter operand, followed by the instruction itself. The result is shown in Figure 9.35, and costs 13 units.

```
Load_Mem          a,R1      ; 3 units
Load_Const        4,R2      ; 1 unit
Mult_Scaled_Reg  8,R1,R2   ; 5 units
Load_Mem          b,R1      ; 3 units
Add_Reg           R2,R1     ; 1 unit
                  Total     = 13 units
```

Fig. 9.35: Code generated by bottom-up pattern matching

The gain over the naive code (cost 17 units) and top-down largest-fit (cost 14 units) is not impressive. The reason lies mainly in the artificially small instruction set of our example; real machines have much larger instruction sets and consequently provide much more opportunity for good pattern matching.

The BURS algorithm has advantages over the other rewriting algorithms in that it provides optimal rewriting of any tree and that it cannot get stuck, provided the set of instruction allows a rewrite at all.

The technique of finding the "best" path through a graph by scanning it in a fixed order and keeping a set of "best" sub-solutions at each node is called **dynamic programming**. The scanning order has to be such that at each node the set of sub-solutions can be derived completely from the information at nodes that have already been visited. When all nodes have been visited, the single best solution is chosen at some "final" node, and working back from there the single best sub-solutions at the other nodes are determined. This technique is a very common approach to all kinds of optimization problems. As already suggested above, it can be seen as a specific implementation of memoization. For a more extensive treatment of dynamic programming, see text books on algorithms, for example Sedgewick [257] or Baase and Van Gelder [23].

Although Figure 9.35 shows indeed the best rewrite of the input tree, given the instruction set, a hand coder would have combined the last two instructions into:

```
Add_Mem b,R2 ; 3 units
```

using the commutativity of the addition operator to save another unit. The BURS code generator cannot do this since it does not know (yet) about such commutativities. There are two ways to remedy this: specify for each instruction that involves a commutative operator two pattern trees to the code generator generator, or mark commutative operators in the input to the code generator generator and let *it* add the patterns. The latter approach is probably preferable, since it is more automatic, and is less work in the long run. With this refinement, the BURS code generator will indeed produce the Add_Mem instruction for our input tree and reduce the cost to 12, as shown in Figure 9.36.

```
Load_Mem          a,R1      ; 3 units
Load_Const        4,R2      ; 1 unit
Mult_Scaled_Reg 8,R1,R2 ; 5 units
Add_Mem           b,R1      ; 3 units
                  Total     = 12 units
```

Fig. 9.36: Code generated by bottom-up pattern matching, using commutativity

9.1.4.4 Pattern matching and instruction selection combined

As we have seen above, the instruction collection phase consists of two subsequent scans: first use pattern matching by tree automaton to find all possible instructions at each node and then use dynamic programming to find the cheapest possible rewrite for each type of destination. If we have a target machine on which the cost functions of the instructions are constants, we can perform an important optimization which allows us to determine the cheapest rewrite at a node at code generator generation time rather than at code generation time. This is achieved by combining both processes into a single tree automaton. This saves compile space as well as compile time, since it is no longer necessary to record the labels with their costs in the nodes; their effects have already been played out at code generator generation time and a single state number suffices at each node. The two processes are combined by adapting the subset algorithm from Section 9.1.4.2 to generate a transition table CostConsciousNextState[ ]. This adaptation is far from trivial, as we shall see.

Combining the pattern matching and instruction selection algorithms The first step in combining the two algorithms is easy: the cost of each label is incorporated into the state; we use almost the same format for a label as in Section 9.1.4.1: $L{\rightarrow}location@cost$. This extension of the structure of a label causes two problems:

1. Input trees can be arbitrarily complex and have unbounded costs. If we include the cost in the label, there will be an unbounded number of labels and consequently an unbounded number of states.
2. Subnodes like #7.1 and #8.1 have no cost attached to them in the original algorithm, but they will need one here.

We shall see below how these problems are solved.

The second step is to create the initial states. Initial states derive from instructions that have **basic operands** only, operands that are available without the intervention of further instructions. The most obvious examples of such operands are constants and memory locations, but the program counter (instruction counter) and the stack pointer also come into this category. As we have seen above, each basic operand is the basis of an initial state. Our example instruction set in Figure 9.23 contains two basic operands—constants and memory locations—and two instructions that operate on them—#1 and #2. Constants give rise to state S_1 and memory locations to state S_2:

State S_1:
    $\rightarrow$cst@0
    #1$\rightarrow$reg@1

State S_2:
    $\rightarrow$mem@0
    #2$\rightarrow$reg@3

We are now in a position to create new states from old states, by precomputing entries of our transition table. To find such new entries, we systematically consider all triplets of an operator and two existing states, and scan the instruction set to find nodes that match the triplet; that is, the operators of the instruction and the triplet are the same and the two operands can be supplied by the two states.

Creating the cost-conscious next-state table The only states we have initially are state S_1 and state S_2. Suppose we start with the triplet $\{'+', S_1, S_1\}$, in which the first S_1 corresponds to the left operand in the input tree of the instruction to be matched and the second S_1 to the right operand. Note that this triplet corresponds to a funny subtree: the addition of two constants; normally such a node would have been removed by constant folding during preprocessing, for which see Section 7.3, but the subset algorithm will consider all combinations regardless of their realizability.

There are three nodes in our instruction set that match the + in the above triplet: #3, #4, and #7. Node #3 does not match completely, since it requires a memory location as its second operand, which cannot be supplied by state S_1, but node #4 does. The cost of the subtree is composed of 1 for the left operand, 1 for its right operand, and 1 for the instruction itself: together 3; notation: #4$\rightarrow$reg@1+1+1=3. So this match enters the label #4$\rightarrow$reg@3 into the label set. The operand requirements of node #7 are not met by state S_1, since it requires the right operand to be #7.1, which is not in state S_1; it is disregarded. So the new state S_3 contains the label #4$\rightarrow$reg@3 only, and CostConsciousNextState['+', S_1, S_1] = S_3.

More interesting things happen when we start calculating the transition table entry CostConsciousNextState['+', S_1, S_2]. The nodes matching the operator are again #3, #4, and #7, and again #3 and #4 match in the operands. Each node yields a label to the new state number S_4:

    #3$\rightarrow$reg@1+0+3=4
    #4$\rightarrow$reg@1+3+1=5

and we see that we can already at this moment (at code generator generation time) decide that there is no point in using rewrite by #4 when the operands are state S_1 and state S_2, since rewriting by #3 will always be cheaper. So state S_4 reduces to $\{$#3$\rightarrow$reg@4$\}$.

But when we try to compute CostConsciousNextState['+', S_1, S_4], problem 1 noted above rears its head. Only one pattern tree matches: #4; its cost is 1+4+1=6 and it creates the single-label state S_5 $\{$#4$\rightarrow$reg@6$\}$. Repeating the process for CostConsciousNextState['+', S_1, S_5] yields a state S_6 $\{$#4$\rightarrow$reg@8$\}$, etc. It seems that we will have to create an infinite number of states of the form $\{$#4$\rightarrow$reg@$C\}$ for ever increasing Cs, which ruins our plan of creating a *finite*-state automaton. Still, we feel that somehow all these states are essentially the same, and that we should be able to collapse them all; it turns out we can.

When we consider carefully how we are using the cost values, we find only two usages:

1. in composing the costs of rewrites and then comparing the results to other such compositions;
2. as initial cost values in initial states.

The general form of the cost of a rewrite by a pattern tree p is

> cost of label n in the left state +
>> cost of label m in the right state +
>> cost of instruction p

and such a form is compared to the cost of a rewrite by a pattern tree s:

> cost of label q in the left state +
>> cost of label r in the right state +
>> cost of instruction s

But that means that only the *relative* costs of the labels in each state count: if the costs of all labels in a state are increased or reduced by the same amount the result of the comparison will remain the same. The same applies to the initial states. This observation allows us to normalize a state by subtracting a constant amount from all costs in the state. We shall normalize states by subtracting the smallest cost it contains from each of the costs; this reduces the smallest cost to zero.

Normalization reduces the various states #4→reg@3, #4→reg@6, #4→reg@8, etc., to a single state #4→reg@0. Now this cost 0 no longer means that it costs 0 units to rewrite by pattern tree #4, but that that possibility has cost 0 compared to other possibilities (of which there happen to be none). All this means that the top of the tree will no longer carry an indication of the total cost of the tree, as it did in Figure 9.34, but we would not base any decision on the absolute value of the total cost anyway, even if we knew it, so its loss is not serious. It is of course possible to assess the total cost of a given tree in another scan, or even on the fly, but such action is not finite-state, and requires programming outside the FSA.

Another interesting state to compute is CostConsciousNextState['*', S_1, S_2]. Matching nodes are #5, #6, #7.1, and #8.1; the labels for #5 and #6 are

    #5→reg@1+0+6=7
    #6→reg@1+3+4=8

of which only label #5→reg@7 survives. Computing the costs for the labels for the subnodes #7.1 and #8.1 involves the costs of the nodes themselves, which are undefined. We decide to localize the entire cost of an instruction in its top node, so the cost of the subnodes is zero. No cost units will be lost or gained by this decision since subnodes can in the end only combine with their own top nodes, which then carry the cost. So the new state is

    #5→reg@7
    #7.1@0+3+0=3
    #8.1@0+3+0=3

which after normalization reduces to

```
#5→reg@4
#7.1@0
#8.1@0
```

We continue to combine one operator and two operand states using the above techniques until no more new states are found. For the instruction set of Figure 9.23 this process yields 13 states, the contents of which are shown in Figure 9.37. The states S_1, S_2, S_3, and S_4 in our explanation correspond to S_{01}, S_{02}, S_{03}, and S_{05}, respectively, in the table.

The state S_{00} is the empty state. Its presence as the value of an entry CostConsciousNextState[op, S_x, S_y] means that no rewrite is possible for a node with operator op and whose operands carry the states S_x and S_y. If the input tree contains such a node, the code generation process will get stuck, and to avoid that situation any transition table with entries S_{00} must be rejected at compiler generation time.

A second table (Figure 9.38) displays the initial states for the basic locations supported by the instruction set.

$S_{00} = \{\}$
$S_{01} = \{\rightarrow cst@0, \#1 \rightarrow reg@1\}$
$S_{02} = \{\rightarrow mem@0, \#2 \rightarrow reg@3\}$
$S_{03} = \{4 \rightarrow reg@0\}$
$S_{04} = \{6 \rightarrow reg@5, \#7.1@0, \#8.1@0\}$
$S_{05} = \{3 \rightarrow reg@0\}$
$S_{06} = \{5 \rightarrow reg@4, \#7.1@0, \#8.1@0\}$
$S_{07} = \{6 \rightarrow reg@0\}$
$S_{08} = \{5 \rightarrow reg@0\}$
$S_{09} = \{7 \rightarrow reg@0\}$
$S_{10} = \{8 \rightarrow reg@1, \#7.1@0, \#8.1@0\}$
$S_{11} = \{8 \rightarrow reg@0\}$
$S_{12} = \{8 \rightarrow reg@2, \#7.1@0, \#8.1@0\}$
$S_{13} = \{8 \rightarrow reg@4, \#7.1@0, \#8.1@0\}$

Fig. 9.37: States of the BURS automaton for Figure 9.23

cst: S_{01}
mem: S_{02}

Fig. 9.38: Initial states for the basic operands

The transition table CostConsciousNextState[] is shown in Figure 9.39; we see that it does not contain the empty state S_{00}. To print the three-dimensional table on two-dimensional paper, the tables for the operators + and * are displayed separately. Almost all rows in the tables are identical and have already been combined in the printout, compressing the table vertically. Further possibilities for horizontal compression are clear, even in this small table. This redundancy is characteristic of BURS transition tables, and, using the proper techniques, such tables can be compressed to an amazing degree [225].

The last table, Figure 9.40, contains the actual rewrite information. It specifies, based on the state of a node, which instruction can be used to obtain the result of the expression in a given location. Empty entries mean that no instruction is required, entries with $-$ mean that no instruction is available and that the result cannot be obtained in the required location. For example, if a node is labeled with the state S_{02} and its result is to be delivered in a register, the node should be rewritten using instruction #2, and if its result is required in memory, no instruction is needed; it is not possible to obtain the result as a constant.

$$
\begin{array}{c|ccccccccccccc}
+ & S_{01} & S_{02} & S_{03} & S_{04} & S_{05} & S_{06} & S_{07} & S_{08} & S_{09} & S_{10} & S_{11} & S_{12} & S_{13} \\
\hline
S_{01} & & & & & & & & & & & & & \\
\text{-} & S_{03} & S_{05} & S_{03} & S_{09} & S_{03} & S_{09} & S_{03} & S_{03} & S_{03} & S_{03} & S_{03} & S_{03} & S_{09} \\
S_{13} & & & & & & & & & & & & &
\end{array}
$$

$$
\begin{array}{c|ccccccccccccc}
* & S_{01} & S_{02} & S_{03} & S_{04} & S_{05} & S_{06} & S_{07} & S_{08} & S_{09} & S_{10} & S_{11} & S_{12} & S_{13} \\
\hline
S_{01} & S_{04} & S_{06} & S_{04} & S_{10} & S_{04} & S_{12} & S_{04} & S_{04} & S_{04} & S_{04} & S_{04} & S_{13} & S_{12} \\
S_{02} & & & & & & & & & & & & & \\
\text{-} & S_{07} & S_{08} & S_{07} & S_{11} & S_{07} & S_{11} & S_{07} & S_{07} & S_{07} & S_{07} & S_{07} & S_{11} & S_{11} \\
S_{13} & & & & & & & & & & & & &
\end{array}
$$

Fig. 9.39: The transition table CostConsciousNextState[ ]

	S_{01}	S_{02}	S_{03}	S_{04}	S_{05}	S_{06}	S_{07}	S_{08}	S_{09}	S_{10}	S_{11}	S_{12}	S_{13}
cst	--	--	--	--	--	--	--	--	--	--	--	--	--
mem	--		--	--	--	--	--	--	--	--	--	--	--
reg	#1	#2	#4	#6	#3	#5	#6	#5	#7	#8	#8	#8	#8

Fig. 9.40: The code generation table

Code generation using the cost-conscious next-state table The process of generating code from an input tree now proceeds as follows. First all leaves are labeled with their corresponding initial states: those that contain constants with S_{01} and those that contain variables in memory with S_{02}, as specified in the table in Figure 9.38; see Figure 9.41. Next, the bottom-up scan assigns states to the inner nodes of the tree, using the tables in Figure 9.39. Starting at the bottom-most node which has operator $*$ and working our way upward, we learn from the table that CostConsciousNextState[$*$, S_{01}, S_{02}] is S_{06}, CostConsciousNextState[$*$, S_{01}, S_{06}] is S_{12}, and CostConsciousNextState[$+$, S_{02}, S_{12}] is S_{03}. This completes the assignment of states to all nodes of the tree. In practice, labeling the leaves and the inner nodes can be combined in one bottom-up scan; after all, the leaves can be considered operators with zero operands. In the same way, the process can easily be extended for monadic operators.

Now that all nodes have been labeled with a state, we can perform the top-down scan to select the appropriate instructions. The procedure is the same as in Section 9.1.4.3, except that all decisions have already been taken, and the results are summarized in the table in Figure 9.40. The top node is labeled with state S_{03} and the table tells us that the only possibility is to obtain the result in a register and that we need instruction #4 to do so. So both node b and the first * have to be put in a register. The table indicates instruction #2 for b (state S_{02}) and instruction #8 for the * node (state S_{12}). The rewrite by instruction #8 sets the required locations for the nodes 4, 8, and a: reg, cst, and reg, respectively. This, together with their states S_{01}, S_{01}, and S_{02}, leads to the instructions #1, none and #2, respectively. We see that the resulting code is identical to that of Figure 9.35, as it should be.

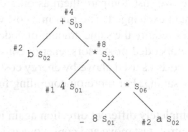

Fig. 9.41: States and instructions used in BURS code generation

Experience shows that one can expect a speed-up (of the code generation process, not of the generated code!) of a factor of ten to hundred from combining the scans of the BURS into one single automaton. It should, however, be pointed out that only the speed of the code generation part is improved by such a factor, not that of the entire compiler.

The combined BURS automaton is probably the fastest algorithm for good quality code generation known at the moment; it is certainly one of the most advanced and integrated automatic code generation techniques we have. However, full combination of the scans is only possible when all costs are constants. This means, unfortunately, that the technique is not optimally applicable today, since most modern machines do not have constant instruction costs.

9.1.4.5 Adaptation of the BURS algorithm to different circumstances

One of the most pleasant properties of the BURS algorithm is its adaptability to different circumstances. We will give some examples. As presented here, it is only concerned with getting the value of the expression in a register, under the assumption that all registers are equal and can be used interchangeably. Suppose, however, that a machine has two kinds of registers, A- and B-registers, which figure differently in the instruction set; suppose, for example, that A-registers can be used as operands in address calculations and B-registers cannot. The machine description will show for each register in each instruction whether it is an A-register or a B-register. This is easily handled by the BURS automaton by introducing labels like #65→regA, #73→regB, etc. A state (label set) {#65→regA@4, #73→regB@3} would then mean that the result could be delivered into an A-register at cost 4 by rewriting with instruction #65 and into a B-register at cost 3 by rewriting with instruction #73.

As a different example, suppose we want to use the size of the code as a tie breaker when two rewrites have the same run-time cost (which happens often). To do so we use a cost pair rather than a single cost value: (run-time cost, code size). Now, when comparing costs, we first compare the run-time cost fields and if they turn out to be equal, we compare the code sizes. If these are equal too, the two sequences are equivalent as to cost, and we can choose either. If, however, we want to optimize for code size, we just compare them as ordered integer pairs with the first and the second element exchanged. The run-time cost will then be used as a tie breaker when two rewrites require the same amount of code.

When compiling for embedded processors, energy consumption is often a concern. Replacing the time costs as used above by energy costs immediately compiles and optimizes for energy saving. For more on compiling for low energy consumption see Section 9.3.

An adaptation in a completely different direction again is to include all machine instructions —flow of control, fast move and copy, conversion, etc.— in the instruction set and take the complete AST of a routine (or even the entire program) as the input tree. Instruction selection and scheduling would then be completely automatic. Such applications of BURS technology are still experimental.

An accessible treatment of the theory behind bottom-up tree rewriting is given by Hemerik and Katoen [119]; for the full theory see Aho and Johnson [2]. A more recent publication on the application of dynamic programming to tree rewriting is by Proebsting [225]. An interesting variation on the BURS algorithm, using a multi-string search algorithm, is described by Aho, Ganapathi, and Tjiang [1]. A real-world language for expressing processor architecture information, of the kind shown in Figure 9.23, is described by Farfeleder et al. [96], who show how BURS patterns, assemblers, and documentation can be derived from an architecture description.

In this section we have assumed that enough registers are available for any rewrite we choose. For a way to include register allocation into the BURS automaton, see Exercise 9.15.

BURS as described here does linear-time optimal instruction selection for trees only; Koes and Goldstein [160] have extended the algorithm to DAGs, using heuristics. Their algorithm is still linear-time, and produces almost always an optimal instruction selection. Yang [308] uses GLR parsing (Section 3.5.8) rather than dynamic programming to do the pattern matching.

This concludes our discussion of code generation by combining bottom-up pattern matching and dynamic programming; it provides optimal instruction selection for trees. We will now turn to an often optimal register allocation technique.

9.1.5 Register allocation by graph coloring

In the subsection on procedure-wide register allocation in Section 7.5.2.2 (page 348) we have seen that naive register allocation for the entire routine ignores the fact that variables only need registers when they are live. On the other hand, when two variables *are* live at the same position in the routine, they need two different registers. We can therefore say that two variables that are both live at a given position in the program "interfere" with each other when register allocation is concerned. It will turn out that this interference information is important for doing high-quality register allocation.

Without live analysis, we can only conclude that all variables have values at all positions in the program and they all interfere with each other. So for good register allocation live analysis on the variables is essential. We will demonstrate the technique of register allocation by graph coloring, using the program segment of Figure 9.42.

```
a := read();
b := read();
c := read();
a := a + b + c;
if (a < 10) {
    d := c + 8;
    print(c);
} else if (a < 20) {
    e := 10;
    d := e + a;
    print(e);
} else {
    f := 12;
    d := f + a;
    print(f);
}
print(d);
```

Fig. 9.42: A program segment for live analysis

This program segment contains 6 variables, a through f; the read() calls symbolize unoptimizable expressions and the print() calls unoptimizable variable use. Its flow graph is shown in Figure 9.43.

In addition, the diagram shows the live ranges of the six variables as heavy lines along the code. A small but important detail is that the live range of a variable starts "half-way" through its first assignment, and stops "half-way" through the assignment in which it is last used. This is of course because an assignment computes the value of the source expression completely before assigning it to the destination variable. In other words, in y:=x*x the live ranges of x and y do not overlap if this is the end of the live range of x and the start of the live range of y.

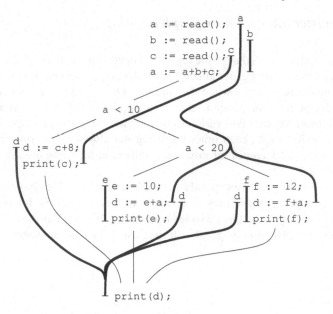

Fig. 9.43: Live ranges of the variables from Figure 9.42

9.1.5.1 The register interference graph

The live ranges map of Figure 9.43 shows us exactly which variables are live simultaneously at any point in the code, and thus which variables interfere with each other. This allows us to construct a **register interference graph** of the variables, as shown in Figure 9.44.

Fig. 9.44: Register interference graph for the variables of Figure 9.42

The nodes of this (non-directed) graph are labeled with the variables, and arcs are drawn between each pair of variables that interfere with each other. Note that this interference graph may consist of a number of unconnected parts; this will happen, for example, in routines in which the entire data flow from one part of the code to another goes through global variables. Since variables that interfere with each other cannot be allocated the same register, any actual register allocation must be subject to the restriction that the variables at the ends of an arc must be allocated different registers. This maps the register allocation problem on the well-known graph coloring problem from graph theory: how to color the nodes of a graph with the lowest possible number of colors, such that for each arc the nodes at its ends have different colors.

Much work has been done on this problem, both theoretical and practical, and the idea is to cash in on it here. That idea is not without problems, however. The bad news is that the problem is NP-complete: even the best known algorithm needs an amount of time exponential in the size of the graph to find the optimal coloring in the general case. The good news is that there are heuristic algorithms that solve the problem in almost linear time and usually do a good to very good job. We will now discuss one such algorithm.

9.1.5.2 Heuristic graph coloring

The basic idea of this heuristic algorithm is to color the nodes one by one and to do the easiest node last. The nodes that are easiest to color are the ones that have the smallest number of connections to other nodes. The number of connections of a node is called its **degree**, so these are the nodes with the lowest degree. Now if the graph is not empty, there must be a node N of degree k such that k is minimal, meaning that there are no nodes of degree $k - 1$ or lower; note that k can be 0. Call the k nodes to which N is connected M_1 to M_k. We leave node N to be colored last, since its color is restricted only by the colors of k nodes, and there is no node to which fewer restrictions apply. Also, not all of the k nodes need to have different colors, so the restriction may even be less severe than it would seem. We disconnect N from the graph while recording the nodes to which it should be reconnected. This leaves us with a smaller graph, which we color recursively using the same process.

When we return from the recursion, we first determine the set C of colors that have been used to color the smaller graph. We now reconnect node N to the graph, and try to find a color in C that is different from each of the colors of the nodes M_1 to M_k to which N is reconnected. This is always possible when $k < |C|$, where $|C|$ is the number of colors in the set C; and may still be possible if $k >= |C|$. If we find one, we use it to color node N; if we do not, we create a new color and use it to color N. The original graph has now been colored completely.

Outline code for this recursive implementation of the heuristic graph coloring algorithm is given in Figure 9.45. The graph is represented as a pair *Graph.nodes, Graph.arcs*; the arcs are sets of two nodes each, the end points. This is a convenient high-level implementation of an undirected graph. The algorithm as described above is simple but very inefficient. Figure 9.45 already implements one optimization: the set of colors used in coloring the graph is returned as part of the coloring process; this saves it from being recomputed for each reattachment of a node.

Figure 9.46 shows the graph coloring process for the variables of Figure 9.42. The top half shows the graph as it is recursively dismantled while the removed nodes are placed on the recursion stack; the bottom half shows how it is reconstructed by the function returning from the recursion. There are two places where the algorithm

```
function ColorGraph (Graph) returning the colors used:
   if Graph = ∅: return ∅;

   — Find the least connected node:
   LeastConnectedNode ← NoNode;
   for each Node in Graph.nodes:
      Degree ← 0;
      for each Arc in Graph.arcs:
         if Node ∈ Arc:
            Degree ← Degree + 1;
      if LeastConnectedNode = NoNode or Degree < MinimumDegree:
         LeastConnectedNode ← Node;
         MinimumDegree ← Degree;

   — Remove LeastConnectedNode from Graph:
   ArcsOfLeastConnectedNode ← ∅;
   for each Arc in Graph.arcs:
      if LeastConnectedNode ∈ Arc:
         Remove Arc from Graph.arcs;
         Insert Arc in ArcsOfLeastConnectedNode;
   Remove LeastConnectedNode from Graph.nodes;

   — Color the reduced Graph recursively:
   ColorsUsed ← ColorGraph (Graph);

   — Color the LeastConnectedNode:
   AvailableColors ← ColorsUsed;
   for each Arc in ArcsOfLeastConnectedNode:
      for each Node in Arc:
         if Node ≠ LeastConnectedNode:
            Remove Node.color from AvailableColors;
   if AvailableColors = ∅:
         Color ← a new color;
         Insert Color in ColorsUsed;
         Insert Color in AvailableColors;
   LeastConnectedNode.color ← Arbitrary choice from AvailableColors;

   — Reattach the LeastConnectedNode:
   Insert LeastConnectedNode in Graph.nodes;
   for each Arc in ArcsOfLeastConnectedNode:
      Insert Arc in Graph.arcs;
   return ColorsUsed;
```

Fig. 9.45: Outline of a graph coloring algorithm

is non-deterministic: in choosing which of several nodes of lowest degree to detach and in choosing a free color from C when $k < |C| - 1$. In principle the choice may influence the further path of the process and affect the total number of registers used, but it usually does not. Figure 9.46 was constructed using the assumption that the alphabetically first among the nodes of lowest degree is chosen at each disconnection step and that the free color with the lowest number is chosen at each reconnection step. We see that the algorithm can allocate the six variables in three registers; two registers will not suffice since the values of a, b and c have to be kept separately, so this is optimal.

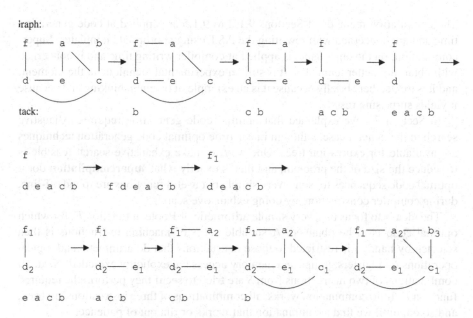

Fig. 9.46: Coloring the interference graph for the variables of Figure 9.42

The above algorithm will find the heuristically minimal number of colors required for any graph, plus the way to use them, but gives no hint about what to do when we do not have that many registers.

An easy approach is to let the algorithm run to completion and view the colors as pseudo-registers (of which there are an infinite number). These pseudo-registers are then sorted according to the usage counts of the variables they hold, and real registers are assigned to them in that order, highest usage count first; the remaining pseudo-registers are allocated in memory locations. If our code had to be compiled with two registers, we would find that pseudo-register 3 has the lowest usage count, and consequently b would not get a register and its value would be stored in memory.

In this section we have described only the simplest forms of register allocation through graph coloring and register spilling. Much more sophisticated algorithms have been designed, for example, by Briggs *et al.* [49], who describe an algorithm that is linear in the number of variables to be allocated in registers. Extensive descriptions can be found in the books of Morgan [196] and Muchnick [197].

The idea of using graph coloring in memory allocation problems was first published by Yershov [310] in 1971, who applied it to the superposition of global variables in a machine with very little memory. Its application to register allocation was pioneered by Chaitin *et al.* [56].

9.1.6 Supercompilation

The compilation methods of Sections 9.1.2 to 9.1.5 are applied at code generation time and are concerned with rewriting the AST using appropriate templates. Supercompilation, on the other hand, is applied at compiler writing time and is concerned with obtaining better templates. It is still an experimental technique at the moment, and it is treated here briefly because it is an example of original thinking and because it yields surprising results.

In Section 7.2 we explained that optimal code generation requires exhaustive search in the general case, although linear-time optimal code generation techniques are available for expression trees. One way to make exhaustive search feasible is to reduce the size of the problem, and this is exactly what **supercompilation** does: optimal code sequences for some very simple but useful functions are found off-line, during compiler construction, by doing exhaustive search.

The idea is to focus on a very simple arithmetic or Boolean function F, for which optimal code is to be obtained. A suitable set S of machine instructions is then selected by hand; S is restricted to those instructions that do arithmetic and logical operations on registers; jumps and memory access are explicitly excluded. Next, all combinations of two instructions from S are tried to see if they perform the required function F. If no combination works, all combinations of three instructions are tried, and so on, until we find a combination that works or run out of patience.

Each prospective solution is tested by writing the N-instruction sequence to memory on the proper machine and trying the resulting small program with a list of say 1000 well-chosen test cases. Almost all proposed solutions fail on one of the first few test cases, so testing is very efficient. If the solution survives these tests, it is checked manually; in practice the solution is then always found to be correct. To speed up the process, the search tree can be pruned by recognizing repeating or zero-result instruction combinations. Optimal code sequences consisting of a few instructions can be found in a few hours; with some luck, optimal code sequences consisting of a dozen or so instructions can be found in a few weeks.

A good example is the function sign(n), which yields $+1$ for n > 0, 0 for n = 0, and -1 for n < 0. Figure 9.47 shows the optimal code sequence found by supercompilation on the Intel 80x86; the sequence is surprising, to say the least.

The cwd instruction extends the sign bit of the %ax register, which is assumed to contain the value of n, into the %dx register. Negw negates its register and sets the carry flag cf to 0 if the register is 0 and to 1 otherwise. Adcw adds the second register

```
; n in register %ax
    cwd                            ; convert to double word:
                                   ;    (%dx,%ax) = (extend_sign(%ax), %ax)
    negw %ax                       ; negate: (%ax,cf) := (–%ax, %ax ≠ 0)
    adcw %dx,%dx                   ; add with carry: %dx := %dx + %dx + cf
; sign(n) in %dx
```

Fig. 9.47: Optimal code for the function sign(n)

plus the carry flag to the first. The actions for $n > 0$, $n = 0$, and $n < 0$ are shown in Figure 9.48; dashes indicate values that do not matter to the code. Note how the correct answer is obtained for $n < 0$: adcw %dx,%dx sets %dx to %dx+%dx+cf = $-1 + -1 + 1 = -1$.

```
                 Case n > 0    Case n = 0    Case n < 0
                 %dx %ax cf    %dx %ax cf    %dx %ax cf
initially:
                  –   n  –      –   0  –      –   n  –
cwd
                  0   n  –      0   0  –     -1   n  –
negw %ax
                  0  -n  1      0   0  0     -1  -n  1
adcw %dx,%dx
                  1  -n  1      0   0  0     -1  -n  1
```

Fig. 9.48: Actions of the 80x86 code from Figure 9.47

Supercompilation was pioneered by Massalin [185], who found many astounding and very "clever" code sequences for the 68000 and 80x86 machines. Using more advanced search techniques, Granlund and Kenner [110] have determined surprising sequences for the IBM RS/6000, which have found their way into the GNU C compiler.

9.1.7 Evaluation of code generation techniques

Figure 9.49 summarizes the most important code generation techniques we have covered. The bottom line is that we can only generate optimal code for all simple expression trees, and for complicated trees when there are sufficient registers. Also, it can be proved that code generation for dependency graphs is NP-complete under a wide range of conditions, so there is little hope that we will find an efficient optimal algorithm for that problem. On the other hand, quite good heuristic algorithms for dependency graphs and some of the other code generation problems are available.

Problem	Technique	Quality
Expression trees, using register-register or memory-register instructions	Weighted trees; Figure 7.28	
with sufficient registers:		Optimal
with insufficient registers:		Optimal
Dependency graphs, using register-register or memory-register instructions	Ladder sequences; Section 9.1.2.2	Heuristic
Expression trees, using any instructions with cost function	Bottom-up tree rewriting; Section 9.1.4	
with sufficient registers:		Optimal
with insufficient registers:		Heuristic
Register allocation when all interferences are known	Graph coloring; Section 9.1.5	Heuristic

Fig. 9.49: Comparison of some code generation techniques

9.1.8 Debugging of code optimizers

The description of code generation techniques in this book paints a relatively moderate view of code optimization. Real-world code generators are often much more aggressive and use tens and sometimes hundreds of techniques and tricks, each of which can in principle interfere with each of the other optimizations. Also, such code generators often distinguish large numbers of special cases, requiring complicated and opaque code. Each of these special cases and the tricks involved can be wrong in very subtle ways, by itself or in combination with any of the other special cases. This makes it very hard to convince oneself *and* the user of the correctness of an optimizing compiler.

However, if we observe that a program runs correctly when compiled without optimizations and fails when compiled with them, it does not necessarily mean that the error lies in the optimizer: the program may be wrong in a way that depends on the details of the compilation. Figure 9.50 shows an incorrect C program, the effect of which was found to depend on the form of compilation. The error is that the array index runs from 0 to 19 whereas the array has entries from 0 to 9 only; since C has no array bound checking, the error itself is not detected in any form of compilation or execution.

In one non-optimizing compilation, the compiler allocated the variable i in memory, just after the array A[10]. When during execution i reached the value 10, the assignment A[10] = 2*10 was performed, which updated i to 20, since it was located at the position where A[10] would be if it existed. So, the loop terminated

```
int i, A[10];

for (i = 0; i < 20; i++) {
    A[i] = 2*i;
}
```

Fig. 9.50: Incorrect C program with compilation-dependent effect

after having filled the array as expected. In another, more optimizing compilation, the variable i was allocated in a register, the loop body was performed 20 times and information outside A[] or i was overwritten.

Also, an uninitialized variable in the program may be allocated by chance in a zeroed location in one form of compilation and in a used register in another, with predictably unpredictable results for the running program.

All this leads to a lot of confusion and arguments about the demarcation of responsibilities between compiler writers and compiler users, and compiler writers have sometimes gone to great lengths to isolate optimization errors.

When introducing an optimization, it is important to keep the non-optimizing code present in the code generator and to have a simple flag allowing the optimization to be performed or skipped. This allows selective testing of the optimizations and any of their combinations, and tends to keep the optimizations relatively clean and independent, as far as possible. It also allows the following drastic technique, invented by Boyd and Whalley [47].

A counter is kept which counts the number of optimizations applied in the compilation of a program; at the end of the compilation the compiler reports something like "This compilation involved N optimizations". Now, if the code generated for a program P malfunctions, P is first compiled with all optimizations off and run again. If the error persists, P itself is at fault, otherwise it is likely, though not certain, that the error is with the optimizations. Now P is compiled again, this time allowing only the first $N/2$ optimizations; since each optimization can be applied or skipped at will, this is easily implemented. If the error still occurs, the fault was dependent on the first $N/2$ optimizations, otherwise it depended on the last $N - N/2$ optimizations. Continued binary search will thus lead us to the precise optimization that caused the error to appear. Of course, this optimization need not itself be wrong; its malfunctioning could have been triggered by an error in a previous optimization. But such are the joys of debugging...

These concerns and techniques are not to be taken lightly: Yang et al. [309] tested eleven C compilers, both open source and commercial, and found that all of them could crash, and, worse, could silently produce incorrect code.

This concludes our treatment of general optimization techniques, which traditionally optimize for speed. In the next sections we will discuss code size reduction, energy saving, and Just-In-Time compilation.

9.2 Code size reduction

Code size is of prime importance to embedded systems. Smaller code size allows such systems to be equipped with less memory and thus be cheaper, or alternatively allows them to cram more functionality into the same memory, and thus be more valuable. Small code size also cuts on transmission times and uses an instruction cache more efficiently.

9.2.1 General code size reduction techniques

There are many ways to reduce the size of generated code, each with different properties. The most prominent ones are briefly described below. As with speed, some methods to reduce code size are outside the compiler writer's grasp. The programmer can, for example, use a programming language that allows leaner code, the ultimate example of which is assembly code. The advantage of writing in assembly code is that every byte can be used to the full; the disadvantage is the nature and the extent of the work, and the limited portability of the result.

9.2.1.1 Traditional optimization techniques

We can use traditional optimization techniques to generate smaller code. Some of the these techniques can be modified easily so as to optimize for code size rather than for speed; an example is the BURS tree rewriting technique from Section 9.1.4. The advantage of this form of size reduction is that it comes at no extra cost at run time: no decompression or interpreter is needed to run the program. A disadvantage it that obtaining a worth-while code size reduction requires very aggressive optimization. Debary *et al.* [79] show that with great effort size reductions of 16 to 40% can be achieved, usually with a small speed-up.

9.2.1.2 Useless code removal

Much software today is constructed from components. Since often these components are designed for general use, many contain features that are not used in a given application, and considerable space can be saved by weeding out the useless code. A small-scale example would be a monolithic print routine that includes extensive code for formatting floating point numbers, used in a program handling integers only; on a much larger scale, some graphic libraries drag in large amounts of code that is actually used by very few programs. Even the minimum C program int main(void) {return 0;} is compiled into an executable of more than 68 kB by *gcc* on a Pentium. Useless code can be found by looking for unreachable code, for example routines that are never called; or by doing symbolic interpretation (Section 5.2), preferably of the entire program. The first is relatively simple; the second requires an extensive effort on the part of the compiler writer.

9.2.1.3 Tailored intermediate code

We can design a specially tailored intermediate code, and supply the program in that code, accompanied by an interpreter. An advantage is that we are free in our design of the intermediate code, so considerable size reductions can be obtained. A disadvantage is that an interpreter has to be supplied, which takes up memory, and perhaps must be sent along, which takes transmission time; also, this interpreter will cause a considerable slow-down in the running program. The ultimate in this technique is threaded code, discussed in Section 7.5.1.1. Hoogerbrugge *et al.* [123] show that threaded code can reach a size reduction of no less than 80%! The slow-down was a factor of 8, using an interpreter written in assembly language.

9.2.1.4 Code compression

Huffman and/or Lempel-Ziv (*gzip*) compression techniques can be used *after* the code has been generated. This approach has many variants and much research has been done on it. Its advantage is its relative ease of application; a disadvantage is that decompression is required before the program can be run, which takes time and space, and requires code to do the decompression. Code compression achieves code size reductions of between 20 and 40%, often with a slow-down of the same percentages. It is discussed more extensively in Section 9.2.2.

9.2.1.5 Tailored hardware instructions

Hardware designers can introduce one or more new instructions, aimed at code size reduction. Examples are ARM and MIPS machines having a small but slow 16-bits instruction set and a fast but larger 32-bits set, and the "echo instruction" discussed in Section 9.2.2.3.

9.2.2 Code compression

Almost all techniques used to compress binary code are adaptations of those used for—lossless—general file compression. Exceptions to this are systems that disassemble the binary code, apply traditional code eliminating optimizations like symbolic interpretation to detect useless code and procedural abstraction, and then reassemble the binary executable. One such system is *Squeeze++*, described by De Sutter, De Bus and De Bosschere [75].

We shall first briefly discuss general compression techniques, and then show some applications to code compression.

9.2.2.1 General compression techniques

The basic operation of a general file compression technique is to replace file segments, called **words**, by shorter segments (sequences of bits), called their **codes**. Decompression then follows by replacing the codes by their corresponding file segments. For this to work, the codes must be **prefix-free**: no code can be the prefix of another code, or we would not be able to decide where a code stops.

General file compression is a mature field about which many books have been written, for example the books by Salomon [247] and by Sayood [252]. The brief discussion below is a crude but practical simplification.

Compression is only possible in the presence of redundancy, of repeating patterns; a completely random file cannot be compressed. To find the redundancy, we either need to do analysis of the file or to know its nature in advance. To exploit the redundancy we need a compression algorithm.

A compression algorithm is characterized by three properties:

- whether the codes are fixed-length or variable-length;
- whether the input words are fixed for all files or are from a file-dependent dictionary;
- whether the mapping from input word to code is fixed for the entire file or changes as the compression process progresses, in which case the algorithm is called **adaptive**.

We will first discuss the variable-length codes and the dictionary algorithm, and then see how they can be made adaptive.

Variable-length codes — Huffman coding A variable-length code maps fixed-length words, usually bytes, onto variable-length sequences of bits, the codes. Compression is achieved by assigning shorter codes to the more frequent input words. The frequency of the words can be determined by scanning the file.

Since there are 256 different bytes, an example using bytes for input words would require tables with 256 entries; we will therefore give an example with words of 2 bits. For our example we suppose the 4 possible words have the frequency distribution shown in Figure 9.51. The table already contains the optimal codes; they

Word	Frequency	Code
00	10%	110
01	60%	0
10	20%	10
11	10%	111

Fig. 9.51: Words and frequencies with their Huffman codes

probably conform to what the reader would come up with after some thought, but the problem for large codes is to how construct them using an algorithm.

That problem was solved by Huffman [126] in 1952, in the following elegant way. Find the two words L_1 and L_2 with the lowest frequencies; combine them into a new virtual word V by adding their frequencies; and solve the now reduced problem in the same way. Then retrieve the code C for V and give L_1 the code $C0$ and L_2 the code $C1$. If there is only one word left, it gets the empty code, and there is no new reduced problem. It can be shown that this procedure creates the optimal code mapping.

We now apply this algorithm to the words of Figure 9.51. The two lowest-frequency words are 00 and 11; we combine them into a new virtual word $\{00,11\}$ called V_1, which gets a frequency of 20%. Next we combine 10 and V_1 into $\{10,V_1\}$ called V_2, with a frequency of 40%. Then we combine 01 and V_2 into the last virtual word V_3, which gets the empty code C_3. Unrolling the process, 01 gets code C_30, which is 0, and V_2 gets C_31, which is $1 = C_2$; the next step assigns code 10 to word $C_20 = 10$, and $C_21 = 11$ to V_1; and finally 00 gets code $C_10 = 110$ and 11 gets $C_11 = 111$. These assignments conform to the codes shown in Figure 9.51. We see that the codes are prefix-free, since whenever a code C_k is duplicated it is followed by a 0 in one resulting code and by a 1 in the other. The decision tree used in the decompression is shown in Figure 9.52.

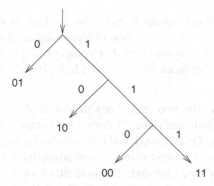

Fig. 9.52: Decoding tree for the Huffman code of Figure 9.51

The 40-bits input '01 00 10 01 01 10 11 01 01 01 10 01 01 01 01 00 01 11 10 01', which has the correct frequency distribution, is compressed to '0 110 10 0 0 10 111 0 0 0 10 0 0 0 0 110 0 111 10 0' (32 bits), a compression of 20% (spaces added for readability). The decoding tree has to be included in the compressed file, but for large files its size is negligible compared to the compressed data itself.

Huffman coding works better for larger input words and less lopsided frequency distributions; on texts it achieves a compression of 30 to 45%. It compresses the 331013 bytes of the text of one version of this chapter to 1577589 bits = 197199 bytes, including the decompression tree, a reduction of 40.4%.

Compressing using a dictionary In its basic form, **dictionary compression** analyses the input to select a number of long and frequent input words, assigns short codes to them and compresses the input by replacing all occurrences of the selected words by their codes; the set of selected words is called the **dictionary**. This descriptions immediately raises several questions. How many words do we keep? What exactly is "a long and frequent word"? And what if the assigned codes also occur in the text? Not surprisingly, actual implementations differ in their answers to these questions.

A simple and intuitive implementation for compression of a natural language text could, for example, define a word as a sequence of letters, select the 255 words with the largest product of length and frequency for the dictionary, and assign the two-byte code (255,N) to the word in position N ($N \in \{0..254\}$) in the dictionary. If the input already contains a byte 255, we replace it by the two-byte code (255,255); this is why we selected 255 words rather than 256. The dictionary can be prepended to the compressed file. The redundancy that is squeezed out lies in the fact that texts often use the same word many times.

Since a dictionary word w of length $|w|$ is replaced by a code of length 2, the profit is actually $|w| - 2$ bytes per occurrence, rather than $|w|$. A program that selected the 255 words from the input with the largest values for $(|w| - 2) \times F(w)$, where $F(w)$ is the frequency of word w, compressed the above mentioned version of this chapter from 331013 bytes to 250066 bytes, + a dictionary of 2274 bytes = 252340 bytes, a reduction of 23.8%.

Subjecting the result to Huffman compression reduces the size further, to 166553 bytes, a total reduction of 49.7%. Often compressing an already compressed file with a different technique again helps. For comparison, the well-known file compression program *gzip* reduces the original file to 101557 bytes, a reduction of 69.4%.

Adaptive algorithms The two techniques described above rely on pre-obtained statistical data that remain the same all during the compression; this requires two scans of the input, which is awkward, and is unsuitable for files with different statistics in different regions. **Adaptive compression** adapts its statistics during the compression action, and updates the code mapping accordingly. For this to work, the decompression program must keep synchronized with the mapping as it is changed by the compression program. This is easily arranged by first encoding the word according to the old mapping and then changing the mapping; the decompression program will then decode the word through the old mapping and use the statistical information from it to update its mapping to match that of the compression program for the next word. The system starts with blank or default statistics.

Adaptive Huffman coding just recomputes the encoding tree after each input word; for adaptive dictionary compression there are several possibilities. The system can drop a word from the dictionary and insert a new one at any moment; it can decide to use longer or shorter words and/or longer or shorter codes; and others, described in the literature. Adaptive dictionary compression is substantially better than non-adaptive; most file compression programs (ZIP, LZ, Deflate, etc.) use an adaptive dictionary scan followed by Huffman compression.

9.2.2.2 Applying general techniques to code compression

The above techniques are, in their unmodified form, unsuitable for code compression. The reason is simple: they allow sequential decompression only, and to execute code we need at least a limited form of random access, to call functions and to jump to labels – unless we decompress the entire program, which available memory may not allow.

The non-adaptive techniques are easily adapted. Huffman coding can just start at a byte boundary for any code position that can be accessed from elsewhere, by inserting filler bits; we then need to make sure that the code in the previous byte ends in a jump, to prevent the filler bits from being decoded. Dictionary compression has no problem in this respect, provided the codes it inserts consist of entire bytes, but its compression ratio is not very good. Liao, Devadas, and Keutzer [178], using advanced dictionary entry selection techniques, achieve code size reductions between 4 and 19%.

Adaptive decompression requires continuous knowledge of statistics constructed from the previous decompressed code, but this information is not readily available when performing a jump to a label in compressed code. There are two ways out of this (in addition to the trivial solution of starting with blank statistics at each label). We can determine general statistics for the entire program and start with them at each label (Latendresse and Feeley [169]). Or we can compute the intersection M of all the mappings that hold when a jump to a given label occurs, and before each such jump emit decompressor instructions to adapt the present mapping to M. An algorithm to do so is described by Gilbert and Abrahamson [105].

Another issue is how much of the code should be decompressed by each invocation of the decompressor. Obvious choices are: one instruction; a basic block; a routine; or the entire program. The first choice may, however, involve too much overhead, and the last one may cause memory problems. Another option is to decompress as much as the instruction cache will hold; then let the program run, catch the cache miss interrupt and fill the cache with new decompressed code. Lefurgy, Piccininni, and Mudge [172] explain how to do this.

9.2.2.3 Special techniques for code compression

Unlike the average file offered for compression, compiled programs are highly structured, and several techniques exploit this structure. We will present these techniques here in arbitrary order, since it is difficult to determine their relative merits; most achieve reductions of between 5 and 20%. Most are used in combination with other techniques, which they may reinforce or just supplement; the reported combined reductions lie between 20 and 45%, usually with a slow-down of a comparable percentage.

- It is well known that it is only a small portion of the code of a program that does most of the work, the so called **hot code**. So decompression time can be saved by compressing the cold code only.
- Instructions consist of three fields: an opcode, some register numbers, and possibly a machine address. Each of these fields has quite different statistical properties, so it is profitable to compress each of these three streams by a separate algorithm. This is called **split-stream code compression** (Ernst *et al.* [95], and Lucco [182]).
- In dictionary compression, the first occurrence of a dictionary word in the text is usually encoded like all the others, but an alternative implementation is to leave it in place in the text, so we can refer back to it from subsequent occurrences. This does away with the entire dictionary, but can make the back reference (its code) longer and more complicated. The technique may be attractive for code compression, since stretches of repeated code occur frequently in a given function while not occurring elsewhere. Since hopefully the function is relatively small, the back references can be short.

  This idea is implemented in the **echo instruction**, a virtual or real machine instruction with two fields, a counter N and an offset O. Its effect is to jump O bytes backwards, execute N instructions, and return to the position after the echo instruction. This instruction can then be issued each time a previously generated code segment would be generated again. Its effect can be simulated by an interpreter, but it is one of the few compression techniques that can be incorporated cheaply in the hardware, at the cost of a counter and a return address. Echo instructions have been researched by Lau *et al.* [171], and Brisk, Nahapetian, and Sarrafzadeh [50].
- In principle most opcodes in instructions can be combined freely with most registers and most condition bits, but generated code usually uses a limited set of combinations only. The elements of this limited set can mapped to special short codes, resulting in code-specific dictionary compression. See Heydemann, Bodin, and Charles [122].

9.2.3 Discussion

There is no "best" code compression algorithm; much depends on the target application. Techniques are difficult to compare, since they are most often used in combination. The largest compression is achieved by threaded code (Section 7.5.1.1), which achieves reductions of up to 80%, at the expense of a slow-down of a factor of 8 or more (Hoogerbrugge *et al.* [123]); threaded code could be considered a form of dictionary compression. The lowest slow-downs, actually speed-ups, are achieved by very aggressive optimization (see Debary *et al.* [79], who achieve reductions of 16 to 40%), or by link-time disassembly, followed by a clean-up and reassembly (see De Bus *et al.* [74], who achieve reductions ranging from 20 to 70%, depending on how wasteful the original code was).

Beszédes *et al.* [38] give a good survey of the possibilities, analysing and comparing 12 code compression techniques.

9.3 Power reduction and energy saving

In those applications in which a reduced code size is important, saving energy is often also an issue. In a sense this is unfortunate, since saving energy correlates much more strongly with speed-up than with code size reduction. The reason for this phenomenon is the following.

Power and energy — Volts, amperes, watts, and joules

The tension (**voltage**) on an electric wire is measured in volts, abbreviated V; it can be thought of as the pressure of the electrons in the wire relative to that in the ground.

When a voltage difference is applied to an appliance, a **current** starts to flow, which is measured in amperes, abbreviated A; it can be thought of as the amount of electrons per second, and its magnitude is proportional to the voltage difference.

An electric current flowing over a voltage difference produces **power**, measured in watts, abbreviated W; the power is proportional to the product of voltage difference and current: $W = V \times A$. The power can be used for purposes like producing light, running a computer, or running an elevator, but in the end almost all power is dissipated as heat.

The longer the power is produced, the more energy results; **energy** is measured in joules, abbreviated J, and we have $J = W \times t$, where t is the time in seconds during which the power was produced.

If any of the above quantities varies with time, the multiplications must be replaced by integration over time.

On the one hand energy is a more intuitive notion than power, just as length is more intuitive than speed; so power is more easily explained as energy per time unit than vice versa. On the other hand the watt is a more usual unit than the joule, which is why electricity bills show the energy in kWh, kilowatt-hours, units of 3600000J (3.6MJ).

Broadly speaking, there are three classes of machine instructions as far as power consumption is concerned (for the difference between power and energy see the Sidebar). First there are the instructions without memory access (Load_Reg R*m*,R*n*; Add_Reg R*m*,R*n*; Mult_Reg R*m*,R*n*, etc.), which all consume roughly the same power, say 600 mW. Next we have those that perform a read memory access, for example Load_Mem n,R*m*, which consume perhaps a third more, say about 800 mW. And finally instructions that write to memory, for example Store_Reg R*m*,n, which consume another third more, say about 1000 mW. So as long as the mix of these three groups remains the same, the power consumption does not change, and energy consumption is directly proportional to the time the program takes to finish[1].

---

[1] Traditionally the "power" consumption of an instruction is measured in mA rather than in mW, but as long as the voltage is kept constant, they are proportional to each other. For a fixed voltage of 1.5V, the above numbers correspond to about 400mA, 530mA and 670mA, respectively.

It may come as a surprise that adding and multiplying take about the same power, even though multiplication is so much more labor-intensive. One has to note, however, that power is energy per time unit, in this case energy per cycle. If the multiplication instruction takes 10 machine cycles and the addition takes one and both take the same power, multiplication costs 10 times as much energy as addition.

As already mentioned at the beginning of this chapter, energy saving is important to increase operation time in battery-powered equipment, and to reduce the electricity bill of wall-powered computers. In addition to energy consumption we have to worry about peak power and step power.

Peak power is the maximum power dissipated during program execution. It strongly influences chip temperature, and high chip temperatures have an exponentially bad effect on reliability, chip lifetime, and power leakage. Also, if the peak power limit is exceeded, the chip may be damaged or even destroyed. The term "peak power" is somewhat misleading. Each instruction uses a particular amount of power, so theoretically the peak power usage of a program is that of the most expensive instruction. One instruction-length peak, however, is too short to have any influence, but enough of them over a short enough period of time cause heat to build up and will do damage in the end. So what is actually meant by "peak power" is the time-decaying average of the power use of the instructions over a time long enough to do damage but short enough for the cooling system to be unable to dissipate the heat. This average can be reduced by using high-power instructions sparingly or intersperse them with lower-power instructions.

Step power is the power consumption variation between successive instructions. Large variations in power consumption are bad for chip reliability and reduce battery span; both chip and battery like a quiet and orderly life. Figure 9.53 summarizes power, peak power, step power and energy consumption of a program run; the area under the curve is the energy consumed.

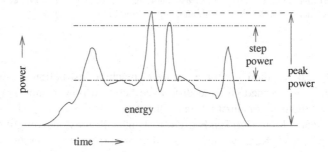

Fig. 9.53: Power, peak power, step power and energy consumption of a program run

We will now turn to some compilation techniques that can assist in obtaining code with low energy consumption and acceptable peak and step power properties.

It should be pointed out that even more than with code size reduction there are possibilities to reduce energy consumption that lie outside the grasp of the compiler writer. We mention economizing on non-CPU resources like disks, memory banks, and screens; using faster and less memory-intensive algorithms and data structures; running energy-consuming parts of the program remotely, on a wall-powered computer; and, above all, writing parts of the program in assembly language. Energy savings between 80 and 94% have been achieved by writing the program partly or entirely in assembly language; see, for example, Roy and Johnson [241].

9.3.1 Just compiling for speed

Just using the speed optimization facilities of the compiler can already help considerably. Valluri and John [285] and Seng and Tullsen [258] found that using the –O1 option of the GNU C compiler *gcc* saved around 20% energy on the average, although savings of 2 and 70% occurred as well; the further optimization levels helped little beyond that. Experiments with a BURS code generator (Tiwari, Malik, and Wolfe [280]) showed that optimizing for energy often yields the same code as optimizing for speed. And Parikh *et al.* [213] found that optimizing for energy with speed as a tie breaker yields code that is as good for speed as code optimized solely for speed.

9.3.2 Trading speed for power

Many processors can be run on several voltage settings. Changing the voltage has the interesting property that the speed of the processor changes linearly with the voltage, but the power consumption is proportional to the square of the voltage. The reason is that the current flowing though an appliance is proportional to the voltage, so when the voltage changes by a factor α, the current also changes by the same factor; and since the power equals $V \times A$, it changes by a factor of α^2 (see the sidebar on power and energy). This phenomenon can be exploited to trade speed for power in a very profitable way (Saputra *et al.* [250]).

In its simplest application we just lower the voltage by, say, 20%. This reduces the power consumption by 36%, but the processor slows down by 20%, which makes the program taken 25% more time. (In the time the processor used to perform 100 cycles, it now performs 80, so we need 1.25 the time to make it perform a 100 again.) So in total the power consumption is reduced by 20%, at the expense of an increase of 25% in processing time.

Now suppose we manage to speed up this program by 25%, using some optimization technique – often a quite feasible task. Then, when lowering the voltage by 20% there is no slow-down with respect to the unoptimized program, and the full 36% gain materializes. So we obtain 36% profit for a 25% optimization speed-up.

This approach also works for those real-time programs for which there is normally no advantage in speeding up the program, since there is no merit in supplying the answer before it is needed. Suppose we have a program whose task it is to produce the bitmap for a new image every 1/25th second, for which it uses P mW power and thus $P/25$ mJ energy; see Figure 9.54(a). Now suppose we improve its speed by 25%; then the program finishes its task in $0.8 \times 1/25$ sec, as shown in Figure 9.54(b). The (peak) power is still P mW, the step power has gone up, and the required energy is reduced by 20% to $0.8P \times 1/25$ mJ, plus the energy spent in idling.

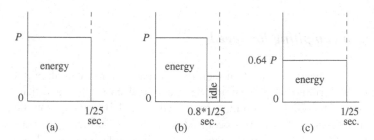

Fig. 9.54: Trading speed for power by lowering the voltage

If we now lower the voltage by the same 20%, we get a completely different picture (Figure 9.54(c)): the power consumption is reduced by 36%, and so is the energy; step power is back to its original level; and no energy is wasted in idling. In addition to increasing battery life time the lower voltage will boost CPU longevity and reliability.

Another way to exploit the beneficial effect of lowering the voltage is finding the time-critical basic blocks in the program, using full voltage for them and lowering the voltage dynamically on the other blocks. See Hsu and Kremer [125] for details.

9.3.3 Instruction scheduling and bit switching

Most code generation methods described in the previous sections have the structure "instruction selection, instruction scheduling, register allocation". Section 9.1.2.1 showed how the AST could be converted to a DAG, using the instruction set of a very simple machine; the ladder algorithm of Section 9.1.2.2 then scheduled the instructions for minimal data movement. The BURS technique (Section 9.1.4) tiled the AST optimally with possibly complex instructions; the scheduling was then done by the simple weighted register allocation algorithm of Section 7.5.2.2. We have also seen that the BURS algorithm can easily be adapted to optimize for energy saving.

In embedded systems it is often profitable to replace the scheduling algorithm in the code generation method by one based on energy saving. The reason lies in a peculiarity of electronic circuits: switching a bit from 0 to 1 or from 1 to 0 takes much more energy than switching from 0 to 0 or from 1 to 1. And since an instruction finds the bits in the processor as they are left by the previous instruction, the energy used by an instruction depends to a certain extent on that previous instruction. The majority of these bits are outside compiler control, but many are not. More in particular, during instruction scheduling the compiler has a certain freedom to rearrange instructions, and during register assignment the compiler can choose the register numbers more or less freely.

Cold scheduling is the name of a collection of techniques that try to minimize bit switching by exploiting this freedom. We will show a simple example here. More can be found in Kandemir, Vijaykrishnan, and Irwin [141], and the references in it.

For our demonstration we return to the 2-address register machine of Figure 7.26. We will assume that the opcodes are 3 bits wide and that the instructions are assigned opcodes 1 (=001) to 6 (=110) in the order in which they are presented in the picture. We also assume that the machine has 4 registers, numbered 0 to 3, so the register fields are 2 bits wide. For our cold scheduling we will concentrate on the bits of the opcode and those of the second operand; the format of the first operand is too variable for a simple example.

Figure 9.55 shows the dependency graph of the instructions of the code for the expression b∗b − 4∗(a∗c); it is similar to Figure 7.33, except that b has been recognized as a common subexpression. Our computer tells us that there are 168 possible schedules (topological sorts obeying the dependencies) for this DAG; combined with the 4!=24 possible register assignments per schedule, there are 168×24 = 4032 possible code sequences.

Probably the most straightforward code sequence is shown in the left-most two columns of Figure 9.56(a); the third column shows the bits of the opcode and second register fields, separated by two dots to show that we ignore the first operand; and the fourth column shows the number of bit switches between consecutive instructions.

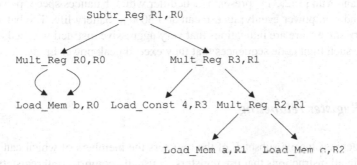

Fig. 9.55: Dependency graph for b∗b − 4∗(a∗c)

We see that the straightforward code sequence generates 20 bit switches. Examining the other code sequences that obey the dependencies, we find that the minimum number of bit switches is 9, reduction of 55%; a code sequence with that property is shown in the right half of Figure 9.56.

On average, cold scheduling reduces the number of bit switches that are under the control of the compiler writer by about 30 to 40%. Because there are also fixed bits in the instruction –constants, addresses–, and because many more bit switches occur in a CPU than just those in the loading of the instruction register, this translates to a 2

Instruction	Opcode, reg. & bit switches		Instruction	Opcode, reg. & bit switches	
Load_Mem b,R0	010..00	3	Load_Mem a,R1	010..01	1
Mult_Reg R0,R0	101..00	4	Load_Mem b,R0	010..00	1
Load_Mem a,R1	010..01	2	Load_Mem c,R2	010..10	3
Load_Mem c,R2	010..10	5	Load_Const 4,R3	001..11	2
Mult_Reg R2,R1	101..01	2	Mult_Reg R2,R1	101..01	0
Load_Const 4,R3	001..11	2	Mult_Reg R3,R1	101..01	1
Mult_Reg R3,R1	101..01	2	Mult_Reg R0,R0	101..00	1
Subtr_Reg R1,R0	100..00		Subtr_Reg R1,R0	100..00	
	Total = 20			Total = 9	
(a), straightforward			(b), optimized		

Fig. 9.56: Reducing bit switching by cold scheduling

to 4% power reduction of the CPU, so it is fair to say that the term "cold scheduling" is very, very relative.

It should also be pointed out that the optimization has also lowered the step power: the standard deviation of the number of bit switches, which is a measure for the step power, is 1.12 for the straightforward code and 0.88 for the optimized code.

The above optimized schedule and register assignment was found through exhaustive search. Larger basic blocks will require heuristic algorithms to find a local optimum; Section 9.3.4 below discusses one such algorithm for reducing bit switching through register relabeling.

Kim and Yun [152, 311] present a scheduler which balances speed, power, peak power and step power evenly; its use can add 30% to battery life. The balancing is necessary since there are indications that very aggressive instruction scheduling can generate such tight code sequences that they exceed peak power limits.

9.3.4 Register relabeling

Most machines have a subset E of the registers the members of which can be used equally in all instructions that use registers; E usually comprises all registers except perhaps the ones with the lowest and/or highest numbers. The registers in E have the property that if we swap two of these registers everywhere in the entire program, the working of the program is unaffected, provided the program does not execute dynamically computed instructions. This effect can be used to do program-wide bit switching reduction.

The algorithm is applied either to the assembly code as produced by the compiler, preferably including that of the libraries, or to the disassembled code of an existing binary executable; note that in the latter case we do not even need the source code. From this code a graph is constructed with the registers as nodes; an edge is drawn between two registers if they occur in the same position in two consecutive instructions, and the edge is labeled with the bit switching cost incurred by the two register numbers. The total register bit switching energy cost is then the sum of the weights on all edges. All unused registers in E are added as unconnected nodes, so they get a chance too of being used.

Next, all pairs of two registers (of which there are $O(n^2)$, where $n = |E|$) are examined, their register numbers swapped, their edges (of which there are $O(n)$) recomputed, the gain assessed, and numbers swapped back. At the end of these $O(n^3)$ steps the swap with the largest gain is accepted and applied to the graph. This process is then repeated until no more improvement is achieved and a local minimum is found. In measurements by Mehta *et al.* [190] this led to about 15% decrease in bit switching, and 4.25% in overall energy saving.

With some minor modification the algorithm can also take into account the fixed non-register bits that occur in register positions in instructions adjacent to ones that do have registers (Woo, Yoon and Kim [307], Kandemir, Vijaykrishnan and Irwin [141]); doing so raises the energy savings to 11-12%.

9.3.5 Avoiding the dynamic scheduler

Many CPUs perform *dynamic instruction scheduling*: they search the instruction stream for instructions that can be performed in parallel in the various function units of the processor. The hardware for this is one of the major energy consumers in the CPU, taking perhaps 30% of the energy, and it is worthwhile to try to avoid it. In the general case dynamic scheduling is useful, since the compiler cannot always determine which instructions should be scheduled when, to obtain maximum throughput. But often the basic block is so simple that the compiler can construct a schedule which causes even the static scheduler to issue the instructions in the proper order to utilize the function units well. We can then, for these blocks, switch off the dynamic scheduler and save energy. Valluri, John, and Hanson [286] show how to do this; they achieve about 25% energy saving, at the expense of a slowdown of a few percents.

9.3.6 Domain-specific optimizations

An important function of embedded systems is image and video processing, which requires intensive matrix manipulation. Processing the matrix is implemented using for-loops, but since the action in the loop body is often tiny, energy (and speed) savings can be obtained by simplifying the surrounding control structure. An example is loop unrolling, in which the body of the loop is repeated in line say 8 times before the test and jump back is performed. Kandemir *et al.* [142] discuss this and many other loop optimizations and give experimental results; they vary considerably

for different programs. Many loop optimizations also affect the size of the program
aversely.

9.3.7 Discussion

A program can be positioned in a space spanned by four dimensions: speed, size,
energy consumption, and peak power dissipation. In this space it is boxed in by
limits: a lower limit on speed and upper limits on the others. Of these limits peak
power dissipation is a hard ceiling: if the peak power dissipation limit is exceeded,
the chip fries, which is bad for Quality of Result. Speed and size dimensions may
also form hard walls: if the image is not ready in 1/25 sec, the movie jitters, which
is bad for user satisfaction; and if the size is too large the application does not fit and
the program is a no-show. Energy consumption is usually the most forgiving: new
energy is no more than the nearest wall socket away — but that may of course be a
problem if the program runs on the Moon.

The program can be moved around inside this box by optimization techniques
and voltage manipulation. Optimization techniques move the program in complicated ways and affect all dimensions simultaneously; voltage manipulation modifies speed, power and energy in a predictable way. In practical applications we want
the program positioned so that it fulfills certain conditions; an example of such a
condition is "best speed under 10kB and under 275 mW". Given the profusion of
optimization possibilities and their complicated interactions it may be difficult to
fulfill such conditions, which is why people have enlisted the help of a computer.
Kadayif et al. [140] describe an energy-aware emulator and use it to do integer linear
programming to select optimizations to satisfy multiple criteria.

An extensive tutorial on power and energy management, featuring many compiler
optimization techniques with examples and analyses, was written by Kremer [162].

9.4 Just-In-Time compilation

Interpreted code has the attractive property that it can be totally independent of the
machine and operating system it runs on: the same program file can be used on any
system that has a working interpreter for it. However, interpreted code runs slower
than compiled code, so there is a clear trade-off here.

One way to largely avoid the overhead of interpretation is to let the interpreter
generate machine code for an interpreter code segment, right before that code is
needed. This is called **Just-In-Time compilation** (**JIT compilation**). Once the code
has been compiled, it is usually kept for the remainder of the run. The advantage of
this approach is that it hides much of the compilation process from the user, and that
the generated code can be adapted to a particular processor and even the particular
execution statistics of the program run. Although the technique has been popularized

by Java implementations, it is by no means restricted to that language. Many earlier interpreters already did some form of compilation, and the techniques of Java JIT implementations are now applied to interpreters for other languages.

Obviously the technique only works if the compilation process is fast enough to be acceptable. Modern JIT implementations use a number of techniques to achieve this: Their compilers have been carefully tuned to be as fast as possible while still producing fast code. They only compile those parts of the code that contribute significantly to the execution time of the program (the "hot spots" of the program). In some cases they even use multiple quality levels: a fast compiler yielding code of moderate quality for the bulk of the code, and a more sophisticated but slower compiler for important hot spots.

As an alternative, Jung, Moon, and Bae [139] evaluate the possibility of preloading extremely optimized code for Java classes onto the embedded device, and then use an interpreter for the actual program. They find this to be a very convenient way of achieving considerable speed-ups. The rationale for this approach is that the "variable" part of the program often consists almost exclusively of method calls.

9.5 Compilers versus computer architectures

One of the reasons that optimization techniques are still evolving is that the machines they target are still evolving. In fact there are a number of trends in computer architecture that make efficient compilation more and more challenging. We will now briefly mention some aspects that have not received attention above.

Over the years there has been a spectacular increase in the number of transistors that can be used in a processor. Initially these extra transistors were used to implement functions such as multiplication and floating-point operations directly in hardware, requiring little change in compilation techniques.

The next development was that on-chip caching was added. For many programs this hides the relatively slow accesses to main memory, but it makes the performance of the machine harder to predict, complicating the job of the compiler writer. For example, changing instruction order can improve or harm the instruction or the data cache performance. Similarly, for machines with an instruction cache it is worth trying to reduce code size, simply because it occupies less cache. Compilers with more sophisticated optimizations, for example modeling the entire cache system in detail, have been developed, but the ever-increasing complexity of computer architectures (e.g. multiple cache levels and sophisticated cache replacement policies) render such sophistication impractical.

Ironically, one of the reasons for the increased complexity is the ineffectiveness of compiler optimizations: since compilers are often unable to predict these performance effects in spite of all efforts, machines increasingly have hardware to optimize the code themselves. An example is the dynamic scheduler mentioned in Section 9.3.5, which reorders instructions to avoid waiting for data that is fetched from slow memory and prefetches instructions. Effectively these machines implement in hardware part of the code optimizations that were traditionally done in the compiler. And of course this more sophisticated behavior of the processor is even harder to model in the compiler.

Over the years the size of the on-chip caches have increased significantly, but at a certain point their effectiveness has decreased so much that it was more effective to use the additional available transistors for other architectural features. Most important was the introduction of multiple execution units. Initially architectures simply allowed the use of independent parts of the execution unit, such as the integer and floating-point units, to be used in parallel. Gradually more parallel units were added, starting with simple integer units, evolving to the point where there are two or three instances of each architectural unit. Such processors are called **super-scalar**. To maintain the illusion of a single processor executing a single stream of instructions, the processor analyzes the data dependencies between the instructions, and executes the instructions on parallel execution units whenever possible.

A modern processor with multiple cache levels, parallel execution units, and sophisticated execution prediction can be very fast, but is far too complicated to allow an accurate prediction of its performance. Moreover, all this sophistication results in a significant energy consumption. Therefore an alternative approach to computer architecture abandons all the sophistication, and simply offers multiple execution units and fast memory banks. Explicitly supplying code to all execution units requires very large instructions, which is why such processors are called Very Large Instruction Word (VLIW) processors. Efficient use of these features is left to the compiler: it is expected to generate instruction streams for all execution units, and to explicitly access faster and slower memory or register banks. Any latency in memory access can only be compensated by placing the memory access early enough in the instruction stream. Obviously, generating efficient code for such an architecture requires a sophisticated compiler.

Generating efficient code for either type of processor is far from trivial, mainly because there is such a large gap between the programming models of mainstream programming languages and those of modern processors. Mainstream programming languages still use the model of the sequential execution of a single stream of instructions, whereas technology forces modern processors to be highly parallel.

Next to the two approaches described above, there is a third approach: to squarely place the burden on the programmer. In this approach we simply offer the user multiple processors, often even on a single chip. The user can only use them efficiently by providing multiple parallel instruction streams, but this is beyond the concerns of the compiler writer.

9.6 Conclusion

Code optimization is an infinitely large, infinitely complex field, in which hardware developments and optimization techniques chase each other, often leaving the compiler designer dizzy. The size of the field is evident even in this book, which is more concerned with general compiler design than with optimization: until this point we have already encountered at least seventeen optimization techniques: (in arbitrary order) function in-lining, common subexpression elimination, code compression, BURS, compilation by symbolic interpretation, constant propagation, data-flow equations, dead code elimination, last-def analysis, register allocation by graph coloring, strength reduction, procedural abstraction, supercompilation, weighted register allocation, peephole optimization, basic block scheduling, and (almost) exhaustive search. The complexity is evident too: the techniques form a motley collection, the items of which are difficult to classify.

It is more or less possible to classify the techniques into two groups: techniques that convert the AST to code with a certain degree optimality (for example, BURS and compilation by symbolic interpretation); and techniques that optimize an existing conversion (for example, constant propagation and dead code elimination). There are only a few of the first, and an almost infinite number of the second.

A more useful classification of optimization techniques is according to their effect: speed, size, energy. Though many techniques affect all three favorably, this is not universally true. For example, function in-lining is good for speed but bad for size. Özer, Nisbet and Gregg [208] show such a classification.

Summary

- Code generation consists of three components, instruction selection, instruction scheduling, and register assignment. Optimization efforts can address one or more of these components; optimizing all three of them at the same time is NP-complete in most situations. Due to this and the complexity of the field, very many optimization techniques have been developed.
- Compilation by symbolic interpretation (compilation on the stack) is somewhat similar to context analysis by symbolic interpretation. As in the latter, we keep a symbolic representation, but now we include both the stack and the registers; more importantly, this time the information in the representation must be exact. The representation is called a regvar descriptor.
- If the effect of a node can be stored exactly in the regvar descriptor, we do so. No code is generated for the node, but its semantics is preserved in the regvar descriptor: old regvar + node = new regvar.
- If the effect of a node is such that we cannot keep the information in the regvar descriptor exact, we generate code to achieve the effect, and record the result in the regvar. So the semantics is preserved in the rewriting of the node: old regvar + node = code + new regvar.
- If we have the information from live analysis available, we can delete all information about a variable from the regvar description the moment we leave its live range.
- A basic block is a maximal part of the control graph that contains no splits (jumps) or combines (labels). A basic block starts at a label or at the beginning

of the routine and ends just before a jump or jump-like node or label or the end of the routine. It contains expressions and assignments only.

- The concept of a basic block separates the concerns of code generation for straight sequences of expressions and assignments from those of flow of control. The separation is especially useful for narrow compilers, since it allows them to do optimized code generation for expression sequences.
- Code generation for basic blocks proceeds in two steps. First the control-flow graph is converted into a dependency graph, which is a "DAG", a directed acyclic graph. We then rewrite the dependency graph to code. The gain lies in the fact that the dependency graph is much less restrictive to instruction scheduling than the control-flow graph.
- The dependency graph of a basic block is formed by two kinds of dependencies: data dependencies inside expressions through operands, and data dependencies through variables that obtain their value in an assignment and whose value is used in an expression further on. The ultimate data dependencies are the values that are still needed after the basic block; these are called the roots of the basic block.
- Emphasizing these data dependencies and removing other flow-of-control dependencies yields a rough data dependency graph that can be simplified by shunting out the assignments and keeping only those nodes that are reachable from the roots. The graph is a DAG, a directed acyclic graph.
- The DAG of a basic block can be reduced further by recognizing common subexpressions. The reduction takes place by merging nodes that have the same operands, operator, and dependencies, repeatedly.
- Traditionally, DAGs of basic blocks are implemented as arrays of triples.
- The nodes in the DAG of a basic block are rewritten to the corresponding machine instructions. The DAG is then linearized by scheduling based on late evaluation of the operands.
- The specific form of late evaluation used for the scheduling of DAGs identifies ladder sequences; such ladder sequences match sequences of register-memory instructions that all have the register in common. Such sequences are very efficient.
- To find the scheduling, first available ladder sequences are isolated and then code from them is generated in last-to-first order, starting with a ladder on which no data from other ladders depend. The ladder is then removed from the DAG and the process is repeated.
- Pointers in expressions in basic blocks can be handled by two simple rules: 1. an assignment under a pointer makes any variable used in a subsequent expression dependent on that assignment; 2. retrieving a value from under a pointer is dependent on all preceding assignments. Extended analysis may allow some of these dependencies to be canceled.
- Optimal rewriting of expression trees (but not of DAGs!) can be obtained through BURS code generation; BURS stands for Bottom-Up Rewriting System.

- The BURS technique allows one to decompose a given input tree of arbitrary complexity into a number of subtrees, each of which is a member of a given set of trees, the pattern trees. The pattern trees may again be of arbitrary complexity.
- To apply BURS to code generation, we equate the input tree with the expression AST and the pattern trees with the ASTs of the machine instructions.
- BURS operates in two scans over the input tree, one bottom-up and one top-down. The bottom-up scan annotates each node of the input tree with references to nodes in the pattern trees. The presence of a reference to a node N with an node I in the input tree means that the tree with I at the top can be rewritten by rewriting its top section by the subtree that has N as its top. This implies that after the rewrite of the top section, all other parts of the tree below I can also be rewritten. The top-down scan can then rewrite the entire tree.
- The bottom-up scan combines sets of fragments of pattern trees that are applicable at a certain node in the input tree much in the same way as a lexical analyzer combines sets of items of regular expressions that are applicable in a certain position in the input stream.
- Like the lexical analyzer, the speed of the BURS pattern matcher can be improved by implementing it as an FSA, a tree automaton in this case, rather than interpretatively.
- Unlike the case of the lexical analyzer, the various patterns have different costs, and we want a minimum-cost rewrite. In the interpreting implementation, cost-based decisions can be handled by using a dynamic programming technique: at each node, only the cheapest way to get the result in a given register type is retained. In the tree automaton implementation, constant costs can be incorporated into the automaton. The resulting transition table are often huge but can be compressed considerably.
- BURS code generation is adapted relatively easily to additional requirements. Examples are code generation for machines with several types of registers and the extension of the method to flow-of-control instructions.
- Two variables which are both live at a given position in the program "interfere" with each other when register allocation is concerned. If we know the live ranges of all variables, we can construct the register interference graph of the variables, in which each node represents a variable and each arc between two node N_1 and N_2 represents overlap of the live ranges of the variables represented by the nodes N_1 and N_2.
- We can find a possible assignment of registers to variables by coloring the graph such that no two nodes of the same color are connected by an arc; each color then represents a register. The optimal register assignment corresponds to a graph coloring with the lowest possible number of colors.
- The problem of optimal graph coloring is NP-complete, but good heuristics exist; for example, temporarily remove a node of minimal degree from the graph, color the remaining graph recursively using the same algorithm, reconnect the removed node and color it.
- In supercompilation, a small but frequently used intermediate code fragment is taken and the best possible code for it is generated using exhaustive search. The

resulting code is then used as a template in a compiler. Surprising code sequences have been found in this way.

- Code compression often uses the traditional file compression techniques Huffman coding and dictionary compression, but has to adapt them to non-sequential decoding required by routine calls and jumps to labels.
- An important question is the unit of decompression: one instruction, one basic block, one routine, or the entire program. Since larger units cause less overhead but require more memory, the answer depends on the details of the application.
- Code-specific techniques are: compression of cold code only; split-stream compression: compressing the different fields of the instructions using tailored algorithms and statistics for each; using an echo instruction, virtual or real; combining opcodes and registers into new, shorter, pseudo-instructions.
- There are four energy aspects to a program: average power consumption, processing time, peak power, and step power. The total energy cost is the product of average power and time.
- The foremost energy saver is speed—make the program finish sooner. The second is lowering the voltage on the CPU when that speed is not needed; it quadratically lowers the power consumed, but slows down the program linearly. Next comes cold scheduling: instruction scheduling for minimal bit switching and low-energy instructions, avoiding memory access wherever possible. Ad-hoc, domain-dependent methods come fourth.
- Just-In-Time (JIT) compilation tries to offer the best of compilation and interpretation, by allowing a program to be stored in a portable execution format, and compiling it shortly before it is used to executable code of the target machine.

Further reading

Much detailed information about the plethora of optimizations that are possible can be found in chapters 9 to 12 of Aho *et al.*'s book [6]. The most important specialized books on optimized code generation are by Muchnick [197], Morgan [196], and Srikant and Shankar [264]. Many developments are reported in the *ACM SIGPLAN Conference on Programming Language Design and Implementation, PLDI*. Much research on optimization for embedded systems is reported in various conferences on the subject, for example the *International Conference on Compilers, Architecture, and Synthesis for Embedded Systems*, and the *International Workshop on Embedded Computer Systems: Architectures, Modeling, and Simulation*. More in particular, power consumption reduction is often discussed in proceedings of the *International Symposium on Low Power Electronics and Design*, and in the journals *IEEE Transactions on VLSI Systems* and *IEEE Transactions on CAD of Integrated Circuits and Systems*. JIT compilation was until recently mostly the domain of Java Virtual Machines (JVMs), and were discussed in the mainstream conferences mentioned above. There are also specialized conference series, such as the *Symposium on JavaTM Virtual Machine Research and Technology*, and workshops, for example

Java Grande, and the *Workshop on Java for High-Performance computing* series. Since IBM has a strong interest in efficient JVMs, their scholarly publications, such as their *IBM Systems Journal*, are also a good source. Aycock [22] describes the history of JIT since 1960.

Exercises

9.1. (▷791) In Section 9.1.2.1, an algorithm is presented to convert the AST of a basic block to a data dependency graph. Step 3 of that algorithm inserts dependencies to reflect the fact that an assignment to a variable replaces its old value. Which other requirement does it also express?

9.2. (▷792) Given the code fragment

```
x := a*a + 2*a*b + b*b;
y := a*a − 2*a*b + b*b;
```

draw the dependency graph before and after common subexpression elimination.

9.3. (▷792) (a) Draw the dependency graph of the C expression *p++.
(b) In the basic block {a = *p++; b = *p++;}, the expression *p++ is not a common subexpression, appearances notwithstanding. How does the common subexpression elimination technique described in Section 9.1.2.1 discover that *p++ is not a common subexpression?

9.4. In Section 1.2 we chose ASTs over lists of instructions for the intermediate code representation. Redo the demo compiler from that section with triples rather than ASTs as intermediate code.

9.5. (▷www) Give the data dependency graph after common subexpression elimination of Exercise 9.2 in triple representation.

9.6. (▷792) Step 2 of the algorithm in the subsection on the scheduling of the data dependency graph in Section 9.1.2.2 features two nodes, S and N. Is the algorithm still correct when S and N happen to be the same node?

9.7. (▷792) Show that there is always at least one available ladder sequence when scheduling the data dependency graph.

9.8. (▷www) Refer to Figure 9.12 concerning the rewriting and scheduling of a ladder sequence. Given the commutativity of the + operator, it is tempting to add the value of b directly to I1 without loading it into register R1 first, thus saving one register and one instruction. Explain why this is not allowed.

9.9. (▷www) Use the ladder-sequence algorithm on page 399 to generate code for the dependency graph of Figure B.8. Draw the updated dependency graph after each coded ladder sequence.

9.10. (▷www) The ladder-sequence algorithm on page 399 always uses R1 as the ladder register in step 3. Better code can be obtained by using the "appropriate" register and so avoiding register-to-register transfers. Discuss ways to choose an "appropriate" register.

9.11. Given a machine with 3 machine instructions:

(1) $R_1 := mem$
(2) $R_1 := R_1 + R_2$
(3) $R_1 := R_1 + mem$

where *mem* denotes the contents of a memory location.
(a) Show the sets that the BURS code generator builds at the nodes of the input tree corresponding to the expression **a + b**, and explain why it does so.
(b) Show the tree or trees that result from the rewriting process.

9.12. (▷www) Refer to Section 9.1.4.3 on instruction selection by dynamic programming. Suppose we indicate associativity of operators to the code generator generator, in addition to commutativity. Would this be useful? Would this cause the code generator generator to add more patterns? Which ones?

9.13. (▷793) Redesign the lexical analysis algorithm to yield the largest number of tokens for a given input string, rather than the longest matches, using dynamic programming in a way similar to the tree pattern matching algorithm. Why is it not good enough to just yield the shortest token all the time?

9.14. Redesign the lexical analysis algorithm to yield the smallest number of matches, rather than the longest matches.

9.15. (▷www) The dynamic programming algorithm sketched in Section 9.1.4.3 assigns cost zero to the label mem, since the label means "value already resides in memory" rather than "value can be brought to memory at cost *C*". Add an instruction Store_Reg R,*x* with cost 3 units to the instruction set of Figure 9.23. This instruction allows any operand that resides in a register to be yielded in memory, at a price. Also, in addition to the cost of a rewrite in a label, we can record the maximum number of registers used.

Redo the computations that led to Figure 9.34, while including the possibility of storing operands in memory and recording the maximum number of registers used. Use the resulting tree to derive an instruction sequence when only one register is available. What happens when two registers are available?

9.16. (▷www) Given the register interference graph for the five variables a, b, c, d, and e:

show the steps the graph coloring algorithm goes through when coloring this graph, and produce the resulting register allocation.

9.17. (▷www) Given the code sequence

```
int  tmp_2ab = 2*a*b;
int  tmp_aa = a*a;
int  tmp_bb = b*b;

x = tmp_aa + tmp_2ab +tmp_bb;
y = tmp_aa − tmp_2ab +tmp_bb;
```

and given that a and b are live on entry and dead on exit, and that x and y are live on exit:
(a) Construct the register interference graph.
(b) Color the graph. How many registers do we need?

9.18. (▷793) Refer to Section 9.1.6 on supercompilation. Suppose we have a modest set of 20 machine instructions, each operating on 2 registers, and 3 machine registers. We want to find a pattern for a given function by trying all combinations of at most N instructions. Under the assumptions that trying a single combination takes ten microseconds, that all but one or two combinations are rejected, and that rejecting takes place on the average after two tests, what would be a reasonable value of N for the search to take a weekend?

9.19. (▷www) Design a good and compact format for the Huffman decoding tree.

9.20. (▷www) To get an impression of heat management on a chip: (a) On the basis of the following rough data, do a back-of-the-envelope computation to estimate how much the execution of an instruction raises the temperature of that instruction's circuit. Current: 666mA; voltage: 1.5V. Instruction time: 1ns (nanosecond, 10^{-9} second). Chip size: 1x1cm; transistor count (instructions per chip): 10^8. Number of transistors per instruction: 1000. Heat capacity: $1J/cm^3$/degree (i.e. 1 Joule raises the temperature of 1 cubic centimeter of the material by one degree Celsius); this is about $1/4$ the heat capacity of water. Assume the thickness of the heat-absorbing part of a transistor to be the same as its length and width.
(b) If each execution of an instruction raises the temperature, why doesn't the chip fry?

9.21. *History of JIT*: Study Brown's early JIT paper [52], entitled "Throw-away Compiling", and write a summary of it.

Part IV
Memory Management

Chapter 10
Explicit and Implicit Memory Management

All compilers and many run-time systems use dynamically sized data. The size of such data is not known in advance and room for it must be found at run time. Examples inside the compiler are symbol tables, strings from the source program, ASTs, register interference graphs for graph coloring, and many others. The examples in run-time systems derive from the nature of the source language: strings, dynamically sized arrays in imperative languages, closures in functional languages, tentative unifications in logic languages, and incoming messages in distributed languages are a few that come to mind.

There was a time when compiler writers could afford to allocate fixed amounts of memory for such data, for example 32 bytes for an identifier, and give an error message or even truncate the data, with or without warning, when the limit was exceeded. With the sometimes awkward memory structures and the limited memory management techniques of those days, such restrictions helped to simplify compiler writing. Also, available memories were so small that nobody expected to be able to use long identifiers or to compile large programs. With present memory sizes and better programming languages, techniques, and algorithms, both arguments have become void, and dynamic memory management is an integral part of both compilers and run-time systems.

When a program is started, most operating systems allocate at least the following three memory segments for it:

- the "code segment", which contains the program code and which is usually read-only or execute-only; it is addressed by the program counter and is next to invisible to the program code itself;
- the "stack segment", which contains the stack and which may come with an overflow and underflow detection mechanism; it is addressed by one or more stack pointers, which are most of the time manipulated automatically by machine instructions;
- the "data segment", which is a single contiguous stretch of memory locations, totally at the disposition of the program for the purpose of storing data; its start location and size are accessible to the program in some way and its contents are

addressable by machine instructions; its use is up to the programmer. When the emphasis is on memory management, the data segment is also called the **heap**.

Some operating systems allow more complicated and sometimes baroque architectures, but we will restrict ourselves to the simple case. Our main interest is in the data segment; we will use it for all our memory management. Usually there is an operating system command or system call to resize the data segment; if the segment has to be moved as a result of this, the operating system makes sure this move is transparent to the program.

It is the task of memory management to hand out and take back subsegments of the data segment in such a way that all subsegments fit inside the data segment and no memory location is ever part of more than one subsegment. These subsegments are usually called "blocks" or "chunks"; for a more precise definition of blocks and chunks see Section 10.1.1. Additional important objectives are that a request for memory should not be refused when there is still a possibility to fulfill it and that the amortized cost of obtaining and freeing memory should be constant or almost constant. See below for an explanation of the notion of "amortized cost". Memory allocation methods in the 1960s and '70s used to require a time proportional to the number of blocks handed out; this resulted in quadratic time requirements and limited the methods to some several thousands of blocks. This was no problem with the limited computer memories in those days but is unacceptable now, and more efficient methods are required.

Amortized costs

The **amortized cost** of steps in a sequence is the average cost of one step, averaged over a long enough period. If, for example, each step normally costs 1 unit but one in five costs 10 units, the amortized cost is 2.8 units, since that is the average per step in the long run.

This way of measuring costs is useful for situations in which we cannot prevent occasional steps from being much more expensive than usual. This is the case in algorithms that require occasional reorganization of their data; it also applies to buying a house.

Allocating memory in the heap is easy enough: we keep a pointer to the first free location in the heap, allocate the requested block from there, and bump the pointer to the next free location. The problem with this scheme is that sooner or later, we run out of heap space; if memory blocks are requested continually and no blocks are released, even the largest memory will fill up eventually. If we decide we want blocks to be released, a new question arises: who is responsible for the release?

The naive answer is "the programmer, of course", but that answer underestimates the complexity of the task: to perform deallocation correctly the programmer must be aware of the lifetime of every memory block, even in the most complicated data structures, and ensure that a block is released only once, and only after its last access.

Many programmers have experienced serious problems with this explicit deallocation. Freeing memory too early by mistake results in a **dangling pointer**, a pointer to freed and thus unprotected memory. Dereferencing such a pointer tends to have weird effects, which makes the error hard to detect and correct. In particular

- the dangling pointer may not be dereferenced until long after the memory has been freed erroneously, obscuring the relation between cause and effect;
- after dereferencing the dangling pointer, the program may proceed with the incorrect data for some time before an inconsistency is observed;
- the freed memory block may be allocated again and the program may accidentally modify the new contents through the dangling pointer;
- by writing under the dangling pointer the program may accidentally damage the administration of the memory manager, which may cause other allocations and deallocations to go wrong, compounding the problem;
- the error may be hard to reproduce, because the exact same sequence of memory allocations and deallocations may be required to cause the observed error; this is especially a problem in interactive systems.

Recent advances in static program analysis can mitigate these problems a bit. For example, Cherem, Princehouse and Rugina [59] describe a specialized control flow graph analysis technique which tracks allocated blocks through the program, to detect missing free() operations, which cause memory leaks, and premature free() operations, which cause dangling pointers.

In addition to the user allocating data, run-time systems often allocate data which have unpredictable lifetimes and of whose existence the programmer is not even aware; generating the freeing instructions for these data can be extremely difficult. Efforts to solve these problems have resulted in techniques for automatically releasing unused data by doing implicit deallocation.

In the following sections we will discuss techniques for data allocation with explicit deallocation by the programmer, and for data allocation with implicit deallocation. Implicit deallocation is usually called "garbage collection". Generally speaking, compilers deallocate their internal data explicitly (or not at all) and run-time systems leave the deallocation of user-allocated data to the user or the garbage collector. More in particular, almost all run-time systems for programs in the functional, logical, and more advanced paradigms feature garbage collectors. Garbage collectors are also used in many applications outside compiler construction. Examples are text editors, word processors, photo editors, and web browsers.

We will therefore discuss the techniques with explicit deallocation in a general and compiler setting and those with implicit deallocation in a run-time system setting.

10.1 Data allocation with explicit deallocation

In most systems, basic memory allocation comes in the form of a routine that finds a block of unused memory of the requested size, marks it as used, and returns a pointer to the block. If no such block is available, the result varies: a null pointer may be returned, an error routine may be called, or the program may be aborted. The requested size is given as a parameter to the routine; the marking prevents the block from being handed out more than once. A second routine can be used to return the block to the system. This routine may simply mark the block as not in use. The implementation of this marking varies; a bit map with one marking bit for each byte suggests itself, but other implementations are possible and perhaps equally usual.

This basic mechanism is available in C as the routines void *malloc (size_t size) and free (void *ptr). The void * construction is a trick to fake polymorphic pointers in C, and need not worry us here. We will discuss the workings of malloc() and free() below.

Although compilers are essentially just normal programs, they have enough in common to consider the allocation and deallocation problems of two classes of data types that are in great demand in compilers. These data types are *linked lists* and *extensible arrays*; both are used to implement sorted or unsorted sets or *bags*. A correct and efficient implementation of these data structures is of the utmost importance for the correctness and the efficiency of the compiler, which is why we will pay attention to them here.

It is true that some modern languages (notably the functional and logic languages, and Java) have automatic data allocation and deallocation mechanisms, but in practice almost all compilers are still written in a traditional language, for example C or C++. Data allocation and deallocation in these languages requires considerable care, and experience has shown that it is very advantageous in compiler writing to organize memory management properly and systematically.

10.1.1 Basic memory allocation

A memory allocation request of N bytes supplies the user with a pointer to the first byte of a block of N free bytes. The memory allocation process requires the block to be embedded in a more complicated data structure since some additional administration is necessary for each block. Memory fragments are called **blocks** if they are in the hands of the user, and **chunks** if they are handled by the memory allocator. A chunk contains a block plus some administration; this administration includes at least the length of the chunk and is usually located just before the block. A user-held pointer to a block points to the first byte available to the user; a chunk pointer points to the beginning of the chunk; in most implementations, there is a small constant difference between the two. Block pointers can occur in many places, including program variables, machine registers, and blocks on the heap. Chunk pointers occur only in chunk administrations, if at all.

The offset between chunk pointer and block pointer needs some attention on machines with alignment requirements (Section 8.1.4). A user who calls malloc() expects to obtain a pointer that is aligned properly for storing any data type in the language. This restricts the pointer to be divisible by the least common multiple of all data alignment requirements of the machine. In practice this means that the numerical value of the block pointer returned by malloc() must be a multiple of 8 or 16, and chunk addresses must be at least 8 or 16 bytes apart.

We will now consider the relation between chunks and the heap. The heap is carved up into a contiguous sequence of chunks, each chunk marked with its size. The last byte of one chunk is followed immediately by the first byte of the next chunk. Since the length of a chunk is known, one can find its end and thus the start of the next chunk. Pointers that reside inside a block are under user control and will point to the start of blocks or be null; pointers inside the allocation administration, if any, are under the control of the allocator and will point to chunks. A typical layout of chunks is shown in Figure 10.1. In addition to the chunk size field, we need a few bits in each chunk for administration purposes. One of the bits is a **free bit**, which indicates if a chunk is free. Usually the free chunks are chained together in a **free list**. On machines with alignment requirements, the size field must be aligned on an integer-alignment boundary; if we allocate 4 bytes for the field, it can probably include the administration bits. For the block pointer to come out on a 16-, 32-, or 64-byte boundary, the chunk must then be allocated on a 16-, 32-, or 64-byte boundary minus 4.

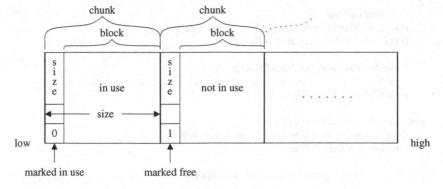

Fig. 10.1: Memory structure used by the malloc/free mechanism

We will now describe a naive implementation of a routine *Malloc(BlockSize)*; it is intuitively very simple and exhibits the basic principles, but is not good enough for practical use; optimizations will be suggested in the next subsection.

To allocate a block B of the required *BlockSize*, *Malloc* steps through the chunks until it finds a chunk C marked "free" that is large enough to accommodate B. The chunk C is then broken into two chunks C_1 and C_2, such that C_1 has the proper size for the block B—unless of course the block happens to fit exactly, in which case no chunk C_2 is created. Now the size fields of C_1 and C_2 are set to their new values, the free bit of C_1 is turned off, that of C_2 is turned on, and a pointer to the block in C_1 is returned to the requester.

To free a block pointed to by a given pointer, the free bit of the corresponding chunk is simply turned on.

If *Malloc* cannot find a chunk that is large enough it first tries to coalesce adjacent free chunks into larger chunks, by scanning the memory looking for such situations. If two adjacent free chunks C_1 and C_2 are found, the size of C_1 is set to the sum of the sizes of C_1 and C_2. The free bit of C_1 need not be modified since it is already set to free; neither do the administration fields in C_2 need adjustment since they are now out of reach of the allocator. This operation can also be performed during any other scan of memory, or upon freeing a block.

If this does not provide a sufficiently large chunk, *Malloc* calls a routine *SolveOutOfMemoryCondition()* in a last attempt to remedy the situation. Below we discuss some ways of obtaining additional memory that could be implemented in the routine *SolveOutOfMemoryCondition()*.

```
FirstChunkPointer ← BeginningOfAvailableMemory;
OnePastAvailableMemory ← BeginningOfAvailableMemory + SizeOfAvailableMemory;

FirstChunkPointer.size ← SizeOfAvailableMemory;
FirstChunkPointer.free ← True;

function Malloc (BlockSize) returning a polymorphic block pointer:
    Pointer ← PointerToFreeBlockOfSize (BlockSize);
    if Pointer ≠ NullPointer: return Pointer;

    CoalesceFreeChunks;
    Pointer ← PointerToFreeBlockOfSize (BlockSize);
    if Pointer ≠ NullPointer: return Pointer;

    SolveOutOfMemoryCondition (BlockSize);
    — if SolveOutOfMemoryCondition returns, there is at least BlockSize space
    return Malloc (BlockSize);

procedure Free (BlockPointer):
    ChunkPointer ← BlockPointer − AdministrationSize;
    ChunkPointer.free ← True;
```

Fig. 10.2: A basic implementation of *Malloc(BlockSize)*

Outline code for the basic *Malloc* is given in Figures 10.2 and 10.3. The pointer *OnePastAvailableMemory* points to the first byte past the end of available memory. This is a useful pointer, but if memory extends to the last byte of addressable memory it may not be representable; in that case additional trickery is needed. The code assumes that data can be accessed at any alignment; if this is not supported by a given machine, the computation of *RequestedChunkSize* in Figure 10.3 must be modified to take the alignment requirements into account (alignment requirements are discussed in Section 8.1.4).

The implementation of the routine *SolveOutOfMemoryCondition()* depends on the system. If the basic memory allocation system coexists with a garbage collector that uses the same chunk structure, the routine can call it, in an attempt to find unused chunks that have not been freed. If this frees space for at least *BlockSize* bytes, *SolveOutOfMemoryCondition()* has succeeded and can return safely.

Another option is to try to increase the amount of memory allotted to the program. The *Malloc* algorithm as stated assumes that the value of *OnePastAvailableMemory* is fixed for any one run of the program, but actually many operating systems feature requests to reset this value and thus extend or restrict the amount of memory available to the program. After all, our memory allocation system is a client to a more basic memory allocation system, that of the operating system. Such requests to bump *OnePastAvailableMemory* can be issued at any moment the routine *PointerToFreeBlockOfSize(BlockSize)* fails to find a block, and it is tempting to do so at the first possible occasion, to avoid the work of coalescing blocks or doing garbage collection. The problem is, however, that some operating systems will extend the available memory almost indefinitely but implement this by supplying paged or virtual memory, which resides completely or partially on disk and is correspondingly slow. Also, operating systems may lower the priority of programs that hog large amounts of memory. It is difficult to give generally applicable advice on this issue, since the final efficiency of the memory allocator depends on three factors, two of which are unknown: the memory allocator itself, the way the program uses it, and the operating system.

The important rules are that *SolveOutOfMemoryCondition()* should not return unless enough memory has been freed, nor should it give up as long as there is one possibility left to continue.

10.1.2 Optimizations for basic memory allocation

There are two efficiency problems with the above implementation; both lie with the free list. First, finding a suitable chunk in the free list requires linear search through the entire memory, which is unacceptable. Second, coalescing is done in a separate phase, performed only when the usual linear search fails; this makes the performance of the algorithm irregular.

The simplest approach to the first problem is to chain the free chunks in a linked list; the link pointers can be accommodated in the unused space following the ad-

```
function PointerToFreeBlockOfSize (BlockSize) returning a polymorphic block pointer:
    -- Note that this is not a pure function: it may split chunks
    ChunkPointer ← FirstChunkPointer;
    RequestedChunkSize ← AdministrationSize + BlockSize;

    while ChunkPointer ≠ OnePastAvailableMemory:
        if ChunkPointer.free:
            LeftOverSize ← ChunkPointer.size – RequestedChunkSize;
            if LeftOverSize >= 0:
                -- large enough chunk found:
                SplitChunk (ChunkPointer, RequestedChunkSize);
                ChunkPointer.free ← False;
                return ChunkPointer + AdministrationSize;
        -- try next chunk:
        ChunkPointer ← ChunkPointer + ChunkPointer.size;
    return NullPointer;

procedure SplitChunk (ChunkPointer, RequestedChunkSize):
    LeftOverSize ← ChunkPointer.size – RequestedChunkSize;
    if LeftOverSize > AdministrationSize:
        -- there is a non-empty left-over chunk
        ChunkPointer.size ← RequestedChunkSize;
        LeftOverChunkPointer ← ChunkPointer + RequestedChunkSize;
        LeftOverChunkPointer.size ← LeftOverSize;
        LeftOverChunkPointer.free ← True;

procedure CoalesceFreeChunks:
    ChunkPointer ← FirstChunkPointer;

    while ChunkPointer ≠ OnePastAvailableMemory:
        if ChunkPointer.free:
            CoalesceWithAllFollowingFreeChunks (ChunkPointer);
        ChunkPointer ← ChunkPointer + ChunkPointer.size;

procedure CoalesceWithAllFollowingFreeChunks (ChunkPointer):
    NextChunkPointer ← ChunkPointer + ChunkPointer.size;
    while NextChunkPointer ≠ OnePastAvailableMemory
          and NextChunkPointer.free:
        -- Coalesce them:
        ChunkPointer.size ← ChunkPointer.size + NextChunkPointer.size;
        NextChunkPointer ← ChunkPointer + ChunkPointer.size;
```

Fig. 10.3: Auxiliary routines for the basic *Malloc(BlockSize)*

ministration area. Chunks can still be split as explained above; chunks that are freed can be prepended to the list. We have thus replaced linear search through all chunks by linear search through the free chunks. This is some improvement, but is likely not to be enough.

A more sophisticated implementation classifies the free chunks according to size and keeps a free list for each interval. Intervals could for example be defined by the powers of 2, and separate linked lists could be kept for all free chunks with sizes between 2^n and $2^{n+1} - 1$, for a sensible set of values of n. Now, when a block is requested of size s, we determine a k such that $2^{k-1} < s <= 2^k$. We now find the linked list for chunks of sizes 2^k through $2^{k+1} - 1$; if that list is empty, we try the list for 2^{k+1} through $2^{k+2} - 1$, and so on, until we find one that is not empty. The first block in that list is guaranteed to have enough room, so allocation takes place in (almost) constant time. The chunk left over in the allocation must of course be linked into the free list of its interval; this can be done in constant time too. The interval boundaries do not need to be powers of 2; depending on the application, a different increasing sequence can be more useful.

Coalescing can be done on the fly, during each call of *Free* if we have easy access to the chunk preceding the one being freed; the one following it is already within easy reach, using the size of the chunk being freed. This access can be obtained simply by copying the size information of each chunk at its end, where it can be found by the *Free* operation. Of course, this duplicate size information costs additional space and must be maintained by all other operations on the chunks.

By combining these two optimizations, a very efficient memory allocator can be constructed. The combination of the two optimizations is not entirely trivial since a chunk being freed may be merged with the preceding and/or following chunks, depending on which of them is free. The surrounding free chunk or chunks must then be detached from their respective free lists, and the chunk resulting from the merge must be inserted in its proper free list.

10.1.3 Compiler applications of basic memory allocation

We will now turn to two special applications of memory allocation in a compiler, linked lists and extensible arrays.

10.1.3.1 Linked lists

Linked lists are used for many purposes in a compiler: identifier lists, symbol tables, string storage, syntax trees, code fragments, etc. The C compiler from the Amsterdam Compiler Kit ACK [271] contains 25 different list types and the Orca compiler contains 17; for Orca, see Bal, Kaashoek and Tanenbaum [27].

Records in these linked lists are added and removed at irregular intervals, and a naive implementation is to request them one by one from the standard memory manager, for example malloc(), and return them using free(). Much efficiency can be gained by batching these records in blocks rather than allocating them one by one. A separate set of blocks is allocated and maintained for each record type T. Each block is an array of a fixed number of records and is obtained from the standard memory manager; suitable sizes are 16 or 32 records per block. A free list is maintained linking the free records in the blocks.

Initially, the system starts with zero blocks and an empty free list. The first allocation request for a record of type T finds the free list empty, allocates a block of type ARRAY OF T, creates a free list linking the free records using the space in the same free records, and hands out the first record. Subsequent allocation requests normally obtain their records directly from the free list, which speeds up the memory management considerably.

Records can be returned to this system and are then reattached to the free list. Blocks are never returned to the standard memory manager. In principle they could be, if an entire block came to consist of free records only, but detecting such an event would require much more administration and the total gain would be limited, as observed in Exercise 10.5.

```
FreeListForT ← NoT;

function NewT () returning a pointer to a T:
    if FreeListForT = NoT:
        — Acquire a new block of records:
        NewBlock [1 .. BlockFactorForT] ← Malloc (SizeOfT × BlockFactorForT);
        — Construct a free list in NewBlock:
        FreeListForT ← address of NewBlock [1];
        for i in [1 .. BlockFactorForT – 1]:
            NewBlock [i].link ← address of NewBlock [i + 1];
        NewBlock [BlockFactorForT].link ← NoT;

    — Extract a new record from the free list:
    NewRecord ← FreeListForT;
    FreeListForT ← NewRecord.link;

    — Zero the NewRecord here, if required
    return NewRecord;

procedure FreeT (OldRecord):
    — Prepend OldRecord to free list:
    OldRecord.link ← FreeListForT;
    FreeListForT ← address of OldRecord;
```

Fig. 10.4: Outline code for blockwise allocation of records of type T

Figure 10.4 shows outline code for the routines *NewT()* and *FreeT(OldRecord)*. The global variable *FreeListForT* is used to hold the beginning of the linked list of free records. When a new record is requested, *FreeListForT* is tested to see if a free record is available. If it is not, a new block is requested from *Malloc()* and the records in the newly obtained block are linked into the free list, which is then no longer empty. The requested record can now be unlinked from the head of the free list, possibly zeroed, and a pointer to it be delivered to the caller. The routine *FreeT ()* links the record to be freed back into the free list; the record is not marked or cleared in any way and if the program uses the pointer to it afterwards, chaos will ensue. The structure of the free list, as it winds through the allocated blocks, is sketched in Figure 10.5.

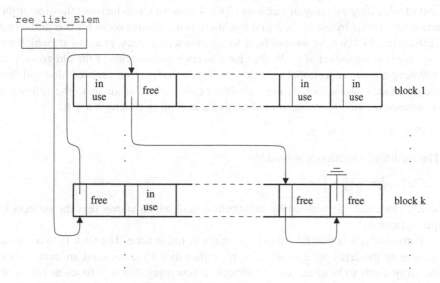

Fig. 10.5: List of free records in allocated blocks

The free list is constructed using *link* fields in the records; since the links are present only in free records, they do not need allocation space of their own and can be stored in the records, in the same space where user data resides when the record is in use. This technique requires the records to be at least as large as a link pointer, a condition that is almost certainly fulfilled for records used in a compiler. It will be clear that this code can easily be generated automatically for all record types T used in dynamic allocation in the compiler or in the compiled program.

10.1.3.2 Extensible arrays

An **extensible array** is an array to which elements can be added at the high-index end. Extensible arrays are used in several places in a compiler: in hash tables; while reading and storing input the length of which is not known in advance; while constructing executable program images in the assembler; etc. Their use in run-time systems is perhaps less common but not exceptional; one application is the *event queue* in simulation programs, when this queue is maintained by *heap sort*. Extensible arrays have advantages over linked lists when random access is needed, or when the elements are small, never change their order, or are never freed again. For example, storing the characters of a string in an extensible array is much more attractive than storing them in a linked list.

The simple-minded approach to extensible arrays would be to first allocate an array of reasonable size, and then, when the array turns out to be too small, to extend it with a reasonable increment, and to repeat this process as needed. Doing so, however, yields a quadratic algorithm, as can be seen as follows. We write the cost of allocating an array of size n as $C(n)$. When we try to increase the size of the array, say with μ bytes, we will find that there is not always room for this at the end of the array. In that case we will have to allocate a new array, at a cost α, which we suppose is independent of n. We then have to copy the contents of the old array; this will have a cost proportional to n, say γn. In C, the function realloc() does all this for us; other systems usually have similar facilities. This leads us to the following recurrence relation for the cost of obtaining a new array of length $n + \mu$:

$$C(n + \mu) = C(n) + \alpha + \gamma n$$

The recurrence relation is solved by

$$C(n) = \tfrac{\gamma}{2\mu} n^2 + (\tfrac{\alpha}{\mu} - \tfrac{\gamma}{2}) n$$

which can easily be verified by substitution, and which shows that the process is quadratic in n.

Fortunately, it *is* possible to extend arrays in linear time. The trick is to increase the size of the array by a constant factor rather than by a constant amount. When the array needs to be extended, we allocate a new array that is β times as big, with $\beta > 1$. Again, this allocation has constant cost α. We then copy the contents of the old array into the new array, at cost γn. This yields the recurrence relation

$$C(\beta n) = C(n) + \alpha + \gamma n$$

which has the solution

$$C(n) = \tfrac{\gamma}{\beta - 1} n + \tfrac{\alpha}{\ln(\beta)} \ln(n)$$

This can again be verified by substitution, and shows that the process indeed requires time linear in n; the logarithmic term is negligible. Intuitively speaking, each reallocation takes β times longer than the previous one, but the results last β times longer.

A disadvantage of almost any scheme for extensible arrays is that sooner or later the array has to be moved. Consequently, no pointers can be kept to entries in the array, and accessing elements of the array using an index involves loading the address of the array first rather than using a fixed starting location. Fortunately, the C syntax allows the same construction for both situations: it is "referentially transparent" in this case since the indexing construct A[i] will work both if A is a fixed allocated array of type T and if A is a pointer to a dynamically allocated array of type T.

The basic allocation scheme embodied by malloc() and free(), the linked list allocation, and the extensible array technique all have one thing in common: deallocation is explicitly indicated by the user. Explicit deallocation is a problem, though, for programmer and compiler alike. We will now turn to automatic methods that remove the need for explicit deallocation.

10.1.4 Embedded-systems considerations

Computer memory is cheap enough these days for many embedded systems to have sufficient memory to allow the standard memory allocation techniques to be applied. But it is often the case that as soon as technology has given us "enough" of something, two kinds of applications come along, one that requires even more, and one that forces us to make do with much, much less. An example of the latter is a **Wireless Sensor Network** (**WSN**), a collection of very small computers that through sensors inspect their environments, correlate their findings with their neighbors, and when necessary report to some higher-up computer.

It may seem that for such a tiny embedded system static memory allocation is enough: if communicating with 10 WSN neighbors is sufficient, just statically allocate 10 records. But even such systems may receive variable-length messages, which must be stored for further processing. A good way to handle such variable-length messages is to cut them into fixed-length segments of say 14 or 30 bytes, append a two-byte link to the next segment or a zero to indicate termination, and store the segments in a linked-list data structure like the one described in Section 10.1.3.1.

A different problem occurs when the embedded system has a reasonable amount of memory and is programmed in Java or another language that uses a garbage collector. If such a system has to obey real-time requirements we may wish to avoid activating the garbage collector to prevent unacceptable delays. But Java has no possibility to switch off the garbage collector, and even if it had, it would not solve the problem: memory would fill up and the application would stop. The problem can be "solved" by implementing a simplified form of malloc/free, as follows.

It is typical of real-time applications that the number of classes they regularly allocate objects from is very small. These "hot" classes are extended with two methods, create() and destroy(). Rather than creating the object through new, using it, and then leaving it to the garbage collector, the program creates it through create(), uses it, and then destroys it, as with malloc/free. When an object is destroyed, destroy() puts it in a free list. The method create() first checks the free list, and if it contains an object, it retrieves it; if not, it allocates a new object using new.

This technique is called **object pooling**. If a program has only one hot class, then after a warm-up period the free list will often have an element available, new will be called only rarely, and garbage collection will be almost entirely avoided. For programs with more than one hot class, the technique approximates this situation.

The use of destroy() partially reintroduces the problems of manual deallocation, but in a more limited form: destroy() applies to one or at most a few classes only, and Java is easier to analyse than most languages. Mohamed and Al-Jaroodi [193] describe a technique to semi-automatically insert calls to the destroy() method.

10.2 Data allocation with implicit deallocation

Implicit deallocation, or **garbage collection** as it is usually called, is the automatic reclamation of memory that is no longer in use by the application program. Programming systems that offer garbage collection relieve the programmer from the error-prone task of reclaiming memory manually by using an explicit free() primitive. Correctly freeing blocks in handwritten code requires a considerable insight into the dynamics of the program. Correctly freeing blocks in generated code is often not feasible, due to the unpredictable lifetimes of the allocated data structures. Therefore, garbage collection is considered to be an important feature of modern programming systems, which reduces programming efforts considerably.

Examples of programming systems that offer garbage collection are object-oriented languages like Java and Smalltalk, functional languages like ML and Haskell, logic languages like Prolog, and scripting languages like awk and Perl.

10.2.1 Basic garbage collection algorithms

In principle, the objective of garbage collection is to reclaim automatically the set of memory chunks that will no longer be used by the program, the **garbage set**. Since, however, no automatic method can determine what the program is going to do, this ideal is in the general case unattainable. Two practical approximations for the garbage set are "the set of all chunks to which there are no pointers", and "the set of all chunks that are not reachable from the non-heap-allocated program data". It will be clear that no chunk in either of these sets can be in use in the program, so these approximations are safe. The "no-pointers" criterion leads to a technique called *reference counting*, and the "not-reachable" criterion is exemplified in this chapter by two techniques, *mark and scan* and *two-space copying*. The three techniques are all very different:

- Reference counting directly identifies garbage chunks. It is simple and reasonably efficient but requires all pointer actions to be monitored during program execution and may not recover all garbage chunks.
- Mark and scan identifies reachable chunks and concludes that the rest is garbage. It is reasonably efficient and does not require pointer monitoring, but is quite complicated. It is the only algorithm that will recover all available memory.
- Two-space copying is not concerned with garbage. It copies the reachable chunks from a memory region called "from-space" to a memory region called "to-space"; the remaining space in to-space is a single free chunk. It is very efficient,

does not require pointer monitoring and is moderately complicated but wastes half of the memory.

Once garbage chunks have been identified by these techniques they must be turned into free memory space to be useful. Garbage chunks found by reference counting or mark and scan must be returned to the free list by the algorithm. Two-space copying automatically creates a fresh free list consisting of a single large chunk that includes all of free memory.

Locating all free chunks and adding them to the free list is not always enough, since it leaves the free memory fragmented in a number of free chunks separated by chunks in use. This phenomenon is called **memory fragmentation**. If the user requests a chunk with a size that is larger than the largest chunk in the free list, the memory allocator will be unable to supply that chunk, even though the total size of free memory may be larger or even much larger than the request. To obtain the free memory in its most valuable form, a single free chunk, we need to do *compaction*. Compaction moves the used chunks to one side, thereby moving the free chunks to the other side, creating a single large free chunk. Compaction is more complicated and time-consuming than just freeing the garbage chunks, but it avoids fragmentation and is the best way to recover all unused memory.

The main problem with compaction is that it involves moving reachable chunks, which may contain pointers to other chunks which are also moved. Needless to say, this has to be orchestrated carefully; a technique for doing so is explained in Section 10.2.6. Reference counting and mark and scan can optionally be followed by a compaction phase; two-space copying does compaction automatically.

Garbage collection algorithms come in three varieties:

- **One-shot**: the garbage collector is started, runs to completion while in full control of all chunks, and then returns, leaving behind a hopefully improved situation. Since the garbage collector is in full control when it runs, it can be fairly simple, but its unexpected activation can be disruptive. This is not much of a problem inside compilers, but it may be so inside application programs, especially interactive ones.

- **On-the-fly** (also called **incremental**): some garbage collector actions are performed at each call of *Malloc* and/or *Free*. These actions make some local modifications to the chunk structure to increase the probability of finding a free chunk when needed. On-the-fly garbage collectors are usually much more difficult to construct than one-shot garbage collectors, but are smoother and less disruptive in their operation. Also, they may still need a one-shot garbage collector as backup for situations in which they cannot cope with the demand.

- **Concurrent**: the garbage collector runs on a second processor, different from the one that runs the program. It runs continuously and concurrently, and tries to keep memory garbage-free. Unfortunately, concurrent garbage collection is sometimes also called on-the-fly, in spite of the fact that this term suggests one agent rather than two.

Reference counting garbage collection is an on-the-fly algorithm. On-the-fly and concurrent variants of mark and scan garbage collection have been known since the late 1970s [35, 85], but have not seen wide application. We will restrict ourselves here to reference counting and the one-shot variants of mark and scan and two-space copying.

Garbage collection needs considerable preparation and support in the compiler, which will be treated in the next section. We will then discuss the three garbage collection techniques mentioned above: reference counting, mark and scan, and two-space copying (Sections 10.2.3 to 10.2.5), followed by an explanation of compaction (Section 10.2.6). It has been found advantageous to restrict most of the garbage collection activations to the most recently allocated set of chunks, the newest generation. A discussion of this optimizing approach, called "generational garbage collection" (Section 10.2.7), concludes this section and this chapter.

10.2.2 Preparing the ground

A chunk is only reachable by the program if the program directly has a pointer to it or can use a pointer to reach the chunk indirectly. The pointers that are directly available to the program can be located in various places, depending on the implementation. These places may include the global variables, local variables, routine parameters, registers, and perhaps others. We will use the term **program data area** for the non-heap memory that is directly accessible to the program code. The set of pointers in the program data area will be referred to as the **root set**. It should be noted that the root set is a conceptual notion rather than a data structure; it is the set of all pointers in the program data area, not a list of their values. The root set is usually not implemented directly but is conceptually present in the program code of the garbage collector.

The pointers in the root set may point to chunks in the heap, which is under control of the garbage collector; such chunks are then reachable. Reachable chunks in the heap can, of course, contain pointers that point to other chunks in the heap, which are then reachable as well.

This decomposes the problem of finding all reachable chucks—and so the problem of garbage collection—into three subproblems:

1. determining the root set by finding all pointers in the program data area, with their types;
2. finding all pointers in a given chunk, with their types;
3. finding *all* reachable chunks using the information of 1 and 2.

Subproblems 1 and 2 require knowledge of the pointer layout of the program data area and of each chunk type. The garbage collector needs compiler support for this; techniques to supply the required information are covered in the next section. Solutions to subproblem 3 constitute the garbage collection algorithms proper, and are usually implemented as run-time system routines.

A constellation of a root set and a heap with reachable and unreachable chunks is shown in Figure 10.6; chunks a and c are reachable from the root set, d and f are reachable from the heap through a and c respectively, and chunks b and e are unreachable. The first pointer from c points into the program data area.

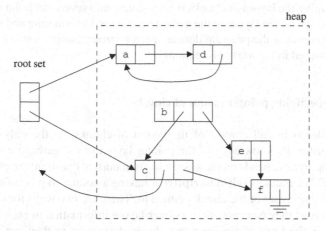

Fig. 10.6: A root set and a heap with reachable and unreachable chunks

Reference counting, which is not based on the concept of reachable chunks, does not require a root set, but it must still be able to find all pointers in a given chunk.

Since the garbage collector will, in principle, follow any pointer, there is still another requirement that the code generated by the compiler has to obey: all pointers must be **valid** which means that they must point to locations the garbage collector can again interpret. This property is usually ensured by the language definition and the compiler. Pointer validity is also called **pointer consistency**.

10.2.2.1 Compiler assistance to garbage collection

The compiler has to provide the root set and information about the pointer layout of each chunk to the garbage collector; the **pointer layout** of a chunk C describes the position of each pointer P in the chunk, together with the type of the chunk that P points to. The compiler also has to make sure that all reachable pointers, both in the program data area and in the heap, are valid when the garbage collector is activated. Providing the root set requires knowledge of the pointer layout of the program data area, and it was already clear that we also need the pointer layout of each chunk type.

Achieving pointer validity is relatively simple. A pointer can only be invalid when it is uninitialized or when it has been ruined by assigning a bad pointer value to it. If the compiler makes sure that each newly allocated pointer of type pointer to T is initialized correctly, no bad pointer values of the type pointer to T can arise. If the source language is type-secure, no values of other types can be assigned to a pointer to type T, and pointer validity is assured. If the source language is not type-secure, pointer validity cannot be achieved and garbage collection can only be based on the pessimistic assumptions of conservative garbage collection; conservative garbage collection is briefly described below in this section.

Determining the layout of chunks is very simple and several techniques are available for specifying the layout to the garbage collector. Determining and maintaining the pointer layout of the program data area can be troublesome, however. Both subjects are covered in the next two sections.

10.2.2.2 Specifying pointer layout of chunks

The compiler is in full control of the layout of chunks, so the only problem is how to transfer the knowledge of the pointer layout to the garbage collector. The method employed depends on the answer to an important question: are chunks "self-descriptive"? A chunk is **self-descriptive** if having a pointer to it is sufficient to obtain the pointer layout of the chunk pointed to. There are two ways for chunks to be self-descriptive: they can carry their pointer layout information in each copy, either directly or in the form of a pointer to a shared descriptor, or they can all have the same layout. The latter situation arises for example in Lisp interpreters, in which each chunk consists of exactly two pointers, one to the car field and one to the cdr field of the Lisp cell.

There are several ways to make the pointer layout of chunks available to the garbage collector.

- The compiler can generate a bit map for each chunk type, specifying which words inside a chunk of that type are pointers to other chunks. With this method, chunks must be self-descriptive, since just having the pointer must be sufficient for the garbage collector to continue. So each chunk must either contain its bit map or a pointer to its bit map. This method requires the collector to interpret the bit map, which might be too expensive.
- The compiler can generate a specific routine for each chunk type, which calls a garbage collector routine passed as a parameter for each pointer inside the chunk. This method avoids the run-time interpretation of bit maps and the need for self-description, since the code can pass the type of the chunk together with the pointer to the garbage collector routine. It also makes handling any chunk of a type that does not contain pointers a null operation, probably a useful optimization. A problem with this method is that such routines tend to be recursive, in which case they require an undetermined amount of stack space, which may or may not be available when the garbage collector is activated. This is one of the rare cases where a significant portion of the run-time system can be generated automatically.
- The compiler can organize the chunks to start off with an array containing all pointers, followed by the other data types. With this organization, the collector only has to know the location of the pointer array and the total number of pointers inside the chunk. If the pointer array is the first field and the total number of

pointers is stored in the chunk's administration, the chunk is self-descriptive at low cost.

Collecting the pointers inside a consecutive region is the most efficient method since it requires the fewest cross calls between compiled code and collector. The language definition may, however, not allow the reorganization of the data items inside a chunk.

In addition to the pointer layout, the collector has to know the size of each chunk. Similar considerations as with the pointer layout apply.

The technique of specifying the pointer layout by routine is described extensively by Goldberg [106], for a strongly typed source language.

10.2.2.3 Specifying the pointer layout of the program data area

The root set is usually supplied by running a library routine that scans the program data area and calls a specific garbage collection routine for each pointer the program data area contains. It is then up to the specific garbage collection routine to see if the pointer is interesting and perform the proper actions. To perform its task, the library routine must be able to find all pointers in the program data area, with their types, and be sure each pointer is valid; in short, it needs the pointer layout of the program data area. The problem is that the pointer layout of the program data area, unlike that of chunks, is complicated and dynamically variable.

The program data area usually consists of the global data area and a stack holding one or more stack frames or activation records. The pointer layout of the global data area is known and constant, although it may be distributed over several source program modules. To know the pointer layout of the stack, the garbage collector has to know which activation records it contains, and what the pointer layout of each activation record is. Both pieces of information are dynamic, so activation records must be self-describing. This is, however, easier said than done: the contents of the activation records change dynamically.

The main obstacles to a pointer-valid program data area of known layout are the working stacks and parameter lists under construction which may occur in the activation records. Working stacks may contain pointers in dynamically differing places and of dynamically differing types depending on the progress of the program, and parameter lists do not correspond to a data type in the language. Also, parameters lists are sometimes constructed on the working stack, which combines the problems.

In both cases the solution lies in defining anonymous data types for all structures that can occur, and keeping track of which one is current. For example, the parameter list of a routine with three formal parameters

```
PROCEDURE Three_Parameters (
    I : integer,
    Tp: treePointer,
    Gp: graphPointer
)
```

can be described by a record type

```
TYPE _anonymous_0001:
   I : integer,
   Tp: treePointer,
   Gp: graphPointer;
```

To get guaranteed pointer validity, the record must be allocated in its entirety before the actual parameters are evaluated, and the pointers in it must be set to null; they are then updated as the actual parameters are obtained. Adding this feature to an existing compiler may require considerable work.

The same technique must be used for the working stack but there the situation is worse: whereas parameter lists are fixed and appear in the program in the form of formal parameter lists, the data structures that appear on the working stack are the results of pushes and pops generated by the code generator, after it has optimized the target code. One source of relief in this awkward situation is that pointer validity is only required at points where the garbage collector can indeed be activated; this is at an explicit use of an allocator and at a routine call. Fortunately, these are exactly the points at which a code generator tends to make sure that all values from registers are stored safely in memory. So we only have to define anonymous data types for the working stack configurations at these points. Still, for a large routine with many expressions that manipulate pointers, this can amount to a considerable number of anonymous data types. Also, the actual data type of the working stack has to be updated at run time.

Similar techniques can be used for data structures with dynamically changing types, for example unions.

Another approach to pointers in the working stack can be followed in implementations in which the working stack is used only to implement expressions. The technique is simple: make sure the working stack is always empty when a garbage collector activation can occur. In fact, it has to be empty when any call occurs, since any call might in the end cause a call to the garbage collector to be made. To achieve this situation, all calls, and all other actions that can have side effects are moved to positions before the expression, using temporary variables. For example, an expression

```
a := (b := c(3)) + d(new Tree);
```

in which the assignment (:=) inside the expression yields the value assigned and new is the record allocator, is transformed into

```
b := c(3);
t1 := new Tree;
t2 := d(t1);
a := (b) + t2;
```

In effect, the "difficult" part of the working stack has been moved to the local variable stack. Since the data type of the local variable stack is constant for a given routine, only one anonymous data type needs to be generated.

Some languages and compilers just cannot supply the pointer layout information and consistency required by garbage collection. An example of such a language is C, in which in principle any piece of data can be stored in any type of variable by using the proper cast. To accommodate such languages and such compilers, another approach to the pointer layout and consistency problem has been devised. In this approach any sequence of bytes in the program data area and the heap that contains a value that could represent a valid pointer is taken to be a valid pointer.

Once this drastic idea has sunk in, two things will become clear. The first is that some recognized pointers may actually be fake. This has two consequences: we have to be very careful in following pointers; and we may occasionally reach a chunk by accident that could not have been reached by following correct pointers. This may cause subsequent algorithms to retain chunks that could be freed. The second is that if all pointers to non-free chunks indeed reside in the program data area and the heap, we will find all non-free chunks. This prevents the algorithm from freeing chunks that should be retained.

This approach is known as **conservative garbage collection**, since it conserves at least as many chunks as it should and probably more; the idea was introduced by Boehm and Weiser [46]. Its implementation requires considerable care; pitfalls are discussed by Wentworth [296] and Boehm [45]. It has been applied successfully in some systems, see for example Moreau and Zendra [194], but should probably still be regarded as experimental, and we will not discuss it any further here.

10.2.2.4 Some simplifying assumptions

Garbage collection is an old and mature subject and many techniques, ranging from straightforward to ingenious to downright sneaky, have been invented in the course of time. A full treatment of garbage collectors could easily fill a book (at least one such book exists, Jones and Lins [136]), so we will make a number of simplifying assumptions for the benefit of the following discussion.

We assume that the garbage collector operates on the same memory structure as and in cooperation with the simple malloc/free mechanism described in Section 10.1.1. We also assume that it is possible both to free blocks explicitly and to have them freed automatically by a garbage collector. This is useful in implementations in which the run-time system itself uses allocated blocks and knows when to free them safely; it also allows the garbage collector to free blocks through this mechanism, thus decreasing the complexity of the garbage collector.

Even with our simplified malloc/free model, the following constitutes an outline only; several issues are swept under the rug. For one thing we assume that all pointers point to the beginning of chunks—or at least to a fixed position inside of them. In some languages the programmer can construct a pointer to a field inside a record; it must then be possible to reconstruct from such a pointer the pointer to the allocated chunk into which it points.

Actual garbage collectors arc full of details required by the peculiarities of the data types of the implemented language, including arrays, unions, and sets of types that may contain pointers. And last, and in this case probably least, in addition to data pointers the administrative pointers that connect activation records must be followed. These pointers are essential especially in functional languages and in imperative languages that feature coroutines, functions as first-class citizens, or tasks.

We also assume that all chunks are self-descriptive, either because they have enough information in them to retrieve the pointer layout, or because they all have the same structure. The algorithms below can usually be reworked easily to operate on non-self-descriptive data, but some benefits of the algorithm may be lost in the process.

As said, the discussion below is concerned with the basic algorithms only, which are relatively simple; actual garbage collectors tend to be complicated and hairy, and, which is worse, error prone. The reasons for this additional complexity are twofold.

The first is that the basic algorithms assume the user data to consist of chunks of known size and type, with all pointers initialized. Worse, many memory management publications use a model in which chunks are all of the same type and in which the heap and the program data area have the same uniform structure. Reality is different. Actual languages have uninitialized pointers, arrays of dynamically alterable size, unions which have dynamic types some of which may contain pointers, exception handlers which may invalidate assumptions about what is on the working stack, tasks that may update data structures concurrently, and other complications. Also the structures of the program data area and the heap are usually vastly different. There is no fundamental reason why all these complications could not be incorporated correctly in an existing garbage collection algorithm, but doing so requires considerable care and increases the complexity of the code.

The second reason is that garbage collection is intuitively considered a waste of valuable computer cycles by many users, and there is pressure on the compiler writer to optimize the garbage collector heavily. Given the baroque structure of the data types in most languages, there is indeed often room for spectacular optimization; for example, knowing that an array consists of elements that do not contain pointers and so does not need to be scanned will improve the speed of the garbage collector.

Also, the target code optimizer may optimize away code that is essential for the garbage collector. It may, for example, decide in a late stage that it can hold a variable in a register all the time and delete all memory accesses to the location reserved for it. This leaves an uninitialized pointer location, which will derail the garbage collector, unless the pointer layout is also updated. Again, this can all be programmed correctly, but tends to heap complication on complication. Each optimization, both of the garbage collector *and* of the generated code, is a threat to garbage collection correctness, and has to be designed and implemented with the utmost care.

Garbage collectors are notoriously difficult to debug, since they do surgery on the nervous system of the running program—the pointers in the activation records and in user data structures in the heap. For the same reason, a bug in the garbage collector will cause unpredictable and incomprehensible failure of the user program. Conversely, once a compiler has a name of having a buggy garbage collector, any failure of any user program using the compiler will first be blamed on the garbage collector, before any other source of error is considered. Even more than is the case with other parts of a compiler, it is important to get a garbage collector right before making it fast.

We will now turn to the actual garbage collection algorithms.

10.2.3 Reference counting

Reference counting is an intuitive garbage collection algorithm that records in each chunk the number of pointers that point to it; when the number drops to zero the chunk can be declared garbage; in a literal sense, reference counting collects garbage, unlike the other garbage collection algorithms, which actually collect reachable chunks. In line with the name "reference counting", we will call pointers "references" in this section.

The reference count is updated in several actions on the chunk. When a chunk is allocated from the heap, its reference count is initialized to one. Whenever a reference to the chunk is duplicated, its reference count is increased by one ("incremented"). Likewise, whenever a reference to the chunk is deleted, its reference count is decreased by one ("decremented"). If the reference count drops to 0, the chunk can be freed because it is no longer reachable. Figure 10.7 shows a heap with a number of chunks with reference counts and the references connecting them; some references come from the global data area. Note that there are no chunks with reference count 0.

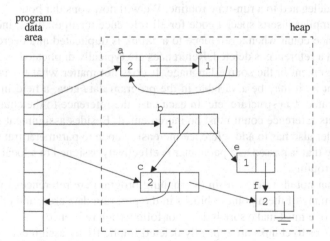

Fig. 10.7: Chunks with reference count in a heap

Simply returning the chunk with a zero reference count to the free list is not enough to reclaim all garbage, since it may contain references to other chunks that may now become garbage as well. For example, by deleting the reference to chunk b in Figure 10.7, chunk e also becomes garbage, but f remains in use, since there is still one reference left and its reference count does not drop to 0. The resulting constellation is shown in Figure 10.8.

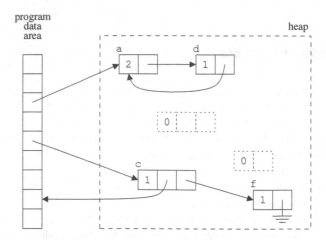

Fig. 10.8: Result of removing the reference to chunk b in Figure 10.7

The two main issues in implementing reference counting are keeping track of all reference manipulations and recursively freeing chunks with zero reference count. The compiler plays an important role in keeping track of references; the recursive freeing is delegated to a run-time routine. We will now consider both.

The compiler inserts special code for all reference manipulations: incrementing the reference count when a reference to a chunk is duplicated and decrementing it when such a reference is deleted. References are typically duplicated as an effect of some assignment in the source language. It does not matter what the target of the assignment is: it may be a variable in the program data area, a field in a dynamically allocated data structure, etc. In each case the reference to the chunk is duplicated, so its reference count must be incremented. Besides assignment statements, the compiler also has to add reference increasing code to parameter transfers, since a reference that is passed as a parameter is effectively assigned to a local variable of the called routine.

Note that not all references in the running program are references to chunks on the heap; many of them point to blocks in the program data area, and all reference-counting code must make sure it does not follow such references.

References to chunks are typically deleted implicitly by assignment statements. An assignment to a reference variable overwrites the current reference with a new value, so before installing the new reference the reference count of the chunk addressed by the current reference should be decremented. Figure 10.9 shows an outline of the code that must be generated for the pointer assignment p:=q; when performing reference counting.

```
if Points into the heap (q):
    Increment q.referenceCount;
if Points into the heap (p):
    Decrement p.referenceCount;
    if p.referenceCount = 0:
        FreeRecursivelyDependingOnReferenceCounts (p);
p ← q;
```

Fig. 10.9: Code to be generated for the pointer assignment p:=q

The other source of reference deletions is passing the end of a scope, at which point all its local variables are deleted. A local variable holding a reference to a chunk should be processed to decrement the associated reference count, and if the scope is that of a routine the same applies to the routine's parameters that hold references.

We have seen that the proper way to reclaim the memory allocated to a chunk is to first decrement recursively the reference counts of all references contained in the chunk, and then return it to the free list. An outline of the code is given in Figure 10.10, in which *Pointer* references the chunk to be freed recursively.

```
procedure FreeRecursivelyUsingReferenceCounts(Pointer);
        if not IsPointerIntoHeap (Pointer): return;
        if Pointer.referenceCount ≠ 0: return;
        for each i in 1 .. Pointer.numberOfPointers:
            if IsPointerIntoHeap (Pointer.pointer [i]):
                Decrement Pointer.pointer [i].referenceCount;
                FreeRecursivelyUsingReferenceCounts (Pointer.pointer [i]);
        FreeChunk(Pointer);          — the actual freeing operation
```

Fig. 10.10: Recursively freeing chunks

Recursion is, however, an unwelcome feature in a garbage collector since it requires an unpredictable amount of stack space. Depending on the run-time system and the operating system, this stack space may be part of the program data area, part of the heap, or a separate memory segment; in any case, its size is limited and may not suffice for the operation of the garbage collector. Having a garbage collector fail for lack of memory is kind of embarrassing, though, and several techniques have been invented to avoid the problem. The best solution is using *pointer reversal*, which will be explained in Section 10.2.4.3. A simpler but still adequate solution is suggested in Exercise 10.11(c). For an even simpler but less effective improvement see Exercise 10.10.

Reference counting is a simple technique that can be implemented easily by modifying the compiler to perform reference manipulation as outlined above. Unfortunately, reference counting has some serious drawbacks that limit its applicability. First, and foremost, reference counting cannot reclaim cyclic data structures. Consider the example in Figure 10.8, in which the reference count of chunk a is 2. If the reference from the root set to chunk a is deleted, the reference count drops to 1 so the chunk is not reclaimed, as shown in Figure 10.11. However, chunk a has become garbage since it is no longer reachable from the root set. Reference counting cannot reclaim chunk a because chunk d, which has also become garbage, holds a reference to it.

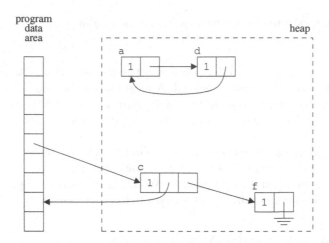

Fig. 10.11: Reference counting fails to identify circular garbage

The problem with reference counting is that it takes its decisions by considering only one node in the graph at a time, and in order to reclaim a cyclic data structure all nodes in the data structure should be considered as garbage together. Once reference counting has failed to reclaim a cyclic data structure, the chunks involved will never be reclaimed. This has the unfortunate effect that free space leaks away, which might even cause the program to run out of free space when other garbage collectors would be able to reclaim the cyclic structures and allow the program to continue.

The second problem with reference counting is efficiency. The compiled code has to monitor all reference manipulations, and each and every reference manipulation requires the adjustment of the associated reference counts. This is a considerable overhead in comparison to other garbage collection techniques that do not monitor any pointer action and reclaim garbage chunks only when needed (see Sections 10.2.4 and 10.2.5).

The final problem with reference counting is memory fragmentation. The free list is augmented with the reclaimed chunks, but it remains fragmented. In principle doing a compaction phase during a reference counting allocation request is possible, but few reference counting garbage collectors go to such lengths.

Despite its problems, reference counting is a popular technique for managing relatively small numbers of dynamically allocated data structures, usually in hand-written software. For example, a UNIX kernel typically uses reference counts to handle the recovery of file descriptors. Its use in generated code is less widespread.

10.2.4 Mark and scan

The **mark and scan** garbage collection algorithm described in this section is the most effective one in that it frees all memory that can be freed (reference counting fails to free circular structures, two-space copying leaves half of the memory unavailable). It is often combined with compaction, and then also provides the largest possible chunk of memory available. The mark and scan algorithm is also sometimes called **mark and sweep**.

The mark and scan garbage collection algorithm consists of two phases. The first, the **marking phase**, marks all chunks that are still reachable; the second, the **scan phase**, scans the allocated memory and considers as free chunks all chunks that are not marked reachable and makes them available again. We will now consider the marking and scanning phases in more detail.

10.2.4.1 Marking

Marking is based on two principles: chunks reachable through the root set are reachable and any chunk reachable from a pointer in a reachable chunk is itself reachable. We assume that the root set resides in a program data area or the topmost activation record, and that a data type description for it has been constructed and made available by the compiler. Now, in its simplest form, marking marks the program data area as reachable, finds the pointers in it using its data type description, and recursively marks all chunks pointed to by these pointers, in a simple depth-first scan. If this recursive process finds a chunk without pointers or a chunk that has already been marked, it backtracks and continues with the next pointer. Since the number of reachable chunks is finite and no chunk is processed more than once, this depth-first scan terminates and takes a time linear in the number of reachable chunks.

Marking requires a second bit in the administration header of the chunk, the **marked bit**, in addition to the free bit. This bit starts off as "cleared".

The main problem with this recursive process is that it needs a stack of unknown size, and the question is where to find room for this stack at a time when memory is in short supply, witness the fact that the garbage collector was activated. It has been suggested to us that in this day and age, in which computers easily have stacks of 1 megabyte or more, the question is no longer relevant. It is our experience that each generation of designers again suggests that "X is certainly enough", and that suggestions like these lead to machines with built-in 640 kB boundaries.

The simplest answer to the question of where to put the stack is: reserve room for the marking stack in each chunk. One pointer and a small counter are sufficient: the pointer points back to the parent chunk which contains the pointer that caused the present chunk to be processed, and the counter counts how many pointers have already been processed in the present chunk. See Figure 10.12, in which the third child is being processed.

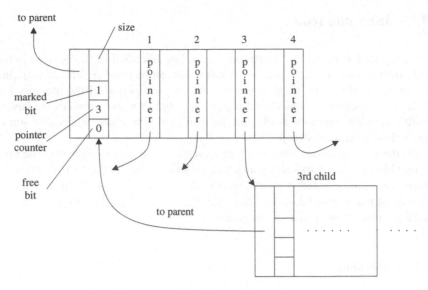

Fig. 10.12: Marking the third child of a chunk

This technique costs room for one pointer, one counter, and one bit per allocated chunk. Whether this is a problem or not depends on the average size of a chunk and on the ease with which the counter and bit can be accommodated. In a Lisp interpreter, in which chunks (called "cells" there) contain two pointers only, the overhead is more than 33%, even though the counter can only have the values 0 and 1; in modern systems, in which the minimum allocation size is perhaps 16 or 32 bytes anyway the overhead is often considerably less. For a way to mark the directed graph of all reachable chunks without using space for the extra pointer, see Section 10.2.4.3.

10.2.4.2 Scanning and freeing

Just freeing the unreachable chunks is now easy: using the lengths noted in the chunks we step through memory, from chunk to chunk. For each chunk C we check if it has been marked reachable; if so, we clear the marked bit of C for the next scan, and if not, we turn on the free bit of C.

We can also exploit this left-to-right scan to combine adjacent free chunks. To this end, we keep a pointer F to the first free chunk we find and note its size. As long as we keep on meeting free blocks, we just add up their sizes until we run into a chunk in use or into end of memory. We then update the administration of the chunk pointed to by F to the total size of the free chunks, thus creating a single larger free chunk, and continue our scan. We repeat this process as soon as we meet another free chunk, and so on.

The result of a mark and scan operation is a heap in which all chunks marked in use are reachable and each pair of free chunks is separated by chunks in use. This is the best one can achieve without moving the chunks. A subsequent compaction phase can combine all the free chunks into one large free chunk, thereby improving the performance even further.

10.2.4.3 Pointer reversal—marking without using stack space

The above marking technique requires an overhead of one pointer plus a few bits in each chunk at all times, even when the garbage collector is not running. This overhead can be avoided almost completely by **pointer reversal**. This ingenious technique has applications outside of the field of garbage collection, since it allows one to visit all nodes of a directed graph without using additional space for a stack. The garbage collection algorithm based on pointer reversal is also called the **Schorr and Waite algorithm** after its inventors [255].

The marking algorithm described above kept a pointer in each chunk C being visited. This pointer pointed to C's parent P in the visiting process and would be followed when the marking algorithm was finished with chunk C. Now, when the marking algorithm is working on chunk C, it finds the pointers in C, which point to children of C and visits them one by one. Imagine that the marking algorithm has gone off visiting the n-th child of C, say D; then after a while it will return from this visit. Upon returning from D to C, the marking algorithm can retain a pointer to D, the chunk it just left. But this pointer also resides in C in the n-th pointer field! This leads to the observation that while visiting the n-th child of C the contents of the n-th pointer field in C are redundant.

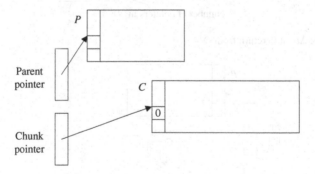

Fig. 10.13: The Schorr and Waite algorithm, arriving at C

The "Schorr and Waite graph marking algorithm" utilizes this redundancy to store the parent pointer which would otherwise go on the stack, as follows. Figure 10.13 depicts the situation when processing the chunk C starts. The algorithm maintains two auxiliary pointers, *ParentPointer* and *ChunkPointer*; *ChunkPointer* points to the chunk being processed, *ParentPointer* to its parent. Moreover, each chunk

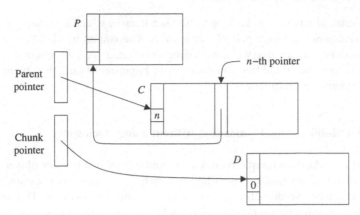

Fig. 10.14: Moving to D

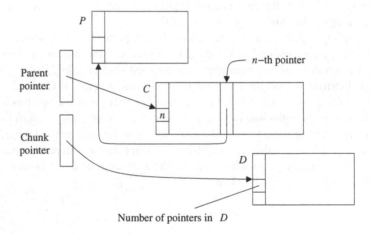

Fig. 10.15: About to return from D

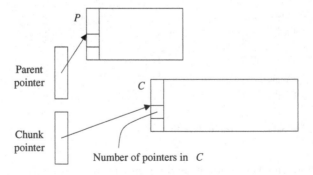

Fig. 10.16: About to return from C

contains a counter field which records the number of the pointer in the chunk that is being followed; the counter starts off at 0 and when it has reached the total number of pointers in the chunk, the chunk has been visited completely.

We assume that the processing of pointers in C proceeds until we reach the n-th pointer, which points to child D. In order to move to D, we shift the contents of *ParentPointer*, *ChunkPointer*, and the n-th pointer field in C circularly, using a temporary variable *OldParentPointer*. Some care is required, since the pointer that addresses C changes in the middle of the code:

— C is pointed to by ChunkPointer.
OldParentPointer ← ParentPointer;
ParentPointer ← ChunkPointer;
— C is pointed to by ParentPointer.
ChunkPointer ← n-th pointer field in C;
n-th pointer field in C ← OldParentPointer;

This results in the return pointer to the parent P of C being stored in the n-th pointer field in C, which normally points to D, as shown in Figure 10.14. As far as *ParentPointer* and *ChunkPointer* are concerned, the situation is now equivalent to that in Figure 10.13, when we first arrived at C, except that C is now the parent and D is the chunk going to be processed.

Figure 10.15 shows the situation when we are about to return from visiting D; the only difference with Figure 10.14 is that the counter in D has now reached the total number of pointers in D. In order to return from D to C, we circularly shift back the pointers:

— C is pointed to by ParentPointer.
OldParentPointer ← ParentPointer;
— C is pointed to by OldParentPointer.
ParentPointer ← n-th pointer field in C;
n-th pointer field in C ← ChunkPointer;
ChunkPointer ← OldParentPointer;
— C is pointed to by ChunkPointer.

and increment the counter in C.

The whole fancy footwork is then repeated for the $n + 1$-th pointer in C, and so on, until all children of C have been visited. We are then ready to return from C, as shown in Figure 10.16. Note that the return pointer to P has by now been stored in and subsequently retrieved from each pointer position in C.

Returning to P from C, the marking algorithm is in a position similar to where it was when returning from D to C. Again, the marking algorithm makes sure it brings along the pointer to its point of departure, C, to restore the pointer in P to C, which for the duration has been replaced by P's return pointer to its parent.

It should be pointed out that the above only describes a clever technique for avoiding a stack while visiting all nodes in a graph. To prevent looping on cycles in the graph, nodes must be marked at the beginning of a visit, and already marked nodes must not be visited again. The same marked bit can then be used during freeing, to indicate that a chunk is reachable.

10.2.5 Two-space copying

The mark phase in a mark and scan garbage collector touches the reachable chunks only, but the scan phase touches all chunks. This makes it expensive, since most chunks have a short lifetime and a very large fraction of the heap consists of garbage chunks when the garbage collector is invoked. **Two-space copying** exploits this important observation by avoiding scanning all chunks and only processing the reachable chunks; it manages to do so at the expense of doubling the memory requirements. With memory becoming cheaper every day, however, it has become reasonable to optimize for time rather than for memory.

The basic two-space copying collector by Cheney [58] works as follows. The available heap space is divided into two equal parts: the **from-space** and the **to-space**, as shown in Figure 10.17. During normal computation new chunks are allocated in from-space by simply advancing a pointer through the from-space. When the heap space in the from-space has been consumed, all reachable chunks are copied to the empty to-space by the garbage collector.

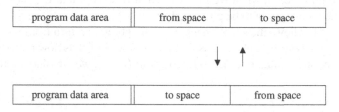

Fig. 10.17: Memory layout for two-space copying

The two-space copying operation starts with copying the chunks in from-space that are referenced by pointers in the root set. The copies are placed in the to-space in consecutive positions, starting right at the beginning. The original of a chunk in the from-space is marked "copied" and a forwarding pointer pointing to the copy in the to-space is stored in it; since the chunk has just been copied, its contents can be destroyed. No pointers are updated in the copies, so the pointers in them still point to chunks in the from-space.

Then the chunks in to-space are scanned from left to right for pointers to chunks in from-space, using a "scan pointer". Suppose a pointer in a chunk P under the scan pointer points to a chunk Q in from-space. Now there are two possibilities: Q is marked "copied", in which case it contains a forwarding pointer which is used to update the pointer in P; or Q is not marked "copied", in which case it must be copied now. After the copy has been made, the original Q is marked "copied" and its contents are replaced by a forwarding pointer to the copy. This process is repeated until the to-space contains no more pointers to chunks in from-space. Then all reachable chunks in the from-space have been copied to to-space and all pointers have been updated to point into to-space. Next, the roles of the two semi-spaces are reversed, and normal computation is resumed.

When scanning, we may also find that the pointer in a chunk P points to the program data area; such pointers need no attention and are ignored. The strict separation of program data and the heap allows the garbage collector to detect efficiently with one compare instruction whether the pointer refers to a chunk in from-space or in program data. The pointer cannot point to a chunk in to-space, since P has just been copied from from-space, which contains no pointers to to-space, and no pointers in it have been updated yet.

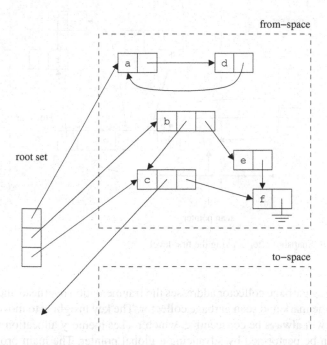

Fig. 10.18: Initial situation in two-space copying

This algorithm does not need a stack to keep track of which chunks contain pointers that still must be traced. Instead it uses a simple scan pointer in the to-space that shows which of the copied chunks have been scanned and which have not. Figure 10.18 shows the from- and to-spaces at the start of a garbage collection operation, Figure 10.19 shows a snapshot after the three chunks directly accessible from the root set have been copied and scanning started, and Figure 10.20 shows the situation after four chunks have been copied and one has been scanned. The forwarding pointers have been shown as dotted lines with hollow arrow heads, to distinguish them from the "real" pointers; in an implementation, the "copied" marker, not shown in the diagrams, serves to distinguish between the two.

We see that the collector copies the graph in breadth-first order, and compacts the chunks automatically (inevitably it also compacts the arrows in the diagram!). It is also easy to see that after all chunks have been copied and scanned, the from-space contains no interesting data any more and can be considered empty.

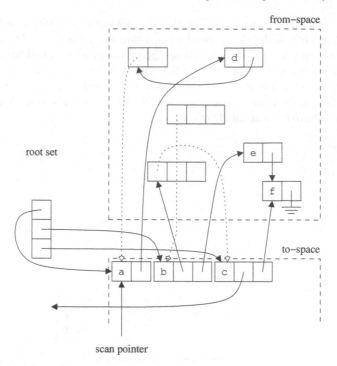

Fig. 10.19: Snapshot after copying the first level

A copying garbage collector addresses the fragmentation overhead and time complexity of the mark and scan garbage collector. The key insight is to move chunks so
free space will always be consecutive, which makes memory allocation very cheap,
since it can be performed by advancing a global pointer. The main problems with
two-space copying garbage collection are that it wastes half of the heap and that its
performance is poor if the heap is nearly full. Two-space copying is a very effective but also very demanding garbage collection algorithm. It is a good choice when
run-time speed is important and memory is not scarce. This is frequently the case
with advanced programming paradigms on modern machines, which is where we
find two-space copying most often.

10.2.6 Compaction

Since the size of the largest free chunk may be considerably smaller than the sum of
the sizes of all free chunks, it is useful to move all used chunks together. Doing so
moves all free chunks together also, so they can be combined into one maximum-
size free chunk. The **compaction** algorithm described below can be performed in
any situation in which there are only two kinds of chunks, chunks marked in use and

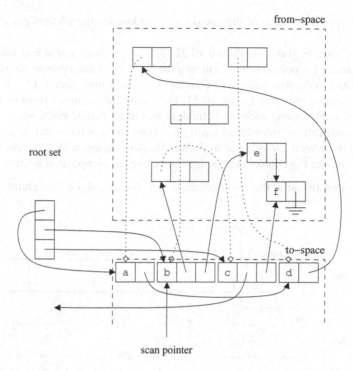

Fig. 10.20: Snapshot after having scanned one chunk

chunks marked free, and the pointers in the chunks marked in use are all consistent. Since this is true even if some of the chunks marked in use are actually unreachable, compaction can, technically speaking, be done at almost any moment: it is largely independent of garbage collection and is just a free-list improving technique. Needless to say, it is most effective just after the garbage collector has run, and in practice it is often integrated with the garbage collector. It is useless after two-space copying, though.

Compaction is most simply done in three left-to-right sweeps through memory, using one additional pointer per chunk. We assume that the used chunks will be moved to the lower end of the heap. For clarity, Figures 10.21 through 10.23, which depict the compaction process, are drawn as if compaction moves the chunks from "old" memory to "new" memory, but actually the "old" and "new" in the diagrams designate the same memory. The first sweep calculates the addresses of the new positions of the chunks, the second updates existing pointers to point to the new positions, and the third actually moves the chunks:

- *Address calculation*, shown in Figure 10.21. The chunks are scanned from low to high and for each used chunk C its new position after compaction is computed; the address corresponding to this position is stored in the administration of C. Since the new position of the first used chunk is known (the lower edge of memory) and the sizes of the chunks are also known, the address calculation is trivial.

- *Pointer update*, shown in Figure 10.22. The program data area and the chunks are scanned for pointers that point into the heap; each such pointer to a chunk C is updated to the new address of C found in the administration of C.

- *Move chunks*, shown in Figure 10.23. The chunks are scanned from low to high through memory and each used chunk is moved to its new position, as found in its administration. Since chunks will only move to the left (or stay in place), this can be done with a single left-to-right scan. All pointers within the chunks now again point to the chunks they pointed to before the compaction started.

All of the memory after the last used chunk now forms a single free chunk.

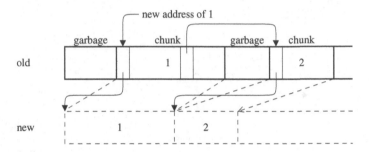

Fig. 10.21: Address calculation during compaction

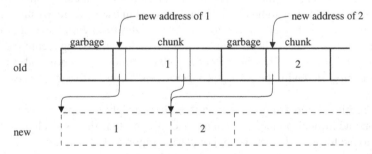

Fig. 10.22: Pointer update during compaction

10.2.7 Generational garbage collection

The statistical properties of allocates and frees are utilized by an optimization called **generational garbage collection**. It is based on the phenomenon that most allocated

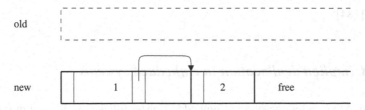

Fig. 10.23: Moving the chunks during compaction

blocks fall out of use almost immediately; conversely, if a block has been around for a while already, chances are that it will stay in business for some time to come. This suggests restricting the—expensive—action of the garbage collector to the most recently allocated chunks only. Especially in a compacting garbage collector these are easy to find: they all lie at addresses past the end of the last compaction. Only if garbage collection on this newest generation fails to free enough memory or to meet some efficiency criterion, is a full garbage collection performed.

Many variants of generational garbage collection exist, some of great sophistication and efficiency, but in its basic form it divides the heap dynamically into two regions, one for an older generation of chunks and one for a younger generation; the routine malloc() hands out chunks from the younger region. As usual, a third region also exists, the program data area. Now a certain large percentage of the garbage collector activations restrict themselves to the younger generation region, using a simple trick. The trick is to consider the older generation region to be part of the program data area, and collect only the chunks in the younger generation region, using any garbage collection algorithm desired. Since the program data area can be seen as an input parameter to any garbage collection process and since it can in principle have any shape and content, it is obvious that this unusual view of what constitutes a program data area still yields correct results. The complementary smaller percentage of the garbage collector activations are full garbage collections, in which the program data area and the heap have their traditional roles. These serve to reclaim any chunks in the older generation region that have become unreachable.

Algorithms differ in the answers they give to the questions of what the exact difference between older and younger is, whether more than two generations are distinguished, exactly when and how often a full garbage collection is done, and what garbage collection algorithm is used. They are often combined with other optimizing techniques, most of which again exploit statistical properties of chunk usage.

For example, it is known that very few pointers to young chunks are stored in old chunks and the program data area, so some algorithms keep a list of such pointers to be used as a root set for garbage collecting the young region. This avoids scanning the possibly large program data area and old region upon such occasions, but requires monitoring all pointer assignments.

Generational garbage collection algorithms are the fastest and most efficient garbage collection algorithms known. For an example of a mature, high-performance garbage collection system using generational garbage collection, see

Ungar [284].

10.2.8 Implicit deallocation in embedded systems

Compared to stand-alone systems, embedded systems have two properties that make garbage collection hard: they have less memory; and they are subject to sometimes stringent real-time constraints.

Having little memory does not in itself make garbage collection more difficult; it just increases the frequency with which the garbage collector is activated and thus the cost per allocation, as the following calculation shows. For simplicity we assume that all chunks are the same size. Suppose that the memory size is M chunks, and that at the end of each garbage collection cycle R chunks remain in use (the "residency"). So the next $M - R$ chunks can be allocated, but then the garbage collector is activated. This activation touches all chunks, costing cM units, where c is the cost per chunk. For a stationary program execution, this activation frees $M - R$ chunks on the average. So $M - R$ allocations cost cM units, which makes the cost per allocation

$$\frac{cM}{M-R} = c + \frac{cR}{M-R}$$

The fraction on the right is the extra cost incurred by the fact that not all chunks are freed by a cycle. As M gets smaller, the denominator gets smaller, so the fraction, and the extra cost, increases.

The answer of some embedded systems to the problem of expensive garbage collection is to assign the task to a co-processor, which runs the garbage collector concurrently, almost without using CPU cycles from the main program. The co-processor can be programmed with any concurrent garbage collection algorithm, as described, for example, by Jones and Lins [136, Ch. 8].

Occasionally an embedded system offers garbage collection options an off-the-shelf system does not: if the co-processor is microprogrammed, special instructions can be implemented which assist the garbage collector. Stanchina and Meyer [265] describe such a system.

The process used in the computation above allocates $M - R$ chunks at little cost, and then performs an expensive garbage collection cycle. In a system with real-time constraints such behavior is unacceptable. Concurrent garbage collection on a co-processor solves the problem, but a simpler solution is available: the use of an on-the-fly garbage collector, which spreads out the cost more or less evenly over all allocations or all pointer accesses. See Jones and Lins [136, Ch. 6].

10.3 Conclusion

This concludes our treatment of memory management with explicit and implicit deallocation. In summary, explicit deallocation is implemented using linked lists of free chunks, and implicit allocation is implemented by computing the transitive closure of the directly accessible chunks and freeing all chunks not in this set.

On-the-fly garbage collectors take the bumpiness out of the process. Concurrent garbage collectors do that, and take load off the main processors, but require additional hardware.

Summary

- All compilers and many compiled programs need dynamic memory allocation—access to memory chunks the number and/or size of which is not known statically.
- Usually, all dynamic memory is allocated from a single contiguous segment of memory, called the data segment or the heap.
- Allocating requested memory chunks is an administrative matter; freeing memory chunks that are no longer needed is both an administrative matter and a programming paradigm issue.
- Data allocation with explicit deallocation by the programmer usually uses a malloc()/free()-like interface. Data allocation with implicit deallocation requires a form of garbage collection.
- Memory fragments are called "blocks" if they are in the hands of the user, and "chunks" if they are handled by the memory allocator. A chunk contains a block plus some administration.
- Memory is allocated in a region called the "heap". It consists of a contiguous sequence of chunks, each chunk marked with its size. A bit tells whether a chunk is in use or free.
- A call of malloc finds a free chunk of sufficient size and returns a pointer to it, after updating some administration. A call of free() frees the chunks supplied to it, and may coalesce adjacent free chunks into a larger one.
- For increased efficiency, the free chunks can be linked into multiple free lists, one for each size interval.
- Compiler data structures that require dynamic allocation are linked lists and extensible arrays. Linked lists of records of a given size can be implemented efficiently by batching the records in larger blocks and maintaining a free list of them. Extensible arrays can be implemented efficiently by increasing the array size by a constant factor.
- Data allocation with implicit deallocation is very useful since explicit deallocation is very difficult for the programmer to do; explicit deallocation in generated code is often so difficult as to be infeasible. Also, memory allocation errors are hard to find and correct.

- Garbage collection should free all chunks that the program will not use any more, but settles for the chunks that are unreachable from the program data area.
- Reference counting garbage collection detects garbage chunks by seeing their reference counts drop to zero. Mark and scan garbage collection identifies all reachable chunks by transitive closure and frees all unreachable chunks. Two-space copying garbage collection copies all reachable chunks to a different space, to-space; the remaining space in to-space is a single free chunk.
- Just returning identified garbage chunks to the free list leaves free memory fragmented; compaction is needed to upgrade the fragmented free list into a single free chunk.
- Garbage collection algorithms can be one-shot, on-the-fly, or concurrent.
- To operate, the garbage collector needs a root set and the pointer layout of all reachable chunks. Also, all reachable pointers must be valid, point to something sensible or be null. Compiler support is needed for all three of these features.
- The root set is extracted from the program data area; pointer layout follows from the chunk data types. The compiler must provide both to the garbage collector in the compiled program.
- Pointer validity can be achieved in a type-secure language by properly initializing all pointers.
- The pointer layout of chunks is known to the compiler; it can be supplied to the garbage collector in the form of a bit map, in the form of a routine, or it can be fixed.
- Chunks can be self-descriptive, in which case the pointer layout can be obtained from each chunk itself. Otherwise the pointer layout must be supplied by the context.
- The pointer layout of the program data area is complicated and dynamically variable. The main villains are the stack with arbitrary activation records and the working stacks and parameter lists under construction in these activation records.
- Pointer layouts must be created by the compiler for every possible activation record that can occur during program execution, and code must be generated that keeps track of which one is current.
- The number of required pointer layouts for activation records may be reduced by using the working stack only for simple expressions. It is then empty when the garbage collector is activated.
- If the language does not allow the root set and/or the pointer layout to be provided or pointer consistency to be achieved, a conservative estimate can be made of the root set and the pointers in each chunk: any value that looks like a pointer is a pointer. If implemented carefully, this works correctly; it may still leave some garbage undetected, though.
- Actual garbage collectors are complicated by baroque language features such as arrays of dynamically alterable size, unions with dynamic types which contain pointers, and exception handlers. The effects of aggressive code optimization can also be a complicating factor.

- Reference counting garbage collection records in each chunk the number of pointers that point to it; when the number drops to zero the chunk is garbage and can be freed.
- To keep the reference count of a chunk current, it must be incremented when a reference to the chunk is copied and decremented when such a reference is destroyed.
- When reference counting frees a chunk, the reference counts of all chunks it refers to must be decremented, and so on, recursively. A recursive implementation can be achieved using pointer reversal.
- Reference counting cannot free unreachable circular data structures. Also, monitoring all pointer manipulation may be expensive.
- Mark and scan garbage collection is the only algorithm that frees all memory that can be freed. It is often combined with compaction, and then also provides the largest possible chunk of memory available.
- The marking phase marks all chunks that are still reachable; the scan phase scans the allocated memory and frees all chunks that are not marked reachable.
- Marking needs a stack of unknown size. This stack can be distributed over the chunks, with each chunk having room for a parent pointer in the marking process. The scan phase can combine adjacent chunks to improve the quality of the free list.
- The overhead of the room for the parent pointer can be eliminated by using pointer reversal, also called the Schorr and Waite algorithm. In pointer reversal, while visiting a child D of a chunk C, the parent pointer of C is stored in the location in C which held the pointer to D. The visit to D returns a pointer to D, which is used to restore the pointer in C by swapping it with the parent pointer. This restores the parent pointer, which can then be swapped with the location of the next pointer in C.
- In two-space copying, the available heap space is divided into two equal parts: the from-space and the to-space. New chunks are allocated in from-space by advancing a pointer. Upon garbage collection, all reachable chunks are copied from the from-space to the empty to-space, while updating all pointers, including those in the program data area.
- Two-space copying copies the graph of reachable chunks in breadth-first fashion: first the chunks that are reachable directly from the program data area, then those reachable in two steps from the program data area, then those reachable in three steps, and so on.
- When a chunk is reached for the first time, through a pointer P, the chunk is copied to the first free position in the to-space, and a forwarding pointer is left in the original, pointing to the copy; the pointer to the copy replaces P. When a chunk is reached again, through a pointer Q, no copying takes place and the forwarding pointer is used to replace Q.
- When all reachable chunks in the from-space have been copied to to-space and all pointers have been updated, the roles of from-space and to-space are flipped, and ordinary computation is resumed.

- Two-space copying does not need a stack; it avoids the fragmentation overhead and time complexity of the mark and scan garbage collector. Its main problem is that it wastes half of the heap. It is a good choice when run-time speed is important and memory is not scarce.
- The size of the largest free chunk may be considerably smaller than the sum of the sizes of all free chunks; this is called fragmentation. Compaction moves all used chunks together; this moves all free chunks together also, so they can be combined into one maximum-size free chunk.
- Compaction is a free-list improving technique rather than a garbage collection technique and is largely independent of garbage collection. It can, technically speaking, be done at almost any moment, but is most effective right after a garbage collection.
- Compaction is done in three left-to-right sweeps through memory: the first sweep calculates the addresses of the new positions of the chunks in the heap; the second updates existing pointers in the program data area and the heap chunks to point to the new positions; and the third actually moves the chunks.
- Generational garbage collection restricts the expensive action of the garbage collector to the most recently allocated chunks only, since these are the most short-lived.
- In its basic form, generational garbage collection divides the heap dynamically into one region for an older generation of chunks and one for a younger generation. Generational garbage collector activations restrict themselves to the younger generation region by considering the older generation region to be part of the program data area. The algorithm then automatically collects only the chunks in the younger generation region.
- Generational garbage collection algorithms are the fastest and most efficient garbage collection algorithms known.
- In summary, explicit deallocation is implemented using linked lists of free chunks, and implicit allocation is implemented by computing the transitive closure of the directly accessible chunks and freeing all chunks not in this set.

Further reading

Detailed information about the garbage collection algorithms described here and many others can be found in the book *Garbage Collection—Algorithms for Automatic Dynamic Memory Management* by Jones and Lins [136]. An extensive bibliography on garbage collection and related topics is supplied by Sankaran [249], and an interesting survey is given by Cohen [65]. Journals to consult are, for example, *ACM SIGPLAN Notices*, *ACM Transactions on Programming Languages and Systems*, and *Software—Practice and Experience*.

Garbage collection has a long history starting in the 1960s with the development of LISP. The original paper on LISP [186] describes mark and scan garbage collection, calling it "reclamation". The early garbage collection algorithms, such as reference counting, imposed a considerable overhead on the execution time of an application, which led to the (mis)conception that garbage collection is more expensive than manual memory management. Recent studies, however, have shown that advanced algorithms such as generational copying garbage collection perform roughly as well as, and sometimes even better than, manual memory management [15, 31].

Recent advances are reported in the proceedings of the *ACM SIGPLAN International Symposium on Memory Management ISMM* and of the *International Workshop on Memory Management*, and in the more algorithmically oriented computer science journals.

Exercises

10.1. (▷www) Modify the outline code for the basic *Malloc* given in Figures 10.2 and 10.3 for the situation that the least common multiple of the alignment requirements of the machine is 32 bytes and the *AdministrationSize* is 4 bytes.

10.2. (▷793) In Section 10.1.1 we suggest calling the garbage collector, if there is one, whenever *Malloc()* runs out of space, hoping that it will free some unused chunks the user has forgotten to free. It would seem, however, that this is incorrect, since the user could free some of these chunks later on in the program, and these chunks would then be freed twice. Why is this not a problem?

10.3. (▷www) In languages with explicit memory deallocation, memory leaks can be a major problem. Memory leaks occur when the programmer forgets to deallocate a block of memory that is no longer used. What can be done to address this problem, apart from using a garbage collector? Answers are supplied by Hastings and Joyce [118], Barach, Taenzer and Wells [30], and in the answers section of this book.

10.4. (a) Using a loop of calls to malloc(), each requesting say 1 Mb, find out how much memory one can obtain on your system.
(b) By timing the access times of random bytes in the chunks thus obtained, find out if the access times of the chunks are all equal. If they are not, what could be the cause?

10.5. (▷www) In Section 10.1.3, it is claimed that returning blocks to the standard memory manager would require much administration. Why is it not enough to have a single counter per block, which holds the number of busy records for that block, and to return the block when it reaches 0?

10.6. (▷794) Where, in the construction of assemblers as explained in Chapter 8, can one make good use of extensible arrays?

10.7. (▷794) Name some properties of garbage collection algorithms that make concurrent garbage collection very hard.

10.8. (▷www) A C programmer (hacker) decides to exploit the fact that addresses on his target machine are always less than $2**31$, and uses the most significant (32nd) bit of some pointer variables as a flag bit, to store some useful information, using code like:

```
int x, *p;
/* set flag bit thus: */
p = ( int  *) ( ( int ) p | 0x80000000);
/* dereference the pointer thus: */
x = * ( int  *) (( int ) p & 0 x7fffffff );
```

What will this do to the garbage collection algorithms? Will conservative garbage collection still work?

10.9. (▷794) In Figure 10.9, the reference count of the chunk under p is incremented *before* that of the chunk under q is decremented. What could conceivably go wrong if the order were reversed? Hint: consider the assignment p:=p.

10.10. (▷www) The stack requirements of a recursive descent node marking algorithm can be reduced somewhat by tail recursion elimination (page 593). Apply this technique to the recursive descent freeing algorithm of Figure 10.10. Why is this a problem?

10.11. (▷www) (a) Implement recursive descent marking. Test your implementation on a large graph of the structure shown in Figure 6.9. What is the complexity of the algorithm? What is the complexity of your implementation? How about memoization?
(b) Implement the Schorr and Waite marking algorithm. Answer the same questions as in part (a).
(c) There is another algorithm for marking a graph without using an unbounded stack: use a *bounded stack* as explained by Knuth [158] in his *Art of Computer Programming*, Algorithm C on page 415. It works as follows. Say, the stack is limited to N entries. When the stack overflows, the oldest entry is discarded, leaving the N most recent return addresses. When the stack becomes exhausted (underflows) the algorithm stops. We call this Algorithm A. The marking algorithm now consists of repeated calls of A, until a call finds no more nodes to mark.
(i) Argue that this works.
(ii) What part of the graph will be marked by a single run of the algorithm A?
(iii) Implement, test, and time the algorithm; hint: you need one more marking bit than for the unbounded stack implementation. What is its complexity?

10.12. (▷www) One possibility to limit the stop-and-go behavior of the mark and scan algorithm is to perform the scan phase incrementally. After the mark phase, we no longer perform a scan of the complete memory, but rather modify the *Malloc()* code in Figures 10.2 and 10.3 to scan until it finds a free chunk of suitable size. Give outline code that implements this incremental scheme.

10.13. (▷794) Consider the pointer reversal algorithm in Section 10.2.4.3 for binary trees in read-only memory, for example on a CD-ROM. The algorithm requires us to store the parent pointer in a node for the purpose of finding the parent upon having finished with the node, but we cannot write that pointer in read-only memory. Suppose now that the tree stores the "exclusive or" ($\otimes$) of the left and right pointers and the parent pointer, rather than the left and right pointers themselves. When returning for the last time to a node, we can then find the parent pointer as follows. The right pointer entry holds right pointer $\otimes$ parent pointer, and since we know right pointer (we just came from there!), we can compute the parent pointer:

right pointer $\otimes$ parent pointer $\otimes$ right pointer
    = parent pointer

using the equalities $A \otimes B \otimes A = A \otimes A \otimes B = 0 \otimes B = B$. Turn this idea into a complete algorithm.

10.14. (▷www) Compaction has occasionally been characterized as "one-space copying", in analogy to two-space copying. Describe the similarities and differences.

10.15. (▷www) *History of memory management*: Study Collins' 1960 paper [66], which introduces reference counting garbage collection, and write a summary of it in modern terminology.

Part V
From Abstract Syntax Tree
to Intermediate Code

Chapter 11
Imperative and Object-Oriented Programs

In the previous chapters we have discussed general methods for performing lexical and syntax analysis, context handling, code generation, and memory management, while disregarding the programming paradigm from which the source program originated. In doing so, we have exploited the fact that much of compiler construction is independent of the source code paradigm. Still, a Java compiler differs considerably from a Prolog compiler: both require paradigm-specific techniques, in addition to general compiler construction techniques. We will explore these paradigm-specific techniques in the next four chapters. Figure 11.1 shows the numbers of the chapters and sections that contain material on the subjects of lexical and syntactic analysis, context handling, and code generation for programs in the four paradigms covered in this book. For each of the three subjects we have already considered the general methods; the paradigm-specific methods are covered as shown in the table.

		Imperative and object-oriented	Functional	Logic	Parallel and distributed
Lexical and syntactic analysis,	general:	Ch. 2 & 3			
	specific:	–			
Context handling,	general:	Ch. 4 & 5			
	identification & type checking:	Sect. 11.1			
	specific:	Ch. 11	Ch. 12	Ch. 13	Ch. 14
Code generation,	general:	Ch. 6–9			
	specific:	Ch. 11	Ch. 12	Ch. 13	Ch. 14

Fig. 11.1: Roadmap to paradigm-specific issues

There are hardly any paradigm-specific lexical and syntactic issues, so the general treatment in Chapters 2 and 3 suffices. One exception is the "offside rule" in some functional languages, in which the text layout plays a role in parsing; it is described in Section 12.1.1. Two aspects of context handling are almost universal: identification and type checking; rather than dedicating a separate chapter to these, we cover them at the beginning of the present chapter, in Section 11.1. The paradigm-specific context manipulations are described where needed in Chapters 11 through 14.

The main differences in compilers for different paradigms lie in the kind of code they generate, and this is the primary reason for having a separate chapter for each of them. Most (but not all) compilers for imperative and object-oriented languages produce code at the level of an assembler or lower, whereas many (but by no means all) compilers for functional, logic, and parallel and distributed languages generate C or C++ code as their target code. The general code generating techniques have been discussed in Chapters 6 through 9. and the specific forms of code to be generated for the four paradigms are treated in Chapters 11 through 14.

Returning to the structure of the present chapter, we first discuss identifier/operator identification and type checking; operator identification requires special attention since in most languages operators are overloaded, and the context is needed to make the final identification. The rest of the chapter concerns code generation for the imperative and object-oriented languages. Since programs in these languages work by specifying direct instructions for the manipulation of explicit data, and since both the instructions and the data are relatively close to those of the hardware, the main issues in code generation for these languages are the mappings of source language data onto bytes and of source language statements to low-level instructions. These issues are covered in Sections 11.2 and 11.4, respectively. An intermediate position is occupied by the activation records and closures (Section 11.3). Activation records are data structures used by the run-time system to represent active ("running" or "suspended") routines; closures are representations of routines that allow some advanced operations on them, most prominently partial parameterization. Both combine data and flow of control.

Although functional, logic, and parallel/distributed programs often require data structures that are not direct mappings of programmer data and instruction sequences that do not derive directly from the program, much of the following discussion is still relevant for the more advanced paradigms.

----------------------------------- **Roadmap** -----------------------------------

11.1 Context handling

The context handling phase follows the lexical and syntactic phases. The latter are concerned with local phenomena and relate each item to its immediate neighbors only: for example, lexical analysis combines letters with adjacent letters and digits into identifiers, and syntax analysis combines adjacent identifiers and operators into expressions. Context handling, on the other hand, is concerned with long-distance relations: for example, it relates the type of a variable in a declaration to its use in an expression and relates the position of a label to its use in a goto statement. The connectors in these long-range relations are the identifiers: all applied occurrences of an identifier i in an expression are plugs which fit in one socket, the declaration for i, and from that socket they obtain information about type, lifetime, and so on.

The first task of the context phase is to take the annotated syntax tree and to find the defining occurrence of each applied occurrence of an identifier or operator in the program.

That done, the context phase can turn to its second task, performing the context checking on each node of the tree, as specified by the rules in the language definition. Most of the context rules in language manuals are concerned with type checking, and will, for example, specify that the condition expression in an if-statement must have type Boolean. Other rules may, for example, forbid a jump to a label inside a for-statement from a goto statement outside that for-statement.

Additionally, context handling may be used to perform the final steps in syntax checking. For example, the syntax of a language as given in the manual may forbid records (structs) with no fields, but it is probably more user-friendly to allow such records in the parser and to issue the error message "No fields found in record type declaration" during context handling than to exclude them syntactically and issue the message "Unexpected closing parenthesis", or something similar, during parsing.

Context handling is also sometimes called **semantic checking**, which emphasizes the checking for correct meaning more than that for correct context use. Of course, correct meaning cannot be fully checked in any formal sense of the word, but often useful warnings about dubious meanings can be given. Examples are the detection of unused variables and routines, infinite loops, non-trivial expressions that have a trivial result (for example EXPR >= 0, where EXPR is an expression of type unsigned integer), and many others.

The problem with this is that much of this information becomes available more or less automatically during code optimization. Issuing the warnings in that phase, however, has the awkward property that the messages fail to appear when the program is compiled without optimizations. Duplicating part of the code optimization effort in the context handler just to give the proper messages is not attractive either. The reasonable compromise—doing the analysis and issuing the messages in the context phase and saving the results for the code generator— complicates the interfaces of all the phases between the context phase and the consumer of the information. Such are the worries of the compiler designer.

Context handling is one of the least "automated" phases of a compiler. For lexical analysis, parsing, and code generation many tools have been developed which generate efficient implementations from formal specifications. Attempts have been made to formalize and automate the context handling, as described in Chapter 4, but in practice this phase is usually hand-crafted, meaning that every restriction in the language specification has its own code to check it, and has its own potential for being wrong.

We will now first turn to two context handling issues that play a direct role in static correctness checking in most languages: identification and type checking.

11.1.1 Identification

At a conceptual level, identification is the process of finding the defining occurrence of a given applied occurrence of an identifier or operator. The **defining occurrence** of an identifier is the place of its main, and usually only, introduction. This introduction supplies information about the identifier: its kind (whether it is a constant, a variable, a module, etc.), its type, possibly an initial or fixed value, possible allocation properties, etc. The other occurrences of an identifier are its **applied occurrences** and are the consumers of this information. For example, in

```
INT month := 1;
WHILE month <= 12 DO
    print_string (month_name[month]);
    month := month + 1;
END WHILE;
```

the month in the first line is the defining occurrence, the others are applied occurrences.

This formulation of the problem does not cover all cases. Some languages allow **forward declarations**, which result in identifiers having more than one introduction. Other languages do not require identifiers to be introduced or declared at all; those languages have the information about the identifiers built in or the information is distributed over all the applied occurrences: type and other properties of an identifier follow from its form and/or use.

At the compiler construction level, these differences disappear: there is an information entry for each named item in the program, in which all information about this item is collected. It is the task of the identification process to connect all occurrences of an identifier to its proper entry. Information can then be inserted in and retrieved from this entry as desired. As explained in Section 2.11, the information base in which all the entries are kept is called the *symbol table* or *name list*.

Not all identifiers must be looked up in the same set of entries: for example, variables must be looked up among the local and global identifiers, field selectors must be looked up among the field selectors of a given type, etc. Each of these sets of entries defines a **name space**, and the syntactic position of an identifier in the program determines which name space it belongs in. The precise rules follow from the language manual, but usually identifiers in the syntactic positions of variable names, routine names, and some others live in one name space, the **general name space**, and field selectors live in special name spaces belonging to record types.

This implies that one can have a variable name i next to a field name i, without the two getting in each other's way, as shown in the C code fragment

```
struct one_int {
    int i ;
} i ;


    ...
    i . i = 3;
```

The first i in i.i is looked up in the general name space, leading to its identification as a variable of type struct one_int. The second i is then looked up in the special name space of the members of the type struct one_int.

Specific questions about the name spaces in a particular language must be answered by the language manual. Examples of such questions are whether labels live in the general name space or in a special label name space, and whether module names have a name space of their own. In principle any position that can be distinguished syntactically or contextually can have its own name space. C has three main name spaces, one containing the names of enums, structs, and unions, one containing the labels, and one containing all the rest; the latter includes variable identifiers, routine identifiers, type identifiers, and enumeration value identifiers. In addition, C has a name space for each struct and each union; these name spaces contain only the field selectors of the corresponding structs and unions.

11.1.1.1 Scopes

Some name spaces, especially those in block-structured languages, are scope-structured. These scopes work in stack fashion: there is a stack of scope elements, one for each scope entered, and all actions are performed on the top element(s). The rules are simple:

- a new empty scope element is stacked upon scope entry;
- declared identifiers are entered in the top scope element;
- applied identifiers are looked up in the scope elements from top to bottom; and
- the top element is removed upon scope exit, thus removing all declarations from that scope.

A naive implementation of a scope-structured name space is shown in Figure 11.2; on the left is the scope stack, on the right the linked lists of declaration information records, one for each name declared in each scope. The capital P in a record for a name stands for the properties attached to the name in the declaration.

Five levels of scope have been shown; they represent a possible constellation for a C program: level 0 is the library level, level 1 the program (routine declaration)

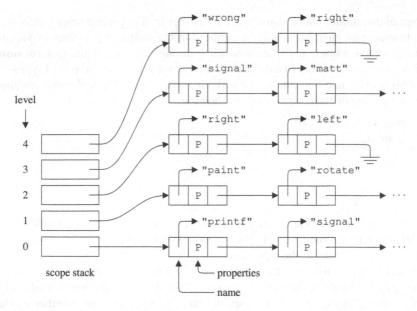

Fig. 11.2: A naive scope-structured symbol table

level, level 2 the formal parameter level, level 3 the local variable level and level
4 a subblock. Such a symbol table might result from the C code in Figure 11.3.
This set-up allows easy insertion of new names and easy removal of entire scopes;
identifiers can be found by performing a simple sequential search.

```
void rotate(double angle) {
    ...
}

void paint(int left , int right) {
    Shade matt, signal;

    ...
    {   Counter right, wrong;
        ...
    }
}
```

Fig. 11.3: C code leading to the symbol table in Figure 11.2

The organization shown in Figure 11.2 is simple and intuitive, but lacks two features essential for use in a practical compiler: it has no provisions for name spaces
and it does not use the fast symbol table access discussed in Section 2.11. We have
seen there that some identifier identification must already be done between the lexi-

cal scan and the parser, long before anything about scope and name spaces is known. This identification is based on the routine *Identify(Name)*, which yields a pointer to a record of type *IdfInfo*, which gives access to all information about the identifier *Name*. The speed of access is obtained using a hash table.

There are several ways to combine hash table identification, name spaces, and scopes in one implementation. We will discuss one possibility here, suitable for C-like languages; for a variation on this implementation, see Exercise 11.2.

Figures 11.4 and 11.5 together show an implementation that utilizes the easy access to names provided by a hash table, provides a fixed number of name spaces at the cost of a single field selection, and allows efficient scope stack operations. To avoid clutter, the diagrams depict a subset of the symbol table from Figure 11.2: only the names paint, signal, and right are shown.

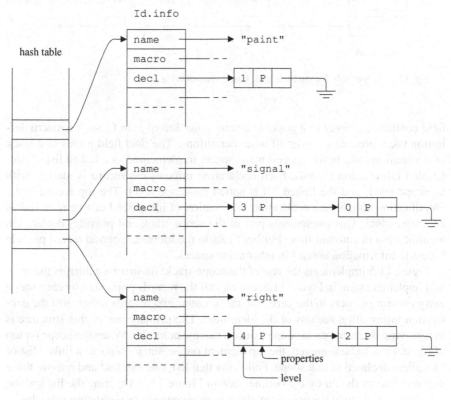

Fig. 11.4: A hash-table based symbol table

Figure 11.4 shows the identification part: the IdentificationInfo records are directly pointed to and accessed by the hash table. The name spaces are implemented as fields in the IdentificationInfo records, as follows. The record for identifier *I* starts with a pointer to the name *I*, for hash collision resolution and error reporting. Each following field represents the contents of a name space with respect to *I*. The first

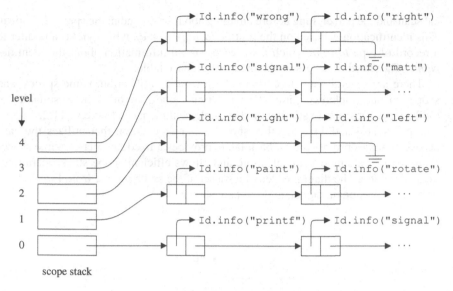

scope stack

Fig. 11.5: Scope table for the hash-table based symbol table

field contains a pointer to a possible macro definition of *I*; in C, such a macro definition takes precedence over all other definitions. The decl field points to a stack of declarations of *I* in the general name space, implemented as a linked list of declaration information records. Each declaration information record is marked with its scope level, and the linked list is sorted on scope level. The top record is the identification sought: the declaration information of identifier *I* can be retrieved as *Identify(I)*.decl. This implements part of the scope stack and provides declaration identification in constant time. Further fields in the IdentificationInfo record provide access to information about *I* in other name spaces.

Figure 11.5 implements the rest of the scope stack: its structure mirrors the original implementation in Figure 11.2, except that the records pointed to by each scope entry contain pointers to the pertinent IdentificationInfo records rather than the declaration information records of the identifiers. The primary use of this structure is in removing declarations at scope exit in a narrow compiler. When the scope on top of the stack is to be removed, the top element on the stack points to a linked list of identifiers declared in that scope. Following that list, one can find and remove these declarations, as shown by the outline code in Figure 11.6. Deleting the list and the top element conclude the operation; the previous scope is restored automatically.

These data structures allow fast and easy addition of identifier declarations and the removal of entire scope information sets. Without these data structures, scope removal would involve scanning the entire symbol table, which may contain hundreds or thousands of identifiers, to find the ones that are declared on the level to be removed.

```
procedure RemoveTopmostScope ():
    LinkPointer ← ScopeStack [TopLevel];
    while LinkPointer ≠ NoLink:
        — Get the next IdentificationInfo record:
        IdfPointer ← LinkPointer.idf_info;
        LinkPointer ← LinkPointer.next;
        — Get its first DeclarationInfo record:
        DeclarationPointer ← IdfPointer.decl;
        — Now DeclarationPointer.level = TopLevel
        — Detach the first DeclarationInfo record:
        IdfPointer.decl ← DeclarationPointer.next;
        FreeRecordPointedAtBy (DeclarationPointer);
    Free (ScopeStack [TopLevel]);
    TopLevel ← TopLevel − 1;
```

Fig. 11.6: Outline code for removing declarations at scope exit

As we have seen, record and module declarations create named subscopes which
themselves live in scopes. In idf.sel, idf is first looked up as an identifier in the
identifier name space. This gives a pointer to a definition of idf, which among others
holds a pointer to a record T describing the type of idf. T, which may be defined in
a different (older) scope than idf itself, is then tested to see if it is a structured type.
If it is not, the expression idf.sel tries to select from a type that has no selectors and
an error message must be given.

In one possible implementation, shown in Figure 11.7, T provides a pointer to
a list of records describing selectors, in which the selector sel can be looked up by
sequential search. This will then lead to the type of the field. In Figure 11.7, it would
be contained in property part P of the second record.

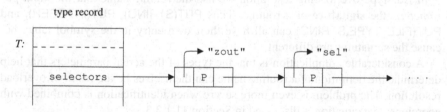

Fig. 11.7: Finding the type of a selector

Removing a level that holds definitions of structured types entails removing both
the type definitions and their fields. This is not particularly difficult, but requires
some care.

11.1.1.2 Overloading

If the source language manual states that all identifiers in a scope hide the identifiers with the same names in older (more outer) scopes, identification is relatively
simple: the definition record pointed at by the decl field in Figure 11.4 provides the
definition sought. In a language with overloading, however, identifiers do not hide
all identifiers with the same name; for example, PUT(s: STRING) does not hide
PUT(i: INTEGER) in Ada. Also, in many languages the operators are overloaded:
the + in 3 + 5 is different from the one in 3.1 + 5.1, since the first has two integers
as operands and the second operates on two floating point numbers.

The ambiguity caused by the overloading is resolved by considering the context
in which the name to be identified occurs. There are two issues here. The first is that
in the presence of overloading the identifier identification process comes up with
a *set* of definitions, rather than with a single identification. These definitions are
selected from the list of definitions supplied by the decl field in Figure 11.4. The
rules for selecting such a set of definitions from the list of all definitions depend on
the source language. The second issue then concerns the reduction of this set to a
single definition. This reduction process is again based on language-specific rules
that consider the context of the identifier. If, as a result of the reduction process, no
applicable definition remains, the identifier is undefined; if more than one definition
remains, the identifier is ambiguous; and if exactly one definition remains, it is the
definition of the identifier in the given context.

Suppose, for example, that the compiler needs to identify the PUT in the Ada
statement PUT("Hello"). In Ada, routine identifiers can be overloaded and the overloading has to be resolved by considering the types of the parameters. This is easily
achieved by generalizing the access key of the symbol table. Normally, a symboltable entry is uniquely identified by its scope and the symbol string. For a language
with Ada-type overloading resolution we use the routine name *and the input parameters*, the **signature** of a routine. Thus PUT(STRING), PUT(INTEGER), and
PUT(FILE_TYPE,STRING) can all have their own entry in the symbol table, because the signatures are different.

A considerable complication is that the types of the actual parameters that help
determine the definition of a routine name can themselves be the result of overload
resolution. The problem is even more severe when identification is combined with
coercions; that situation is discussed in Section 11.1.2.3.

Now that we have seen how we can still identify names in the presence of overloading, we consider its consequences for removing the top scope upon block exit.
The main change is that there can now be more than one definition with the same
level in the definition record chains in Figure 11.4. It is easy to remove them all
rather than just the first one, when visiting the *IdfInfo* record in the code in Figure
11.6.

11.1.1.3 Imported scopes

Some programming languages feature constructs that introduce copies of scopes from other places. Examples are the scope resolution operator in C++, the with-statement in Pascal and Modula-2, and the import declaration in Modula-2, Ada, and other languages with modules or packages. The details of these scope importers differ from language to language. In C++, a scope resolution operator x:: preceding a function definition introduces the field selectors of the class x in a scope around that function definition. The Pascal and Modula-2 construct WITH x DO ... END is similar: it starts a new scope in which the field selectors of the record x are available as identifiers in the general name space. The FROM module IMPORT declaration of Modula-2 and the use declaration of Ada, however, do not introduce a new scope but rather merge the new names into the present scope. Name clashes must be prevented in Modula-2 by explicitly selecting the imported names, and are avoided automatically in Ada by the overloading mechanism and the visibility rules associated with the use declaration. In all cases the result is that, with some identifiers, the programmer can just write sel, instead of idf.sel, or more importantly PUT("Text") instead of TEXT_IO.PUT("Text").

The obvious implementation of this feature is of course to retrieve the scope S to be imported, and to collect all names in it. Next, this collection is filtered as required, and a new scope is created and stacked if the semantics of the importing construct prescribes so. Each name N is then defined in the top-level scope in the usual fashion, with its properties derived from its entry in S. The time required by this technique is proportional to the number of names imported.

11.1.2 Type checking

The previous section has shown us that looking up an identifier leads to a declaration information record—a container for the properties of the object that the identifier identifies. The most basic and obvious, but therefore somewhat inconspicuous, property is the **kind** of the object—whether it is a constant, a variable, a routine, a type, a module, etc.; and the first step in checking the proper use of the identifier is checking this kind. Kind checking in itself is almost—but not entirely—trivial: for example, when the context requires a module identifier, it is simple to test if a module identifier has been supplied, using the declaration information. Some of the kinds, however, specify objects that involve values, for example constants, variables, and routines. These values belong to **types** —sets of values and operations— and their use is subject to often complicated and intricate rules, and has to be checked. This type checking is not at all trivial; we will therefore first concentrate on type checking, and address one issue in kind checking at the end of this section. For a comprehensive treatment of types in programming languages see Pierce [222].

Type checking is valuable because it can be seen as a simple but practical form of **formal verification** of a program: the programmer states that the value of variable is always element of a particular set, and the compiler verifies that this is so. Type systems are often intricate to get the most of this desirable property while still being comfortable for the programmer.

Type checking is involved in large parts of the annotated syntax tree. For example, the language rules usually specify which types can be combined with a certain operator; there are rules for formal and actual parameter types in a routine call; and assigning an expression value to a variable restricts the allowed types for the expression. Type information in a compiler has to be implemented in such a way that all these and many other checks can be performed conveniently.

Types are usually introduced by name through **type declarations**, as in

    TYPE Int_Array = **ARRAY** [Integer 1..10] **OF** Integer;

which defines the type Int_Array, but they may also be introduced **anonymously**, as in the following variable declaration:

    VAR a: **ARRAY** [Integer 1..10] **OF** Real;

When a type is introduced anonymously, it does not have a name in the source program, but for uniformity it needs one. Therefore, the compiler must use its imagination to invent a unique name, for example producing such internal names as #type01_in_line_35. So the above declaration of a is seen as an abbreviation of

    TYPE #type01_in_line_35 = **ARRAY** [Integer 1..10] **OF** Integer;
    VAR a: #type01_in_line_35;

Type declarations often refer to other type identifiers. In some languages they are allowed to refer to type identifiers that have not been declared yet; such references are called **forward type references**. Forward type references enable the user to define mutually recursive types, for example:

    TYPE Ptr_List_Entry = **POINTER** TO List_Entry;
    TYPE List_Entry =
        RECORD
            Element: Integer;
            Next: Ptr_List_Entry;
        END RECORD;

where the first occurrence of List_Entry is a forward type reference. However, forward type references also add some complications to the work of the compiler writer:

- The forward type references usually must be resolved. When, during processing, a forward type reference is met, the identifier in it is added to the symbol table, and marked as forward. Next, when a type declaration for this identifier is met, its symbol table entry is modified to represent the actual type.
- A check must be added for loose ends. At the end of a scope in which forward type references occur, the forward type references all must have been resolved if the language manual says so (and it usually does). This check can be implemented by checking all symbol table entries of the scope for being marked forward. If a forward type reference is met, it is a loose end, and must be reported.

• In some languages, a check must be added for circularity. The consequence of allowing forward type references is that the user can now write a circular type definition:

```
TYPE x = y;
TYPE y = x;
```

which probably is illegal. We will see below how to deal with this problem. (C and family do not suffer from this problem since they do not allow forward references to types. They do support forward references to union/structure tags, which is sufficient in practice.)

11.1.2.1 The type table

All types in a compilation unit are collected in a **type table**, with a single entry for each type. For each type, the type table entry might, among others, contain the following:

• its type constructor ("basic", "record", "array", "pointer", and others);
• the size and alignment requirements of a variable of the type;
• the types of the components, if applicable.

Various information is being recorded for types:

• for a basic type: its precise type (integer, real, etc.);
• for a record type: the list of the record fields, with their names and types;
• for an array type: the number of dimensions, the index type(s), and the element type;
• for a pointer type: the referenced type;
• for other type constructors: the appropriate information.

The type table entry must contain all the type information required to perform the type checking and code generation. The exact content therefore depends on the source language at hand. The representation in the compiler, on the other hand, depends on the implementation language, the language in which the compiler is written. In an imperative implementation language, the representation of a type usually is a record with a variant part (or a union) for those items that depend on the type constructor. In an object-oriented implementation language, a type would be an object class with all fields and methods that all type constructors share, and each type constructor would have its own subclass, with extensions specific for the type constructor at hand.

To demonstrate how the type table is built, let us now consider a simple language with record and pointer as the only type constructors, and one built-in type: integer. Also, for the sake of simplicity, let us assume that there is only one, global, scope for type identifiers. In this language, the built-in type integer is a predefined identifier indicating an integer type. The compiler places the identifier in the symbol table and its type in the type table, before it starts processing the input. This results in

```
type table:          symbol table:
TYPE 0: INTEGER "integer": TYPE 0
```

where the type table is indexed by values of the form TYPE n (implemented as integers or pointers) and the symbol table is indexed by strings.

Because of possible forward type references, it is not possible to just build the type table as input is processed. One possible solution is to add identifier references to the type table, which must be resolved when all input has been processed. For example, let us process the following type declarations:

TYPE a = b;
TYPE b = **POINTER** TO a;
TYPE c = d;
TYPE d = c;

Processing the first type declaration, TYPE a = b;, might result in the following type table and symbol table:

```
type table:          symbol table:
TYPE 0: INTEGER    "integer": TYPE 0
TYPE 1: ID_REF "b" "a": TYPE 1
                   "b": UNDEFINED_TYPE
```

Then, processing TYPE b = POINTER TO a; results in another type table entry for a (because references to identifiers have not been resolved yet). So, we add TYPE 2: ID_REF "a" to the type table and process TYPE b = POINTER TO TYPE 2. The UNDEFINED_TYPE symbol table entry for b is now resolved, and we obtain:

```
type table:                  symbol table:
TYPE 0: INTEGER              "integer": TYPE 0
TYPE 1: ID_REF "b"          "a": TYPE 1
TYPE 2: ID_REF "a"          "b": TYPE 3
TYPE 3: POINTER TO TYPE 2
```

The last two lines of the input are processed in the same way, and our type table and symbol table now look as follows:

```
type table:                        symbol table:
TYPE 0: INTEGER                    "integer": TYPE 0
TYPE 1: ID_REF "b"                "a": TYPE 1
TYPE 2: ID_REF "a"                "b": TYPE 3
TYPE 3: POINTER TO TYPE 2 "c": TYPE 4
TYPE 4: ID_REF "d"                "d": TYPE 5
TYPE 5: ID_REF "c"
```

Now that the input has been processed, all identifier references must be resolved. There are two reasons for doing this, the more important one being cycle detection. The other reason is that it is convenient to have each type referred to by a single, unique, index in the type table.

The first step in resolving the identifier references is to replace the identifier references in the type table by type references: a reference to an entry in the symbol table which refers to an entry in the type table is replaced by a direct reference to this type table entry. Our modified type table now has the following contents:

type table:
TYPE 0: INTEGER
TYPE 1: TYPE 3
TYPE 2: TYPE 1
TYPE 3: POINTER TO TYPE 2
TYPE 4: TYPE 5
TYPE 5: TYPE 4

Now, cycles can be detected by the closure algorithm presented in Figure 11.8. The algorithm also resolves type references to type references: when it has finished, a type table entry can still be a TYPE, but the entry it then refers to is no longer a TYPE—unless it is a cyclic definition. The algorithm constructs a set *Cyclic* containing all type table entries describing a type with a cycle. After executing this algorithm, our type table looks as follows:

type table:
TYPE 0: INTEGER
TYPE 1: TYPE 3
TYPE 2: TYPE 3
TYPE 3: POINTER TO TYPE 2
TYPE 4: TYPE 4
TYPE 5: TYPE 4

and the *Cyclic* set contains both TYPE 4 and TYPE 5. For all members in the *Cyclic* set, an error message must be produced. Also, these type table entries can be replaced with a special ERRONEOUS_TYPE entry.

Data definitions:
  1. T, a type table that has entries containing either a type description or a reference (TYPE) to a type table entry.
  2. *Cyclic*, a set of type table entries.
Initializations:
  Initialize the *Cyclic* set to empty.
Inference rules:
  If there exists a TYPE type table entry t_1 in T and t_1 is not a member of *Cyclic*, let t_2 be the type table entry referred to by t_1.
  1. If t_2 is t_1 then add t_1 to *Cyclic*.
  2. If t_2 is a member of *Cyclic* then add t_1 to *Cyclic*.
  3. If t_2 is again a TYPE type table entry, replace, in t_1, the reference to t_2 with the reference referred to by t_2.

Fig. 11.8: Closure algorithm for detecting cycles in type definitions

A good next step is to replace any type table reference TYPE n, where the corresponding type table entry n contains TYPE m, with a type table reference TYPE m. Note that there may be many of these references, in the symbol table, in the type table itself, as well as in other data structures in the compiler. This action converts our type table and symbol table to

type table:	symbol table:
TYPE 0: INTEGER	"integer": TYPE 0
TYPE 1: TYPE 3	"a": TYPE 3
TYPE 2: TYPE 3	"b": TYPE 3
TYPE 3: POINTER TO TYPE 3	"c": TYPE 4
TYPE 4: ERRONEOUS_TYPE	"d": TYPE 5
TYPE 5: ERRONEOUS_TYPE	

and may make similar changes to other data structures in the compiler.

Another option is to have a function *ActualType( )* in the compiler, which is called whenever a type table reference is required and which resolves a TYPE, for example:

```
function ActualType (TypeIndex) returning a type index:
    IF TypeTable [TypeIndex] is a TYPE reference:
        return TypeTable [TypeIndex].referredIndex;
    else — TypeTable [TypeIndex] is a direct type:
        return TypeIndex;
```

This avoids the extra pass over the internal compiler data structures used by the first approach, but requires calls of *ActualType( )* to be inserted in many places in the compiler code, which may be error prone.

For a different approach to scope table management see Assmann [20].

11.1.2.2 Type equivalence

When type checking an expression or the formal and actual parameters of a routine call, often two types must be compared to see if they match in the given context. For example, a routine may be declared to have a parameter of a floating point type, and a call to this routine may have an integer parameter. The compiler has to detect this situation, and produce an error message if the language rules do not allow this. Which combinations are allowed in which context is specified by the language manual. For example, the routine call of the example above is allowed in (ANSI) C, but not in Modula-2.

An important part of comparing two types concerns the notion of **type equivalence**. When two types are equivalent, values of these types have the same representations: one can be used where the other is required, and vice versa. The language manual, again, specifies when two types are equivalent. There are two kinds of type equivalence, structural equivalence and name equivalence. Since structural equivalence is tricky to define and implement well, modern languages tend to use name equivalence whenever possible. However, in some cases, for example for array equivalence, using structural equivalence makes for a much more useful language.

Name equivalence Two types are **name-equivalent** when they have the same name. Note that this requires every type to have a name (either user-declared or anonymously assigned by the compiler). In a language with name equivalence, the two types t1 and t2 in

```
TYPE t1 = ARRAY [Integer] OF Integer;
TYPE t2 = ARRAY [Integer] OF Integer;
```

are not equivalent since they have different generated names, but the following two types are:

    TYPE t3 = ARRAY [Integer] OF Integer;
    TYPE t4 = t3 ;

Implementing a name equivalence check is easy: name-equivalent types have the same index in the type table, once the ID_REF entries as described above have been resolved.

Structural equivalence Two types are **structurally equivalent** when variables of these types can assume the same values (when the two types have the same structure) and allow the same operations. This makes the types

    TYPE t5 = RECORD c: Integer; p: POINTER TO t5; END RECORD;
    TYPE t6 = RECORD c: Integer; p: POINTER TO t6; END RECORD;
    TYPE t7 =
        RECORD
            c: Integer;
            p: POINTER TO
                RECORD
                    c: Integer;
                    p: POINTER TO t5;
                END RECORD;
        END RECORD;

all equivalent.

Testing for structural equivalence is difficult. The algorithm basically works as follows: first, all types are placed into a single equivalence class. Then, repeatedly, attempts are made to split each equivalence class E into two equivalence classes E_1 and E_2, by selecting a single type T as a pivot from E and putting all types that can be shown to be not equivalent to T in E_1 and all types that cannot be shown to be not equivalent to T in E_2, according to certain rules.

11.1.2.3 Coercions

Type equivalence is only a building block in, not the complete answer to, type checking. In type checking, we want to answer the following question: if we expect a value of type T_1 at a particular position in the program, but we find a value of type T_2, is that acceptable? In this context, the type expected is sometimes called the **a posteriori type** and the type found the **a priori type**, but the terms "type expected" and "type found" are more intuitive and less error-prone. If T_1 and T_2 are equivalent, the type check certainly succeeds; if they are not equivalent the rules are language-dependent. For example, if a is a variable of type real, we expect a value of type real in the right-hand side of an assignment to a. However, the assignment a:=5 may have to be dealt with as well. Some languages do not allow any type mismatch, others require the compiler to insert a data conversion from integer to real. Such an implicit data and type conversion is called a **coercion**.

Exactly which coercions the compiler can insert depends on the language. In general, more than one coercion may have to be applied. For example, in the assignment xx := 5 where xx is of type complex, a coercion from integer to real and then a coercion from real to complex may be required. In many languages, the possible coercions also depend on the context. For example, in C, the context "right-hand side of an assignment expression" differs from the context "operand of a binary operator". In the former context, a coercion from real to integer is allowed, in the latter it is not: in

    int i = 2.7;

the 2.7 is coerced to integer (which in C involves truncation, so the value becomes 2), and in

    1 + 2.7

the 1 is coerced to real rather than the 2.7 to integer, to allow the + to be identified as a floating point addition.

As the above example already shows, the presence of coercions complicates operator and routine identification: operand and result types may need to be coerced to other types, before a matching identification can be found. Also, unrestricted application of coercions may lead to ambiguities. For example, the + in the expression 2+3 indicates integer addition, but if a coercion of the operands from integer to floating point is allowed, it could also indicate floating point addition.

Finding the proper coercions in an AST, for a language with arbitrary sets of types, contexts, and coercions, is a very difficult problem, for which no solution has yet been found. The approach presented here is similar to the one used in Section 11.1.1.2 to handle overloading of identifiers, and works for moderately complicated coercion rules. It is based on two closure algorithms, to be applied in succession. The first finds all types in each node that might play a role, the second crosses out all inapplicable types; the details depend on the source language rules. If in the end any type set in a node is empty, no identification could be made, and if any of the type sets contains more than one element, an ambiguity has been detected.

The closure algorithms are given in Figures 11.9 and 11.10. The sets with which the type sets of the nodes are initialized can be built in (as for a leaf 3.14) or supplied by the identification mechanism. Note that even the leaf nodes get type sets, since they too may be overloaded (for example enumeration values in Ada), and/or coerced. The inference rule in Figure 11.9 adds all types reachable by coercions; usually there are very few of these. The inference rules in Figure 11.10 then remove all types that are upward or downward incompatible. Note that the algorithm only determines the types; applying the necessary modifications to the expressions requires separate code.

As said before, the algorithm presented here is not the answer to all identification problems in the presence of overloading and coercions. In fact, as it stands, it is not even capable of handling operator identification in C. The basic problem is mainly one of language design and can be sketched as follows.

Data definitions:

1. *S* of a node, a variable type set attached to that node in the expression.
2. *C* of a node, a non-variable context associated with that node.

Initializations:

The type set *S* of each operator node contains the result types of all identifications of the operator in it; the type set *S* of each leaf node contains the types of all identifications of the node. The context *C* of a node derives from the language manual.

Inference rules:

For each node N with context C, if its type set S contains a type T_1 which the context C allows to be coerced to a type T_2, T_2 must also be present in S.

Fig. 11.9: The closure algorithm for identification in the presence of overloading and coercions, phase 1

Data definitions:

S of a node, a type set attached to that node in the expression.

Initializations:

Let the type set *S* of each node be filled by the algorithm of Figure 11.9.

Inference rules:

1. For each operator node N with type set S, if S contains a type T such that there is no operator identified in N that results in T and has operands T_1 and T_2 such that T_1 is in the type set of the left operand of N and T_2 is in the type set of the right operand of N, T is removed from S.
2. For each operand node N with type set S, if S contains a type T that is not compatible with at least one type of the operator that works on N, T is removed from S.

Fig. 11.10: The closure algorithm for identification in the presence of overloading and coercions, phase 2

Suppose a language has two types, int and real, and two +-operators, with types (int, int) → int and (real, real) → real. To accommodate expressions like 3.14 + 5 the language has to allow a coercion from int to real in operand context, to reach the expression 3.14 + (real)5, which identifies the second +. But having such a coercion in operand context makes the expression 3 + 5 ambiguous, since it allows both 3 + 5 to identify the first + and (real)3 + (real)5 to identify the second +.

This problem in language design is solved by having rules like "In operand context, a value can only be coerced to real if the other operand is real without using a coercion". Such rules make the coercions allowed in one syntactic position dependent on what is found in another syntactic position. This kind of longer-range relationship is not supported by the algorithm presented here and has to be coded separately, either as a third scan over the expression or as ad-hoc code in the inference rule in Figure 11.10.

Another potential problem with the algorithm is that phase 1 will not terminate for certain coercion rules. This happens, for example, with the coercion rules of Algol 68, where the inference rule in Figure 11.9 will continue forever to require new types. Fortunately very few programming languages have such a complicated coercion mechanism as Algol 68, so this phenomenon is usually not a problem.

11.1.2.4 Casts and conversions

Some languages allow the use of casts. A **cast** specifies the required type explicitly. For the compiler, it just introduces a different context, with usually different and stronger coercion rules. A cast differs from an explicit **conversion** in that it still uses the coercion system of the language. In contrast, an explicit conversion is a function which transforms data of one type to that of another type, and the types of its operands and result are subject to the normal source language type rules. Of course, the function could be a built-in function of the language, in which case the compiler must know about it. On the other hand, it could just be a library function.

11.1.2.5 Kind checking

With one exception, kind checking is trivial, as explained at the start of this section. The exception concerns constants and variables, and the complication arises from the fact that the actual kinds we are concerned with are locations and values rather than constants and variables. We will now examine the relationships between these notions.

In the assignment *destination:=source*, we expect a location on the left and a value on the right. If we adhere to the idea that the assignment operator, like all operators, requires values as input, we expect a value which is the address of a location on the left and a (normal) value on the right. Based on the topology of the assignment statement, the first is called an **lvalue** (pronounced "el-value") and the second is called an **rvalue**.

In the assignment p := q;, in which p and q are variables, we expect an lvalue for p and an rvalue for q. Since p is a variable, it has a location and its address is the lvalue; one even says that "a variable is an lvalue". On the other hand, q is an lvalue too, but in its position an rvalue is required. The kind checking system solves this by inserting a coercion which retrieves the contents of the location addressed by an lvalue. This coercion is similar to the dereferencing explained below, but is less conspicuous because it is usually incorporated in the machine instructions. Although the AST for the assignment p := q;, as amended by kind checking, contains a dereference node (Figure 11.11, in which the arrows show the dependencies), this node is not reflected explicitly in the corresponding code sequence:

```
Load_Mem q,R1
Store_Reg R1,p
```

It is hidden inside the machine instruction Load_Mem, as explained in the introduction to register machines at the beginning of Section 7.5.2.

We are now in a position to formulate the kind checking rules for lvalues and rvalues. The table in Figure 11.12 shows the basic rules; a – indicates that no action

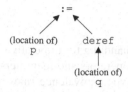

Fig. 11.11: AST for p := q with explicit deref

is required. The lvalue/rvalue attribute propagates bottom-up in the AST of an expression, according to language-dependent, but usually obvious, rules. Some of the rules are stated in the table in Figure 11.13, for C or a similar language; *V* stands for lvalue or rvalue.

The combined rules state, for example, that a[1] is an lvalue if a is a variable; type checking then tells us that a must be an array. This means that a[1] can be used as the destination in an assignment, since an lvalue is expected in that position. Suppose, however, that the expression a[1] is used as an index, for example in a[a[1]]; here an rvalue is required, so the lvalue needs to be dereferenced. On the other hand, 3 := 4 is erroneous, since 3 is an rvalue, and an lvalue is required; and so is &x := 7, for the same reason.

		Expected	
		lvalue	rvalue
Found	lvalue	--	deref
	rvalue	error	--

Fig. 11.12: Basic checking rules for lvalues and rvalues

Expression construct	Resulting kind
constant	rvalue
identifier (variable)	lvalue
identifier (otherwise)	rvalue
&lvalue	rvalue
*rvalue	lvalue
V[rvalue]	*V*
V.selector	*V*
rvalue + rvalue	rvalue
lvalue := rvalue	rvalue

Fig. 11.13: lvalue/rvalue requirements and results of some expression constructs

11.1.3 Discussion

The main problem in context handling for imperative and object-oriented languages is the identification of types, operators and identifiers. The problem is complicated by forward type references, type equivalence rules, routine and operator identification rules, overloading of identifiers and operators, and context-dependent coercions. No hard-and-fast general algorithm is available, but for almost all practical languages the problem can be solved by some form of inference rules working on type sets in the nodes of the expressions, and for many languages much simpler approaches involving only one type per node are possible.

11.2 Source language data representation and handling

In this section we discuss some of the data structures that represent source language data at run time, and the run-time manipulation needed to deal with the source language operations on these data. In the source language, a data item has a type, which may be a basic, built-in type of the language, or a constructed type, built using one of the type constructors in the language. The target language data types are usually limited to single bytes, integers of various sizes, address representations, and floating point numbers of several sizes.

Every source language data type is mapped to a particular combination of target language data types, and the run-time representation of a source language data item is the result of the application of this mapping. It is the task of the compiler writer to create such a mapping. We assume here that the target language has the common arithmetic, comparison, and copy operations, and has a byte-addressable memory; this assumption is almost universally justified.

11.2.1 Basic types

The usual **basic types** in a source language are characters, integers of several sizes, and floating point numbers of several sizes. The source language operations on these typically are arithmetic operations, assignment and comparison. The arithmetic operations include addition, subtraction, multiplication, division, and remainder. All these can be mapped directly to the target language data types and operations. Often the same instructions are used for signed and unsigned arithmetic, but the comparison instructions usually differ. Traditionally, characters were mapped to single bytes using the ASCII encoding, but many modern source languages support Unicode [277], and require two or four bytes to represent all possible character values.

Some source languages also have a **void type**, corresponding to no value at all. In some other languages a void type is present, but only implicitly. Representation of the void type in the target language is usually trivial or not necessary at all.

Floating-point numbers are in principle amenable to all the usual expression optimizations and simplifications, but due to their complicated arithmetic rules a number of obvious optimizations are incorrect. For example, the "obvious" simplification of v*0 to 0.0 fails, because for v = ∞ the result of the multiplication should be ∞. See Exercise 11.8 for more pitfalls in floating-point optimizations.

Modern processors invariably implement the floating point arithmetics specified in the IEEE 754 standard [128], and consequently modern language definitions support, or even mandate, IEEE 754 floating point semantics.

11.2.2 Enumeration types

An **enumeration type** defines a set of names to be the values of the new data type. The run-time representation is an integer, with values usually ranging from 0 to the number of enumeration values minus 1, although some languages allow the programmer to specify the integer values corresponding to the names of the enumeration type. In any case, the range of values is known at compile time, so an integer type of suitable size can be chosen to represent the values.

Operations allowed on enumerations usually are limited to copying, comparison for equality, comparison for greater/smaller, and sometimes increment/decrement, all of which are readily available in the target language for the integer representation chosen.

An enumeration type which is available in many languages, including some that do not have explicit enumeration types, is the **Boolean type**, with false and true as enumeration literals. An implementation with 0 for false and 1 for true suggests itself, but in many cases representing the Boolean value can be avoided, as shown in Section 11.4.1.1.

11.2.3 Pointer types

Most imperative and object-oriented languages support a **pointer type** of some kind. Pointers represent the addresses of source language data structures. The run-time representation of a pointer is an unsigned integer of a size large enough to represent an address. The integer operations for copying, assignment, comparison, etc. are available for pointers as well, and some target machines have special instructions or addressing modes for dealing with pointers.

The one operation that is particular to pointers is **dereferencing**, which consists of obtaining the value of the data structure that the pointer refers to. If the value to be obtained is small enough to fit in a register, dereferencing can usually be implemented as a single machine instruction. If the value is larger, though, as in dereferencing a pointer to a record or array, it is more efficient to find out what the final destination of the value is and to copy it to that place directly. For example, the assignment

```
q = *p;
```

in which q is the name of a record variable of type T and p is a pointer to a record of the same type, may be translated to a call of a library routine byte_copy():

```
byte_copy(&q, p, sizeof (T));
```

or the loop inside byte_copy may be in-lined.

An obvious optimization is available when the record obtained by dereferencing is used only for field selection. The language C has a special notation for this situation, ptr–>field, but other languages require the programmer to use the notation (*ptr).field. Literal implementation of the latter would indeed dereference the record under the pointer ptr to the top of the working stack and then replace the top of the working stack by the selected field. But when the compiler recognizes the situation it can first compute the pointer to the field and then dereference that pointer: (*ptr).field is translated as *(&(ptr–>field)).

The above applies when the context requires an rvalue. When the context requires an lvalue for a field selection, for instance in an assignment to ptr–>field, the required address can be obtained by adding the offset of field within the record to the pointer ptr.

Most languages that support pointers actually support **typed pointers**, for example POINTER TO INTEGER. In addition, there is often a **generic pointer type**, one that can be coerced to any other pointer type. For example, C has a "pointer to void" type, Modula-2 has a "pointer to byte" type. Coercing such a generic pointer type to another pointer type is a compile-time action, for which no run-time code is required.

11.2.3.1 Bad pointers

In the above we have assumed that a pointer indeed points to a valid value present in memory. In an incorrect program this need not be the case. Although the compiler can usually make sure that *if* the pointer refers to a value, that value will be of the right type, there are a number of situations in which the pointer does not refer to a value:

1. the pointer was never initialized;
2. the pointer is a null pointer, normally used to indicate the absence of a value, but the programmer forgot to check;
3. the pointer once referred to a value, but that value was located on the heap and has been removed since by a free() operation, leaving the pointer dangling;
4. the pointer once referred to a value, but that value was located in the activation record of a routine that has since been terminated, leaving the pointer dangling.

These dangers make pointers hard to use, as anyone with programming experience in C can confirm.

Languages differ in their approach to bad pointers. In C, the actions of an incorrect program are undefined, and the best one can hope of any of the above errors is that the program crashes before it produces incorrect results. The memory management units (MMUs) of most processors will generate an exception or trap if the pointer to be dereferenced is null, thus catching error 2 above, but their behavior on uninitialized pointers (error 1) will be erratic, and since errors 3 and 4 involve perfectly good pointers whose referents have gone away, no MMU assistance can be expected for them.

Language designers sometimes take measures to tame the pointer. Several approaches suggest themselves. Avoiding pointers at all is a good way to solve pointer problems (as done, for example, in functional and logic languages) but requires a lot of alternative programming support. In Java, pointers have been tamed by not allowing pointer arithmetic and limiting the way they can be obtained to object creation methods. Also, objects cannot be explicitly removed: as long as a pointer to an object exists, the object is alive. However, null-pointer dereferencing is still possible in Java.

Automatic initialization of pointers eliminates uninitialized pointers (error 1). The dereferencing of null pointers (error 2) can be eliminated in the language design by having two kinds of pointer-like type constructors, "pointers", which may point to a value or be null, and "references", which are guaranteed to point to a value. References can be dereferenced safely. Pointers cannot be dereferenced and can only be used in a test for null; if the pointer is not null, a reference is obtained, which can then, of course, be dereferenced safely. Having a garbage collector and disallowing calls to free() eliminates dangling pointers to the heap (error 3). And disallowing pointers to local variables eliminates other dangling pointers (error 4).

Although these possibilities are language design issues rather than compiler design issues, they are still relevant to compiler design. Implementing automatic initialization of pointers is easy, and symbolic interpretation can often establish that a pointer cannot be null. This is especially important in translating generated code, in which care has already been taken never to dereference null pointers. Also, there is a technique that avoids dangling pointer errors due to returning routines *without* disallowing pointers to local variables. Aspects of this technique are important for the run-time systems of some imperative and many functional and logic languages, which is why we will discuss these aspects here.

11.2.3.2 Pointer scope rules

Of the four types of errors, error 4 is the most problematic, since a good pointer turns into a dangling pointer through a routine exit, an action that is only remotely associated with the pointer. Following the saying that an ounce of prevention is worth a pound of cure, a set of rules has been developed to prevent dangling pointers from arising in the first place, the so-called "scope rules". Although no language except Algol 68 has put these rules in the hands of the programmer, they play a considerable role in the more advanced forms of routine construction and calling, and in the implementation of functional and logic languages. Because the possibilities and restrictions of passing routines as parameters and returning them as values are difficult to understand without these scope rules, it seems advisable to treat them here, in their more easily understandable data structure version.

Values located in activation records have limited "lifetimes", where the **lifetime** of an entity is the time in the run of the program during which the entity exists. The lifetime of a value is the same as that of the activation record in which it resides. Therefore, pointers to local values have limited "validity spans"; the **validity span** of a pointer is equal to the lifetime of the value it points to. For historic reasons, the validity span of a pointer is called its **scope**, and the rules for avoiding dangling pointers are called the **scope rules**. This terminology is unfortunate, since it inevitably causes confusion with the terms "scope of an identifier" and "scope rules", as discussed in Section 11.1.1, but we will conform to it to keep in line with the literature. Where necessary, a distinction can be made by using the terms "identifier scope" and "pointer scope".

The values that pointers refer to can be located in activation records or on the heap; for the purpose of this discussion, the global data area can be considered as the oldest activation record.

The lifetime of a value is equal to that of the container it is located in. For values on the heap, the lifetime is infinite; this does not mean that the data will be kept infinitely long, but rather that it is impossible to ever find out that its lifetime may not be infinite.

The lifetime of an activation record is governed by the routine calling mechanism; if the call is a simple subroutine call, the lifetime of the resulting activation record is enclosed in the lifetime of the activation record of the caller. If we call the lifetime of an activation record its "scope", as we did before with pointers, we see that one scope can lie completely inside another scope. We will call a scope P smaller than a scope Q $(P < Q)$ if P lies entirely inside Q. This imposes an ordering on scopes, but we will see that some scopes, for example those in different threads, are incommensurable, so the ordering is a partial one in principle.

In summary, the lifetime of a value is the time span during which the value exists, the scope of a value is the time span during which the value is valid. The purpose of the scope rules is to make sure that any value will be valid during its entire lifetime.

We are now in a position to formulate the scope rules [299]:

- The scope of a location on the heap is infinite; the scope of a location in an activation record is that of the activation record.
- The scope of the activation record of the program is infinite; the scopes of the other activation records depend on the calling mechanism and the implementation.
- The scope of a value is the smallest scope of any pointer it contains or infinite if it does not contain pointers.
- The scope of a pointer is that of the location into which it points.
- A value with scope V may be stored only in a location with scope L if $V >= L$; in other words, p := q requires "scope of p <= scope of q".

It is incorrect to express the last rule as "A value with scope V may not be stored in a location with scope L if $V < L$". The assignment is also forbidden if V and L cannot be compared, since that would imply the possibility that part of the lifetime of L falls outside the lifetime of V.

Together these rules ensure that values remain valid as long as they exist, so no dangling pointers can originate from routines returning. If activation records are put on a stack, the scope of the activation record of a called routine is smaller than that of the activation record of the caller. An immediate consequence of that is that data on the heap cannot contain pointers to the stack, except perhaps to the global activation record.

Another consequence is that a local pointer variable in a routine R cannot point to data local to a routine called by R. This effectively prevents the notorious dangling pointer caused in C by assigning the address of a local variable to a pointer passed as a parameter, as shown in Figure 11.14. Here the scope of &actual_buffer is that of the activation record of obtain_buffer(), and that of *buffer_pointer is that of do_buffer(), which is larger. This assignment constitutes a scope rule violation; if it is allowed to pass unchecked, as it is in C, the following happens. When obtain_buffer() returns, actual_buffer[] disappears, but a pointer to it remains in buffer, which is passed to use_buffer(). When use_buffer() then uses its now invalid parameter, the scope rule violation takes its toll.

```
void do_buffer(void) {
    char *buffer;

    obtain_buffer(&buffer);
    use_buffer(buffer);
}

void obtain_buffer(char **buffer_pointer) {
    char actual_buffer[256];

    *buffer_pointer = &actual_buffer;
    /* this is a scope-violating assignment: */
    /* scope of *buffer_pointer > scope of &actual_buffer */
}
```

Fig. 11.14: Example of a scope violation in C

In principle the scopes of pointers, locations, and values could be maintained and checked at run time, but doing so is awkward and inefficient. If the need arises, as it does in Algol 68, symbolic interpretation can be used to avoid generating checks where they are not needed. In practice the scope rules are used at compiler design time, to design efficient implementations of advanced routine operations in all paradigms with the property that no dangling pointers will ever be generated. These implementations are designed so that they never store a short-lived value in a longer-lived container. We will see several examples in Section 11.3.

A run-time approach to pointer safety is taken by Austin *et al.* [21], who discuss a method for the detection of all pointer and array access errors by replacing all pointers by so called "safe pointers". Oiwa [207] describes the extensive effort that went into the design and construction of a memory-safe full ANSI-C compiler, *Fail-Safe C*. Programs compiled with this compiler are on the average 5 times slower than with *gcc*.

11.2.4 Record types

A **record**, also called a **structure**, is a data item in which a fixed number of members, also called "components", of possibly different types are grouped together. In the target language, these members are represented consecutively in a memory area that is large enough to contain all members. What constitutes "large enough" depends on the sizes of the members and the alignment requirements of the target machine.

For example, a variable of the C structure

```
struct example {
    int member1;
    double member2;
};
```

is—in principle—represented as follows:

| member1 |
| member2 |

As explained in Section 8.1.4, some processors impose address alignment requirements on certain data accesses. For example, the SPARC processor requires an int (a 4-byte quantity) to have an address that is a multiple of 4 (is 4-byte aligned), and a double (an 8-byte quantity) to be 8-byte aligned. member1 of the example above thus must be 4-byte aligned, which is easily accomplished if the structure itself is 4-byte aligned, but member2 must be 8-byte aligned, and this can be accomplished by first making sure that it is 8-byte aligned within the structure by inserting a gap of 4 bytes between member1 and member2, and then making sure that the structure itself is 8-byte aligned. This way, member2 will also always be 8-byte aligned.

In general, gaps must be inserted between the structure members to make sure that each member is aligned properly within the structure, and then the size and the alignment requirement for the structure itself must be computed. This alignment requirement is the lowest common multiple (LCM) of the member alignment requirements. Often this is just the largest member alignment requirement, because alignment requirements usually are small powers of 2 (and thus one is either a multiple or a divisor of the other). Also, a gap can be inserted at the end of the structure to make sure that the size of the structure is a multiple of its alignment requirement.

This is convenient when the structure is used to build other data types, such as an array of these structures.

To get back to our example structure, on a SPARC it will be represented as follows:

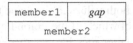

and it must be aligned on 8-byte boundaries. If x is a variable of this type, it has size 16, x.member1 lies at offset 0 from the start of x, and x.member2 lies at offset 8 from the start of x.

The mandatory operations on record types are **field selection** and copying; comparison for equality is not always required. The selection of a field from a record is accomplished in the target language by computing the address of the field, and then accessing the field through that address. This is done by adding the offset of the field within the record, which is known to the compiler, to the address of the record. The resulting address is the lvalue of the field (if it has one in the context at hand). To obtain the rvalue of the field, the address must be dereferenced. Record copying can be accomplished by either copying all fields individually or by copying the whole record, including the contents of any gaps. The latter may be more efficient if there is an efficient memory block copy instruction or routine available in the target language.

The possible presence of gaps makes record comparison more complicated than record copying. The contents of a gap usually are undefined, so they must be disregarded when comparing records. Therefore, record comparison has to be done field by field. For the example record type above, the compiler could generate a routine, returning 1 if the records are equal, and 0 if they are not, according to the following C scheme:

```
int compare_example(struct example *s1, struct example *s2) {
    if (s1->member1 != s2->member1) return 0;
    if (s1->member2 != s2->member2) return 0;
    return 1;
}
```

and then generate code that calls this routine whenever two records of this type must be compared. It could also generate in-line code to perform the comparison.

11.2.5 Union types

A **union type** is a data type of which the values are of one of a set of types. For example, a variable a of type

```
union {
    int i ;
```

```
    float f ;
};
```

in C can either hold a value of type int or a value of type float. To access the value of
type int, the programmer uses a.i; to access the value of type float the programmer
uses a.f. A union cannot hold both values at the same time. In C, the programmer is
responsible for keeping track of which of the union fields is present: the union is not
"discriminated". Some other languages have a special field, called the **union tag**,
which is always present in unions and indicates which variant the union currently
holds: the union is "discriminated". Each variant of the union has its own (constant)
value of the union tag. The type of the union tag usually is an enumeration type, and
each variant is associated with a particular enumeration value.

The run-time representation of an undiscriminated union is very simple: it is like
a record, except that all fields overlap. Therefore, its size is equal to the aligned size
of the largest variant, and its alignment requirement is equal to the lowest common
multiple of the alignment requirements of its variants. Field selection of an undiscriminated union is simple: the field always resides at offset 0 from the start of the
union. Copying consists of a memory copy of the size of the union. Comparison is
not available for undiscriminated unions.

The representation of a discriminated union is that of a record containing two
fields: the union tag and the—undiscriminated—union of the variants, as above. The
generated code can access the union tag to check which variant is current; whether
the programmer can also do so is source-language dependent. In principle a check
must be generated for each union-field access to make sure that the selector matches
the current variant of the union, and if it is not, a run-time exception must be produced. In an optimizing compiler this check can often be avoided by doing static
analysis, for example using symbolic interpretation as explained in Section 5.2.

11.2.6 Array types

An **array type** describes data structures which consist of series of items (also called
elements) of the same type. An array can have one or more dimensions. An array
element is indicated through one or more index expressions, one for each dimension of the array. The run-time representation of the array consists of a consecutive
sequence of the representation of the elements; the address of the first element is
called the **base address** of the array. For example, a one-dimensional array

A: **ARRAY** [1..3] **OF** Integer;

will be stored as

A[1]
A[2]
A[3]

and a two-dimensional array

  B: **ARRAY** [1..2, 1..3] **OF** Integer;

can be stored in either **row-major order**, which means that the elements are stored row after row (Figure 11.15(a)), or in **column-major order**, which means that the elements are stored column after column (Figure 11.15(b)). These schemes can easily be extended to more than two dimensions. Below, we will assume row-major order, as this is the order most often used.

B[1,1]
B[1,2]
B[1,3]
B[2,1]
B[2,2]
B[2,3]

(a)

B[1,1]
B[2,1]
B[1,2]
B[2,2]
B[1,3]
B[2,3]

(b)

Fig. 11.15: Array B in row-major (a) and column-major (b) order

  Note that, as long as the compiler makes sure that the element size is a multiple of the alignment requirement of the element, there will be no gaps *between* the array elements. This is important for the implementation of array comparison, as well as the implementation of element selection, as discussed below.

  As with records, array copying can be done either element by element or through a memory block copy. Array comparison, if the source language allows it, can be done through a direct memory comparison if the array elements do not have any gaps, and element by element otherwise.

  All languages that support arrays also support **element selection**, which is usually called **indexing**. Assume an n-dimensional array A with base address $base(A)$, where dimension k has lower bound LB_k and upper bound UB_k. The number of elements along dimension k is then $LEN_k = UB_k - LB_k + 1$. Now suppose that the location of element $A[i_1, i_2, \ldots, i_n]$ must be computed. Given the base address $base(A)$ and the size el_size of the array elements in bytes, the location of the required element is obtained by multiplying el_size with the number of elements in front of the required element, and adding the result to $base(A)$. For a one-dimensional array this location is $base(A) + (i_1 - LB_1) \times el\_size$. In general, for an n-dimensional array, the location of the element $A[i_1, i_2, \ldots, i_n]$ is:

  $base(A) + ((i_1 - LB_1) \times LEN_2 \times LEN_3 \times \ldots \times LEN_n$

  $+ (i_2 - LB_2) \times LEN_3 \times \ldots \times LEN_n$

  $\ldots$

  $+ (i_n - LB_n)) \times el\_size$

This is a lot of computation just to determine the location of one element. Fortunately, a large part of it can be precomputed. Reorganizing the expression results in

$$base(A) - (LB_1 \times LEN_2 \times LEN_3 \times \ldots \times LEN_n$$

$$+ LB_2 \times LEN_3 \times \ldots \times LEN_n$$

$$+ \ldots$$

$$+ LB_n) \times el\_size$$

$$+ (i_1 \times LEN_2 \times LEN_3 \times \ldots \times LEN_n + i_2 \times LEN_3 \times \ldots \times LEN_n + \ldots + i_n) \times el\_size$$

All lines of this expression except the last are independent of the indices in the element selection and depend only on the array A. In fact, the first n lines of the expression contain the location of the element $A[0, 0, \ldots, 0]$, the **zeroth element**.

Of course, it is quite possible that the zeroth element does not exist inside the array, because 0 may not be a member of the interval $LB_k \ldots UB_k$ for some k; this does not prevent us, however, from using its location, $zeroth\_element$, in address computations. The $LEN_k \times \ldots \times LEN_n$ products in the last line are also independent of the indices, and we can compute them in advance. If we designate the product $LEN_k \times \ldots \times LEN_n$ by $LEN\_PRODUCT_k$, we have:

$$LEN\_PRODUCT_n = el\_size$$

$$LEN\_PRODUCT_k = LEN\_PRODUCT_{k+1} \times LEN_{k+1} \quad \text{for } n > k >= 1$$

$$zeroth\_element(A) = base(A) - (LB_1 \times LEN\_PRODUCT_1$$

$$+ LB_2 \times LEN\_PRODUCT_2$$

$$+ \ldots$$

$$+ LB_n \times LEN\_PRODUCT_n)$$

With these values precomputed, the location of the element $A[i_1, i_2, \ldots, i_n]$ can be computed by the formula

$$zeroth\_element(A) + i_1 \times LEN\_PRODUCT_1 + \ldots + i_n \times LEN\_PRODUCT_n$$

All these precomputed values for the array can be stored in an **array descriptor**. This descriptor should also contain the array bounds (or the lower bound and the length) themselves, so array bound checks can be generated. An example of an array descriptor is shown in Figure 11.16.

The computation described above results in the location of an array element. When an lvalue is required in the context at hand, this location serves as one. When the rvalue of the array element is required, the location (a pointer) must be dereferenced. Again, this dereferencing may be implicit in the selected machine instructions.

When the array does not change size during its lifetime, and the bounds are known at compile time, it is called a **static array**. In contrast, when the array may change size during its lifetime, or its bounds are determined at run time, it is called

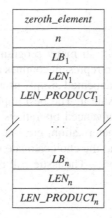

Fig. 11.16: An array descriptor

a **dynamic array**. For static array access the array descriptor does not actually have to be used at run time. Instead, the compiler can compute all the values the array descriptor would contain and use them as constants in index expressions, with the exception of *zeroth_element*. The compiler *can*, however, compute the offset of *zeroth_element* from the first element of the array itself, and use that to compute the value of *zeroth_element* when needed.

11.2.7 Set types

Some languages have **set types**, which are usually limited to sets of a small subrange of integers. These are probably best implemented as bitsets. In a **bitset**, each value in the subrange is represented by a single bit: if the bit is set, the value is a member of the set; if the bit is not set, the value is not a member of the set. Bitsets can be stored conveniently in target machine words. For example, the set of the integers ranging from 0 to 31 can be represented by a single 32-bit word.

The usual set operations are implemented by means of bit operations: set union is implemented with a bitwise OR, set intersection is implemented with a bitwise AND, symmetric set difference is implemented with a bitwise EXCLUSIVE OR, and set difference is implemented with a bitwise NOT followed by a bitwise AND.

Some languages allow sets of any type for which comparison for equality exists. Some possible representations of such sets are linked lists [275], trees, and hash tables [251].

11.2.8 Routine types

Routines are not considered data in many programming languages, and in these
languages the question of how to represent routines as a data type does not arise. In
C, a routine as data can be implemented simply as a pointer to its code; an indirect
routine call is then used to activate it. The best implementation of routines as data
in languages that allow more advanced operations on routines—nesting, routines
as first-class data, partial parameterization, etc.—depends in complicated ways on
the exact operations allowed and the choices made in the implementation as to the
allocation of the activation records. The issue will be covered integrally in Section
11.3.

11.2.9 Object types

An **object** is a record with built-in methods, with some additional features. Its type
is usually called a **class**. In some languages, an object is similar to an *abstract data
type* in which only the methods are visible from outside and the object fields can
only be accessed from within the method bodies. In other languages, the object
fields can be accessed like record fields.

The basic operations on objects are "field selection", "copying", and "method
invocation". Although many object-oriented languages do not allow direct access to
the fields of an object, field selection is needed for the access from inside methods in
the object. Copying is trivial and will not concern us here. For **method invocation**,
first the method must be identified, and then the call must be made.

The method call is similar to a routine call, but to make the object fields directly
accessible from within the method body, a pointer to the object is passed implicitly
as an additional parameter. Within the method the object is usually visible under
a reserved name such as self or this; the method can then access the object fields
through this name. In this section we will focus on method selection; the actual
routine or method invocation is discussed in Section 11.4.2.

In most object-oriented languages, objects also have **constructors** and **destruc-
tors**, which are methods that are to be invoked on object creation and object removal,
respectively. As far as the following discussion is concerned, these are methods
which are invoked like any other method.

If this was all there was to it, implementation of objects would be quite simple.
Suppose that we have an object class A with methods m1 and m2 and fields a1 and
a2. The run-time representation of an object of class A then consists of a record
containing the fields a1 and a2:

a1
a2

In addition, the compiler maintains a compile-time table of methods for class A:

m1_A
m2_A

where we have appended "_A" to the method names, to indicate that they operate on an object of class A, rather than on a different class that also defined methods with names m1 or m2. In this simple model, field selection is implemented as record field selection, and object copying is implemented as record copying; method selection is done by the identification phase in the compiler. Methods are implemented as routines with one additional parameter, a pointer to the object. So the method m2_A could be translated to the C routine

```
void m2_A(Class_A *this, int i) {
    Body of method m2_A, accessing any object field x as this->x
}
```

assuming that m2_A() has one integer parameter and returns no value and where Class_A is the C type name for class A. The method invocation a.m2(3); is then translated to m2_A(&a, 3);.

The problem is, however, that all object-oriented languages have at least some of the features discussed below. They make objects much more useful to the programmer, but also complicate the task of the compiler writer. These are the features that distinguish objects from abstract data types.

11.2.9.1 Feature 1: Inheritance

Inheritance, present in all object-oriented languages, allows the programmer to base a class B on a class A, so that B inherits the methods and fields of A, in addition to its own fields and methods. This feature is also known as **type extension**: class B extends class A with zero or more fields and methods. Class A is the **parent class** of class B, and class B is a **subclass** of class A. Now suppose that class B extends class A by adding a method m3 and a field b1. The run-time representation of an object of class B is then:

a1
a2
b1

In addition, the compile-time table of methods for class B is:

m1_A
m2_A
m3_B

This can still be implemented using the means for abstract data types described above.

11.2.9.2 Feature 2: Method overriding

When a class B extends a class A, it may redefine one or more of A's methods; this feature is called **method overriding**. Method overriding implies that when a parent class *P* defines a method, all classes based directly or indirectly on *P* will have that method, but the implementations of these methods in these subclasses may differ when overridden by redefinitions. Put more precisely, the method is *declared* in the class *P*, and then *defined* in class *P* and possibly redefined in any of its subclasses.

We use the phrase "the declaration of *X*" here as a statement saying that *X* exists, and "the definition of *X*" as a statement telling exactly what *X* is; this usage is in accordance with but somewhat stricter than the traditional usage in programming languages, where one speaks for example of "forward declarations" rather than of "forward definitions".

Now assume that class B in the example above redefines method m2, which was already defined for objects of class A. Then the definition of method m2 in A is both its only declaration and its first definition; that in class B is a redefinition. Some languages, for example C++ and Java, allow the method declaration to occur without a definition; the method is then a **virtual** or a **abstract method** (terminology depending on the language at hand), and a class in which at least one virtual method occurs is an **abstract class**. The actual methods must then be defined in classes that extend the abstract class.

We will rename the methods so that the name reflects both the class in which it is declared and the class in which it is defined. The names consist of three parts, the method name, the class it is declared in, and the class it is defined in; the parts are separated by underscores (_). So a name m2_A_B is used to designate a method m2 declared in class A and defined in class B.

Method overriding affects the compile-time table of methods. Under the above assumption that class B redefines method m2, which was already declared and defined in class A, the method table of class A now becomes:

m1_A_A
m2_A_A

and the method table of class B becomes:

m1_A_A
m2_A_B
m3_B_B

Now suppose a is an object of class A, and b is an object of class B. A method call a.m2(...) will then be translated with a call to m2_A_A, whereas a method call b.m2(...) will be translated to a call to m2_A_B. This differentiates clearly between m2_A_A, which was declared in class A and defined in class A, and m2_A_B which was also declared in class A but defined in class B.

If inheritance is the only other object-oriented feature in the language, the type of the translation of m2_A_A is

```
void m2_A_A(Class_A *this, int i);
```

and that of m2_A_B is

```
void m2_A_B(Class_B *this, int i);
```

11.2.9.3 Feature 3: Polymorphism

When a class B extends a class A and the language allows a pointer of type "pointer to class B" to be assigned to a variable of type "pointer to class A", the language supports **polymorphism**: a variable of type "pointer to class A" may actually refer to an object of class A or any of its extensions. The implementation of this feature requires a new operation, **pointer supertyping**: converting a pointer to an object of subclass B to a pointer to an object of a parent class A. This operation is used in assignments, for example:

```
class B *b = ...;
class A *a = b;
```

in which the second line is translated into

```
class A *a = convert_ptr_to_B_to_ptr_to_A(b);
```

For now, the routine convert_ptr_to_B_to_ptr_to_A() is a compile-time type operation. Because an object of class B starts with the fields of class A, the value of the pointer need not be changed and the only effect consists of changing the type of the pointer:

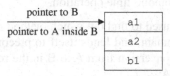

But note that we now have identical pointers to objects of different classes.

11.2.9.4 Feature 4: Dynamic binding

Now that a pointer p of type class A * can actually refer to an object of class B, a question arises about the methods that apply. If the source program applies method m2 to the object referred to by p, should the translation invoke m2_A_A or m2_A_B? There are two possible answers to this question: **static binding**, which maintains that statically p refers to an object of class A, so m2_A_A should be called; and **dynamic binding**, which maintains that if the object is actually of class B we should apply m2_A_B, and if the object is actually of class A, we should apply m2_A_A.

Static binding is trivial to implement, but most object-oriented languages use dynamic binding, for various important programming language design reasons. Dynamic binding has two significant consequences:

- There are two kinds of As out there, "genuine" As which use m2_A_A and As "embedded" in Bs, which use m2_A_B, and the two cannot be distinguished statically. It follows that from now on, the object representation must include dynamic type information, telling if it is an A or a B.
- B's methods require a pointer to a B to obtain access to all of B's fields. As m2 may, however, be called through a pointer of type "pointer to A" that dynamically points to an object of class B, we need yet another operation, **pointer (re)subtyping**, which reconstructs a pointer to B from the pointer to A. The method invocation p->m2(3), where p is statically a pointer to an object of class A, could then be translated to

```
switch (dynamic_type_of(p)) {
    case Dynamic_class_A: m2_A_A(p, 3); break;
    case Dynamic_class_B:
        m2_A_B(convert_ptr_to_A_to_ptr_to_B(p), 3); break;
}
```

where the dynamic type information is an enumeration type with the values Dynamic_Class_A and Dynamic_Class_B. When p is statically a pointer to B, we could translate the invocation p->m2(3) immediately to

```
m2_A_B(p, 3);
```

Note that this code is consistent with the declarations void m2_A_A(Class_A *this, int i) and void m2_A_B(Class_B *this, int i). We will see, however, that a better translation is possible. For now, pointer subtyping is again a compile-time operation.

The switch statement used to find out which method routine to call is a function that works on a small domain, and lends itself to precomputation. To this end we incorporate the pointer conversion from A to B in the routine for m2_A_B, which now accepts a pointer to A:

```
void m2_A_B(Class_A *this_A, int i) {
    Class_B *this = convert_ptr_to_A_to_ptr_to_B(this_A);
    Body of method m2_A_B, accessing any object field x as this->x
}
```

More in general, every method translation m_X_Y gets as its first parameter a pointer to Class_X, which is then immediately converted to a pointer to Class_Y by applying convert_ptr_to_X_to_ptr_to_Y(). If X and Y are the same, the conversion can be omitted.

With this modification to m2_A_B(), the method invocation p->m2(3), where p is statically a pointer to an object of class A, can be translated as

```
(dynamic_type_of(p) == Dynamic_class_A ? m2_A_A : m2_A_B)(p, 3);
```

which features a computed function which is called with the parameter list (p, 3). Rather than computing the function from the dynamic type information of p each time an operation on p is performed, we can incorporate the resulting function address in the dynamic type information. The type information for an object of class B is then a record with three selectors, m1_A, m2_A, and m3_B, containing the addresses of the routines to be called for methods m1, m2, and m3. These are m1_A_A(), m2_A_B(), and m3_B_B(); each of these routines has as its first parameter a pointer to an object of class A. Such a record with addresses of method routines is called a **dispatch table** and the type information in each object is implemented as a pointer to its dispatch table, as shown in Figure 11.17.

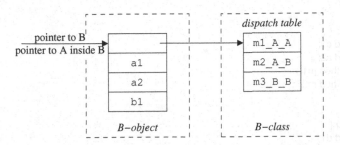

Fig. 11.17: The representation of an object of class B

The type information for an object of class A is a two-field dispatch table containing the addresses of the routines m1_A_A() and m2_A_A(), both of which have a pointer to an object of class A as their first parameter. So in both dispatch tables the selector m1_A selects routines of the same type; the same applies to m2_A. This in turn means that the selection p–>dispatch_table–>m2_A, where p is of type class A *, yields the proper routine with the proper type, regardless of whether p points to an object of class A or one of class B. The method invocation p–>m2(3) can now be translated very efficiently as

(p–>dispatch_table–>m2_A)(p, 3);

As we have modified the routine m2_A_B(), the translation given above for the invocation p–>m2(3), when p is statically a pointer to B, is no longer correct. The routine now expects a pointer to A, and must be given one:

m2_A_B(convert_ptr_to_B_to_ptr_to_A(p), 3);

Until now, the effect of the conversion routines has been that of type conversion only; no actual code was involved. We will now turn to another object-oriented feature that requires the conversion routines to have substance.

11.2.9.5 Feature 5: Multiple inheritance

So far, we have only discussed **single inheritance**, in which an object class may only inherit from a single parent class. In this section, we will discuss the consequences of allowing objects to extend more than one parent class. This feature is called **multiple inheritance**, and is supported by several important object-oriented programming languages. Suppose, for example, that we have an object class C with fields c1 and c2 and methods m1 and m2, an object class D with field d1 and methods m3 and m4. Next an object class E is defined which extends both C and D, adds a field e1, redefines methods m2 and m4, and adds a method m5. All this is shown in Figure 11.18.

```
class C {
    field c1;
    field c2;
    method m1();
    method m2();
};

class D {
    field d1;
    method m3();
    method m4();
};

class E extends C, D {
    field e1;
    method m2();
    method m4();
    method m5();
};
```

Fig. 11.18: An example of multiple inheritance

Unlike the situation with single inheritance, it is no longer possible to represent an object as a pointer to a dispatch table followed by all object fields. In particular, the "D inside E" object must start with a pointer to its dispatch table, followed by its object fields. It is still possible to combine the dispatch tables for E, "C inside E", and "D inside E". However, they are no longer all indexed by the same pointer. The dispatch table for E becomes:

```
m1_C_C
m2_C_E
m3_D_D
m4_D_E
m5_E_E
```

so the dispatch tables for E and "C inside E" still have the same address, but the pointer to the dispatch table for "D inside E" refers to the third entry (that of m3_D_D of the dispatch table for E. Moreover, this pointer has to be represented explicitly between the object fields of E. The representation is summarized in Figure 11.19.

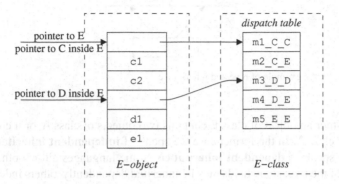

Fig. 11.19: A representation of an object of class E

This has consequences when viewing an object of class E as an object of class D, and vice versa. The pointer supertyping and pointer subtyping operations, which up to this point did not require code, now in some cases get substance:

supertyping:
    convert_ptr_to_E_to_ptr_to_C(e) ≡ e
    convert_ptr_to_E_to_ptr_to_D(e) ≡ e + sizeof (class C)

subtyping:
    convert_ptr_to_C_to_ptr_to_E(c) ≡ c
    convert_ptr_to_D_to_ptr_to_E(d) ≡ d − sizeof (class C)

When an object class E inherits from both class C and class D, an ambiguity may arise. For example, C and D may both contain a method with the same name. Class E inherits both these methods, but when applying a method with this name to an object of class E, only one method can be applied, and it may not be clear which version is intended. The language rules should indicate when a conflict or ambiguity arises, and the compiler has to detect these situations. Often the compiler task is complicated enough to warrant specific publications, for example Ramalingam and Srinivasan [230] or Boyland and Castagna [48]. These are very language-specific problems, however, and we will not discuss them here.

11.2.9.6 Feature 6: Dependent multiple inheritance

An important issue that arises with multiple inheritance, one which we have ignored in the discussion above, is **repeated inheritance**. For example, if both class C and D of the example above are extensions of a class A, as depicted in Figure 11.20, then what does "A inside E" mean? Depending on the language, this can mean one of two

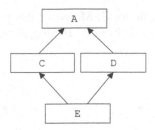

Fig. 11.20: An example of repeated inheritance

things: either an object of class E contains two objects of class A, or it contains one object of class A. In the former case we speak of **independent inheritance**, in the latter we speak of **dependent inheritance**. Some languages allow both, or even a mixture of the two: some fields may be inherited dependently, others independently.

Independent multiple inheritance is implemented exactly as described above. The only complication is in the identification, and the language rules should prescribe when and how the programmer should use qualification, exactly as if the fields and/or methods of class A resulted from different classes, but with the same names.

Now let us turn to dependent inheritance. The added complexity here is not in the method selection, but in the representation of the object data. We can no longer use the "parent objects first" scheme, because, in the example above, we would get two copies of the data of A. So, we will have to arrange the object data so that it only has one copy of the A data. We can accomplish that by placing the components of the object data in the object in the following order: the first entry is the pointer to dispatch table of E (and of "C inside E"); the next entries are the fields of A; then follow all fields of C not inherited from A; the entry after that is the pointer to dispatch table of "D inside E" (which points to within E's dispatch table); next are all fields of D not inherited from A; and, finally, all fields of E not inherited from C or D.

This order is correct for the E object and the "C inside E" object, but what about the "D inside E" object? The compiler has to decide what a D object looks like when compiling the D object class, at a time when it does not know about either C or E. Assuming that a D consists of a pointer to its dispatch table followed by its fields will not work, since when a D resides inside an object of type E, the fields it inherits from A are some distance ahead of the dispatch table pointer and D's own fields follow it. So when producing code to access the object fields, the compiler has no idea where they are. As usual, the answer to this kind of problem is a run-time descriptor. This descriptor should allow a method to find the object fields, given a pointer to the object itself. For each field, the descriptor must contain the offset of the field from the object pointer. We enumerate the object fields, so we can use the enumeration index as an index in an **offset table**. In addition to a pointer to the dispatch table, the object representation now must also contain a pointer to the offset table. Since we do not know beforehand which object classes will be involved in multiple inheritance, we must follow this two-pointer scheme for all objects.

Now let us return to our example of Figure 11.18, and extend it by assuming that both object class C and object class D extend an object class A, which has fields a1 and a2 and methods m1 and m3. So, object class C redefines method m1, and object class D redefines method m3; see Figure 11.21.

```
class A {
    field a1;
    field a2;
    method m1();
    method m3();
};

class C extends A {
    field c1;
    field c2;
    method m1();
    method m2();
};

class D extends A {
    field d1;
    method m3();
    method m4();
};

class E extends C, D {
    field e1;
    method m2();
    method m4();
    method m5();
};
```

Fig. 11.21: An example of dependent multiple inheritance

An object of class E has the representation depicted in Figure 11.22. Assuming that all pointers and fields have size 1, field a1 has offset 2 from the E pointer, field a2 has offset 3, etc., and the offset table of class E contains

2 3 4 5 8 9

The offset table of the "D inside E" class contains

−4 −3 2

Note that for an object of class E, there is an ambiguity on m1 as well as m3. The language rules or the programmer will have to specify which m1 and m3 are intended when applying it to an object of class E.

By now it may be clear why some languages (notably Java) do not allow multiple inheritance: it causes many complications and adds some method invocation overhead. On the other hand, the benefit is added flexibility.

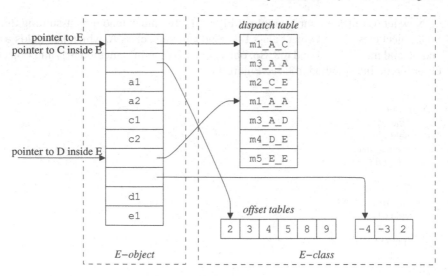

Fig. 11.22: An object of class E, with dependent inheritance

11.2.9.7 Optimizations for method invocation

All the manipulations discussed above make a method invocation more expensive
than a routine call: the method is called through a dispatch table, and the method
itself may have to adjust the object pointer that is passed to it. Therefore, some
languages have a mechanism for indicating that a method may not be redefined by a
subclass. Such an indication allows the compiler to identify the method directly, as
it would identify any routine; the compiler can then use the routine call mechanism
instead of the dispatch table. In Java, a method can be marked "'final'", indicating
that it may not be redefined. In C++, methods that may be redefined must be marked
"virtual".

Static analysis can also be of assistance in allowing the compiler to find out
exactly to which subclass a method is applied. It may also be able to determine the
method called, and generate a direct routine call.

More information about the implementation of inheritance can be found in papers
by Templ [276], which covers independent multiple inheritance only, and Vitek and
Horspool [289], which covers implementation of dynamic binding in dynamically
typed object-oriented languages.

11.2.10 Interface types

Java has incorporated an extension that relieves the limitations of single inheritance
somewhat, without adding the complexity (and all the power) of multiple inheri-

tance. The extension consists of so-called interfaces. An **interface** is like an object class in that it consists of a number of method specifications. In contrast to an object class, however, it cannot have non-constant object fields and all methods must be abstract. An interface may extend a single parent interface.

An interface is not instantiated like an object, but one can declare Java variables of an interface type, and invoke methods from the interface specification on them; Java variables are actually pointers to objects. The trick is that an object class may specify that it implements one or more of those interfaces, and that an interface type is compatible with any object type that implements this interface. So, for example, given an interface

```
public interface Comparable {
    public int compare(Comparable o);
}
```

it is possible to define an object class that implements this interface, while it still can extend another object class.

The compiler must generate a separate dispatch table for each interface that an object class implements. This separate interface dispatch table only contains entries for methods that are specified in the interface specification, but the entries refer to methods of the object type. A variable of an interface type can be represented by a record containing two pointers, one to the interface dispatch table, and one to the object. Method invocation on an interface then goes through the pointer to the interface dispatch table. Conversion from an interface value to an object class value requires a run-time check to ensure that the object class actually corresponds to the type of the object referred to by the interface value, or is a parent class of it. The reverse conversion, from a class to an interface, consists of a compile-time check that the object class actually implements the interface type.

11.3 Routines and their activation

Routines have been with us since the first programs were written and will probably continue to serve us for a very long time. It is therefore amazing to see how complicated these seemingly basic entities are. A routine call is a combination, a successful combination one must admit, of at least four loosely related features:

1. supplying a new computing environment containing at least some temporary memory, the local variables;
2. passing information to the new environment, the parameters;
3. transfer of the flow of control to the new environment, with—in normal circumstances–an eventual return to the caller;
4. returning information from the new environment, the return value(s).

Some of these features are available in isolation in some languages. Creating a new environment (1) is available in C and many other languages as block entrance. Code that can be transferred to with guaranteed return (3) without creating a new environment is known as a "refinement" [26]. But the package deal of the routine call has been far more important.

11.3.1 Activation records

The list of the four features above shows that the basic ingredient of a routine activation is the new environment. The data structure supporting the new environment is the **activation record**, also called **frame**. An activation record holds the data pertinent to an invocation of a routine or object method; it represents an activated and not yet terminated routine. In particular, it contains user data—local variables, parameters, return values, register contents—and administration data—code addresses, pointers to other activation records. Managing the user data is discussed in Section 11.4.2.2.

In non-concurrent code, only one of the activation records represents a running routine; all the others are suspended: no instructions of those routine activations are being executed. The instruction being executed is located in the code of the running routine and the **program counter**, PC, points at it, or—more usually—just after it, depending on hardware conventions. The activation record of the running routine is indicated by a **frame pointer**, FP. The frame pointer, which usually resides in a dedicated register, is used at run time to access the contents of the activation record of the running routine; its use is explained in more detail in Section 11.4.2.2.

Depending on the language and function that is being compiled, the offset from the stack pointer to the frame pointer may be known at compile time. In such cases it may be more efficient to not maintain a frame pointer, but use the stack pointer instead.

In this section we concern ourselves with allocating, deallocating, and otherwise organizing the activation records in efficient ways. In many languages, routines are activated in a strictly last-in-first-out order: when a routine *A* invokes a routine *B*, *A* cannot continue until *B* has finished. For such languages a stack is the preferred allocation scheme for activation records. In other languages complications exist, due to features like nested routines, iterators, coroutines, routines passed as parameters, routines returned as routine results, partially parameterized calls, non-local gotos, and continuations. Such features complicate the use of a stack for the activation records. In our implementations, we will try to use stack allocation as long as possible, for efficiency reasons.

We will first discuss the contents of activation records. Next, we consider several forms of routines and make an inventory of the operations available on routines. Finally we consider implementations of these operations on the various forms of routines.

11.3.2 The contents of an activation record

Although the contents of an activation record depend on the source language, the compiler, and the target machine, the dependency is not a strong one, and all types of activation records have much in common. They almost invariably include the following components:

- the local variables of the routine;
- the parameters of the routine;
- the working stack; and
- an administration part.

The first three components correspond closely to the local variables, parameters, and intermediate results in the source program. These components will be examined in more detail in Section 11.4.2.2, where we discuss the actual routine call. Some aspects of the administration part are discussed further on in this subsection.

Figure 11.23 shows a possible structure for an activation record. The peculiar order of the components is helpful in the creation of activation records in routine calls and in addressing the user values they contain. It is the most natural order on most machines and it is the order used in our treatment of routine calls in Section 11.4.2.2. Other orders are possible, though, and may have their advantages, especially when they are supported by special stack manipulation instructions.

An activation record is accessed through its frame pointer. In our treatment this frame pointer points to the last byte of the administration part, just before the first local variable. This is convenient since it allows addressing local variable k by FP + offset(k) and parameter p by FP + sizeof (administration part) + offset(p), regardless of how many parameters or local variables there are. The offsets of local variables are negative, those of the parameters positive. The direction of low to high addresses is in accordance with that on most machines.

The exact contents of the administration part of an activation record A resulting from the invocation of a routine R are machine- and implementation-dependent. They always include either return or continuation information, and a "dynamic link"; they may include a "lexical pointer". In some implementations, the administration part also contains copies of values kept in registers, but since these again

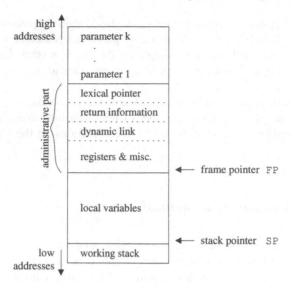

Fig. 11.23: Possible structure of an activation record

represent local variables, parameters, and intermediate results from the source program, their treatment is also deferred to Section 11.4.2.2. **Return information** consists of a return address, which is the code address in the caller of R to which the flow of control will return when R terminates. **Continuation information** consists of a continuation address, which is the code address in R at which the flow of control will continue when R is resumed. Which of the two is present depends on the implementation, as explained in the next few paragraphs. In both cases the **dynamic link** is the frame pointer of the caller of R.

The issue of storing return addresses in the activation records of callees or continuation addresses in the activation record of callers may be confusing and a few words are in order. In principle, any operation that suspends a routine R for whatever reason can store the continuation (resumption) information in the activation record of R; the information can then serve to continue R when that is required. Such operations include calling another routine, suspending in an iterator, transferring to another coroutine, and even a thread switch (Section 14.1.2). Storing continuation information about R in the activation record of R has the advantage of keeping R as a conceptual unity.

Storing return information in the activation record of the callee has a much more limited applicability: it supports only routine calling. The reason is simple: only the callee can get at the information and the only thing it can do with it is to use it to return to the caller. Hardware support is, however, much stronger for storing return information than for storing continuation information, and in virtually all implementations the call to a routine S stores return information in the activation record of S.

The administration part may contain another important entry: the "lexical pointer", also called "static link"; this is the frame pointer of the enclosing visible scope. The lexical pointer allows access to the local variables of the lexically enclosing routine and to its lexical pointer, as will be explained in Section 11.3.6. For some languages, no lexical pointer is needed. In C, for example, routines can only be defined on the top level, so a routine has only one enclosing visible scope, the global scope, in addition to its own local scope. The frame pointer of the global activation record is constant, though, and need not be stored; it can be incorporated into the machine addresses of the global items. The frame pointer of the local activation record is available as the current frame pointer FP.

Activation records can be allocated on a stack or on the heap. Stack allocation is cheaper but limits the usability of the activation records. As said before, we will try to use stack allocation as long as possible in our implementation.

11.3.3 Routines

A routine is just a piece of code, reachable through a pointer to its first instruction, its **code address**. When a routine R is called (invoked, activated) an activation record is created for it and the flow of control is transferred to its first instruction by setting the program counter to the routine code address; the routine is now **running**. When R calls a routine S, an activation record for S is created and the flow of control is transferred to the first instruction of S; S is now running and R is **suspended**. R is then the **parent** of S, and S is the **child** of R. When S finishes, it is **terminated**, and R is **resumed**. The **ancestors** of a routine R are defined as the parent of R and the ancestors of the parent of R. Routines that are running or suspended have activation records; they are called **active**. A routine can be active more than once simultaneously, in which case it is recursive; only one invocation can be running at any given time. When a routine returns, its activation record is removed. When the last activation record of a routine has been removed, the routine becomes **inactive** again.

The above is the behavior of the classical **subroutine**; there are several other kinds of routines, which exhibit additional features. The simplest is the **iterator**, a routine that can suspend itself temporarily and return to its parent without losing its activation record. This allows the iterator to continue where it suspended itself, when it is called again. As a result, the iterator can yield a succession of values; hence its name. The temporary return statement is usually called "suspend" or "yield".

An example application of an iterator in C notation is given in Figure 11.24. The iterator next_fibonacci() is started by the first call to it in the routine use_iterator(). After initializing a and b, the iterator immediately suspends itself on the yield a statement, yielding the value 0. The second call to next_fibonacci() continues just after the yield a statement, and again suspends immediately, yielding a 1. The third and further calls require the computation of further elements of the Fibonacci sequence, which are then yielded by the second yield b statement. (The construction for (;;) is C idiom for an infinite loop.) In languages that lack iterators, programmers usually implement them with global variables or by introducing additional parameters, as shown for example in Section 1.4.2, but the general implementation requires the retention of the activation record. A well-known example of an iterator is the UNIX routine getchar().

```c
void use_iterator(void) {
    for (;;) {
        printf ("%d\n", next_fibonacci ());
    }
}

int next_fibonacci(void) {
    int a = 0; int b = 1;
    yield a;
    yield b;
    for (;;) {
        int tmp = a; a = b; b = tmp + b;
        yield b;
    }
}
```

Fig. 11.24: An example application of an iterator in C notation

A third variety of routines is the **coroutine**. Like the iterator it can suspend itself, but unlike the iterator suspending does not imply a return to the parent but rather transfers the control to a named coroutine, which is then resumed. This form of flow of control is often used in simulation programs, and was introduced by Simula 67 [41]. There the coroutine transfer statement is called "resume". The statement resume(C) in a coroutine X leaves X temporarily and resumes the coroutine C at the same point the last resume statement in C left C temporarily. A simplified example application in a C-like notation concerns producer/consumer communication, as shown in Figure 11.25. The example shown there is overly simple, since in practice the resume(Consumer) statements may be hidden in routines called directly or indirectly by Producer(), and a subsequent resume(Producer) must continue inside those calls, with the complete environments intact. This requires retaining the activation records of those calls and all calls that lead to them.

Independently of these variants, routines can be global or nested. The code in a **global routine** only has access to global entities and to its own local entities. The code of a **nested routine**, declared on the same level as local variables, has access to these same global and strictly local environments, but also to entities declared in lexically intervening routines, as shown in Figure 11.26. Since j, k, and m reside in different activation records, providing access to them requires some thought.

```
char buffer[100];

void Producer(void) {
    while (produce_buffer()) {
        resume(Consumer);
    }
    empty_buffer();        /* signal end of stream */
    resume(Consumer);
}

void Consumer(void) {
    resume(Producer);
    while (!empty_buffer_received()) {
        consume_buffer();
        resume(Producer);
    }
}
```

Fig. 11.25: Simplified producer/consumer communication using coroutines

```
int i;

void level_0(void) {
    int j;

    void level_1(void) {
        int k;

        void level_2(void) {
            int m;

            ...              /* code has access to i, j, k, m */
            k = m;
            j = m;
        }

        ...                  /* code has access to i, j, k */
        j = k;
    }

    ...                      /* code has access to i, j */
}
```

Fig. 11.26: Nested routines in C notation

11.3.4 Operations on routines

In addition to declaring a routine, which specifies its name, parameter types, and return type and which is a compile-time action, several operations of increasing complexity can be performed on routines.

First of all, a routine can be **defined**. This differs from declaring a routine in that defining it supplies the code of the routine. Also, defining may be a run-time action: when the routine level_1() in Figure 11.26 is recursive, each recursive invocation defines a different routine level_2(), each having access to a different incarnation of variable k. A routine definition results in a defined routine, possibly represented at run time as a routine value.

No doubt the most important operation on a defined routine is **calling** it. Calling a defined routine creates an activation record for it and transfers control to its code. Details of routine calling, which include parameter passing, passing back a return value and returning from the routine, are covered in Section 11.4.2.2.

Once a defined routine is seen as a value, two more operations on it become possible: **passing it as a parameter** to a routine in a call, and **returning it as a value** from a routine call. An important difference between these two operations is that passing a routine value as a parameter introduces the value into a *smaller* pointer scope, whereas returning a routine as a value introduces the value into a *larger* scope. (Pointer scopes were treated in Section 11.2.3.2.) Consequently, returning routines as values is fundamentally more difficult to implement than passing them as parameters. It turns out that once we have implemented returning routines as values, we can also store them in arbitrary data structures, more in particular in global variables. Routines passed as parameters are important in the implementation of logic languages, routines stored in data structures are essential for functional languages. Both occur in some imperative languages, for example Icon and Algol 68.

Routine values resulting from these two operations must allow the same operations as any other defined routine. In particular, it must be possible to call them, to pass them on as parameters, and to return them as values.

A less frequent operation is **jumping out of a routine**. The destination of such a jump, also called a **non-local goto**, is a **non-local label**. A non-local label is a label in another routine. A variation on the code from Figure 11.26 is shown in Figure 11.27. The routine level_2() contains a non-local goto statement to label L_1 in routine level_1(). The goto L_1 statement terminates the activation of level_2() and transfers control to L_1 in routine level_1(); if level_2() is recursive, several invocations of level_2() will have to be terminated. If level_1() is recursive, each incarnation defines a different non-local label L_1.

In addition to being directly visible, the non-local label can also be passed to the running routine as a parameter. When the non-local label is returned as a value or stored in a data structure with a scope not smaller than that of the label itself, it is called a **continuation**. Continuations allow side branches of computations to be resumed, and support a remarkable programming paradigm [16].

Designing a non-local goto mechanism requires finding a representation for the non-local label that supports transfer of control, being passed as a parameter, and

```
void level_0(void) {

    void level_1(void) {

        void level_2(void) {

            ...
            goto L_1;
            ...
        }

        ...

    L_1:...
        ...
    }

    ...
}
```

Fig. 11.27: Example of a non-local goto

being returned as a value. Note that this representation does not need to be the same
as that of a routine value.

The last operation on routines we will discuss in this section is **partial parameterization**. In partial parameterization, one or more actual parameters are supplied
to a defined routine, but the routine is not called, even if all actual parameters have
been supplied. Instead, a new defined routine results, with $n - m$ parameters, if the
original routine had n parameters, of which m have been supplied; again, m can be
equal to n. An example in C notation would be:

```
extern int add(int i, int j);      /* yields i + j */
int (*inc)( int i );               /* a routine variable inc */

int main(void) {
    ...
    inc = add(, 1);                /* supply the second parameter */
    ...
    printf ("%d\n", inc (5));
    ...
}
```

in which an external routine add(int, int) is parameterized with 1 as its second parameter, to yield a new one-parameter routine, inc(). No call is involved, just the
creation of a new defined routine. The last line of the code calls inc() with one parameter, 5, to print the result 6.

There is a simpler form of partial parameterization, in which parameters are supplied one by one in order from left to right. This form is called "currying" and plays
a important role in functional languages, as shown in Sections 12.1.7 and 12.4.4.

Since partially parameterized routines are just ordinary routines, it is important that such routines be implemented so that all operations available on routines are available on them. This includes calling, further parameterization, being a parameter, being a return value, and perhaps others.

11.3.5 Non-nested routines

We will first discuss the implementation of non-nested routines since they are simpler than nested routines. Non-nested routines can be implemented using stack allocation exclusively, except when partial parameterization is among the required operations.

A non-nested routine is represented at run time simply by the start address of its code. When called, a new activation record is stacked, as described in Section 11.4.2.2. If the code address is known at compile time, a routine call instruction can be used to transfer control to the routine; if the address results from run-time computation, an indirect routine call instruction must be used. A non-nested running routine has access to two environments only: the global data area and its own activation record. The global data area is addressed directly. The routine's own activation record is accessible through the frame pointer FP, which is kept pointing to the activation record of the running routine. Direct addressing and the frame pointer together provide access to the complete environment of a running non-nested routine.

A non-nested routine can be passed on as a parameter or returned as a value by just passing on or returning its code address. The same operations are possible on this passed or returned routine as on the original routine, since in both cases the code address is all that is needed.

Jumping out of a non-nested routine is not a natural concept, since besides the routine's own code there is no other syntactically visible code to jump to. Still, it is occasionally useful to terminate a running routine and transfer control to a marked code location in an ancestor routine. Two possible applications are: stopping a recursive search when an answer has been found; and handling exceptions (Section 11.4.3.2). The C programming language has the **setjmp/longjmp mechanism** for this. A call to the built-in routine setjmp(env) saves information about its code position and stack environment in a "jump buffer" pointed to by the parameter env, and returns 0; it marks a possible place in the execution of the program to which control may be transferred by performing the non-local goto. A later call to the built-in routine longjmp(env, val) restores the environment saved by the last call of setjmp(env), and returns from the call to setjmp() as if it returned val. This effectively implements a non-local goto, with the jump buffer representing the non-local label. A condition for the proper functioning of this mechanism is that the routine that called setjmp must still be active at the time the corresponding longjmp is called.

The mechanism is demonstrated in Figure 11.28. The routine find_div_7() implements a recursive search for a number divisible by 7, and is symbolic for any

such search process. When a number divisible by 7 has been found, a longjmp()
is performed to the label (*jmpbuf_ptr) passed as a parameter, otherwise the search
continues with the next higher number. Without the longjmp call, the search recurses
into infinity.

```
#include <setjmp.h>

void find_div_7(int n, jmp_buf *jmpbuf_ptr) {
    if (n % 7 == 0) longjmp(*jmpbuf_ptr, n);
    find_div_7(n + 1, jmpbuf_ptr);
}

int main(void) {
    jmp_buf jmpbuf;          /* type defined in setjmp.h */
    int return_value;

    if ((return_value = setjmp(jmpbuf)) == 0) {
        /* setting up the label for longjmp() lands here */
        find_div_7(1, &jmpbuf);
    }
    else {
        /* returning from a call of longjmp() lands here */
        printf ("Answer = %d\n", return_value);
    }
    return 0;
}
```

Fig. 11.28: Demonstration of the setjmp/longjmp mechanism

The driver establishes the "non-local label" by calling setjmp(); the actual label
is not textually visible and is located after the else. The driver then initiates the
search, starting at 1; the non-local label is passed as a parameter. When the solution
is found, find_div_7 performs the non-local goto, which lands at the else branch.

Note that the traditional C programming technique of allocating the jmp_buf data
structure among the global variables constitutes a violation of the pointer scope
rules. The jump buffer will contain pointers to the activation record of the routine
that fills it, so its scope is smaller than that of the global data area. If the jump
buffer is filled in the routine main() in C the problem disappears, since there is no
code on a global level that could access the jump buffer, but if the jump buffer is
filled in a subroutine, a pointer scope violation can easily occur, resulting in a jump
to a routine that has already been terminated. Passing the jump buffer address as
a parameter to all interested routines as in Figure 11.28 solves the problem and is
safe, but annoying.

Now that we have seen the feature and its use, we turn to its implementation.
The implementation of setjmp(env) must at least save the frame pointer of its
caller and its own return address in the jump buffer env. The implementation of
longjmp(env, val) retrieves the destination activation record frame pointer and the

return address from the jump buffer env. It then unstacks activation records until it finds the destination activation record and transfers to the return address. The implementation must also deliver val in the function result register.

Partial parameterization of non-nested routines cannot be implemented substantially more simply than that of nested ones. We will therefore postpone its discussion to the next section.

11.3.6 Nested routines

Not all operations on nested routines can be implemented using stack allocation for the activation record, but much can still be done to preserve the stack regime.

In addition to the usual code address, the routine descriptor used to represent a defined nested routine R must contain enough information to provide access to the data that are visible from the point of its definition. These are the constants, variables, parameters, routines, etc., of the lexically enclosing routines of R and reside in activation records of these routines. The straightforward way to provide this access is to include the frame pointer of the invocation of the routine in which R is defined (another solution, using "closures" is discussed below, in Section 11.3.6.5). This pointer is called the **lexical pointer** or **static link**. Referring to Figure 11.26, the descriptor of the routine level_2() consists of the code address of level_2() and a lexical pointer, the frame pointer of the enclosing routine level_1(). Figure 11.29 shows such a two-pointer routine descriptor.

lexical pointer
routine address

Fig. 11.29: A routine descriptor for a language that requires lexical pointers

Several points are worth noting here. The first is that it is conceptually convenient to imagine the definition of a routine to correspond to run-time code, which produces a correctly filled local routine descriptor in the activation record, just as the definition int i = 5; produces a correctly filled local integer variable. Figure 11.30 shows possible code for the construction of a routine descriptor for the routine level_2() from Figure 11.26. Further optimization may of course render the explicit construction of the routine descriptor superfluous, just as constant propagation can remove the allocation of i from the program if i turns out not to be modified anywhere. Also, the value level_2_as_a_value could be constructed on the fly when calling routine A() in Figure 11.30.

A second point is that if level_1() is recursive, each incarnation has a different activation record with a different address, so the routine descriptors for the different level_2()s in them differ, as they should.

```
void level_1(void) {
    int k;

    void level_2(void) {
        int l;

        ...
    }
    routine_descriptor level_2_as_a_value = {
        FP_of_this_activation_record(),   /* FP of level_1() */
        level_2                           /* code address of level_2() */
    };

    A(level_2_as_a_value);   /* level_2() as a parameter */
}
```

Fig. 11.30: Possible code for the construction of a routine descriptor

Another point is that when nested routines have a two-pointer descriptor, it is next to necessary to use them for non-nested routines for reasons of uniformity. The top-level routine descriptors can get a null lexical pointer, since all data visible from outside a top-level routine is accessible by direct addressing and the lexical pointer will never be consulted.

Since the code of routine level_2() has access not only to the data of level_1() but also to those of level_0(), it would seem that supplying a lexical pointer to just the activation record of level_1() is not enough. We will see now, however, that it is.

11.3.6.1 Calling a nested routine

When a routine R defined by a two-pointer routine descriptor D is called, a new activation record is created; the present program counter PC, the frame pointer FP and the lexical pointer from D are stored in the administration area of the new activation record; FP is made to point to the new activation record; and control is transferred to the code address from D. See Figure 11.31.

As said, the point of having a lexical pointer is the access it allows to all lexically enclosing environments. We will now first see how the access to l and k in the statement k = l in Figure 11.26 can be obtained. The variable l is located in the activation record of the running routine, so it can be reached through the frame pointer: l is *(FP + offset(l)), where offset(X) is the offset of entry X from the frame pointer of the activation record. The variable k is located in the activation record of the immediately enclosing routine, which can be reached through the lexical pointer, which in turn can be found through the frame pointer: k is *(*(FP + offset(lexical_pointer)) + offset(k)) in routine level_2(). (Of course, k is *(FP + offset(k)) in routine level_1().) So the assignment k = l is translated to intermediate code as shown in Figure 11.32. The translation of the statement j = l is

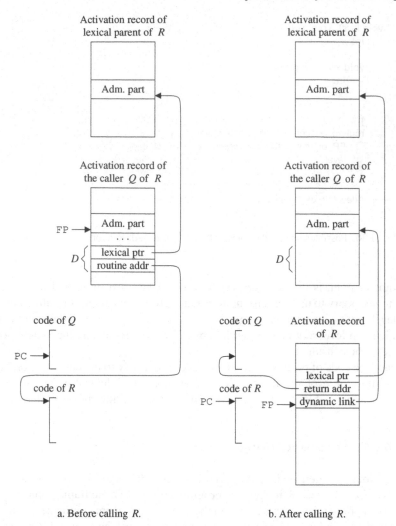

a. Before calling *R*.   b. After calling *R*.

Fig. 11.31: Calling a routine defined by the two-pointer routine descriptor *D*

similar, except that j must be found by following the lexical pointer twice (Figure 11.32). These translations may look imposing, but BURS techniques can often find good code for such forms, by exploiting advanced addressing modes.

We see that storing the lexical pointer to the activation record of the lexically enclosing routine in the activation record of the running routine builds a linked list of those activation records that hold the data visible from the running routine. The length of the list is equal to the lexical nesting depth of the running routine.

The number of times the lexical pointer must be followed to reach an entry in a routine *R* from a routine *S* is equal to the difference in lexical nesting depth be-

```
*(
    *(
        FP
        +
        offset ( lexical_pointer )
    )
    +
    offset (k)
) =
*(FP + offset ( l ))
```

Fig. 11.32: Intermediate code for the non-local assignment k = l

```
*(
    *(
        *(  FP
            +
            offset ( lexical_pointer )
        )
        +
        offset ( lexical_pointer )
    )
    +
    offset ( j )
) =
*(FP + offset ( l ))
```

Fig. 11.33: Intermediate code for the non-local assignment j = l

tween S and R. It is therefore convenient to represent local addresses in the compiler as pairs of nesting difference and offset; since the nesting difference cannot be negative, a value of -1 can be used to code direct addressing. So, inside routine level_2(), l is represented as [0, offset(l)], k as [1, offset(k)], j as [2, offset(j)], and i as [-1, offset(i)]. Note that the nesting difference is a compile-time constant.

11.3.6.2 Passing a nested routine as a parameter

Passing a nested routine as a parameter is simple now: just pass the two-pointer descriptor. No matter to what static or dynamic depth the routine level_2() is passed on, when it is finally called the above calling scheme constructs an activation record with a lexical pointer that indicates the activation record of level_1() and thus restores the proper environment for a call of level_2(); see Figure 11.34.

Since the two-pointer routine descriptor contains a pointer of possibly limited scope, the lexical pointer, we have to consider the pointer scope rules. The scope of the routine descriptor is the same as that of the activation record in which the routine was declared. When passing the routine descriptor to a child routine, it is passed into an environment of smaller scope, so no scope violation can occur, regardless of

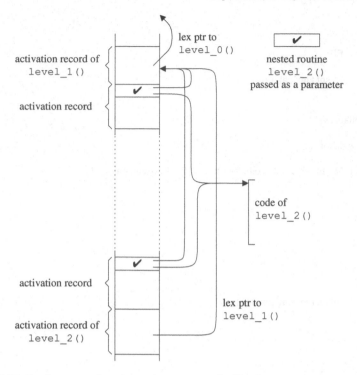

Fig. 11.34: Passing a nested routine as a parameter and calling it

whether we use a heap or a stack for the activation records.

11.3.6.3 Returning a nested routine as a value

Returning a nested routine as a value is equally simple: just return the two-pointer descriptor. Now, however, the two-pointer descriptor is passed to an environment of potentially larger scope, so there is the danger of a pointer scope violation. The violation will indeed occur under a stack regime: when routine level_1() returns routine level_2() as a value to its parent level_0(), and this parent calls the returned routine, the call will construct an activation record for level_2() whose lexical pointer refers to the activation record of level_1(), which is long gone! We see that returning a nested routine as a value is incompatible with the stack regime; it requires the activation records to be allocated on the heap.

Heap allocation indeed solves the problem. Since all environments have the same infinite scope, no data is introduced into environments of larger scope, and no pointer scope violation can occur. More in detail, the activation record of the call of routine level_1() in our example will be retained automatically after the call has terminated, since it is still accessible from the program data area: FP, which is in the root set, points to the activation record of level_0(), which contains the routine value level_2(), which contains the frame pointer of level_1() as the lexical pointer. Such operations may seem weird in a C-like language, but are commonplace in functional languages, and in some imperative languages, for example Icon and some variants of Algol 68.

11.3.6.4 Jumping out of a nested routine

The main operation a non-local label in a given routine invocation I must support is the non-local goto. Performing a non-local goto to this label terminates zero or more routine invocations until routine invocation I surfaces and then transfers control to the local label.

This can be implemented by representing the non-local label as a two-pointer descriptor containing the frame pointer of the routine invocation that holds the label, and the code address of the label. The implementation of a non-local goto to a non-local label L must then travel back through the activation record chain as defined by the dynamic links, until it finds the activation record with a frame pointer that is equal to that in L. Each activation record met on the way must be released, since the activation of the corresponding routine is terminated implicitly by the non-local goto. Once the proper activation record has been found, FP is made to point to it and execution proceeds at the code address indicated in L.

If routine level_1() in Figure 11.27 is recursive, each invocation defines a different label L_1. Their representations differ by pointing to different activation records; performing non-local gotos on them will terminate different numbers of active routines.

The two-pointer non-local label descriptor can be passed as a parameter or returned as a value in the same way as a routine descriptor can, and the same pointer scope considerations hold. The two are, however, fundamentally different: a routine descriptor holds a pointer to an activation record that will be the parent of a new running routine and a code address to be jumped to by a routine call instruction, a non-local label descriptor holds a pointer to an activation record that will itself be running again and a code address to be jumped to by a jump instruction.

As with routine definitions, it is often convenient to allocate the non-local label descriptor as a constant entry in the activation record, as shown in Figure 11.35. Again, however, values like L_1_as_a_value may be constructed on the fly.

11.3.6.5 Partial parameterization

The data structure representing a partially parameterized routine must be capable of holding an indeterminate number of actual parameters, so the above two-pointer descriptor does not suffice and will have to be extended. The extension consists of space for all its parameters, plus a mask indicating which parameters have al-

```
void level_1(void) {
    non_local_label_descriptor L_1_as_a_value = {
        FP_of_this_activation_record(),   /* FP of level_1() */
        L_1      /* code address of L_1 */
    };

    void level_2(void) {

        ...
        non_local_goto(L_1_as_a_value); /* goto L_1; */
        ...
    }

    ...
    L_1 :...
    ...
}
```

Fig. 11.35: Possible code for the construction of a label descriptor

ready been filled in. Figure 11.36 shows the result of partially parameterizing a 5-parameter routine with its second and fourth parameter values.

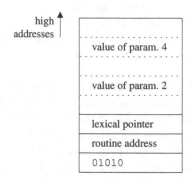

Fig. 11.36: A closure for a partially parameterized routine

This representation of a partially parameterized routine is called a **closure**; unfortunately it is the same term as used in "transitive closure" and "closure algorithm", with which it has nothing to do. The closure can be allocated on the stack or on the heap, with different consequences for the pointer scope rules.

Once we have this representation, implementing the desired operations on it is simple.

Further parameterization of a closure is implemented by scanning the mask to find the locations of the free parameters and filling them in. The required type checking has already been done since the corresponding routine just has a new routine type with a subset of the original parameters. If the language specifies that parameters are always supplied one at the time from left to right, the mask can be replaced by a counter and finding the location of the first free parameter is trivial. This "currying" style of partial parameterization occurs in many functional languages, and is explained in more detail in Section 12.1.7.

Once all parameters of the routine have been supplied, it can, but need not be invoked, since a fully parameterized routine can be treated as a parameterless routine (see page 563).

The invocation of a fully parameterized routine can be done remarkably efficiently: allocate room for the activation record and block-copy the closure into it. If the layout is chosen properly, the parameters and the lexical pointer are already in place, and the mask can be overwritten by the dynamic link; such a layout is already shown in Figure 11.36.

Passing a routine represented by a closure as a parameter or returning it as a value can be implemented in the obvious way: pass or return a copy of the closure. Since the closure contains the required lexical pointer, it can be invoked in the same way as described above. This implementation requires that *all* routines be treated as partially parameterized and closures must be used everywhere instead of two-pointer routine descriptors.

11.3.6.6 Discussion

In this subsection we have considered representations for nested routines and implementations for the operations on them. Some of these operations, notably passing them as parameters and returning them as values, give rise to new routines and we have been careful to ensure that our implementations of the operations also work on them.

Most operations on routines and non-local labels are compatible with a stack regime, except returning them as values, which requires heap-allocated activation records. Since heap allocation of the activation records slows down the calling mechanism, it is important to seek ways to avoid it and maintain a stack regime. We will now discuss such a way.

11.3.7 Lambda lifting

The problem with two-pointer routine descriptors is that they contain a lexical pointer, which points into the stack and which reduces its pointer scope. As a result, two-pointer routine descriptors cannot be moved around freely, which in turn limits their usability. One simple solution was given above: allocate all activation records on the heap. We will now consider another simple solution: do away with lexical pointers and make all routines global. This immediately reintroduces the original problem: how to gain access to the non-local data; but we now give a new answer: pass pointers to them as parameters.

Figure 11.37 shows the result of this transformation on the routines of Figure
11.26. At the top we see the innermost routine level_2(), which used to have access to two non-local non-global variables, j and k, and which now has two pointer
parameters. When called (in level_1()), the actual parameters are supplied from j,
which level_1() has received as a parameter, and the address of k. A similar explanation applies to the call of level_1() in level_0(). It is clear that the two assignments
*k = l and *j = l assign the value of l to the proper locations.

```
int i;

void level_2(int *j, int *k) {
    int l;

    ...     /* code has access to i, *j, *k, l */
    *k = l;
    *j = l;
}

void level_1(int *j) {
    int k;

    ...     /* code has access to i, *j, k */
    level_2(j, &k);    /* was: level_2(); */
    A(level_2);    /* level_2() as a parameter: */
        /* this  is a problem */
}

void level_0(void) {
    int j;

    ...     /* code has access to i, j */
    level_1(&j);   /* was: level_1(); */
}
```

Fig. 11.37: The nested routines from Figure 11.26 lambda-lifted (in C notation)

The transformation shown here is called **lambda lifting**. The name derives from
the lambda expressions in Lisp and other functional languages that are lifted to
global level by it, but the technique has been in use with C programmers for ages.

Lambda lifting has effectively rid us of two-pointer routine descriptors with their
limited scopes, but the moment we try to pass a lifted routine as a parameter, we
run into a new problem: how do we pass on the extra parameters that result from
the lambda lifting? When passing level_2() as a parameter, how do we pass the j and
&k that go with it? There is a stunning answer to this question: use partial parameterization! Rather than passing the code address of level_2(), we pass a closure C
containing the code address, j, and &k. Note that these closures, unlike the earlier
closures, do not contain lexical pointers. When the routine parameter corresponding

to C is finally called, the run-time system recognizes it as a closure and performs a closure invocation.

The scope of closure C is determined by the scope of &j, which, unfortunately is again that of the activation record of the lexically enclosing routine, level_1(). This still prevents the closure from being returned as a value, due to pointer scope problems. This problem is solved by another drastic measure: all local data that is used non-locally is allocated on the heap and the corresponding local entries are replaced by pointers. Figure 11.38 shows the final result. In particular, the closure passed in the call of A() has infinite scope: it contains a code address and two heap pointers. Thus, the closure can be moved to any environment and called wherever needed. The activation record of level_1() may long have disappeared; the required "locals" in it still exist on the heap.

```c
int i;

void level_2(int *j, int *k) {
    int l;

    ...                      /* code has access to i, *j, *k, l */
    *k = l;
    *j = l;
}

void level_1(int *j) {
    int *k = (int *)malloc(sizeof (int ));

    ...                      /* code has access to i, *j, *k */
    level_2(j, k);           /* was: level_2 (); */
    A(closure(level_2, j, k)); /* was: A(level_2); */
}

void level_0(void) {
    int *j = (int *)malloc(sizeof (int ));

    ...                      /* code has access to i, *j */
    level_1(j);              /* was: level_1 (); */
}
```

Fig. 11.38: Lambda-lifted routines with additional heap allocation in C notation

We have now achieved an implementation in which the stack mechanism is used for the routine invocation administration and the strictly local variables, and in which variables that are used non-locally are allocated on the heap. Such an implementation is advantageous for languages in which efficient routine calling and free movement of routine variables are very important. The implementation is especially profitable for languages that require partial parameterization anyway; in short, for implementing functional languages and advanced imperative languages. The main property of the implementation is that routines are represented by closures that do not carry lexical pointers; this gives them the opportunity to acquire infinite scope.

11.3.8 Iterators and coroutines

The above techniques give us enough material to implement both iterators and coroutines in a simple way. The two implementations are almost identical. The invocation of an iterator or coroutine creates an activation record in the usual way, and its address is stored in a variable, allocated for the purpose; the activation record will have to be allocated on the heap, unless the functionality of the iterator or coroutine is restricted severely. When either is suspended, continuation information is stored in that activation record. The iterator returns temporarily to its caller, whose activation record can be found by following the dynamic link; the coroutine transfers to another coroutine, whose activation record can be found in its coroutine variable. When the iterator or coroutine is resumed the continuation information is retrieved and acted upon. When the iterator or coroutine terminates, its activation record is deleted, and the iterator or coroutine variable zeroed.

This concludes our discussion of non-nested and nested routines and the implementation of several operations applicable to them. The basic data structures in all the implementations are the activation record and the routine representation. The latter exists in two variants, the two-pointer routine descriptor and the closure. The detailed allocation design decisions are based on the pointer scope rules explained in Section 11.2.3.2.

11.4 Code generation for control flow statements

In Chapters 7 and 9 we discussed code generation for expressions and basic blocks. In this section, we will concentrate on code generation for statements that affect the flow of control, and thus demarcate the basic blocks. Three levels of flow of control can be distinguished:

- local flow of control, which determines the statement inside a routine or method to be executed next (Section 11.4.1);
- routine calls and method invocations, which perform the parameter transfer and flow-of-control manipulation needed to activate a new routine (Section 11.4.2);
- non-local jumps, which transfer the flow of control out of the currently running routine into an ancestor routine (Section 11.4.2.3).

We assume that all source code expressions, with one exception, have already been evaluated and that the results have been stored in an appropriate place, usually a register. The exception is formed by Boolean expressions used for flow control, for example the control expressions in if-statements; they are treated separately in Section 11.4.1.1. In addition, we assume the existence of a mechanism in the compiler for allocating temporary variables and labels. This description is intentionally not very precise; details always depend on the source and target languages.

To describe the code generation for the flow of control, we will use the four statement types below, written in a Pascal-like notation. Each has a straightforward equivalent on virtually all processors.

- A simple goto statement: GOTO *label*; the address of the destination is the constant value *label*.
- An indirect goto statement: GOTO *label_register*; the address of the destination is the contents of *label_register*.
- A conditional goto statement, in two forms:
  IF *condition_register* THEN GOTO *label*
  and
  IF NOT *condition_register* THEN GOTO *label*.
- An assignment statement: *destination* := *source*, used to compute temporary values needed for the flow of control.

We will sometimes write simple expressions where registers appear in the above statements, especially when these expressions derive from the code generation mechanism itself rather than from the source code; this increases the readability of the code samples.

Roadmap

11.4.1 Local flow of control

The two main mechanisms for influencing the local flow of control in imperative and object-oriented languages are "selection" and "repetition". Selection causes a piece of code to be selected for execution, based on the value of some expression. Repetition causes a piece of code to be executed zero or more times, based on the value of some expression or expressions. More often than not these expressions are Boolean expressions, and in many cases it is useful to translate them in special ways. We will therefore first consider code generation for Boolean expressions used in controlling program execution, and then turn to code for selection and repetition statements.

11.4.1.1 Boolean expressions in flow of control

Fundamentally, Boolean expressions are no different than other expressions: evaluating one yields a Boolean value. Most Boolean expressions are, however, used to affect the flow of control rather than to produce a value; we will call Boolean expressions used in that way **Boolean control expressions**. There are two reasons to treat Boolean control expressions specially.

The first reason has to do with two properties of machine instructions. Boolean expressions often consist of comparisons and the comparison instructions of most machines produce their results in special condition registers in a special format rather than as 0/1 integer values on the stack or in a register; so an additional conversion is required to obtain a genuine Boolean value. And the most usual way of affecting the flow of control is by using a conditional jump, and the machine instructions for conditional jumps base their decisions on condition registers rather than on 0/1 integer values; so jumping on a Boolean value requires an additional conversion of the Boolean value to a value in a condition register. Obviously, the naive code sequence for Boolean control expressions

```
/* code for the Boolean expression: */
comparison code, yielding a condition value
conversion from condition value to Boolean
/* code for the conditional jump: */
conversion from Boolean to condition value
jump on condition value
```

is to be avoided.

The second reason for treating Booleans specially is related to a property of some programming languages. Several programming languages (for example C, Ada, Java) feature lazy Boolean operators, operators that evaluate operands only when their value is needed. Examples are the && and || operators in C. Such operators do not fit the translation model discussed in Sections 7.5.2.1 and 7.5.2.2: $expr_1$ && $expr_2$ cannot be translated as

```
code to compute expr₁ in loc₁
code to compute expr₂ in loc₂
code for the && operator on loc₁ and loc₂
```

since that would result in the unconditional evaluation of both expressions. Instead, code intermingled with conditional jumps must be generated; again these conditional jumps react to values in condition registers. In short, Boolean control expressions are tightly interrelated with conditional jumping.

This relationship can be exploited conveniently when we know the labels to which control must be transferred when the Boolean expression yields true or false, before we generate the code. We can then use a code generation technique like the one shown in Figure 11.39. The procedure *GenerateCodeForBooleancontrolexpression* gets two parameters, *TrueLabel* and *FalseLabel*, in addition to the usual *Node* pointer. A special value *NoLabel* is available for these parameters, to indicate that control must continue at the end of the expression: the control must "fall through" to the end. We assume a single condition register here, although most machines have several of them, with assorted semantics.

```
procedure GenerateCodeForBooleanControlExpression (Node, TrueLabel, FalseLabel):
    select Node.type:
        case ComparisonType:           -- <, >, ==, etc. in C
            GenerateCodeForComparisonExpression (Node.expr);
            -- The comparison result is now in the condition register
            if TrueLabel ≠ NoLabel:
                Emit ("IF condition_register THEN GOTO" TrueLabel);
                if FalseLabel ≠ NoLabel:
                    Emit ("GOTO" FalseLabel);
            else -- TrueLabel = NoLabel:
                if FalseLabel ≠ NoLabel:
                    Emit ("IF NOT condition_register THEN GOTO" FalseLabel);
        case LazyAndType:              -- the && in C
            -- Create EndLabel to allow left operand fall-through:
            EndLabel ← NewLabel ();
            if FalseLabel = NoLabel:
                -- The lazy AND should fall through on failure
                LeftOperandFalseLabel ← EndLabel;
            else -- The lazy AND should fail to the original FalseLabel:
                LeftOperandFalseLabel ← FalseLabel;
            GenerateCodeForBooleanControlExpression
                (Node.left, NoLabel, LeftOperandFalseLabel);
            GenerateCodeForBooleanControlExpression
                (Node.right, TrueLabel, FalseLabel);
            Emit ("LABEL" EndLabel ":");
        case LazyOrType:               -- the || in C
            ...
        case NegationType:             -- the ! in C
            GenerateCodeForBooleanControlExpression
                (Node.left, FalseLabel, TrueLabel);
```

Fig. 11.39: Code generation for Boolean expressions

If the node represents a (numeric) comparison operator, we generate code for this operator; this leaves the result in the condition register. Then, depending on the presence or absence of the true and false labels, we generated zero, one or two jump instructions.

The use of the value *NoLabel* is shown in the entry for the lazy && operator. First we generate code for the left operand of the && operator, such that when it succeeds, control falls through to reach the code of the right operand of the && operator. What happens when the left operand fails is more complicated. We cannot just transfer control to the *FalseLabel* since it could be *NoLabel*, in which case we have to lead the control on to the end of the code generated for the &&. The auxiliary label *LeftOperandFalseLabel* take care of this.

Similar entries can be constructed for the || and ?: operators of C. The last entry in Figure 11.39 shows that the implementation of the negation operator comes free of charge: we just swap the true and false labels.

As an example, the call

GenerateCodeForBooleanControlExpression (Parse ("i > 0 && j > 0"), NoLabel, Else label)

in which we assume that *Parse(string)* produces the parse tree for *string*, yields the code sequence

```
Compare_greater i, 0
IF NOT condition_register THEN GOTO Else label
Compare_greater j, 0
IF NOT condition_register THEN GOTO Else label
```

There are also occasions when we have to construct a genuine Boolean value, for example to assign it to a variable or to pass it as a parameter. We can then use conversion instructions if the target machine has them, or use the above scheme to produce code to jump to places where the proper values are constructed.

11.4.1.2 Selection statements

The two most common selection statements are the if-statement and the case statement. The if-statement selects one of two statement sequences (one of which may be absent), based on the value of a Boolean expression; the case statement (also sometimes called a "switch statement" or a "selection statement") selects one out of several statement sequences, based on the value of an integer or enumeration expression.

The if-statement The general form of an **if-statement** is:

IF *Boolean_expression* THEN *true_sequence* ELSE *false_sequence* END IF;

which results in the AST

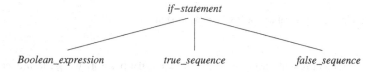

Code generation for an if-statement is simple: create two new labels, false_label and end_label, and generate the following code:

```
BooleanControlCode (Boolean_expression, 0, false_label)
    code for true_sequence
    GOTO end_label;
false_label:
    code for false_sequence
end_label:
```

where *BooleanControlCode* is the code generated by the procedure *GenerateCodeForBooleanControlExpression* with the parameters shown (*NoLabel* is represented by 0).

If the else-part is absent (or empty), the false_label is not needed and we generate

```
    BooleanControlCode (Boolean_expression, 0, end_label)
    code for true_sequence
end_label:
```

The case statement We will consider **case statements** of the form:

```
CASE case_expression IN
    I₁: statement_sequence₁
    ...
    Iₙ: statement_sequenceₙ
    ELSE else-statement_sequence
END CASE;
```

where $I_1 \ldots I_n$ are **case labels** —integer or enumeration values representing compile—time constants. The expression *case_expression* must be evaluated. If its value is equal to one of the values $I_1, \ldots, I_n$, the corresponding statement sequence is executed. If not, the statement sequence of the else-part is executed.

There are many code generation schemes for case statements and it is the task of the compiler to select an efficient one for the statement at hand. The choice depends on the number of case entries, the range (or reach) of the case labels, and on the density of the case labels within the range.

The following is a simple scheme that works well when there are only a few case entries (n being small, say 10 or less). First, $n + 2$ labels are allocated: label_1 through label_n, label_else, and label_next. Also, a temporary variable is allocated for the case expression. Then, the code of Figure 11.40 is generated. This scheme implements a linear search through all the case labels. Note that we allocate a temporary variable for the case expression. Usually, the language manual specifies that the case expression must be evaluated only once, and, even if the language manual does not, it may still be more efficient to do so.

```
    tmp_case_value := case_expression;
    IF tmp_case_value = I₁ THEN GOTO label_1;
    ...
    IF tmp_case_value = Iₙ THEN GOTO label_n;
    GOTO label_else;                    -- or insert the code at label_else
label_1:
    code for statement_sequence₁
    GOTO label_next;
    ...
label_n:
    code for statement_sequenceₙ
    GOTO label_next;
label_else:
    code for else-statement_sequence
label_next:
```

Fig. 11.40: A simple translation scheme for case statements

The execution time of the above scheme is linear in n, the number of cases in the case statement. Case selection in constant time is possible using a **jump table**, as follows. First the compiler computes the lowest case label I_{low} and the highest case label I_{high}. Then the compiler generates a table of $I_{high} - I_{low} + 1$ entries, to be indexed with indices ranging from 0 to $I_{high} - I_{low}$. The entries in this table are code labels: label_k for an entry with index $I_k - I_{low}$, for k ranging from 1 to n, and label_else for all others. Finally the following code is generated:

```
tmp_case_value := case_expression;
IF tmp_case_value < Ilow THEN GOTO label_else;
IF tmp_case_value > Ihigh THEN GOTO label_else;
GOTO table [tmp_case_value − Ilow];
```

If $I_{high} - I_{low}$ is much larger than n, many of the jump table entries contain label_else, and the table may be deemed too space-inefficient. In that case, the case labels can be organized into a balanced binary tree, in which each node of the tree represents one case label I, the right branch indicates a subtree with case labels larger than I, and the left branch indicates a subtree with case labels smaller than I. For each node node_k in the binary tree, the following code is generated:

```
label_k:
    IF tmp_case_value < Ik THEN
        GOTO label of left branch of node_k;
    IF tmp_case_value > Ik THEN
        GOTO label of right branch of node_k;
    code for statement_sequencek
    GOTO label_next;
```

If the left branch and/or the right branch does not exist, the corresponding GOTO is replaced by GOTO label_else.

Many more advanced translation schemes for case statements exist. Several translation schemes for the case statement were analyzed and compared by Sale [245]. Very sophisticated techniques for producing good code for the case statement are described by Hennessy and Mendelsohn [120], Bernstein [36], and Kannan and Proebsting [143].

11.4.1.3 Repetition statements

The most common repetition statements are the while statement and the for-statement. The while statement executes a statement sequence an indeterminate number of times (including 0 times), as long as the while expression remains fulfilled. The for-statement executes a statement sequence a fixed number of times.

The while statement The **while statement**

```
WHILE Boolean_expression DO statement_sequence END WHILE;
```

can be processed by allocating two labels: end_label and test_label, and generating the following code:

```
test_label:
    BooleanControlCode (Boolean_expression, 0, end_label);
    code for statement_sequence
    GOTO test_label;
end_label:
```

In many cases, however, the following scheme results in more efficient code: allocate two labels: sequence_label and test_label, and generate the following code:

```
    GOTO test_label;
sequence_label:
    code for statement_sequence
test_label:
    BooleanControlCode (Boolean_expression, sequence_label, 0);
```

This scheme is usually more efficient when there are several iterations, because it only executes a single conditional jump instruction per iteration, whereas the first scheme executes a conditional jump instruction and an unconditional jump instruction per iteration. If *Boolean_expression* evaluates to false the first time, there will be no iterations, and the first scheme is more efficient.

Which scheme is more efficient also depends on the target processor. Note that the branch in the conditional goto statement of the first scheme is actually taken only once. On many processors, in particular processors that maintain an instruction look-ahead cache, a conditional branch instruction is more expensive when the branch is taken than when it is not, because when it is, the instruction look-ahead cache must be flushed. On the other hand, some modern processors perform look-ahead at the target of the branch instruction as well, and/or have a sophisticated branch prediction mechanism.

The for-statement We will first consider the following type of **for-statement**:

```
FOR i IN lower_bound..upper_bound DO
    statement_sequence
END FOR;
```

where i is the controlled variable of the for-statement; the implicit step size is 1; and *lower_bound* and *upper_bound*, both inclusive, are to be evaluated once upon starting the for-statement. Code generation for a for-statement is quite tricky, because care must be taken that the controlled variable of the for-statement does not cause overflow.

The intuitive approach is to allocate a temporary variable tmp_ub for the upper bound, and generate the following code:

```
i := lower_bound;
tmp_ub := upper_bound;
WHILE i <= tmp_ub DO
    code for statement_sequence
    i := i+1;                    -- WRONG: may cause overflow
END WHILE;
```

where the while statement is handled as described above. Unfortunately, this scheme will not always work. In particular, the computation of *upper_bound* may produce the largest value representable for the type of the controlled variable i. After a while i will reach the value of tmp_ub. Then, on machines that detect overflow, the increment of the controlled variable will cause an exception. On machines that do not detect overflow, the for-statement will never terminate, because i can never become larger than the largest value representable for its type, and can thus never become larger than tmp_ub.

Therefore, the loop termination test must compare the controlled variable i with tmp_ub for equality, and be executed after the statement sequence, but before the increment of the controlled variable. However, moving the loop termination test to the end of the statement sequence means that another test is required to determine if the loop should be entered at all. This leads to the following, improved, scheme (with the temporary variable tmp_ub allocated as above, and labels loop_label and end_label):

```
    i := lower_bound;
    tmp_ub := upper_bound;
    IF i > tmp_ub THEN GOTO end_label;
loop_label:
    code for statement_sequence
    IF i = tmp_ub THEN GOTO end_label;
    i := i + 1;
    GOTO loop_label;
end_label:
```

In this generation scheme, the first IF clause makes sure that the statement sequence will never be executed when *lower_bound* is larger than *upper_bound*. Also, the controlled variable i will never be incremented beyond *upper_bound*, thus preventing overflow and its consequences.

An issue that we have ignored until now is what value the controlled variable i should have after the loop is finished. In some languages, the for-loop declares the controlled variable implicitly, so it no longer exists after the loop. Some other languages do not specify what value the controlled variable should have afterwards, or explicitly specify that it is not specified (so that programs that depend on it are erroneous). When the language manual does specify the value, the implementation should of course follow the manual, if necessary by adding the proper assignment at the end_label.

Many languages offer more general forms of for-statements, for example providing an explicit step size. An explicit step size causes additional complications, as is illustrated by the following for-statement:

FOR i **IN** 1..6 **STEP** 2 **DO** ... **END FOR**;

The complication here is that the controlled variable never becomes exactly equal to the upper bound of the for-statement. Therefore, the scheme described above fails miserably. With an explicit step size, we cannot compare the upper bound and the controlled variable for equality, and, as we have seen above, we cannot compare for greater/smaller either, because of possible overflow problems.

A solution lies in computing first the number of times the loop will be executed. An extra temporary variable is needed to hold this number. Note that this temporary loop count must have a range that is large enough to represent the difference between the maximum value and the minimum value representable in the type of the controlled variable. For example, if the controlled variable is of type integer, the value MAX(integer) − MIN(integer) must be representable in this temporary variable. Remarkably, this can be accomplished by making the loop count an unsigned integer of the same size as the integer: if the representable values of an integer range from -2^n to $2^n - 1$, then the representable values of an unsigned integer of the same size range from 0 to $2^{n+1} - 1$, which is exactly large enough. This does not work for a step size of 0. Depending on the language this exception can be detected at compile-time. Also, if the step size expression is not a constant, the step size needs a temporary variable as well.

All of this leads us to the scheme of Figure 11.41. Note that, although we no longer use the controlled variable to detect whether the for-statement is finished, we still have to keep its value up-to-date because it may be used in the *statement_sequence* code. Also note that the compiler can switch to the simpler and more efficient scheme discussed earlier when it can determine that the step size is 1.

```
i := lower_bound;
tmp_ub := upper_bound;
tmp_step_size := step_size;
IF tmp_step_size = 0 THEN
    ... probably illegal; cause run-time error ...
IF tmp_step_size < 0 THEN GOTO neg_step;
IF i > tmp_ub THEN GOTO end_label;
-- the next statement uses tmp_ub - i
--    to evaluate tmp_loop_count to its correct, unsigned value
    tmp_loop_count := (tmp_ub - i) DIV tmp_step_size + 1;
    GOTO loop_label;
neg_step:
IF i < tmp_ub THEN GOTO end_label;
-- the next statement uses i - tmp_ub
--    to evaluate tmp_loop_count to its correct, unsigned value
    tmp_loop_count := (i - tmp_ub) DIV (-tmp_step_size) + 1;
loop_label:
    code for statement_sequence
    tmp_loop_count := tmp_loop_count - 1;
    IF tmp_loop_count = 0 THEN GOTO end_label;
    i := i + tmp_step_size;
    GOTO loop_label;
end_label:
```

Fig. 11.41: Code generated for a general for-statement

Sometimes, what looks like a for-statement actually is not. Consider, for example, the C for-loop of Figure 11.42. Here, expr1 and expr3 may contain any expression, including none at all. The expression expr2 may be absent (in which case we have an infinite loop), but if it is present, it must return a value of a type that is allowed in a condition context. If expr2 is present, the C for-loop is almost, but not quite, equivalent to the while loop of Figure 11.43; for a difference see Exercise 11.29.

```
for (expr1; expr2; expr3) {
    body;
}
```

Fig. 11.42: A for-loop in C

```
expr1;
while (expr2) {
  body;
  expr3;
}
```

Fig. 11.43: A while loop that is almost equivalent to the for-loop of Figure 11.42

Code generation for repetition statements is treated in depth by Baskett [32].

Optimizations for repetition statements As can be seen from the above, the administration overhead for for-loops can be considerable. An effective optimization that reduces this overhead, at the cost of increasing code size, is loop unrolling. In **loop unrolling**, the body of the loop is replaced by several copies of it, and the administration code is adjusted accordingly. For example, the loop

```
FOR i := 1 TO n DO
    sum := sum + a[i];
END FOR;
```

can be replaced by the two for-loops shown in Figure 11.44. In this example, we have chosen an **unrolling factor** of 4. Note that, in general, we still need a copy of the original loop, with adjusted bounds, to deal with the last couple of iterations. If the bounds are compile-time constants, it may be possible to avoid this copy by choosing the unrolling factor to be a divisor of the loop count.

This optimization is particularly effective when the body is small, so the unrolled loop still fits in the instruction cache. It may also be used to increase the size of the basic block, which may improve chances for other optimizations.

It is sometimes useful to generate separate code for the first or last few iterations of a loop, for example to avoid a null pointer check in every iteration, to ensure memory accesses in the main loop are aligned, or to avoid special code in the main loop for the final, potentially partial, iteration of the loop. This optimization is called **loop peeling**.

```
FOR i := 1 TO n–3 STEP 4 DO
   –– The first loop takes care of the indices 1 .. (n div 4) * 4
   sum := sum + a[i];
   sum := sum + a[i+1];
   sum := sum + a[i+2];
   sum := sum + a[i+3];
END FOR;

FOR i := (n div 4) * 4 + 1 TO n DO
   –– This loop takes care of the remaining indices
   sum := sum + a[i];
END FOR;
```

Fig. 11.44: Two for-loops resulting from unrolling a for-loop

11.4.2 Routine invocation

Until now we have discussed code generation for statements that affect the local flow of control. In this section, we will discuss routine calls and object method invocations. Execution of a *routine call* transfers the flow of control to the start of the called routine. The called routine will eventually return the flow of control to just after the routine call. Two important issues in calling a routine are routine identification —finding out which routine to call— and how to perform the call and return. A third operation connected with the flow of control in and around routines is the non-local goto statement, which terminates the running routine and transfers control to a labeled code location in an ancestor of the running routine. This deviates from the simple call–return scheme described above, since the call is not terminated by the expected return.

In object-oriented languages, we invoke methods on objects. The effect of a method invocation with regard to the flow of control is identical to that of a routine call. Method invocation and routine call differ in degree in that the routine to be called is almost always determined statically and the method to be invoked is often only determined at run time, by using a dispatch table. An additional difference is that a method has direct access to the fields of the object. This access is implemented by passing a pointer to the object as an additional parameter, as discussed in Section 11.2.9. We will now first consider what to call and then how to call it.

11.4.2.1 Routine identification—what to call

Before we can translate a routine call, the routine must be identified. Usually this has already been done during semantic checking. A routine name may be overloaded, but if the input program is correct, the language rules allow the compiler to identify a single routine to be called.

In languages that allow routine variables, the routine to be called may be the result of an expression. In this case, the compiler will not be able to identify the routine to be called, and must produce code to evaluate the expression. This should result in a (run-time) routine value, as discussed in Section 11.2.8; the routine value can then be called through an (indirect) routine call, for which an instruction is available on all reasonable target machines.

In object-oriented languages, method identification is not so simple. As we have seen in Section 11.2.9.4, in many cases a dispatch table must be consulted at run time to find the method to be invoked. The result of this consultation is again a routine value.

11.4.2.2 Routine calls—how to call it

Calling a routine is not just a transfer of control to the code of the routine; the **calling sequence** must also create the components of an activation record, as described in Section 11.3.2. Part of the calling sequence is performed at the routine call site and part is performed at the entry point of the called routine.

Before creating the components of the activation record, space for the activation record itself must be allocated. If a stack is used to store activation records, the space is allocated more or less automatically: the components are pushed onto the stack in the right order. If the allocation is explicit, the caller must allocate a chunk of memory of a suitable size, large enough to contain all components. This means that the required size must somehow be made available to the caller, for example as a run-time constant.

In the following discussion we will assume that activation records are allocated on a stack; this is the most usual situation. Heap allocation of activation records can be derived easily from the discussion below; where special measures are required, these are described.

A **stack** is a memory area onto which items can be pushed and from which items can be popped. Associated with a stack is a **stack pointer**, SP, which points to the "top" of the stack; the stack pointer resides in a dedicated register.

There is some confusion about which way stacks grow in memory. In abstract descriptions of stack machines, the usual convention is that pushing an item onto the stack raises the stack pointer; we used this convention in the pure stack machine of Section 7.5.2. On almost all real-world machines, however, pushing an item onto the stack *lowers* the numerical value of the stack pointer. This implies that the stack grows from high-numbered addresses to low-numbered addresses. Since we are considering code for real machines here, we will follow the hardware convention in this section.

There is an independent confusion about drawing stacks on paper: which way do they grow on paper? Although the word "stack" would suggest otherwise, stacks traditionally grow downwards in drawings, and we will follow that convention. Together the two conventions imply that memory addresses decrease from top to bottom in drawings, as was already illustrated in Figure 11.23.

The major advantage of using a stack for the activation records is that they do not have to be explicitly allocated and deallocated, thus saving considerably on allocation and deallocation times. Another advantage is that the working stack of the caller and the parameter area of the callee can be combined, which may save some time and space, as parameter values no longer have to be copied.

We will now discuss the individual components of the activation record, in the order in which they are usually created.

The parameter area and parameter transfer   The parameters of the routine must be stored in or pushed to the location in which the callee expects them. The compiler must impose a rule for accomplishing this. An example of such a rule is: when parameters are passed on the stack, the last parameter is pushed first. Such a rule is suitable for languages that allow a variable number of parameters to be passed in a routine call and results in the **parameter area** shown in Figure 11.23 when the activation record is constructed on the stack. The compiler could also reserve a fixed number of registers for parameter passing and push the rest of the parameters onto the stack. Whatever scheme is chosen, it is essential that the caller stores the parameters in locations where the callee can access them.

If the routine returns a result, the parameter area may also contain a pointer to the location in which this result must be stored.

In some languages, a value can have a dynamic component, a component the size of which can only be determined at run time; the prime example is a dynamic array. For a parameter with a dynamic component, the dynamic component is allocated on the heap. The parameter part of the activation record then contains a pointer to the component, or a descriptor of known size with a pointer to the component.

Usually, the language manual specifies which parameter passing mechanism is to be used. The simplest and most common parameter passing mechanism is **call by value**: the rvalue of the actual parameter is used as the initial value of the corresponding formal parameter.

Many languages also support some form of output parameters, allowing a routine to change the values of some of its actual parameters by assigning to the corresponding formal parameters. There are two common mechanisms for this: **call by reference**, in which the change is effected immediately, and **call by result**, in which the change is effected upon return from the call. Both call by reference and call by result can be implemented by passing the lvalue of the actual parameter instead of its rvalue. The usual context condition here is that the actual parameter has an lvalue. In call by reference, an assignment to the formal parameter is implemented as an assignment to this lvalue. Call by result is implemented by allocating a local variable for the parameter, using this local variable throughout the routine, and assigning this local variable through the corresponding lvalue parameter in the return sequence.

Another common parameter passing mechanism is **call by value-result**, which is a combination of call by value and call by result. It is implemented using the scheme of call by result, with the addition that the local variable allocated for the parameter is initialized with the value of the actual parameter.

The administration part   The **administration part** includes the frame pointer of the caller, which represents the dynamic link, and the return or continuation address. In languages that require so, it may also contain the frame pointer of the lexically enclosing routine, which represents the static link. During the initialization of the administration part, control is transferred to the callee, after saving the return address in the activation record of the callee or the continuation address in the activation record of the caller. Sometime during this phase, the old frame pointer is stored in the administration part and FP is set to indicate the new activation record.

The administration part also often contains space to save some machine registers. For example, sometimes machine registers are used for local variables and temporaries. When this is the case, these registers must be saved on routine call entry and restored on routine exit. There are two frequently used schemes for register saving and restoring: "caller saves" and "callee saves". In the **callee-saves scheme**, the routine entry code of the callee saves all registers that may be corrupted by the callee's code. In the **caller-saves scheme**, the routine call code contains code which saves the registers that the caller requires to be unharmed upon continuing after the call. In this scheme, the callee is free to use and corrupt all machine registers, since the caller has saved the ones it needs.

The caller-saves scheme usually requires fewer register saves and restores during run time, because it only has to save the registers active at the call, whereas in the callee-saves scheme all registers used by the routine need to be saved. On the other hand, the caller-saves scheme may require more instruction space, because every calling sequence needs to contain code to save and restore registers, whereas the callee-saves scheme only has code for this purpose at the routine entry and routine exit. Note that in the caller-saves scheme, the registers are saved in the caller's activation record, whereas in the callee-saves scheme, they are saved in the callee's activation record.

The local variable area   Once control has been transferred to the callee, the callee can start building the **local variable area**, the part of the activation record in which local variables and compiler temporaries reside. The compiler can determine the size of this component from the sizes and alignment requirements of the local variables; it may even reorder variables with different alignment requirements to minimize the total size. The compiler also knows what temporary variables are required for the code of the routine, by keeping track of their number, size and alignment requirements during the code generation phase for this routine. This information is very dependent on the details of the code generation process, since optimizations may introduce or remove temporary variables. Space for the local variable area is allocated by decreasing the stack pointer by the proper amount.

As with parameters, one or more of the local variables may have a dynamic component; this dynamic component can be allocated on the heap, but for local variables there is another option, allocating it in the "dynamic allocation part" of the activation record, as explained below.

The working stack   The local variable area is followed by the **working stack**, which is used for anonymous intermediate results from expressions. It may also be used for the bounds of for-statements, although it is more common to put these in temporaries.

Going through the code of a routine, the compiler can easily keep track of the size of the working stack and record its maximum size. At the end of the scan, the maximum size of the working stack for the routine is known; it can then be incorporated as a fixed-size block in the activation record.

The top of the working stack is indicated by the stack pointer as left by the allocation of the local variable area, and the working stack itself is the space below it. Machine instructions with push and pop properties can be used to access the working stack.

The dynamic allocation part If the target language allows activation records of dynamically extensible size, the activation record may also have a separate **dynamic allocation part** for local variables. These dynamic parts are then stored in the dynamic allocation part instead of on the heap. Since the dynamic allocation part is the only part the size of which cannot be determined statically, it has to come at the end of the activation record, as shown in Figure 11.45. In this set-up, the stack pointer points to the "top" of the dynamic allocation part.

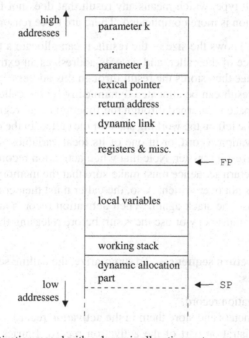

Fig. 11.45: An activation record with a dynamic allocation part

Some processors do not allow dynamic allocation parts, because they require the size of the activation record to be specified when it is created, by the compiler. For example, the SPARC processor has a save/restore mechanism for creating new activation records; the save part of the mechanism requires the size as a parameter. If the target language allows it, however, storing the dynamic part of local variables or parameters in the activation record has the advantage that it does not have to be deallocated explicitly on routine exit. Instead, its deallocation is implicit in the deallocation of the activation record. Also, allocation on the stack is much faster, since it only involves resetting the stack pointer.

A disadvantage is that the hardware stack pointer SP is now no longer available for manipulating the working stack. The remedy is to allocate the working stack somewhere in the activation record, and implement its stack pointer in software, for example in a normal register. It is not necessary to check this software pointer for stack overflow, since the size of the working stack is known in advance, and sufficient space can be guaranteed to be available.

Returning function results If the callee returns a value, the result can be made available to the caller in several ways. For a "simple" result type, such as an integer, real, or pointer, the compiler usually uses a machine register, called the **function result register**. The callee simply stores the result in this register, and the caller accesses this register to obtain the result. This register may serve other purposes as well, for example as a scratch register in the evaluation of expressions. For a "compound" result type, which means any result that does not fit naturally[1] into a register, the situation is more complicated. There are three reasonable solutions:

- If the compiler knows the size of the result, it can allocate a temporary variable in the data space of the caller, and pass its address as an extra parameter to the callee. The callee then stores the result through this address.
- Space for the result can be allocated dynamically by the callee, and a pointer to the allocated space is returned through the function result register.
- The result can be left on the working stack of the callee, in the dynamic allocation part of its activation record, or in one of its local variables, with a pointer to it in the function result register. Note that when activation records are allocated on the stack, the return sequence must make sure that the memory area in which the result resides is not overwritten. Also, the caller must then copy or use the result before it can use the stack again. When activation records are allocated on the heap, the caller must copy or use the result before releasing the activation record of the callee.

The calling and return sequences To summarize, the calling sequence consists of the following steps:

- Create an activation record.
- Evaluate parameters and store them in the activation record.
- Fill the administration part of the activation record. Entries include the frame pointer of the caller and the return address. They may also include the lexical pointer if required, probably some machine registers, and possibly also the old stack pointer.
- Transfer control to the callee.
- Make the frame pointer FP point to the activation record of the callee.

---

[1] Some data types, for example a record with just four character fields, fit unnaturally into a register. Most compilers will consider such result types "compound".

- Update the stack pointer SP, allowing enough space for the local variable part.

The dynamic allocation part, if present, is filled as the values of the local variables are computed.

The return sequence consists of the following steps:

- If the callee has a return value, store the result in the area designated for it.
- Restore the machine registers that were saved in the administration part.
- Update the stack pointer SP so that it indicates the frame pointer FP.
- Restore the frame pointer FP from the administration part.
- Transfer control to the caller, using the saved return address. Note that the administration part can still be accessed, because SP now indicates the activation record.
- Release the activation record of the callee.

Activation records and stack layout A typical layout of a stack with activation records is shown in Figure 11.46; the diagram depicts two activation records, that of a caller and that of its callee. We see that the two activation records overlap partially, since they share the parameter area. The caller evaluates the actual parameters of the call one by one, in last-to-first order, using its working stack. After evaluating a parameter, the result is left on the working stack, and the next one is evaluated on top of it. In this way, when all parameters have been evaluated, their values lie on the top of the caller's working stack. The working stack of the caller can now be used as the parameter area of the callee, resulting in overlap between the two activation records.

In this set-up, local variables are addressed through the frame pointer FP using negative offsets, parameters are addressed through FP using positive offsets, and the working area is addressed through the stack pointer SP. The position of SP in Figure 11.46 indicates an empty working stack.

If the implementation places activation records on the heap instead of on the stack, some of the techniques described above are not possible. Since activation records on the heap are separate entities, they cannot overlap and the working stack in one cannot serve as the parameter area in the other. Since records on the heap cannot be extended, activation records on the heap cannot have dynamic allocation parts.

Routine calling and parameter passing have received ample attention in the early literature; some pertinent papers are by Wichmann [298] and by Kowaltowski [161]. A very informative paper with strong opinions on the subject is by Steele [266].

Optimizations for routine invocations Several optimizations for routine invocations have already been mentioned above, the most important but at the same time most inconspicuous one being the allocation of the activation records on a stack rather than on the heap. Some others are the additional allocation of dynamic data on the stack, the precomputation of the size of the working area, and the overlapping actual and formal parameters.

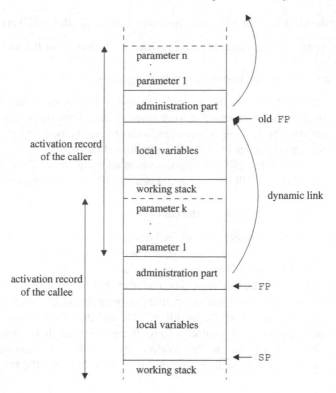

Fig. 11.46: Two activation records on a stack

There is another important optimization for routine invocations, which has more to do with flow of control than with activation records: tail call elimination. In its simplest form, the compiler replaces the code sequence

```
Call    routine
Return
```

with

```
Jump routine
```

This not only saves code and processor cycles, but it also unburdens the stack. When activation records come into play, the optimization becomes more complicated, but the concept remains the same.

A **tail call** is any routine call that is the last executed statement in a routine body. Routine bodies can contain more than one tail call; for example, in Figure 11.47 both gcd(b, a) and gcd(a-b, b) are tail calls. Tail calls are important for a combination of reasons: they occur frequently; they are easily detected; and, most importantly, they can be eliminated relatively easily, leading to sometimes considerable speed-up.

Although the frequency of tail calls in user programs of course depends on the subject, the programmer and the language, inspection of a few programs will quickly show that a sizeable number of routines end in a tail call. The code for quicksort,

```
PROCEDURE QuickSort(A: ArrayType);
  VAR Low, High: ArrayType;
BEGIN
  Split (A, Low, High);
  QuickSort(Low);
  QuickSort(High)
END
```

is a simple example, showing one tail call and two non-tail calls. The frequency of tail calls is even higher in generated code for functional and logic languages, as we will see in Chapters 12 and 13.

Tail calls are easy to detect in the control flow graph: they correspond to routine call nodes whose successor is a return node.

Much of the administration involved in a tail call is superfluous and can be eliminated. There are several reasons for this. First, there is no reason to return to the routine R that made the call (the *caller*) when the routine C that was called (the *callee*) has finished, since there is no additional code in the caller that needs to be executed. So there is no need for a return address when C exits, nor was there any need to store one when C was called: the transfer to C can be effected by a simple jump instruction. Second, the formal and local variables of the caller R are no longer required as soon as the parameters of the tail callee C have been computed, provided these parameters do not contain pointers to the formals or locals of R. And third, now that we have seen that the formals and locals can be abandoned and there is no need for a return address, most or all of the activation record of R is free just before the call and, with possibly some data juggling, can be used as the activation record of C.

```
int gcd(int a, int b) {
    if (b == 0) return a;
    if (b == 1) return 1;
    if (b > a) return gcd(b, a);
    return gcd(a-b, b);
}
```

Fig. 11.47: Recursive implementation of Greatest Common Divisor

When R and C are the same routine, we have a direct recursive tail call. We will discuss this situation first, using the Greatest Common Divisor (Figure 11.47)[2] as an example. The routine body contains two recursive tail calls. To eliminate the calls and reuse the activation record, we need to assign the new parameters to the

---

[2] There are much better algorithms for the GCD.

```
int gcd(int a, int b) {
 L_gcd:
         if (b == 0) return a;
         if (b == 1) return 1;
         if (b > a) {      /* return gcd(b, a); */
                  int tmp_1 = b, tmp_2 = a;
                  a = tmp_1, b = tmp_2;
                  goto L_gcd;
         }
         {         /* return gcd(a−b, a); */
                  int tmp_1 = a−b, tmp_2 = b;
                  a = tmp_1, b = tmp_2;
                  goto L_gcd;
         }
}
```

Fig. 11.48: Iterative implementation of GCD by tail call elimination

```
int gcd(int a, int b) {
 L_gcd:
         if (b == 0) return a;
         if (b == 1) return 1;
         if (b > a) {      /* return gcd(b, a); */
                  int tmp_2 = a;
                  a = b,  b = tmp_2;
                  goto L_gcd;
         }
         {         /* return gcd(a−b, a); */
                  a = a−b;
                  goto L_gcd;
         }
}
```

Fig. 11.49: Iterative implementation of GCD after basic bloc optimization

old ones, and replace the call by a jump. The first is most easily done by introducing temporary variables. The new parameters are assigned to the temporaries, and then the temporaries are assigned to the old parameters; this avoids problems with overlaps. The jump requires a label at the start of the routine body. This leads to the code of Figure 11.48. Basic block optimization can then be used to simplify the assignment sequences; this yields the code of Figure 11.49.

When R and C are not the same routine, there is still a simple way of eliminating the call to C: in-lining it. If that results in one or more directly recursive calls, R and C were mutually recursive, and we can eliminate the calls as explained above. If not, we can repeat the process, but all the caveats of in-lining (Section 7.3.3) apply. This approach fails if not all source code is available, for example, when calling a separately compiled (library) function. Most mutually recursive functions, however, occur in the same module.

When generating assembly code, eliminating the call is even easier, since the start of the code of C is available. The parameter values of C are written over the activation record of R, using temporary variables as needed; the activation record then looks like a proper activation record for C, and a simple jump to the start of the code of C suffices for the transfer of control.

Tail recursion removal was introduced in 1960 by McCarthy [186], to assist in the translation of LISP. A good description of tail recursion removal with examples and an evaluation is given by Bailey and Weston [25]. Formal foundations of tail recursion elimination are presented by Clements and Felleisen [63].

11.4.2.3 Non-local gotos

The flow-of-control aspects of non-local goto statements have already been covered in Section 11.3.6.4. We will consider here the data handling aspects.

The main data issue of the implementation of a non-local goto statement is that the registers that were saved in the intervening activation records must be restored when these activation records are destroyed. In the absence of special measures there is no proper way to do this, because there is no way to find out which registers to restore from a given activation record. A special measure that can be taken to prevent this problem is to record in each activation record which saved registers it contains. Restoring the registers then becomes trivial, at the cost of some extra book-keeping at each routine call. For some target machines, it may be feasible to always, in each activation record, save and restore the same set of registers, so that it is not required to record which registers are saved. Another option is not to use register variables in routines that can be the target of a non-local goto. These routines must then also save all registers on routine entry, and restore them on routine exit. This technique allows the implementation not to restore registers from intervening activation records.

We will now turn to a form of control flow in which the non-local goto plays a significant role.

11.4.3 Run-time error handling

There are many ways a program can get into trouble. Some examples of problems are: integer overflow, an array bound error, memory exhaustion, and power failure. Depending on circumstances, the generated code, the run-time system, the operating system, or the hardware may detect the error, and then some level of the system will probably cause some error message to be displayed and the program to be terminated. Or the error may go unnoticed. Since this is often not the desired situation, some languages allow the programmer to specify which errors must be caught and also to specify the actions to be performed upon the occurrence of these errors or exceptional situations. So, handling of a run-time error consists of two parts: the error must be detected and the actions for the error must be performed. Both have their problems: detecting the error may be difficult and some of the required actions are very inconvenient.

11.4.3.1 Detecting a run-time error

A run-time error can be caused either by the program itself or by external circumstances. Detecting a run-time error caused by external circumstances is very system-specific. For example, a memory failure—the malfunction of a memory section—may or may not be made available to the program. It is up to the run-time system to make errors caused by external circumstances available if it can.

Often, the operating system makes exceptional external circumstances available to the run-time system by causing an interrupt. For example, on the UNIX operating system, a user can interrupt a running program by typing a control-C or similar keystroke. The default action on an interrupt is to terminate the program, but UNIX includes a mechanism for making the interrupt available to the program. The program can then detect that an interrupt has occurred, and take appropriate action.

Examples of run-time errors caused by the program itself are: integer overflow, array bound errors, division by zero, and dereferencing a null pointer. Some of these errors cause the operating system to give an interrupt, but often the compiler must generate checks to detect these run-time errors. Several error conditions can be checked for by examining certain bits in the processor status word. For example, there is usually an overflow bit, indicating that the last instruction performed caused an overflow. Similarly, a library or the program itself may also detect run-time errors, for example file access errors, or program-specific problems such as illegal user input, internal errors, or security violations.

Most processors lack special facilities for higher-level error conditions, for example array or range bound errors. If such errors are to be detected, the compiler must generate code to perform a check, testing that a certain integer falls within a range. Such a check basically looks as follows:

```
IF (val < lowerbound) OR (val > upperbound) THEN
    THROW range_error;
END IF;
```

where THROW is a basic statement to signal an error. These checks can be quite expensive, which is why many compilers have a switch that disables the generation of these checks.

11.4.3.2 Handling a run-time error

When a programming language does not have facilities to allow the user to deal with run-time errors, the story ends here. The run-time system can make sure that it produces an intelligible error message, and then may terminate the program, producing some kind of memory image, usually called a "memory dump", which can then be examined using a post-mortem debugger. Many languages, however, include a mechanism for dealing with run-time errors. We will now discuss two such mechanisms, signal routines and exceptions.

Signal handlers A simple mechanism for dealing with run-time errors is the **signal statement**. A signal statement binds a specific class of error conditions to a specific user-defined routine, the **signal handler**. Whenever a run-time error occurs, the corresponding signal handler is called. The signal handler might then close open files, free system resources, print a message, and terminate the program. Alternatively, it could deal in some other way with the error, and just return. In the latter case, the program will resume just after the point where the error occurred. To implement the signal statement, the run-time system maintains a program-wide list of (error condition class, signal handler) pairs, so it can call the corresponding signal handler when a run-time error occurs.

Sometimes it is convenient to have the program continue at a point different from where the run-time error occurred. For example, a program could be in a main loop processing commands. A run-time error in one of the commands should then cause the program to print an error message and continue with the main loop. The programmer can implement this by using a non-local goto statement in the signal handler to transfer to the main loop of the program. In a non-nesting language like C, the setjmp/longjmp mechanism can be used, as shown in Figure 11.50.

```
#include <setjmp.h>

jmp_buf jmpbuf;            /* type defined in setjmp.h */

void handler(int signo) {
    printf ("ERROR, signo = %d\n", signo);
    longjmp(jmpbuf, 1);
}

int main(void) {
    signal(6, handler);        /* install the handler ... */
    signal(12, handler);       /* ... for some signals */
    if (setjmp(jmpbuf) == 0) {
        /* setting up the label for longjmp() lands here */
        /* normal code: */
        ...
    } else {
        /* returning from a call of longjmp() lands here */
        /* exception code: */
        ...
    }
}
```

Fig. 11.50: An example program using setjmp/longjmp in a signal handler

Exception handlers A more flexible feature, available in many modern programming languages, is the facility to specify "exception handlers". An **exception handler** specifies a particular error condition and a set of statements that will be executed should this error condition occur. This allows an exception handler to access the local variables of the block or routine in which the error condition occurred. The statements in the exception handler replace the rest of the statements in the block or routine, should the corresponding error condition, or "exception", occur.

Usually, each block of statements or each routine can have its own exception handler. It can even have several exception handlers, for different error conditions.

When an exception E occurs, the chain of activation records is followed, releasing activation records on the way as in the implementation of a non-local goto, until one is found that has a handler for the exception E. This handler is then executed, and execution resumes at the end of the block or routine that the handler is associated with—unless the exception handler terminates the program or causes another exception.

For each exception handler, the compiler generates the code corresponding to the statements in the exception handler, terminating it with a jump to the end of the block associated with the handler, and labels this code with a unique handler label. Also, for each block or routine with exception handlers it generates a table of (exception, handler label) tuples, with one entry for each exception handler.

In addition, the administration part of each activation record must contain a pointer to the table of exception handlers currently installed for its routine. If the exception handlers are associated with a routine, this is a constant; if they are associated with a block, the pointer must be updated as blocks with exception handlers are entered and left. Now, when an exception E occurs, the chain of activation records is examined as follows, most recent activation record first:

1. The pointer to the table of exception handlers is extracted from the currently examined activation record.
2. The table referenced is searched for a handler for exception E. If such a handler H is found, step 3 is performed. If not, step 1 is performed on the parent activation record (the one of the caller). If there are no more activation records, the program is terminated, possibly after printing a message.
3. A non-local goto to the exception handler H is performed. This automatically releases all examined activation records that turned out not to have a handler for exception E. Note that the generated code for the exception handler takes care of the continuation of the program execution, once the handler is finished.

The discussion above leads us to the important observation that routines with exception handlers can be the target of a non-local goto. So, depending on the implementation of non-local gotos, the compiler may or may not keep variables of routines with exception handlers in registers, in accordance with the preceding discussion on non-local gotos.

A disadvantage of the method described above is that, depending on the implementation of the non-local goto, activation records may be examined twice, once to find a handler, and once to perform the non-local goto. An optimization to this approach is to restore information from an examined activation record when it turns out not to have a handler for the exception, and to then discard the activation record.

The exception handler mechanism is more flexible than the signal handler mechanism. Its increased flexibility comes, however, at the cost of a slight increase in the number of instructions required to perform a routine call or block entrance; these instructions are necessary for the construction of the exception handler table. Other exception handler implementations are feasible, of which we will discuss one example.

An alternative implementation replaces the (exception, handler label) pairs mentioned above by a program-wide list of tuples (exception, handler label, start address, end address). Here "start address" indicates the beginning of the block protected by the handler, and "end address" indicates the end of that block. When an exception occurs, the run-time system uses this list of tuples to determine which handler should be invoked, as follows. First, the value of the program counter at the time the exception occurred is compared with the start and end addresses of blocks protected by a handler for the exception at hand. If it falls within a start address–end address range, a handler is found, and a non-local goto is performed, as discussed above. If not, the return address is extracted from the activation record at hand. This return address represents the position in the code where the caller currently is. This position may again be protected by a handler, so, again, it is compared with the start and end addresses of blocks protected by a handler for the exception at hand. Again, as above, if a handler is found, a non-local goto is performed. If not, the return address of the caller is extracted, etc. Ultimately, either a return address (and an activation record) with a handler is found, or execution terminates.

This scheme is more efficient as long as no exceptions occur. However, searching for a handler may be more expensive, depending on the exact implementation of the exception handler table.

11.5 Code generation for modules

Modules (also called "packages") are syntactic structures in which a number of related items are grouped together. They often restrict access to their contents by providing an explicit interface, which is then the only means of accessing the module. The related items in a module could for example be variables and routines affecting these variables. Modules are somewhat similar to objects, but there are also considerable differences. In some respects they are simpler: they usually cannot be created dynamically, and lack all the object-oriented features discussed in Section 11.2.9. On the other hand, modules are compilation units and it must be possible to compile them separately; second, modules often require an explicit initialization.

Regarding code generation, modules introduce two problems to the compiler writer:

- The target language usually has one, flat, name space. Therefore, the compiler must make sure that if two different modules export an item of the same name,

they have a different name in the generated code.
- The compiler must generate code to perform the module initialization; a complication here is that at module initialization modules may use items from other modules, so these other modules must be initialized first.

11.5.1 Name generation

Usually, the rules that the characters in a name must obey are more strict in the source language than in the target language. Often, there is a character c that is allowed in names in the target language but not in names in the source language; examples are the . (dot) and the $ sign. If so, this feature can be used to create unique names for items in a module: simply concatenate the item name to the module name, using c as a separator. Note that this assumes that module names are unique, which they usually are.

If there is no such character, there may be some other rules in the source language that can be exploited in the compiler to produce a unique name. If all else fails, the compilation process could have a phase that analyzes the complete program and does name generation.

11.5.2 Module initialization

Most source languages allow modules to have explicit **initialization code**, for example for global variables. Even if this is not the case, a language might require implicit initialization of these variables. Note that a module, and more specifically the initialization code of a module, could use items from other modules. This means that those modules should be initialized earlier. This can be accomplished by having the initialization code of each module call the initialization code of all the modules that it uses. Then, the whole initialization phase can be started by calling the initialization phase of the module that contains the main program.

When adopting this solution, there are two issues one should be aware of: avoiding multiple initializations and detecting circular dependencies.

11.5.2.1 Avoiding multiple initializations

If module *A* uses module *B* and module *C*, and module *B* also uses module *C*, the initialization code of module *A* calls that of module *B* and that of module *C*. The initialization code of module *B* also calls that of module *C*, so *C*'s initialization will get called twice. This can be prevented by having a module-specific variable *ThisModuleHasBeenInitialized* in each module, which is set to true once its initialization code is called. The initialization of a module then becomes:

```
if not ThisModuleHasBeenInitialized:
    ThisModuleHasBeenInitialized ← True;
    — call initialization of the modules used by this module
    — code for this module's own initializations
```

11.5.2.2 Detecting circular dependencies

Circular dependencies between module *specifications* are usually detected by the compiler. When compiling a module specification *A* that imports a module specification *B*, the compiler usually demands that module specification *B* is present for examination or has already been compiled. If module specification *B* then requires module specification *A*, the compiler can easily detect that it already was compiling *A*, and deal with this according to what the language manual prescribes (which is probably to disallow this).

For module *implementations* the situation is different. When compiling a module implementation *A*, which uses module specification *B*, the compiler can see what module specifications are used by the module specification for *B*, but it cannot know what module specifications are used by *B*'s implementation, since the latter need not even be available yet. Now suppose the present or a future *B* implementation uses *A*'s specification. Then we have a circular dependency, which is not detected at compile time, because when compiling *B*'s implementation, the compiler only reads *A*'s specification, which in our example does not use *B* at all.

One way to detect circular dependencies is to postpone this check to run time, during module initialization. Each module then has a module-wide Boolean variable *ThisModuleIsBeingInitialized*, and the initialization code then becomes:

```
if ThisModuleIsBeingInitialized:
    — circular dependency; deal with it
if not ThisModuleIsInitialized:
    ThisModuleIsInitialized ← True;
    ThisModuleIsBeingInitialized ← True;
    — call initialization of the modules used by this module
    ThisModuleIsBeingInitialized ← False;
    — code for this module's own initializations
```

A disadvantage of this approach is that the error does not become apparent until the compiled program is run. A more elegant solution to this problem is to have the compiler produce a list of the modules that each module uses. A separate compilation phase, which is invoked after all module implementations have been compiled, may then read these lists and detect circular dependencies.

Such a phase could also be used to determine a global initialization order, by imposing a relation $<$ on the modules, such that $A < B$ means that the initialization of A must be called before the initialization of B. In the absence of circular dependencies, a topological sort then gives the global initialization order. The presence of such a phase allows the generation of an initialization routine, to be called at program startup, which calls the module initializations in the right order. The module initializations themselves then only perform the initialization of the module itself. It is, however, not always convenient or practical to have such a phase.

11.5.3 Code generation for generics

Many languages offer generic units. A **generic unit** is a recipe for generating actual versions of the unit; it is parameterized with one or more generic parameters, usually types. Generic units are usually limited to routines, modules, and object classes. A generic unit must be instantiated by supplying the actual parameters to produce an instance of the generic unit, which can then be used like any other unit in the program. Section 2.12.3 presented the classic example of a generic list.

When generating code for a generic unit, we are faced with the question of how to implement a generic parameter, especially when it is a type. There are two fundamental ways to deal with this problem. The first way is to not produce code for the generic unit itself, but rather to produce code for every instantiation. This can be viewed as expanding the generic unit as if it were a macro, as already suggested in Section 2.12.3 in the context of macro processing. Alternatively, the compiler writer can design run-time representations of the generic parameters whatever they are, and pass them as normal parameters during run time. Given the unusual nature of generic parameters, they have unusual representations, called "dope vectors".

11.5.3.1 Instantiation through expansion

In **instantiation through expansion**, no code is generated for the generic unit, which remains available as an AST only. Suppose we have a generic unit G with a generic parameter type T, and suppose the generic unit is instantiated with actual parameter type tp. The instantiation then consists of the following steps:

- Create a copy of the AST of the generic unit G.
- In the copy of the AST, replace every occurrence of identifier T which is identified as the generic parameter type T by the type indicated by the identifier tp at the instantiation point.
- Process the resulting AST as if it were an ordinary AST, resulting from an ordinary unit.

An important issue that must be treated with care is name generation, also discussed in Section 11.5.1. Usually, the target language has a single, flat, name space. Therefore, the compiler must generate a unique name for each instantiation. We cannot just use the generic unit's name—which is supposed to be unique—since a generic unit may be instantiated more than once. However, the instantiation probably also has a name, and the unit in which the instantiation takes place also has a name. A combination of all these names allows the compiler to produce a unique name for the items in the instantiated unit.

Instantiation through expansion is relatively easy to implement and there is no run-time overhead. It may, however, increase the size of the generated code significantly, especially when a generic unit contains instantiations of its own. Of course, the compiler could keep track of which instantiations it has already performed and reuse those when possible, but this will not always help, because all instantiations may be with different parameters.

11.5.3.2 Instantiation through dope vectors

In **instantiation through dope vectors**, the compiler actually produces code for the generic unit from the AST. The generated code will have to utilize run-time descriptors for the instantiation parameters. The run-time descriptor of an instantiation parameter must contain enough information to support all possible usages of a generic parameter of its kind: for a constant, it should contain its value; for a routine, it should contain its address and a lexical pointer, if applicable; and for a type, it should contain a so-called **dope vector**.

If a generic parameter is a type tp, the compiler will have to generate code to allocate, initialize, and deallocate variables of type tp, and to perform operations that involve tp, for example assignment, comparison, copying, and possibly arithmetic operations of various lengths. Since these are operations that very much depend on the nature of the type tp, it is convenient for the compiler to generate calls to routines which perform these operations. The addresses of these routines can then be found in the run-time descriptor of the instantiation parameter, the dope vector. This makes a dope vector very similar to a method table with entries for a constructor, a destructor, a copy routine, etc.

So, the dope vector has an entry for each operation that is allowed on a value or variable of a generic parameter type, including allocation, deallocation, and copying. Each entry indicates a routine implementing the specific operation, as depicted in Figure 11.51.

The main advantage of the use of dope vectors is that the executable code of the generic unit is shared by all its instantiations. A disadvantage is the added overhead: often, dynamic allocation schemes must be used for types for which simple static allocation would be sufficient. Also, there is the routine call overhead for simple operations such as assignment and comparison. Note that this overhead cannot be eliminated by in-lining the call, since the routine to be called is not known until run time.

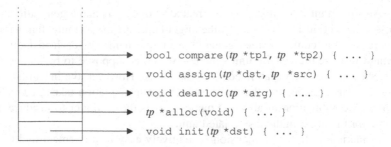

```
          ─────────────────▶  bool compare(tp *tp1, tp *tp2) { ... }
          ─────────────────▶  void assign(tp *dst, tp *src) { ... }
          ─────────────────▶  void dealloc(tp *arg) { ... }
          ─────────────────▶  tp *alloc(void) { ... }
          ─────────────────▶  void init(tp *dst) { ... }
```

Fig. 11.51: A dope vector for generic type *tp*

11.6 Conclusion

This brings us to the end of our discussion of the strongly interrelated issues of intermediate code generation and code generation for run-time systems, for imperative and object-oriented languages. We have seen that the most important run-time data structure is the activation record: it allows both data and the flow of control to move from routine to routine. Code for its manipulation can be generated in-line or be contained in run-time library routines. The design of other run-time data structures, which derive from source language type constructors, is fairly straightforward. We have seen that all source language flow of control is expressed by simple unconditional and conditional jumps in the intermediate code; the generation of code for expressions has already been covered in Chapters 7 and 9. Special attention was paid to the selection of the proper method to call in an object-oriented method invocation; dispatch tables of varying complexity are used to implement specific object-oriented features. Another area in which intermediate code and run-time system are interwoven is exception handling. Finally we have discussed issues in the implementation of modules and of generics.

Summary

Summary—Context handling

- Static correctness checking during context handling consists mostly of two issues: identification and type checking.
- Identification matches an applied occurrence of an identifier or operator with its defining occurrence, and with a symbol table entry, in which the information about the item is collected.
- A scope stack allows fast and easy manipulation of scope information sets.
- Some languages allow identifiers or operators to have several different definitions through overloading. Overload resolution is the process of reducing the set of

possible definitions of an operator or identifier to a single one.
- Type checking is the process that determines which type combinations in the source program are legal according to the rules of the source language. It does so by determining which types are equivalent, and deciding which coercions are allowed in which context.
- Each node in the AST of an expression represents either an lvalue (a location) or an rvalue (a value). These attributes propagate bottom-up, according to language-dependent, but usually intuitive, rules.

Summary—Data representation and routines

- Characters, integers, floating point numbers, enumerations, and pointers all have an obvious corresponding data type in virtually all target languages.
- The target representation of a record type consists of the consecutive target representations of its members, possibly separated by gaps to obey alignment requirements of the target machine.
- The target representation of an array type consists of the consecutive target representations of its elements, either in row-major or column-major order. In addition, a run-time array descriptor is required for dynamic arrays.
- The run-time representation of an object consists of two parts: (1) a pointer to a table for the present implementation of the object type, and (2) a record holding the object fields. The table is a dispatch table for the methods, and possibly an offset table for the fields.
- Inheritance and polymorphism make it necessary to enumerate object methods, and use the enumeration index of a method to obtain its address at run time from the dispatch table. Dependent multiple inheritance requires a similar technique to find the offset of a field within an object representation, using the field offset table.
- An activation record holds the data pertinent to the invocation of a routine or object method. It includes the parameters, an administration part, local variables, and a working stack.
- If routines are activated in a strictly last-in-first-out order, a stack can be used to store the activation records.
- An activation record is accessed through a frame pointer, which usually resides in a dedicated machine register.
- A routine is a piece of code, reachable through its code address. When a routine is called, an activation record is created for it and flow of control is transferred to its first instruction.
- The above actually is a subroutine. Other kinds of routines are iterators and coroutines.
- An iterator yields a succession of values.
- A coroutine can suspend itself, and does so by transferring control to another coroutine, which then resumes at the point where it was last suspended.

- Routines can be global or nested. A global routine can only access global entities and its own local entities. A nested routine can access those, and can in addition access entities in lexically intervening routines.
- Operations on routines include declaring a routine (specifying its name, parameter types, and return type), defining a routine (declaring it and supplying its code), calling a routine, passing a routine as parameter, returning a routine as a value, jumping out of a routine (a non-local goto), and partial parameterization (creating a new routine with some of the parameters of the original routine already supplied).
- Nested routines require access to lexically intervening routines. This can be implemented by means of a lexical pointer, which is a copy of the frame pointer of the lexically enclosing scope.
- Passing a nested routine as a parameter or returning it as a result requires a two-pointer value: a lexical pointer and a routine address. Returning a nested routine as a result may violate pointer scope rules.
- A closure is a representation of a partially parameterized routine, with space for all parameters plus a mask indicating which parameters have been filled in.
- A nested routine can be lifted out of its parent by isolating the activation record of the parent routine as a data structure and passing it to the lifted routine. This allows all the access the nested routine had.
- Any place a lifted routine is called, the activation record of its parent must be passed to it. In particular, if a lifted routine is passed around, the activation record of its parent must be passed along with it; they form a (routine address, activation record address) pair.

Summary—Code generation

- The two main mechanisms for local flow of control are selection (if- and case statements) and repetition (for- and while statements). Code is generated for them by mapping them to lower-level target language constructs, such as conditional jumps and assignments.
- Code for if-statements is trivial, using true and false labels. The jump can be integrated into the Boolean expression by passing the true and false labels to the routine that generates code for it.
- Case statements can be implemented as linear lists of tests, jump tables, balanced binary trees, and others.
- Code for the while statements is similar to that for the if-statement, including the incorporation of the jump into the Boolean expression.
- The for-statement poses two problems: in a naive implementation the controlled variable may overflow where it should not, and for non-unit step size, the upper bound may be overstepped. Both problems are remedied by a careful implementation; the resulting code is surprisingly complex.

- The code for repetition statements can be optimized by "unrolling the loop", generating the code for the loop body multiple times.
- The translation of a routine call or method invocation consists of two steps: identifying the routine or method called, and performing the call.
- The routine to be called can be a named routine, a routine variable or a method. The first two identify themselves, the third is looked up in the dispatch table.
- A routine is called in three steps: an activation record is allocated, it is partly filled with information, and control is transferred to the start of the code of the routine; filling the activation record may then continue. Many detailed decisions are required to design a complete routine call protocol.
- The information stored in the activation record may include parameters, return or continuation information, a lexical pointer, a dynamic link (old frame pointer), dumped register values, local variables, working stack, dynamic allocation part, etc.
- Storing of register values may be done by the caller ("caller saves") or by the callee ("callee saves"), with subtly different effects. In both cases it is the register values of the caller that get saved.
- A dynamic allocation part may be present to hold the dynamic parts of local variables and perhaps parameters.
- In most languages activation records can be allocated on the stack. If routines can be returned as values (functional languages), or if more than one thread is present (coroutines) this is not possible and heap allocation must be used.
- A return value can be delivered in a function result register, on the top of the working stack, or under a pointer passed as an input parameter.
- An important optimization on routine calls is tail call elimination, which can often optimize away the entire routine call.
- When generating assembly code, the tail call inside a routine R can be optimized into a stack adjustment plus jump to the new routine, C.
- In C we can only jump to the start of the current routine. This allows us to optimize the important case of directly tail-recursive functions by overwriting the parameters with the values of the tail call and jumping back to the start of function R.
- While performing a non-local goto, the registers stored in the activation records that are removed must be restored. Special code is required for this.
- Run-time error handling (exception handling) consists of two parts, detecting the error and processing the error.
- Detection of run-time errors depends in complicated ways on language properties, the operating system, the run-time system, and compiler-generated checks. Two different mechanisms for dealing with run-time errors are: signal handlers, and exception handlers.
- A signal statement binds a specific class of error conditions to a specific user-defined routine, the signal handler. Whenever a run-time error occurs, the corresponding signal handler is called.
- To implement the signal statement, the run-time system maintains a program-wide list of (error condition class, signal handler) pairs, so it can call the cor-

responding signal handler when a run-time error occurs. Signal handlers often perform a non-local goto.

- An exception handler specifies a particular error condition and a set of statements that will be executed should this error condition occur. The statements in the exception handler replace the rest of the statements in the block or routine, should the corresponding error condition, or exception, occur.

- When an exception E occurs, the chain of activation records is followed, releasing activation records as in the implementation of a non-local goto, until one is found that has a handler for the exception E. This handler is then executed, and execution resumes at the end of the block or routine that the handler is associated with.

- The administration part of each activation record contains a pointer to the table of exception handlers currently installed for its routine. If the exception handlers are associated with a block, the pointer must be updated as blocks with exception handlers are entered and left.

- The presence of modules in a source language forces the compiler to generate unique names, because the target language usually has a flat name space.

- The initialization phase must make sure that modules are initialized in the proper order, obeying module dependencies.

- The two common implementations for instantiation of generic units are expansion, in which the compiler processes the generic unit at the instantiation point as if it were an ordinary unit, and dope vectors, in which the compiler generates run-time descriptors, the so-called dope vectors, for the generic parameters of the generic unit.

Further reading

For many years, the only programming languages in existence were imperative ones. Examples of imperative programming languages are: FORTRAN, Algol 60, Pascal, Algol 68, Modula-2, C, Ada, and many, many more. Several of these languages are still quite popular. Consequently, all compiler construction books discuss the implementation of imperative programming languages.

The first object-oriented language was Simula. It introduced classes, inheritance, and polymorphism. It was originally designed specifically for simulation problems (hence the name), but was later developed into a complete programming language. Other better-known object-oriented languages are Smalltalk, C++, and Java. There seem to be no books that are specifically about the compilation of object-oriented languages, although both Appel [18] and Wilhelm, Seidl and Hack [113, 300–302] pay considerable attention to the subject. For the more theoretically inclined, Duran *et al.* [91] describe an algebraic formalism for the derivation of compilers for object-oriented languages.

Many advances in the compilation of imperative and object-oriented languages are reported in the conference proceedings of the *ACM SIGPLAN Conference on*

Programming Language Design and Implementation - PLDI, the *Conference on Object-Oriented Programming Systems, Languages and Applications - OOPSLA*, the *IEEE International Conference on Computer Languages - ICCL*, and the *European Conference on Object-Oriented Programming - ECOOP*.

Exercises

11.1. (▷www) Why is the result of the expression EXPR >= 0 trivial, when EXPR is an expression of type unsigned integer?

11.2. (▷794) In Section 11.1.1, Figure 11.4, we first follow the hash table and then split according to the name space desired. Perhaps a more intuitive way of implementing name spaces is to have a separate hash table for each name space, and pass a pointer to it as a parameter to the routine *Identify()*. A call *Identify (NameSpace, Name)* would then return a pointer to the proper *DeclarationInfo*. Discuss the pros and cons of this idea.

11.3. (▷www) The following declarations are given for a language that uses name equivalence:

```
A, B: array [1..10] of int;
C: array [1..10] of int;
D: array [1..10] of int;
```

Explain which of these four variables have the same type and which have different types.

11.4. Explain the transformations the type of a routine undergoes in partial parameterization.

11.5. Determine which nodes carry lvalues, which carry rvalues and where dereference operators have to be added, in the AST for the expression a[a[1]] := s[0].sel; assume that a is an integer array variable and s is a variable array of structures.

11.6. (▷794) Design rules for the lvalue/rvalue checking of the C conditional expression *condition*?*expr₁*:*expr₂*. Compare your rules with the behavior of the GNU C compiler, with and without –ansi and –pedantic flags.

11.7. (▷794) One of the scope rules in Section 11.2.3.2 says "The scope of a value is the smallest scope of any pointer it contains or infinite if it does not contain pointers." What if the value contains pointers with incommensurable scopes?

11.8. (▷794) Why are the following expression modifications incorrect for IEEE 754 floating-point computations:

1. a+(b+c) → (a+b)+c
2. a∗(b∗c) → (a∗b)∗c

3. v == v → `true`

11.9. (▷www) In C, why is it that assignment (=) *is* defined for structs and equality (==) is not? (Hint: this *is* a compiler construction question.)

11.10. (▷www) Given the C structure

```
struct example2 {
    int member1;
    double member2;
    int member3;
}
```

where an int is 4 bytes and a double is 8 bytes, and an int must be 4-byte aligned, and a double must be 8-byte aligned.
(a) What is the size and alignment of struct example2?
(b) What happens if fields member2 and member3 are interchanged?
(c) Could an optimizing compiler consider reorganizing record fields to achieve minimal size?

11.11. (▷www) Section 11.2.6 suggests that the compiler can compute the offset of *zeroth_element* from the first element of the array itself. Let us call this offset *zeroth_offset*. Give the formula for *zeroth_offset*(A) and the formula for the address of $A[i_1, \ldots, i_n]$ using *base*(A) and *zeroth_offset*(A) instead of *zeroth_element*(A).

11.12. (▷www) Given a three-dimensional array and a three-deep nested set of arrays (i.e. an array of arrays of arrays), with all arrays bounds-checked and starting at element 0, compute for both how many multiplications, additions, comparisons, and memory dereferences are needed. What if the arrays do not start at element 0?

11.13. (▷www) Show that it is possible to implement a bounds check of a Java array with only one comparison.

11.14. (▷www) Refer to Section 11.2.7 on set types. Discuss the implementation of set union and set intersection when implementing a set as a linked list.

11.15. (▷www) Consider the following classes (presented in a Java-like syntax):

```
abstract class Shape {
    boolean IsShape() { return true; }
    boolean IsRectangle() { return false; }
    boolean IsSquare() { return false; }
    abstract double SurfaceArea();
}

class Rectangle extends Shape {
    double SurfaceArea() {
        ...
    }
    boolean IsRectangle() { return true; }
}
```

```
class Square extends Rectangle {
    boolean IsSquare() { return true ; }
}
```

Give the method tables of the classes Rectangle and Square.

11.16. (▷794) When a language supports polymorphism, as described in Section 11.2.9.3, it is sometimes necessary to examine the actual type of the object at hand. The example of Exercise 11.15 has methods like IsSquare that enable the user to do this. Some languages have a built-in operator for this. For instance, Java has the instanceof operator. The expression A instanceof C is a Boolean expression yielding true if A indicates an object that is an instance of class C. Design an implementation for this operator.

11.17. (▷794) Refer to Figures 11.18 and 11.19 concerning multiple inheritance. Given an object e of class E, give the compiled code for the calls e.m1(), e.m3(), and e.m4().

11.18. (▷www) Refer to Figures 11.21 and 11.22 concerning dependent multiple inheritance. Suppose method m5 in class E is defined as

```
void m5() {
    e1 = d1 + a1;
}
```

where all fields have type int. Give the compiled C code for m5.

11.19. (▷795) Explain why the "caller saves" scheme usually requires fewer register saves and restores at run time than "callee saves".

11.20. Given the GNU C routine:

```
void A(int A_par) {
    void B(void) {
        printf("B called, A_par = %d\n", A_par);
    }
    void C(int i) {
        if (i == 0) B(); else C(i–1);
    }
    C(5);
}
```

(a) Draw the stack that results from the call A(3).
(b) How does the final call of B() access the parameter A_par of A?
(c) Repeat parts (a) and (b) for the routine

```
void A(int A_par) {
    void C(int i) {
        void B(void) {
            printf("B called, A_par = %d\n", A_par);
        }
        if (i == 0) B(); else C(i–1);
    }
    C(5);
}
```

11.21. (▷www) (F.E.J. Kruseman Aretz, mid-1960s) Write a program that reads an array of integers terminated by a zero, and prints its middle element, *without* using an array, linked list, or otherwise allocated data. Hint: Read the elements of the array recursively, on each level of recursion prepare a routine element(int i), which returns the i-th element, and pass this routine to the next level.

11.22. (▷www) Why is it that the closure must be *copied* to the activation record in the invocation of a routine represented by a closure? If the closure is allocated in an extensible array on the heap, it could itself be turned into an activation record, could it not?

11.23. Study the coroutine mechanism of Simula 67 [41], and design intermediate code sequences for the new, detach and resume commands.

11.24. What code should be generated for the Boolean assignment b := x > y, in which b is a Boolean variable with the representation true = 1 and false = 0, and x > y translates to Compare_greater x, y, which leaves the result in the *condition_register*?

11.25. (▷www) The discussion of case statements in Section 11.4.1.2 mentions using a balanced tree for the case labels as a possible implementation for the case statement. Why does the tree have to be balanced?

11.26. (▷www) Discuss the translation of a case statement by means of a hash table.

11.27. (▷www) A repeat statement allows the programmer to execute a sequence of statements an indeterminate number of times, until a *Boolean_expression* is fulfilled. Give a translation of the statement

REPEAT *statement_sequence* UNTIL *Boolean_expression* END REPEAT;

to intermediate code. Note that the *statement_sequence* is executed at least once.

11.28. (▷www) The C language has a break and a continue statement. The break statement terminates the closest enclosing loop, and the continue statement proceeds with the next iteration. In fact, these are both jumps. In the code generation schemes of Section 11.4.1.3, where would these go to? In other words, where should the compiler place the break_label, and where the continue_label?

11.29. (▷www) Why is the C while loop of Figure 11.43 not exactly equivalent to the for-loop of Figure 11.42? Hint: consider the effect of a continue statement inside the body.

11.30. (▷795) Refer to Figure 11.41. What goes wrong if one generates

```
(1)     i := i + tmp_step_size;
(2)     IF tmp_loop_count = 0 THEN GOTO end_label;
(3)     GOTO loop_label;
end_label:
```

in which statements (1) and (2) are interchanged with respect to the original?

11.31. (▷www) The optimization explained in the last subsection of Section 11.4.1.3 replaces a loop with a step size of 1 by a loop with a step size of 4, thus apparently introducing all the complexity of the code of Figure 11.41. Devise a simpler code scheme for such loops. Make sure it is still overflow-resistant.

11.32. (▷795) In Section 11.4.2.2 we claim that pushing the last parameter first onto a stack is a technique suitable for languages that allow a variable number of parameters to be passed in a routine call. Explain.

11.33. *Routine invocation implementation project.*
(a) Study the routine call and routine exit instructions of a machine and assembler available to you.
(b) Design an activation record layout, simple parameter passing and routine call and routine exit sequences for recursive routines, and test your design by running the translation (manual or otherwise) of, for example, the mutually recursive routines

```
void A(int i) {
    showSP("A.SP.entry");
    if (i > 0) {B(i−1);}
    showSP("A.SP.exit");
}

void B(int i) {
    showSP("B.SP.entry");
    if (i > 0) {A(i−1);}
    showSP("B.SP.exit");
}
```

Here showSP() is an ad-hoc routine which allows you to monitor the progress by showing the value of the stack pointer in some way; you will probably have to improvise. Start by calling A(10).
(c) Design a format for routines as parameters and test your design with

```
void A(int i, void C()) {
    showSP("A.SP.entry");
    if (i > 0) {C(i−1, A);}
    showSP("A.SP.exit");
}

void B(int i, void C()) {
    showSP("B.SP.entry");
    if (i > 0) {C(i−1, B);}
    showSP("B.SP.exit");
}
```

Start by calling A(10, B).
(d) Design a format for labels as parameters and test your design with

```
void A(int i, label L) {
    showSP("A.SP.entry");
    if (i > 0) {B(i−1, exit); return ;}
    exit : showSP("A.SP.exit"); goto L;
}

void B(int i, label L) {
    showSP("B.SP.entry");
    if (i > 0) {A(i−1, exit); return ;}
    exit : showSP("B.SP.exit"); goto L;
}
```

11.34. (▷795) 1. Explain how a deterministic FSA can be implemented on a compiler with tail recursion elimination, by having a routine for each state. 2. Would you recommend this technique? 3. Why doesn't this work for non-deterministic FSAs?

11.35. (▷www) Refer to the subsection on signal handlers in Section 11.4.3.2 on handling run-time errors. Consider the following code fragment in a language that allows a exception handler to resume at the point where the error occurred:

```
X := A / B;
Y := A / B;
```

An optimizing compiler wants to transform this code into:

```
X := A / B;
Y := X;
```

Explain why, if an exception handler is defined for the code fragment, this optimization is incorrect.

11.36. (▷795) A language designer is designing a programming language that features, among other things, generic routines with generic type parameters. He/she considers adding generic routines as generic parameters (non-generic routines can already be passed as normal parameters in the language) and comes to you, a compiler designer, for advice. Evaluate the proposed addition from a compiler construction point of view.

11.37. *History of imperative language implementation*: Study Sheridan's 1959 paper [260] on the IBM FORTRAN compiler, and identify and summarize the techniques used.

Chapter 12
Functional Programs

Functional languages are based on the idea that a program is a function with one input parameter, its input, and one result, its output. Running a program is seen as the application of a function to the input, resulting in the output. This computational model of function application, simple as it is, is very expressive and builds upon the results of mathematical research into computable functions.

The mathematical world view of functional languages shows up in a number of places. For example, syntactical constructs have been included in the language to ease the specification of sets and recursive functions. More important, however, is the idea that a programmer should not be bothered with implementation details of a certain function, but should rather concentrate on specifying its input–output relation. In particular, a programmer should specify *what* to compute, rather than *how*, *where*, and *when*. Consequently, there are no ;-operators, for-loops, or other statements that specify how the computation proceeds from one statement to the other; more specifically, there are no statements at all. Also, there is no assignment operator specifying a variable or memory location where a computation must be stored.

The difference in approach to computing is illustrated by the following example, which lists program sections for the factorial function fac in the functional language Haskell (Figure 12.1) and the imperative language C (Figure 12.2). The functional

```
fac 0 = 1
fac n = n * fac (n−1)
```

Fig. 12.1: Functional specification of factorial in Haskell

specification of fac is a good example of how recursion is used to tackle problems. The function is defined by two equations. The first equation states that $0! = 1$, while the second equation states that $n! = n \times (n-1)!$. Unfolding the recursion then leads to $n! = n \times (n-1) \times (n-2) \times \ldots \times 1$. This definition of factorial is also the basis for the C code, but this is not directly visible because of the interleaving

```
int fac(int n) {
    int product = 1;

    while (n > 0) {
        product *= n;
        n--;
    }
    return product;
}
```

Fig. 12.2: Imperative definition of factorial in C

of control statements and computation rules. The C code uses a while loop to avoid expensive recursive function calls; the intermediate results produced by the loop are accumulated in the local variable product.

Efficiency considerations often lead imperative language programmers to compromise on the readability of their code. Functional language programmers, on the other hand, put the burden of finding an efficient computation order on the compiler. Fortunately, compiler technology for functional languages has matured enough to handle cases like factorial: the techniques discussed in the remainder of this chapter are capable of generating C code from the Haskell specification that is equivalent in efficiency.

Functional languages raise the level of abstraction at which programmers should be concerned about performance. Functional programmers must still be concerned about $O(n^2)$ versus $O(n \ln n)$ algorithms, but need no longer worry about reducing the number of function calls, managing memory efficiently, and other low-level programming aspects. A consequence is that the interpreter or compiler must handle these issues and must handle them efficiently. The first functional language compilers were not up to this task, and generated very slow code; a slow-down of a factor of 100 compared to C was no exception. Fortunately, today's compilers are capable of generating code quality that matches, and sometimes even exceeds, that of plain C for a considerable class of programs.

On the one hand, compilers for functional languages are more complicated than their imperative counterparts. The front-end has to handle additional syntactic constructs capturing concise mathematical notations, and the back-end has to handle the higher level of abstraction. On the other hand, functional languages compilers are simpler than their imperative counterparts. The simple and regular syntax leads to a small and clean front-end without the many exceptional cases typically found in imperative compilers, and the functional paradigm eases many of the advanced analyses employed by an optimizing back-end, since, for example, no memory aliasing can occur.

Before discussing the additional techniques employed in a functional language compiler, we present a short tour of the programming language Haskell [219] to highlight the aspects of functional languages that require special care. Haskell was defined by an international standard committee. It is representative of the "purely functional lazy languages" and contains most features from the functional languages developed so far.

12.1 A short tour of Haskell

The following sections emphasize the aspects of functional languages that raise the level of abstraction above that of imperative languages. Some aspects, such as pattern matching, have a modest impact on the compiler and are typically handled in the lexical analyzer and parser. This so-called **syntactic sugar** includes: the offside rule, list notation, list comprehension, and pattern matching. Other aspects of functional languages like lazy evaluation cannot even be handled completely at compile time and require considerable run-time support. The syntax of function application is explained below.

Function application

The Haskell syntax for function application is very concise, but possibly misleading for the unwary. Applying a function f to the two arguments 11 and 13 is written in Haskell as:

    f 11 13

Note that there are no brackets around the arguments to f, nor are the arguments separated by a comma. The reason for simply juxtaposing function and arguments is that it allows currying to be expressed naturally, as shown in Section 12.1.7.

Function application binds stronger than any operator, so g n+1 is parsed as (g n) + 1 rather than g (n+1) as the layout may suggest. Also, it is left-associative, so g g n is parsed as (g g) n, rather than as g (g n), and parentheses are required to obtain the other interpretation.

12.1.1 Offside rule

The layout of a Haskell program matters to parsing. Consider the following definition of divide, which handles divisions by zero:

    divide x 0 = inf
    divide x y = x/y

The definition consists of two equations. An **equation** consists of a left-hand side, followed by the = token, followed by the right-hand side. Note that there is no explicit token to denote the end of each equation. In many languages a line break is treated as ordinary white space, which would allow incorrect parses such as:

```
(divide x 0 = inf divide x)
(y = x/y)
```

On the other hand, treating every line break as a equation terminator is very inconvenient since a long expression may need to span several lines for clarity. The **offside rule** controls the bounding box of an expression. Everything below and to the right of the = token is defined to be part of the expression that makes up the right-hand side of the equation. The right-hand side terminates just before the first token that is "offside"—to the left—of the = position. The offside rule has to be applied recursively when handling nested equations, as in:

```
fac n = if  (n == 0) then 1 else prod n (n−1)
        where
           prod acc n = if  (n == 0) then acc
                        else prod (acc∗n) (n−1)
```

Tab stops are 8 characters apart; A tab character causes the insertion of enough spaces to align the current position with the next tab stop.

The offside rule can be handled conveniently in the lexical analyzer by having it insert explicit end-of-equation tokens (the ; in Haskell), as follows. The lexical analyzer maintains a stack of offside markers. When the lexical analyzer detects a token with associated offside semantics such as =, it pushes the current character position onto the marker stack. Upon detecting a line break, the lexical analyzer skips all white space and records the character position of the next token. It compares the position against the top of the marker stack. If the new position is less than the marker, the lexical analyzer pops the marker and returns the end-of-equation token. It continues popping markers and returning end-of-equation tokens until the stack is empty or the position is greater than the top marker.

12.1.2 Lists

The **list** is a powerful data structure that has been part of functional languages from day one with the introduction of the list processing language LISP by McCarthy in 1960 [186]. Since lists are used so frequently, Haskell includes special notation for them. The empty list, also known as "Nil", is denoted by []. Non-empty lists are written as an opening bracket [, the elements separated by commas, and a closing bracket], as shown in the examples below:

```
[ ]
[1]
[1,  2,  3,  4]
[4,  3,  7,  7,  1]
["red",  "yellow",  "green"]
[1  ..  10]
```

Strings are actually just lists of characters, so "red" is a convenient notation for ['r', 'e', 'd']. The last example shows a shorthand notation named **arithmetic sequence** for the list [1, 2, 3, 4, 5, 6, 7, 8, 9, 10]. The elements of a list can be of any type —integers, strings, user-defined types, etc.— but all elements of a given list must be of the same type; the polymorphic typing of Haskell, discussed in Section 12.1.5, does not allow lists to contain elements of different types.

Lists can also be constructed element by element using the : infix operator. This operator combines an element and a list into a new list. For example, the list [1, 2, 3] is equivalent to the expression

```
(1 : (2 : (3 : [ ])))
```

As a second example, consider the range function, which constructs the arithmetic sequence [n .. m] dynamically:

```
range n m = if  n>m then [ ]
               else  (n : range (n+1) m)
```

12.1.3 List comprehension

A **list comprehension** is a syntactical construct that closely matches mathematical set notation. For example, the set of squares of all odd numbers up to 100, defined mathematically by

$$S = \{n^2 \mid n \in \{1,\ldots,100\} \land \text{odd } n\}$$

can be expressed in Haskell as follows:

```
s = [n^2 | n <- [1..100], odd n]
```

where the <- symbolizes the element sign "$\in$" rather than an arrow. The list comprehension is read as "n square, such that n is an element of 1 to 100 and n is odd".

List comprehension is convenient for developing programs that can be expressed in terms of sets. Note, however, that list comprehension, as the name suggests, generates lists rather than sets: ordering is important and elements may occur multiple times in list comprehensions. It is especially convenient to use when generating new lists from old ones. For example, the quicksort algorithm can be specified concisely using list comprehensions as follows:

```
qsort [ ]    = [ ]
qsort (x:xs) = qsort [y | y <- xs, y < x]
               ++ [x]
               ++ qsort [y | y <- xs, y >= x]
```

Here the pivot of the quicksort is taken to be the head of the input list; it is isolated from this list by using pattern matching on the infix operator : (see below). The list comprehension for all elements that go left of the pivot x iterates over the tail of the input list xs filtering out all elements less than x. The second list comprehension filters out all elements greater or equal to x. Both are then sorted recursively and concatenated with the pivot using the concatenating function ++.

List comprehension is considered syntactic sugar since it can be transformed relatively easily into a simpler expression. This transformation will be discussed in Section 12.4.3.

12.1.4 Pattern matching

Pattern matching is a convenient way to express recursive functions. In fact, we have already met a case of pattern matching, the factorial function in Figure 12.1 reproduced here:

```
fac 0 = 1
fac n = n * fac (n−1)
```

The first equation defines the base case of the recursive specification, which matches the argument with pattern 0; the match will only succeed if the actual parameter has the value 0. The second equation covers all arguments by matching against the pattern n; this match will always succeed. Another example is the length function

```
length [ ]    = 0
length (x:xs) = 1 + length xs
```

which computes the length of a list by pattern matching on the empty list [ ] and on the infix list constructor :.

In general a function is specified by several equations containing patterns at argument positions in the left-hand side. A pattern can be a constant such as 0 and [ ], a variable such as n or x, or a constructor whose elements are themselves patterns such as (x:xs). Function equations are matched from top to bottom; the patterns in them are matched from left to right.

Function definitions based on pattern matching can be translated easily into equivalent definitions based on if-then-else constructs. For example, the fac function without pattern match can be defined as

```
fac :: int −> int
fac n = if (n == 0) then 1
        else n * fac (n−1)
```

The length function requires some more work since the pattern in the second equation (x:xs) introduces two identifiers that are subsequently used in the right-hand side of the equation. We use the let-expression of Haskell to introduce the local definitions we need:

```
length list = if ( list  == [ ]) then 0
        else let
             x  = head list
             xs = tail  list
           in
                 1 + length xs
```

Further technical details of translating pattern matching will be presented in Section 12.4.2.

12.1.5 Polymorphic typing

Haskell, like most functional languages, is a strongly typed language. This means that for each expression or definition we can check at compile time whether or not it obeys the typing rules of the language. Haskell supports the usual *monomorphic* types consisting of basic types, for example Char and Int, and user-defined structured types, for example records and unions. In addition, Haskell supports **polymorphic types**. An expression is said to be polymorphic if it "has many types". For example, the empty list [] has many types: list of characters, list of numbers, list of lists of characters, and an infinite number of others. The exact type depends on the context in which [] is used. An important source of polymorphism is the class of list handling functions that operate on any type of list. Consider the length function again:

```
length [ ]   = 0
length (x:xs) = 1 + length xs
```

The function length can be applied to any type of list since the individual list elements are not used; the element x pattern-matched in length's second equation does not appear in the corresponding right-hand side. Type declarations, which are optional in Haskell, consist of an identifier, a type declaration sign "::" and a type specification. The type of length is:

```
length ::  [a]  −> Int
```

where a is a **type variable** that stands for an arbitrary type. Thus, length takes an arbitrary list ([a]) as input and returns (−>) an integer (Int) as its output. We can derive instances of a polymorphic type by replacing type variables with specific types. For example, by replacing a with Int or [Char] we see that

```
[ Int ]  −> Int
[[ Char]]  −> Int
```

are instances of the type [a] −> Int. These instances typically appear when length is used in larger expressions and the context imposes additional constraints of the type of length, as for example in length [1, 2, 3] + length ["red", "yellow", "green"]

The main advantage of polymorphic typing is that functions and data structures can be reused for any desired type instance. The same definition of length can be used to compute the length of a list of integers and a list of strings. Languages without a polymorphic type system would require the specification of two length functions: one that operates on lists of integers and another that handles lists of strings. C allows the programmer to resort to pointers and write a single length function that operates on generic lists, where elements are present as void * pointers. The handling of pointers, however, is error-prone and the use of the void * device discards valuable type information.

Type checking in polymorphic languages like Haskell is more difficult than in traditional monomorphic type systems. In particular, the equality of types involving type variables is harder to determine and requires **unification**, as will be explained in Section 12.3.

12.1.6 *Referential transparency*

By definition, a function in Haskell defines a fixed relation between inputs and output: whenever a function f is applied to the argument value arg it will produce the same output no matter what the overall state of the computation is. Haskell, like any other pure functional language, is said to be "referentially transparent" or "side-effect free." This property does not hold for imperative languages, where assignments to global variables and through pointers may cause two function calls f arg to yield different results, even when the argument value arg is the same in both calls.

The good thing about referential transparency is that it simplifies program analysis and transformation since a closed expression always denotes the same value independent of the context, and may be moved around freely. A closed expression is an expression that contains no references to external names other than global identifiers. The bad thing is that it prevents the programmer from writing space-efficient programs that use in-place updates. For example, adding 1 to all elements of a list in Haskell requires a complete new list to be constructed:

add_one [ ]   = [ ]
add_one (x:xs) = x+1 : add_one xs

Each application of the list constructor ":" allocates a fresh node.

In an imperative language, we can update the input list in-place, in which case we require the caller to create a copy of the input beforehand if the original is still needed later. In simple cases the functional language compiler can determine that the input list is indeed no longer needed after the call to add_one, so it can generate in-place updates too. Unfortunately, whenever the input list is passed as part of a larger data structure the compiler probably cannot infer the last-use requirement, and must conservatively allocate a new list.

Functional programs are notorious for allocating huge amounts of memory. Therefore garbage collection is a very important part of the run-time system. It allows the run-time system to present the user with an unlimited amount of memory, but requires the compiler to insert the necessary hooks in the code, as discussed in Section 10.2.2. Given the fast rate at which functional programs typically allocate and, implicitly, deallocate memory, garbage collection techniques that only examine the live data, like two-space copying (Section 10.2.5), perform best.

12.1.7 Higher-order functions

A fundamental concept of modern functional languages is that functions are "first-class citizens": functions may be passed as arguments, returned as results, and kept in data structures, just like ordinary data values such as integers. A function that takes a function as an argument, or delivers one as a result, is referred to as a **higher-order function**. With some notable exceptions (e.g., Python, Algol 68) imperative languages barely support higher-order functions: functions may perhaps be passed as parameters, but in most languages it is impossible to create new functions at run time.

The ability to construct new functions out of existing ones provides great abstractive power to the user, and is common in mathematics. The differential operator D, for example, is a higher-order function which takes a function as argument and returns another function, its derivative, as the result:

$$\mathrm{D}f = f' \text{ where } f'(x) = \lim_{h \downarrow 0} \frac{f(x+h) - f(x)}{h}$$

Similarly, Haskell allows the definition of functions that have one or more functions as parameters, and that yield new functions. For example, the standard Haskell function foldl takes a function F of two operands and an initial value I as its parameters, and yields a function of one operand L which applies F left-to-right successively to all elements of the list L, starting with the initial value I: it "folds" the list from the left. So the definition

```
sumlist lst = foldl add 0 lst
  where
  add a b = a + b
```

defines a function that yields the sum of all elements of a list. Thus, the call

```
sumlist [3,4,7]
```

yields the sum of the values 0+3+4+7, 14.

The point of the example is that foldl returns as its result a new function, which uses an already existing function, add, as its parameter. This is a very powerful mechanism, because it allows separation of concerns. For one thing, it allows the enumeration of the elements of lists, sets, and trees to be separated from the precise computations to be done on the elements.

The notion of higher-order functions allows a very interesting and non-obvious observation: any function with multiple parameters can be treated as a higher-order function by applying the parameters one by one. Working from left to right through the parameter list, each parameter application yields another function, which requires one parameter less, until all parameters have been applied and a parameterless function remains. For example, if a function add takes two parameters, and yields the sum of its parameters, applying just a constant 1 to add yields a new function that adds 1 to its (single) parameter. The process of transforming a multiparameter function into a higher-order function in this way is called **currying**, after Haskell B. Curry, who applied this principle to functional languages. (And yes, the programming language Haskell is also named after him.) Currying a function is useful because it provides a new powerful mechanism to define functions; it is a special case of partial parameterization, which was discussed in Section 11.3.4.

As a consequence of the curried function notation, the computation sumlist[3,4,7] => 14 can be viewed as a 4-step process, performed by feeding foldl its parameters one by one. First we define

```
addlist = foldl add
  where
  add a b = a + b
```

Next we supply the initial value:

```
addlist0 = addlist 0
```

And finally we supply the list to be summed:

```
sumlist347 = addlist0 [3,4,7]
```

We can now call the parameterless function sumlist347 and obtain our answer, 14. Note that foldl is no longer a function with two parameters, F and I, which yields a function with one parameter, L, which yields an integer; it is now a function with one parameter F, which yields a function with one parameter I, which yields a function with one parameter L, which yields a function with no parameters, which yields an integer. Also note that there is no semantic difference between the definitions of sumlist and addlist0: both versions always yield exactly the same result.

Currying complicates compiler construction since we need additional run-time support to represent functions with only part of their parameters applied, and to eventually evaluate these functions. This will be discussed in detail in Section 12.5.

Since we need to represent unevaluated function applications anyway, we may as well extend that to complete function applications, and treat them as parameterless function applications. We did this for function sumlist347 above. It is not necessary to immediately evaluate the function: it may be passed unevaluated as long as the called function is prepared to carry out the evaluation when needing the value. Lazy evaluation, which is to be discussed next, uses exactly this approach and does not evaluate a parameterless function until its value is needed.

12.1.8 Lazy evaluation

Functional languages lack explicit control flow and are based solely on expressions constructed out of values and function applications. Evaluating a non-trivial expression amounts to evaluating some subexpressions and combining the partial results into the final answer by applying a built-in operator or user-defined function. It is up to the compiler and run-time system to determine which subexpressions to evaluate in which order. In contrast, imperative languages prescribe to a large extent how and when expressions should be evaluated. For example, expressions at argument positions must be evaluated before calling the function. **Lazy evaluation** relaxes these constraints by specifying that a subexpression will only be evaluated when its value is needed for the progress of the computation. In contrast, the evaluation order of imperative languages is called **eager evaluation**. The difference can be demonstrated by the following example:

```
main = take 100 [1..]
```

The function take *n lst* is a standard Haskell function, which takes the first *n* elements from the list *lst*. Lazy evaluation does not start by evaluating the 100 and the entire list [1..], as would happen in a comparable imperative program, but rather invokes take with unevaluated parameters. Lazy evaluation works by invoking the top node of the expression tree first, rather than one of the lower nodes, and take is the function at the top of the expression tree for main. Upon invoking, take evaluates the 100 and then proceeds to evaluate its second argument step by step until the first 100 list elements are known.

We could of course just as easily have generated a list of 100 elements directly, but in general lazy evaluation makes it much easier to express algorithms that work on lists of arbitrary, including infinite, length. For example, the function

```
both lst [ ] = [ ]
both [ ] lst = [ ]
both (a:ta) (b:tb) = if  a == b then a:(both ta tb)
                     else if a < b  then (both ta (b:tb))
                     else (both (a:ta) tb)
```

takes two lists with monotonously increasing element values, and returns a list of all elements that occur in both lists. The function works on lists of finite or infinite length, without the programmer having to worry about list lengths. A possible call is:

```
double = [n | n <− [1..], n 'rem' 2 == 0]
triple  = [n | n <− [1..], n 'rem' 3 == 0]

main = both double triple
```

which prints the list of integers that are both even and divisible by 3.

Another example of the usefulness of lazy evaluation is in constructing parsers based on attribute grammars. An attribute grammar translates into a set of functions, one for each production rule, specifying how each attribute is to be computed. These functions can be used for parsing immediately: lazy evaluation automatically evaluates the attributes in the right order. See Johnsson [132] for a detailed description.

The expressiveness of lazy evaluation burdens the functional language implementation, which must support delaying and resuming computations. Section 12.5 discusses graph reduction, which is the basis of modern implementations of functional languages. In essence a function application translates into a heap-allocated data structure containing the function and its argument. When needed, such a suspended function can be activated by taking the code pointer and calling it with the arguments stored in the heap.

12.2 Compiling functional languages

The short tour of Haskell has highlighted the functional language features that require additional work in the compiler. For reference, Figure 12.3 lists which compiler phase handles which aspect of Haskell. Note that the handling of the most difficult aspects—higher-order functions and lazy evaluation—is deferred to the run-time system. Consequently, the run-time system of a functional language is considerably larger than that of most imperative languages and includes routines for garbage collection (see Chapter 10), dynamic function creation/invocation, and suspension/resumption of lazy computations.

12.2.1 The compiler structure

Compiler phase	Language aspect
Lexical analyzer	Offside rule
Parser	List notation
	List comprehension
	Pattern matching
Context handling	Polymorphic type checking
Run-time system	Referential transparency
	Higher-order functions
	Lazy evaluation

Fig. 12.3: Overview of handling functional language aspects

The general structure of a functional language compiler is given in Figure 12.4.

The high-level source language is simplified through several transformations into a small functional core, which contains all essential functional aspects but no syntactic sugar. The functional core requires explicit typing of functions to ease code generation, so for languages like Haskell where type declarations are not mandatory, the compiler front-end has to derive them from the source code (Sections 12.3 and 12.4).

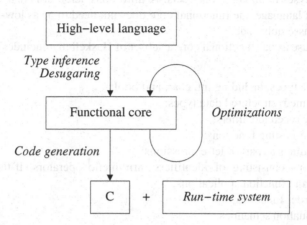

Fig. 12.4: Structure of a functional compiler

After the initial translation of the high-level language into the functional core, numerous optimizations are applied to improve code quality (Section 12.7). Many of these optimizations are also present in imperative compilers; examples are constant folding, function in-lining, and common subexpression elimination. In the final step, code generation takes the functional core and transforms it into the target code (Section 12.6). C is usually selected as the target language, since this offers the possibility to leverage imperative compiler technology for free. ANSI C programs are portable across a wide range of hardware platforms and C compilers are good at the complicated task of generating machine code: they include fancy algorithms for register allocation and instruction scheduling. C compilers, however, are not capable of optimizing memory references and function calls as much as required by functional programs, so code generation in a functional language compiler still requires some work.

The resulting C program is then compiled with an ordinary C compiler and linked with the run-time system into an executable. The run-time system takes care of handling those aspects of a functional language that cannot be handled at compile time, like lazy evaluation and higher-order functions (Section 12.5).

12.2.2 The functional core

The definition of what constitutes the **functional core** requires some thought. On the one hand, it must be high-level enough to serve as an easy target for the front-end that compiles the syntactic sugar away. On the other hand, it must be low-level enough to allow concise descriptions of optimizations, which are often expressed as case analyses of all core constructs. A third consideration is that when using C as the target language, the functional core does not need to be as low-level as when generating assembly code.

We will use as our functional core a subset of Haskell that includes the following constructs:

- basic data types, including int, char, and bool;
- (user-defined) structured data types;
- explicitly typed identifiers;
- typed non-nesting functions;
- local bindings as part of let-expressions;
- expressions consisting of identifiers, arithmetic operators, if-then-else compounds, and function applications;
- higher-order functions;
- lazy evaluation semantics.

These constructs, except for the last two, can be easily mapped onto C constructs. For example, the factorial function without pattern matching

```
fac  ::  int  −> int
fac n = if  (n == 0) then 1
             else n * fac (n−1)
```

maps into:

```
int  fac( int  n) {
      return  (n == 0 ? 1 : n * fac(n−1));
}
```

Since most of the functional core can be mapped easily to C, code generation concentrates on making higher-order functions and lazy evaluation explicit by generating calls to the run-time system.

The remaining sections of this chapter discuss the various parts of a functional compiler as outlined in Figure 12.4. First we briefly discuss type checking (Section 12.3), followed by the desugaring transformations, which translate Haskell into the functional core (Section 12.4). Next, we discuss the run-time system (Section 12.5), which takes care of handling higher-order functions and lazy evaluation by means of an interpreter known as the graph reducer. This graph reducer is the target of the code generator described next (Section 12.6); when generating C, difficult functional core constructs like higher-order functions are translated into calls to the run-time system. The most important optimizations performed on the functional core that reduce the number of calls to the run-time system by performing part of the

interpretation at compile time are covered in Section 12.7. Finally, we discuss some
advanced graph manipulation techniques aimed at reducing memory consumption
(Section 12.8). Such reduction also improves the speed of the compiled program,
due to better cache behavior and reduced garbage collector activity.

Where-clauses are not part of the functional core, since they have been removed
by lambda lifting as described in Section 11.3.7. It is, in principle, feasible to eliminate let-expressions the same way, but since they are semantically simpler, a more
efficient translation is possible, as explained in Section 12.6 (Figures 12.22 and
12.23).

<hr>

Roadmap

<hr>

12.3 Polymorphic type checking

The polymorphic type system of Haskell makes **type checking** more difficult than
for imperative (monomorphic) languages as discussed in Chapter 11. The simple notion of type equivalence needs to be redefined when polymorphic types like [a] and
[b −> c] are compared. Another complication is that type declarations in Haskell are
optional. Although good programming practice dictates that users explicitly provide
the types of their functions, the Haskell type checker must be capable of deriving
type information solely from the function definition. It is not immediately obvious
how to do this, since it is a property of a polymorphic function that it has many types.
For example, consider the higher-order function map, which applies a function f to
all elements of a list:

```
map f [ ]    = [ ]
map f (x:xs) = f x : map f xs
```

From the [ ] pattern in the first equation we derive that the second argument of map
is a list. Likewise the result of map is a list too. Note that both list types are not
related, so the first equation constrains the type to

```
map :: a  −> [b]  −> [c]
```

where a, b, and c are type variables representing arbitrary types. The second equation contains the subexpression f x, which reveals that f is a function. The general
type of a function is $\alpha -> \beta$. We know, however, that x is an element of the argument

list with type [b] and that f x is part of map's result list with type [c]. Therefore, we conclude that the type of f is b->c. The type of map is now constrained to

    map :: (b —> c) —> [b] —> [c]

The brackets around b –> c are necessary since the –> operator is right-associative, which is consistent with currying. We cannot refine the type further without compromising on the generality of map. For example, narrowing the type to (a –> a) –> [a] –> [a]) excludes the use of functions like ord, which transform values from one type into another (Char to Int). When inferring types, the type checker should derive from the constraints the most general instance of the type, which represents the complete set of types that the function covers.

Type checking in Haskell boils down to handling function application, which is the essential building block of expressions, and may involve a polymorphic function as well as a polymorphic argument. When encountering an anonymous function application like

    fun expr

the type checker introduces type variables so it can express typing constraints:

    fun :: a —> b
    expr :: c

In imperative languages function application is dealt with by checking whether or not the type of an expression at some argument position (c) is "equal" to the type of the corresponding formal parameter (a). In Haskell it is not required that types a and c are equal in that they represent the same set of types, but only that they can be unified to a subset that is common to both. Consider, for example, the type declarations of functions map and length:

    map :: (a —> b) —> [a] —> [b]
    length :: [c] —> Int

In the expression

    map length

the type checker must unify the type of length, which is [c] –> Int, with the type of map's first argument, a –> b. This results in a becoming the list [c] and b becoming Int, which allows the type checker to conclude that the type instance of map in map length is

    map :: ([c] —> Int) —> [[c]] —> [Int]

and so the type of map length itself is

    map length :: [[c]] —> [Int]

This result can be used to determine that the expression

    map length ["red", "yellow", "green"]

is well-typed: the types [[c]] and [[Char]] are unifiable, with c = Char. An expression like map length [1 .. 100], however, is invalid: the unification of [[c]] and [Int] fails, because it would require [c] and Int to be unified, which is impossible because Int is not a list.

The details of unification are deferred to Chapter 13, since unification is the basic mechanism used to implement logic programming languages.

For type-checking it suffices to notice that the unification of two polymorphic types essentially results in a substitution of the type variables involved. These substitutions are easily accommodated in the type-table structure suggested in Section 11.1.2. When type checking an n-ary function f, n fresh types t_i are added, one for each argument, and the type of f is set to

$$f \; :: \; t_1 \; -> \; \ldots \; -> \; t_n \; -> \; t_r$$
$$a_i \; :: \; t_i$$

A function definition may comprise multiple equations, which are to be type checked one after the other. Each equation may contain some patterns at argument positions. A pattern is handled by introducing fresh types for its components and unifying the top-level type with the corresponding argument type t_i. For example, the pattern (x:xs) requires two additional entries in the type table, one for x, say t_x, and another for xs, say t_{xs}. The type of (x:xs) is then $[t_x]$, which must be unified with type t_i.

Type checking then proceeds bottom up through the AST for the right-hand side of the equation. Constants simply propagate their corresponding type, which may be polymorphic. This is, for example, the case with the empty list [ ]. We create a fresh entry in the type table to hold a new instance of the type [a]. It is important that each occurrence of [ ] gets its own type so the type checker can handle cases like

```
length (1:[ ]) + length ('a':[ ])
```

where the first occurrence of [ ] has type [Int] and the second (unrelated) occurrence is of type [Char]. Global identifiers like length must also be assigned a fresh type on each occurrence, since they may be used in different contexts. In the example above length has types [Int] -> Int and [Char] -> Int, respectively. For local identifiers like parameter names, on the other hand, the type checker must use a single entry in the type table to catch type errors like

```
f xs = length xs + xs
```

Type checking fails since the two types for xs —[a] and Int— cannot be unified. The intermediate nodes in the AST are essentially all function applications, and require a unification as outlined above.

12.4 Desugaring

The next step after type checking is to remove the syntactic sugar from a Haskell program and transform it into its functional-core equivalent. In this section we focus on translating *lists*, *pattern matching*, *list comprehension*, and *nested functions* to core constructs.

12.4.1 The translation of lists

List notations contain three forms of syntactic sugar: the :, , and .. infix operators. The operator : constructs a node with three fields: a type tag Cons, an element, and a list. So the form x : xs is transformed to (Cons x xs), and the list [1, 2, 3] is transformed to

(Cons 1 (Cons 2 (Cons 3 [ ])))

Lists like [1..100] and [1..] are usually translated to calls of library functions that express these lists in terms of : and [ ]. An example of such a function is the function range, already encountered in Section 12.1.2:

```
range n m = if  n>m then [ ]
                 else  (n : range (n+1) m)
```

12.4.2 The translation of pattern matching

Pattern matching is a notational convenience for expressing recursive functions that contain several cases distinguished by patterns occurring at parameter positions. The general layout of such a function is shown in Figure 12.5. The n-ary function fun is specified as m equations with patterns constraining the arguments. The equations are matched from top to bottom; the patterns are matched from left to right.

fun $p_{1,1}$ $\cdots$ $p_{1,n}$ = $expr_1$
fun $p_{2,1}$ $\cdots$ $p_{2,n}$ = $expr_2$
$\vdots$

fun $p_{m,1}$ $\cdots$ $p_{m,n}$ = $expr_m$

Fig. 12.5: The general layout of a function using pattern matching

As exemplified by the function take

```
take  ::  Int  —> [a]  —> [a]
take 0 xs     = [ ]
take n [ ]    = [ ]
take n (x:xs) = x : take (n−1) xs
```

which returns the first n elements of a list, three types of patterns exist:

* constant patterns, such as 0 and [ ],

- variable patterns, like n and xs, which match any argument, and
- constructor patterns, like (x:xs), which is really syntactic sugar for (Cons x xs).

A constructor pattern matches a specific case of a structured type. A constructor may contain several fields, each being a pattern itself. Examples are x:(y:s), which matches any list of length two or more, and x:(y:[ ]), which matches any list of exactly length two. Such nested patterns may impose additional constraints, and introduce variables that may be referenced in the expression part of the equation. The generalized pattern-matching function of Figure 12.5 is compiled into the code of Figure 12.6. Here $cond_i$ specifies the conditions imposed by the patterns for equation i, and $defs_i$ defines all the variables that occur in the patterns $p_{i,1} \ldots p_{i,n}$. In short, $cond_i$ tests the structure and $defs_i$ retrieves the contents if the structure matches. The last line of code is added to catch the case that all patterns fail, which signals an error in the specification of the function; the error routine prints a message and then halts execution. The translated code for the take function is shown in Figure 12.7. Trans-

```
fun a₁ ... aₙ ⇒ if (cond₁) then let defs₁ in expr₁
                else if (cond₂) then let defs₂ in expr₂
                    ⋮
                else if (condₘ) then let defsₘ in exprₘ
                else error "fun: no matching pattern"
```

Fig. 12.6: Translation of the pattern-matching function of Figure 12.5

```
take a1 a2 = if  (a1 == 0) then
                 let xs = a2 in [ ]
             else if  (a2 == [ ]) then
                 let n = a1 in [ ]
             else if  (_type_constr a2 == Cons) then
                 let
                     n  = a1
                     x  = _type_field 1 a2
                     xs = _type_field 2 a2
                 in
                     x : take (n−1) xs
             else
                     error "take: no matching pattern"
```

Fig. 12.7: Translation of the function take

lating constant and variable patterns to functional core constructs is easy: a constant yields an equality test, and a variable imposes no constraint at all. Constructor patterns, on the other hand, require additional support to provide type information at run time. We must be able to verify that an argument (a2) matches the constructor specified in the pattern (Cons). For simplicity we require the run-time support to provide the _type_constr function, which returns the constructor tag of an arbitrary structured type element. In addition, we must be able to reference the fields in the constructor type. Again we assume that the run-time support will assist us by providing the generic _type_field*n* function, which returns the *n*th field of any structured type. These two functions are straightforward to implement if the run-time system uniformly encodes structured types as records with a common header and a variable number of fields.

The simplistic approach of translating pattern matches away by generating code for the individual equations results in non-optimal code. It can be improved in several ways, all of which require the handling of multiple equations at once. For example, recursive functions typically perform a case analysis of all constructors that might occur as a certain argument, as exemplified in Figure 12.7. Since the code has already been type-checked at compile time, any second argument in a call of take is guaranteed to be a list. So the last equation need not verify that the argument matches the constructor pattern, and consequently, the error guard can be omitted too. This simplifies take to the code shown in Figure 12.8. Another optimization

```
take a1 a2 = if  (a1 == 0) then
                 let  xs = a2 in  [ ]
               else if  (a2 == [ ]) then
                 let  n = a1 in  [ ]
               else
               let
                  n  = a1
                  x  = _type_field 1 a2
                  xs = _type_field 2 a2
               in
                  x : take (n−1) xs
```

Fig. 12.8: Optimized translation of the function take

concerns the occurrence of the same pattern in multiple equations. Consider the function last, which returns the last element in a list:

```
last :: [a] −> a
last [x]    = x
last (x:xs) = last xs
```

The first pattern, [x], is syntactic sugar for (Cons x [ ]), whereas the second pattern, (x:xs), stands for (Cons x xs). When generating code for each equation separately, both equations will check that their argument points to a Cons constructor node. The check in the second equation can be optimized away by proper book-keeping, resulting in the translation shown in Figure 12.9. Note that the check for the constructor pattern cannot be optimized away as it could with take above, since the patterns do not cover all the patterns of the list type; the pattern [ ] is missing, leaving last [ ] undefined. An alternative method of implementing pattern matching consists

```
last a1 = if (_type_constr a1 == Cons) then
          let
              x  = _type_field 1 a1
              xs = _type_field 2 a1
          in
              if (xs == [ ]) then
                 x
              else
                 last xs
          else
              error "last : no matching pattern"
```

Fig. 12.9: Translation of the function last

of generating one finite state automaton for all the patterns of a function definition and using it at run time to determine the correct right-hand-side expression [217].

12.4.3 The translation of list comprehension

List comprehensions can be transformed away just after type checking has been performed. For readability the transformation is presented as a source-to-source translation, although in reality it operates on ASTs. Our running example will be the following list comprehension, which computes all Pythagorean triangles with sides less than or equal to n:

```
pyth n = [(a,b,c) | a <- [1 .. n],
                    b <- [a .. n],
                    c <- [b .. n],
                    a^2 + b^2 == c^2]
```

Note that the numbers b and c are not drawn from the range $[1 .. n]$, but from $[a .. n]$ and $[b .. n]$ respectively. Doing so improves the efficiency of the algorithm and prevents the generation of equivalent triples like $(3, 4, 5)$ and $(4, 3, 5)$.

In general, a list comprehension

list comprehension → expression '|' qualifier ',' ... ',' qualifier

consists of an expression and a number of qualifiers separated by commas, where a **qualifier** is either a generator or a filter. A **generator** is of the form var '<-' list expression; it introduces a variable iterating over a list, which may be used in later qualifiers. A **filter** is a Boolean expression, which constrains the variables generated by earlier qualifiers.

The transformation of list comprehensions works by processing the qualifiers from left to right one at a time. This approach naturally leads to a recursive scheme as presented in Figure 12.10. Transformation rule (1) covers the base case where no

more qualifiers are present in the list comprehension. The result is a single element
list holding the expression *expr*.

T{ [*expr* |] } $\Rightarrow$ [*expr*]   (1)

T{ [*expr* | *F*, *Q*] } $\Rightarrow$ **if** (*F*) **then** T{ [*expr* | *Q*] } (2)
                            else [ ]

T{ [*expr* | *e* <– *L*, *Q*] } $\Rightarrow$ mappend f_Q *L*   (3)
                            where
                                f_Q *e* = T{ [*expr* | *Q*] }

Fig. 12.10: Translation scheme for list comprehensions

The filter qualifier is handled in transformation rule (2), where *F* stands for the
filter and *Q* for the remaining sequence of qualifiers. The filter is transformed into
a conditional expression. If the condition in *F* holds, we can compute the remainder of the list comprehension by recursively invoking the transformation scheme T;
otherwise the computation is terminated by returning the empty list.

The generator qualifier *e* <– *L* is covered in rule (3). The generator produces
zero or more elements *e* drawn from a list *L*. We must generate code to iterate
over all elements *e* of *L*, compute the remainder *Q* of the list comprehension for
each value of *e*, and concatenate the—possibly empty—result lists into a single
list. The key idea is to generate a nested function (f_Q), which takes element *e* and
produces the list of values that *Q* (the remainder of the list comprehension) can
assume for that element *e*. This function f_Q is then called with each element of *L*
as an argument and the resulting lists are concatenated, yielding the desired result.
We rely on the scoping rules of Haskell to have all external references to *e* present
in "T{[*expr* | *Q*]}" refer to the argument *e* of our new function f_Q. To avoid name
clashes the function name f_Q must be a (new) name that does not occur in the list
comprehension.

This leaves us with the problem of calling a given function for all elements in a
list and concatenating the elements of the resulting lists into one list. We cannot use
the map function for this purpose since it simply concatenates the results of function
applications, and would yield a list of lists in this case. But a small modification of
map suffices:

```
mappend :: (a –> [b]) –> [a] –> [b]
mappend f [ ]    = [ ]
mappend f (x:xs) = f x ++ mappend f xs
```

Each call to function f returns a list of values, which are appended (++) together
by mappend into one big list, rather than Cons-ed into a list of lists. The function
mappend provides exactly the functionality we need to transform the generator in
rule (3).

Applying the transformation to the Pythagorean list comprehension produces the
code shown in Figure 12.11.

```
pyth n = mappend f_bc2 [1..n]
   where
      f_bc2 a = mappend f_c2 [a .. n]
         where
            f_c2 b = mappend f_2 [b .. n]
               where
                  f_2 c = if  (a^2 + b^2 == c^2)
                          then [(a,b,c)]
                          else [ ]
```

Fig. 12.11: The code for Pythagorean list comprehension desugared

12.4.4 The translation of nested functions

The transformation of list comprehensions generates "nested functions", as do several other transformations. The functional core deliberately excludes nested functions, functions that are local to other functions, since most target languages of functional compilers (for example, C and assembly code) do not support nested routines. As explained in Section 11.3.6, the standard approach in non-functional compilers is to parameterize the nested routine with a lexical pointer, the frame pointer of the lexically enclosing function. Through this pointer, the generated code can access variables in outer scopes.

Using lexical pointers to activation records in combination with higher-order functions and lazy evaluation causes dynamic scope violations, however, since a call to a nested function may escape its lexical scope at run time, rendering its lexical pointer invalid. For example, a nested function can be returned as the result of a higher-order function; lazy evaluation can delay the execution of a call to the nested function until long after the caller has returned its value, which contains a reference to the suspended call. The latter case is exemplified by the function sv_mul shown in Figure 12.12. The sv_mul function defines the multiplication of a scalar and a

```
sv_mul scal vec = let
                     s_mul x = scal * x
                  in
                     map s_mul vec
```

Fig. 12.12: A function returning a function

vector, which is represented by a list. It calls the higher-order function map to apply the nested function s_mul to each element in the vector list. At run time, however, the interpreted code for sv_mul returns a graph holding the unevaluated expression map s_mul vec. Since this graph includes a pointer to s_mul, which is defined in the activation record of sv_mul, its dynamic scope (pointer scope) is that of the activation record. Returning the graph to an environment of larger scope constitutes a scope violation, as explained in Section 11.2.3.2. If we return the routine value map s_mul vec, the activation record of sv_mul will be removed before the nested function s_mul is ever applied.

A potential solution is to allocate activation records from the heap instead of allocating them on the stack. The obvious disadvantage, however, is the higher cost. Also, the overhead of allocating and initializing activation records, passing and dereferencing lexical pointers, is relatively large for most nested functions, which usually only reference one or two non-local entries. Therefore, modern functional language compilers use lambda lifting to unnest nested routines, as explained in Section 11.3.7. The functional core, however, directly supports currying, so we do not need to generate closures and take care of allocating (part of) the activation records in the heap, as in the imperative case. Translating a nested routine f to a global routine is just a matter of extending it with additional parameters $p_1 \ldots p_a$ that capture the out-of-scope pointers; each usage of the nested function f must be replaced with a curried call: $f\, p_1 \ldots p_a$.

Returning to our scalar-vector multiply example of Figure 12.12, we lift the nested s_mul function into a global function named sv_mul_dot_s_mul as follows (we use the identifier sv_mul_dot_s_mul rather than the intended sv_mul.s_mul since Haskell does not allow dots in identifiers). We extend the function heading with an additional parameter named scal, which captures the pointer to the scal parameter of the outer sv_mul function. Next, all calls of s_mul in the body of sv_mul are replaced by the expression sv_mul_dot_s_mul scal. The result is shown in Figure 12.13, in which the function sv_mul now returns an expression in which names either refer to parameters (passed by value) or to global names. For nested func-

```
sv_mul_dot_s_mul scal x = scal * x
sv_mul scal vec = map (sv_mul_dot_s_mul scal) vec
```

Fig. 12.13: The function of Figure 12.12 with s_mul lambda-lifted

tions with a single out-of-scope pointer, lambda lifting is definitely cheaper than using heap-allocated activation records. Passing one additional parameter is as expensive as passing a lexical pointer, while no activation record has to be allocated and initialized. In most other cases lambda lifting outperforms activation records too. Activation records are only beneficial when shared between multiple nested functions so the initialization overhead can be amortized; this case rarely occurs in practice.

Now that we have seen how the front-end can remove all syntactic sugar from the source program and leave just program text in the functional core, we can turn to the problem of translating this functional core text to runnable code. The main issues are higher-order functions and lazy evaluation. The usual translation of functional core code is a hybrid one: the generated code creates data structures, graphs, which are handled further by an interpreter. The next section introduces the graphs and treats the interpreter, the "graph reducer". The generation of the code that produces these graphs is explained in Section 12.6. There are a multitude of possibilities to short-circuit this two-stage process of first creating graphs and then reducing them, each leading to better code but a more complicated code generator. The most prominent of these are covered in the last few sections of this chapter.

12.5 Graph reduction

The **graph reducer** is the heart of the run-time system and deals with higher-order functions and lazy evaluation. It will be used extensively by the code generator, described in the next section, to handle the applications of both standard and higher-order functions to their arguments. The graph reducer is an interpreter which operates on heap-allocated data structures representing expressions that are part of the functional program being executed. Expressions may be simple basic values such as integers and Booleans, structured types such as lists, and function applications. A function application can either represent a curried function consisting of a function and some of its arguments, or a lazy function application with all arguments present whose value may or may not be needed during the remainder of the computation.

Recall that currying depends on the observation that

$$f\ e_1\ e_2 \dots e_n$$

is syntactic sugar for the chain of unary function applications written as

$$(^n f\ e_1)\ e_2) \dots e_n)$$

or, more explicitly, as

$$(^n f\ @\ e_1)\ @\ e_2) \dots e_n)$$

in which the function application operator @ has been made visible. Graph reduction takes this observation literally, by representing a function application as a linked list of application nodes, an **application spine**:

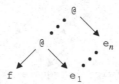

The @-operator denotes an application node holding a function pointer and an argument pointer. With this explicit representation of function application, higher-order functions can be passed around as ordinary pointers, and can be instantiated by allocating and initializing the required application nodes.

The execution of a functional program starts with the construction of the graph representing the initial expression whose value must be computed. Next, the graph reducer repeatedly selects a part of the graph that represents an expression that can be simplified by applying a function definition. Such an expression is called a **reducible expression**, or a **redex** for short. The selected redex is then reduced and the process is repeated. The graph reducer stops when it can no longer find a reducible expression. Finally, the resulting graph is returned as the result of the initial expression.

Each step of the graph reducer is commonly referred to as a **reduction**, because an expression is reduced to a simpler one. Note, however, that applying a function usually enlarges the graph since the number of nodes representing the body usually exceeds the number of nodes holding the application spine. Nevertheless, applying a function is considered to yield a simpler expression since one level of abstraction—the function—is peeled off.

The fully reduced expression resulting from a nested expression is just returned as its result. The result of the top-level expression is printed by the driver, as the result of the program. The driver prints the expression through a depth-first visit of all nodes, performing a case analysis on the type of each node. A basic value can be printed immediately; a function node has an associated name; a structured value is handled by recursively invoking the graph reducer on each field; and a curried function is printed as first the function name (f) and then recursively the arguments one by one. Note that finding a curried function is not an error since functions are first-class citizens and may be the result of any expression, even of the main program.

As an example of the operation of the graph reducer, consider the reduction of the following expression:

```
let
    twice f x = f (f x)
    square n = n*n
in
    twice square 3
```

The higher-order function twice applies the function square passed as an argument twice to the value 3. The graph reducer starts off with building the initial expression twice square 3:

$$(1)$$

The next step is to select a function application that can be reduced. The initial expression contains just one redex, the application of twice to its two parameters, square and 3. Now the declaration

```
twice f x = f (f x)
```

says that we can replace the subgraph

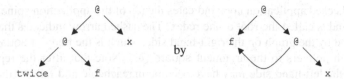

for any substitution of f and x. By taking square for f and 3 for x, we can replace
graph (1) by

(2)

Likewise, the declaration

square n = n*n

allows us to replace the subgraph

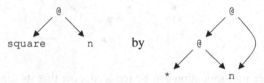

which, applied to graph (2) by taking square @ 3 for n, yields

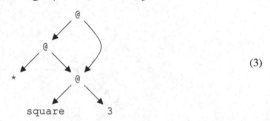

(3)

Since graphs can become arbitrarily large it is inconvenient to draw the complete
graph after each reduction, especially since reductions only involve small subgraphs.
Therefore a reduction is shown by clearly marking the redex and its replacement.
This is also exactly in line with the underlying implementation, which does not
copy the complete graph at each reduction, as the diagrams may suggest, but only
replaces the small part under reduction. For example, the application of square that
transformed graph (2) into graph (3) is written as

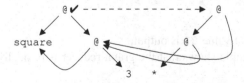

The checked application node indicates the top of the application spine under reduction and is called the root of the redex. The dashed arrow indicates that the root is replaced by the graph on the right-hand side, which is the body of square instantiated with pointers to the argument square @ 3. Note that after the replacement (part of) the left-hand side may have become unreachable and falls to the garbage collector.

Continuing the reduction process, we must select the next redex. There are two candidate function applications: the multiplication (∗) spine and the square spine, each having all their arguments present. The multiplication spine, however, cannot be reduced because its arguments are not in the proper format; the built-in operator can only perform the multiplication when both arguments point to a number. Therefore, the graph reducer selects the square spine for the third reduction step:

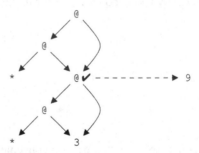

Next, the inner multiplication can be reduced, now that its arguments *are* in the proper format:

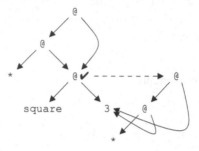

Finally, the remaining multiplication can be reduced to complete the computation:

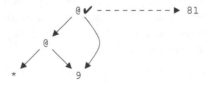

after which the final value **81** is output.

The above example shows that the graph reducer is basically a three-stroke engine:

- select a redex consisting of a function and its arguments,
- instantiate the right-hand side of the function, and
- update the root of the redex.

The update in the last step is essential to avoid duplication of work. If the update was omitted, each dereference of one of the pointers to the root would have to redo the instantiation in step 2. In the worst case this causes an exponential overhead. Selecting the redex (step 1) is an important issue since it steers the computation and, therefore, is the key to implementing lazy evaluation.

Note that in step 2 the right-hand side of a function is not "evaluated" in the imperative sense, since all function applications contained in it are translated to application spines in the graph. Depending on the selection criteria such function applications may or may not be evaluated in the future, whereas in imperative programs they are evaluated to a single value as soon as they are met.

Nevertheless, even in functional languages it is sometimes necessary to immediately evaluate a function argument completely. In particular, such "strict arguments" are required for many built-in operators: operators like + and * require that both their arguments are numbers so that they can perform the addition or multiplication, respectively. In many functional languages users are also allowed to annotate their function arguments to be strict, and compilers internally also add this annotation. Why that is useful is explained in Section 12.7.1.

12.5.1 Reduction order

In general the computation graph contains many redexes that can be selected for reduction. Although the graph reducer can select any redex, it is important to select one that is essential for computing the final result, or else the reducer may spend all its time reducing non-essential redexes and never terminate. For example, it may try to construct an infinite list before it passes it to a function that only requires the first element. Thus, the safest strategy for a graph reducer is to always only reduce essential redexes.

This brings up the next problem: how to reliably find an essential redex. To do so we observe that if the initial expression is not a value, we know we must reduce it, so at some moment that expression will be part of an essential redex. However, before it can be reduced, it may be necessary to first reduce some of its sub-expressions, which makes these expressions essential too. In particular, we may have to evaluate the left-hand side of an application expression to know which function must be applied.

These observations lead to the following reduction algorithm: We start at the root node of the initial expression. If the root node is not an application node, we have done our job and stop. If the root is an application node, it must be reduced. To determine the extent of the redex, we traverse the application spine down to the left to find the function, say f, that we must apply; see Figure 12.14. We check whether or not the application spine contains the necessary number of arguments for the function f. If it does not, we have detected a curried function that cannot be applied, and we stop. If the spine contains more than the necessary number of arguments, only part of the spine is involved in the immediate reduction, and the result of that reduction must be a new function that can be applied to the unused arguments.

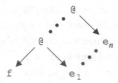

Fig. 12.14: Identifying an essential redex

If all n arguments of f are present in the spine from the root, we have located a function application whose value is needed. However, before we can reduce this redex, we must first evaluate any strict arguments to the function. After that, we can apply f: the application node in the spine pointing to the last argument of f (the node pointing to e_n in the diagram) will be replaced by the evaluated expression. Since the replacement expression is also essential for the final result, we don't have to return to the root, but can search the application spine from this point for a new function to apply.

The process of developing the graph and finding the next redex to be evaluated in the computation is called **unwinding**. The unwind procedure outlined above always selects the "leftmost outermost" redex. This reduction order is also known as **normal-order reduction**. It is the underlying mechanism to implement lazy evaluation. Imperative languages use a different strategy for evaluating expressions: **applicative-order reduction**; they evaluate expressions at argument positions before invoking the function. The following example illustrates the difference:

```
let
   const c x = c
in
   const 1 (2+3)
```

The corresponding graph is:

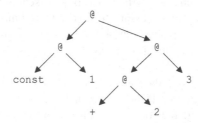

Normal-order reduction selects the leftmost outermost redex, the root of which is the top application node in our example. This application of const reduces to 1 immediately, without ever touching the second argument of const. Applicative-order reduction, on the other hand, evaluates the graph in depth-first order, and evaluates parameters from left to right. In this case the first redex it evaluates, the **leftmost innermost** redex, is the addition that yields 5. Another reduction is needed to reduce const 1 5 to the final result 1. This example shows that applicative-order reduction sometimes needs more reduction steps than normal-order to derive the result. In the worst case, however, applicative-order reduction may start evaluating a non-terminating computation that is not needed and, consequently, fail to produce the result obtained with normal-order reduction. More strongly: since normal-order reduction always only selects redexes that are essential for the final result, it is the best reduction strategy to avoid non-termination: if a program does not terminate under normal-order reduction, there is no reduction strategy that will make it terminate. Another consequence of the difference in reduction order is that for example the expression const 1 (1/0) will generate a run-time "division by zero" error under applicative-order reduction, while no error occurs under normal-order reduction.

12.5.2 The reduction engine

This section provides the C code for a simple reduction engine based on the previous discussion. The reduction engine operates on four types of graph nodes: numbers, lists, function applications, and function descriptors. Figure 12.15 shows the header file declaring the structure of graph nodes: a tag and a union holding one of the four node types.

A function descriptor contains the arity of the function, its name for printing and debugging purposes, and a pointer to the actual C code. An integer is represented directly by its value. A list node holds one CONStructor consisting of pointers to the head and tail of the list; the empty list contains no further information besides the NIL tag. And a (binary) application node holds pointers to the function and argument. The function pointer may point to a function descriptor or another application node.

Nodes can be created by invoking the associated constructor function, which calls the memory manager to allocate a fresh node in the heap. Figure 12.16 shows such a constructor function, for APPL nodes. Since nodes are manipulated almost exclusively through pointers, the data type Pnode is the predominant data type in the reduction engine.

The eval function in Figure 12.17 implements the three-stroke reduction engine. It takes a pointer to an arbitrary graph node and performs a case analysis on the tag to find out what to do next. Application nodes and function descriptors require further processing, while all other tags stop the reduction engine since a basic value can be returned as is.

An application spine must be unwound to identify the function and arguments constituting a redex that needs evaluation. Since the arguments are needed when executing the function, the reduction engine pushes them onto a stack so it can refer to

```
typedef enum {FUNC, NUM, NIL, CONS, APPL} node_type;

typedef struct node *Pnode;

typedef Pnode (*unary)(Pnode *arg);

struct function_descriptor {
    int  arity ;
    const char *name;
    unary code;
};

struct node {
    node_type tag;
    union {
        struct function_descriptor  func;
        int  num;
        struct {Pnode hd; Pnode tl;} cons;
        struct {Pnode fun; Pnode arg;} appl;
    } nd;
};

/* Constructor functions */
extern Pnode Func(int arity, const char *name, unary code);
extern Pnode Num(int num);
extern Pnode Nil(void);
extern Pnode Cons(Pnode hd, Pnode tl);
extern Pnode Appl(Pnode fun, Pnode arg);
```

Fig. 12.15: Declaration of node types and constructor functions

```
Pnode Appl(const Pnode fun, Pnode arg) {
    Pnode node = (Pnode) heap_alloc(sizeof(*node));

    node->tag = APPL;
    node->nd.appl.fun = fun;
    node->nd.appl.arg = arg;
    return node;
}
```

Fig. 12.16: The node constructor function for application (@) nodes

```
#include "node.h"
#include "eval.h"

#define STACK_DEPTH 10000

static Pnode arg[STACK_DEPTH];
static int top = STACK_DEPTH;                    /* grows down */

Pnode eval(Pnode root) {
    Pnode node = root;
    int frame, arity ;

    frame = top;
    for  (;;)  {
        switch (node->tag) {
        case APPL:                               /* unwind */
            arg[--top] = node->nd.appl.arg; /* stack argument */
            node = node->nd.appl.fun;   /* application node */
            break;

        case FUNC:
            arity = node->nd.func.arity;
            if (frame-top < arity) {             /* curried function */
                top = frame;
                return root ;
            }
            node = node->nd.func.code(&arg[top]);  /* reduce */
            top += arity ;                  /* unstack arguments */
            *root = *node;                  /* update root pointer */
            break;

        default:
            return node;
        }
    }
}
```

Fig. 12.17: Reduction engine

them directly. After unwinding the application nodes the arguments are conveniently stacked as shown in Figure 12.18.

When the reduction engine detects a function descriptor it checks if all arguments are present. If this is not the case then the root points to a curried function, which cannot be reduced, so reduction stops and the arguments are unstacked before returning. The caller decides on what to do with the curried function; for example, the top-level driver will print it. If, however, all arguments are found present, the pointer to the function code is retrieved from the descriptor and the function is called. The arguments of the function are passed as an array. When the call returns the arguments are popped off the stack and the result is copied into the root node, so all future references will find the result immediately and need not repeat the call. This

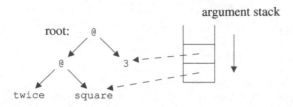

Fig. 12.18: Stacking the arguments while searching for a redex

completes the current reduction step, and the next reduction cycle is started.

The reduction engine is accompanied by several routines implementing the semantics of the built-in arithmetic and list operators. Each built-in operator is wrapped in a function descriptor, which includes a pointer to the code performing the actual reduction. Figure 12.19 shows the code of the built-in multiplication operator mul. The basic routine mul() evaluates its arguments, extracts the numbers from them, multiplies the numbers and creates a node for the result. The basic routine is unsuitable for calling by the interpreter since the latter supplies the arguments as an array; the prelude routine _mul bridges the gap. The function description __mul represents the function mul as a graph node, to be used when a graph for a call of mul must be constructed.

```
Pnode mul(Pnode _arg0, Pnode _arg1) {
    Pnode a = eval(_arg0);
    Pnode b = eval(_arg1);

    return Num(a->nd.num * b->nd.num);
}

Pnode _mul(Pnode *arg) {
    return mul(arg[0], arg [1]);
}

struct node __mul = {FUNC, {{2, "mul", _mul}}};
```

Fig. 12.19: Code and function descriptor of the built-in operator mul

We see that the mul routine starts by calling eval on both arguments, to ensure that these point to numbers rather than to unevaluated application nodes. This leads to a situation where eval indirectly calls itself, thus stacking the arguments of multiple function applications on top of each other. An example is shown in Figure 12.20, which presents a snapshot taken from the evaluation of the expression twice square 3. The depth of the stack of eval calls depends on the program being executed and is in principle unbounded. To avoid memory corruption, the stack can be implemented as an extensible array (Section 10.1.3.2).

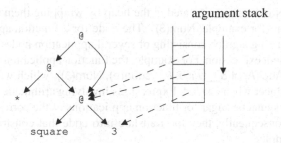

argument stack

Fig. 12.20: A more complicated argument stack

12.6 Code generation for functional core programs

With the graph reducer in place, generating C code for functional core programs becomes almost trivial, since the only task of the C code is to create graphs for the interpreter eval(). For each function definition in the program, we generate a function descriptor and the necessary code to build the right-hand-side graph. For example, the higher-order function

twice f x = f (f x)

can be easily transformed into the code

```
Pnode twice(Pnode _arg0, Pnode _arg1) {
    Pnode f = _arg0;
    Pnode x = _arg1;

    return Appl(f, (Appl(f, x )));
}

Pnode _twice(Pnode *arg) {
    return twice(arg[0], arg[1]);
}

struct node __twice = {FUNC, {2, "twice", _twice}};
```

It may not be immediately obvious, but the introduction of the two local variables f and x that pick up the arguments is the result of—trivial—pattern matching on the arguments f and x.

Generating code from a user-defined function that instantiates the right-hand-side graph at run time is straightforward. The graph reducer (eval) knows how to handle function applications, so we will simply translate each core construct into a function call, as follows.

Expressions form the heart of the functional core and consist of identifiers, numbers, function applications, arithmetic operators, if-then-else compounds, and let-expressions. Identifiers need no further processing since we can use the same names in the C code. Numbers are allocated in the heap by wrapping them with their constructor function (for example, Num(3)). The code for a function application boils down to constructing a graph consisting of several application nodes holding pointers to the argument expression. For example, the function application twice square 3 translates into Appl(Appl(&__twice, &__square), Num(3)), which will be evaluated by the graph reducer when needed. Expressions involving arithmetic infix operators are regarded as syntactic sugar for function applications of the corresponding built-in operators. Consequently, they too translate into code that constructs a piece of graph. For example,

n * fac (n−1)

becomes

Appl(Appl(&__mul, n), Appl(&__fac, Appl(Appl(&__sub, n), Num(1))))

Translating the if-then-else construction in the functional core is less straightforward. It cannot be translated into the if-then-else of C, because the latter is a statement and cannot occur as part of an expression. The conditional expression in C (cond ? x : y) *can* be used in expressions, but it is not suitable either, because lazy evaluation requires that nothing be evaluated before it is needed. Without further analysis we cannot be sure that the condition tested in a (nested) if-then-else compound is needed. Therefore we translate the if-then-else compound into a call to the built-in conditional primitive shown in Figure 12.21. Note that Booleans are handled as numbers by the run-time system, just as in C.

```
Pnode conditional(Pnode _arg0, Pnode _arg1, Pnode _arg2) {
    Pnode cond = _arg0;
    Pnode _then = _arg1;
    Pnode _else = _arg2;

    return eval(cond)−>nd.num ? _then : _else;
}

Pnode _conditional(Pnode *arg) {
    return conditional(arg[0], arg[1], arg[2]);
}

struct node __conditional =
    {FUNC, {3, "conditional", _conditional}};
```

Fig. 12.21: Code and function descriptor of the built-in conditional operator

The final construct that can be used to form an expression in the functional core is the let-expression. An example of a let-expression is shown in Figure 12.22. The main property of let-expressions is that they introduce local bindings. These bindings are translated into assignments to local variables in C. Such a local variable holds a pointer to the graph node representing the named expression, which can even be a (curried) function. The translation of the function f is shown in Figure 12.23; the usual definitions of _f and __f are not shown. Dependencies between

```
f a = let
        b = fac a
        c = b * b
      in
        c + c
```

Fig. 12.22: Example of a let-expression

```
Pnode f(Pnode _arg0) {
    Pnode a = _arg0;
    Pnode b = Appl(&__fac, a);
    Pnode c = Appl(Appl(&__mul, b), b);

    return Appl(Appl(&__add, c), c);
}
```

Fig. 12.23: Translation of the let-expression of Figure 12.22

local bindings are resolved by topologically sorting the bindings before emitting code; the case of bindings that refer to each other is handled in Exercise 12.13. Let-expressions may occur at the top level or nested inside other expressions. Since C does not allow local variables to be declared inside expressions, such nested let-expressions require some more work. We can float the nested locals to the beginning of the C function if we resolve name clashes caused by merging the nested scopes. This is easily accomplished by renaming nested identifiers to unique names.

12.6.1 Avoiding the construction of some application spines

The performance of the interpreted core programs is rather poor. The construction and interpretation of the graphs is the main source of overhead. For example, a simple multiplication already requires the allocation of two apply nodes making up the function call and a number node to store the result. Fortunately, a simple optimization, "short-circuiting a function application", requires no further program analysis and can significantly reduce the graph handling overhead. It can be applied to top-level expressions and to the arguments of many built-in functions, as we will see. Section 12.7 covers optimizations that require more extensive compile-time program analysis.

The code generation scheme discussed above treats all function calls equally and generates code to allocate a spine of application nodes. When such an application spine is returned as the result of a function, the graph reducer immediately unwinds this spine to locate the function and arguments, followed by a call to that function. As an example consider the function average:

average a b = (a+b) / 2

the C translation of which is shown in Figure 12.24. When average() (or actually _average()) is invoked by the graph reducer we know that its value is needed under the lazy evaluation mechanism. Therefore we can **short-circuit** the construction of the application spine for the top-level call and call the div() routine directly, as shown in Figure 12.25. Note that the arguments to div() are still unevaluated.

```
Pnode average(Pnode _arg0, Pnode _arg1) {
    Pnode a = _arg0;
    Pnode b = _arg1;

    return
        Appl(
            Appl(
                &__div,
                Appl(
                    Appl(&__add, a),
                    b
                )
            ),
            Num(2)
        );
}
```

Fig. 12.24: Translation of the function average

```
Pnode average(Pnode _arg0, Pnode _arg1) {
    Pnode a = _arg0;
    Pnode b = _arg1;

    return div(Appl(Appl(&__add, a), b), Num(2));
}
```

Fig. 12.25: Suppressing the top-level spine in the translation of the function average

More in general, if the top-level expression in a right-hand side is an application of a function F with n arguments, the standard code segment for this application

$$\text{Appl(Appl(}^{n-1} \text{ \&\_\_}F, A_1), \ldots A_n)$$

which builds an application spine of length n, can be short-circuited to $F(A_1, \ldots A_n)$ which calls F directly.

This optimization is not restricted to top-level expressions and can be applied to any position in which an application spine is constructed which we know will be unwound immediately by the interpreter. One such position is in the strict arguments of built-in operators. Most built-in operators require their arguments to be evaluated before the actual operation can be performed, so they invoke eval on their strict arguments. Thus, if a built-in operator is called directly then we know that it will invoke eval for its strict arguments. The default code generation scheme translates each function application into an application spine to preserve lazy evaluation semantics. Constructing application spines for expressions that are strict arguments of a built-in operator, however, is unnecessary and the application spine may be replaced by a direct call. So, short-circuiting can be applied not only to top-level calls in right-hand sides of function definitions but also to function calls that are strict arguments of built-in operators.

The effect on the average code is that the lazy addition spine is replaced by a direct call to the built-in add operator, resulting in the optimized code shown in Figure 12.26. Note that all arguments are still unevaluated; what we save is constructing the spine, unwinding it to an array, extracting _add() from the node __add, and calling _add(), which retrieves the arguments from the array and calls add().

```
Pnode average(Pnode _arg0, Pnode _arg1) {
    Pnode a = _arg0;
    Pnode b = _arg1;

    return div(add(a, b), Num(2));
}
```

Fig. 12.26: Suppressing the argument spine to div in Figure 12.25

The performance effect of these optimizations depends on the program being interpreted, but improvements of a factor of two or more are quite common.

12.7 Optimizing the functional core

The performance of the interpreter-based approach outlined in the previous sections is way off compared to the performance of imperative codes, even if we include the optimizations for short-circuiting of application nodes and exploit the strictness of built-in operators described in the previous section. To achieve acceptable performance, close to that of imperative programs, state-of-the-art functional language compilers apply a host of advanced optimizations, all of which require program-wide knowledge. Typically these optimizations are performed on the AST after the source language has been simplified to an intermediate code like our functional core.

We will now discuss four important optimizations that occur at the functional-core level. Low-level optimizations are left to the C compiler, which is used as a portable optimizing assembler. The first two optimizations, strictness analysis and boxing analysis, tackle the overhead of manipulating graph nodes. The other two optimizations, tail call elimination and accumulating arguments, address the (recursive) function call overhead introduced by the functional programming style, which structures programs as a composition of many small functions. Together these four optimizations allow us to generate code for the recursive factorial function that is as efficient as its imperative loop-based counterpart (see Figure 12.2).

12.7.1 Strictness analysis

By default, lazy evaluation causes expressions at argument positions in a function call to be passed unevaluated as a graph of application nodes. Building the graph is quite expensive, and becomes pure overhead when the called function will in all cases evaluate the (lazy) argument to proceed its computation. Some functions *always* need to evaluate some of their arguments. If a function always needs the value of argument a_i, the function is said to be **strict** in argument a_i. The purpose of **strictness analysis** is to determine for all user-defined functions which arguments are strict. Then the code generator can exploit strictness information by evaluating expressions at strict argument positions before calling the function, to save the overhead of building the graph structure by the caller and the call to the graph reducer by the callee.

The basic scenario for analyzing the strictness of a function is to propagate the strictness of built-in operators and other user-defined functions bottom-up through the AST. As an example, consider the function

    safe_div a b = if (b == 0) then 0
                      else a/b

The AST of this function, annotated with the flow of the strictness information, is shown in Figure 12.27.

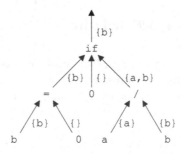

Fig. 12.27: Flow of strictness information in the AST of safe_div

We start by constructing the basic sets of strict identifiers at the leaves of the AST. A parameter p yields the set $\{p\}$, since when the reduction engine reaches p, the value of p will be needed. Likewise, a local variable v, defined in some let-expression, yields the set $\{v\}$. Constants, data constructors, and function names yield the empty set $\{\ \}$. The strictness information sets are propagated up the AST according to the rules shown in Figure 12.28. Note that the italic capitals (L, R, C, etc.) represent language constructs in the left column and the sets of strict variables occurring in these language constructs in the right column.

Language construct	Set to be propagated	
L operator R	$L \cup R$	
if C then T else E	$C \cup (T \cap E)$	
$\text{fun}_m\ @\ A_1\ @\ \dots\ @\ A_n$	$\bigcup_{\text{strict(fun},i)} {}_{i=1}^{\min(m,n)} A_i$	, if $n >= m$
$F\ @\ A_1\ @\ \dots\ @\ A_n$	F	
let $v = V$ in E	$(E \backslash \{v\}) \cup V$	, if $v \in E$
	E	, otherwise

Fig. 12.28: Rules for strictness information propagation

Arithmetic operators need both their arguments, so we simply take the union of the left and right sets. The if-then-else construct tests the condition and then selects the then- or else-part. All strict arguments in the condition are needed. In addition we propagate the parameters that are needed both in the then- and else-part, since, whichever way the conditional goes, these will be needed. Next, we consider the two propagation rules to handle calls to user-defined functions. The first rule covers the case that the function identifier is a global name (fun_m), so we know exactly which function is called and what the properties of its arguments are. The second rule covers the case that the function being invoked is described by some expression (F), which could be as simple as a function parameter or as complicated as an intermediate result computed by a higher-order function.

When a global function is called with enough parameters ($n >= m$), the union of all argument sets occurring at strict parameter positions is propagated. The strictness predicate "strict(fun, i)" is used to filter which argument sets (A_i) are part of the result set. The number of arguments supplied (n) may exceed the number of parameters (m), so the union is over m arguments only.

For function expressions (the second rule) no strictness information about the arguments can be derived. We can do better than propagating the empty set, however, since we do know that the function itself will be needed, so we return the set F holding the function parameter.

The final rule in Figure 12.28 covers the usage of local variables in let-expressions. If a local variable is strictly needed for the evaluation of the result expression it will be part of the set E of strict identifiers. In that case, we remove it from the set and add all strict identifiers occurring in the value expression V associated with variable v. Otherwise, we simply pass set E.

Determining the strictness of a function by floating up sets of strict arguments requires knowledge about the strictness of the functions used in the body. We can be conservative and have the strictness predicate return false for functions that we have not processed yet, but a better solution is to use a closure algorithm. Before presenting this algorithm, however, we address recursive functions since they require special trickery.

12.7.1.1 Strictness analysis for recursive functions

The approach of floating up strictness information may fail to infer the strictness of certain arguments of recursive functions. The problem is that, even with a closure algorithm, the bottom-up traversal starts with conservative information about the strictness of the recursive function's arguments. This prevents the discovery of strict arguments like b in the following example:

```
f a b = if (a == 0) then b
        else f (a−1) (b+1)
```

The function f is representative for a class of functions that iterate until some termination condition is met: $a == 0$. Each step performs an operation on some intermediate result: $b+1$. When the recursion stops, the result of all computation steps, b, is returned. It is clear that f is strict in both its arguments, but without any knowledge about the strictness of f beforehand propagating the strict arguments along the AST identifies only a as being a strict argument.

The solution is to optimistically assume that a recursive function is strict in *all* its arguments, propagate the strict arguments under this assumption, and then check if the derived set of strict arguments includes all arguments. This is the case for f as Figure 12.29 shows. The optimistic assumption that f is strict in both arguments is signaled with the (+, +) annotation and holds true since the result set that floats out the AST is {a, b}.

In the general case, the result set R may not contain all arguments. In that case, we know that the initial assumption (A) was too optimistic; the best we can hope for is that the function is strict in R. Therefore, we narrow the strictness assumption to R and propagate the sets through the AST again. Narrowing the strictness assumption A continues until the result set R equals the assumption A.

As an example, consider the function

```
g x y z = if (z == 0) then x
          else g y x (z−1)
```

The optimistic approach in the case of g needs three steps:

step	assumption	result
1	{x, y, z}	{x, z}
2	{x, z}	{z}
3	{z}	{z}

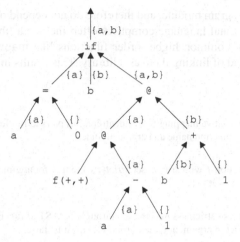

Fig. 12.29: Optimistic strictness analysis of the function f

This is the correct result, since g returns either x or y depending on whether or not z is even. In general, the optimistic approach is guaranteed to produce the correct set of strict arguments for any recursive function f that terminates. Only for recursive functions that may fail to terminate once invoked, the optimistic scheme may report arguments to be strict that are not. An obvious but ugly example is the function

    f x = f x

The optimistic approach derives that f is strict in x in one step. Although this is strictly speaking incorrect, since the value will never be needed, the error has no serious consequences in practice. Evaluating an expression in a non-strict context has two potential consequences: (1) the evaluation may not terminate, or (2) an invalid operation is being performed. Since the call to f would not terminate anyway, the only difference is that in case (2) a run-time error is reported instead of looping indefinitely.

Now that we have shown how to handle self-recursive functions, it is easy to generalize the optimistic approach to cover mutually recursive functions calling each other. The closure algorithm in Figure 12.30 does exactly that. It starts off with a set of strictness assumptions, one for each function involved, and iterates until the corresponding result sets match their assumptions.

The algorithm of Figure 12.30 is capable of identifying any strict argument, but requires all ASTs to be available at once. This is not very practical (separate compilation), nor feasible (proprietary libraries). Some compilers therefore store strictness information in associated info files, which will be consulted when a function is used in another program module. Whenever an info file is updated, all modules depending on it must be recompiled to identify as many strict arguments as possible. In the case of a library, recompiling to update the info file is usually not an option and, consequently, strict arguments may be missed. This, however, is only a problem for higher-order library functions that operate on user functions; all other functions cannot call back the program module, and therefore do not depend on external strictness information. Functional language compilers often include a library file containing the source code of common higher-order functions like map and mappend with each user file instead of linking them as a library. This results in better analysis and, hence, better code.

Data definitions:
   1. *Strict*, an associative mapping from (identifier, int) pairs to Booleans, where each pair describes a function name and argument index.

Initializations:
   1. For each function f with arity m set $Strict[f, i]$ to true for arguments i ranging from 1 to m.

Inference rules:
   1. If propagation of strictness information through the AST of function f shows that f is not strict in argument i, then $Strict[f, i]$ must be false.

Fig. 12.30: Closure algorithm for strictness predicate

12.7.1.2 Code generation for strict arguments

Expressions occurring at strict argument positions may be evaluated immediately without constructing a graph. Section 12.6.1 already showed the advantage of exploiting the strictness of the arguments of built-in operators. Now we can also exploit strictness of user-defined functions. For example, consider the factorial function fac:

```
fac :: int  −> int
fac n =  if  (n == 0) then 1
            else n * fac (n−1)
```

Without strictness information about itself fac compiles into the code shown in Figure 12.31. Note that the strictness of the built-in multiplication mul is already used to call fac directly. Also, the conditional has been expanded in-line, and the strictness of its first argument has been used to call equal directly. The argument of fac, however, is passed lazily as a graph. Using the fact that fac is strict in its argument n allows us to remove the last spine construction, leading to the code of Figure 12.32.

Until now we have used the strictness information to avoid constructing applications spines, but we can go one step further. In addition to generating a routine fac() which expects one unevaluated argument in which it is strict, we can generate a second routine fac_evaluated(), which expects an evaluated argument. We can then replace fac(n) by

```
fac_evaluated(eval(n))
```

```
Pnode fac(Pnode _arg0) {
    Pnode n = _arg0;

    return equal(n, Num(0))->nd.num ? Num(1)
        : mul(n, fac(Appl(Appl(&__sub, n), Num(1))));
}
```

Fig. 12.31: Lazy translation of the argument of fac

```
Pnode fac(Pnode _arg0) {
    Pnode n = _arg0;

    return equal(n, Num(0))->nd.num ? Num(1)
        : mul(n, fac(sub(n, Num(1))));
}
```

Fig. 12.32: The first step in exploiting the strictness of the argument of fac

and, if we know that n has already been evaluated, leave out the call to eval(). We can do the same for the built-in operators, leading to the introduction of add_evaluated(), equal_evaluated(), etc. The code for fac that uses this optimization is shown in Figure 12.33; note that the code for fac() itself has been left in place, and now calls fac_evaluated() after evaluating the argument. Now, when generating a direct call of fac, the code generation has a choice between two translations: calling fac_evaluated() if fac is known to be strict and the argument is known to be evaluated, and calling fac() otherwise. (The options of calling _fac() when arguments are in an array and of creating a node using __fac are still open as well.) This code uses at most one call of eval() for each call of fac(n); this is a great improvement over the code from Figure 12.32, which called eval() 6 · n times.

```
Pnode fac_evaluated(Pnode _arg0) {
    Pnode n = _arg0;

    return equal_evaluated(n, Num(0))->nd.num ? Num(1)
        : mul_evaluated(n, fac_evaluated(sub_evaluated(n, Num(1))));
}

Pnode fac(Pnode _arg0) {
    return fac_evaluated(eval(_arg0));
}
```

Fig. 12.33: Exploiting the strictness of fac and the built-in operators

With strictness analysis we avoid constructing and interpreting application spines at strict positions. The overall effect on performance is strongly program dependent, since the quality of the strictness analyzer and the laziness of the program determine which fraction of the application spines can be optimized away. The strictness analysis discussed so far only considers arguments of functions, but many expressions are part of data structures. Some progress has been made with analyzing the strictness of data structures like lists [54], but in general it is a hard nut to crack, so most strictness analyzers simply do not address the issue at all.

To alleviate the problem of strictness analysis failing to determine the strictness of certain expressions compilers often have provisions for the programmer to manually indicate strictness. Haskell provides the standard function seq (for "sequence"), which can be used in seq x y to ensure that x is evaluated before running y. This function can easily be used to mark strict expressions, but also plays an important role in programming interactive programs where actions should happen in a precise order.

12.7.2 Boxing analysis

For simplicity the graph reducer requires all data to be "boxed" in a graph node containing a tag for identification, as outlined in Figure 12.15. Although this allows a uniform treatment of pointers when interpreting the computation graph, it is also a source of inefficiency. For example, the strict version of the function fac in Figure 12.33 still allocates a considerable number of graph nodes to hold the intermediate results produced by the built-in operators equal, mul, and sub, even in their _evaluated forms. These intermediate nodes are passed on to another operator or call of fac, both of which are only interested in the numerical contents, not in the box surrounding it.

The function mul_evaluated()

```
Pnode mul_evaluated(Pnode a, Pnode b) {
    return Num(a−>nd.num * b−>nd.num);
}
```

simply dereferences the argument pointers without even inspecting the node tag, and does not use the pointers otherwise. It is obvious that we can pass the numbers directly, instead of boxed in graph nodes. In general, we can pass any basic value unboxed at strict argument positions. Once strictness analysis is performed, it takes little analysis to find out which arguments are suited for unboxing. This analysis is called **boxing analysis**.

The effect on the fac example is shown in Figure 12.34, which features the routine fac_unboxed(). The built-in operators are no longer needed, and the corresponding C operators are invoked directly. The function fac_evaluated() was adapted to take care of unboxing the argument before calling fac_unboxed(), and boxing the result in a number node. Boxing the result is necessary since fac_evaluated() has to return a boxed value as before.

After applying the boxing analysis to fac, it no longer allocates any graph node. This is, however, an exception since most functions in a Haskell program of reason-

```
int fac_unboxed(int n) {
    return (n == 0 ? 1 : n * fac_unboxed(n−1));
}

Pnode fac_evaluated(Pnode _arg0) {
    Pnode n = _arg0;

    return Num(fac_unboxed(n−>nd.num));
}

Pnode fac(Pnode _arg0) {
    return fac_evaluated(eval(_arg0));
}
```

Fig. 12.34: Strict, unboxed translation of the function fac

able size do not operate on strict arguments with basic types. Nevertheless boxing
analysis can have a noticeable effect on performance: the unboxed factorial runs
about 10 times faster than its boxed counterpart.

12.7.3 Tail calls

The last statement in a routine in code generated for functional languages is often
a function call, and it is often recursive. One reason is that repetition is expressed
using recursion in functional languages, but we will see in Chapter 13 that the same
phenomenon occurs in code generated for logic programs, as Figures 13.16, 13.20,
and even 13.15 and 13.18 amply attest. Especially the recursive tail calls are a problem, since they may lead to stack overflow. A tail-recursive routine working on a
linked list of N elements will reach a stack depth of N just before finishing; and
when it finishes, it spends a time proportional to N in unstacking the activation
records. An iterative routine working on the same N-element list would have a stack
depth of 1 and a one-level unstacking operation would suffice upon termination. So
the tail call elimination techniques from Chapter 11 (page 593) are a great help.

As an example consider the following function, which drops the first n elements
from a list:

```
drop n lst  = if  (n == 0) then  lst
                 else  drop (n−1) (tail  lst )
```

Using strictness information and boxing analysis we would normally generate the
C-code

```
Pnode drop_unboxed(int n, Pnode lst) {
    if  (n == 0) {
        return  lst ;
    } else {
```

```
        return drop_unboxed(n−1, tail(lst));
    }
}
```

The tail call can easily be transformed into a back jump:

```
Pnode drop_unboxed(int n, Pnode lst) {
L_drop_unboxed:
    if (n == 0) {
        return lst ;
    } else {
        int    _tmp0 = n−1;
        Pnode _tmp1 = tail(lst );

        n = _tmp0; lst = _tmp1;
        goto L_drop_unboxed;
    }
}
```

The tricky part of overwriting the parameters with the new values of the tail call is left to the C compiler by introducing a set of temporary variables _tmp0 and _tmp1.

12.7.4 Accumulator transformation

Although we have seen above how to transform direct tail recursion into efficient C code, many self-recursive functions do not end in a tail call, but require a little postprocessing of the result of the recursive call. An example is again the function fac:

```
fac :: int −> int
fac n = if (n == 0) then 1
           else n * fac (n−1)
```

The problem is that in this code the multiplication is performed *after* the recursive call, resulting in a stack of n recursive calls. Another transformation is required to reduce the required stack space to a single frame. If the operator using the recursive result is associative, as is the case for multiplication, we can transform the code to use an accumulating argument, as shown in Figure 12.35. The local

```
fac n = if (n == 0) then 1 else prod n (n−1)
           where
               prod acc n = if (n == 0) then acc
                               else prod (acc*n) (n−1)
```

Fig. 12.35: Tail-recursive fac with accumulating argument

function prod accumulates the results of the multiplications along the way in its first argument acc: the call prod p q computes p*q*(q-1)*...*1. So the desired product n*(n-1)*...*1 is computed by the call prod n (n-1), except for n equals 0, which has to be caught as a special case.

Since prod is a tail-recursive function being strict in both arguments, the code generator may now produce the code shown in Figure 12.36. Note that the local function prod is lifted to the top and has been renamed to fac_dot_prod. The tail call to itself has been transformed into a jump, which makes the code as efficient as the handwritten imperative version of Figure 12.2.

```
int fac_dot_prod_unboxed(int acc, int n) {
L_fac_dot_prod_unboxed:
    if (n == 0) {
        return acc;
    } else {
        int _tmp0 = n * acc;
        int _tmp1 = n-1;

        acc = _tmp0; n = _tmp1;
        goto L_fac_dot_prod_unboxed;
    }
}

int fac_unboxed(int n) {
    if (n == 0) {
        return 1;
    } else {
        return fac_dot_prod_unboxed(n, n-1);
    }
}
```

Fig. 12.36: Accumulating translation of fac, with tail recursion elimination

The transformation to an accumulating argument depends on the compiler being able to recognize the recursive pattern and to determine that the operations performed on the results are associative. In other words, the top-level node in the AST should be an associative operator and one of its children should be a self-recursive call. Figure 12.37 gives the translation scheme for a general right-recursive function: if a function definition matches the first line in the table, it can be replaced by the other two functions. In this scheme, $\oplus$ denotes an associative operator, F is the function name, and $B, V, E, E_1 \ldots E_n$ denote arbitrary expressions. An additional constraint is that the $\oplus$ operator should be strict, to avoid building a chain of unevaluated expressions through the accumulating argument. Note that the test B in the replacement code of F is evaluated in a different environment than the B in the code for F'; so the code of B is duplicated in this transformation, but its actions are not.

$$F\ x_1 \ldots x_n = \text{if } B \text{ then } V \text{ else } E \oplus F\ E_1 \ldots E_n$$
$$\Rightarrow$$
$$F\ x_1 \ldots x_n = \text{if } B \text{ then } V \text{ else } F'\ E\ E_1 \ldots E_n$$
$$F'\ x\_acc\ x_1 \ldots x_n = \text{if } B \text{ then } x\_acc \oplus V \text{ else } F'\ (x\_acc \oplus E)\ E_1 \ldots E_n$$

Fig. 12.37: Accumulating argument translation scheme

The function fac, given as

```
fac :: int -> int
fac n = if (n == 0) then 1
           else n * fac (n-1)
```

matches the conditions in the translation scheme, with F = fac, n = 1, $\oplus$ = *, B = (n == 0), V = 1, E = n, and E_1 = (n–1). This results in its replacement by the functions

```
fac n = if (n == 0) then 1 else fac_prime n (n-1)

fac_prime x_acc n = if (n == 0) then x_acc * 1
                       else fac_prime (x_acc * n) (n-1)
```

which, after the arithmetic simplification x * 1 $\Rightarrow$ x, matches the code in Figure 12.35.

Translation of the functional core code of Figure 12.35 to C yields the code of Figure 12.36. In-lining and a few other optimizations discussed in Chapter 9 yield code that is comparable to that in Figure 12.2. In summary, the following optimizations were required to transform the definition of fac in Figure 12.1 to C code equivalent to that of Figure 12.2:

- top-level short-circuiting of the if-statement and its branches
- short-circuiting of == and * due to known strictness of their arguments
- strictness analysis which yields that fac is strict in its argument
- short-circuiting the – operator, which is now allowed
- translation to C
- unboxing the argument
- accumulating the argument
- in-lining and further optimizations performed by the C compiler

12.7.5 Limitations

The optimizations presented in this section showed that it is possible to generate efficient code for the factorial example. Likewise, many simple mathematical functions can be compiled into efficient C code. In general, however, strictness analysis breaks down on symbolic code that manipulates user-defined data structures; it is very difficult to determine whether or not certain fields inside a record are strict, especially when infinite data structures and higher-order functions are involved. Aggressive in-lining and constant propagation before carrying out strictness analysis reduces the problem somewhat, since all cases of known functions passed as an argument then reduce to ordinary, non-higher-order, functions. Nevertheless, the daily practice is that most data structures are passed lazily, which causes a significant amount of time being spent in the run-time system. The graph reducer and garbage collector may take more execution time than the user-defined code bits in the worst case.

12.8 Advanced graph manipulation

As mentioned several times before, the performance of functional programs is strongly dependent on the amount of graph manipulation involved. Streamlining the handling of graph nodes therefore has a noticeable impact on performance. In this section we discuss a few advanced techniques employed by several reduction engines at the lowest level.

12.8.1 Variable-length nodes

The basic graph reducer discussed in Section 12.5.2 uses a single graph node type (Figure 12.15) to represent the different possibilities. Although this uniform coding eases the interpretation of graph nodes, it also wastes memory. For example, a simple number takes up as much space as a function descriptor holding three attributes (its arity, name, and code address). The obvious improvement is to use **variable-length graph nodes**, where each node consists of a tag followed by a number of fields depending on the node type. The impact on the graph reducer, and the garbage collector as well, is minimal since the code in Figure 12.17 is based on a case analysis of the node tag. The performance effect is that less heap space will be allocated, resulting in fewer garbage collections. Another effect is that cache performance increases since unused parts of the uniform nodes no longer take up precious cache space.

12.8.2 Pointer tagging

Graph nodes are quite small, so the node tag field consumes relatively much memory. Note that a graph node is always identified through a pointer, or else it is garbage, so we can lift the tag from the node and put it in the pointer itself. The least significant bits in a pointer are "free", because of alignment constraints for the nodes. Typically nodes are aligned on word (4 bytes) boundaries, allowing 2 bits for tagging. Four tags is precisely what we need to encode the node types used by the basic graph reducer; the node_type defined in Figure 12.15 enumerates five values, but we can easily represent "Nil" as a constant (null) pointer. If more tags are needed the most significant bits in a pointer can be used for tagging too. This reduces the maximal addressable memory space, but, when using 32-bit pointers, taking two bits off still leaves 1 Gbyte, and 64-bit pointers are even less problematic. In combination with the two least significant bits, this provides 16 different tags, which is enough to represent the (most common) node types in any graph reducer.

Pointer tagging saves one word per graph node, which reduces the pressure on the cache and garbage collector. Another advantage is that inspecting the tag now consists of selecting a few bits from the pointer instead of dereferencing it. The selection can be accomplished with a simple binary AND operation, and is cheaper than the memory lookup required before. Nothing comes for free, of course, but the price of pointer tagging is small: before dereferencing a tagged pointer the tag bits must be zeroed to convert it into a "clean" pointer. It typically requires one binary AND operation to zero the tag bits, so the benefits far outweigh the costs.

12.8.3 Aggregate node allocation

The basic code generation scheme from Section 12.6 translates a function into a sequence of calls to constructor functions like Num() and Appl() to build the graph representing the body of the function. This simplistic approach causes the nodes to be allocated one by one. It is more efficient to allocate them all at once. **Aggregate node allocation** can be arranged, but requires some analysis of the AST to compute the total amount of heap space needed for the complete expression. Note that the compiler can no longer generate code that calls the constructor functions of the run-time system, but must generate the proper code for filling in the specific node type itself.

12.8.4 Vector apply nodes

The usage of binary application nodes supports the concepts of currying and higher-order functions very well, but has the drawback of generating long application spines for functions with many arguments. Calling an n-ary function in a lazy context requires n application nodes. Although aggregate allocation of the nodes at once reduces the costs of building the spine somewhat, more can be gained by representing the spine as a single vector of pointers to the arguments. A **vector apply node** is a variable-length graph node consisting of a function pointer, a length field, and n argument pointers. The length field is needed by both the graph reducer and the garbage collector to function properly. The vector apply node is more space efficient than a spine of binary application nodes if the number of arguments exceeds two ($2 + n$ versus $2n$). Another advantage of using vector nodes is that unwinding becomes cheaper, because the pointers in the application spine need not be traversed.

Vector apply nodes frequently represent delayed function calls in which all function arguments are present; the number of arguments matches the arity of the function. In this case the vector apply node is in fact a self-contained closure. The graph reducer can improve performance by discriminating closures from curried applications. Normally the graph reducer unwinds an apply node by stacking the argument list before finally invoking the function through its code address. The arguments are passed as an array of pointers. Inside a closure the arguments already appear as an array, so the graph reducer can skip the unwind phase and invoke the function directly. This saves processing as well as stack space. It is an important optimization since most vector apply nodes hold closures and currying is used (relatively) sparingly in most functional programs.

12.9 Conclusion

This concludes the chapter on compiling functional programs. We saw that the increased level of abstraction provided by functional languages over traditional imperative languages puts a burden on the compiler writer. Some features, like pattern matching and list comprehension, are considered syntactic sugar and can be handled quite easily in the front-end. Fundamental features like currying, higher-order functions, and lazy evaluation, however, require substantial effort from the compiler back-end even when C is used as the target language. Lazy evaluation implies an execution order (normal order reduction) that is different from the strict model offered by the target machine (applicative order reduction in C).

Therefore the language run-time system centers around an interpreter, the graph reducer, which repeatedly searches for the next computation step (reduction) in a graph of unevaluated expressions. To increase performance, the functional language compiler exploits several optimizations to minimize or even circumvent interpretation overhead (for example, graph manipulation). Strictness analysis is the most important optimization since it identifies which expressions must always be evaluated, so traditional code can be generated for them. Unfortunately, strictness analysis on symbolic code involving user-defined data structures is notoriously difficult. As a consequence a large fraction of the computation goes through the interpreter. This also explains why the garbage collector, discussed in Section 10.2, is another important component of the run-time system of a functional language.

Summary

- Functional languages promote a declarative style, in which programmers specify only *what* to compute. It is up to the compiler and run-time system to decide *how*, *where*, and *when* to compute (sub-)results.

- Functional languages include special syntax (for example, list comprehension) and programming constructs (for example, higher-order functions) to raise the level of abstraction. This complicates the compiler and the run-time system.
- Syntactic sugar is handled by the lexical analyzer and parser. This includes the offside rule, list notation, list comprehension, and pattern matching.
- The more fundamental issues concern polymorphic typing, referential transparency, higher-order functions, and lazy evaluation.

Summary—The front-end

- A functional language compiler is typically structured as a front-end that transforms the complete source language to an intermediate language that contains only the essential features: basic data types, structured data types (lists), non-nesting functions, local bindings (lets), expressions, higher-order functions, and lazy evaluation semantics.
- Numerous optimizations are performed on the intermediate code (or actually the AST), before code is generated. Most compilers build on imperative compiler technology by generating C; C is used as a portable optimizing assembler.
- Pattern matching is handled by generating a simpler function which includes a sequence of if-then-else constructs to explicitly check whether or not actual arguments match a specific constant or type constructor.
- List comprehension is handled by a translation scheme that transforms the (semi-)mathematical notation into a set of higher-order functions that iterate over lists and filter out the right elements.
- Nested functions are floated to the top by the lambda-lifting transformation. Pointers to identifiers in outer scopes are translated into pointers to additional arguments that are passed to the lifted functions explicitly.
- Type checking of functional languages is complicated by polymorphic types; functions and expressions may have multiple types. Also, types need not be specified explicitly, so the compiler must infer the type of arbitrary expressions using type inference techniques.
- Type inference first determines the constraints that are imposed by the body of the function at hand. The set of constraints is then solved by unification, which results in the most general instance of the type of the function.

Summary—Graph reduction

- Higher-order functions and lazy evaluation are tackled by an interpreter known as the graph reducer, which explicitly manipulates application nodes representing (partial) function calls. A function call with n argument expressions is represented as a spine of n application nodes, each holding a function and argument

pointer. An application spine that holds a function and all its arguments is known
as a "redex" (for "reducible expression").

- The graph reducer is a three-stroke engine that repeatedly selects a redex, instantiates the right-hand side of the function, and updates the root of the redex.
  Instantiating the right-hand side of the function builds the graph representing the
  body and replaces the formal parameters with pointers to the actual arguments.
- The reduction order controls the selection of the next redex. Normal-order reduction always selects the leftmost outermost redex and, consequently, only reduces
  what is needed to progress the computation; this is lazy evaluation. Applicative-
  order reduction is used by imperative languages and evaluates the leftmost innermost redex first; expressions at argument positions are evaluated before calling
  the function.
- Normal-order reduction can handle a larger class of programs. It allows programmers to specify infinite data structures as long as they only use a finite part
  of them.
- The code generator emits C code, which will be invoked by the graph reducer, to
  instantiate the body of a user-defined function at run time.
- Expressions are translated into a sequence of application nodes. The if-then-else
  construct translates into a call to the conditional function supplied by the run-
  time system. Local bindings (let-expressions) translate into assignments to local
  variables in C.
- If a function f directly calls another function g (with some arbitrary argument
  expressions) then control can be transferred directly to g without using application nodes. This optimization short-circuits top-level function applications. Expressions occurring as operands to a built-in strict operator may be evaluated
  immediately instead of being transformed into a (lazy) piece of graph.
- A broad compiler, which has access to the AST of all functions, is needed
  to achieve acceptable performance. Strictness analysis and boxing analysis are
  program-wide analyses that avoid the manipulation of graphs in many cases.
- Strictness analysis identifies for each function which arguments will always be
  evaluated, so corresponding argument expressions need not be passed as a graph
  of function applications, but may be evaluated safely before the call.
- Determining the strict arguments of a function proceeds bottom-up through the
  AST. Function application is handled by looking up the strict arguments of the
  called function and passing the sets of strict arguments in the AST at the corresponding positions upward. The strictness properties of a recursive function are
  optimistically set to true. Then the strict arguments are determined by repeatedly
  propagating sets along the AST, until a fixed point is reached.
- Once strictness analysis is performed it is no longer necessary to pass strict arguments as graph nodes. Boxing analysis determines which arguments may be
  passed by value and takes care of changing between boxed and unboxed representations when switching from interpreted to compiled code.
- Tail call elimination is a useful optimization in code fro functional programs.
- Often recursive functions do not end in a tail call, but in an operator that processes the result returned by the tail call. The accumulating transformation may

be applied when the operator is associative and the tail call is recursive. The body of the function is reorganized to take an additional argument, which accumulates partial results in a strictly tail-recursive manner; the operation is performed as input to the accumulating argument of the tail call.

- The end result is that state-of-the-art compilers for functional languages can emit code that is similar to traditional imperative counterparts for the class of numerical algorithms. Optimizing symbolic and inherently lazy programs is much more difficult, though.
- The last drop of performance can be gained by streamlining the graph reducer itself. We discussed four advanced graph-manipulation techniques: variable-length nodes, pointer tagging, aggregate node allocation, and vector apply nodes (or closures).

Further reading

Functional programming differs considerably from imperative programming. The books by Bird [40] and Thompson [279] provide a gentle introduction into the world of higher-order functions, currying, and lazy evaluation. Both books use the Haskell language, which is the *de facto* standard functional language with lazy semantics and which succeeds early lazy languages like SASL, Miranda, and LML. Standard ML [192] on the other hand, is the prominent functional language with strict, or non-lazy, semantics. It is quite popular, and the book by Paulson [215] is a good place to start. LISP, originating in the early sixties, is still alive, with Scheme [92] being the prominent representative.

Detailed information about the implementation of functional languages can be found in the proceedings of the annual *International Conference on Functional Programming - ICFP*, which combines the former biennial *Functional Programming and Computer Architecture - FPCA* and *Lisp and Functional Programming - LFP* conferences. The *Implementation of Functional Languages* workshops are also a rich source of information. Journals to consider are the *Journal of Functional Programming*, and *Higher-Order and Symbolic Computation* (formerly: *LISP and Symbolic Computation*). A systematic study of functional language implementations is given by Douence and Fradet [87].

This chapter discussed the modern approach of compiling functional languages using C as the universal assembler. This approach is the most recent stage in the historical development of implementing functional languages, which progressed from poorly performing interpreters (SKI combinators) [281] through supercombinators (G-machine) [131] to native code generation. The standard reference to the early work is Peyton Jones's *The Implementation of Functional Programming Languages* [218]. The follow-up *Implementing Functional Languages* [220] is especially useful for practitioners since it describes the *spineless tagless G-machine* that forms the heart of the state-of-the-art Haskell compiler from Glasgow University.

The Glasgow Haskell Compiler (GHC) is available from the Internet (`http://www.haskell.org/ghc`), and comes with a complete set of sources. It is structured such that "others can plug in their own strictness analyzer, profiler, front-end, back-end, or other special pass". This open structure, and the availability of all source code, eases experimentation with the compiler, although learning the GHC's internals is quoted to be "a fairly substantial exercise".

A more recent Haskell compiler, UHC, is described by Dijkstra, Fokker and Swierstra [84]. The compile time transformations on the program tree are implemented through attribute grammars, and the aspect-oriented structure allows language variants and extensions to be implemented easily. It compiles to C or Java.

Exercises

12.1. In Section 12.3, the type of map is described as map :: (b -> c) -> [b] -> [c] "since the -> operator is right-associative, which is consistent with currying". Explain why the right-associativity of the -> operator is consistent with currying and what would be wrong if the type of map were specified as map :: b -> c -> [b] -> [c].

12.2. (▷www) Derive the type of the following function foldr, which folds a right-associative operator into a list of values:

```
foldr  op val [ ]      = val
foldr  op val (x:xs) = op x ( foldr  op val xs)
```

12.3. (▷www) Haskell uses the dot operator (.) to denote function composition (f.g). What is the polymorphic type of this built-in composition operator?

12.4. (▷www) Give equivalent functional-core expressions for the following lists:

```
" list "
[1..481]
```

12.5. (▷www) Pattern matching is considered syntactic sugar that can easily be compiled away. Transform the function

```
unique (a:b:cs) = if  (a == b) then  a : unique cs
                              else  a : unique (b:cs)
unique cs       = cs
```

which contains a nested pattern, into an equivalent functional-core function.

12.6. (▷796) The pattern translation in Figure 12.6 contains code to catch cases in which all patterns fail.
(a) Argue that the activation of this code signals an error in the specification of the function.
(b) Argue that it signals an error in the use of the function.

12.7. *Pattern matching by repeated variables; advanced topic*: Some functional languages (for example Miranda, but not Haskell) allow another form of pattern matching, pattern matching by **repeated variables**. This pattern allows an argument name to occur more than once in the left-hand side of a function definition and requires these occurrences to have the same value for the match to succeed. This allows, for example, definitions like

```
equal x x = 1
equal x y = 0
```

(a) Find out the precise semantics of this form of pattern matching in Miranda, with an eye to, for example, f (x:(y:xs)) (y:(x:ys)).
(b) Design a translation technique for the translation of these patterns to the functional core.
(c) Design the strictness computation rules for the code resulting from these patterns.

12.8. (▷www) The definition of the quicksort function from Section 12.1.3 uses list comprehensions. Use the translation scheme in Figure 12.10 to derive a version that uses higher-order functions instead.

12.9. (▷www) The transformed qsort function in Exercise 12.8 uses local functions. Use the lambda-lifting transformation to float these functions out.

12.10. (▷www) Applicative-order reduction may compute expressions that are not needed. Give an example where applicative-order reduction even fails to terminate, while normal-order reduction succeeds in returning a result (by being lazy).

12.11. (▷796) The three-stroke reduction engine ends each reduction step by updating the root with the result. Omitting the update may lead to exponential overhead. Give an example program that demonstrates this.

12.12. (▷www) The reduction engine in Figure 12.17 updates the root node by copying the value into it. This approach does not work if we extend the reducer to handle user-defined data structures, which can be of arbitrary size. The usual work-around is to introduce indirection nodes that consist of a tag and a pointer to the true value. Discuss the changes of the eval() code that are required to incorporate such indirection nodes.

12.13. (▷www) Recursive definitions inside let-expressions cannot be translated into assignments to local C variables. Explain. A solution is to use a two-phase approach. First, generate code for the recursive definition while using a blank entry for each forward reference. Second, generate code to backpatch the blank entries. Give the translation for the function

```
rep n = let
            lst  = n :  lst
        in
            lst
```

which generates an infinite list of ns.

12.14. Explain the optimizations in Section 12.6.1 as examples of partial evaluation.

12.15. (▷www) What are the strict arguments of the following function?

```
f x y z 0 = x + z
f x y z p = f y 0 0 (p−1) + f z z 0 (p−1)
```

12.16. (▷www) Explain the unboxing transformation of Figure 12.33 to Figure 12.34 as an example of partial evaluation.

12.17. (▷www) In the last few paragraphs of Section 12.7.3 we examined the problem of filling a parameter record with values, some of which possibly derive from that same parameter record. If, for simplicity, we assume that all values have the same size, we can formalize the problem as follows. Given the set A of assignments

```
P_new[1] := f₁(...);
P_new[2] := f₂(...);
...
P_new[N] := f_N(...);
```

in which P_new[ ] is an array, and the function arguments (...) may contain any combination of the elements of an array P_old, give an algorithm for generating code for the assignments in A that works correctly even if P_new and P_old are actually the same array. These assignments do what is called *in situ replacement*.

12.18. (▷796) The mappend function given in Section 12.4.3 looks like a suitable candidate for the accumulating argument transformation, but it is not. Explain. Hint: consider the performance consequences.

12.19. (▷796) Discuss the benefits of using vector apply nodes when evaluating the following expression:

```
take 100 (from 1)
where
    take 0 xs     = [ ]
    take n (x:xs) = x : take (n−1) xs

    from n = n : from (n+1)
```

12.20. *History of functional language implementation*: Study Landin's 1964 paper [168] on the mechanical evaluation of expressions, and identify and summarize the concepts and techniques described.

Chapter 13
Logic Programs

In the previous chapter we have seen that the compilation of functional programs is basically simple, once the idea of a closure is understood. For logic programs the situation is different: even implementing the basic mechanisms already poses considerable problems.

Logic programming is based on the specification of "relations" between "terms", "facts" using these relations, and "rules" for "inferring" new facts from existing facts. Some of the terms involved in these facts and rules may be or may contain logical variables. Facts and rules together are called "clauses". A program in a logic language consists of a "list of clauses".

The point of logic programming is that it is possible to request specific inferred facts by doing "queries". Such inferred facts are obtained by the program by searching through the clauses, combining them in various ways and doing backtracking when the combinations lead nowhere, and often even when they *do* lead to a desired fact. During this search, the variables in the rules may be **bound** tentatively to various terms, and these bindings will have to be undone during backtracking. The terms tried for variables may be constants, but may also be other variables or structures; these structures may hold constants, bound or unbound variables and/or further structures. Also, the variables are themselves terms. For these reasons, the usual means of binding variables to values, the assignment, is out of the question, and the binding is performed by a process called "unification", to be explained further on in this chapter.

Note that "a variable is bound to a value", whereas "a value is assigned to a variable". The reason for using the verb "to bind" in this way is that, unlike traditional variables, logic variables can be unbound—have no binding—or bound—have a binding—and that if they have a binding, that binding leads to a value (or another variable).

An example of a relation is "is a parent of". Facts using this relation might be "Arne is a parent of Sachiko" and "Sachiko is a parent of Rivka". Another example of a relation is "is a grandparent of", and the two relations might be linked in a rule "X is a grandparent of Z if there is a Y such that X is a parent of Y and Y is a parent of Z", in which X, Y, and Z are logical variables. The system should then be able to infer from the above facts the new fact "Arne is a grandparent of Rivka".

The first logic language processors were interpreters, and in fact there has long been serious doubt if logic language programs could be compiled profitably at all. Today, for problems of a logic programming nature, logic programs compiled by high-end logic-language compilers achieve speeds that approach those obtained for the corresponding imperative implementations to within a factor of 2 or 3. Compilation of full backtracking search over the clauses and of unification of the terms require substantial implementation effort even in their non-optimized form, but modern Prolog compilers achieve the remarkable speed of their object code by doing extensive optimizations. Fortunately, many optimizations consist of specializations of more general code and can be understood easily on the basis of that code.

We will first explain the full backtracking search mechanism by showing a very simple and inefficient interpreter for it (Section 13.2). This is followed by a discussion of the unification of two terms (Section 13.3). We then concentrate on a general compilation technique for full recursive backtracking search over the clauses combined with full recursive backtracking unification of the terms. Its main property is that it is a uniform implementation of a logic programming model that is slightly more general than is required by Prolog, and from which more specialized implementations can be derived (Section 13.4). Often, some of the search code can be performed at compile time and part of the remainder can be generated as chunks of in-line code. This often allows us to avoid calling upon the general search mechanism. This optimization is discussed in Section 13.4.3.

Next, we restrict ourselves to unification as used in Prolog, which does not require backtracking; this yields a more imperative implementation of unification (Section 13.5). As with the search code, often some of the unification code can be performed at compile time and some of the remainder can be generated as chunks of in-line code. Finally, we apply one optimization to the unification code: "Read"/"Write" mode (Section 13.5.4).

Some compilers for logic languages simplify life by generating C code rather than assembly code, and so will we in this chapter. There is a problem with this approach, however: the most natural expression of full backtracking search requires nested routine declarations, which standard C does not allow. Fortunately, one of the most important C implementations, the GNU C compiler, has an extension that allows exactly these nested routines. Also, nested routines are available in a few other imperative languages. Some compilers for advanced logic languages take the level of the target code another step higher and generate Prolog code [77].

Whereas few intermediate codes for imperative languages have reached more than local fame, there exists a more or less well-known intermediate code for Prolog: the **Warren Abstract Machine** or **WAM**; this may reflect on the complexity of the task of compiling Prolog. The WAM document defines 39 instructions that together allow an efficient compiled implementation of Prolog, including the "cut" operator but excluding assert, retract, and the numeric operators [291]. The instructions deal with such things as selecting the proper clause to use in inferring a fact, unifying under various circumstances, and backtracking. Each instruction corresponds reasonably closely to a node in the AST of a Prolog program; this makes intermediate code generation relatively easy.

The WAM does all memory allocation, for which it uses five stacks; it can do its own deallocation, but efficiency can be increased by using an internal compacting garbage collector on some of the stacks. The machine incorporates quite a number of optimizations to the basic Prolog execution model. Many of these optimizations interact with each other, with the result that most WAM instructions cannot be understood in isolation: several readings of the defining document are required to understand the purpose and applicability of the instructions. The WAM report gives translations of the WAM instructions into an abstract assembly code, which allows WAM to target code generation almost by macro processing. Aït-Kaci has written a tutorial on the WAM [8].

The WAM is too detailed for treatment in this book. We will first concentrate on the basic execution model for logic languages and then derive a few WAM-like instructions from it, with optimizations. This approach avoids the complications inherent in interacting optimizations and may also be helpful in designing WAM-like instruction sets for other logic languages. For another derivation of some WAM instructions see Kursawe [164].

―――――――――――――― **Roadmap** ――――――――――――――

13.1 The logic programming model

We will recall here briefly the principle and some of the concepts of logic programming, mainly to review the terminology and to introduce a simple working example.

13.1.1 The building blocks

Logic programming is based on named **relations** between terms, facts stating such relations, and rules for inferring new facts from established facts. A **fact** consists of the name of the relation and its terms, in some syntactic notation; it is an instance of the named relation. An example of a relation is parent/2, which notation means that the relation is named parent and governs 2 terms; in other words, it is a **binary relation**. The number of terms may be important in a given logic language to identify the relation: a logic language might allow another relation parent/1, which would then govern 1 term and be a **unary relation**. A few examples of facts using the relation parent/2 are:

```
parent(arne, james).
parent(arne, sachiko).
parent(koos, rivka ).
parent(sachiko, rivka ).
parent( truitje , koos).
```

It is more than likely that the first fact is intended to mean that Arne is a parent of James, and that similar meanings should be attached to the other four facts, but of course such an interpretation is in no way necessary for a logic program to function.

Given the above facts, a **query** could be

```
?– parent(X, rivka).
```

in which X is an **unbound variable**. Conventionally, names of variables begin with a capital letter, and names of constants begin with a small letter. The query ?– parent(X, rivka) asks the system to scan the facts, to find those which match the query, and to show the values of the variables for which the matches occur; note the plural "matches", since more than one match may occur. The body of the query, parent(X, rivka) is our initial **goal** of the search. A fact **matches** a goal if there is a binding for the variables in the goal and the fact that makes goal and fact equal. The above goal results in two successive bindings, X = sachiko and X = koos, since the first makes the goal equal to the fact parent(sachiko, rivka) and the second to parent(koos, rivka).

Queries do not need to contain variables: the query ?– parent(koos, rivka) results in yes and the query ?– parent(rivka, arne) results in no. On the other hand, facts may contain variables: the fact parent(X, rivka) means that X is a parent of Rivka for any value of X. The fact parent(X, rivka) can be considered as shorthand for an infinite number of facts: parent(a, rivka), parent(b, rivka), ... This feature is useful, for example to express the fact equal(X, X) which says that X equals X for any value of X.

An example of a **rule** is

```
grandparent(X, Z) :– parent(X, Y), parent(Y, Z).
```

which means that when we have established the facts parent(X, Y) and parent(Y, Z) for some values of X, Y, and Z, we may infer the fact grandparent(X, Z). Another interpretation of this rule is that we may replace the goal grandparent(X, Z) by the goal list parent(X, Y), parent(Y, Z), for any bindings of X, Y, and Z. The part before the :– token is called the **head** of the rule, the part after the :– token is called the **body** of the rule. We see that the comma in the body can be interpreted as a logical AND.

Again the rule may be seen as a summary of infinitely many rules, obtained by infinitely many different bindings for X, Y, and Z:

```
grandparent(a, c) :– parent(a, b), parent(b, c).
      with X=a, Y=b, Z=c
grandparent( truitje , rivka) :–
    parent( truitje , koos), parent(koos, rivka ).
      with X=truitje, Y=koos, Z=rivka
grandparent(arne, rivka) :–
    parent(arne, koos), parent(koos, rivka ).
      with X=arne, Y=koos, Z=rivka
    ...
```

Note that the facts required by the second example have been established above and that we may therefore infer the fact grandparent(truitje, rivka); this is not the case in the first and the third example.

Actually, facts and rules are not as different in nature as it seems: rules establish facts conditionally upon other facts, facts do so unconditionally. It is therefore convenient to play down the difference and combine them in the notion **"clause"**.

13.1.2 The inference mechanism

Now suppose the system is presented with the query

?– grandparent(arne, X).

which asks for an X of which arne is a grandparent, and makes grandparent(arne, X) our initial goal. The system then tries to find or infer the goal for some binding for X. There are no grandparent facts directly, but there *is* a rule for inferring them, the clause

grandparent(X, Z) :– parent(X, Y), parent(Y, Z).

To get an applicable instance of this clause, we make a copy of it with fresh variables in it:

grandparent(X1, Z1) :– parent(X1, Y1), parent(Y1, Z1).

and try to make the goal grandparent(arne, X) and the head of this clause equal by binding the variables in them; this is the unification process we mentioned above. It is easy to see that the bindings X1=arne and Z1=X do the job; note that we can bind a variable (Z1) to a variable (X). This unification transforms the clause copy into

grandparent(arne, X) :– parent(arne, Y1), parent(Y1, X).

We can now replace our goal grandparent(arne, X) by a new goal list:

parent(arne, Y1), parent(Y1, X).

Next, we try to unify the first part, parent(arne, Y1) with a fact and find that there are two possibilities, parent(arne, james) (with Y1=james) and parent(arne, sachiko) (with Y1=sachiko). The first transforms our goal list into parent(arne, james), parent(james, X).

but no fact can be unified with parent(james, X), so this is a dead end; the second transforms our goal list into

parent(arne, sachiko), parent(sachiko, X).

and now we find that parent(sachiko, X) can be unified with the fact parent(sachiko, rivka) by using the binding X=rivka. So we have shown that our query can be reduced to a list of known facts by the binding X=rivka, and the answer to the query

?– grandparent(arne, X).

is

grandparent(arne, rivka).

This corresponds to the fact "Arne is a grandparent of Rivka" mentioned at the beginning of this chapter. The process by which it was derived is an example of an **inference technique**.

The above covers the basics of the logic paradigm. All logic languages have many additional features, usually including structures, lists, and other more advanced data types, integer arithmetic, string manipulation, ways to influence the search order, and ways to abort a search. We will only consider two of these additional features in this chapter, both from Prolog: structures and the "cut" mechanism.

13.2 The general implementation model, interpreted

We can use a more precise version of the above inference technique to explain the workings of a very simple interpreter for logic languages. This interpreter is not intended as a serious implementation and serves as a model only; also, it implements only the bare bones of the logic paradigm, as explained above.

The main data structure of this interpreter is the **goal list stack**. Each of the goal lists on the stack is a separate possibility to satisfy the query, independent of the other goal lists: the semantics of the stack is the logical OR of all its elements. This set-up is depicted in Figure 13.1.

The interpreter works on the top goal list on the stack only. It pops it off the stack, processes it, and pushes zero, one, or more new goal lists back onto the stack. The stack starts with one entry: the body of the query, followed by a special **display goal** named << that has the variables in the query and their names as terms. When the stack is empty, all answers to the query have been found and the processing stops.

The goal list notation is extended with the construct $[\,P\,?=\,Q\,]$, which signifies a request to unify P and Q, and the construct $[\,P == Q\,]$, which signifies that P and Q have been unified successfully. These constructs are used as follows. As we have seen above, unification serves to adapt a copy of a clause to a given goal list by

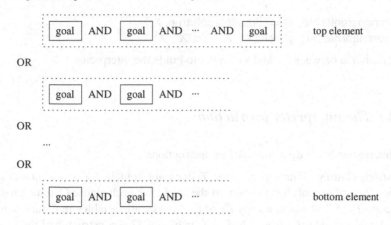

Fig. 13.1: The goal list stack

finding the minimal substitution that will make the head of the clause and the first goal in the goal list equal. For example, the (clause copy, goal list) pair

    grandparent(X1, Z1) :− parent(X1, Y1), parent(Y1, Z1).
    grandparent(arne, X), <<("X", X).

is unified by the substitutions X1=arne and Z1=X:

    grandparent(arne, X) :− parent(arne, Y1), parent(Y1, X).
    grandparent(arne, X), <<("X", X).

Note that unification is always performed between one term from the head and one term from the goal, never between two terms from a head or from a goal. Once an appropriate substitution for the unification has been found and performed throughout the clause copy and the goal list, we can replace the first goal in the goal list by the body of the clause copy:

    parent(arne, Y1), parent(Y1, X), <<("X", X).

We will write the (clause copy, goal list) pair as a single goal list by provisionally inserting the clause copy after the first goal, and enclosing the first goal and the head of the clause copy in a [?=] construct:

    [grandparent(arne, X) ?= grandparent(X1, Z1)],
        parent(X1, Y1), parent(Y1, Z1), <<("X", X).

This can be read as "If grandparent(arne, X) can be unified with grandparent(X1, Z1), the goal list parent(X1, Y1), parent(Y1, Z1), «("X", X) after substitution is valid". The concatenation of the body of the clause copy and the original goal list tail is automatic in this notation; also, the substitution involved in the unification can be performed in one sweep over the extended goal list. After successful unification, the ?= is changed to ==:

[grandparent(arne, X) == grandparent(arne, X)],
    parent(arne, Y1), parent(Y1, X), <<("X", X).

The difference between ?= and == serves to guide the interpreter.

13.2.1 The interpreter instructions

The interpreter is iterative and has four instructions:

- "Attach clauses". The top goal list T does not contain ?= or ==, nor is it the special display goal; it is popped off the stack. For each clause C in the program, a copy T_1 of T is made, a copy C_1 of C is made, all variables in C_1 are replaced by fresh variables, C_1 is attached to T_1 using the [?=] construct, and the result is pushed onto the stack. The process is depicted in Figure 13.2.
- "Unify". The top goal list T contains ?= and is popped off the stack. An attempt is made to unify the goal and the clause head in T in the [?=] construct, resulting in zero or more substitutions. For each substitution S a copy of T is made, and S is applied to all goals in the copy. The zero or more resulting goal lists are stacked. (In Prolog at most one goal list results.) If the unification is completed in any of them, the ?= separator is replaced by the == separator.
- "Match". The top goal list T contains == and is popped off the stack. The [==] construct, which contains the two unified goals, is removed from it and the resulting goal list is pushed back onto the stack.
- "Succeed". The top goal list T is the special display goal and is popped off the stack. Its terms are displayed in answer to the query.

It is easy to see that in each situation only one interpreter instruction is applicable.

clause head :– clause body.
                                        } [first goal ?= clause head], clause body, other goals.
first goal, other goals.

Fig. 13.2: The action of "Attach clauses" using one clause

We will now show how this interpreter processes the query ?– grandparent(arne, X). To keep the example small, we reduce the program to four clauses:

pa(arne, james)
pa(arne, sachiko)
pa(sachiko, rivka)
gp(X, Z) :– pa(X, Y), pa(Y, Z)

in which we abbreviate parent and grandparent to pa and gp, respectively, and leave out the (Prolog) dot at the end of each clause. We show the stack with one entry to a line. The initial stack is

```
gp(arne,X),<<("X",X)
```

The applicable instruction is "Attach clauses" and since there are four clauses, this results in four entries:

```
[gp(arne,X) ?= pa(arne,james)],<<("X",X)
[gp(arne,X) ?= pa(arne,sachiko)],<<("X",X)
[gp(arne,X) ?= pa(sachiko,rivka)],<<("X",X)
[gp(arne,X) ?= gp(X1,Z1)],pa(X1,Y1),pa(Y1,Z1),<<("X",X)
```

A copy of each of the four clauses has been inserted after the first goal, using the [?=] construct. Note that the variables in the clause for gp have been renamed. Note also that the entire goal list has been copied four times.

The instruction applicable to the top goal list is "Unify", but it fails immediately since not even the names of the relations to be unified (gp and pa) match; so this goal list is rejected. The same happens to the next two goal lists. This leaves us with one goal list:

```
[gp(arne,X) ?= gp(X1,Z1)],pa(X1,Y1),pa(Y1,Z1),<<("X",X)
```

The unification attempt of gp(arne,X) and gp(X1,Z1) succeeds when we substitute arne for X1 and X for Z1:

```
[gp(arne,X) == gp(arne,X)],pa(arne,Y1),pa(Y1,X),<<("X",X)
```

The next applicable instruction is "Match", which removes the two unified goals:

```
pa(arne,Y1),pa(Y1,X),<<("X",X)
```

Applying "Attach clauses" results in

```
[pa(arne,Y1) ?= pa(arne,james)],pa(Y1,X),<<("X",X)
[pa(arne,Y1) ?= pa(arne,sachiko)],pa(Y1,X),<<("X",X)
[pa(arne,Y1) ?= pa(sachiko,rivka)],pa(Y1,X),<<("X",X)
[pa(arne,Y1) ?= gp(X2,Z2)],pa(X2,Y2),pa(Y2,Z2),pa(Y1,X),<<("X",X)
```

The top entry unifies by putting Y1 equal to james; "Match" then removes the unified goals:

```
pa(james,X),<<("X",X)
[pa(arne,Y1) ?= pa(arne,sachiko)],pa(Y1,X),<<("X",X)
[pa(arne,Y1) ?= pa(sachiko,rivka)],pa(Y1,X),<<("X",X)
[pa(arne,Y1) ?= gp(X2,Z2)],pa(X2,Y2),pa(Y2,Z2),pa(Y1,X),<<("X",X)
```

It is important to note that the substitution of Y1 takes place in the top entry only; this keeps the entries completely independent. "Attach clauses" yields

```
[pa(james,X) ?= pa(arne,james)],<<("X",X)
[pa(james,X) ?= pa(arne,sachiko)],<<("X",X)
[pa(james,X) ?= pa(sachiko,rivka)],<<("X",X)
[pa(james,X) ?= gp(X,Z)],pa(X,Y),pa(Y,Z),<<("X",X)
[pa(arne,Y1) ?= pa(arne,sachiko)],pa(Y1,X),<<("X",X)
[pa(arne,Y1) ?= pa(sachiko,rivka)],pa(Y1,X),<<("X",X)
[pa(arne,Y1) ?= gp(X2,Z2)],pa(X2,Y2),pa(Y2,Z2),pa(Y1,X),<<("X",X)
```

Four unification attempts fail, leaving

```
[pa(arne,Y1) ?= pa(arne,sachiko)],pa(Y1,X),<<("X",X)
[pa(arne,Y1) ?= pa(sachiko,rivka)],pa(Y1,X),<<("X",X)
[pa(arne,Y1) ?= gp(X2,Z2)],pa(X2,Y2),pa(Y2,Z2),pa(Y1,X),<<("X",X)
```

Again, a unification attempt succeeds, with Y1=sachiko this time, and after matching results in

```
pa(sachiko,X),<<("X",X)
[pa(arne,Y1) ?= pa(sachiko,rivka)],pa(Y1,X),<<("X",X)
[pa(arne,Y1) ?= gp(X2,Z2)],pa(X2,Y2),pa(Y2,Z2),pa(Y1,X),<<("X",X)
```

The top entry again requires an "Attach clauses":

```
[pa(sachiko,X) ?= pa(arne,james)],<<("X",X)
[pa(sachiko,X) ?= pa(arne,sachiko)],<<("X",X)
[pa(sachiko,X) ?= pa(sachiko,rivka)],<<("X",X)
[pa(sachiko,X) ?= gp(X3,Z3)],pa(X3,Y3),pa(Y3,Z3),<<("X",X)
[pa(arne,Y1) ?= pa(sachiko,rivka)],pa(Y1,X),<<("X",X)
[pa(arne,Y1) ?= gp(X2,Z2)],pa(X2,Y2),pa(Y2,Z2),pa(Y1,X),<<("X",X)
```

The attempts at unification on the first two entries fail, removing the entries, but the third succeeds with X=rivka:

```
[pa(sachiko,rivka)  == pa(sachiko,rivka)],<<("X",rivka)
[pa(sachiko,X) ?= gp(X3,Z3)],pa(X3,Y3),pa(Y3,Z3),<<("X",X)
[pa(arne,Y1) ?= pa(sachiko,rivka)],pa(Y1,X),<<("X",X)
[pa(arne,Y1) ?= gp(X2,Z2)],pa(X2,Y2),pa(Y2,Z2),pa(Y1,X),<<("X",X)
```

"Match" removes the unified goals, leaving us for the first time with a display goal:

```
<<("X",rivka)
[pa(sachiko,X) ?= gp(X3,Z3)],pa(X3,Y3),pa(Y3,Z3),<<("X",X)
[pa(arne,Y1) ?= pa(sachiko,rivka)],pa(Y1,X),<<("X",X)
[pa(arne,Y1) ?= gp(X2,Z2)],pa(X2,Y2),pa(Y2,Z2),pa(Y1,X),<<("X",X)
```

The interpreter instruction "Succeed" now displays the binding X=rivka in answer to the query, and removes the entry. The next three unifications fail, leaving an empty stack. Reaching the bottom of the stack signals the end of our search for answers to the query.

It will be clear that an interpreter performing the four instructions "Attach clauses", "Unify", "Match", and "Succeed" can be written easily, but it will be equally clear that the interpreter has two glaring inefficiencies: "Attach clauses" generates large numbers of goal lists that are obviously dead ends, and many goals in the goal lists are copied many times. Also, the treatment of unification has been rather vague. We will now turn to these problems, not with an eye to improving the interpreter, which is a cardboard model anyway, but because any serious compiled code based on the above model will exhibit the same problems if we do not solve them here.

13.2.2 Avoiding redundant goal lists

The "Attach clauses" instruction generates inordinate numbers of redundant goal lists because it attaches any clause to the goal list being processed even if it is obvious that the subsequent unification will fail. An example is

[gp(arne,X) ?= pa(arne,james)],<<("X",X)

in which an instance of the relation gp/2 can never match an instance of the relation pa/2. A more subtle example is

[pa(arne,Y1) ?= pa(sachiko,rivka)],pa(Y1,X),<<("X",X)

in which the relation names match, but the first term differs. If the names of the relations are known at compile time, the first redundancy can be diagnosed and avoided easily at compile time. The second example is less straightforward: whereas the term sachiko is known at compile time, the corresponding term arne is the result of a binding at run time. So a run-time check is required, but the possibility of this check can be determined at compile time. The C code we will generate uses the identification mechanism of C to avoid the first redundancy (the beginning of Section 13.4) and some simple run-time code to avoid the second (Section 13.4.3).

13.2.3 Avoiding copying goal list tails

A simple way to avoid copying the entire goal list N times for N applicable clauses in "Attach clauses" suggests itself: copy the first goal and the clause only, and represent the rest of the goal list by a pointer to the original copy:

```
[pa(arne,Y1)  ?= pa(arne,james)],
[pa(arne,Y1)  ?= pa(arne,sachiko)],
[pa(arne,Y1)  ?= pa(sachiko,rivka)],        pa(Y1,X),
[pa(arne,Y1)  ?= gp(X2,Z2)],pa(X2,Y2),pa(Y2,Z2),   <<("X",X)
```

This solves the efficiency problem, but introduces a new problem, which becomes apparent when we do the unification on the top goal list, binding the variable Y1 to the constant james:

```
[pa(arne,james)  ?= pa(arne,james)],
[pa(arne,Y1)  ?= pa(arne,sachiko)],
[pa(arne,Y1)  ?= pa(sachiko,rivka)],        pa(james,X),
[pa(arne,Y1)  ?= gp(X2,Z2)],pa(X2,Y2),pa(Y2,Z2),   <<("X",X)
```

The data structure now suggests that pa(james,X),«("X",X) will be the goal list tail for the other three unifications as well. But we know from the above analysis that the top goal list will eventually fail, and that the goal list tail that leads to success is actually pa(sachiko,X),«("X",X). So by the time the unification [pa(arne,Y1) ?= pa(arne,sachiko)]) is being done, the old goal list tail

pa(Y1,X),«("X",X) must have been restored. The problem is solved by recording the
fact that the binding Y1=james was performed tentatively and then undoing it —
backtracking over it—when the goal list is dropped. This is the first moment in our
discussion of the execution of logic programs that the idea of **backtracking** actually
pops up: the need for backtracking originates from our wish to avoid copying the
entire partial solution at each and every choice point.

How exactly tentative bindings are recorded and undone depends on the implementation details of the unification process. Also, we have left the unification process underspecified in the above example of the processing of a logic query. It is
therefore time now to turn to unification in more detail.

13.3 Unification

Until now we have seen only the simplest form of unification, involving only constants and variables. Even then there are already three possibilities:

- unification between two constants: the unification succeeds if the two constants
  are equal and fails otherwise;
- unification between an (unbound) variable and a constant: the constant is bound
  to the variable and the unification succeeds;
- unification between two (unbound) variables: the variable in the head is bound to
  that in the goal and the unification succeeds.

We do not treat the case of a bound variable separately. A bound variable can
be bound to a constant, in which case it is treated as that constant, or it can be
bound to an unbound or bound variable, in which case it is treated as that unbound
or bound variable. The interpreter or the generated code must contain code to find
out what a variable is bound to; this code is said to "dereference" the variable. The
unification of two variables requires some thought and will be discussed in more
detail in Section 13.3.3.

It is important to implement unification in such a way that it is possible to undo
bindings, since this is required by backtracking. This is quite difficult in general, but
we will see that in the traditional implementation it is simple to undo the *most recent
binding*; this rule applies recursively, so bindings B_1, B_2, ..., B_n can be undone
cheaply in the order B_n, B_{n-1}, ..., B_1. Fortunately, that is all that the usual backtrack
techniques require. We will return to this subject in Section 13.5.

13.3.1 Unification of structures, lists, and sets

Most logic languages allow other terms in addition to constants and variables. Examples are structures, lists, and sets. Structures are named lists of a fixed number of
components; times(2, X) is an example of a structure with the name times and the

components 2 and X. The name of a structure is also called its **functor**; the above example explains why. Note that structures look like facts, but they do not express a relation; they just represent data structures and the structure times(2, X) above could well represent the mathematical formula $2x$.

Structures can only be unified with variables or other structures. Two structures are unified by the same rules as a (head, goal) pair is: their names must be equal, the number of components contained in them must be equal, and these components must be unifiable pairwise by finding the proper bindings, recursively if necessary, in top-down fashion. So times(2, X) and times(2, times(Y, Z)) can be unified by binding X to times(Y, Z), since the substitution X=times(Y, Z) turns both structures into times(2, times(Y, Z)).

There is a rather subtle difficulty here: suppose we try to unify the two structures times(2, X) and times(2, times(Y, X)). Straightforward unification binds X to times(Y, X)), but the corresponding substitution X=times(Y, X) turns the first structure into times(2, times(Y, X)) and the second into times(2, times(Y, times(Y, X)))! The reason is of course that we bound the variable X to a structure in which that same variable X occurs, causing a circularity. In this case, the unification is not possible, and the system should reject it. Diagnosing this situation is called the **occur check**. The occur check is perceived as expensive, since it seems to require scanning the structures involved, and many Prolog systems forgo it, accepting the incorrect binding. Remarkably, this almost never leads to incorrect results; Plaisted [223] has tried to find an explanation of this phenomenon. Martelli and Montanari [184] give an efficient bottom-up implementation of unification, which performs the occur check free of charge.

Many logic languages feature lists as terms. An example is the Prolog list

[X, plus(1, X), times(2, X)]

Actually, a list is just a nested set of binary structures with functor "|", and the above list denotation is shorthand for

"|"(X, "|"(plus(1, X), "|"(times(2, X), "[ ]")))

in which "[ ]" is the empty list. In principle, lists can be implemented as structures using the "|" functor, but in practice systems use tailored code for them for efficiency reasons. Unification of lists follows the same rules as that of structures; for example,

[X, plus(1, X), times(2, X)]

and

[a, plus(1, Y), times(2, a)]

can by unified by X=a and Y=a.

Another type of term is the set, as occurring for example in the fact

pa({koos|sachiko},rivka).

which summarizes

pa(koos,rivka).
pa(sachiko,rivka).

This seems a harmless abbreviation, but now the goal list

[pa(X,rivka) ?= pa({koos|sachiko},rivka)],<<("X",X)

yields two possible unification results:

[pa(koos,rivka) ?= pa({koos|sachiko},rivka)],<<("X",koos)
[pa(sachiko,rivka) ?= pa({koos|sachiko},rivka)],<<("X",sachiko)

This requires extending the "Unify" instruction. Since this multiplication of goal lists may occur to different degrees for each of the term pairs in the head and the first goal, the idea suggests itself to perform the unification one term pair at a time, rather than for the entire (head, goal) pair. The "Unify" instruction then turns

[pa(→X,rivka) ?= pa(→{koos|sachiko},rivka)],<<("X",X)

in which the term pair to be unified is marked with a preceding →, into

[pa(koos,→rivka) ?= pa({koos|sachiko},→rivka)],<<("X",koos)
[pa(→X,rivka) ?= pa({koos|→sachiko},rivka)],<<("X",X)

Another application of "Unify" then turns the top goal list into

[pa(koos,rivka) == pa({koos|sachiko},rivka)],<<("X",koos)

by unifying the second term. Now the question mark has been removed and the "Match" instruction can be applied to remove the matching head and goal. After reporting the binding X=koos, the system proceeds with the next goal list on the goal list stack:

[pa(→X,rivka) ?= pa({koos|→sachiko},rivka)],<<("X",X)

The idea of performing the unification stepwise by term–term pairs simplifies its implementation and also renders unification of structures and of lists easier to understand. Consider, for example, the unification of

[X, plus(1, X), times(2, X)]

and

[a, plus(1, Y), times(2, b)]

Working top-down, which is from left to right in our notation, X and a are unified by binding X to a, next plus and plus are found equal, and 1 and 1 are unified trivially. Then X and Y are unified, but X is dereferenced first, and yields a, so Y is bound to a; of course Y is dereferenced too, but since it is not bound, the dereferencing yields the variable Y again. After successfully unifying the subterms times and 2, we try to unify X and b; X is dereferenced and yields a, which cannot be unified with b, so the unification fails. This implies that the backtracking mechanism must undo the bindings Y=a and X=a, in that order.

13.3.2 The implementation of unification

A reasonable set of C data types for the construction of terms is shown in Figure
13.3. Starting at the last definition, we find Term defined as a discriminated union
of constant, variable, and structure; we have left out the other term types since they
offer little new.

```
struct variable {
    char *name;
    struct term *term;
};

struct structure {
    char *functor;
    int arity ;
    struct term **components;
};

typedef enum {Is_Constant, Is_Variable, Is_Structure} Term_Type;
typedef struct term {
    Term_Type type;
    union {
        char *constant;                /* Is_Constant */
        struct variable variable ;     /* Is_Variable */
        struct structure structure ;   /* Is_Structure */
    } term;
} Term;
```

Fig. 13.3: Data types for the construction of terms

A constant is represented by a pointer to its value, stored as a string. A variable
is represented simply by a pointer; we also keep its name. For a bound variable the
pointer points to the term to which the variable is bound; an unbound variable is
marked by a zero (null) pointer. A structure is implemented as a record with three
fields, specifying the functor, the number of components N (its **arity**) and a pointer
to an array of N components. Assembly-code implementations may leave out the
pointer and put the array directly into the record, but this is difficult to do in C due
to allocation problems.

Unification (Figure 13.4) immediately distinguishes two situations: unification
involving a variable, and unification of two non-variable terms. To take care of any
bound variables, the routine unify_terms() dereferences both terms; if a term remains
a variable after an attempt at dereferencing, it is unbound. The routine then calls
unify_unbound_variable() (Figure 13.6) or unify_non_variables() (Figure 13.7), depending on whether an (unbound) variable is involved. The routine deref() is shown
in Figure 13.5; it follows the pointer chain until it finds a non-variable or a variable
with a zero pointer.

```
int unify_terms(Term *goal_arg, Term *head_arg) {
    /* Handle any bound variables: */
    Term *goal = deref(goal_arg);
    Term *head = deref(head_arg);

    if (goal->type == Is_Variable || head->type == Is_Variable) {
        return unify_unbound_variable(goal, head);
    }
    else {
        return unify_non_variables(goal, head);
    }
}
```

Fig. 13.4: C code for the unification of two terms

```
Term *deref(Term *t) {
    while (t->type == Is_Variable && t->term.variable.term != 0) {
        t = t->term.variable.term;
    }
    return t;
}
```

Fig. 13.5: The function deref()

The routine unify_unbound_variable() (Figure 13.6) starts by identifying a spe-cial case, the situation that both unbound variables are the same; in this case unifi-cation is trivial *and* must be treated separately since we would otherwise bind the variable to itself. Next the term that is the variable is bound to the other term. It is all right if that second term is again a variable; we will consider that case in more detail in Section 13.3.3. The binding is registered by calling trail_binding(), so it can be undone later during backtracking. Note that it is not necessary to record the old value to be restored; unlike in general backtracking, the value to be restored is always "unbound". Exactly when the corresponding restore operation takes place depends on the clause search mechanism, which will be covered in Section 13.5.

The code for the routine unify_non_variables() (Figure 13.7) is straightforward: if the two terms are of different type the unification fails, otherwise the proper routine for the data type is called. Two constants can be unified when a string comparison on their values succeeds, as shown in Figure 13.8. The routine unify_structures() (Figure 13.9) first checks that the two structures have the same arity, and then calls unify_terms() for each pair of terms. If all this succeeds, the unification of the two structures succeeds; otherwise it fails.

It will be clear that similar routines can be written for lists and other logical data types. For a way to implement multiple unifications, which may, for example, arise when using sets as terms, see Section 13.3.1.

We observe that the only place where a binding is made is in the routine unify_unbound_variable() (Figure 13.6). We will now consider binding of variables and backtracking over it in more detail.

```
int unify_unbound_variable(Term *goal, Term *head) {
    /* Handle identical variables: */
    if (goal == head) {
        /* Unification of identical variables is trivial */
    }
    else {
        /* Bind the unbound variable to the other term: */
        if (head->type == Is_Variable) {
            trail_binding (head);
            head->term.variable.term = goal;
        }
        else {
            trail_binding (goal);
            goal->term.variable.term = head;
        }
    }
    return 1;        /* variable unification always succeeds */
}
```

Fig. 13.6: C code for unification involving at least one unbound variable

```
int unify_non_variables(Term *goal, Term *head) {
    /* Handle terms of different type: */
    if (goal->type != head->type) return 0;

    switch (goal->type) {
    case Is_Constant:            /* both are constants */
        return unify_constants(goal, head);
    case Is_Structure:            /* both are structures */
        return unify_structures (
                &goal->term.structure, &head->term.structure
        );
    }
}
```

Fig. 13.7: C code for the unification of two non-variables

```
int unify_constants(Term *goal, Term *head) {
    return strcmp(goal->term.constant, head->term.constant) == 0;
}
```

Fig. 13.8: C code for the unification of two constants

```
int unify_structures(struct structure *s_goal, struct structure *s_head) {
    int counter;

    if (s_goal->arity != s_head->arity
    || strcmp(s_goal->functor, s_head->functor) != 0
    ) return 0;

    for (counter = 0; counter < s_head->arity; counter++) {
        if (!unify_terms(
            s_goal->components[counter], s_head->components[counter]
        )) return 0;
    }

    return 1;
}
```

Fig. 13.9: C code for the unification of two structures

13.3.3 Unification of two unbound variables

Unification between two variables is unlike anything that happens to variables in imperative languages: the variables are associated with each other in such a way that both are still unbound, and that when one of them is bound to a constant or a third variable, so is the other. The usual implementation of this association is to bind one of the variables to the other, and to dereference any variable before use to find out what it is actually bound to. There is a slight conceptual problem with this, though, since binding an unbound variable B to an unbound variable A results in B still being unbound.

Figure 13.10(b) shows the result of a sequence of four variable–variable bindings: B to A, C to B, D to B, and E to C. Although one would expect this sequence to produce the binding tree shown in Figure 13.10(a), this is not what happens. Binding B to A results in a simple binding of B to A, but binding C to B starts by dereferencing B (and C), only to find that B is actually A. So, in the implementation, C is bound to A rather than to B. The same happens to the bindings D to B, and E to C.

As we have seen above, the binding of an unbound variable V to a term T is implemented as a pointer in V to T. Undoing the binding is easy if we know the position of this pointer: store a zero pointer in it. It is important to note that only the most recent binding can be undone easily this way, for the following reason. Since both variables are dereferenced before binding, the decision of which pointer is stored into which variable can depend on any of the previous bindings. In the above example, the binding of C to B resulted actually in C being bound to A because B was already bound to A. If we were now to attempt to undo the binding of B to A, we would have to unbind C from A and bind it to B, but the data structure in Figure 13.10(b) gives us no possibility to do so. The most recent binding is the only binding that has the property that no other bindings depend on it, so it can be removed without problems. Figure 13.10(a) contains enough information to undo

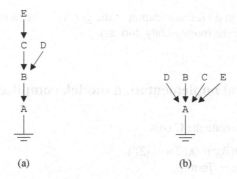

(a)   (b)

Fig. 13.10: Examples of variable–variable bindings

any binding at any moment, but is much less efficient. Most logic languages, including Prolog, undo only the most recent binding and thus allow us to use the more efficient implementation of Figure 13.10(b).

More complicated trees of bindings can also occur. If, for example, C in Figure 13.10(b) is bound to an unbound variable Z, a pointer to Z is written into A, and A is registered for undoing purposes. This results in the tree of Figure 13.11(a). Now, when the binding of C to Z is undone, the pointer in A is zeroed, restoring the situation to that of Figure 13.10(b). Note that neither of these actions affected C, the variable that was bound.

The tree shown in Figure 13.11(b) could result from binding W to A; the tree of which W is part could have been created by binding V to W and then W to X. More in particular, a binding of *any* variable in the tree V,W,X to *any* variable in the tree A-E,Z ends up as a binding from X to Z. Undoing such a binding just zeroes the pointer in X.

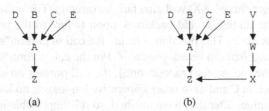

(a)   (b)

Fig. 13.11: Examples of more complicated variable–variable bindings

This concludes our discussion of interpreted unification of logic terms; interpreted search was explained already in Section 13.2. We will now look at compiled search and will return to compiled unification in Section 13.5. Although it is possible to generate code for statically recognizable unification operations, compiled code will still have to do full unification in the general case. So even compiled code will have to include the routine unify_terms().

13.4 The general implementation model, compiled

It is tempting to generate the C code

```
int grandparent(Term *X, Term *Z) {
    Term *Y = new_Term();

    Y->type = Is_Variable;
    return parent(X, &Y) && parent(&Y, Z);
}
```

for the inference rule

```
grandparent(X, Z) :- parent(X, Y), parent(Y, Z).
```

much the same way we generated the C code

```
int expression(void) {
    return term() && rest_expression();
}
```

in Figure 3.5 for the grammar rule

```
expression → term rest_expression
```

from Figure 3.4. That would be wrong, however, as the simple call grandparent("arne", &X) shows. The resulting call parent("arne", &Y) will successfully set Y to "james", but the subsequent call parent("james", Z) will fail; so the query grandparent("arne", &X) will also fail, incorrectly. The reason is that to function properly, the routine should backtrack upon failure to the position where the latest choice was made. This position is *inside* the call of parent("arne", &Y), where another value (sachiko) can be assigned to Y. For the call parent("james", Z) to start in the body of the routine for grandparent(), the call parent("arne", &Y) must have finished, however. In C and most other imperative languages, no local information is preserved for routines after they have finished, so it is impossible in these languages to backtrack to the indicated position inside the call parent("arne", &Y) *after* that call has finished. One imperative language in which this *is* possible, is Icon.

The translation of the grammar rule in Figure 3.5 works only by virtue of the fact that the routine term() cannot succeed in more than one way in deterministic top-down parsing. It can match the input in zero or one way, but not in more than one way, so once it succeeds, there is no reason ever to return to it, since it will not succeed a second time. Consequently it contains no latest choice position. It is this property that is formalized into the LL(1) property in Section 3.4.1.

There is a second suggestion that is implicit in the above example: clauses correspond to routine definitions, and goals correspond to routine calls. More in particular, all clauses with the same relation name correspond to a single routine, which will be called when a goal of that name is to be unified and substituted. If we include the number of terms of the relation in the routine name, the C identifier identification mechanism will already restrict any unification attempt to relations with the same name and the same number of terms. In order to follow this idea, however, we have to come up with a representation of the stack of goal lists.

We will first introduce a technique that allows a routine to "return" more than one value in succession. We will then see that that technique, quite remarkably, also solves the second problem.

13.4.1 List procedures

Functions that return a value do so because the caller wants to do something with the returned value V, say some action $A(V)$. Putting it this way leads to the idea that the function could call $A(V)$ directly, rather than returning V. This idea allows the function to return more than one value: rather than writing

```
int return_two_values(void) {
    return 11 and then return 13;
}
    ...
    A(return_two_values());    /* use the values */
```

which is impossible in C and almost all other imperative languages (except Icon), we can write

```
void two_values(void (*Act_on)(int )) {
    (*Act_on)(11); (*Act_on)(13);
}
    ...
    two_values(A);              /* use the values */
```

which *is* possible in C and any other imperative language that allows routines as parameters. The routine two_values() is called a **list procedure**, since it represents a list, [11, 13]. When it is called with the routine A() as a parameter, it performs the actions A(11) followed by A(13).

List procedures are part of a nameless programming paradigm in which a composite data item is represented as a one-parameter routine that applies its parameter, an **action routine**, to each of the components of the data item.

An example of a list procedure is shown in Figure 13.12. The routine number_pair_list() represents the list of integer pairs [(1, 3), (4, 6), (7, 3)]; the type "list of integer pairs" is already suggested by the type of the routine. Note that the routine specifies the list of numbers only and gives no indication of the action(s) to be performed on them. It is data only.

The routine number_pair_list() can be used to define another routine which finds and prints all pairs in number_pair_list that sum up to a given parameter sum. One way to do so is shown in Figure 13.13. To use the number list routine, an action routine to be applied to each pair must be defined; this is fs_test_sum(), which gets the values of the pair as parameters and does the checking. Neither number_pair_list() nor fs_test_sum() can have additional parameters without damaging the general applicability of number_pair_list() as a list procedure. So the parameter of find_sum(int sum) must be passed by storing it in a global variable, fs_sum. A call find_sum(10) makes its parameter available globally and then lets number_pair_list() call fs_test_sum() for each pair of integers that number_pair_list() represents. Finally, fs_test_sum() tests the required property using the global variable fs_sum. The output is

```
Solution found: 4, 6
Solution found: 7, 3
```

```
void number_pair_list(void (*Action)(int v1, int v2)) {
    (*Action)(1, 3);
    (*Action)(4, 6);
    (*Action)(7, 3);
}
```

Fig. 13.12: An example of a list procedure

```
int fs_sum;

void fs_test_sum(int v1, int v2) {
    if (v1 + v2 == fs_sum) {
        printf ("Solution found: %d, %d\n", v1, v2);
    }
}

void find_sum(int sum) {
    fs_sum = sum;
    number_pair_list(fs_test_sum);
}
```

Fig. 13.13: An application of the list procedure

The code in Figure 13.13 definitely lacks elegance; worse, the approach does not scale. Any serious program using this technique will contain many action routines, each belonging to a find_sum-like routine. If we are not careful, their names will clash and we are already trying to avoid such future name clashes by using the prefix fs_ on the global names. This is not good enough, however, since the global variable fs_sum prevents the routine find_sum() from being used recursively. Suppose in some problem the action routine fs_test_sum() needs to call find_sum(42) to decide whether the pair of integers it is called with constitute a solution. This cannot be programmed conveniently in the style of Figure 13.13, since a call of find_sum(42) would overwrite the value of fs_sum.

A good approach to program structure problems is often to keep the scope of names as small as possible. In our case this means that both fs_test_sum() and fs_sum should be local to find_sum(), as shown in Figure 13.14. This allows each find_sum-like routine to have its own action routine named test_sum() without the danger of name clashes; moreover, and more importantly, the global variable fs_sum has disappeared completely, allowing full recursion. The problem with the code in Figure 13.14 is that it is not ANSI C: it uses a nested routine. Fortunately, one of the most important C implementations, the GNU C compiler, has an extension that allows exactly these nested routines. Also, nested routines are available in a few other imperative languages.

```
void find_sum(int sum) {
    void test_sum(int v1, int v2) {
        if (v1 + v2 == sum) {
            printf ("Solution found: %d, %d\n", v1, v2);
        }
    }

    number_pair_list(test_sum);
}
```

Fig. 13.14: An application of the list procedure, using nested routines

It should be noted that action routines differ from *continuations* as explained in Section 11.3.4. Continuations represent the entire rest of the program, do not return to the caller, and consequently are usually called at the end of a routine. Action routines *do* return, and can be called freely at any place in a routine. They only represent that part of the program that is dependent on the data the action routine is called with—although in some programs that may of course include almost the entire rest of the program.

We now have enough techniques to tackle the compiled implementation of logic languages.

13.4.2 Compiled clause search and unification

We translate each clause for a given relation into a routine, and then create a single list procedure for that relation, which calls each of the clause routines in succession. Goals of the relation are translated as calls to the corresponding list procedure. Both the list procedure and the clause translations get a special action routine parameter in such a call. This action routine is to be called for each successful unification of the goal and one of the clauses for the relation. In fact, the action routine represents the goal list tail used in the interpreter in Section 13.2. We see that using list procedures solves both the problem of routines returning multiple values and the problem of the duplicated goal lists, as promised at the end of the introduction to this section.

For example, the relation parent/2 in Section 13.1 translates into the list procedure shown in Figure 13.15. This routine calls five clause routines to establish the logical OR of the five clauses. The clause routines are local to and nested inside the routine parent_2(). They can therefore access its parameters as non-local variables. And when they have met with success, they will call the action routine goal_list_tail(). One of these clause routines, the one for parent(arne, sachiko), is shown in Figure 13.16; it will be discussed in the next paragraph.

```
void parent_2(Term *goal_arg1, Term *goal_arg2, Action goal_list_tail) {

    ... /* the local routines parent_2_clause_[1–5]() */

    /* OR of all clauses for parent/2 */
    parent_2_clause_1();    /* parent(arne, james). */
    parent_2_clause_2();    /* parent(arne, sachiko). */
    parent_2_clause_3();    /* parent(koos, rivka). */
    parent_2_clause_4();    /* parent(sachiko, rivka). */
    parent_2_clause_5();    /* parent( truitje , koos). */

}
```

Fig. 13.15: Translation of the relation parent/2

Suppose we have a query ?– parent(arne, X), resulting in the initial goal list parent(arne, X), «("X", X) as shown in the explanation of the interpreter. To expand the first goal parent(arne, X) in this goal list, we issue the call parent_2("arne", X, goal_list_tail), in which the action routine goal_list_tail() corresponds to the goal list tail «("X", X). Since parent_2() will call each clause for parent/2 and since each clause will call goal_list_tail() whenever it succeeds, this results effectively in the same actions as the interpreter performs on the stack of goal lists

```
[parent(arne,X)  ?= parent(arne,james)],
[parent(arne,X)  ?= parent(arne,sachiko)],
[parent(arne,X)  ?= parent(koos,rivka)],           << ("X",X)
[parent(arne,X)  ?= parent(sachiko,rivka)],
[parent(arne,X)  ?= parent(truitje,koos)],
```

We see that the action routine provides a very convenient and effective way to avoid copying the goal list tail.

The code generated for parent_2_clause_2() and shown in Figure 13.16 goes through the same motions as the interpreter. It is best read from the bottom up-

```
/* translation of 'parent(arne, sachiko).' */
void parent_2_clause_2(void) {

    /* translation of 'arne, sachiko).' */
    void parent_2_clause_2_arg_1(void) {

        /* translation of 'sachiko).' */
        void parent_2_clause_2_arg_2(void) {

            /* translation of '.' */
            void parent_2_clause_2_body(void) {
                goal_list_tail ();
            }

            /* translation of head term 'sachiko)' */
            unify_terms(goal_arg2, put_constant("sachiko"),
                        parent_2_clause_2_body
            );
        }

        /* translation of head term 'arne, ' */
        unify_terms(goal_arg1, put_constant("arne"),
                    parent_2_clause_2_arg_2
        );
    }

    /* translation of 'parent(' */
    parent_2_clause_2_arg_1();
}
```

Fig. 13.16: Generated clause routine for parent(arne, sachiko)

wards, due to the "declaration before use" rule of C. Parent_2_clause_2() calls the nested routine parent_2_clause_2_arg_1() for the first argument. That routine attempts to unify the first argument goal_arg1 with its own first head argument arne by calling unify_terms(); the data structure for the head argument was created by calling put_constant(). In addition to the arguments, parent_2_clause_2_arg_1() also passes the routine parent_2_clause_2_arg_2() as the action routine to unify_terms(), in the understanding that unify_terms() will call its action routine when the unification has succeeded.

Reading upwards, we see that parent_2_clause_2_arg_2(), nested within parent_2_clause_2_arg_1(), tries to unify the second argument goal_arg2 with its own head argument sachiko in the same manner. The only difference is that the action routine that is passed on is now parent_2_clause_2_body() rather than parent_2_clause_2_arg_3(), since the closing parenthesis after the head term sachiko signifies that the head of the clause is finished. The code for parent_2_clause_2_body() is very simple: since there is no body with goals that have to be satisfied, it just calls goal_list_tail().

We see that there is a close relationship between the Prolog code and the C code: a comma as a separator after a head term translates into an action routine name ending in _arg_*N*, a closing parenthesis into an action routine name ending in _body, and a dot into a call of goal_list_tail().

The code for the version of unify_terms() that uses an action routine is very similar to that shown in Figures 13.4, 13.6, 13.7, and 13.9. The main difference is that where these routines do a return 1 to show that they succeed, the version in this section calls the action routine goal_list_tail(), passed to it as its third parameter, and proceeds to find more matches. The only interesting point is that since the searching routines do not return until all searching involving their results has finished, they can undo the variable bindings themselves on the way back and there is no need to record the bindings by calling trail_binding(). The code for unify_unbound_variable() (Figure 13.17) shows how first the variable is bound by setting variable.term, then the search is continued with this binding, and finally the binding is undone by setting variable.term to zero.

```
void unify_unbound_variable(Term *goal_arg, Term *head_arg, Action goal_list_tail) {
    if (goal_arg == head_arg) {
        /* Unification of identical variables succeeds trivially */
        goal_list_tail ();
    }
    else {
        /* Bind the unbound variable to the other term: */
        if (head_arg->type == Is_Variable) {
            head_arg->term.variable.term = goal_arg;
            goal_list_tail ();
            head_arg->term.variable.term = 0;
        }
        else {
            goal_arg->term.variable.term = head_arg;
            goal_list_tail ();
            goal_arg->term.variable.term = 0;
        }
    }
}
```

Fig. 13.17: C code for full backtracking variable unification

Code that could be generated for the query ?– parent(arne, X) is shown in Figure 13.18. Actually, since queries are entered dynamically, if such code is generated, it will have to be compiled on the fly. It is, however, more likely that the input processing section of the compiled program performs the top level of the query interpretively. Section 13.4.5 suggests how this can be done efficiently.

The displaying entry in the goal list «("X", X) is represented by the nested routine display_X(). It will be passed on through several calls of parent_2...() and unify_terms(), until at some point all requirements for the query are fulfilled and it is called; the search then continues, until all possibilities have been tested. The output of the compiled query is indeed

```
void query(void) {
    Term *X = put_variable("X");

    void display_X(void) {
        print_term(X);
        printf ("\n");
    }

    parent_2(put_constant("arne"), X, display_X);
}
```

Fig. 13.18: Possible generated code for the query ?– parent(arne, X)

```
X = james
X = sachiko
```

As an aside, we note that much of the visual complexity of the code of Figure 13.16 is due to the absence of routine denotations in C. A **routine denotation** is a notation for the formal parameters and the body of a routine; such a notation, known as a *lambda expression* in functional languages, acts as a literal or constant and is available in some imperative languages as well, for example in Algol 68 and Icon. For lack of such a device in C we are forced to name all intermediate routines, which could just as well remain anonymous. For example, Figure 13.19 shows the Algol 68 code for parent_2_clause_2(), in which

```
procedure void parent 2 clause 2 = (
    unify terms(goal arg1, put constant("arne"),
        void: unify terms(goal arg2, put constant("sachiko"),
            void: goal list tail
        )
    )
);
```

Fig. 13.19: Algol 68 code for parent_2_clause_2()

```
void: unify terms(goal arg2, put constant("sachiko"),
    void: goal list tail
)
```

is a routine denotation, and so is "**void**: goal list tail". These routine denotations are passed as the third parameter to two different calls of the procedure "unify terms".

The clause parent(arne, sachiko) has no body, so the code in Figure 13.16 shows how to do head matching only; there are no goal calls. We will therefore now look at the translation of grandparent— see Figure 13.20. This figure shows all the code for the translation of the clauses for grandparent/2. The structure is very similar to that of Figure 13.16. Starting from the bottom, we find a list of calls to all clauses for grandparent/2, of which there is only one: grandparent(X, Z) :- parent(X, Y), parent(Y, Z). The nested routine grandparent_2_clause_1() unifies the two terms X and Z in the usual way and passes the action routine grandparent_2_clause_1_body() to the last unification, rather than goal_list_tail(), since the clause has a body. The translation of the body follows the same pattern, adapted to goals: rather than calls to unify_terms(), calls to the routines representing the goals are dispatched; again the last call passes on the action routine goal_list_tail().

Code for the head variables X and Z and for the free variable Y is generated in the appropriate routines, using the library routine put_variable(). The routine put_variable() allocates space for a variable and initializes that space with an unbound variable of the given name. The routine names put_variable, and put_constant used above, derive from the corresponding WAM instructions.

The close match between Prolog code and translation is even more visible here than in Figure 13.16: each next nested routine represents the translation of a smaller piece of the clause, and the one call in it handles the difference between the two nested routines, as the comments show.

The above paints an elegant and idealized picture of compiled Prolog code; real-world compiled Prolog code is much more hairy, due to optimizations. The code segment shown in this section suggests already several optimizations, for example the in-line substitution of several routines that are called only once, but much stronger optimizations are possible. We will now look at one specific optimization.

13.4.3 Optimized clause selection in the WAM

The code for the relation parent/2 shown in Figure 13.15 calls the routines for all five clauses for parent/2, regardless of the values of the arguments goal_arg1 and goal_arg2. If we do a little analysis, however, we can often see that a certain call is doomed to fail, or even that the entire call of parent_2() will never succeed. For example, if one of the parameters is not a constant or an unbound variable, the call will never succeed. Also, if one of the parameters *is* a constant, we can compare it to the corresponding constant in each clause in turn and if they do not match it is futile to call the routine for that clause. So two optimizations are possible here, one on the type of an argument, and, if that argument is a constant, another on the value of that constant. The WAM supports these optimizations for the first argument only, and we will see now how this is done.

Optimized clause selection proceeds in two steps. First, the type of the first argument is used to jump to the label of the code that handles terms of that type for the given routine; this multiway jump is performed by the WAM instruction switch_on_term. Second, for constants and structures, there are further switch instructions to lead the flow of control to specific pieces of code that are appropriate for the specific first argument.

The use of the switch_on_term instruction can be seen in Figure 13.21. The header and code for the clauses themselves are the same as in Figure 13.15, but the OR list of calls to the routines parent_2_clause_[1–5]() is replaced by a call on

```
void grandparent_2(Term *goal_arg1, Term *goal_arg2, Action goal_list_tail) {
   /* translation of 'grandparent(X,Z):−parent(X,Y),parent(Y,Z).' */
   void grandparent_2_clause_1(void) {

      /* translation of 'X,Z):−parent(X,Y),parent(Y,Z).' */
      void grandparent_2_clause_1_arg_1(void) {
      Term *X = put_variable("X");

         /* translation of 'Z):−parent(X,Y),parent(Y,Z).' */
         void grandparent_2_clause_1_arg_2(void) {
         Term *Z = put_variable("Z");

            /* translation of body 'parent(X,Y),parent(Y,Z).' */
            void grandparent_2_clause_1_body(void) {
            Term *Y = put_variable("Y");

               /* translation of 'parent(Y,Z).' */
               void grandparent_2_clause_1_goal_2(void) {
                  parent_2(Y, goal_arg2, goal_list_tail );
               }

               /* translation of 'parent(X,Y),' */
               parent_2(goal_arg1, Y, grandparent_2_clause_1_goal_2);
            }

            /* translation of head term 'Z):−' */
            unify_terms(goal_arg2, Z, grandparent_2_clause_1_body);
         }

         /* translation of head term 'X,' */
         unify_terms(goal_arg1, X, grandparent_2_clause_1_arg_2);
      }

      /* translation of 'grandparent(' */
      grandparent_2_clause_1_arg_1();
   }

   /* OR of all clauses for grandparent/2 */
   grandparent_2_clause_1();
}
```

Fig. 13.20: Clause routine generated for grandparent/2

switch_on_term. This call dereferences the first argument goal_arg1, retrieves its type and jumps to one of the labels L_Variable, L_Constant, or L_Structure. The corresponding WAM instruction receives these labels as parameters; it has another label parameter for lists, but since we don't do lists, we have omitted it here. Code segments labeled by L_Variable, L_Constant, and L_Structure follow; they are discussed in the following paragraphs. Note that first arguments for which the flow of control is led to L_Variable correspond to *unbound variables*, due to the dereferencing. The position at the end of the routine is labeled by L_fail; actually a jump to this label means that there are no more possibilities rather than that the routine failed, but the WAM uses the term "fail" in these cases and so will we.

```
void parent_2(Term *goal_arg1, Term *goal_arg2, Action goal_list_tail) {

    ...  /* the local routines parent_2_clause_[1−5]() */

    /* switch_on_term(L_Variable, L_Constant, L_Structure) */
    switch (deref(goal_arg1)−>type) {
    case Is_Variable:   goto L_Variable;
    case Is_Constant:   goto L_Constant;
    case Is_Structure:  goto L_Structure;
    }

L_fail :;
}
```

Fig. 13.21: Optimized translation of the relation parent/2

If the first argument is an unbound variable, this variable can certainly be bound to the first argument of the head in each clause, so the code labeled by L_Variable just calls all clause routines in succession, just as the unoptimized routine parent_2() did; see Figure 13.22.

```
L_Variable:
    /* OR of all clauses for parent/2 */
    parent_2_clause_1();   /* parent(arne, james). */
    parent_2_clause_2();   /* parent(arne, sachiko). */
    parent_2_clause_3();   /* parent(koos, rivka ). */
    parent_2_clause_4();   /* parent(sachiko, rivka ). */
    parent_2_clause_5();   /* parent( truitje , koos). */
    goto L_fail ;
```

Fig. 13.22: Code generated for the label L_Variable

The code labeled by L_Constant is shown in Figure 13.23. It uses the WAM instruction switch_on_constant to implement the second optimization and direct the flow of control to the proper code segment for the constant. For the optimization to be effective, checking the argument before calling must be much faster than calling the routine and doing the checking in the traditional way. To this end all constants in the program are stored in a *hash table*, and a function entry(const char *constant, int table_size, const char *table[ ]) is made available that returns the entry index for constant in table[ ]; these entry indexes are constants, available to the program in some form, for example as a set of identifiers ENTRY_*C* for each constant *C* in the program. The table_size must be a power of two in the WAM, and we conform to that requirement here.

```
L_Constant:
    /* switch_on_constant(8, constant_table) */
    switch (
        entry(deref(goal_arg1)->term.constant, 8, constant_table)
    ) {
    case ENTRY_arne: goto L_Constant_arne;
    case ENTRY_koos: goto L_Constant_koos;
    case ENTRY_sachiko: goto L_Constant_sachiko;
    case ENTRY_truitje: goto L_Constant_truitje;
    }
    goto L_fail;

L_Constant_arne:
    parent_2_clause_1();    /* parent(arne, james). */
    parent_2_clause_2();    /* parent(arne, sachiko). */
    goto L_fail;

L_Constant_koos:
    parent_2_clause_3();    /* parent(koos, rivka). */
    goto L_fail;

L_Constant_sachiko:
    parent_2_clause_4();    /* parent(sachiko, rivka). */
    goto L_fail;

L_Constant_truitje:
    parent_2_clause_5();    /* parent( truitje , koos). */
    goto L_fail;
```

Fig. 13.23: Code generated for the labels L_Constant_...

```
L_Structure:
    goto L_fail;
```

Fig. 13.24: Code generated for the label L_Structure

The compiler, having seen all clauses for parent/2, knows that all of them have constants for their first arguments and it knows what these constants are. So a switch statement over just these values can be constructed. The index of the constant in the hash table constant_table[ ] is retrieved and used to jump to the proper code. If the constant is not in the switch statement, there is no possibility that parent_2() succeeds and a jump to L_fail is taken. Although there are only 6 constants in the program, the hash table constant_table[ ] has size 8, to conform to the WAM requirements.

Each label of the form L_Constant_C labels a list of calls to clause routines for those clauses that have C as their first argument. That list is one or more calls long, as we can see in Figure 13.23. There is no need for the labels L_Constant_james or L_Constant_rivka; they do not occur in the switch statement, since no clause for parent/2 has james or rivka as its first argument. Each list of calls ends in goto L_fail, since at that point all possibilities have been exhausted.

Since there are no clauses for parent/2 with a structure as first argument, the label L_Structure directly leads to L_fail (Figure 13.24). This jump to a jump could have been cut short by having

> **case** Is_Structure: **goto** L_fail ;

in Figure 13.21.

The first argument switch optimization for clause selection is quite effective, although the effect of course depends on the program code. In our example, it reduces the number of calls to the clause routines parent_2_clause_[1–5]() from 105 to 24, for the query ?– parent(arne, X).

The WAM has several other instructions for optimizing clause selection; these are primarily concerned with avoiding administrative and routine call overhead. There is a set of three clause routine call instructions, try_me_else, retry_me_else, and trust_me_else, which are used for the first call, the middle calls, and the last call, respectively, of the clause routines in OR lists, both in top-level routines (Figure 13.15) and after L_Variable and L_Constant_... labels. The first instruction incorporates the routine call and entry administration of parent_2(), the last the routine exit administration. There is a corresponding set try, retry, and trust, which are used for call lists after L_Constant and L_Structure labels. These instructions call simplified versions of the clause routines that assume that the first argument already matches completely (L_Constant) or partially (L_Structure). These combined optimizations complicate the WAM considerably, but do increase its efficiency.

13.4.4 Implementing the "cut" mechanism

Prolog allows the search space to be reduced explicitly by using "cuts". The **cut operator** is an argumentless goal that always succeeds; it is written as an exclamation mark: !. Its property is that if it succeeds in a clause C for a relation R, it commits the relation R to the search space described by the part after the cut in clause C; the rest of the search space of C and the search spaces of the other clauses for R are ignored.

In other words, once the search has passed a cut in a clause for a relation R, then backtracking over that cut causes further processing of the goal R to be skipped.

The cut is surprisingly simple to implement: after having called the action routine for the part of the clause after the cut, jump to the end of the routine for the relation. The technique is shown in Figure 13.25, which contains the translation of the clause

first_grandparent(X, Z) :− parent(X, Y), !, parent(Y, Z).

In this figure, the relation name first_grandparent was abbreviated to first_gp to avoid overly long lines. The clause tries to say that X is a first-grandparent of Z if Z is a child of the first child of X, assuming that the relation parent/2 mentions the children in chronological order. It is actually an unfortunate way of expressing that idea, since it will not solve queries like first_grandparent(X, rivka) except by accident, and only serves here as an example of a clause with a cut.

The translation of the cut is in the middle of the text, and consists of a call to the action routine first_gp_2_clause_1_goal_3() representing the rest of the clause, followed by a jump to L_cut. This label is positioned entirely at the end of the routine for first_gp_2, after the label L_fail. The reason for having two separate labels will become evident in the next section. Normal backtracking would backtrack into first_gp_2_clause_1_body() when first_gp_2_clause_1_goal_3() is finished, to find other bindings for goal_arg1 and Y, but the jump to L_cut cuts this attempt short, in accordance with the semantics of the cut mechanism. The label L_cut has been declared at the beginning of its scope, as is required for non-local labels in GNU C.

13.4.5 Implementing the predicates *assert* and *retract*

Some logic languages (in particular Prolog) feature the possibility to add and remove clauses during program execution, using extra-logical predicates, predicates that do not express relations. The extra-logical predicate assert(Clause) dynamically adds the term Clause as a clause to the program. There are no restrictions on the relation expressed by this clause: it may be a program-defined relation, already occurring statically in the program, it may be a relation that is known only from assert calls, or it may be a brand new one. Conversely, the extra-logical predicate retract(Clause) dynamically removes the clause Clause from the program. Again, there are no restrictions on the kinds of clauses that may be retracted: in particular it is permitted to retract program-defined clauses. The question is how to incorporate such additions and removals to compiled code and how to activate the new clauses, preferably without compromising the efficiency of the program-defined clauses.

A brute-force solution immediately suggests itself: upon adding or removing a clause for the relation R, recompile and relink the routine for R, and update the table of constants. Apart from requiring a pretty heavy machinery, this may not be cost-effective: some Prolog programs start by asserting large numbers of facts, each of which would cause a recompilation. We will therefore discuss a more hybrid

```
void first_gp_2(Term *goal_arg1, Term *goal_arg2, Action goal_list_tail) {
__label__ L_cut;  /* label declarations required by GNU C for non-local jump */

  /* translation of 'first_gp(X,Z):-parent(X,Y),!,parent(Y,Z).' */
  void first_gp_2_clause_1(void) {
    /* translation of 'X,Z):-parent(X,Y),!,parent(Y,Z).' */
    void first_gp_2_clause_1_arg_1(void) {
    Term *X = put_variable("X");
    /* translation of 'Z):-parent(X,Y),!,parent(Y,Z).' */
      void first_gp_2_clause_1_arg_2(void) {
      Term *Z = put_variable("Z");
      /* translation of body 'parent(X,Y),!,parent(Y,Z).' */
      void first_gp_2_clause_1_body(void) {
        Term *Y = put_variable("Y");
        /* translation of '!, parent(Y,Z).' */
        void first_gp_2_clause_1_goal_2(void) {
          /* translation of 'parent(Y,Z).' */
          void first_gp_2_clause_1_goal_3(void) {
            parent_2(Y, goal_arg2, goal_list_tail );
          }
          /* translation of '!,' */
          first_gp_2_clause_1_goal_3();

          goto L_cut;
        }
        /* translation of 'parent(X,Y),' */
        parent_2(goal_arg1, Y, first_gp_2_clause_1_goal_2);
      }
      /* translation of head term 'Z):-' */
      unify_terms(goal_arg2, Z, first_gp_2_clause_1_body);
    }
    /* translation of head term 'X,' */
    unify_terms(goal_arg1, X, first_gp_2_clause_1_arg_2);
  }
  /* translation of 'first_gp(' */
  first_gp_2_clause_1_arg_1();
}
/* OR of all clauses for first_gp/2 */
first_gp_2_clause_1();

L_fail :;
L_cut:;
}
```

Fig. 13.25: Clause routine generated for first_grandparent/2

technique here, in which we switch to an interpreter for the asserted clause but switch back to compiled routines as soon as possible.

In this approach, we keep the asserted clauses in symbolic form, possibly augmented with some mechanism that allows fast access to the asserted clauses for a given relation. This makes the assert and retract operations themselves simple, and the remaining question is how to activate the newly added clauses. We first consider the case that the asserted clause refers to a program-defined relation. We also assume that asserted clauses are to be activated *after* the program-defined clauses; this corresponds to assertz() in Prolog. The case for asserta(), which adds clauses to be activated *before* the program-defined ones, is similar.

To absorb the asserted clause into the search process, we return to the routine generated for parent/2 (Figure 13.15) and add the code shown in Figure 13.26 to call the interpreter. This code checks a global counter to see if any asserted clauses for parent/2 are present at this moment that should be activated after the program-defined clauses; such global counters must be maintained for all relations by assert and retract, and serve to avoid calling the interpreter unnecessarily. If there is at least one asserted clause for parent/2 to be activated now, the name of the relation and the two arguments are stacked in inverse order on the interpreter stack; the name of the relation must be stacked last since it is the first piece of information the interpreter will be interested in. Then the interpreter is called, with the original action routine of parent_2() as its only parameter. The interpreter calls this action routine each time it finds a way to satisfy the goal just stored on the interpreter stack; each such call implies a return to compiled code. Note that the values "parent/2", goal_arg1, goal_arg2, and goal_list_tail together represent the goal list stack introduced in the interpreter in Section 13.2. The process is depicted in Figure 13.27.

We now see the reason for having two separate labels L_fail and L_cut: a jump to L_fail signals exhaustion of the program-defined clauses; a jump to L_cut signals abandoning all further clauses for the relation, including those added by assertz().

The code in Figure 13.26 handles the assertion of clauses and the retraction of clauses that have been asserted. The retraction of program-defined clauses is implemented by preceding each call of a clause routine *C* by a test using a global Boolean retracted_C. Many Prolog implementers decide that this causes so much useless overhead that the implementation does not allow program-defined clauses to be retracted unless they are specifically declared as retractable.

The goal lists in asserted clauses may contain goals with relations that occur only in other asserted clauses, in which case the processing of these goals has to be left to the interpreter, but they may also contain goals with program-defined relations. Since a routine has been compiled for such a goal, it is profitable to call that routine to process the goal, rather than leaving it entirely to the interpreter. This requires the run-time conversion of the name of a routine to a call to that routine. To effect this, we use the same entry() routine used in selecting code for unifying a constant shown in Figure 13.23, and apply it here to the name of the relation and a fixed table of names of program-defined clauses. The dispatch routine do_relation() is shown in Figure 13.28 and uses the name of the relation and the fixed table of relation names to select a code sequence for that relation. The code sequence for parent/2

```
void parent_2(Term *goal_arg1, Term *goal_arg2, Action goal_list_tail) {

    ... /* the local routines parent_2_clause_[1−5]() */

    /* guarded OR of all clauses for parent/2 */
    if (!retracted_parent_2_clause_1)
        parent_2_clause_1();   /* parent(arne, james). */
    if (!retracted_parent_2_clause_2)
        parent_2_clause_2();   /* parent(arne, sachiko). */
    if (!retracted_parent_2_clause_3)
        parent_2_clause_3();   /* parent(koos, rivka). */
    if (!retracted_parent_2_clause_4)
        parent_2_clause_4();   /* parent(sachiko, rivka). */
    if (!retracted_parent_2_clause_5)
        parent_2_clause_5();   /* parent( truitje , koos). */
L_fail :
    if (number_of_clauses_added_at_end_for_parent_2 > 0) {
        stack_argument(goal_arg2);
        stack_argument(goal_arg1);
        stack_argument(put_constant("parent/2"));
        interpret ( goal_list_tail );
    }
L_cut:;

}
```

Fig. 13.26: Translation of **parent/2** with code for controlling asserted and retracted clauses

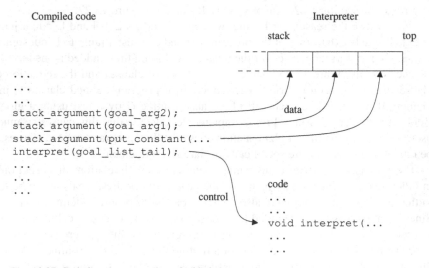

Fig. 13.27: Switch to interpretation of added clauses

unstacks the goal arguments from the interpreter stack and passes them and an action routine to the compiled routine parent_2(); the other code sequences are similar. If the requested relation is not program-defined, the flow of control is directed to an interpreter routine interpret_asserted_relation(), which searches relations that stem from asserted clauses only.

```
void do_relation(const char *relation, Action goal_list_tail ) {
    switch (entry( relation , N, relation_table )) {
    case ENTRY_...:
    case ENTRY_parent_2:
        goal_arg1 = unstack_argument();
        goal_arg2 = unstack_argument();
        parent_2(goal_arg1, goal_arg2, goal_list_tail );
        break;
    case ENTRY_grandparent_2:
        ...
        break;
    case ENTRY_...:
        ...
    default:
        interpret_asserted_relation ( relation ,   goal_list_tail );
        break;
    }
}
```

Fig. 13.28: Dispatch routine for goals in asserted clauses

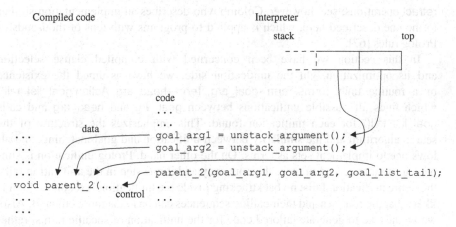

Fig. 13.29: Switch to execution of compiled clauses

The action routine passed to do_relation() is an internal routine in the interpreter. It processes the goals still left on the interpreter stack and then calls the action routine originally passed to the interpreter in Figure 13.26. If we assume that the goal list stack is maintained explicitly in the interpreter, the relation name to be passed to do_relation() is found on the top of the stack and do_relation() is called as follows:

    do_relation(unstack_argument()−>name, internal_goal_list_tail);

The process is depicted in Figure 13.29.
    The unstack_argument() call

    unstack_argument()−>name

in the above call of do_relation() and those in

    goal_arg1 = unstack_argument();
    goal_arg2 = unstack_argument();

in Figure 13.28 unstack a goal, just as the inverse sequence in Figure 13.26 stacked a goal. Note, however, that this is not the same goal. The code in Figure 13.26 is located in the compiled Prolog program and stacks a goal from the compiled program, to be tried with one or more asserted clauses by the interpreter; the code in Figure 13.28 is located in the interpreter and unstacks a goal from an asserted and interpreted clause, to be tried either with a compiled routine if one is available, or with asserted clauses.

The interplay between interpreter and compiled code allows the **assert** and **retract** operations to be implemented reasonably efficiently. Maintaining this mechanism is not such an imposition as it would seem to be, since much of it is needed anyway to process run-time queries. The behavior of the **assert** and **retract** operations with respect to backtracking is examined in Exercise 13.12.

There is very little published material on the implementation of the **assert** and **retract** operations; see, however, Colomb who describes an implementation similar to the one described here, which is applied to programs with tens of thousands of Prolog rules [67].

In this section we have been concerned with compiled clause selection and its optimization. On the unification side, we have assumed the existence of a routine unify_terms(Term *goal_arg, Term *head_arg, Action goal_list_tail), which finds all possible unifications between goal_arg and head_arg and calls goal_list_tail() for each unification found. This emphasizes the structure of the search algorithm and the similarity between unification and goal matching, and allows one to implement sets as terms. On the other hand, Prolog unification is simpler: it cannot succeed in more than one way and if one step in the unification fails, the entire unification fails; no backtracking inside the unification is required. So it is likely that the routines and their calling sequences can be made more efficient. Also, we would like to generate tailored code for the unification of specific terms, rather than call the general library routine. We will now see how to do this.

13.5 Compiled code for unification

Since unification in Prolog either succeeds or fails, we can use the implementation described in Section 13.3.2, which does exactly that. This requires a little rewriting of the parent/2 and grandparent/2 routines. The basic structure of these routines is the same as shown in Figures 13.15 and 13.20; they still have an action routine as their last parameter, and they still act as OR list procedures. But the clause routines require some modification; the one for parent(arne, sachiko) is shown in Figure 13.30. The entire code for the head unification has been replaced by a simple set of calls to the Boolean function unify_terms(), which receives no action routine. Each tests one unification, and if they all succeed we can go on and call the function for the body parent_2_clause_2_body(), which is again identical to that in Figure 13.16.

```
/* translation of 'parent(arne, sachiko).' */
void parent_2_clause_2(void) {
    Trail_Mark trail_mark;

    set_trail_mark(&trail_mark);
    /* translation of '(arne, sachiko)' */
    if (unify_terms(goal_arg1, put_constant("arne"))
    && unify_terms(goal_arg2, put_constant("sachiko"))
    ) {
        /* translation of '.' */
        void parent_2_clause_2_body(void) {
            goal_list_tail ();
        }

        /* translation of '.' */
        parent_2_clause_2_body();
    }
    restore_bindings_until_trail_mark(&trail_mark);
}
```

Fig. 13.30: Clause routine with flat unification for parent(arne, sachiko)

The code in Figure 13.30 shows the use of the **trail**. The trail is one of the stacks of the WAM; it is used to store pointers to variables that have been bound. Each clause routine R that calls unify_terms() declares a stack marker, and records in it the present stack level by calling set_trail_mark(). Each time unify_terms() or one of its subroutines binds a variable, it stacks its address by calling trail_binding() (Figure 13.6). At the end, when all possibilities for this binding have been examined, the routine R unstacks all addresses of variables from the stack until the original level is reached again, by calling restore_bindings_until_trail_mark() on the same stack marker. Note that it is not possible to know statically how many variables have been bound: the calls of unify_terms() may have failed immediately, have failed just before the end or may have succeeded; so a dynamic record must be kept.

Now that we have "flattened" the unification we can take the next step towards compiled unification. Since the heads of the clauses are known from the program, we often find ourselves generating calls of unify_terms() with constant parameters; examples are

```
unify_terms(goal_arg1, put_constant("arne"))
```

from Figure 13.30, and

```
unify_terms(goal_arg,
    put_struct_2(
        "times",
        put_constant("2"),
        put_variable("X")
    )
)
```

used to unify the head structure times(2, X) and the goal argument. In such cases it seems unnecessary to invoke the heavy interpretive unification mechanism of unify_terms(), and the code looks the more clumsy because it creates complicated data structures just for the purpose of comparing them. One could try to remove that inefficiency by creating all fixed data structures at compile time and passing them to unify_terms(), but still the full interpretive unification mechanism would be employed. Also, this technique would fail for structures with constants and variables inside.

13.5.1 Unification instructions in the WAM

Both inefficiencies can be removed simultaneously by directly incorporating the information about the head arguments in the compiled unification code. This leads to the unification "instructions" UNIFY_CONSTANT, UNIFY_VARIABLE, UNIFY_STRUCTURE, and several others. As with any interface, there are two sides to these instructions: how they are used and how they are implemented. Their use is demonstrated in Figure 13.31, which features two applications of UNIFY_CONSTANT. These applications are to be seen as macros, and for that reason they are written in capital letters, following C convention. They expand into code that falls through if the unification succeeds —and then it establishes the proper bindings—and jumps to the label L_fail when it does not. Note that the UNIFY_... instructions are code segments rather than routines, in that the flow of control can leave them by falling through and jumping out. This jump-on-failure fits in with the WAM instructions for clause selection, as seen, for example, in Figure 13.23.

As to the implementation of these instructions, we can of course design the code that implements them by hand, but it is more instructive, and perhaps also safer, to derive them by partially evaluating the corresponding call to unify_terms(). The code to be substituted for UNIFY_CONSTANT (goal_arg, head_text) is shown in

```
/* optimized translation of 'parent(arne, sachiko).' */
void parent_2_clause_2(void) {
    Trail_Mark trail_mark;

    set_trail_mark(&trail_mark);
    /* optimized translation of '(arne, sachiko)' */
    UNIFY_CONSTANT(goal_arg1, "arne");        /* macro */
    UNIFY_CONSTANT(goal_arg2, "sachiko");     /* macro */

    /* optimized translation of '.' */
    goal_list_tail ();
L_fail :
    restore_bindings_until_trail_mark(&trail_mark);
}
```

Fig. 13.31: Clause routine with compiled unification for parent(arne, sachiko)

Figure 13.32; g is a temporary variable of type Term ∗, which loses its meaning at the end of the code segment. The code was derived semi-automatically by partially evaluating the call

    unify_terms(goal_arg, put_constant(head_text))

Since partial evaluators for C are still experimental and not widely available, this particular partial evaluation was performed by hand, as demonstrated in the next section.

```
g = deref(goal_arg);
if (g->type == Is_Variable) {
    trail_binding (g);
    g->term.variable.term = put_constant(head_text);
}
else {
    if (g->type != Is_Constant) goto L_fail;
    if (strcmp(g->term.constant, head_text) != 0) goto L_fail;
}
```

Fig. 13.32: The unification instruction UNIFY_CONSTANT

The code for UNIFY_CONSTANT (Figure 13.32) holds no surprises (fortunately!). On the one hand, it is similar to what a programmer might have written for the task; on the other hand one recognizes fragments from the general unification code from Figures 13.6 and 13.7. A similar process produces the code for UNIFY_VARIABLE (Figure 13.33). It differs somewhat because the head variable may already be bound.

```
v = deref(head_var);          /* head_var may already be bound */
g = deref(goal_arg);
if (v->type == Is_Variable) {
    if (g != v) {
        trail_binding (v);
        v->term.variable.term = g;
    }
} else {
    /* no further compilation possible; call the interpreter */
    if (!unify_terms(g, v)) goto L_fail;
}
```

Fig. 13.33: The unification instruction UNIFY_VARIABLE

13.5.2 Deriving a unification instruction by manual partial evaluation

As said above, the code for the unification instruction UNIFY_CONSTANT from Figure 13.32 was derived by manual partial evaluation. We will now show how such optimized instructions can be derived with only minor effort. In the case of UNIFY_CONSTANT, the derivation basically consists of in-lining the subroutines of unify_terms(), replacing the parameter head_arg by put_constant(head_text) and then repeatedly applying simplifications and deleting unreachable code. The process required the following six editing operations of an almost mechanical nature.

1. *Code in-lining.* Start from unify_terms() (Figure 13.4) and in-line unify_non_variables() (Figure 13.7) and unify_unbound_variable() (Figure 13.6). This is easy to do since they all have the same parameters; just inserting the code suffices. The test for constants is already in-line; we do not in-line unify_structures() since we foresee we will not need it. The result is still correct running C; see Figure 13.34.
2. *Specialization to "constant" as head.* Remove the useless head = deref(head_arg) statement, since head_arg is not a variable. Change the heading to int unify_constant(Term *goal, char *head_text) and replace head by (put_constant(head_text)) throughout the body. See Figure 13.35.
3. *Property substitution.* We replace (put_constant(head_text))->type by Is_Constant, (put_constant(head_text))->term.constant by head_text, and then (put_constant(head_text))->term.* by ERRONEOUS. The code no longer compiles, due to the presence of ERRONEOUS. See Figure 13.36.
4. *Constant propagation.* We replace Is_Constant == Is_Variable by 0, goal == (put_constant(head_text)) by 0 since goal->type is Is_Variable in that context, and goal->type by Is_Constant in the switch statement, since that is its value in that context. The code again does not compile, due to the presence of ERRONEOUS. See Figure 13.37.
5. *Dead code elimination.* Remove the ineffective operations (|| 0) and the unreachable code (if (0)) The code compiles again since all occurrences of ERRONEOUS

```
int unify_terms(Term *goal_arg, Term *head_arg) {
    /* Handle any bound variables: */
    Term *goal = deref(goal_arg);
    Term *head = deref(head_arg);

    if (goal->type == Is_Variable || head->type == Is_Variable) {
        /* Handle identical variables: */
        if (goal == head) return 1;

        /* Bind the unbound variable to the other term: */
        if (head->type == Is_Variable) {
            trail_binding (head);
            head->term.variable.term = goal;
        }
        else {
            trail_binding (goal);
            goal->term.variable.term = head;
        }
        return 1;                    /* always succeeds */
    }
    else {
        /* Handle terms of different type: */
        if (goal->type != head->type) return 0;

        switch (goal->type) {
        case Is_Constant:              /* both are constants */
            return strcmp(goal->term.constant, head->term.constant) == 0;
        case Is_Structure:             /* both are structures */
            return unify_structures (
                &goal->term.structure, &head->term.structure
            );
        }
    }
}
```

Fig. 13.34: Deriving the instruction UNIFY_CONSTANT, stage 1

were located in unreachable code, as desired. See Figure 13.38.

6. *Convert to WAM interface.* Replace return 1 by fall-through and return 0 by goto L_fail, to match the WAM flow of control. Remove superfluous parentheses. This is the final product. See Figure 13.39.

This process of partially evaluating a part of an interpreter to obtain an optimized intermediate code instruction can be applied in many situations. More in particular, it provided the code segments for UNIFY_VARIABLE (Figure 13.33) and UNIFY_STRUCTURE (see below).

```
int unify_constant(Term *goal_arg, char *head_text) {
   Term *goal;

      /* Handle bound goal_arg: */
      goal = deref(goal_arg);

      if (goal->type == Is_Variable
      || (put_constant(head_text))->type == Is_Variable
      ) {
          /* Handle identical variables: */
          if (goal == (put_constant(head_text))) return 1;

          /* Bind the unbound variable to the other term: */
          if ((put_constant(head_text))->type == Is_Variable) {
              trail_binding ((put_constant(head_text)));
              (put_constant(head_text))->term.variable.term = goal;
          }
          else {
              trail_binding (goal);
              goal->term.variable.term = (put_constant(head_text));
          }
          return 1;              /* always succeeds */
      }
      else {
          /* Handle terms of different type: */
          if (goal->type != (put_constant(head_text))->type) return 0;

          switch (goal->type) {
          case Is_Constant:              /* both are constants */
              return
                  strcmp(
                      goal->term.constant,
                      (put_constant(head_text))->term.constant
                  ) == 0;
          case Is_Structure:              /* both are structures */
              return unify_structures (
                  &goal->term.structure,
                  &(put_constant(head_text))->term.structure
              );
          }
      }
}
```

Fig. 13.35: Deriving the instruction UNIFY_CONSTANT, stage 2

```
int unify_constant(Term *goal_arg, char *head_text) {
    Term *goal;

    /* Handle bound goal_arg: */
    goal = deref(goal_arg);

    if (goal->type == Is_Variable || Is_Constant == Is_Variable) {
        /* Handle identical variables: */
        if (goal == (put_constant(head_text))) return 1;

        /* Bind the unbound variable to the other term: */
        if (Is_Constant == Is_Variable) {
            trail_binding ((put_constant(head_text)));
            ERRONEOUS = goal;
        }
        else {
            trail_binding (goal);
            goal->term.variable.term = (put_constant(head_text));
        }
        return 1;                /* always succeeds */
    }
    else {
        /* Handle terms of different type: */
        if (goal->type != Is_Constant) return 0;

        switch (goal->type) {
        case Is_Constant:            /* both are constants */
            return strcmp(goal->term.constant, head_text) == 0;
        case Is_Structure:           /* both are structures */
            return unify_structures(
                &goal->term.structure, ERRONEOUS
            );
        }
    }
}
```

Fig. 13.36: Deriving the instruction UNIFY_CONSTANT, stage 3

13.5.3 Unification of structures in the WAM

Deriving the code for UNIFY_STRUCTURE along the lines explained above is straightforward most of the way, but the resulting code ends in a loop to unify the components, which does not fit the notion of an "instruction". The WAM instruction for unifying structures only unifies the functor and the arity; separate instructions must be generated for unifying the components. We use the same separation here, but some care is required. The code for UNIFY_STRUCTURE can be found in Figure 13.40. Figure 13.41 shows an application of it in the compiled code for the head times(2, X).

```
int  unify_constant(Term *goal_arg, char *head_text) {
     Term *goal;

     /* Handle bound goal_arg: */
     goal = deref(goal_arg);

     if  (goal->type == Is_Variable || 0) {
          /* Handle identical variables: */
          if  (0) return 1;

          /* Bind the unbound variable to the other term: */
          if  (0) {
               trail_binding ((put_constant(head_text)));
               ERRONEOUS = goal;
          }
          else {
               trail_binding (goal);
               goal->term.variable.term = (put_constant(head_text));
          }
          return 1;              /* always succeeds */
     }
     else {
          /* Handle terms of different type: */
          if  (goal->type != Is_Constant) return 0;

          switch (Is_Constant) {
          case Is_Constant:            /* both are constants */
               return strcmp(goal->term.constant, head_text) == 0;
          case Is_Structure:           /* both are structures */
               return unify_structures (
                    &goal->term.structure, ERRONEOUS
               );
          }
     }
}
```

Fig. 13.37: Deriving the instruction UNIFY_CONSTANT, stage 4

The compiled code first establishes the presence of the structure, then acquires a local variable goal_comp pointing to the component list and then steps through the list, unifying the components in turn. As usual, if any of the unifications fails, the instruction executes a jump to the label L_fail.

We see from Figures 13.32 and 13.40 that when the goal argument is an unbound variable, the corresponding constant or structure must be created and the variable bound to it. This is necessary to allow further unification and/or reporting of the value in answer to a query. There is a problem here, though: whereas put_constant() creates the entire constant, put_structure() creates only the record for the structure, fills in the functor, and the arity, but leaves the component entries empty. This matches the behavior of the second part of the code for UNIFY_STRUCTURE, which checks only the type, the functor and the arity but leaves testing the com-

```
int unify_constant(Term *goal_arg, char *head_text) {
    Term *goal;

    /* Handle bound goal_arg: */
    goal = deref(goal_arg);

    if (goal->type == Is_Variable) {
        trail_binding (goal);
        goal->term.variable.term = (put_constant(head_text));
        return 1;            /* always succeeds */
    }
    else {
        if (goal->type != Is_Constant) return 0;
        return strcmp(goal->term.constant, head_text) == 0;
    }
}
```

Fig. 13.38: Deriving the instruction UNIFY_CONSTANT, stage 5

```
int unify_constant(Term *goal_arg, char *head_text) {
    Term *goal;

    goal = deref(goal_arg);
    if (goal->type == Is_Variable) {
        trail_binding (goal);
        goal->term.variable.term = put_constant(head_text);
    }
    else {
        if (goal->type != Is_Constant) goto L_fail;
        if (strcmp(goal->term.constant, head_text) != 0) goto L_fail;
    }
    return 1;
L_fail :
    return 0;
}
```

Fig. 13.39: Deriving the instruction UNIFY_CONSTANT, final result

ponent entries to the code following it. This code (Figure 13.41) cannot, however, handle uninitialized component entries, as would be supplied by the first part if the goal variable is an unbound variable. We solve this problem by initializing the components with anonymous variables in the call to initialize_components() in Figure 13.40; these variables can then be bound to the components of the structure by the instructions for the entries.

Figures 13.42 and 13.43 show the effects of the code of Figure 13.41 when goal_arg is an unbound variable Y, represented as a null pointer. Figure 13.42 shows the result of the instruction UNIFY_STRUCTURE (goal_arg, "times", 2). Three allocations have taken place: one for the structure times/2, one for an array of two components, and one for two "anonymous" variables, which were named

```
g = deref(goal_arg);
if  (g->type == Is_Variable) {
    trail_binding (g);
    g->term.variable.term =
        put_structure(head_functor, head_arity);
    initialize_components(g->term.variable.term);
}
else {
    if  (g->type != Is_Structure) goto L_fail;
    if  (g->term.structure.arity != head_arity
    ||   strcmp(g->term.structure.functor, head_functor) != 0
    ) goto L_fail;
}
```

Fig. 13.40: The unification instruction UNIFY_STRUCTURE

```
/* match times(2, X) */
UNIFY_STRUCTURE(goal_arg, "times", 2);          /* macro */
{   /* match (2, X) */
    Term **goal_comp = deref(goal_arg)->term.structure.components;

    UNIFY_CONSTANT(goal_comp[0], "2");          /* macro */
    UNIFY_VARIABLE(goal_comp[1], X);            /* macro */
}
```

Fig. 13.41: Compiled code for the head times(2, X)

_A01 and _A02 here. The instructions UNIFY_CONSTANT (goal_comp[0], "2") and
UNIFY_VARIABLE (goal_comp[1], X) are referred to these anonymous variables
and bind them to their respective arguments, as shown in Figure 13.43. We see
that the same instructions can perform unification with data structures from the goal
when these are present *and* construct them when they are not.

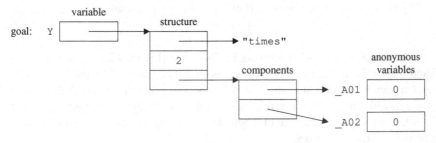

Fig. 13.42: The effect of the instruction UNIFY_STRUCTURE

We are now in a position to generate in-line code for the unification of constants, variables, and structures as head arguments, with goal arguments; unification
of lists as head arguments is very similar to that of structures. Compiled unifica-

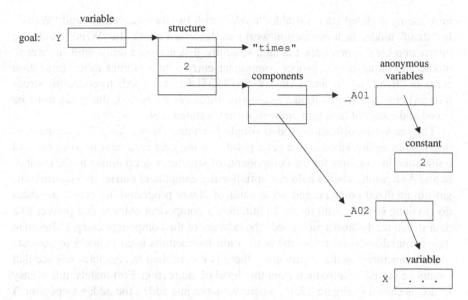

Fig. 13.43: The effect of the instructions of Figure 13.41

tion performs effectively the same operations on the data structures as interpreted unification does, with the exception of the introduction of anonymous variables as structure components. It is much faster, since many of the decisions have been taken at compile time. Note also that compiled unification is applied to all arguments, whereas the optimized clause selection (Section 13.4.3) examines the first argument only.

The WAM features several additional optimizations on the unification instructions; we will discuss one of them in some detail in the next section and briefly mention some others in the section thereafter.

13.5.4 An optimization: read/write mode

There is a second solution to the problem of the uninitialized component entries, already suggested in the wording above: leave the entries uninitialized and modify the unification instructions so they can handle that situation. This solution is especially attractive because the anonymous variables are clearly an artifact of our implementation and continue to add at least one level of indirection to all operations on the structure; avoiding them will result in considerable speed-up, since many Prolog programs manipulate structures and lists extensively.

The solution cannot be implemented as it stands, however, and requires two modifications. The first is simple: the unification instructions on the components have to be notified that the component entries have not been initialized. This is done by introducing a global state variable "mode" with two values, "Read" and "Write". In "Read" mode, each instruction works as described above. In "Write" mode the instruction creates precisely the data structure that it would unify with in "Read" mode, and initializes the proper component entry with a pointer to it. Unification starts in "Read" mode, and a UNIFY_STRUCTURE that needs to create the structure switches to "Write" mode. Since structures can be nested, the mode must be saved at the start of structure unification and restored at the end of it.

The second modification is also simple but more far-reaching. The unification instructions as described above get a pointer to the goal argument to work on, and unification instructions for the components of structures get pointers to the components. As a result, when we do not initialize the component entries, the instructions get uninitialized pointers, and no amount of clever programming can make them do anything sensible with them. To initialize a component entry with a pointer to a data structure, the instruction needs the *address* of the component entry, rather than its—uninitialized—value. So the unification instructions need pointers to pointers to data structures; as the saying goes, there is no problem in computer science that cannot be solved by introducing another level of indirection. Fortunately, this is easy to do, as shown in Figure 13.44, where we have just added the address operator & to the goal arguments. The code saves the mode in mode_1 before calling the read-/write version of UNIFY_STRUCTURE, since that instruction may set the mode to "Write", to warn the following instructions. The mode is restored when all structure components have been unified. Nested structures will need more than one temporary mode_*N* to save nesting modes and more than one temporary goal_comp to address the various component lists.

```
/* match times(2, X) */
mode_1 = mode;              /* save mode */
UNIFY_STRUCTURE(&goal_arg, "times", 2); /* macro */
       /* saves read/write mode and may set it to Write_Mode */
{    /* match (2, X) */
    register Term **goal_comp =
        deref(goal_arg)->term.structure.components;

    UNIFY_CONSTANT(&goal_comp[0], "2"); /* macro */
    UNIFY_VARIABLE(&goal_comp[1], X); /* macro */
}
mode = mode_1;
```

Fig. 13.44: Compiled code with read/write mode for the head times(2, X)

Now that we have seen how the new instructions are used, we can look into their implementation. The read/write version of UNIFY_CONSTANT is shown in Figure 13.45 and is representative of the general approach. The code for "Read" mode is the same as that for the original UNIFY_CONSTANT (Figure 13.32), except that there is an extra dereference operation on the pointer to the goal argument. The code for "Write" mode creates the constant and stores a pointer to it under the goal argument pointer, which in "Write" mode will be an entry in a component list of a goal structure.

```
if (mode == Read_Mode) {
    g = deref(*goal_ptr);
    if (g->type == Is_Variable) {
        trail_binding (g);
        g->term.variable.term = put_constant(head_text);
    }
    else {
        if (g->type != Is_Constant) goto L_fail;
        if (strcmp(g->term.constant, head_text) != 0) goto L_fail;
    }
}
else {   /* mode == Write_Mode */
    *goal_ptr = put_constant(head_text);
}
```

Fig. 13.45: The instruction UNIFY_CONSTANT with read/write mode

The code for UNIFY_STRUCTURE (Figure 13.46) follows this pattern with the exception that it sets the mode to "Write" rather than initializing the components, when the goal argument is an unbound variable.

```
if (mode == Read_Mode) {
    g = deref(*goal_ptr);
    if (g->type == Is_Variable) {
        trail_binding (g);
        g->term.variable.term =
            put_structure(head_functor, head_arity);
        mode = Write_Mode;   /* signal uninitialized goals */
    }
    else {
        if (g->type != Is_Structure) goto L_fail;
        if (g->term.structure.arity != head_arity
        ||  strcmp(g->term.structure.functor, head_functor) != 0
        ) goto L_fail;
    }
}
else {   /* mode == Write_Mode */
    *goal_ptr = put_structure(head_functor, head_arity);
}
```

Fig. 13.46: The instruction UNIFY_STRUCTURE with read/write mode

Figures 13.47 and 13.48 show the effects of the code of Figure 13.41 with goal_arg an unbound variable Y, now using read/write mode. Figure 13.47 shows that the instruction UNIFY_STRUCTURE (goal_arg, "times", 2) has now left the component array entries uninitialized, avoiding the overhead of the construction of the anonymous variables. The instructions UNIFY_CONSTANT (goal_comp[0], "2") and UNIFY_VARIABLE (goal_comp[1], X) recognize this situation and fill in the component array entries with their respective arguments, as shown in Figure 13.48. Compiled unification with read/write mode creates exactly the same data structure

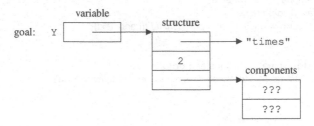

Fig. 13.47: The effect of the instruction UNIFY_STRUCT with read/write mode

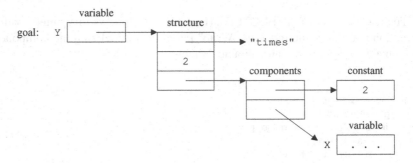

Fig. 13.48: The effect of the instructions of Figure 13.41 with read/write mode

as a set of calls to the put_... routines, except that only that part of the data structure is created that is not already present in the goal argument.

13.5.5 *Further unification optimizations in the WAM*

The above UNIFY_... instructions are simpler than the actual WAM instructions, which feature several further optimizations. We will briefly discuss them here; for a full treatment see the tutorial by Aït-Kaci [8].

We saw that the unification of structures is somewhat complicated by the fact that they can nest. This necessitates saving the mode as shown in Figure 13.44, and leads to the use of several component pointers at the same time, each of which we would like to allocate in a machine register. The WAM avoids these complications in a drastic way: it forbids nested structures. If the head argument consists of a nested structure, it must be unified in top-down breadth-first fashion: the goal and head top-level structures are unified first, skipping any substructures. Next, the second level of structures is unified, skipping any subsubstructures, etc. Since deeply nested head arguments to clauses are rare, this restriction is not much of a problem in practice. The restriction has several advantages: saving the mode has become superfluous; only one goal_comp pointer is needed, which can easily be placed in a register; and the door is opened to other optimizations, which we will describe now.

Since only the UNIFY_STRUCTURE instruction can set the mode to "Write", the mode is guaranteed to be "Read" in any unification not inside a structure. Since simpler code can be generated in "Read" mode (for example the code of Figure 13.32) than when the mode is unknown (Figure 13.45), the WAM has special instructions GET_... to be used instead of UNIFY_... whenever "Read" mode is guaranteed statically; so GET_CONSTANT would be used instead of UNIFY_CONSTANT in Figure 13.31. Note that since no structure unification is ever started inside a structure, there is no UNIFY_STRUCTURE in the WAM, just a GET_STRUCTURE.

Since there is only one pointer to the component list, goal_comp, it can be implicit in the machine and need not be passed explicitly to the instructions. And since the unification instructions for structure components (the UNIFY_... instructions) are differentiated from those used outside structures (the GET_... instructions), GET_STRUCTURE can set the pointer goal_comp and the UNIFY_... instructions can use it and then increment it, to reach the next component. This also removes the need for the extra indirection described above. As a result, the compiled unification code of Figure 13.44 reduces to

```
GET_STRUCTURE(goal, "times", 2); /* macro */
UNIFY_CONSTANT(2);               /* macro */
UNIFY_VARIABLE(X);               /* macro */
```

Note that UNIFY_CONSTANT and UNIFY_VARIABLE each have one parameter now, the head argument known from the rule head; the goal argument is implicit.

A different optimization concerns the instructions GET_VARIABLE and UNIFY_VARIABLE. The first use of a free variable X is guaranteed to be unbound, so the instruction reduces to

```
v = head_var;
g = deref(goal);
trail_binding (v);
v->term.variable.term = g;
```

for GET_VARIABLE and to

```
v = head_var;
if (mode == Read_Mode) {
    g = deref(*goal_comp++);
    trail_binding (v);
    v->term.variable.term = g;
}
```

```
        else {    /* mode == Write_Mode */
            *goal_comp++ = v;
        }
```

for UNIFY_VARIABLE; note the use of the goal component entry pointer goal_comp in the latter, since it is used only during structure unification. The original GET_VARIABLE and UNIFY_VARIABLE instructions are renamed to GET_VALUE and UNIFY_VALUE, although these names are somewhat misleading. The second and further uses of a head variable need not represent a value at all since it may have become bound to an unbound variable.

This concludes our discussion of some optimizations of compiled unification in the WAM, and of compiled unification in general. We have seen that the building blocks for compiled unification can to a large extent be derived semi-automatically by the partial evaluation of calls to the interpreter. This method was already applied to the imperative languages in Section 7.5.1.2, but the gain was limited there. The difference is that here the method is applied manually and to a relatively simple interpreter. Professional compilers for functional and logic languages combine these or similar techniques and use them in combination with optimized clause selection (Section 13.4.3) and tail call elimination (Section 12.7.3), and such traditional optimization techniques as constant propagation, in-lining, and cloning. The resulting code can come within a factor of two or three with respect to the speed of a similar program in an imperative or object-oriented language.

13.6 Conclusion

A logic program consists of a set of deduction rules parameterized with logic variables; the deduction rules are applied by a predefined search mechanism and the logic variables are processed by the unification mechanism. Some deduction rules are unconditional and thus define facts. In response to a user query, the search mechanism applies the deduction rules to deduce new facts (conclusions) that are compatible with the query.

There is a simple implementation of the search mechanism, which duplicates the set of partial solutions at each choice point; optimization of this process leads in a natural way to the concept of backtracking. Prolog defines the search mechanism as depth-first search. This search can be performed by interpretation, but it is also possible to produce a recursive-descent translation by using the backtracking implementation of the search.

Logic variables can be bound, and then they hold information, or unbound, and then they do not hold information. Unification combines the information in two similar structures containing logic variables into a new structure representing the combined information in both. Like the search process, the unification process can be implemented as recursive descent code, resulting in an elegant translation of logic programs.

Components of the recursive descent code are isolated as WAM instructions; at the same time the recursion stack is made explicit. This allows easier translation to machine code.

Summary

- Logic programming is based on (1) the specification of relations between terms, (2) facts using these relations, and (3) rules for inferring new facts from existing facts. Specific inferred facts can be requested by doing queries.
- Facts and rules together are called clauses; they can contain logic variables.
- A logic variable can be (1) unbound; (2) bound to a value, in which case it represents that value; or (3) bound to another variable, in which case it represents whatever that variable represents. A binding of a variable in a clause gives a new clause; the new clause is called an instantiation of the more general clause.
- Clauses can be used to infer new facts, as follows. A clause consists of a head and a list of goals; dependencies between the head and goals are expressed by logic variables. If in an instantiation of a clause all goals are established facts, the head of the clause can be inferred as a fact.
- Answering a query means finding bindings for the variables in it that turn the query into a known or inferred fact.
- To infer a goal fact F, a clause is sought that might infer F, given proper variable bindings. Possible proper bindings are found by unifying F with the head of the clause. The clause is then instantiated using these bindings; the instantiated goal list yields new goals. Some of these may be known facts, others may need to be inferred. If all goals are eventually reduced to known facts or empty, F is inferred.
- The state of the search for clauses and bindings can be recorded in a stack of extended goal lists. An extended goal list is a list of goals and unification requests.
- The inference process considers the top stack entry only. If the top stack entry is empty, we have found an answer to the query and report it, using the instruction "Succeed". If the top stack entry contains unification requests, an attempt is made to satisfy these, using the instructions "Unify" and "Match"; if this fails the top entry is removed. Otherwise, clauses are located that might infer the first goal in the top entry. The instruction "Attach clauses" is used to make copies of the top entry and insert unification requests with these clauses in them.
- All Prolog interpreters and compiled Prolog programs work with this inference process or optimizations of it.
- The inference process acts only on the topmost entry and mainly on its first goal, except for variable binding, which acts on the whole topmost entry. The non-first goals in the non-topmost entries are almost exclusively copies of those in the topmost stack entry, and it is an essential optimization to combine them. However, once combined, variable binding in the topmost entry affects them all. To undo this effect when the topmost entry is removed, all bindings are recorded

when performed and undone when the topmost entry is removed. This is called backtracking.

- Unification is a top-down process on two terms, one from a head term and one from a goal term. The terms are viewed as trees. For unification to succeed, the two top nodes must be equal and have the same number of children, and the pairwise unification of the children of both terms must succeed.

- An unbound variable is unified with a value or variable by binding it to that value or variable. The binding is recorded for backtracking purposes.

- Structures, lists, and sets are unified by the same rules as terms. Variables in them are unified by the rules for variable unification.

- Most Prolog compilers generate either C code or WAM code. The Warren Abstract Machine code is an assembly level macro code that allows convenient optimizing Prolog compilation.

- In a compiled Prolog program, each relation is implemented as a routine, and so is each clause.

- The first goal in the routine for a clause C is processed by a call G to the routine compiled for the relation in that first goal. This routine gets an action routine as a parameter that will be called whenever G succeeds in finding a proper set of bindings. The action routine is constructed to process the rest of the goals of C and then call C's action routine. This implements the AND component of inference. The technique requires nesting routine declarations.

- The routine compiled for a relation R successively tries all clauses for R, passing to them the action routine it obtained from its caller. Copying the goal list has been replaced by copying the action routine. This implements the OR component of inference.

- Static and dynamic analysis can show that many of the calls to clauses for a relation cannot succeed, and should be avoided. The WAM has special instructions for this.

- The WAM has an instruction for clause selection based on the nature of the first goal argument: constant, variable, structure, or list; it effects a four-way jump. Next, for constants and structures as goal arguments it has instructions which perform N-way jumps, based on the value of the constant or the functor of the structure. The code positions reached through these jumps are occupied by calls to exactly the clauses that can have first head arguments with the selected properties.

- Exhaustion of the search possibilities is implemented as a jump to a fail label in the WAM.

- The Prolog "cut" is implemented by jumping to the fail label when backtracking over it.

- Assert is implemented by conditionally calling the interpreter at the beginning and the end of each routine for a relation. Retract is implemented by conditionally calling the clause routines.

- If the interpreter finds in an asserted clause a goal for which a compiled routine exists, it switches back to the compiled code.

- Naive compiled code for unification is inefficient because it often compares known constants to known constants and because it often creates data structures just to compare them.
- To avoid the inefficiencies, the WAM has special instructions for unification with head arguments that are constants, variables, structures, and lists. These instructions are partial evaluations of the general unification routine for head arguments, specialized for constants, variables, structures, and lists. They apply to all head arguments, first or otherwise.
- If a WAM unification instruction meets a goal value, it compares the value to its built-in value. If the two match, the instruction continues; otherwise it jumps to the fail label.
- If a WAM unification instruction meets a goal variable, it creates a copy of its internal value, binds the variable to it, and continues.
- The WAM unification instructions for structures and lists create the top nodes of the structure or list only. The creation of the children is left to further unification instructions, which are notified of this situation by turning from "Read" mode to "Write" mode.
- Using the above and many other optimizations, compiled logic programs can come within a factor of two or three with respect to the speed of equivalent programs in imperative and object-oriented languages.

Further reading

Information about the implementation of logic languages can be found in journals like the *Journal of Logic Programming* and *ACM Transactions on Programming Languages and Systems*, and in the proceedings of, for example, the *International Conference on Logic Programming* and the *ACM SIGPLAN Conference on Programming Language Design and Implementation - PLDI*.

The original explanation of the Warren Abstract Machine is given by Warren [291]. Aït-Kaci [8] has written a tutorial on the WAM.

The definitive survey of sequential Prolog implementation, both historically and technically, was written by Van Roy [242]. it contains an extensive literature list. Diaz *et al.* [83] describe the GNU Prolog compiler, which compiles Prolog into stand-alone executables.

Exercises

13.1. (▷www) Prolog tries the different subgoals in the body of a clause from left to right. In theory, other evaluation orders are also possible, for example from right to left. For each of the two queries

?– grandparent(arne, Z).
?– grandparent(X, rivka).

determine whether left-to-right or right-to-left order is more efficient (using the grandparent relation of Section 13.1). What can we learn from this?

13.2. (▷www) In Section 13.2.1 we showed how the interpreter processes the query ?– gp(arne, X). Process this query again, but now using the optimizations discussed in Section 13.2.2.

13.3. Given the following relations:

author(grune, parsingTechniques).
author(jacobs, parsingTechniques).
author(grune, programmingLanguageEssentials).
author(bal, programmingDistributedSystems).
author(bal, programmingLanguageEssentials).
coauthor(X,Y) :– author(X, Book), (Y, Book).

(a) Show how the interpreter described at the beginning of Section 13.2 processes the query:

?– coauthor(bal, grune).

(b) Describe which code will be generated for these relations using the techniques of Section 13.4.2.
(c) Describe which code will be generated for the relations using the optimized clause selection technique described in Section 13.4.3.

13.4. (▷796) *Project:* In Section 13.2 we presented an implementation model in which the goal lists are kept in a queue which acts like a stack since the "Attach clauses" instruction manipulates it in a last-in-first-out fashion.

Explore the effects of changing the "Attach clauses" instruction so as to manipulate the queue entries in a first-in-first-out fashion: it removes the top goal list, but adds the new goal lists at the bottom. Which of the optimizations discussed here are still applicable?

13.5. (▷www) A language designer proposes to allow queries in which relation names can be variables as well. Discuss the consequences for the general interpreted implementation model.

13.6. (a) Show how the interpreter processes unification of p(X, [2, X, 4]) and p(3, [A, B, 4]), using the techniques described in Section 13.3.
(b) Describe which code will be generated for this unification using the techniques described in Section 13.5.

13.7. (▷www) Write a unification routine unify_lists() for lists as described in Section 13.3.1. Why is this code an improvement over direct application of unify_structures()?

13.8. (▷www) In Section 13.3.3 we explain that the unification sequence B to A, C to B, D to B, E to C, leads to the binding tree in Figure 13.10(b) rather than the one in Figure 13.10(a). Is there a binding sequence that *would* lead to the tree in Figure 13.10(a), and if so, what is it?

13.9. (▷796) Refer to the example at the beginning of Section 13.4.1 on list procedures. The procedure return_two_values() could also return a list with both values it wants to return, and let the caller consume the results one at a time. Why will this not work in general?

13.10. (▷www) Write a list procedure that accepts two list procedures specifying integer lists and that implements the intersection of both lists.

13.11. (▷www) Construct code for a clause with two cuts in it:

first_first_grandparent (X, Z) :− parent(X, Y), !, parent(Y, Z), !.

which tries to say that X is a first-first-grandparent of Z if Z is the first child of the first child of X.

13.12. (▷796) Find out from the Prolog manual how assert and retract should behave with respect to backtracking, and verify if the approach from Section 13.4.5 supports this behavior.

13.13. Design an implementation of optimized clause selection and retracted clause handling in an integrated fashion using bit vectors. Hint: see Colomb [67].

13.14. (▷www) (a) The meta-logical operator var(X) in Prolog is defined to succeed if X is currently an unbound variable and to fail otherwise. How can this operator be implemented in compiled Prolog?
(b) The meta-logical arithmetical infix operator is in Prolog requires its right operand to be a structure E that represents an arithmetic expression in some specific format. All variables in E must be bound. If V is currently an unbound variable, the operation succeeds and V is bound to the arithmetic value of E. If V is bound and its value is equal to the arithmetic value of E, the operation succeeds. Otherwise it fails. How can this operator be implemented in compiled Prolog? Assume the existence of a routine Term *evaluate_expression() that evaluates an expression in the specific format to a term of type Constant, or gives an error message if the expression is in error. Also assume single-length integer arithmetic.

13.15. (▷www) Suppose one introduces in Prolog an arithmetic operator between with the syntax

V between E_1 and E_2

which evaluates E_1 and E_2 as in Exercise 13.14. If V is unbound, the operation succeeds with V bound successively to all arithmetic values between E_1 and E_2 inclusive (of which there may be zero!). If V is bound and its value lies between E_1 and E_2 inclusive, the operation succeeds. Otherwise it fails. How can this operator be implemented in compiled Prolog?

13.16. Derive a unification instruction UNIFY_LIST for unifying lists, similar to the one in Figure 13.40.

13.17. *History of logic language implementation*: Study Robinson's 1965 paper [237], which introduces unification as an essential part of theorem proving and logic programming (requires considerable mathematical sophistication), or his 1971 paper [238], which concerns the implementation of unification, and write a summary of it.

Chapter 14
Parallel and Distributed Programs

Parallel and distributed systems consist of multiple processors that can communicate with each other. Languages for programming such systems support constructs for expressing concurrency and communication. In this chapter, we will study how such languages can be implemented. As we will see, the presence of multiple processors introduces many new problems for a language implementer.

We will first define what we mean by a parallel system and what by a distributed system. In a **parallel system**, the goal is to solve a given problem as fast as possible, using multiple processors. These processors cooperate to solve a single problem. Parallel processing typically features in applications that would take a huge amount of compute time, often weeks or months, on a single processor. So, the reason for using a parallel system is to obtain performance improvements.

A **distributed system** also contains multiple processors, but now the processors work on many different tasks from many users. There is normally no single problem involved. A simple and small-scale example is a system with one workstation per user, plus some additional processors providing a file service or a time-shared compute service. The processors in such a system are autonomous and are connected by a network. There are many reasons for using such a distributed system instead of a single, centralized machine: a distributed system is more cost-effective, potentially more fault-tolerant, and it is easier to extend the system incrementally. Modern distributed systems often are very large and also are geographically distributed. A good example are so-called *grids*, which have many computing- and data-resources that are shared by different organizations. Another example are computational clouds, which provide remote resources that can be hired, using a pay-on-demand model.

Interestingly, it is possible to use a distributed system as a parallel one. In fact, many research groups have studied how to use a collection of (idle) workstations for running parallel programs. This approach is attractive, because many institutes already have the workstations installed. Also, parallel computing on grids has been studied extensively, either by scheduling different parallel jobs on different resources or even by running a single parallel program on many distributed resources at the same time.

An important issue in compiling parallel and distributed programs is the architecture of the target system. During the past decades, many architectures for parallel and distributed systems have been designed. In this chapter, however, we focus on only two widely-used machine models: "multiprocessors" and "multicomputers". The difference between these two architectures is that with a multicomputer processes on different processors run in different address spaces, whereas with a multiprocessor at least part of the address space is shared (see Figure 14.1). In a **multiprocessor**, all processors have access to a single, shared memory. The processors communicate by reading and writing variables in the shared memory. Multiprocessors can be constructed, for example, by connecting several processors to a single bus. Other, more scalable, methods also exist.

Almost all modern processors in fact are multiprocessors, as they contain multiple *compute cores* that can communicate through shared memory or shared caches. A **multicomputer** consists of several processors connected by a network. The processors communicate by sending messages over this network to each other. The network can either be especially designed for the multicomputer, as in the IBM Blue Gene, or it can be an off-the-shelf local area network (LAN), such as Ethernet, Myrinet or Infiniband. A multicomputer built out of off-the-shelf processors and networks is also called a **cluster**.

Multiprocessors and multicomputers also can be mixed in a single system. In fact, many modern clusters consist of many compute nodes connected by a network, where each compute node is a PC with multiple processors, each with multiple cores. For example, a dual quad-core node has 8 cores that can communicate through shared memory or shared caches.

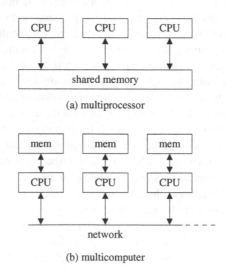

Fig. 14.1: Multiprocessors and multicomputers

Many models and languages have been proposed for parallel and distributed programming and a great amount of research has been done on how to implement these languages efficiently. In this chapter, we necessarily cover only a small fraction of all this work. Rather than trying to give a broad overview of compilation techniques for many different paradigms, we will focus on a few important models. We will focus on language constructs for parallel programming, although many constructs, for example message passing, can be used just as well for writing distributed applications. For distributed applications, additional language constructs exist, such as atomic transactions, but these will not be discussed here.

The parallel programming models we discuss are: *shared variables*, *message passing*, *objects*, *Tuple Space*, and *data-parallel programming*. The first two models, shared variables and message passing, are low-level communication mechanisms that reflect the underlying hardware. Objects, Tuple Space, and data parallelism are high-level constructs that allow communication to be expressed at a higher level of abstraction. The models are described in Section 14.1. Their implementation is based on the notions *process* and *thread*, which are treated in Section 14.2. In Sections 14.3 to 14.6 we discuss implementation techniques for shared variables, message passing, objects, and Tuple Space. In Section 14.7, we look at automatic parallelization, which tries to generate data parallel programs from sequential programs.

We should emphasize that much interesting research is done on other programming paradigms too, in particular on functional and logic languages, and on other parallel programming models, for example collective communication. Also, we will restrict ourselves to compilation techniques for multiprocessors and multicomputers built out of simple microprocessors. Much research has also been done on alternative forms of parallel hardware, for example vector computers and Graphical Processing Units (GPUs). We will not cover these in this book.

Roadmap

A few general remarks can be made about the implementation of parallel languages. Even more than with logic and functional languages, much of the implementation comes in the form of a large run-time system, rather than compiler support. Some of the more popular parallel programming systems (for example PVM and MPI) are even implemented entirely as libraries that are linked with a program written in a traditional language, such as C or FORTRAN. These programming systems need no direct compiler support whatsoever. A problem with this approach is that the programmer is responsible for making the correct library calls, since there is no compiler that checks the calls. Incorrect usage of the library occurs, for example, when a process sends a message containing an integer value, while the receiver expects a floating point value. The type error will not be caught, and will result in incorrect and unpredictable program behavior. This approach is comparable to programming in assembly, where the library calls are regarded as machine instructions of the underlying system.

Many other programming systems are designed as relatively small extensions to existing languages. Often, they are implemented using compilers that do check for errors such as the one described above. Compilers for such languages usually are fairly simple, however, and most of the language implementation consists of a complex run-time system.

An interesting area where compilers do play an important role concerns languages with implicit parallelism. In most languages, the programmer is required to express parallelism explicitly, and to use statements to coordinate the parallel activities (for example by using message passing). In languages with **implicit parallelism**, on the other hand, the compiler tries to parallelize the program automatically. This also requires the compiler to automatically generate communication code. Such compilers are very hard to build and are sometimes even referred to as **heroic compilers**. We study such compilers in Section 14.7.

One problem in studying parallel run-time systems is that the boundary between the Operating System (OS) and the run-time system is often fuzzy. Many primitives, such as processes and communication, can be implemented either in the OS or in the run-time system. A recent trend is to move functionality from the OS to the run-time system. The advantages are that it saves expensive interactions with the OS and that it gives the compiler writer more control over the implementation of the functionality. An extreme form used in some systems is to map devices, for example the network interface, in user space and to let the run-time system control the device without any involvement from the OS. In our discussions, we will always make clear which functionality we assume the OS to provide.

14.1 Parallel programming models

A parallel programming model provides support for expressing parallelism as well as communication and synchronization between parallel tasks. Below we briefly describe the programming models used in this chapter.

14.1.1 Shared variables and monitors

Perhaps the simplest parallel programming model is that of a collection of processes communicating through shared variables. A **process** is an abstraction of a physical processor. Each process executes program code sequentially. Conceptually, a process may be thought of as containing a virtual processor, which supplies the processing power, and an **address space**, which stores data; so an address space is an abstraction of physical memory. The concepts of process and address space are used in many other parallel programming models (discussed later) as well.

A program can create multiple processes to obtain parallelism. A new process is created with the **fork statement**, as in

fork sort(A, 1, 10);

which forks off a copy of sort() as a new process and passes three parameters to it.

With the shared-variable programming model, at least part of the address spaces of the processes overlap, so multiple processes can access the same variables. Such variables are called **shared variables**. A given shared variable can be read and written by some or all processes, and can thus serve as a mechanism for communication between these processes.

An important problem with this programming model is synchronizing the access to the shared variables. If multiple processes simultaneously try to change the same data structure, the result will be unpredictable and the data structure may be left in an inconsistent state. A typical example is two processes that simultaneously try to increment a shared variable X by executing:

X: **shared integer**;

X := X + 1;

Assume that X initially contains the value 5. Clearly, if both processes increment the variable, the resulting value of X should be 7. What may happen instead, however, is that both processes will read the original value (5) and compute the new value (6) based on the original value. Next, both processes will write this new value into X. As a result, the variable is assigned the value 6 twice, instead of being incremented twice.

To prevent such undesirable behavior, **synchronization primitives** are needed that make sure only one process can access a certain shared variable at any given time. This form of synchronization is called **mutual exclusion synchronization**. A simple primitive is a **lock variable**, which has indivisible operations to *acquire* (set) and *release* the lock. If a process tries to acquire a lock that has already been acquired, this process will block until the lock has been released. Lock variables can thus be used to restrict the access to a given shared data structure to a single process only. The example above would be written as follows using lock variables:

```
X: shared integer;
X_lock: lock;

Acquire_Lock(X_lock);
X := X + 1;
Release_Lock(X_lock);
```

Now, only one of the processes can execute the increment statement at a given time. Unfortunately, this method is rather low-level and error-prone. For example, the programmer should guard *all* accesses to shared variables by locks. If the increment statement occurs in several places in the program, and one occurrence is not protected by lock statements, the program is still in danger of behaving incorrectly.

A more structured and higher-level solution to the synchronization problem, which we use in this chapter, is the monitor. A **monitor** is similar to an Abstract Data Type in that it is a type that contains data *and* the operations to access the data. The data encapsulated by a monitor are shared by multiple processes. The key idea of a monitor is to allow only one operation inside the monitor at any given time. Thus, all monitor operations are executed in a mutually exclusive way.

Besides mutual exclusion, a second form of synchronization is needed, called **condition synchronization**. With condition synchronization, a process can be blocked until a specific condition occurs, for example until a certain process has produced a result that is required to continue the computation. With monitors, condition synchronization usually is expressed with **condition variables**, which are shared variables of type Condition, on which two indivisible operations are defined: **wait()** and **signal()**. The operation wait(c) on a condition variable c blocks the invoking process; a signal(c) wakes up one process blocked in a wait on the same condition variable. The two primitives can only be invoked from within a monitor operation. An important feature of the wait operation is that a process that blocks in a wait operation is temporarily lifted out of the monitor, so another process may enter the monitor.

A simple example of a monitor is given in Figure 14.2. The monitor contains a variable representing a "bin" and operations to put data in the bin and take data out of it. The put() operation blocks if the bin already contains data and the get() operation blocks if the bin does not yet contain data. When the operations wake up after being blocked, they recheck the status of the bin, because the status may have changed again since the signal operation was issued.

14.1.2 Message passing models

The shared variable programming model is primarily intended for programming shared memory multiprocessors, machines with physical shared memory. The model is less suitable for multicomputers, since such machines do not have a shared memory for storing shared variables. An alternative programming model, message passing, is suitable for both multiprocessors and multicomputers.

```
monitor BinMonitor;
   bin: integer;
   occupied: Boolean := false;
   full, empty: Condition;

   operation put(x: integer);
   begin
      while occupied do          # wait if the bin already is occupied
         wait(empty);
      od;
      bin := x;                  # put the item in the bin
      occupied := true;
      signal(full);             # wake up a process blocked in get
   end;

   operation get(x: out integer);
   begin
      while not occupied do      # wait if the bin is empty
         wait(full);
      od;
      x := bin;                  # get the item from the bin
      occupied := false;
      signal(empty);            # wakeup a process blocked in put
   end;
end;
```

Fig. 14.2: An example monitor

With message passing, each process can access only its own local data. Processes can exchange data by sending messages to each other. The basic model uses two primitives, the **send statement** and the **receive statement**, as illustrated below:

```
process1:
   send message to process2;
process2:
   receive message from process1;
```

Here, the first process sends a message to the second process. The receive() command blocks the second process until the message has arrived. The format of a message depends on the programming system. In low-level systems a message usually is just an array of bytes. In higher-level languages, a message can be a record-like structured value, with fields of different types.

Many variations of this basic send/receive model exist. One issue is how the sender and receiver address each other. In the basic model, the sender and receiver specify the name of each other. A more flexible method is to let the receiver accept messages sent by any process in the program. This method is useful if the receiver does not know in advance who is going to send the next message. Another way of increasing flexibility is to avoid specifying process names at all, by using indirect names. Many languages use **port** names for this purpose. A message sent to a specific port is delivered at a process that issues a receive statement on the corresponding port name. It is up to the system to match senders and receivers.

Another important issue concerns the question of when exactly the sending process is allowed to continue. With **asynchronous message passing** the sender continues immediately. With **synchronous message passing** the sender waits until the receiver has accepted the message. Synchronous message passing is more restrictive, but it has the advantage that when the sender continues it knows that the message has been delivered.

In some languages, the receiver is given control over which messages to accept. For example, the receiver may specify which kinds of messages it wants to accept, or in which order to handle messages if multiple messages are available:

```
receive print(size, text) suchthat size < 4096;
    # only accept print messages with a small size
```

or

```
receive print(size, text) by size;
    # order the messages by increasing size
```

We have so far assumed that messages are received by an explicit receive statement. An alternative method, called **implicit receipt**, is to create a new thread for each incoming message. A **thread** is a lightweight subprocess, with its own program counter and stack. A thread executes in the context of a process and can access the address space of this process: a thread does not have an address space of its own. This thread will execute a **message handler**, a routine that is defined by the programmer for each type of message. After executing the handler, the thread terminates. With implicit receipt, multiple threads may thus be executing within a single process. All these threads can access the global variables of that process.

Threads can also be used for other purposes. For example, if a process wants to send a request to a remote process, it can create a separate thread to send a message and wait for the result. In the mean time, the original thread (for example the main program) can continue processing. Threads have become an important concept in many parallel programming systems, and will be discussed in Section 14.2.

In this book we assume that the threads of a process execute in a pseudo-parallel way, which means that each executes in turn on the (single) processor on which the process runs; this is also called **concurrent execution**. Alternatively, multiple CPUs of a shared-memory multiprocessor could be assigned to the process, in which case the threads can execute physically in parallel. If the synchronization mechanisms described for shared variables (for example locks and monitors) are used for synchronizing access to the global variables of the process, the program will execute correctly in both cases.

14.1.3 Object-oriented languages

Shared variables and message passing are low-level models that directly reflect the shared-memory and distributed-memory machine architectures. Many other parallel programming languages have been designed that are based on more abstract models.

Examples include parallel functional, logic, and object-oriented languages. In this chapter, we will discuss the latter category, which contains many languages [305].

The key idea of object-oriented programming is to "encapsulate" the data in objects. The data inside an object can only be accessed through **operations** (or **methods**) defined on the object. Other important concepts are classes, inheritance, and polymorphism [26], but we need not discuss these here. One of the greatest advantages claimed for object-oriented programming is that it results in well-structured programs, making the technique suitable for writing large programs and easing the reuse of software components. These advantages are just as important for parallel programming as for sequential programming, which explains the large interest in parallel object-oriented languages.

Parallelism can be introduced by allowing several objects to execute at the same time, possibly on different processors, by letting a process execute inside the object. Communication between objects is expressed through operation invocations: an object can invoke an operation on another object, possibly located on a remote processor. Operation invocation is similar to message passing, but it is more cleanly integrated in the language semantics. Just as with message passing, there are many alternatives for invoking and servicing an operation. Synchronous invocations wait until the operation has been executed, while asynchronous invocations continue immediately. The receiving object can accept invocations explicitly or implicitly.

Many parallel object-oriented languages allow the process inside an object to consist of multiple threads of control. A popular model is to have one thread for the main process of the object and to create an additional thread for each operation invocation; this implements implicit receipt. Synchronization of these threads can be expressed using a monitor. Many parallel object-oriented languages are based on monitors.

14.1.4 The Linda Tuple space

Another approach to obtain a more high-level, abstract programming model is through an appropriate communication data structure: the **Tuple Space**. Tuple Space was designed as part of the **Linda** system. Linda is a small set of simple primitives that can be added to an existing sequential language, resulting in a new parallel language. This idea has been applied to several base languages, resulting in parallel languages like C/Linda, FORTRAN/Linda, and Lisp/Linda. Although the Linda model is quite old, its concepts are still used over and over again in new programming systems, so it is still worth discussing the Tuple Space implementation here.

The Tuple Space is a conceptual shared memory that is addressed "associatively", as follows. Tuple Space can be regarded as a box of tuples—records— that can be accessed by all processes in the program, regardless of the processor on which they run. In this sense, Tuple Space is a shared memory; the point is, however, that Tuple Space can also be implemented reasonably efficiently on a distributed-memory system, as we will see.

Three operations are defined on Tuple Space:

* **out** adds a tuple to the Tuple Space;
* **read** reads a matching tuple in Tuple Space;
* **in** reads a matching tuple in Tuple Space and simultaneously removes the tuple from Tuple Space.

For example, using C/Linda, the call

    out("item", 4, 5.48);

generates a tuple with three fields (a string, an integer, and a floating point number) and deposits it in Tuple Space. The read() and in() operations search for a tuple in Tuple Space. For each field of the tuple, they can specify either

* an **actual parameter**, which is an expression passed by value, or
* a **formal parameter**, which is a variable preceded by a ? symbol and which is passed by reference.

The terms "actual" and "formal" are used with this meaning in the Linda literature; they should not be confused with the traditional use of "actual and formal parameters" in programming languages. For example, the call

    float f;

    in("item", 4, ? &f);

specifies two actual parameters (a string and an integer) and one formal parameter (of type float). This call tries to find a tuple T with three fields, such that:

* the actual parameters in the call have the same types and values as the corresponding fields in tuple T;
* the formal parameters in the call have the same types as the corresponding fields in tuple T.

This process is called **tuple matching**. If a tuple T is found that matches, any formal parameters in the call get the values of the corresponding tuple fields of T, and the tuple T is removed from Tuple Space; all this is performed as an *indivisible operation* (also called *atomic action*). If the matching tuple was generated by the call

    out("item", 4, 5.48);

the variable f will get the value 5.48. If more than one tuple exists in the Tuple Space that matches, one is selected arbitrarily. If no matching tuple exists, the call to in() or read() blocks: the calling process is suspended until another process adds a matching tuple.

The Tuple Space primitives are *indivisible operations* in the sense that if two processes simultaneously try to in the same tuple, only one of them will succeed; the other one will block. Linda does not contain any primitives to modify a tuple while it is in Tuple Space. Instead, the tuple must be taken out of Tuple Space, modified locally, and then put back. The advantage of this approach is that it automatically provides mutual exclusion synchronization on the Tuple Space.

As an example, suppose we want to increment the second field of the tuple shown above. We can then use the following code:

```
int n;
float f;

in("item", ? &n, ? &f);
out("item", n + 1, f);
```

The first statement gets the tuple and removes it from Tuple Space. The second statement increments the second field and puts back the new tuple. If two or more processes try to execute this code at the same time, only one process will succeed in inning the tuple. The others will block until the tuple is back. This achieves the right synchronization behavior.

The above example shows how simple shared data structures can be built in Tuple Space. More complicated data structures can be built using a similar approach. The Linda model resembles the shared variable model, but an important difference is that Tuple Space is addressed associatively. A tuple does not have an address, as a word in memory has. The read() and in() primitives specify a description for a tuple, and the system has to find a tuple that matches this description.

14.1.5 Data-parallel languages

Another important parallel programming model is **data parallelism**. With data parallelism, all processors execute the same algorithm (and code), but operate on different parts of a data set, which usually is an array. In contrast, in a parallel program using processes, different processors can execute different algorithms. The latter kind of parallelism is generally known as **task parallelism**. Data parallelism is more restrictive and less flexible than task parallelism, but it is also easier to use, since only a single algorithm has to be defined for all processors.

A usual approach is to let the programmer define *what* can be executed in parallel, and let the compiler distribute the computations and the data among the different processors. Some parallel languages do this by providing built-in data-parallel operations. Fortran 90, for example, supports operations on matrices that can be executed in a data-parallel way. The simplest explicit language construct for data-parallel programming is the **parallel loop statement**. For example, matrix multiplication can be expressed as follows using data parallelism:

```
parfor i := 1 to N do
    parfor j := 1 to N do
        C[i, j] := 0;
        for k := 1 to N do
            C[i, j] := C[i, j] + A[i, j] * B[j, k];
        od;
    od;
od;
```

This example specifies that the steps of the two outer loops can be executed in parallel, leaving it to the compiler to actually distribute the computations over the different processors. An important advantage of data parallelism is that, due to their simple structure, data-parallel programs are easier to analyze by a compiler. We will discuss this in more detail in Section 14.7, when we look at automatic parallelization. Figure 14.3 summarizes the five parallel programming models.

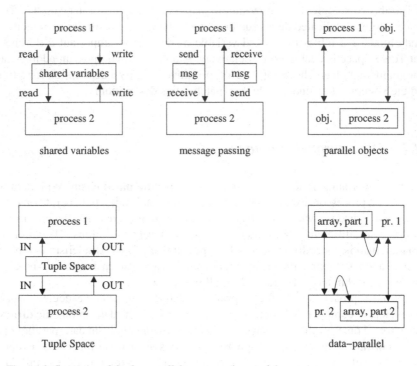

Fig. 14.3: Summary of the five parallel programming models

14.2 Processes and threads

We will now begin our discussion of the implementation of the five parallel programming models discussed above. All these models use processes and many also use threads in addition to processes. Therefore, in this section, we first discuss the implementation of processes and threads.

The first important thing to note is that modern operating systems already provide a *process abstraction*. This should come as no surprise, since a process is essentially an abstraction of a physical processor, and it is the task of the OS to provide abstractions of hardware entities. Unfortunately, using OS processes for implementing language-level processes often has a high overhead. In particular, a context switch from one OS process to another is often expensive, since it requires intervention from the OS kernel. Also, creating OS processes is usually expensive, because such processes are heavyweight; they carry a large amount of state information, such as open file descriptors and accounting information.

An alternative way to implement language-level processes is to use a single OS process per physical processor, and implement all language-level processes on that processor as threads. This approach is used in many parallel languages, since it often is far more efficient than using multiple OS processes. If the language itself also provides a threads abstraction, language-level threads can then be implemented in the same way as language-level processes. Below, we discuss how to implement threads.

Many—but not all—operating systems provide threads in addition to processes. A *thread* carries much less state information than a process, so it is more lightweight. Still, if threads are managed by the OS, all thread operations (creation, context switching, deletion) have to go through the OS, which is still expensive. An alternative solution is to implement threads in *user space*. In general, this is easy to do, and in fact many user-level thread packages exist. The only complicated operation is a thread **context switch**, which requires saving the current program counter, stack pointer, and registers and replacing them with the previously saved values from another thread. Since this operation cannot be expressed in most high-level languages, a few lines of assembly code are usually needed for implementing thread context switches.

A fundamental problem with user-level threads concerns blocking calls to the OS kernel. If one thread invokes a blocking operation (for example a receive statement), another thread in the same process should be allowed to continue. If the OS does not know about the existence of user-level threads, however, the OS will block the entire process, thus preventing other threads from running. Fortunately, several solutions to this problem have been invented [13].

The basic idea is to let the OS know about the existence of threads, but to avoid involving the OS in each and every thread operation. This idea, called **scheduler activations**, is supported in several modern operating systems, for example Solaris. We assume in the remainder of this chapter that the run-time system uses user-level threads.

Each user-level thread is represented by a **thread control block**, which has room to save the status information (see Figure 14.4). Depending on the threads package, the control block may have additional fields. In the example, the Stack limits field indicates the beginning and end of the stack that is assigned to the thread. The Status field indicates whether the thread is "running" (it is the current thread), "runnable" (it is not the current thread, but it can execute), or "blocked" (it cannot execute because it is suspended).

| Status |
| Program counter |
| Stack pointer |
| Stack limits |
| Registers |
| Next-pointer |

Fig. 14.4: Structure of a thread control block

Sometimes a threads package contains a **scheduler** thread that determines which runnable thread should be allowed to execute next. The scheduler uses the status fields to determine which threads can execute. If multiple threads are runnable, two scheduling regimes are possible: either the current thread executes until it (voluntarily) blocks, or the scheduler **preempts**, the running thread after a certain period of time and schedules another thread. The scheduler also takes care of doing the actual context switch to the new thread. A disadvantage of using a special scheduler thread is that the context switches to and from the scheduler thread add run-time overhead. Many thread packages therefore avoid using an explicit scheduler thread. Instead, a thread can call a library routine that selects the next thread to run and does a context switch directly to the selected thread.

Thread control blocks sometimes need to be manipulated as list items. A monitor, for example, can maintain a list of threads that want to enter the monitor. As another example, the scheduler thread may use a list of runnable threads, so it does not need to inspect the Status field of every thread when it wants to select another runnable thread. For this reason, control blocks usually contain one or more pointer fields that are used to link them into lists.

This concludes our introduction to the five parallel programming models and our discussion of processes and threads. In the following sections we turn to the implementation of the five models, where we will primarily look at the implementation of communication primitives.

14.3 Shared variables

On a shared-memory multiprocessor, a shared variable can be implemented simply by storing it in the shared memory. The compiler has to know which part of the memory address space is shared, so it can assign shared variables to locations in shared memory. On many multiprocessors, all of the memory is shared, so this task is trivial. On a distributed-memory multicomputer, shared variables are of course much more difficult to implement. Techniques have been developed to simulate a virtual shared memory on top of a distributed-memory system [148, 177]. Just as virtual memory moves pages between main memory and the disk, virtual shared memory moves pages between the memories of different processors. This technique is outside the scope of this book, however.

14.3.1 Locks

The main difficulty with the shared-variable model is how to implement the synchronization primitives. Let us first look at lock variables. A lock variable has two operations, to acquire and release the lock, that look deceptively simple. The hard problem, however, is implementing these operations *indivisibly*. If several threads try to execute an operation on the same lock variable, only one of them should be allowed to execute at any one same time. This problem has been studied extensively in the operating systems literature.

One solution for making the primitives indivisible is by implementing them in the OS, but this has a high overhead. Fortunately, most processors have hardware instructions that are intended to allow an efficient user-level implementation of locks. A frequently used instruction is **test-and-set**. This instruction checks if a given variable is equal to zero, and if so it sets the variable to one; either way, the original value of the variable is returned. The hardware guarantees the instruction to be indivisible.

With such an instruction, it becomes possible to implement indivisible operations on a lock. A lock variable holds a zero if it is free and a one if it is taken. To acquire the lock, a test-and-set instruction on this variable is executed. If the result is zero, the lock was free, and the variable is now set to one. If multiple threads try to acquire the lock simultaneously, only one of the test-and-set instructions will return zero, since the instruction is indivisible; the others will see that the variable was already set to one. Thus, there can be no confusion about which thread obtained the lock.

If a thread fails to acquire a lock, it should block until the lock becomes free; this happens when it is set to zero again by some other thread. A simple way to implement this blocking is to repeatedly try acquiring the lock. This approach is called **busy waiting** (or **spinning**). It wastes CPU time, however, which in general should be avoided. A better solution is to maintain a list of blocked threads with each lock variable, as shown in Figure 14.5. With this approach, when a thread needs to block on a lock, its control block is added to this list, its status is set to "not runnable", and another (runnable) thread is selected by the scheduler (see Figure

14.5(b)). Whenever a thread releases a lock, it can make the first thread on the list "runnable" again, so the scheduler will eventually select it for execution again (see Figure 14.5(c)). Note that releasing a lock now becomes more complicated than just resetting the lock variable to zero; for further details see Exercise 14.4.

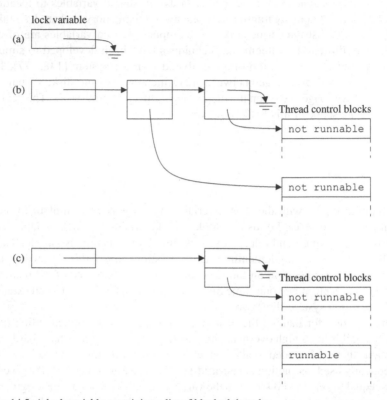

Fig. 14.5: A lock variable containing a list of blocked threads

14.3.2 Monitors

Let us now look at the second synchronization primitive described in Section 14.1.1: the monitor. A monitor is a higher-level mechanism than a lock. It is usually implemented with some support from the compiler. In particular, the compiler helps in making all monitor operations mutually exclusive. First of all, it automatically generates a lock variable for each monitor, called the **monitor lock**. Also, the compiler generates code at the start of every monitor operation to acquire the monitor lock; likewise, it generates code at the end of the operation to release the lock. These statements ensure that only one thread can be in the monitor at a time; if other threads also try to execute an operation on the same monitor, they will be blocked on the monitor lock.

The compiler also generates code to implement the wait and signal operations. For this purpose, a separate list is used for each condition variable, containing the control blocks of threads that are blocked in a wait() operation on that condition variable. The wait operation adds the control block of the current thread to this list, marks the current thread as "not runnable", releases the monitor lock, and finally allows the scheduler to resume another thread. A signal() operation makes one of the threads in the list runnable and removes its control block from this list. Depending on the precise semantics of the monitor, a signal operation may or may not do a context switch to the signaled thread. If no context switch is done, the signaled thread will eventually be selected by the scheduler. When that moment arrives, the thread will first obtain the monitor lock again, and then continue executing its operation.

14.4 Message passing

We will now discuss how to implement message passing on a distributed-memory machine. The implementation depends on which of the communication protocols provided by the operating system is being used. Many languages are implemented on top of a reliable communication protocol, such as TCP/IP. For efficiency reasons, some language implementers prefer a lighter-weight, unreliable protocol, such as UDP, or even use their own communication protocols. An unreliable protocol usually is more efficient than a reliable one; this implies that it obtains a lower latency and higher throughput. The disadvantage is of course that the language run-time system then needs to implement its own protocol to make the language-level operations reliable. Since this protocol can be tailored to what the run-time system needs, the overall performance may be better than that on top of a reliable OS protocol [27].

In the extreme case, some languages are implemented by letting the OS map the network device in user space, and running the entire network protocol as part of the run-time system. This approach only uses the OS during program initialization (to map the network device), but avoids using the OS for communication, so it has a low overhead [39]. In general, the more functionality is implemented in user space, the more flexibility the run-time system has. This often results in performance gains, but at the cost of a more complicated run-time system. For our discussion, however, we assume that the run-time system is built on top of a reliable communication protocol provided by the OS.

Even with this simplification, there still are many issues the run-time system has to take care of. The issues we discuss are: locating the receiver, marshaling, type checking, and message selection. For the purpose of our discussion, assume we have two processes, Sender and Receiver, that are running on different processors and that want to communicate with each other as shown in Figure 14.6. Process Sender thus sends a message multiply(A, B) with two arrays of 100 floating point numbers to process Receiver; process Receiver waits for such a message to arrive and then

```
(* Process Sender: *)
    A, B: array[1..100] of float;
    initialize A and B;
    send multiply(A, B) to Receiver;

(* Process Receiver: *)
    A, B: array[1..100] of float;
    receive multiply(A, B);
    multiply A and B, print result;
```

Fig. 14.6: Sender and Receiver communicating

services it.

14.4.1 Locating the receiver

The first question to answer is how the sender manages to get the message delivered
at the right destination process. At the language level, identifiers such as Sender
and Receiver are used to identify processes, but the OS communication protocol
clearly does not know anything at all about such identifiers. Typically, OS protocols
only know about processor names. Thus, the first task of a run-time system is to
maintain an administration of where each language process runs. In languages that
implement language-level processes as threads, an often-used approach is to have
one **communication daemon thread** per processor. A message intended for process
Receiver is then first sent to the daemon of the processor on which Receiver runs,
using the OS communication protocol; the daemon then hands the message to the
thread that implements the destination process (as described later).

14.4.2 Marshaling

Another issue is how to transmit the message over the network. In the example
above, the message is a structured value containing two arrays of floating point numbers. The OS communication protocol, however, does not know about data types
like arrays or floating point numbers. A typical protocol merely provides a primitive to send and receive flat **message buffers**, which are untyped arrays of bytes.
Therefore, procedures are needed that will convert a language-level message to a
flat buffer at the sending side and to convert such a buffer back at the receiving
side. Such procedures are known as **marshaling** and **unmarshaling** routines. The
conversion process is also called **(de)serialization**.

An example of these conversions is shown in Figure 14.7. Here, a record has
to be marshaled that contains the string "John" and the integer 26. The message
buffer containing the marshaled data starts with a length field in a fixed format (4

bytes), denoting the number of bytes to follow (9). Next, the string is stored in the buffer, in null-terminated ASCII form. Finally the four bytes of the integer value are stored in the buffer, with the least significant byte at the rightmost (highest) address, which also happens to be the format used by the sending processor. At the receiving side, the string and integer value are extracted from the buffer. Note that, in the example, the receiving processor uses a different data representation for integers than is used for the buffer, and stores the least significant byte at the *leftmost* address. An important advantage of marshaling is that such differences in machine representations can be masked. All that is needed is that the sender and receiver agree upon the format of the marshaled data in the buffer. As an optimization, it is also possible to always store the data in the format of the sender, and include a description of this format, for example specifying the byte order in the buffer. The receiver can then check whether the format in the buffer is different from its own format. This scheme avoids doing conversions when the sender and receiver have the same data format.

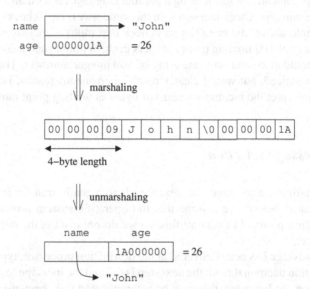

Fig. 14.7: Marshaling

In a library-based programming system, the user often has to write the marshaling routines by hand. With parallel languages, the routines are usually generated automatically by the compiler from the type definitions of the values sent and received. The marshaling routine for a message containing simple data structures, for example arrays, is easy to generate. The routine simply allocates a buffer of the right size and copies the arrays into the buffer. For complicated, pointer-based data structures (such as lists, trees, and graphs), however, automatic generation is not always possible, because the compiler cannot know what constitutes the entire data structure or how to deal with cycles in data structures. Many languages therefore restrict the data types that can be used in messages to scalars, records, and arrays, and disallow data types that contain pointers.

An interesting approach to marshaling is taken by Java RMI, the Java Remote Method Invocation. Any object can be marshaled automatically, provided its class implements the Serializable interface. The Java library contains generic routines that can marshal and unmarshal any serializable object. The routines are written in Java and check dynamically what the types of the object parameters are, using an object-oriented feature called reflection. This approach is highly flexible, but unfortunately the run-time inspection also has a tremendous overhead. It has been shown [183] that specialized compiler-generated routines can be orders of magnitude faster.

14.4.3 Type checking of messages

Another important advantage of using a parallel language rather than a library is that the compiler can type-check messages, in the same way it type-checks routine calls. In the example above, the compiler can check that multiply messages always contain two arrays of 100 floating point numbers each. Without such a compiler-check, the sender could also send, say, one array of 400 integer numbers. The discrepancy would go unnoticed, but would clearly result in erroneous results, because the receiver will interpret the incoming stream of bytes as floating point numbers.

14.4.4 Message selection

After marshaling the message, the next step is to actually transfer it over the network. As stated before, we assume that the operating system provides a reliable communication protocol to achieve this, so we do not discuss the details of such a protocol here.

Once a message has been delivered at the destination processor, typically using a communication daemon thread, the next step is to hand the message to a local thread. Depending on the language, this may be a complicated task, because programmers often are given control over the order in which incoming messages are serviced. In the simplest case (used in our example above), the receiver only indicates the type of message it wants to receive (such as a multiply). In this case, the run-time system can store incoming messages in separate lists, based on the message type. Each receive statement then blocks until the list for the specified type is non-empty.

Some languages, however, give the user more flexibility about which messages to accept, and in which order. In SR, for example, the receiver can specify a predicate on the message:

    receive msg(A, N) **suchthat** N < 50;

In this case, the run-time system has to traverse the list of incoming messages of type msg and check if there is any message whose second field is smaller than 50. Whenever a new message arrives, it also has to be checked in this way. Features like these make the language more expressive, but they clearly also complicate the language implementation.

Our discussion so far has assumed that messages are accepted using an explicit receive statement. An alternative form is implicit message receipt. Conceptually, this approach creates a new thread of control within the receiving process that executes a message handler. To implement this, the run-time system may indeed create a new thread of control for each message. Since message handlers generally take little execution time, however, the overhead of creating and destroying these threads will be high.

To reduce the overhead, several techniques can be used. One idea is to have the communication daemon thread execute the message handler for each incoming message, without creating a new thread. Although this will work in most cases, sometimes a message handler routine may need to block. For example, it may want to acquire a lock that is already taken. Clearly, the communication daemon thread should not block, since it would prevent other incoming messages from being serviced. If message handlers are allowed to block, it follows that they need to be executed by a separate thread.

A second and more general idea is to use a **pool** of message handling threads. When a thread has finished executing a handler, it is returned to the pool instead of being destroyed. When another message comes in, it can be handled by one of the threads in this pool. If the pool is empty when a message arrives, a new thread is created. In this way, many expensive thread creation and destruction operations can be avoided.

14.5 Parallel object-oriented languages

To a large extent, parallel object-oriented languages can use similar implementation techniques as imperative languages. As we have seen, many object-oriented languages are based on ideas like threads and monitors, whose implementation we have already described. Below, we discuss three additional implementation techniques that have been developed more specifically for object-oriented languages: how to locate objects, how to migrate objects, and how to replicate objects.

14.5.1 Object location

The first issue we discuss concerns naming and locating of objects. A parallel or distributed program uses many objects, located on several processors, which can access each other. Typically, an object in such a program is defined by an **object identi-**

fier or **OID**. An OID is similar to a pointer. Unlike normal pointers in C or Pascal, however, an OID is valid network-wide. An object on one processor may contain a reference to an object on another processor. There is no syntactic distinction between invoking an operation on a local object—an object on the same processor as the invoker— or on a remote object. In other words, concurrent object-oriented languages provide a global, program-wide, name space for all objects.

A key question is how to implement this global name space for objects on a distributed-memory machine. A traditional pointer, as used for example in C or Pascal, is represented as a memory address; such a pointer, however, only has meaning for a single address space. An OID, on the other hand, identifies an object on any processor, independent of its location. Typically, some bookkeeping is used on each processor to map an OID onto a physical processor and a memory address within that processor. For example, an OID can be represented as two words: one identifying the processor on which the object resides and one containing its address within that processor (assuming each processor runs a single process).

As an example, suppose an object X contains a reference to another object Y. The reference of X to Y is then stored as a 2-word OID, as shown in Figure 14.8. Suppose X invokes an operation on Y, as in:

```
Y->Determine_Value("Diamond");
```

The run-time system then first determines on which processor Y is stored, by looking at the first word in the OID. Next, it sends a message to this processor containing the operation, the address, and the parameters.

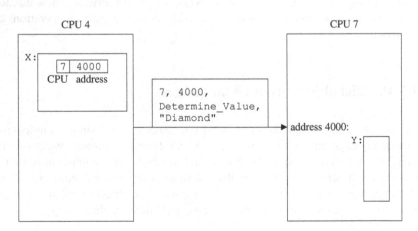

Fig. 14.8: Using object identifiers for remote references

Unfortunately, treating every object in this way is very expensive. For remote objects, the overhead of determining the location of the object is small compared to the time needed to issue a remote operation. For local objects, however, the overhead can be substantial. One solution is to require the programmer to distinguish between local objects—objects that cannot be accessed from a remote processor—and shared or global objects. In Java, for example, remote objects have to implement the Remote interface. Another solution, chosen in the Emerald system, is to let the compiler figure out which objects are used only locally; the others are assumed to be shared.

14.5.2 Object migration

Several object-oriented languages allow objects to be moved dynamically from one processor to another. This technique, called **object migration**, has several advantages. For example, suppose an object X is going to execute a sequence of operations on a remote object Y. Without object migration, each invocation would result in communication. An alternative scheme is to first migrate object Y to the processor on which X runs, then invoke all operations there, and finally, if desired, migrate object Y back to its original location. If Y does not contain much data, this scheme may result in less communication overhead. Object migration can also be used to improve the load balance of a program. The Emerald language provides several notations for expressing object migration and for requesting the system to keep certain groups of objects together on the same processor.

To implement object migration, several challenging problems have to be solved. The data of the object have to be transferred to its new location, using the marshaling and unmarshaling techniques described earlier. For objects containing one or more threads of control, these threads also have to be moved, which is complicated. Finally, if objects are allowed to migrate, it becomes far more complicated to locate an object, given its OID. Our scheme described above assumed that an OID contains the location of the object, encoded as a processor number and a local address. If objects can migrate, this scheme no longer works.

One solution to this problem is to keep track of all references to each object. If an object X migrates from processor A to processor B, all references to X are then changed on all processors. Unfortunately, maintaining all this information in a coherent way is very hard. An alternative scheme that does not need this information works as follows (see Figure 14.9). Instead of updating all references, only the reference on processor A is updated. The run-time system on processor A stores a **forwarding address** (processor B) for object X (see Figure 14.9(b)). Whenever another processor, say C, tries to invoke an operation on X, it will send a message to the run-time system on processor A, because processor C is not yet aware of the new location of X. The run-time system of processor A will notice that X has moved and use the forwarding address for X to determine its current location (processor B); the message is then forwarded to this processor. The run-time system of processor B will execute the operation, return the result to processor C, and also inform the run-time system of processor C of the new location of X. All subsequent invocations from processor C on object X will go straight to processor B, as shown in Figure 14.9(c). In theory, an object can move multiple times, so many forwarding addresses may

have to be followed to find a given object. For this reason, the technique is known
as **pointer chasing**.

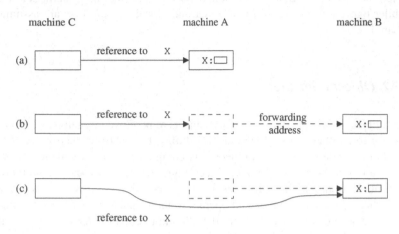

Fig. 14.9: Pointer chasing

14.5.3 Object replication

Besides object migration, some languages also support **object replication**. With this
technique, copies of an object are stored in the local memories of several processors.
The advantage of object replication is that operations that read the state of the object but do not modify it can be executed using the local copy, without doing any
communication. Thus, if an object is mainly read and seldom modified, object replication can substantially reduce the communication overhead [29]. Some languages
also use replication to make programs more fault-tolerant.

A key issue is what to do when an object is modified. Clearly, if the operation
is applied only on the local copy of the object, all other copies in the system will
become out-of-date. Two solutions to this problem are possible. One is to *invalidate*
all other copies, by asking each processor to delete its copy. The problem with this
is that a processor whose copy has been invalidated needs to get a new copy of the
object when it again needs to invoke an operation on the object. If the object is
large, this will have a high communication overhead. The alternative is to *update* all
copies, for example by sending the operation and its parameters and applying the
operation to all copies of the object.

The most fundamental problem with object replication in general is how to guarantee consistency of all copies. We illustrate this using the update protocol. Assume
that processes on two processors, M_1 and M_2, simultaneously want to do an operation on an object X that contains an integer with initial value 0. For example, M_1

wants to set the integer to 10 and M_2 wants to set it to 20, both using an operation assign():

```
M₁: X->assign(10);
M₂: X->assign(20);
```

If M_1 and M_2 both send their operation to all processors, there is a risk that these messages may arrive in a different order at different processors. Some processors may receive the message from M_1 first and then the message from M_2, so the final value of the integer becomes 20. Other processors may receive the messages the other way round, resulting in a final value of 10. As a result, the replicas of the object will become inconsistent. Many solutions have been proposed for keeping the replicas of objects consistent. The solution taken in the Orca system is to use **totally-ordered group communication**, which guarantees that all messages arrive at all destination processors in the same order [29]. With this primitive, either all processors receive the message from M_1 first, or all processors receive the message from M_2 first. Mixtures are guaranteed not to occur. This communication primitive can be implemented either by the OS or by a user-space protocol.

14.6 Tuple space

The next programming model we discuss is the Linda Tuple Space. Tuple Space provides a particularly interesting challenge for language implementers. Recall that the Tuple Space is a kind of associative shared memory. We will discuss how the Tuple Space can be implemented on a distributed-memory system.

```
int n, year;
float f;
...                                    /* code initializing n and f */

(1) in("Olympic year", 1928);
(2) in("Classic movie", "Way out West", 1937);
(3) in("Classic movie", "Sons of the desert", 1933);
(4) in("Classic movie", "Sons of the desert", ? &year);
(5) in("Popular number", 65536);
(6) in("Popular number", 3.14159);
(7) in("Popular number", n);
(8) in("Popular number", f);
```

Fig. 14.10: A demo program in C/Linda

A trivial way of implementing Tuple Space would be to store the entire Tuple Space as a list on a single processor (the "Tuple Space server"), and search this entire list whenever a tuple is read. Obviously, this approach will be highly inefficient. First, it requires a linear search of the entire Tuple Space. Second, every Tuple Space operation will communicate with the Tuple Space server, making this processor a communication bottleneck. Thus, an efficient Tuple Space implementation has to address two issues:

- how to avoid the overhead of associative addressing;
- how to implement the shared memory model on a system that does not provide shared memory.

These problems can be solved using a combination of compile-time and run-time techniques. The **Linda preprocessor** translates Linda programs into the target language (for example C) and also analyzes the usage of Tuple Space operations, as discussed below. The **Linda kernel** is a run-time system that is linked with the compiled target language code. The preprocessor and the kernel cooperate to address the two issues discussed above.

14.6.1 Avoiding the overhead of associative addressing

We first discuss how to avoid the overhead of associative addressing of the Tuple Space model. This problem has to be addressed for any implementation of Linda, whether it runs on a multiprocessor or a multicomputer. To simplify our discussion, we assume here that the Tuple Space is implemented using the shared memory of a multiprocessor. A distributed implementation is discussed in the next subsection.

The Linda preprocessor analyzes all calls to Tuple Space primitives in the program text. It partitions all these calls into disjoint sets, called **partitions**. The partitioning is done in such a way that Tuple Space calls in different partitions cannot affect each other. For this purpose, the compiler looks at the number of parameters of the calls, the types of the parameters, and the values of the parameters if they are compile-time constants.

For example, assume a C/Linda program with the declarations and statements as shown in Figure 14.10. It is clear that the first two calls cannot affect each other, because they have a different number of parameters: the first call ins a tuple with two fields and the second call ins a tuple with three fields, so they access different tuples. The second and third calls both have three parameters, but the compiler can determine statically that the last two parameters are different, so these calls cannot affect each other either. Likewise, the fifth and sixth calls differ in their second parameter. The third and fourth calls clearly do affect each other, since the tuple

("Classic movie", "Sons of the desert", 1933);

can be inned by both calls.

The last two calls are more interesting, because they have actual parameters whose values are not known at compile time. Note that the parameters are variables, but since they are not preceded by a ? they are *actual* parameters that are evaluated at run time. Still, the seventh and eight calls cannot affect each other, because the types of their second parameter are different: the seventh call features an integer parameter and the eight call a floating point parameter.

It is not clear at compile time whether the fifth and seventh calls will affect each other, since that depends on the run-time value of the variable n. Likewise, the sixth and eight calls may or may not affect each other, depending on the value of f. In such cases, the compiler is conservative and puts both calls in the same partition.

The compiler performs the analysis that we informally described above and uses it to generate the five partitions shown in Figure 14.11 for the demo C/Linda program of Figure 14.10. In this example we have used in calls everywhere, but the analysis is the same if out or read primitives (or some combination) are used.

Partition 1:
    (1) in("Olympic year", 1928);

Partition 2:
    (2) in("Classic movie", "Way out West", 1937);

Partition 3:
    (3) in("Classic movie", "Sons of the desert", 1933);
    (4) in("Classic movie", "Sons of the desert", ? &year);

Partition 4:
    (5) in("Popular number", 65536);
    (7) in("Popular number", n);

Partition 5:
    (6) in("Popular number", 3.14159);
    (8) in("Popular number", f);

Fig. 14.11: The partitions for the demo C/Linda program in Figure 14.10

An immediate advantage of this analysis is that the entire Tuple Space can now be split up into different sections, one for each partition. Since calls in two different partitions cannot affect each other, a call need only search the section of the Tuple Space that is reserved for its partition. So, instead of an exhaustive search of the entire Tuple Space, a call need only search a small part of the Tuple Space.

The result of the Tuple Space analysis can be used for more advanced optimizations as well. In particular, the Linda preprocessor analyzes all calls within a partition and then determines a **storage representation** that is optimized for that partition. We illustrate this idea with several examples.

Assume a given partition contains the three calls in the following fragment:

```
string title, SomeTitle;
int year, SomeYear;

out("Classic movie", "Sons of the desert", 1933);
out("Classic movie", SomeTitle, SomeYear);
in("Classic movie", ? &title, ? &year);
```

So, no other calls in the program produce or consume tuples of this form. The tuples of this form will be stored in a separate section of Tuple Space. Since all tuples in this section of Tuple Space will always have the constant "Classic movie" as their first field, there is no need to do run-time matching on this field. In other words, the compiler can determine statically that the first field of the out operation and the in operation will always match. Hence, this field need not be stored in the tuple at run-time, which saves memory and the costs of a run-time string comparison. Also, the second and third parameters of the in call are formal parameters of the right type, so they will always match the actual parameters.

In conclusion, there is no need to do any run-time matching at all for the in call. If tuples of this form exist, resulting from one or more out calls, the run-time system can just take such a tuple and return it. A simple way to implement this is to store the tuples of this partition in a queue. The out call adds a tuple to this queue and the in call waits until the queue is not empty and then returns the first element.

So, the following data structure is used for this partition:

Q: **queue of record**
    string title;
    int year;

A call like out("Classic movie", title, year) is translated into:

    enqueue(Q, [title, year]);

and a call like in("Classic movie", ? &title, ? &year) is translated into:

    [title, year] := dequeue(Q);

where dequeue blocks while the queue is empty. The result is that during run time the Tuple Space need not be searched at all: it is sufficient to do an operation on a queue data structure. The overhead of the associative memory model has thus been eliminated in this case.

As another example, assume the programmer changes the in statement into

    in("Classic movie", ? &title, 1940);

to search for classic movies produced in 1940. This small change has a major impact on the representation scheme. Clearly, this call still belongs to the partition described above, since it has the right number and types of elements. So, we now have a partition with these calls:

    out("Classic movie", "Sons of the desert", 1933);
    out("Classic movie", SomeTitle, SomeYear);
    in("Classic movie", ? &title, 1940);

The new in call cannot be translated into a simple dequeue statement, because it requires that the third field contains the value 1940. One solution would be to search the entire queue until a tuple is found whose last field contains 1940. Unfortunately, if the queue contains many elements, as for example in a complete list of all classic movies, this search may take a long time. The Linda preprocessor therefore switches to an alternative representation scheme for partitions like these, based on a hash table. Each tuple that is added by the out operation is inserted into a hash table, using the last field of the tuple as a hash key. The in operation likewise uses the last field as a hash value, so a linear search is avoided.

If both in calls are used in the same program, things become more complicated again. Assume the program contains the following two statements;

```
in("Classic movie", ? &title, ? &year);
in("Classic movie", ? &title, 1940);
```

The problem is that the first call does not have an actual parameter (a value) that can be used for hashing. Instead, the first call must search the hash table. The hash table thus must have an interface that allows this operation.

To summarize, the Linda preprocessor partitions all Tuple Space calls in a program into disjoint sets and then selects a representation scheme for each set that is tailored to that set. The result is that a Tuple Space call seldom needs to search the complete Tuple Space.

14.6.2 Distributed implementations of the tuple space

The second problem that a Linda implementation has to address is how to represent the Tuple Space on a hardware system that does not have a shared memory. On a shared-memory multiprocessor, the entire Tuple Space can simply be stored in this shared memory. On a distributed-memory machine, however, other representations have to be found.

Several approaches exist to represent Tuple Space on a distributed-memory machine. One approach is based on hashing. As described above, many Tuple Space calls contain a field that has a hash value associated with it. We have described how this hash field can be used to avoid searching the Tuple Space. In a distributed implementation, the hash field can also be used to determine on which processor to store the tuple. To continue our earlier example, a statement like

```
out("Classic movie", "The Music Box", 1932);
```

can use the last field (1932) as a hash value. Assume we have a hash function $h()$ which returns a value between 1 and P, where P is the number of processors in the system. The above statement then sends a message to processor $h(1932)$ and stores the tuple

```
("Classic movie", "The Music Box", 1932)
```

on that processor. (As described earlier, the first field can actually be optimized away, but we will ignore this optimization for our current discussion.) In this way, all tuples in the partition get randomly distributed among all processors, thus preventing one processor from becoming a communication bottleneck.

When a statement like

```
in("Classic movie", ? &title, 1940);
```

is executed, a message is sent to processor $h(1940)$ to ask it for a tuple that matches the in call.

A problem occurs if the program contains in calls that do not have an actual parameter for the last field, as in

in("Classic movie", ? &title, ? &year);

In this case, the Linda preprocessor can determine that the last field is not suitable as a hash value. The second field has the same problem. Instead, the preprocessor can use the first field as hash value. Unfortunately, this means that all tuples that have "Classic movie" as their first field will be stored on the same processor. If there are many such tuples, this processor may become a bottleneck.

The hash-based solution thus tries to distribute all tuples randomly among all processors. The advantage is that it is less likely that any one processor becomes a bottleneck. The disadvantage is that almost all Tuple Space calls result in communication. Also, if a processor P_1 wants to send data to another processor P_2 (using a tuple), chances are that the data go through another (random) processor P_3, because the tuple containing the data is hashed onto processor P_3. In this case, two messages (instead of one) are required to get the data from the source to the destination.

A completely different approach than hashing is to use a **uniform distribution**, which comes in several variants. One option is to broadcast all out calls and store the new tuple at all processors. The entire Tuple Space thus becomes *replicated* on all processors. The advantage is that read calls can be executed locally, using the local copy of Tuple Space, so they do not require any communication at all. In calls can first check the local Tuple Space to see if a matching tuple is available, but they also need communication to inform the other processors that they have to delete the tuple.

The second form of uniform distribution is the inverse of the above scheme: all out calls are executed without doing communication and the new tuple is generated in the local Tuple Space. The entire Tuple Space thus is *partitioned* among all processors. Whenever a tuple needs to be found (using read or in operations), the run-time system first checks if a matching tuple is available in the local partition. If not, it broadcasts a request to all processors. Each processor then checks if a matching tuple is available in its partition. If multiple processors have a matching tuple, further communication is needed to select one of the tuples.

Yet another uniform distribution scheme organizes all processors in a two-dimensional grid. If a processor P executes an out call, the call is sent to all processors in the same *row* as P. A read or in call is sent to all processors in the same *column* of the sender. Since a row and a column always intersect at exactly one point, a read or in call will always find the tuple (at the processor at the intersection point) if it exists.

To summarize, many different representations of the Tuple Space on a distributed system are possible. The best scheme in general depends on the application. For example, if an application frequently reads a given tuple (for example the global bound in a branch-and-bound algorithm), the best performance is obtained if the tuple is replicated. Thus, the first uniform distribution scheme, which replicates the Tuple Space, is most efficient. If tuples are read infrequently, however, this scheme is less efficient. The best scheme also depends on the underlying hardware. For example, if the hardware supports multicast (sending the same message to multiple processors), for example an Ethernet network, replicating the Tuple Space becomes more attractive.

A general problem with this variety of implementation techniques is that the performance model is not clear to the programmer. For example, on some implementations read operations may be cheap while in and out operations are expensive. On other implementations, out operations are cheap and read and in operations are expensive. In other words, the performance of a Linda program will be hard to predict without knowing more about the underlying hardware and Linda implementation. This makes it hard to write programs that are not only portable but also efficient on a wide range of systems.

In conclusion, Linda provides an abstract, high-level programming model. Implementing Linda efficiently is a challenging task, and many novel techniques have been developed to avoid the overhead of associative addressing and to implement the Tuple Space on a distributed-memory system. The high level of abstraction also makes it more difficult for the programmer to understand the performance behavior of the Linda primitives. Nonetheless, the Linda model has had quite some impact on parallel processing research since its introduction in 1985, and is still being studied and used. For example, JavaSpaces [102] is based on a model somewhat similar to Tuple Space.

14.7 Automatic parallelization

The techniques described so far in this chapter are intended for implementing languages with explicit constructs for expressing parallelism. An interesting question is whether we need such languages at all. Parallel programming is more difficult than sequential programming, so for the programmer it would be much easier if the language implementation would take care of the parallelization. The holy grail in parallel processing is to design a compiler that takes as input any sequential program written in a given language and produces as output an efficient parallel program. In this way, programmers could write their programs in sequential languages and would not be bothered with expressing parallelism, communication, or synchronization. In addition, existing sequential programs could be run on a parallel computer without any effort from the user.

The key issue is of course whether such an automatically parallelizing compiler can be implemented. No such compiler exists yet, and it is hard to tell if one ever will. For many applications, clever ideas are required to parallelize them efficiently. Many research papers and Ph.D. theses have been devoted to describing such ideas for specific applications. It remains to be seen whether a compiler will ever be able to parallelize all these applications automatically. On the other hand, substantial progress has been made with automatic parallelization. Rather than trying to predict the future, we will describe the technical problems of automatic parallelization and illustrate some of the techniques that have been developed so far.

Most of the work on automatic parallelization is targeted for specific classes of parallel architectures. We initially assume that the target machine is a shared-memory multiprocessor. In Section 14.7.4 we shall look at distributed-memory multicomputers. Much research has been done on compilers for vector computers and Very Long Instruction Word (VLIW) machines, but we do not discuss such work here. Also, we assume that the source program is written in a Pascal-like, imperative language. In the real world, most parallelizing compilers are designed for Fortran.

14.7.1 Exploiting parallelism automatically

The first question to ask is what kind of parallelism a compiler should try to exploit. In theory, it could look all over the input program and try to find sections of code that can be executed concurrently. Unfortunately, this often results in very fine-grained parallelism that is not suitable for most parallel processors. For example, the two statements

```
A := B * C;
X := Y + Z;
```

can be executed in parallel, but it is unlikely that the overhead of sending the statements to different processors will be outweighed by the performance gain of using parallelism. Some machines (for example VLIWs) are designed to exploit such fine-grained parallelism efficiently, so for such architectures this approach makes sense. The gain to be expected is modest, however.

To exploit larger-scale parallelism and to increase the grain size, a good idea is to look only at loops in the program, since this is where programs usually spend most of their time. This observation is especially true for numerical programs. Most parallelizing compilers therefore exploit loop parallelism. As an example, consider the following statements:

```
print("start computing");
for i := 1 to 1000 do
    A[i] := sqrt(i);
od;
print(A);
```

This code computes 1000 square-roots. All iterations can be executed in parallel, since the calls to sqrt are independent of each other and the results are written to different elements of array A. Moreover, since the calls are expensive, it is worth while to execute them in parallel. Assuming the compiler knows about the sqrt function (for example because it is built into the language) and knows that it has no side effects, it can easily determine that the calls can and should be executed in parallel.

A compiler could convert the above code to a parallel program as follows. Initially, one processor (for example CPU 0) starts executing the program. After executing the first print statement, it arrives at the for-loop. It then splits up the 1000 iterations among all processors. If there are, say, 10 processors, CPU 0 executes iterations 1 to 100, CPU 1 executes iterations 101 to 200, and so on. Each processor writes part of the array A, which is stored in shared memory. After all processors are done, they synchronize and wait until the last one is finished. Finally, CPU 0 prints the value of A[ ].

This execution model is used by most parallelizing compilers. Except for the sequential code (which is executed by one CPU), all processors execute the same code, but on different parts of the data. The model therefore is known as "Single Program Multiple Data" ("SPMD") parallelism [144]. We do not discuss the details of the work distribution and synchronization here, but assume the compiler generates code for it, using traditional communication mechanisms (for example shared variables or message passing) whenever needed. If different iterations do different amounts of computation, the work distribution can become quite complicated, and advanced scheduling techniques may be needed to give every processor an equal amount of work.

In general, programs may contain a large number of loops, so a relevant question is which loops to parallelize. If there are several consecutive loops (each with independent iterations) in the program, they can all be parallelized, one after each other. For example, parallelizing the following code:

```
for i := 1 to 1000 do
    A[i] := sqrt(i);
od;
print(A);
for i := 1 to 5000 do
    B[i] := arctan(i);
od;
print(B);
```

just applies the technique described earlier to both loops in turn. If the loops are "nested" inside each other, however, we have a different situation. For example, consider the following code, which adds the matrices A[,] and B[,]:

```
for i := 1 to 500 do
    for j := 1 to 1000 do
        C[i, j] := A[i, j] + B[i, j];
    od;
od;
```

There are (at least) two ways to parallelize this code. One way is to repeatedly distribute the inner loop over all processors. With 10 processors, each processor will execute 100 (= 1000/10) additions and then synchronize; this process is repeated 500 times (for all values of i). An alternative approach is to distribute the outer loop. All 10 processors will then execute 50 000 (= 50 × 1000) additions before they synchronize. Clearly, the latter approach has a lower overhead, because it requires fewer work-distributions and synchronization steps. Parallelizing compilers therefore try to parallelize "outer loops". Put in other words, they try to exploit large-grained parallelism, whenever possible.

An alternative to this compiler analysis is to allow the programmer to indicate which loops should be executed in parallel. This is what data-parallel languages do, using the parfor construct discussed in Section 14.1.5.

14.7.2 Data dependencies

In the examples given so far, all iterations of the loops are independent of each other. Most loops in actual programs, however, do not have this property. This is where the problems for parallelizing compilers begin. To illustrate, consider a slightly different version of our earlier example:

```
for i := 2 to 1000 do
    A[i] := sqrt(A[i-1]);
od;
```

The iterations of the loop now can no longer be executed in parallel. For example, during iteration 2 (i = 3), the value of A[2] is required. The value of A[2] must be computed before iteration 2 can start. Since the value is computed during the first iteration (i = 2), iteration 1 must be executed before iteration 2. This is called a **loop-carried dependence**. The argument applies to all iterations, so the loop iterations must be executed one by one. In other words, the loop is sequential and cannot be parallelized.

Parallelizing compilers are faced with two challenges. First, they should determine as precisely as possible whether a given loop may or may not be executed in parallel. When in doubt, they must be "conservative" and execute the loop sequentially; otherwise the parallel program might produce different results than the original sequential program. Second, whenever a compiler discovers a loop that cannot be parallelized, it should try to transform it into a loop that can be parallelized. We discuss such transformations in the next subsection. Below, we look at the first issue.

In general, there can be several different reasons why a given loop cannot be parallelized. We illustrate the most important cases with the following code fragment:

```
for i := 1 to 1000 do
    (1)  A[i] := ...;
    (2)  ... := A[i-1];

    (3)  ... := B[i];
    (4)  B[i-1] := ...;

    (5)  C[i] := ...;
    (6)  C[i-1] := ...;
od;
```

Statement 1 assigns a variable (A[i]) whose value will be used in statement 2 during the next iteration of the loop; this is called a **flow dependence**. Statement 3 uses a variable whose value will be changed in statement 4 during the next iteration; this is called an **anti-dependence**. Statement 5 assigns a variable that will be reassigned in statement 6 during the next iteration; this is called an **output dependence**. In each case, the dependence prevents the loop from being parallelized.

The examples above used very simple subscript expressions. We used either i or i–1 as index, where i is the loop variable. In practice, programs use far more complicated subscript expressions, which makes the dependence analysis harder. Still, an accurate dependence analysis may make the difference between being able to parallelize a loop and having to run it sequentially. As an example, consider the following code fragment:

```
for i := 1 to 250 do
    A[4*i] := ...;
    ... := A[4*i – 1];
od;
```

At first sight, one might say that the code looks similar to statements 1 and 2 of our previous example, so there is a flow dependence. More careful inspection of the code reveals that this is not the case. The first statement will assign the array entries 4, 8, 12, and so on, while the second statement will read the entries 3, 7, 11, and so on. Thus, there is no dependence and the loop can be parallelized. On the other hand, the loop

```
for i := 1 to 200 do
    A[5*i] := ...;
    ... := A[4*i – 1];
od;
```

does have a dependence. For example, iteration 3 (i = 3) will assign to A[15] while iteration 4 will read this element. Several techniques, often based on algebraic manipulation, have been developed for testing whether a given loop contains any dependencies.

Several other problems exist that make loop analysis and parallelization even harder. If a loop contains a routine call, this routine will have to be analyzed to determine its effects on any variables that it can access. So, interprocedural analysis is required here. Another hard problem concerns pointer variables. The code below, for example, contains an indirect assignment through a pointer variable p:

```
for i := 1 to 250 do
    *p := ...;
    ... := A[4*i];
od;
```

If p points to an element of A[], this assignment may cause a loop-carried dependence. Unfortunately, it is often difficult to determine during compile time whether p points into A[], let alone determining to which specific element p points. Often, this depends on run-time conditions, and cannot be determined during compile time. Still, several techniques have been developed that try to estimate the possible targets of pointer variables and use this information to parallelize conservatively loops containing pointer-dereferences [127].

An alternative to this compiler analysis is to let the programmer indicate which loops can safely be run in parallel. Data-parallel languages often use a construct like the parfor statement for this purpose. This construct thus may indicate that it is both desirable and legal to run a given loop in parallel. Of course, this also takes away an important advantage of automatic parallelization.

14.7.3 Loop transformations

The for-loops written by the programmer often have a form that make compiler optimization and parallelization difficult. Optimizing compilers for parallel machines therefore exploit techniques to transform loops into other forms, that are either more efficient or easier to parallelize. Dozens of such **loop restructuring transformations** have been designed and each compiler typically uses a bag of such "tricks." Some transformations are not related to parallelism, but try to increase sequential performance, for example by improving the **caching behavior** of the program; they strive to increase the hit ratio for the CPU cache. Rather than trying to give a complete overview of loop transformations, we will illustrate the general idea by describing two transformations that are designed specifically for parallel machines.

We start with a simple example, shown below:

```
for i := 1 to 250 do
    A[4*i] := sqrt(i);
    T := A[4*i - 1];
    ...
od;
```

This code is similar to one of our earlier examples, but an important difference is that it contains an assignment to a scalar variable T. The problem is that this assignment creates an output dependence, since every iteration of the loop will do an assignment to that same T. A compiler can easily transform this loop to an equivalent loop that does not have this dependence. The idea is to let every iteration assign to a different (temporary) variable. After the loop has been executed, the value of the last (250th) iteration is assigned to T. We can implement this idea using an extra array, called Tmp[ ].

```
for i := 1 to 250 do
    A[4*i] := sqrt(i);
    Tmp[i] := A[4*i - 1];
    ...
od;
T := Tmp[250];
```

This transformation is called **scalar expansion**. It eliminates the output dependence and thus allows the transformed loop to be parallelized. On a distributed-memory machine, a slightly different approach is to give every processor its own scalar variable, stored in its local memory. The Tmp[ ] array then essentially is distributed over the local memories. This transformation is known as **privatization**.

Another important transformation is **loop interchange**, which works on nested loops, such as the loops shown below:

```
for i := 2 to 500 do
    for j := 1 to 1000 do
        A[i, j] := A[i–1, j] + B[i, j];
    od;
od;
```

This code is similar to the matrix addition code shown earlier, but the left-hand side of the assignment statement now is an element of A[,]. This assignment statement causes a loop-carried dependence. For example, iteration 2 (i = 3) of the outer loop uses the elements A[2, 1] to A[2, 1000], which are computed during iteration 1 (i = 2). We could parallelize the inner loop, but, as we have discussed before, this generates fine-grained parallelism, which is less efficient. We can solve this problem by transforming the code as follows:

```
for j := 1 to 1000 do
    for i := 2 to 500 do
        A[i, j] := A[i–1, j] + B[i, j];
    od;
od;
```

Note that the inner and outer loops have been exchanged. We can now parallelize the outer loop into 1000 tasks that each execute the inner loop sequentially.

A parallelizing compiler must of course make sure that the original and transformed program are equivalent. The compiler is only allowed to do transformations such as scalar expansion and loop interchange that do not change the result of the programs. We do not discuss the analysis that is required for this.

14.7.4 Automatic parallelization for distributed-memory machines

If the target machine is a distributed-memory multicomputer rather than a shared-memory multiprocessor, automatic parallelization becomes even more difficult, because the compiler now also has to generate communication statements: message sends and receives. We look at some of the additional problems for multicomputers here.

To execute parallel loops efficiently on a multicomputer, it is required to distribute the arrays being accessed over the memories of the different processors. To explain this, consider our earlier example of matrix addition again:

```
for i := 1 to 500 do
    for j := 1 to 1000 do
        C[i, j] := A[i, j] + B[i, j];
    od;
od;
```

On a shared-memory machine, the three arrays can be stored in the shared memory, where they can be accessed by all processors. On a multicomputer, this no longer is the case. One solution would be to store the arrays in the memory of one processor, say CPU 0. All other processors can then access these data by sending messages to CPU 0, asking it to read or write certain elements of the arrays. CPU 0 would thus implement a (very slow) shared memory. Clearly, this approach would generate a huge amount of communication overhead, which would far outweigh the gains of parallelism and thus be unacceptable.

An acceptable solution, avoiding a large part of the communication overhead, can be obtained by distributing the arrays over the different processors, in such a way that each processor contains those elements that it accesses most frequently. In the above example, this distribution actually is quite simple. Assuming that we parallelize the outer loop over 10 processors, each processor accesses 50 rows of the three arrays. For example, CPU 0 accesses rows 1 to 50, CPU 1 accesses rows 51 to 100, and so on, as shown in Figure 14.12. So, by distributing the arrays row-wise we can reduce the communication.

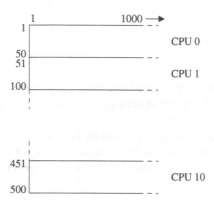

Fig. 14.12: An array distributed over 10 CPUs

Unfortunately, this example is overly simplistic. In general, programs do need to communicate. To illustrate this, suppose the matrix addition code is followed by the (sequential) statement:

```
A[1, 1] := A[125, 1] + A[175, 1];
```

With the row-wise distribution described above, the two operands are stored on CPUs 2 and 3, respectively. If CPU 0, which contains A[1, 1], executes the statement, it thus has to communicate with these two processors to get the current values of the two elements. A slightly more complicated example is the following code:

```
for i := 2 to 499 do
    for j := 1 to 1000 do
        A[i, j] := B[i–1, j] + B[i+1, j];
    od;
od;
```

Most of the assignments can be executed without doing communication, using the distribution described above. For example, processor 0 can assign B[1, 1] + B[3, 1] to A[2, 1], since it contains all these elements. For some assignments, however, data from a remote processor are needed. For example, the assignment to A[50, 1] requires B[51, 1], which is stored on CPU 1. In general, each processor requires the last row of its left neighbor and the first row of its right neighbor (except for the leftmost and rightmost processor).

The task of the compiler is to generate the communication statements needed to implement these data transfers. In simple cases like the one above, the compiler can compute precisely which elements each processor needs, so it can insert send and receive statements in the code to transfer these elements. Figure 14.13 shows in a pseudo-notation what the code generated by the compiler might look like. Each processor is assigned a number of rows of the matrices, ranging from lower_bound to upper_bound. A processor allocates space for these parts of the array, and some extra space to contain two additional rows of B; the initialization of the arrays is not shown. At the start of the execution, each processor checks to see if it should send its first and last rows to its neighbors; we use the notation B[i, *] to denote a row of B. Next, each processor checks if it should receive rows from its neighbors. The send commands can be synchronous or asynchronous, the receive commands are synchronous. Finally, each processor performs its share of the work.

```
INPUT:
    int ID: number of this processor (ranging from 0 to P−1)
    int lower_bound: number of first row assigned to this processor
    int upper_bound: number of last row assigned to this processor

real A[lower_bound..upper_bound, 1000],
    B[lower_bound−1 .. upper_bound+1, 1000];

if ID > 0 then send B[lower_bound, *] to processor ID−1;
if ID < P−1 then send B[upper_bound, *] to processor ID+1;
if ID > 0 then receive B[lower_bound−1, *] from processor ID−1;
if ID < P−1 then receive B[upper_bound+1, *] from processor ID+1;
for i := lower_bound to upper_bound do
    for j := 1 to 1000 do
        A[i, j] := B[i−1, j] + B[i+1, j];
    od;
od;
```

Fig. 14.13: Generated (pseudo-)code

In more complicated cases, the data to be transferred can only be computed at run time. As an example, for the statement

A[1, 1] := B[X, 1];

it depends on the run-time value of X from which processor the element must be fetched. In this case, the compiler generates code to determine this processor (at run time) and to send a request message to it; the run-time system on this processor will then reply with the requested value. Note that this exchange needs two messages over the network, a request and a reply, so it is less efficient than the earlier example.

Finally, there are many important optimizations a compiler can apply to reduce the communication overhead. For example, **message combining** (or **message aggregation**) combines multiple small messages into a single large message, which is more efficient on most systems. Another optimization is to exploit special hardware primitives, such as broadcasting. We do not discuss such optimizations here. Suffice it to say that the task of generating efficient message passing code makes the already very challenging task of automatic parallelization even more difficult.

The data distribution has a huge impact on the performance of the parallel program, since it determines to a large extent which data transfers will take place. The optimal distribution depends on how the arrays are used in the most time-consuming parts of the program. Since it is very difficult for a compiler to determine the optimal distribution, languages like High Performance Fortran allow the programmer to help the compiler. HPF defines a collection of compiler directives that programmers can use to specify distributions of arrays. For example, the following HPF code fragment

```
!HPF$ processors pr(4)
real A(100, 100)
!HPF$ distribute A(BLOCK,*) onto pr
```

declares a two-dimensional array A that is distributed row-wise over four processors.

Many other types of distributions, for example cyclic or column-wise, can also be expressed in HPF. The compiler can use this information as hints about how to distribute the data structures. The speed-ups achieved by supplying hints depend completely on the nature of the problem and the quality of the hints; they can easily make the difference between an infeasible computation and a readily doable one.

14.8 Conclusion

This concludes our discussion of compilation and processing techniques for parallel and distributed programs. We have seen that such programs may express the parallelism explicitly or may rely on automatic parallelization by some language processor. Five models for explicit parallelism have been introduced and their implementations discussed; the Linda Tuple Space can profit more from compiler support than the other four. Automatic parallelization still is a challenging problem, especially for distributed-memory machines. Some languages therefore use a combination of compiler analysis and directives from the user.

Summary

- The goal of parallel systems is to solve a given problem as fast as possible, using multiple processors. A distributed system contains multiple autonomous processors that are connected by a network and that work on many different tasks from many users.

- A process is an abstraction of a physical processor. A process contains an address space that stores data.
- Many models and languages exist for programming parallel and distributed systems. The programming models discussed in this chapter are shared variables, message passing, shared objects, Tuple Space, and data-parallelism.
- Shared variables are variables that can be accessed by multiple processes. Mutual exclusion synchronization mechanisms (for example locks) and condition synchronization mechanisms (for example monitors) are used to synchronize access to the shared variables.
- Message passing uses two primitives, send and receive, to transfer data from one process to another process. Languages differ in the way processes are addressed, and the way messages are sent (synchronous or asynchronous) and received (explicitly or implicitly).
- Parallel object-oriented languages encapsulate shared data in objects.
- Linda provides a globally shared data structure called the Tuple Space, which is addressed associatively.
- With data-parallel programs, all processors execute the same algorithm, but operate on different parts of the data set. Automatically parallelizing compilers usually try to generate data-parallel programs.
- Many parallel and distributed languages are implemented mainly using a run-time system rather than extensive compiler support.
- Language-level processes can be implemented using operating system processes, but a more efficient approach is to use lightweight threads.
- The main problem in implementing shared variables on a shared-memory multiprocessor is how to execute the synchronization primitives indivisibly, and without using busy waiting. Indivisible operations usually are implemented on top of an indivisible hardware instruction, such as test-and-set. Busy waiting is avoided by maintaining a list of blocked threads.
- For message passing, there are many implementation issues. Many different communication protocols exist (for example, UDP, TCP/IP, and custom user-level protocols).
- The receiver of a message is located using an administration of where each language process runs.
- Marshaling and unmarshaling are used to convert between data structures and a linear buffer (an array of bytes) that can be sent over the network.
- One of the advantages of a parallel language over a library is that its implementation can type-check messages.
- Languages that give the programmer control over the order in which messages are serviced need a more complicated run-time system, which maintains a list of incoming messages that is inspected whenever the application wants to receive a message.
- For parallel object-oriented languages, one issue is how to locate objects; if objects can migrate, pointer chasing techniques can be used.

- Languages that support object replication must use a protocol for keeping the replicas of an object consistent. When an object is modified, such a protocol can either invalidate the copies of the object or it can update all copies, for example using totally-ordered group communication.
- The Linda Tuple Space is based on associative addressing; Linda compilers reduce the associated overhead by selecting the right storage representation for each tuple.
- On a distributed-memory multicomputer, Tuple Space can use a hash-based partitioning or a uniform distribution scheme (replicating or partitioning the Tuple Space). The most efficient scheme depends on the application and the underlying hardware.
- Automatic parallelization is a challenging problem. Parallelizing compilers try to find outer loops with iterations that are independent from each other. To eliminate loop dependencies, they can apply loop restructuring transformations. For machines without shared memory, the compiler also has to distribute the data structures over the different processors and generate communication statements when processors need remote data. Message combining is an important optimization to reduce the communication overhead. High Performance Fortran (HPF) also uses information (hints) from the programmer to improve performance.

Further reading

There are several general introductions to parallel processing [11,109,121,227,304]. A good book on distributed systems is Tanenbaum [273]. Two survey papers about parallel and distributed programming languages are by Bal, Steiner and Tanenbaum [28] and Skillicorn and Talia [263].

A survey of the parallel computing landscape is given by Asanovic *et al.* [19]. The book by Wilson and Lu [305] focuses on object-oriented parallel languages based on C++. Survey papers on distributed shared memory systems are Stumm and Zhou [268] and Nitzberg and Lo [203]. Object migration and replication are discussed extensively in papers by Jul *et al.* [138] and Bal *et al.* [29] respectively. Linda is described in several research papers [7, 55]. A technical report describes implementation issues of Linda [43].

The literature contains several overviews of compiler transformations for automatic parallelization [24, 191, 306]. Examples of automatically parallelizing compilers include Polaris [44] and SUIF [114]. High Performance Fortran is described by Loveman [181]; a historical evaluation of HPF is given by Kennedy [149].

Exercises

14.1. (▷796) Message passing can be implemented on both shared-memory and distributed-memory machines, whereas shared variables are difficult to implement on machines without shared memory. Does this imply that shared variables and monitors are superfluous?

14.2. (▷www) The Linda Tuple Space can be used to simulate both message passing and shared variables. Describe how both sending/receiving messages and reading/writing shared variables can be simulated using Linda.

14.3. (▷www) Explain why the costs of a thread switch depend very much on the CPU architecture.

14.4. (▷797) As discussed in Section 14.3, busy waiting can be avoided by using an administration (a list of control blocks) for blocked threads. This administration, however, also has to be protected by locks, to make the operations on it indivisible. So, to implement a lock without busy waiting, we need another lock. Will this result in an endless implementation loop?

14.5. (▷www) Some run-time systems acquire locks using a combination of busy waiting and thread switching, to avoid wasting CPU cycles while still reducing the overhead of thread switches. Can you think of a useful combination?

14.6. (▷797) (a) Explain what happens if two processes simultaneously try to execute a monitor operation that just reads and returns data protected by the monitor (but without modifying any data).
(b) Design an—optimized—implementation of monitors that will allow multiple readers, while preserving the original monitor semantics as perceived by the programmer.

14.7. (▷www) Many message passing languages that use ports as explained in Section 14.1 allow only a single process at a time to receive from any given port. Why would this restriction be imposed?

14.8. Write marshaling and unmarshaling routines for the following procedure:

```
procedure f(x: float; y: integer; z: array[1..100] of integer);
```

14.9. (▷www) Some message passing languages (for example Ada, SR) support a "select statement", with which a receiver can wait for different types of messages from different senders, depending on which one arrives first. Very few languages support the opposite: a statement with which a sender can wait until one of the receivers is willing to accept its message (is waiting in a receive statement). Can you think of a reason for this?

14.10. (▷797) Section 14.4.4 explained that message handlers that may block should be executed by a newly created thread rather than by a daemon thread. Someone suggests the following idea: let the daemon thread simply start executing the message handler. Only if the handler actually needs to block, create a new thread dynamically, copy the current stack of the daemon to the newly created thread, and let the new thread continue the execution of the handler. Why is this hard to implement?

14.11. (▷797) In Section 14.5.2 we discussed the possibility of migrating an object from one processor to another processor. Suppose an object X invokes an operation on an object Y that is located on a different processor. Further suppose X contains a thread of control, but Y does not. Two different options for object migration now exist: X could be moved to the processor of Y, or Y could be moved to the processor of X. What are the advantages and disadvantages of both options?

14.12. (▷www) Someone suggests a new update protocol for implementing replicated objects that does not need totally-ordered group communication. The scheme works as follows. For each replicated object, one processor (containing a replica) is designated as the primary copy. If a processor wants to do a write operation on a replicated object, it sends the operation to the primary copy of the object. The primary copy broadcasts the operation to all other processors that contain a copy. Why is this scheme incorrect?

14.13. (▷www) The operation Maximum is defined as follows. Each processor performs the following procedure call:

    result = Maximum(value);

where value may be different for each processor. Each processor waits (blocks) until every processor has started this call. Next, every processor gets as result the maximum of all the value parameters.
Figure 14.14 shows how the operation can be implemented in C/Linda, for a fixed number of processors P:
(a) Analyze the performance of the operation for the three different distributed implementations of Tuple Space described in Section 14.6.2.
(b) Design an optimized operation, using handwritten message passing. Compare the optimized implementation with the Linda version.

14.14. (▷www) Some implementations of Tuple Space support an extra primitive fetch_all(t), with which all tuples that match t can be obtained in one indivisible operation. Explain why this primitive is difficult to implement.

14.15. (▷www) Does the following code contain a loop dependency? If so, what kind of dependency is it?

```
for i := 2 to 9 do
    A[7*i] := i*i;
    A[9*i – 2] := i*i*i;
    A[11*(i–1)+7] := i*i*i*i;
od;
```

```
int Maximum(int value) {
    if (mycpu == 1) {
        /* the first CPU creates the tuple */
        out("max", value, 1);
    } else {
        /* other CPUs wait their turn */
        in("max", ? &max, mycpu);
        if (value > max) max = value;
        out("max", max, mycpu + 1);
    }
    /* wait until all CPUs are done */
    read("max", ? &max, P);
    return max;
}
```

Fig. 14.14: C/Linda code for the operation Maximum

14.16. (▷www) Loop interchanges as described in Section 14.7.3 may also have performance disadvantages. Consider the following example:

```
for i := 1 to 1000 do
    for j := 1 to 1000 do
        A[i, j] := A[i, j] + 1;
    od;
od;
```

The sequential performance of this code may decrease substantially if the two loops are interchanged. Explain.

14.17. *History of parallel and distributed language implementation*: Study Karp's 1987 paper [144], which points out the difficulties of parallel programming and introduces the concept of SPMD parallelism, and summarize its main points.

Appendix A
Machine Instructions

This appendix lists and specifies the pseudo-instructions that are used throughout this book to illustrate machine-code generation. The instructions do not correspond to any particular real processor, but were chosen to be representative for mainstream processors.

There are data manipulation instructions and flow control instructions. In data manipulation instructions the last argument is the location of the result; it is not named in the instruction name. Instructions starting with "Load_" yield their result in a register; those starting with "Store_" store their result in a memory location; those starting with "SetPar_" store their result in a parameter location; all others yield their result in a register.

Instruction	Operand(s)	Effect

Multi-register machines:

Instruction	Operand(s)	Effect
Load_Const	c,R_n	$c \to R_n$
Load_Addr	a,R_n	$a \to R_n$
Load_Mem	x,R_n	$M[x] \to R_n$
Store_Reg	R_n,x	$R_n \to M[x]$
Store_Indirect_Reg	R_n,R_d	$R_n \to M[R_d]$
Store_IndirectMem_Reg	R_n,x	$R_n \to M[M[x]]$
Add_Const	c,R_n	$R_n + c \to R_n$
Add_Reg	R_m,R_n	$R_n + R_m \to R_n$
Subtr_Reg	R_m,R_n	$R_n - R_m \to R_n$
Mult_Reg	R_m,R_n	$R_n \times R_m \to R_n$
Div_Reg	R_m,R_n	$R_n / R_m \to R_n$
Add_Mem	x,R_n	$R_n + M[x] \to R_n$
Subtr_Mem	x,R_n	$R_n - M[x] \to R_n$
Mult_Mem	x,R_n	$R_n \times M[x] \to R_n$
Add_Scaled_Reg	c,R_m,R_n	$R_n + (c \times R_m) \to R_n$
Mult_Scaled_Reg	c,R_m,R_n	$R_n \times (c \times R_m) \to R_n$
Shift_Left	c,R_n	$R_n << (c{\geq}0\ ?\ c : -c) \to R_n$
SetPar_Const	c,i	$c \to Par[i]$
SetPar_Reg	R_n,i	$R_n \to Par[i]$
Call	a	call routine at address a
Load_Par	i,R_n	$Par[i] \to R_n$
Return		returns from routine
Comp_Neq	R_m,R_n	$(R_m \neq R_n) \to$ Cond
Goto	a	$a \to$ PC
Goto_False	a	**if** $\neg$ Cond: $a \to$ PC

Advanced addressing modes (for Section 7.2):

Instruction	Operand(s)	Effect
Load_Elem_Addr	$A[R_i],c,R_d$	$A + (R_i \times c) \to R_d$
Load_Offset_Elem	$(A+R_o)[R_i],c,R_d$	$M[A + R_o + (R_i \times c)] \to R_d$

One-register machines:

Instruction	Operand(s)	Effect
Add_Constant	c	$R + c \to R$

Stack machines (zero-register machines):

Instruction	Operand(s)	Effect
Push_Const	c	
Push_Local	i	
Store_Local	i	
		see page 336
Add_Top2		
Subtr_Top2		
Mult_Top2		

Appendix B
Hints and Solutions to Selected Exercises

Answers to more exercises can be found on the book's Web site. These exercises are marked with ▷www, just as exercises whose answers are shown in this Appendix are marked by ▷ followed by a page number.

1.1 *Advantages:* Assuming the language is still being designed, writing a major piece of software in it is an excellent shake-down for the language design. Compiling the compiler may be a good way to debug the compiler (but there is a problem here: how defensible is debugging by using not well-debugged tools?) Any improvement to the compiler benefits the compiler writers themselves, which gives them an incentive to improve the compiler more. It shows that they consider their own language and implementation good enough to write a major program in.

Disadvantages: Bootstrapping problems: there is no compiler to compile the first version with. Any changes to the language may necessitate many modifications to the compiler, as both the implementation *and* the source language change. The compiler may unwittingly be tuned to constructions used specifically in the compiler.

1.9 In data structures outside the while statement, as with any while statement.

1.11 See Figure B.1.

1.13 First a subset is created by taking away some features; the language is then extended by adding new features. An example would be a C compiler which does not implement floating point numbers but does have built-in infinite-length integer arithmetic. The sarcasm comes from the fact that everything is an extended subset of everything else, which makes the term meaningless.

1.19 The grammatical production process stops when the sentential form consists of terminals only; to test this situation, we have to be able to tell terminals and non-terminals apart. Actually, this is not entirely true: we can scan the grammar, declare all symbols in left-hand sides as non-terminals and all other symbols as terminals. So context condition (1) actually provides redundancy that can be checked.

1.20 Suppose there were two different smallest sets of information items, S_1 and

Buffered_a ← False;

```
procedure AcceptFromPreviousModule (Ch):
    if Buffered_a:
        — See if Ch is a second 'a':
        if Ch = 'a':
            — We have 'aa':
            Buffered_a ← False;
            OutputToNextModule ('b');
        else — Ch ≠ 'a':
            Buffered_a ← False;
            OutputToNextModule ('a');
            OutputToNextModule (Ch);
    else if Ch = 'a':
        Buffered_a ← True;
    else — not Buffered_a and Ch ≠ 'a':
        OutputToNextModule (Ch);

procedure Flush():
    if Buffered_a:
        Buffered_a ← False;
        OutputToNextModule ('a');
    FlushNextModule ();
```

Fig. B.1: The filter aa → b as a post-main module

S_2. Then S_1 and S_2 must have the same size (or one would not be the smallest) and each must contain at least one item the other does not contain (or they would not be different). Call one such differing item in S_1 X. Since both sets started with the same initial items, X cannot be an initial item but must have been added by some application of an inference rule. This rule clearly did not apply in S_2, so there must be at least one other item Y that is present in S_1 and absent from S_2. By induction, all items in S_1 must differ from all items in S_2, but this is impossible since both started with the same initial items.

2.5 Close cooperation between lexical and syntax analyzer is required. As a kludge, preliminary skipping of the dynamic expression based on counting nested parentheses could be considered. Error recovery is a nightmare.

2.8 They both mean the same as a*. They are not fundamentally erroneous but may draw a warning from a processor, since they are probably not what the programmer intended. Ambiguity is not a concept in lexical analysis, so they are not ambiguous.

2.12 Let him/her implement it and then feed an object file or jpeg picture as source file to the compiler; admire the crash. Or, more charitably, explain this intention to the inventor.

2.18 Each round adds at least one dotted item to *ClosureSet* and there is only a finite number of dotted items.

2.25 It isn't as simple as that. It depends on the amount of interaction of the macro processing with the lexical analysis of larger units, for example strings and comments. In C the scheme is hare-brained since it would require the macro processor to do almost full lexical analysis, to avoid substituting inside strings and comments. But in a language in which macro names have an easily recognizable form (for example in PL/I, in which macro names start with a %), there is no such interference, and a better structuring of the compiler is obtained by a separate phase. But the loss in speed and the large memory requirements remain. Also, with full macro processing preceding compilation, it is very difficult to reconstruct the source text as the compiler user sees it.

3.4 See Hanson [116].

3.8 (a) LL(1) and ε-free. (b) Predictive is still more efficient.

3.12 The recursion stack consists of a list of activation records, each of which defines an active routine; only the top one is running. Each activation record contains a continuation address (often called return address) telling where the routine should continue when it becomes the top node. The code from the continuation address to the end of the routine consists of zero or more routine calls. These calls represent what is being predicted and the corresponding grammar symbols are part of the prediction stack. Thus each activation record represents part of the prediction stack; the total prediction stack is the concatenation of all these parts, in the order of the activation records. Additional exercise: draw a picture that illustrates the above explanation in a clear way.

3.15 The acceptable set of a non-terminal N is the union of FIRST(N) and the acceptable set of the shortest alternative of N. So, the acceptable sets of all non-terminals can be precomputed using a closure algorithm. Now, if the prediction stack is available directly (as an array or a linked list), we can traverse the stack and compute the union of the acceptable sets of the symbols in it. In *LLgen*, however, the prediction stack is just the C stack and is not available for traversal. *LLgen* keeps an integer array indexed by grammar symbols counting how many times a given symbol is present on the stack. This information is easily maintained and suffices to compute the acceptable set.

3.19 (a) When the ACTION table calls for a "reduce using rule $N \rightarrow \alpha$", the item set corresponding to the state on the top of the stack contains the item $N \rightarrow \alpha \bullet$. The dot can only be at the end of α when it has just passed over the last member of α, which must therefore be just below the top state on the stack. This reasoning applies successively to all other members of α, which must therefore also be on the stack.
(b) The item set preceding α on the stack must contain the item $N \rightarrow \bullet \alpha$, or no α would be recognized and no item $N \rightarrow \alpha \bullet$ would eventually be found. The item $N \rightarrow \bullet \alpha$ must have originated from some item $P \rightarrow \beta \bullet N \gamma$. The presence of this item guarantees that a transition on N is possible, leading to a state that includes $P \rightarrow \beta N \bullet \gamma$.

3.20 A value "shift" in an ACTION table entry does not conflict with another "shift" value in that same entry, but a "shift" and a "reduce" do. So do a "reduce" and another "reduce", since they are actually two different "reduces": "reduce to M" and "reduce to N".

3.22 The tree has the form $[\, (x \,]^{n-1} \, (x) \,)^{n-1}$ and the last x is the first handle, in any bottom-up parser. So all the $[\, (x \,]^{n-1}$ must be stacked.

3.25 After rule 2, add: "If t and u are the same operator: if the operator is left-associative, reduce, otherwise shift."

3.27 The set of grammars which can produce infinitely many parse trees, i.e. the infinitely ambiguous grammars; they cause the GLR parse not to terminate. A simple example is $A \rightarrow A|\varepsilon$, which produces the empty string in infinitely many ways.

3.29

```
if  (x > 0) {  if  (y > 0) p = 0; }  else  q = 0;
```

Adding the phrase "on the same nesting level" would solve the problem.

3.31 In a pure bottom-up parser no such pointers exist: trees are constructed before their parents, and the only pointer to a tree is the one on the stack that is used to discard the tree; the stack entry that contains it is removed by the recovery process. If other pointers have been created outside the parsing mechanism, these must be found and zeroed.

3.32 Figure B.2 shows an LALR(1) suffix grammar for the grammar of Figure 3.36.

```
%token IDENTIFIER
%token EoF
%%

input_suffix  :
    expression_suffix EoF | EoF ;
expression :
    term | expression '+' term ;
expression_suffix  :
    term_suffix | expression_suffix '+' term | '+' term ;
term :
    IDENTIFIER | '(' expression ')' ;
term_suffix  :
    expression ')' | expression_suffix ')' | ')' ;
}
```

Fig. B.2: An LALR(1) suffix grammar for the grammar of Figure 3.36

4.2 For a non-terminal N, some of its production rules could set some attributes and other rules could set other attributes. Then the attributes in a tree with a node for N in it could be evaluable for one production (tree) of that N, and not for another. This destroys the composability of context-free grammars, which says that anywhere an N is specified, any production of N is acceptable.

4.5 See Figures B.3 and B.4.

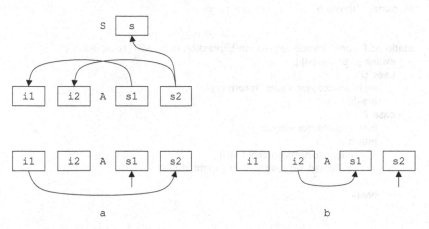

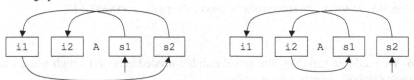

Fig. B.3: Dependency graphs for S and A

IS–SI graph set of A:

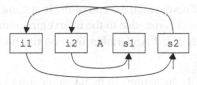

merged IS–SI graph of A:

Fig. B.4: IS-SI graph sets and IS-SI graph of A

4.8 The fact that no intervening visits to other children are needed shows that the production rule already has all the information for the second visit. This may, however, not be the case in all production rules that have this type of child, so other production rules may require two non-consecutive visits.

5.3 See Figure B.5, and note that the code is a simplification over that from Figure 5.2.

```
#include    "parser.h"    /* for types AST_node and Expression */
#include    "thread.h"    /* for self check */

                              /* PRIVATE */
static AST_node *Thread_expression(Expression *expr, AST_node *succ) {
    switch (expr->type) {
    case 'D':
        expr->successor = succ; return expr;
        break;
    case 'P':
        expr->successor = succ;
        return
            Thread_expression(expr->left,
                Thread_expression(expr->right, expr)
            );
        break;
    }
}
                              /* PUBLIC */
AST_node *Thread_start;

void Thread_AST(AST_node *icode) {
    Thread_start = Thread_expression(icode, 0);
}
```

Fig. B.5: Alternative threading code for the demo compiler from Section 1.2

5.6 We need two variables, the actual number needed here and a high-water mark. Simple symbolic interpretation suffices.

5.7 The successor of the then-part is the merge node at the end of the if-statement rather than its else-part, and it is correct that we enter that node with an empty list during symbolic interpretation, since we will never reach the end of the if-statement from the end of the then-part when the program is run, due to the intervening jump. Full symbolic interpretation works on the threaded AST rather than on the linear program text.

5.9 It violates requirement 4 in Section 5.2.1: the actions to be taken on constants do not subsume those taken on variables. Quite to the contrary, any constant can be handled by code generated for variables but not the other way around.

5.12 x becomes initialized. *Con:* It sounds unreasonable and counterintuitive to get a variable initialized by assigning the value of an uninitialized variable to it. *Pro:* The error in the program is probably the lack of initialization of y; the further usage of x is independent of this error. Since a warning is already given on the assignment, no further warnings on subsequent—probably correct—uses of x seem appropriate.

5.14 Consider any routine with a flow-of-control graph that is a linear list from routine entry to routine exit. Whatever the contents of the *KILL* and *GEN* sets, the *IN* and *OUT* sets will be computed in one scan through the list, and there is no way to transport the information about the routine exit back to the last use of a variable.

7.4 The structure of a self-extracting archive is very similar to that of the "compiler" of Section 7.4. Where it contains both the AST and the interpreter, a self-extracting archive contains both the contents of the archive and the extraction code. Often, the archive is compressed, and the extraction code also contains decompression code.

7.5 The program:

```
int  Program[] = {'D',7,'D',1,'D',5,'P','+','P','*','!',0};
```

The interpreter:

```
int  main(void) {
    int  PC = 0;
    int  Instruction ;

    while ((Instruction  = Program[PC++]) != 0) {
        switch ( Instruction ) {
        case 'D': Expression_D(Program[PC++]); break;
        case 'P': Expression_P(Program[PC++]); break;
        case '!': Print (); break;
        }
    }
    return  0;
}
```

7.9 See Figure B.6; the "then" gets 0.7, the "else" 0.3; loop skipping gets 0.1, loop entering 0.9; the cases get 0.4, 0.4, 0.2. Traffic at routine entry is arbitrarily set to 1. The first column gives the 17 equations; all can be solved by simple substitution, except those for e, f, and g, which need elimination. The results are given in the second column. Note that we predict that for every time the routine is called, the loop body A will be executed 6.3 times. Also note that the traffic out of the routine is again 1; what goes in must come out.

8.2 Advantages of PC-relative addressing modes and instructions are:
—they require no relocation, thus reducing the work of the linker;
—they allow **position-independent code**, code that can be loaded anywhere in memory, without any modifications;
—they may allow shorter instructions: an offset may fit in a byte whereas a full address usually does not. Even if it does, the assembler still has to reserve space for a full address, because the linker may modify it.

9.1 These dependencies also express the requirement that all assignments to a variable are executed in sequential, left-to-right order.

Equation	Value
a = 1	1.0
b = 0.7 a	0.7
c = 0.3 a	0.3
d = b	0.7
e = 0.1 (d+f)	0.7
f = g	6.3
g = 0.9 (d+f)	6.3
h = c	0.3
i = 0.4 h	0.12
j = 0.4 h	0.12
k = 0.2 h	0.06
l = i	0.12
m = j	0.12
n = k	0.06
o = e	0.7
p = l+m+n	0.30
q = o+p	1.0

Fig. B.6: Traffic equations and their solution for Figure 7.41

9.2 See Figures B.7 and B.8.

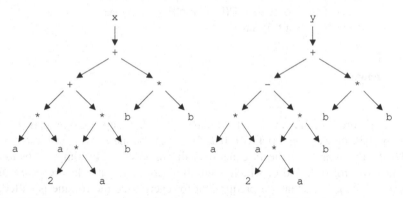

Fig. B.7: The dependency graph before common subexpression elimination

9.3 (a) See Figure B.9.

(b) The input p of the second *p++ is dependent on the output p of the first *p++ and so its dependencies differ from those of the input p of the first *p++.

9.6 S and N cannot be the same node, since that would make the dependency graph contain a cycle because S refers to N.

9.7 A ladder sequences starts at each graph root, except when that root has an incoming dependency. Not all roots can have incoming dependencies, or the dependency graph would be cyclic.

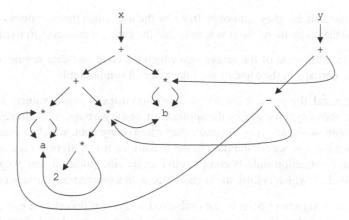

Fig. B.8: The dependency graph after common subexpression elimination

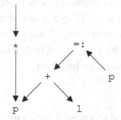

Fig. B.9: The dependency graph of the expression *p++

9.13 Suppose the token set { a, bcd, ab, c, d } and the input **abcd**. Immediately returning the a yields 2 tokens, whereas 3 can be achieved, obviously.

Assume the entire input is in memory. Record in each item its starting position and the number of tokens recognized so far. At each reduce item that says that N tokens have been recognized, add the *InitialItemSet* with token counter N + 1 and the present location as starting point. Having arrived at the end of the input, find the reduce item with the largest token counter and isolate the token it identifies. Work backwards, identifying tokens.

9.18 For the first instruction in the sequence we have 20 × 2 = 40 combinations, using R1,R1 and R1,R2, or more compactly {R1},{R1,R2}. For the second instruction we have 20 × 2 × 3 = 120 combinations, using {R1,R2},{R1,R2,R3}; for the further instructions we have 20 × 3 × 3 = 180 combinations each. In total $4800 \times 180^{N-2}$ combinations.

Estimating a weekend at 2.5 days, each of about 80000 seconds, we have about 2×10^{11} μseconds, or 2×10^{10} tests. So we want the largest N for which $4800 \times 180^{N-2}$ is smaller than 2×10^{10}. Now, $4800 \times 180^{4-2} = 1.5 \times 10^8$ and $4800 \times 180^{5-2} = 2.7 \times 10^{10}$, so N = 4.

10.2 The garbage collector will free chunks only when they are unreachable. If they are unreachable they cannot be freed by the user since the user does not have a pointer to them any more. So it is safe to call the garbage collector from *Malloc()*.

10.6 In the allocation of the arrays into which the code and data segments will be compiled; perhaps in the allocation of the external symbol table.

10.7 In general, the garbage collection algorithms inspect pointer values, which will be (simultaneously) changed by the application. Some garbage collection algorithms (for example two-space copying and compaction) copy data, which is dangerous if the application can access the data in the meantime. Some algorithms assume that the garbage collection only becomes active at specific points in the program (see Section 10.2.2), which is difficult to guarantee with a concurrent garbage collection.

10.9 If the assignment p:=p is not optimized away, if p points to a chunk P with reference count 1, if P contains a pointer to another chunk Q and if the reference count of Q is also 1, then first decreasing the reference count of P causes P to be freed, which causes Q to be freed. Subsequently increasing the reference count of P will not raise the reference count of Q again and the pointer to Q in P will be left dangling. Also, on some systems freeing P might cause compaction to take place, after which the chunk P would be gone entirely and incrementing its reference count would overwrite an arbitrary memory location.

10.13 See Siklóssy [261].

11.2 In most languages we need to know if an identifier is a keyword or the name of a macro, long before its name space is known. If we want to postpone the identification to the time that the proper name space is known, we will need other mechanisms to solve the keyword and macro name questions.

11.6 We have rvalue?V:$V \rightarrow$ rvalue. In principle, rvalue?lvalue:lvalue could yield an lvalue, but ANSI C defines it to yield an rvalue. In GNU C an lvalue results, but a warning is given under the –pedantic flag.

11.7 That is not possible. The last scope rule forbids the creation of such values.

11.8

1. Due to rounding different results for e.g. $a = 1e - 20$ $b = 1.0$ $c = -1.0$.
2. One evaluation order may yield ∞ while the other does not. Example: $a = 1e160$ $b = 1e160$ $c = 1e - 160$.
3. When v is not-a-number, the comparison should yield false.

11.16 At run time, a class may be represented by a class descriptor which contains, among others, the method table of the class. Such a class descriptor could also contain a pointer to the class descriptor of its parent class. An object then contains a reference to its class descriptor instead of a reference to the method table. Then, the implementation of the instanceof operator becomes easy, see Figure B.10.

11.17 The code for these calls is:

```
function InstanceOf (Obj, Class) returning a boolean;
    ObjectClass ← Obj.class;
    while ObjectClass ≠ NoClass:
        if ObjectClass = Class:
            return True;
        else — ObjectClass ≠ Class:
            ObjectClass ← ObjectClass.parent;
    return False;
```

Fig. B.10: Implementation of the instanceof operator

```
(*(e–>dispatch_table[0]))(e);
(*(e–>dispatch_table[2]))((class D *)((char *)e + sizeof(class C)));
(*(e–>dispatch_table[3]))((class D *)((char *)e + sizeof(class C)));
```

Note that although m4 is redefined in class E, it still requires a pointer to an object of class D.

11.19 For example, when the caller calls several routines consecutively, the "caller saves" scheme allows saving and restoring only once, whereas the "callee saves" scheme has no option but to do it for every call. Also, in the "callee saves" scheme the callee has to save and restore all registers that might be needed by any caller, whereas the "caller saves" scheme allows for saving and restoring only those registers that are needed for this particular caller, at this particular call site.

11.30 This may cause overflow, because the controlled variable may then be incremented beyond the upper bound (and thus possibly beyond the maximum representable value).

11.32 Pushing the last parameter first makes sure that the first parameter ends up on the top of the stack, regardless of the number of parameters. Unstacking the parameters will therefore yield them in textual order.

11.34 1. An FSA in state S_i reads a token and decides to jump to state S_j. In the tail recursive implementation, the routine S_i reads a token and decides to call routine S_j, using a tail call. This tail call is eliminated and the stack is not involved. 2. It depends. The advantage is that semantic actions can be incorporated very easily, but the program may fail when compiled with a compiler that does not support tail call elimination. 3. In a non-deterministic FSA we may need to return to routine S_i, so some of the S_j will not be tail calls.

11.36 Two new operations must be supported: instantiation of a generic routine which is a parameter, and passing a generic routine as a parameter to an instantiation. The consequences from a compiler construction point of view are modest. When implementing instantiation through expansion, the first instantiation to be dealt with resides within a non-generic unit. Therefore, a generic routine parameter is available as an AST, which can be copied and processed just as the AST of an ordinary generic unit. One issue that must be dealt with, whether the language has generic routine parameters or not, is cycle detection: when one generic unit contains an instantiation of another generic unit, the result is a chain of instantiations, which must be terminated by the instantiation of a generic unit which does not contain further instantiations. If this is not the case, the implementation through expansion scheme will fail. Without generic routine parameters, detecting this situation is easy: when a generic unit occurs twice on the instantiation chain, there is a cycle. With generic routine parameters, when an identical instantiation (same generic unit and same instantiation parameters) occurs twice on the instantiation chain, there is a cycle. When implementing instantiation through dope vectors, a generic routine has a code address, and can be passed as a parameter, just like an ordinary routine.

12.6 (a) One should not write functions that fail for some arguments (but sometimes one has to). (b) One should not call a function with arguments for which it will fail (but that is sometimes hard to know).

12.11 The following program uses the value of the expression fac 20 2^{10} times:

```
tree 0 val  = val
tree n val  = let  t = tree  (n−1) val in  t ∗ t

main = print  (tree 10 (fac 20))
```

12.18 Although the ++ (append) operator is associative, the amount of work differs for a ++ (b ++ c) and (a ++ b) ++ c. This is a consequence of the append operator, which essentially creates a copy of its first argument to "replace" the null pointer with a pointer to the second list. In (a ++ b) ++ c the list a is copied twice, whereas only one copy is required for a ++ (b ++ c). Transforming mappend into an accumulating argument function would cause the sublists to be copied many times (depending on their position).

12.19 There is no reduction in heap space since all lazy expressions allocated in the heap consist of a (built-in) function with two arguments, which is the break-even point. The benefit is in the graph reducer, which does not need to unwind application spines, but can call the suspended function immediately.

13.4 The new paradigm implements breadth-first search rather than depth-first search. This usually takes (much) more time, but will find a solution if one exists, unlike depth-first search which may work itself in an infinite branch of the search tree. The discussed optimizations are all applicable to some degree.

13.9 The number of values returned in general is unbounded, so an infinite list may have to be returned.

13.12 The asserts and retracts should not be undone by backtracking. Since the data structure in which the asserted clauses are kept and the corresponding counters (for example, number_of_clauses_added_at_end_for_parent_2 in Figure 13.26) are global variables, no backtracking will occur, as required.

14.1 No; shared variables are easier to use than message passing. Also, on a shared-memory machine, shared-variable programs often get better performance than message passing programs, because message passing programs do more copying.

14.4 No; the lock that is used to protect the administration can use spinning, because the operations on the list are very simple and will not block for a long time.

14.6 (a) The first operation that succeeds in acquiring the monitor lock will continue. The second operation, however, will block on the monitor lock, and thus cannot continue until the first operation has released the lock. Thus, although the two operations could in principle be executed simultaneously, the implementation of a monitor runs them sequentially.
(b) 1. Use symbolic interpretation to find those operations that are read-only. 2. Use a multi-state lock to protect the monitor: nobody inside, some readers inside, some readers inside and one or more writers waiting, and one writer inside.

14.10 It is difficult to copy the stack of a thread, because there may exist variables that point into the stack. In C, for example, it is possible to take the address of a local variable (stored on the stack) and store this value in a global variable. If the stack is copied to a new region in memory, the global variable will still point to the location in the original stack. So, migrating a stack from one memory region to another is hard to implement transparently.

14.11 Since X contains a thread, it is harder to migrate, since threads always have a state that has to be migrated (for example, a stack); moreover, thread migration has the same implementation difficulty as stack migration, as described in the answer to Exercise 14.10. Migrating object Y is easier and less expensive, since it does not contain a thread. On the other hand, if multiple active objects (like X) located on different processors do operations on object Y, object Y will repeatedly be moving between these processors. In this case, it may be more efficient to move the active objects to the processor of Y.

References

1. Aho, A., Ganapathi, M., Tjiang, S.: Code generation using tree pattern matching and dynamic programming. ACM Trans. Programming Languages and Systems **11**(4), 491–516 (1989)
2. Aho, A., Johnson, S.: Optimal code generation for expression trees. J. ACM **23**(3), 488–501 (1976)
3. Aho, A., Johnson, S., Ullman, J.: Code generation for expressions with common subexpressions. J. ACM **24**(1), 146–160 (1977)
4. Aho, A., Sethi, R., Ullman, J.: Compilers: Principles, Techniques and Tools. Addison-Wesley (1986)
5. Aho, A., Ullman, J.: The Theory of Parsing, Translation and Compiling, Vol. I: Parsing, Vol. II: Compiling. Prentice Hall (1973)
6. Aho, A.V., Lam, M.S., Sethi, R., Ullman, J.D.: Compilers: Principles, Techniques, and Tools. Addison Wesley (2006). 2nd Ed.
7. Ahuja, S., Carriero, N., Gelernter, D.: Linda and friends. IEEE Computer **19**(8), 26–34 (1986)
8. Aït-Kaci, H.: Warren's Abstract Machine—A Tutorial Reconstruction. MIT Press (1991)
9. Op den Akker, R., Sluiman, E.: Storage allocation for attribute evaluators using stacks and queues. In: H.A..B. Melichar (ed.) Attribute Grammars, Applications and Systems, no. 545 in Lecture Notes in Computer Science, pp. 140–150. Springer-Verlag (1991)
10. Alblas, H.: Attribute evaluation methods. In: H. Alblas, B. Melichar (eds.) Attribute Grammars, Applications and Systems, *Lecture Notes in Computer Science*, vol. 545, pp. 48–113. Springer (1991)
11. Almasi, G., Gottlieb, A.: Highly Parallel Computing, 2nd edn. Benjamin/Cummings (1994)
12. Anderson, J.: A note on some compiling algorithms. Comm. ACM **7**(3), 149–150 (1964)
13. Anderson, T., Bershad, B., Lazowska, E., Levy, H.: Scheduler activations: Effective kernel support for the user-level management of parallelism. In: E.D. Lazowska (ed.) 13th ACM Symp. on Operating Systems Principles, pp. 95–109. ACM (1991)
14. Anonymous: Des Freiherrn von Münchhausen wunderbare Reisen und Abentheuer zu Wasser und zu Lande. Dieterichsche Buchhandlung, Göttingen (1840)
15. Appel, A.: Garbage collection can be faster than stack allocation. Information Processing Letters **25**, 275–279 (1987)
16. Appel, A.: Compiling with Continuations. Cambridge University Press (1992)
17. Appel, A., Supowit, K.: Generalizations of the Sethi-Ullman algorithm for register allocation. Software—Practice and Experience **17**(6), 417–421 (1987)
18. Appel, A.W.: Modern Compiler Implementation in C/ML/Java. Cambridge University Press, Cambridge (2004)
19. Asanovic, K., Bodík, R., Demmel, J., Keaveny, T., Keutzer, K., Kubiatowicz, J., Morgan, N., Patterson, D.A., Sen, K., Wawrzynek, J., Wessel, D., Yelick, K.A.: A view of the parallel computing landscape. Commun. ACM **52**(10), 56–67 (2009)

20. Assmann, W.: Another solution of scoping problems in symbol tables. In: U. Kastens, P. Pfahler (eds.) Compiler Construction, 4th International Conference, CC'92, no. 641 in Lecture Notes in Computer Science, pp. 66–72. Springer-Verlag (1992)

21. Austin, T., Breach, S., Sohi, G.: Efficient detection of all pointer and array access errors. ACM SIGPLAN Notices **29**(6), 290–312 (1994)

22. Aycock, J.: A brief history of Just-In-Time. ACM Comput. Surv. **35**(2), 97–113 (2003)

23. Baase, S., Van Gelder, A.: Computer Algorithms Introduction to Design and Analysis. Addison-Wesley, Reading, Mass. (2000). 3rd Edn.

24. Bacon, D., Graham, S., Sharp, O.: Compiler transformations for high-performance computing. ACM Computing Surveys **26**(4), 345–420 (1994)

25. Bailey, M.W., Weston, N.C.: Performance benefits of tail recursion removal in procedural languages. Tech. Rep. TR-2001-2, Hamilton College, Clinton, NY (2001)

26. Bal, H., Grune, D.: Programming Language Essentials. Addison-Wesley (1994)

27. Bal, H., Kaashoek, M., Tanenbaum, A.: Orca: A language for parallel programming of distributed systems. IEEE Trans. Software Engineering **18**(3), 190–205 (1992)

28. Bal, H., Steiner, J., Tanenbaum, A.: Programming languages for distributed computing systems. ACM Computing Surveys **21**(3), 261–322 (1989)

29. Bal, H.E., Bhoedjang, R., Hofman, R.F.H., Jacobs, C.J.H., Langendoen, K., Rühl, T.: Performance evaluation of the Orca shared-object system. ACM Trans. Computer Systems **16**(1), 1–40 (1998)

30. Barach, D., Taenzer, D., Wells, R.: A technique for finding storage allocation errors in C-language programs. ACM SIGPLAN Notices **17**(5), 16–23 (1982)

31. Barrett, D., Zorn, B.: Garbage collection using a dynamic threatening boundary. ACM SIGPLAN Notices **30**(6), 301–314 (1995)

32. Baskett, F.: The best simple code generation technique for while, for, and do loops. ACM SIGPLAN Notices **13**(4), 31–32 (1978)

33. Bates, R.M.: Logic of lemmings in compiler innovation. Commun. ACM **52**(5), 7 (2009)

34. Bell, J.: Threaded code. Commun. ACM **16**(6), 370–372 (1973)

35. Ben-Ari, M.: Algorithms for on-the-fly garbage collection. ACM Trans. Programming Languages and Systems **6**(3), 333–344 (1984)

36. Bernstein, R.: Producing good code for the case statement. Software—Practice and Experience **15**(10), 1021–1024 (1985)

37. Bertsch, E., Nederhof, M.J.: On failure of the pruning technique in 'Error repair in shift-reduce parsers'. ACM Trans. Programming Languages and Systems **21**(1), 1–10 (1999)

38. Beszédes, Á., Ferenc, R., Gyimóthy, T., Dolenc, A., Karsisto, K.: Survey of code-size reduction methods. ACM Comput. Surv. **35**(3), 223–267 (2003)

39. Bhoedjang, R., Rühl, T., Bal, H.: User-level network interface protocols. IEEE Computer **31**(11), 53–60 (1998)

40. Bird, R.: Introduction to Functional Programming using Haskell, 2nd edn. Prentice-Hall Europe (1998)

41. Birtwistle, G., Dahl, O.J., Myhrhaug, B., Nygaard, K.: SIMULA begin. Petrocelli/Charter (1975)

42. Biswas, S., Aggarwal, S.K.: A technique for extracting grammar from legacy programs. In: M.H. Hamza (ed.) IASTED Conf. on Software Engineering, pp. 652–657. IASTED/ACTA Press (2004)

43. Bjornson, R., Carriero, N., Gelernter, D., Leichter, J.: Linda, the portable parallel. Tech. Rep. RR-520, Yale University (1988)

44. Blume, W., Doallo, R., Eigenmann, R., Grout, J., Hoeflinger, J., Lawrence, T., Lee, J., Padua, D.A., Paek, Y., Pottenger, W.M., Rauchwerger, L., Tu, P.: Parallel programming with Polaris. IEEE Computer **29**(12), 78–83 (1996)

45. Boehm, H.J.: Space-efficient conservative garbage collection. ACM SIGPLAN Notices **28**(6), 197–206 (1993)

46. Boehm, H.J., Weiser, M.: Garbage collection in an uncooperative environment. Software—Practice and Experience **18**(9), 807–820 (1988)

47. Boyd, M., Whalley, D.: Isolation and analysis of optimization errors. ACM SIGPLAN Notices **28**(6), 26–25 (1993)
48. Boyland, J., Castagna, G.: Parasitic methods—implementation of multi-methods for Java. ACM SIGPLAN Notices **32**(10), 66–76 (1997)
49. Briggs, P., Cooper, K., Kennedy, K., Torczon, L.: Coloring heuristics for register allocation. ACM SIGPLAN Notices **24**(7), 275–284 (1989)
50. Brisk, P., Nahapetian, A., Sarrafzadeh, M.: Instruction selection for compilers that target architectures with echo instructions. In: H. Schepers (ed.) Software and Compilers for Embedded Systems, 8th International Workshop, *Lecture Notes in Computer Science*, vol. 3199, pp. 229–243. Springer (2004)
51. Brooker, R., MacCallum, I., Morris, D., Rohl, J.: The compiler compiler. Annual Review Automatic Programming **3**, 229–322 (1963)
52. Brown, P.J.: Throw-away compiling. Softw., Pract. Exper. **6**(3), 423–434 (1976)
53. Bruno, J., Sethi, R.: Code generation for a one-register machine. J. ACM **23**(3), 502–510 (1976)
54. Burn, G.: Lazy Functional Languages: Abstract Interpretation and Compilation. Research Monographs in Parallel and Distributed Computing. Pitman (1991)
55. Carriero, N., Gelernter, D.: How to write parallel programs: A guide to the perplexed. ACM Computing Surveys **21**(3), 323–357 (1989)
56. Chaitin, G.J., Auslander, M.A., Chandra, A.K., Cocke, J., Hopkins, M.E., Markstein, P.W.: Register allocation via coloring. Computer Languages **6**(1), 45–57 (1981)
57. Chapman, N.: LR Parsing: Theory and Practice. Cambridge University Press (1987)
58. Cheney, C.: A non-recursive list compacting algorithm. Commun. ACM **13**(11), 677–678 (1970)
59. Cherem, S., Princehouse, L., Rugina, R.: Practical memory leak detection using guarded value-flow analysis. In: J. Ferrante, K.S. McKinley (eds.) ACM SIGPLAN 2007 Conference on Programming Language Design and Implementation PLDI'07, pp. 480–491. ACM (2007)
60. Cifuentes, C.: Structuring decompiled graphs. In: T. Gyimóthy (ed.) Compiler Construction, 6th International Conference, CC'96, *Lecture Notes in Computer Science*, vol. 1060, pp. 91–105. Springer (1996)
61. Cifuentes, C., van Emmerik, M.: Recovery of jump table case statements from binary code. Science of Computer Programming **40**(2-3), 171–188 (2001)
62. Cifuentes, C., John Gough, K.: Decompilation of binary programs. Softw., Pract. Exper. **25**(7), 811–829 (1995)
63. Clements, J., Felleisen, M.: A tail-recursive machine with stack inspection. ACM Trans. Program. Lang. Syst. **26**(6), 1029–1052 (2004)
64. Cocke, J., Kennedy, K.: An algorithm for reduction of operator strength. Commun. ACM **20**(11), 850–856 (1977)
65. Cohen, J.: Garbage collection of linked data structures. ACM Computing Surveys **13**(3), 341–367 (1981)
66. Collins, G.: A method for overlapping and erasure of lists. Commun. ACM **3**(12), 655–657 (1960)
67. Colomb, R.: Assert, retract and external processes in Prolog. Software—Practice and Experience **18**(3), 205–220 (1988)
68. Conway, M.: Design of a separable transition-diagram compiler. Commun. ACM **6**(7), 396–408 (1963)
69. Cooper, K., Hall, M., Torczon, L.: Unexpected side effects of inline substitution: A case study. ACM Letters on Programming Languages and Systems **1**(1), 22–32 (1992)
70. Cooper, K.D., Harvey, T.J., Waterman, T.: An adaptive strategy for inline substitution. In: L.J. Hendren (ed.) 17th International Conference on Compiler Construction, CC 2008, *Lecture Notes in Computer Science*, vol. 4959, pp. 69–84. Springer (2008)
71. Davidson, J., Fraser, C.: Automatic generation of peephole optimizations. ACM SIGPLAN Notices **19**(6), 111–116 (1984)
72. Davidson, J., Fraser, C.: Code selection through object code optimization. ACM Trans. Programming Languages and Systems **6**(4), 505–526 (1984)

73. Davidson, J., Whalley, D.: Quick compilers using peephole optimizations. Software—Practice and Experience **19**(1), 79–97 (1989)
74. De Bus, B., Kästner, D., Chanet, D., Van Put, L., De Sutter, B.: Post-pass compaction techniques. Commun. ACM **46**(8), 41–46 (2003)
75. De Sutter, B., De Bus, B., De Bosschere, K.: Link-time binary rewriting techniques for program compaction. ACM Trans. Program. Lang. Syst. **27**(5), 882–945 (2005)
76. De Sutter, B., De Bus, B., De Bosschere, K., Keyngnaert, P., Demoen, B.: On the static analysis of indirect control transfers in binaries. In: H.R. Arabnia (ed.) International Conference on Parallel and Distributed Processing Techniques and Applications, PDPTA 2000. CSREA Press (2000)
77. Debray, S.: Implementing logic programming systems—the quiche-eating approach. In: E. Tick, G. Succi (eds.) Implementations of Logic Programming Systems, pp. 65–88. Kluwer Academic (1994)
78. Debray, S., Muth, R., Watterson, S.: Software power optimization via post-link-time binary rewriting (2001). URL \url{http://www.tortolaproject.com/papers/poweropt.pdf}
79. Debray, S.K., Evans, W.S., Muth, R., De Sutter, B.: Compiler techniques for code compaction. ACM Trans. Program. Lang. Syst. **22**(2), 378–415 (2000)
80. DeRemer, F.: Simple LR(*k*) grammars. Commun. ACM **14**(7), 453–460 (1971)
81. DeRemer, F.: Lexical analysis. In: F. Bauer, J. Eickel (eds.) Compiler Construction, An Advanced Course, no. 21 in Lecture Notes in Computer Science, pp. 109–120. Springer-Verlag (1974)
82. Dewar, R.: Indirect threaded code. Commun. ACM **18**(6), 330–331 (1975)
83. Diaz, D., Abreu, S., Codognet, P.: On the implementation of gnu prolog. Theory and Practice of Logic Programming **12**(1-2), 253–282 (2012)
84. Dijkstra, A., Fokker, J., Swierstra, S.D.: The architecture of the utrecht haskell compiler. In: S. Weirich (ed.) 2nd ACM SIGPLAN Symposium on Haskell, Haskell 2009, pp. 93–104. ACM (2009)
85. Dijkstra, E., Lamport, L.: On-the-fly garbage collection: An exercise in cooperation. Commun. ACM **21**(11), 966–975 (1978)
86. Dolgova, E.N., Chernov, A.V.: Automatic reconstruction of data types in the decompilation problem. Programming and Computer Software **35**(2), 105–119 (2009)
87. Douence, R., Fradet, P.: A systematic study of functional language implementations. TOPLAS **20**(2), 344–387 (1998)
88. Dreweke, A., et al.: Graph-based procedural abstraction. In: Fifth International Symposium on Code Generation and Optimization CGO 2007, pp. 259–270. IEEE Computer Society (2007)
89. Driesen, K., Hölzle, U.: Minimizing row displacement dispatch tables. ACM SIGPLAN Notices **30**(10), 141–155 (1995)
90. DuJardin, E., Amiel, E., Simon, E.: Fast algorithms for compressed multimethod dispatch tables. ACM Trans. Programming Languages and Systems **20**(1), 116–165 (1998)
91. Duran, A., Cavalcanti, A., Sampaio, A.: An algebraic approach to the design of compilers for object-oriented languages. Formal Asp. Comput. **22**(5), 489–535 (2010)
92. Dybvig, R.: The Scheme Programming Language: ANSI Scheme, 2nd edn. Prentice Hall (1996)
93. Earley, J.: An efficient context-free parsing algorithm. Commun. ACM **13**(2), 94–102 (1970)
94. Engelfriet, J., de Jong, W.: Attribute storage optimization by stacks. Acta Informatica **27**, 567–581 (1990)
95. Ernst, J., Evans, W.S., Fraser, C.W., Lucco, S., Proebsting, T.A.: Code compression. In: ACM SIGPLAN Conference on Programming Language Design and Implementation, PLDI'97, pp. 358–365. ACM (1997)
96. Farfeleder, S., Krall, A., Steiner, E., Brandner, F.: Effective compiler generation by architecture description. In: M.J. Irwin, K.D. Bosschere (eds.) ACM SIGPLAN/SIGBED Conference on Languages, Compilers, and Tools for Embedded Systems (LCTES'06), pp. 145–152. ACM (2006)

97. Farrow, R.: Sub-protocol-evaluators for attribute grammars. ACM SIGPLAN Notices **19**(6), 70–80 (1984)
98. Farrow, R., Yellin, D.: A comparison of storage optimizations in automatically generated attribute evaluators. Acta Informatica **23**, 393–427 (1986)
99. Feijs, L., van Ommering, R.: Abstract derivation of transitive closure algorithms. Information Processing Letters **63**(3), 159–164 (1997)
100. Fortes Gálvez, J.: Generating LR(1) parsers of small size. In: U. Kastens, P. Pfahler (eds.) Compiler Construction, 4th International Conference, CC'92, no. 641 in Lecture Notes in Computer Science, pp. 16–29. Springer-Verlag (1992)
101. Fraser, C., Hanson, D.: A Retargetable C Compiler—Design and Implementation. Benjamin/Cummings, Redwood City, Ca. (1995)
102. Freeman, E., Hupfer, S., Arnold, K.: JavaSpaces—Principles, Patterns, and Practice. Addison-Wesley (1999)
103. Freiburghouse, R.: Register allocation via usage counts. Commun. ACM **17**(11), 638–642 (1974)
104. Garey, M.R., Johnson, D.S.: Computers and Intractability: A Guide to the Theory of NP-Completeness. W. H. Freeman (1979/1983)
105. Gilbert, J., Abrahamson, D.M.: Adaptive object code compression. In: S.H. *et al.*(ed.) International Conference on Compilers, Architecture, and Synthesis for Embedded Systems, CASES 2006, pp. 282–292. ACM (2006)
106. Goldberg, B.: Tag-free garbage collection for strongly typed programming languages. ACM SIGPLAN Notices **26**(6), 165–176 (1991)
107. Gómez-Zamalloa, M., Albert, E., Puebla, G.: Modular decompilation of low-level code by partial evaluation. In: Eighth IEEE International Working Conference on Source Code Analysis and Manipulation (SCAM 2008), pp. 239–248. IEEE (2008)
108. Gosling, J., Joy, B., Steele, G., Bracha, G.: The Java™ Language Specification, 3rd edn. Addison-Wesley Professional (2005)
109. Grama, A., Gupta, A., Karypis, G., Kumar, V.: Introduction to Parallel Computing, 2nd edn. Pearson (2003)
110. Granlund, T., Kenner, R.: Eliminating branches using a super-optimizer and the GNU C compiler. ACM SIGPLAN Notices **27**, 341–352 (1992)
111. Griswold, R., Griswold, M.: The Implementation of the Icon Programming Language. Princeton University Press (1986)
112. Grune, D., Jacobs, C.J.H.: Parsing Techniques: A Practical Guide, 2nd edn. Springer Verlag (2008)
113. Hack, S., Wilhelm, R., Seidl, H.: Compiler Design: Code Generation and Machine-Level Optimization. Springer (2013)
114. Hall, M.W., Anderson, J.A.M., Amarasinghe, S.P., Murphy, B.R., Liao, S.W., Bugnion, E., Lam, M.S.: Maximizing multiprocessor performance with the SUIF compiler. IEEE Computer **29**(12), 84–89 (1996)
115. Hall, M.W., Padua, D.A., Pingali, K.: Compiler research: The next 50 years. Commun. ACM **52**(2), 60–67 (2009)
116. Hanson, D.: Compact recursive-descent parsing of expressions. Software—Practice and Experience **15**(12), 1205–1212 (1985)
117. Hartmann, A.: A Concurrent-Pascal compiler for minicomputers. No. 50 in Lecture Notes in Compter Science. Springer-Verlag (1977)
118. Hastings, R., Joyce, B.: Purify—fast detection of memory leaks and access errors. In: E. Allman (ed.) Winter '92 USENIX Conference, pp. 125–136. USENIX Association (1992)
119. Hemerik, C., Katoen, J.: Bottom-up tree acceptors. Science of Computer Programming **13**, 51–72 (1990)
120. Hennessy, J., Mendelsohn, N.: Compilation of the Pascal case statement. Software—Practice and Experience **12**(9), 879–882 (1982)
121. Herlihy, M., Shavit, N.: The Art of Multiprocessor Programming. Morgan Kaufmann Pub (2008)

122. Heydemann, K., Bodin, F., Charles, H.P.: A software-only compression system for trading-off performance and code size. In: K.M. Kavi, R. Cytron (eds.) 9th International Workshop on Software and Compilers for Embedded Systems SCOPES 2005, *ACM International Conference Proceeding Series*, vol. 136, pp. 27–36 (2005)

123. Hoogerbrugge, J., Augusteijn, L., Trum, J., van de Wiel, R.: A code compression system based on pipelined interpreters. Softw., Pract. Exper. **29**(11), 1005–1023 (1999)

124. Hopcroft, J., Ullman, J.: Introduction to Automata Theory, Languages, and Computation. Addison-Wesley (1979)

125. Hsu, C.H., Kremer, U.: The design, implementation, and evaluation of a compiler algorithm for CPU energy reduction. In: ACM SIGPLAN 2003 Conference on Programming Language Design and Implementation 2003, pp. 38–48. ACM (2003)

126. Huffman, D.A.: A method for the construction of minimum-redundancy codes. Proceedings of the Institute of Radio Engineers **40**(9), 1098–1101 (1952)

127. Hummel, J., Hendren, L., Nicolau, A.: A framework for data dependence testing in the presence of pointers. In: K. Tai (ed.) International Conference on Parallel Processing (Vol. II), 1994, pp. 216–224. CRC Press (1994)

128. IEEE Computer Society Standards Committee. Working group of the Microprocessor Standards Subcommittee, American National Standards Institute: IEEE standard for binary floating-point arithmetic. ANSI/IEEE Std 754-1985. IEEE Computer Society Press (1985)

129. Jazayeri, M., Pozefsky, D.: Space efficient storage management for attribute grammars. ACM Trans. Programming Languages and Systems **3**(4), 388–404 (1981)

130. Johnson, W., Porter, J., Ackley, S., Ross, D.: Automatic generation of efficient lexical processors using finite state techniques. Commun. ACM **11**(12), 805–813 (1968)

131. Johnsson, T.: Efficient compilation of lazy evaluation. ACM SIGPLAN Notices **19**(6), 58–69 (1984)

132. Johnsson, T.: Attribute grammars as a functional programming paradigm. In: G. Kahn (ed.) 3rd Functional Programming Languages and Computer Architecture Conference, no. 274 in Lecture Notes in Computer Science, pp. 154–173. Springer-Verlag (1987)

133. Johnstone, A., Scott, E.: Suppression of redundant operations in reverse compiled code using global dataflow analysis. In: H. Schepers (ed.) 8th International Workshop on Software and Compilers for Embedded Systems, SCOPES 2004, *Lecture Notes in Computer Science*, vol. 3199, pp. 92–106. Springer (2004)

134. Jones, C.: Estimating Software Costs. McGraw-Hill (1998)

135. Jones, N., Gomard, C., Sestoft, P.: Partial Evaluation and Program Generation. Prentice Hall (1993)

136. Jones, R., Lins, R.: Garbage Collection—Algorithms for Automatic Dynamic Memory Management. John Wiley (1996)

137. Jourdan, M.: Strongly non-circular attribute grammars and their recursive evaluation. ACM SIGPLAN Notices **19**(6), 81–93 (1984)

138. Jul, E., Levy, H., Hutchinson, N., Black, A.: Fine-grained mobility in the Emerald system. ACM Trans. Computer Systems **6**(1), 109–133 (1988)

139. Jung, D.H., Moon, S.M., Bae, S.H.: Evaluation of a java ahead-of-time compiler for embedded systems. The Computer Journal **55**(2), 232–252 (2012)

140. Kadayif, I., Kandemir, M., Chen, G., Vijaykrishnan, N., Irwin, M.J., Sivasubramaniam, A.: Compiler-directed high-level energy estimation and optimization. Trans. on Embedded Computing Sys. **4**(4), 819–850 (2005)

141. Kandemir, M., Vijaykrishnan, N., Irwin, M.J.: Compiler optimizations for low power systems. In: R. Graybill, R. Melhem (eds.) Power Aware Computing, Series in Computer Science, pp. 191 – 210. Springer Verlag (2002)

142. Kandemir, M.T., Vijaykrishnan, N., Irwin, M.J., Ye, W.: Influence of compiler optimizations on system power. IEEE Trans. VLSI Syst. **9**(6), 801–804 (2001)

143. Kannan, S., Proebsting, T.: Correction to 'producing good code for the case statement'. Software—Practice and Experience **24**(2), 233 (1994)

144. Karp, A.: Programming for parallelism. IEEE Computer **20**(5), 43–57 (1987)

145. Kastens, U.: Lifetime analysis for attributes. Acta Informatica **24**, 633–652 (1987)
146. Kastens, U., Hutt, B., Zimmermann, E.: GAG: A Practical Compiler Generator. No. 141 in Lecture Notes in Computer Science. Springer-Verlag (1982)
147. Katayama, T.: Translation of attribute grammars into procedures. ACM Trans. Programming Languages and Systems **6**(3), 345–369 (1984)
148. Keleher, P., Cox, A., Dwarkadas, S., Zwaenepoel, W.: TreadMarks: Distributed shared memory on standard workstations and operating systems. In: J. Mogul (ed.) Winter 94 USENIX Conference, pp. 115–132. USENIX Association (1994)
149. Kennedy, K., Koelbel, C., Zima, H.: The rise and fall of High Performance Fortran: an historical object lesson. In: Third ACM SIGPLAN conference on History of programming languages, pp. 7.1–7.22. ACM (2007)
150. Kernighan, B.W., Ritchie, D.: The C Programming Language, 2nd edn. Prentice-Hall (1988)
151. Keßler, C., Bednarski, A.: A dynamic programming approach to optimal integrated code generation. ACM SIGPLAN Notices **36**(8), 165–174 (2001)
152. Kim, J., Yun, H.S.: Low power software & systems techniques (2002). URL \url{davinci.snu.ac.kr/courses/emb/2002-2/doc/LowPowerOverview\%201.pdf}
153. King, J.: Symbolic execution and program testing. Commun. ACM **19**(7), 385–394 (1976)
154. Klint, P.: Interpretation techniques. Software—Practice and Experience **11**(9), 963–973 (1981)
155. Knuth, D.: On the translation of languages from left to right. Inform. Control **8**, 607–639 (1965)
156. Knuth, D.: Semantics of context-free languages. Math. Syst. Theory **2**(2), 127–145 (1968)
157. Knuth, D.: Semantics of context-free languages—correction. Math. Syst. Theory **5**(1), 95–96 (1971)
158. Knuth, D.: The Art of Computer Programming—Vol 1: Fundamental Algorithms, 2nd edn. Addison-Wesley (1973)
159. Knuth, D., Stevenson, F.: Optimal measurement points for program frequency counts. BIT **13**, 313–322 (1973)
160. Koes, D.R., Goldstein, S.C.: Near-optimal instruction selection on DAGs. In: M.L. Soffa, E. Duesterwald (eds.) Sixth International Symposium on Code Generation and Optimization (CGO 2008), pp. 45–54. ACM (2008)
161. Kowaltowski, T.: Parameter passing mechanisms and run-time data structures. Software—Practice and Experience **11**(7), 757–765 (1981)
162. Kremer, U.: Compilers for power and energy management (2003). URL http://www.cs.rutgers.edu/~uli/PLDI03.tutorial.pdf
163. Kristensen, A.: Template resolution in XML/HTML. Computer Networks and ISDN Systems **30**(1-7), 239–249 (1998)
164. Kursawe, P.: How to invent a Prolog machine. New Generation Computing **5**, 97–114 (1987)
165. LaLonde, W., Lee, E., Horning, J.: An LALR(*k*) parser generator. In: C. Freiman (ed.) IFIP Congress 71, pp. 153–157. North-Holland (1971)
166. Lämmel, R., Verhoef, C.: Semi-automatic grammar recovery. SP&E **31**(15), 1395–1438 (2001)
167. Lämmel, R., Zaytsev, V.: An introduction to grammar convergence. In: M. Leuschel, H. Wehrheim (eds.) IFM 2009, Integrated Formal Methods, *Lecture Notes in Computer Science*, vol. 5423, pp. 246–260. Springer (2009)
168. Landin, P.: The mechanical evaluation of expressions. Computer J. **6**(4), 308–320 (1964)
169. Latendresse, M., Feeley, M.: Generation of fast interpreters for Huffman compressed bytecode. Sci. Comput. Program. **57**(3), 295–317 (2005)
170. Lattner, C.: LLVM and Clang: Next generation compiler technology. In: BSD Conference, BSDCan 2008. University of Ottawa,, Ottawa, Canada (2008)
171. Lau, J., Schoenmackers, S., Sherwood, T., Calder, B.: Reducing code size with echo instructions. In: J.H. Moreno (ed.) International Conference on Compilers, Architectures and Synthesis for Embedded Systems, pp. 84–94. ACM (2003)

172. Lefurgy, C., Piccininni, E., Mudge, T.N.: Reducing code size with run-time decompression. In: Sixth International Symposium on High-Performance Computer Architecture, pp. 218–227. IEEE (2000)

173. Lemkin, P.: PSAIL: A portable SAIL to C compiler—description and tutorial. ACM SIGPLAN Notices 23(10), 149–171 (1988)

174. Levine, J., Mason, T., Brown, D.: Lex and Yacc, 2nd edn. O'Reilly (1992)

175. Levine, J.R.: Linkers and Loaders. Morgan-Kaufmann (2000)

176. Lewis II, P., Stearns, R.: Syntax-directed transduction. J. ACM 15(3), 465–488 (1968)

177. Li, K., Hudak, P.: Memory coherence in shared virtual memory systems. ACM Trans. Computer Systems 7(4), 321–359 (1989)

178. Liao, S.Y., Devadas, S., Keutzer, K.: A text-compression-based method for code size minimization in embedded systems. ACM Trans. Design Autom. Electr. Syst. 4(1), 12–38 (1999)

179. Lichtblau, U.: Decompilation of control structures by means of graph transformations. In: International Joint Conference on Theory and Practice of Software Development (TAPSOFT'85), Lecture Notes in Computer Science, vol. 185, pp. 284–297. Springer (1985)

180. Linz, P.: An Introduction to Formal Languages and Automata. Jones and Bartlett (1997)

181. Loveman, D.: High performance Fortran. IEEE Parallel and Distributed Technology 1(1), 25–42 (1993)

182. Lucco, S.: Split-stream dictionary program compression. In: ACM SIGPLAN Conference on Programming Language Design and Implementation, PLDI 2000, pp. 27–34. ACM (2000)

183. Maassen, J., Nieuwpoort, R.V.v., Veldema, R., Bal, H., Kielmann, T., Jacobs, C., Hofman, R.: Efficient Java RMI for parallel programming. ACM Transactions on Programming Languages and Systems 23(6), 747–775 (2001)

184. Martelli, A., Montanari, U.: An efficient unification algorithm. ACM Trans. Programming Languages and Systems 4(2), 258–282 (1982)

185. Massalin, H.: Superoptimizer: A look at the smallest program. ACM SIGPLAN Notices 22(10), 122–126 (1987)

186. McCarthy, J.: Recursive functions of symbolic expressions and their computation by machine. Commun. ACM 3(4), 184–195 (1960)

187. McCreight, E.M.: A space-economical suffix tree construction algorithm. J. ACM 23(2), 262–272 (1976)

188. McKenzie, B., Yeatman, C., De Vere, L.: Error repair in shift-reduce parsers. ACM Trans. Programming Languages and Systems 17(4), 672–689 (1995)

189. Meduna, A.: Elements of Compiler Design. Auerbach (2008)

190. Mehta, H., Owens, R.M., Irwin, M.J., Chen, R.Y., Ghosh, D.: Techniques for low energy software. In: B. Barton, et al. (eds.) International Symposium on Low Power Electronics and Design, ISPLED 1997, pp. 72–75. ACM (1997)

191. Midkiff, S.P.: Automatic Parallelization—An Overview of Fundamental Compiler Techniques. Synthesis Lectures on Computer Architecture. Morgan & Claypool Publishers (2011)

192. Milner, R., Tofte, M., Harper, R., MacQueen, D.: The Definition of Standard ML, revised edn. MIT Press (1997)

193. Mohamed, N., Al-Jaroodi, J.: Eliminating garbage collection for embedded real-time software. In: L.T. Yang, et al. (eds.) 2005 International Conference on Embedded Systems and Applications, ESA 2005, pp. 10–16. CSREA Press (2005)

194. Moreau, P.E., Zendra, O.: Gc^2: A generational conservative garbage collector for the ATImage library. J. Log. Algebr. Program. 59(1-2), 5–34 (2004)

195. Morel, E.: Data flow analysis and global optimization. In: B. Lorho (ed.) Methods and Tools for Compiler Construction, pp. 289–315. Cambridge University Press (1984)

196. Morgan, R.: Building an Optimizing Compiler. Digital Press/Butterworth-Heinemann (1998)

197. Muchnick, S.: Advanced Compiler Design and Implementation. Morgan Kaufmann (1997)

198. Muchnick, S., Jones, N.: Program Flow Analysis. Prentice Hall (1981)

199. Naur, P.: Checking of operand types in ALGOL compilers. BIT 5, 151–163 (1965)

200. Nethercote, N., Seward, J.: How to shadow every byte of memory used by a program. In: C. Krintz, S. Hand, D. Tarditi (eds.) 3rd International Conference on Virtual Execution Environments, VEE 2007, pp. 65–74. ACM (2007)

201. Nethercote, N., Seward, J.: Valgrind – a framework for heavyweight dynamic binary instrumentation. In: J. Ferrante, K.S. McKinley (eds.) ACM SIGPLAN 2007 Conference on Programming Language Design and Implementation, PLDI'07, pp. 89–100. ACM (2007)
202. Nguyen, T.T., Raschner, E.: Indirect threaded code used to emulate a virtual machine. ACM SIGPLAN Notices 17(5), 80–89 (1982)
203. Nitzberg, B., Lo, V.: Distributed shared memory: A survey of issues and algorithms. IEEE Computer 24(8), 52–60 (1991)
204. Nolan, G.: Decompiling Java. Apress, Berkeley, CA (2008)
205. Noonan, R.: An algorithm for generating abstract syntax trees. Computer Languages 10(3/4), 225–236 (1985)
206. Nuutila, E.: An efficient transitive closure algorithm for cyclic digraphs. Information Processing Letters 52(4), 207–213 (1994)
207. Oiwa, Y.: Implementation of the memory-safe full ansi-c compiler. In: M. Hind, A. Diwan (eds.) ACM SIGPLAN Conference on Programming Language Design and Implementation, PLDI 2009, pp. 259–269. ACM (2009)
208. Özer, E., Nisbet, A.P., Gregg, D.: Classification of compiler optimizations for high performance, small area and low power in FPGAs. Tech. rep., Trinity College, Dublin, Ireland (2003)
209. Pagan, F.: Converting interpreters into compilers. Software—Practice and Experience 18(6), 509–527 (1988)
210. Pagan, F.: Partial Computation and the Construction of Language Processors. Prentice Hall (1991)
211. Pager, D.: The lane-tracing algorithm for constructing LR(k) parsers and ways of enhancing its efficiency. Inform. Sci. 12, 19–42 (1977)
212. Paige, R., Koenig, S.: Finite differencing of computable expressions. ACM Trans. Programming Languages and Systems 4(3), 402–452 (1982)
213. Parikh, A., Kim, S., Kandemir, M., Vijaykrishnan, N., Irwin, M.J.: Instruction scheduling for low power. J. VLSI Signal Process. Syst. 37(1), 129–149 (2004)
214. Parr, T., Quong, R.: ANTLR: A predicated-LL(k) parser generator. Software—Practice and Experience 25(7), 789–810 (1995)
215. Paulson, L.: ML for the Working Programmer, 2nd edn. Cambridge University Press (1996)
216. Pemberton, S.: Comments on an error-recovery scheme by Hartmann. Software—Practice and Experience 10(3), 231–240 (1980)
217. Pettersson, M.: A term pattern-match compiler inspired by finite automata theory. In: U. Kastens, P. Pfahler (eds.) Compiler Construction, 4th International Conference, CC'92, no. 641 in Lecture Notes in Computer Science, pp. 258–270. Springer-Verlag (1992)
218. Peyton Jones, S.: The Implementation of Functional Programming Languages. Prentice Hall (1987)
219. Peyton Jones, S., Hughes, J.: Haskell 98: A non-strict, purely functional language. Internet (1999). URL http://www.haskell.org/onlinereport
220. Peyton Jones, S., Lester, D.: Implementing Functional Languages. Prentice Hall (1992)
221. Peyton Jones, S.L., Ramsey, N., Reig, F.: C−−: A portable assembly language that supports garbage collection. In: G. Nadathur (ed.) Principles and Practice of Declarative Programming PPDP'99, *Lecture Notes in Computer Science*, vol. 1702, pp. 1–28. Springer (1999)
222. Pierce, B.C.: Types and Programming Languages. The MIT Press (2002)
223. Plaisted, D.: The occur-check problem in Prolog. New Generation Computing 2, 309–322 (1984)
224. Poonen, G.: Error recovery for LR(k) parsers. In: B. Gilchrist (ed.) Information Processing 77, pp. 529–533. North Holland (1977)
225. Proebsting, T.: BURS automata generation. ACM Trans. Programming Languages and Systems 17(3), 461–486 (1995)
226. Purdom Jr., P.: A transitive closure algorithm. BIT 10, 76–94 (1970)
227. Quinn, M.: Parallel Computing—Theory and Practice. McGraw-Hill (1994)
228. Rabin, M.O., Scott, D.: Finite automata and their decision problems. IBM J. Research and Development 3, 114–125 (1959)

229. Räihä, K.J., Saarinen, M.: Testing attribute grammars for circularity. Acta Informatica **17**, 185–192 (1982)
230. Ramalingam, G., Srinivasan, H.: A member lookup algorithm for C++. ACM SIGPLAN Notices **32**(5), 18–30 (1997)
231. Regehr, J., Reid, A.: HOIST: A system for automatically deriving static analyzers for embedded systems. In: S. Mukherjee, K.S. McKinley (eds.) 11th International Conference on Architectural Support for Programming Languages and Operating Systems, ASPLOS 2004, pp. 133–143. ACM (2004)
232. Rekers, J.: Generalized LR parsing for general context-free grammars. Tech. Rep. CS-R9153, CWI, Amsterdam (1991)
233. Reps, T.: Maximal-munch tokenization in linear time. ACM Trans. Programming Languages and Systems **20**(2), 259–273 (1998)
234. Révész, G.: Introduction to Formal Languages. McGraw-Hill (1985)
235. Richter, H.: Noncorrecting syntax error recovery. ACM Trans. Programming Languages and Systems **7**(3), 478–489 (1985)
236. Ritter, T., Walker, G.: Varieties of threaded code for language implementation. BYTE **5**(9), 206–227 (1980)
237. Robinson, J.: A machine-oriented logic based on the resolution principle. J. ACM **12**(1), 23–41 (1965)
238. Robinson, J.: Computational logic: The unification computation. Mach. Intell. **6**, 63–72 (1971)
239. Rodriguez-Cerezo, D., Cabezuelo, A.S., Sierra-Rodríguez, J.L.: Implementing attribute grammars using conventional compiler construction tools. In: M.G. *et al.*(ed.) Federated Conference on Computer Science and Information Systems - FedCSIS 2011, pp. 855–862 (2011)
240. Röhrich, J.: Methods for the automatic construction of error correcting parsers. Acta Informatica **13**(2), 115–139 (1980)
241. Roy, K., Johnson, M.C.: Software design for low power. In: J. Mermet, W. Nebel (eds.) Low Power Design in Deep Sub-micron Electronics, pp. 433–459. Kluwer Academic Press (1996)
242. van Roy, P.: 1983-1993: The wonder years of sequential Prolog implementation. J. Logic Programming **19-20**, 385–441 (1994)
243. Runeson, J., Nyström, S.O., Sjödin, J.: Optimizing code size through procedural abstraction. In: J.W. Davidson, S.L. Min (eds.) Languages, Compilers, and Tools for Embedded Systems, ACM SIGPLAN Workshop LCTES 2000, *Lecture Notes in Computer Science*, vol. 1985, pp. 204–205. Springer (2001)
244. Rutishauser, H.: Automatische Rechenplanfertigung bei programmgesteuerten Rechenanlagen. Birkhäuser Verlag, Basel (1952). In German: Automatic Computation Plan Construction for Program-Controlled Computation Devices
245. Sale, A.: The implementation of case statements in Pascal. Software—Practice and Experience **11**(9), 929–942 (1981)
246. Saloman, D.: Assemblers and Loaders. Ellis Horwood (1992)
247. Salomon, D.: Data Compression: The Complete Reference, 4th edn. Springer Verlag (2006)
248. Samelson, K., Bauer, F.: Sequential formula translation. Commun. ACM **3**(2), 76–83 (1960)
249. Sankaran, N.: A bibliography on garbage collection and related topics. ACM SIGPLAN Notices **29**(9), 149–158 (1994)
250. Saputra, H., Kandemir, M.T., Vijaykrishnan, N., Irwin, M.J., Hu, J.S., Hsu, C.H., Kremer, U.: Energy-conscious compilation based on voltage scaling. In: Joint Conference on Languages, Compilers, and Tools for Embedded Systems & Software and Compilers for Embedded Systems (LCTES'02-SCOPES'02), pp. 2–11. ACM (2002)
251. Sassa, M., Goto, E.: A hashing method for fast set operations. Information Processing Letters **5**(2), 31–34 (1976)
252. Sayood, K.: Introduction to Data Compression, 3rd edn. Morgan Kaufmann (2005)
253. Schäckeler, S., Shang, W.: Procedural abstraction with reverse prefix trees. In: Seventh International Symposium on Code Generation and Optimization, CGO 2009, pp. 243–253. IEEE Computer Society (2009)

254. Schnorr, C.: An algorithm for transitive closure with linear expected time. SIAM J. Comput. **7**(2), 127–133 (1978)
255. Schorr, H., Waite, W.: An efficient machine-independent procedure for garbage collection in various list structures. Commun. ACM **10**(8), 501–506 (1967)
256. Scott, E., Johnstone, A.: GLL parse-tree generation. Science of Computer Programming (2012)
257. Sedgewick, R.: Algorithms. Addison-Wesley (2002)
258. Seng, J.S., Tullsen, D.M.: The effect of compiler optimizations on Pentium 4 power consumption. In: 7th Annual Workshop on Interaction between Compilers and Computer Architecture (INTERACT-7 2003), pp. 51–56. IEEE Computer Society (2003)
259. Sethi, R., Ullman, J.: The generation of optimal code for arithmetic expressions. J. ACM **17**(4), 715–728 (1970)
260. Sheridan, P.B.: The arithmetic translator-compiler of the IBM FORTRAN automatic coding system. Commun. ACM **2**(2), 9–21 (1959)
261. Siklóssy, L.: Fast and read-only algorithms for traversing trees without an auxiliary stack. Information Processing Letters **1**(4), 149–152 (1972)
262. Sippu, S., Soisalon-Soininen, E.: Parsing Theory, Vol. I: Languages and Parsing; Vol. II: LL(k) and LR(k) Parsing. EATCS Monograph on Theoretical Computer Science. Springer-Verlag (1988/1990)
263. Skillicorn, D., Talia, D.: Models and languages for parallel computation. ACM Computing Surveys **30**(2), 123–169 (1998)
264. Srikant, Y.N., Shankar, P.: The Compiler Design Handbook: Optimizations and Machine Code Generation. CRC Press, Boca Raton, Fl. (2002)
265. Stanchina, S., Meyer, M.: Exploiting the efficiency of generational algorithms for hardware-supported real-time garbage collection. In: Y. Cho, et al. (eds.) 2007 ACM Symposium on Applied Computing (SAC), pp. 713–718. ACM (2007)
266. Steele Jr., G.L.: Debunking the 'expensive procedure call' myth, or, procedure call implementations considered harmful. In: ACM National Conference, pp. 153–162 (1977)
267. Stirling, C.: Follow set error recovery. Software—Practice and Experience **15**(3), 239–257 (1985)
268. Stumm, M., Zhou, S.: Algorithms implementing distributed shared memory. IEEE Computer **23**(5), 54–64 (1990)
269. Sudkamp, T.: Languages and Machines—An Introduction to the Theory of Computer Science, 2nd edn. Addison-Wesley (1997)
270. Sysło, M., Dzikiewicz, J.: Computational experiences with some transitive closure algorithms. Computing **15**, 33–39 (1975)
271. Tanenbaum, A., van Staveren, H., Keizer, E., Stevenson, J.: A practical toolkit for making portable compilers. Commun. ACM **26**(9), 654–660 (1983)
272. Tanenbaum, A., van Staveren, H., Stevenson, J.: Using peephole optimization on intermediate code. ACM Trans. Programming Languages and Systems **4**(1), 21–36 (1982)
273. Tanenbaum, A., van Steen, M.: Distributed Systems: Principles and Paradigms, 2nd edition, 2nd ed. edn. Prentice Hall (2006)
274. Tarditi, D., Lee, P., Acharya, A.: No assembly required: Compiling Standard ML to C. ACM Letters on Programming Languages and Systems **1**(2), 161–177 (1992)
275. Tarjan, R.: Efficiency of a good but not linear set merging algorithm. J. ACM **22**(2), 215–225 (1975)
276. Templ, J.: A systematic approach to multiple inheritance. ACM SIGPLAN Notices **28**(4), 61–66 (1993)
277. The Unicode Consortium: The Unicode Standard, Version 5.0. Addison-Wesley (2006). URL `http://linguistlist.org/pubs/books/get-book.cfm?BookID=21316`
278. Thompson, K.: Regular expression search algorithm. Commun. ACM **11**(6), 419–422 (1968)
279. Thompson, S.: Haskell: The Craft of Functional Programming, 2nd edn. Addison-Wesley (1999)
280. Tiwari, V., Malik, S., Wolfe, A.: Power analysis of embedded software: A first step towards software power minimization. IEEE Trans. VLSI Syst. **2**(4), 437–445 (1994)

281. Turner, D.: A new implementation technique for applicative languages. Software—Practice and Experience **9**, 31–49 (1979)
282. Uhl, J.S., Nigel Horspool, R.: Flow grammars—a flow analysis methodology. In: P.A. Fritzson (ed.) Compiler Construction: 5th International Conference, CC '94, no. 786 in Lecture Notes in Computer Science, pp. 203–217. Springer-Verlag (1994)
283. Ukkonen, E.: On-line construction of suffix trees. Algorithmica **14**(3), 249–260 (1995)
284. Ungar, D.: Generation scavenging: A non-disruptive high performance storage reclamation algorithm. ACM SIGPLAN Notices **19**(5), 157–167 (1984)
285. Valluri, M., John, L.: Is compiling for performance == compiling for power? In: 5th Annual Workshop on Interaction between Compilers and Computer Architectures, p. 10 (2001)
286. Valluri, M.G., John, L.K., Hanson, H.: Exploiting compiler-generated schedules for energy savings in high-performance processors. In: I. Verbauwhede, H. Roh (eds.) International Symposium on Low Power Electronics and Design, 2003, pp. 414–419. ACM (2003)
287. Verbrugge, C., Co, P., Hendren, L.: Generalized constant propagation—a study in C. In: T. Gyimóthy (ed.) Compiler Construction: 6th International Conference, CC'96, no. 1060 in Lecture Notes in Computer Science, pp. 74–90. Springer-Verlag (1996)
288. Vigna, G.: Static disassembly and code analysis. In: M. Christodorescu, *et al.* (eds.) Malware Detection, *Advances in Information Security*, vol. 27, pp. 19–41. Springer (2007)
289. Vitek, J., Horspool, R.: Compact dispatch tables for dynamically typed object-oriented languages. In: T. Gyimóthy (ed.) Compiler Construction: 6th International Conference, CC'96, no. 1060 in Lecture Notes in Computer Science, pp. 309–325. Springer-Verlag (1996)
290. Waddle, V.: Production trees: A compact representation of parsed programs. ACM Trans. Programming Languages and Systems **12**(1), 61–83 (1990)
291. Warren, D.: An abstract Prolog instruction set. Tech. Rep. Technical Note 309, Artificial Intelligence Center, SRI (1983)
292. Warshall, S.: A theorem on Boolean matrices. J. ACM **9**, 11–12 (1962)
293. Wegbreit, B.: Property extraction in well-founded property sets. IEEE Trans. Software Engineering **SE-1**(3), 270–285 (1975)
294. Weiser, M.: Program slicing. IEEE Trans. Software Eng. **10**(4), 352–357 (1984)
295. Wendt, A.: Fast code generation using automatically generated decision trees. ACM SIGPLAN Notices **25**(6), 9–15 (1990)
296. Wentworth, E.: Pitfalls of conservative garbage collection. Software—Practice and Experience **20**(7), 719–727 (1990)
297. Wheeler, D.: Programme organization and initial orders for the EDSAC. Proc. Roy. Soc. A **202**, 573–589 (1950)
298. Wichmann, B.: How to call procedures, or second thoughts on Ackermann's function. Software—Practice and Experience **7**(3), 317–329 (1977)
299. van Wijngaarden, A., Mailloux, B.J., Peck, J.E.L., Koster, C.H.A., Sintzoff, M., Lindsey, C.H., Meertens, L.G.L.T., Fisker, R.G.: Revised report on the algorithmic language Algol 68. Acta Informatica **5**, 1–236 (1975)
300. Wilhelm, R., Seidl, H.: Compiler Design: Virtual Machines. Springer (2011)
301. Wilhelm, R., Seidl, H., Hack, S.: Compiler Design: Analysis and Transformation. Springer (2012)
302. Wilhelm, R., Seidl, H., Hack, S.: Compiler Design: Syntactic and Semantic Analysis. Springer (2012)
303. Wilken, K., Liu, J., Heffernan, M.: Optimal instruction scheduling using integer programming. ACM SIGPLAN Notices **35**(5), 121–133 (2000)
304. Wilkinson, B., Allen, M.: Parallel Programming—Techniques and Applications Using Networked Workstations and Parallel Computers, 2nd edn. Pearson Education (2005)
305. Wilson, G., Lu, P.: Parallel Programming Using C++. MIT Press (1996)
306. Wolfe, M.: High Performance Compilers for Parallel Computing. Addison-Wesley (1996)
307. Woo, S., Yoon, J., Kim, J.: Low-power instruction encoding techniques. In: SoC (Systems on Chips) Design Conference, p. 6. Seoul (2001)

308. Yang, W.: A fast general parser for automatic code generation. In: C.H. Hsu, V. Malyshkin (eds.) Methods and Tools of Parallel Programming Multicomputers, MTPP 2010, *Lecture Notes in Computer Science*, vol. 6083, pp. 30–39. Springer (2010)

309. Yang, X., Chen, Y., Eide, E., Regehr, J.: Finding and understanding bugs in c compilers. In: ACM SIGPLAN 2011 Conference on Programming Language Design and Implementation PLDI'11, pp. 283–294. ACM (2011)

310. Yershov, A.: The Alpha Automatic Programming System. Academic Press (1971)

311. Yun, H.S., Kim, J.: Power-aware modulo scheduling for high-performance VLIW processors. In: E. Macii, V. De, M.J. Irwin (eds.) International Symposium on Low Power Electronics and Design, ISLPED 2001, pp. 40–45. ACM (2001). DOI http://doi.acm.org/10.1145/383082.383091

312. Yuval, G.: The utility of the CDC 6000 registers. Software—Practice and Experience **7**(4), 535–536 (1977)

313. Zhou, X., Yan, L., Lilius, J.: Function inlining in embedded systems with code size limitation. In: Y.H. Lee, et al. (eds.) Third International Conference on Embedded Software and Systems, ICESS 2007, *Lecture Notes in Computer Science*, vol. 4523, pp. 154–161. Springer (2007)

Index

∅, **39**
⊥, **141**
ε, **35**
ε-closure, 82, 83, 160, 161, 174
ε-move, 76, **77**, 113, 160
⊢, **225**
ε-rule, **38**, 168, 185, 249
2-pass compiler, **28**
2-scan compiler, **28**

a posteriori type, **527**
a priori type, **527**
abstract class, **546**
abstract data type, 544, 545
abstract method, **546**
abstract syntax tree, **10**, 23, 55, 57, 209
acceptable partitioning, **237**
acceptable-set method, **144**
accumulating arguments, 664, 675
acquiring a lock, 741, 751, 752, 757, 779
action routine, **697**
ACTION table, **166**, 176, 204
activation record, 316, 481, 534, **556**
active node, **305**
active routine, 316, **559**, 571, 787
active-node pointer, **305**, 330
actual parameter, in Linda, **746**
Ada, 520, 779
adaptive compression, **440**
adaptive, of a compression algorithm, **438**
address descriptor, **388**
address space, 364, 738, **741**, 744, 751
administration part, 557, 559, **589**, 600
aggregate node allocation, **668**
Algol 68, 529, 530, 536, 537, 562, 571, 703
Algol 68 format, **112**

alignment requirements, **366**, 467, 505, 538, 612
alternative, **37**, 118, 120
ambiguous grammar, **38**, 116, 185, 529
amortized cost, **464**, 640
analysis–synthesis paradigm, **6**
ancestor routine, **559**, 564
annotated abstract syntax tree, **10**, 57, 299
annotation, **10**, 99, 209
anonymous type declaration, **522**
anti-dependence, **770**
ANTLR, 137
application spine, **641**, 653, 796
applicative-order reduction, **646**, 674
applied occurrence, 214, 369, 514, **514**
arithmetic sequence construct, **621**
arithmetic simplification, **322**, 325, 666
arity, 647, 667, **691**, 721
array descriptor, **542**
array type, 523, **540**
array without array, 614
assembly code, **355**, 368, 369, 597, 749
asserta(), 711
assertz(), 711
assignment, 270, 486, 530, 537, 612
assignment operator, 389
assignment under a pointer, 402, 771
associative addressing, 745
AST, **10**
asynchronous message passing, **744**, 775
atomic action, 746
Attach clauses instruction, 684
attribute, **10**, 99, 141, 249, 628
attribute evaluation rule, **211**, 213, 226, 237, 238, 241, 256
attribute evaluator, 212, **217**, 219, 245
attribute grammar, 7, 210, **210**, 627

Printed in the United States
By Bookmasters